D0166338

Understanding ICD-10-CM and ICD-10-PCS Coding:

A Worktext

Understanding ICD-10-CM and ICD-10-PCS Coding:

A Worktext

Mary Jo Bowie
MS, BS, AAS, RHIA, RHIT

Regina Schaffer
BS, AAS, RHIT, CPC

DELMAR
CENGAGE Learning™

Australia • Brazil • Japan • Korea • Mexico • Singapore • Spain • United Kingdom • United States

DELMAR
CENGAGE Learning™

**Understanding ICD-10-CM and
ICD-10-PCS Coding: A Worktext**
Bowie, Mary Jo and Schaffer, Regina M.

Vice President, Career and Professional
    Editorial: Dave Garza

Director of Learning Solutions:
    Matthew Kane

Senior Acquisitions Editor:
    Rhonda Dearborn

Managing Editor: Marah Bellegarde

Product Manager:
    Jadin Babin-Kavanaugh

Editorial Assistant: Lauren Whalen

Vice President, Career and Professional
    Marketing: Jennifer Baker

Marketing Director: Wendy Mapstone

Senior Marketing Manager:
    Nancy Bradshaw

Marketing Coordinator: Erica Ropitzky

Production Director: Carolyn Miller

Production Manager: Andrew Crouth

Content Project Manager: Anne Sherman

Senior Art Director: Jack Pendleton

Technology Project Manager: Patti Allen

© 2011 Delmar, Cengage Learning

ALL RIGHTS RESERVED. No part of this work covered by the copyright herein may
be reproduced, transmitted, stored, or used in any form or by any means graphic,
electronic, or mechanical, including but not limited to photocopying, recording,
scanning, digitizing, taping, Web distribution, information networks, or information storage and retrieval systems, except as permitted under Section 107 or 108
of the 1976 United States Copyright Act, without the prior written permission of
the publisher.

For product information and technology assistance, contact us at
Cengage Learning Customer & Sales Support, 1-800-354-9706

For permission to use material from this text or product,
submit all requests online at **www.cengage.com/permissions**.
Further permissions questions can be e-mailed to
permissionrequest@cengage.com

Library of Congress Control Number: 2010920698

ISBN-13: 978-14354-8158-9

ISBN-10: 1-4354-8158-5

Delmar
5 Maxwell Drive
Clifton Park, NY 12065-2919
USA

Cengage Learning is a leading provider of customized learning solutions with
office locations around the globe, including Singapore, the United Kingdom,
Australia, Mexico, Brazil, and Japan. Locate your local office at: **international.
cengage.com/region**

Cengage Learning products are represented in Canada by
Nelson Education, Ltd.

To learn more about Delmar, visit **delmar.cengage.com**
Purchase any of our products at your local college store or at our preferred online
store **www.CengageBrain.com**

Notice to the Reader

Publisher does not warrant or guarantee any of the products described herein or perform any independent analysis
in connection with any of the product information contained herein. Publisher does not assume, and expressly
disclaims, any obligation to obtain and include information other than that provided to it by the manufacturer. The
reader is expressly warned to consider and adopt all safety precautions that might be indicated by the activities
described herein and to avoid all potential hazards. By following the instructions contained herein, the reader
willingly assumes all risks in connection with such instructions. The publisher makes no representations or
warranties of any kind, including but not limited to, the warranties of fitness for particular purpose or
merchantability, nor are any such representations implied with respect to the material set forth herein, and the
publisher takes no responsibility with respect to such material. The publisher shall not be liable for any special,
consequential, or exemplary damages resulting, in whole or part, from the readers' use of, or reliance upon, this
material.

Printed in the United States of America
1 2 3 4 5 6 7 12 11 10

To my husband, Bill, who is my encouragement and who will get a new sports car if this book is a success! To my daughters Sarah and Bethannie, who are the joy of my life. Thanks for all you do to allow me the time to write. To my parents for making sure that you gave me all the opportunities to become who I am today.

—Mary Jo

To my son Mike and his beautiful wife Maria, who had to endure my presence at the computer for endless hours—your support was truly appreciated. To my "baby girl" Marie, who kept telling mom: "Please take a day off for yourself" (Now I can.) To my Marine Matt, no mother could be more proud than I am—thank you for your support and please be safe. Dad, you're the best. To the man who gave me the three most precious gifts ever and to the mom who was always there for me, you will always be in my heart.

And to MJB and Bill—what would I do without you!

—Regina

To Jadin Babin-Kavanaugh, who always keeps us moving in the right direction and who is truly a delight to work with. To Rhonda Dearborn, who facilitated the opportunity for us to write this book, we are forever grateful. To all of our Cengage family, who work to make our books happen.

—Mary Jo Bowie and Regina Schaffer

Contents

Preface

Understanding ICD-10-CM and ICD-10-PCS: A Worktext provides a comprehensive textbook to learn and master ICD-10-CM and ICD-10-PCS coding. This book can be used to instruct learners in both academic and clinical settings. Its design helps coders transition to the new coding system.

The *ICD-10-CM Official Coding Guidelines for Coding and Reporting* are highlighted in various book chapters, and the complete guidelines are contained in the appendix. Numerous clinical examples and case studies are used throughout the book to provide opportunities for learners to practice with real-life scenarios. Frequently encountered diseases are highlighted to enable the learner to become familiar with common disease signs and symptoms, clinical testing, and treatments.

Organization of the Worktext

Several features are incorporated into the chapters to facilitate learning:

- A **chapter outline** gives a brief overview of chapter content.
- **Learning objectives** familiarize the learner with chapter objectives.
- **Key terms** are listed at the start of each chapter and then highlighted and defined within the chapter.
- Many clinical **examples** are used throughout the text.
- **Illustrations** of human anatomy appear, based on the concept that learning is enhanced through visual tools.
- **Coding assignments** and **case studies** are used to determine comprehension of the material and to provide real-world practice.
- **Internet links** provide additional reference materials for the learner and take learning beyond the textbook.
- **Chapter summaries** review the main ideas for review purposes.
- **Chapter reviews** contain questions to reinforce content presented.
- The **StudyWare CD-ROM** includes features, quizzes, and activities for each chapter, plus coding case studies.
- The **EncoderPro Free Trial CD-ROM** includes ICD-10 codes as well as a mapping tool.

Supplements

The following supplements are available with the textbook to enhance the classroom experience:

Instructor's Manual

The *Instructor's Manual* contains answers to the exercises, chapter reviews, coding assignments, and case studies, as well as sample syllabi and course preparation information. (ISBN 1435481593)

Instructor Resources CD-ROM

These resources are available on CD-ROM and also at the Online Companion site for this book. The *Instructor Resources to Accompany Understanding ICD-10-CM and ICD-10-PCS Coding* includes:

- The **Instructor's Manual**, with lesson plans and complete answer keys.
- The **Computerized Test Bank** makes generating tests and quizzes a snap, with over 1,000 test questions to choose from and online testing capability.
- Customizable presentations for each chapter, written in **PowerPoint**™.

To access these great resources online, go to **delmarlearning.com/companions**. In the search field in the upper right corner, search by author, title, or ISBN. A number of titles may come up, so make sure to choose the correct edition of the book. Instructor resources are password-protected; please consult your instructor's manual for the user identification and password information. (ISBN 1435481615)

WebTutor on Blackboard

WebTutor is an Internet-based course management and delivery system designed to be used with the textbook. The WebTutor contains:

- Online chapter quizzes.
- Online glossary with flash cards.
- PowerPoint slides for each chapter.
- A preloaded computerized test bank.
- Discussion topics.

(ISBN 1435481607)

How to Use the StudyWare CD-ROM™

The StudyWare™ software helps you learn terms and concepts presented in *Understanding ICD-10-CM and ICD-10-PCS*. As you study each chapter in the text, be sure to complete the activities for the corresponding content areas on the CD-ROM. Use StudyWare™ as your own private tutor to help you learn the material in your textbook.

When you open the software, be sure to enter your first and last names so the software can properly track your quiz results. Then choose a content area from the menu to take a quiz, complete an activity, or complete a coding case.

Menus

You can access any of the menus from wherever you are in the program. The menus include chapter quizzes, activities, and Coding Cases 1–10.

Quizzes and Activities

Quizzes include multiple choice, image labeling, true/false, matching, and fill-in-the-blank questions. You can take the quizzes in both Practice Mode and Quiz Mode.

Use Practice Mode to improve your mastery of the material. You have multiple tries to get the answers correct. Instant feedback tells you whether you are right or wrong and helps you learn quickly by explaining why an answer is correct or incorrect.

Use Quiz Mode when you are ready to test yourself and keep a record of your scores. In Quiz Mode, you have one try to get the answers right, but you can take each quiz as many times as you want. You can view your last scores for each quiz and print out your results to submit to your instructor. Remember to enter your first and last names each time you enter StudyWare so that the program can track your results every time.

Copyright © 2011 Delmar, Cengage Learning. ALL RIGHTS RESERVED.

Copyright © 2011 Delmar, Cengage Learning. ALL RIGHTS RESERVED.

Concentration and Coding Case Studies

Concentration is a memory game you can play with one or two players to help review the key terms and concepts covered in each chapter.

There are also ten Coding Cases in the StudyWare, each paired with a video. Watch the video, read the case notes, then enter the correct ICD-10 codes for each case, in diagnosis order.

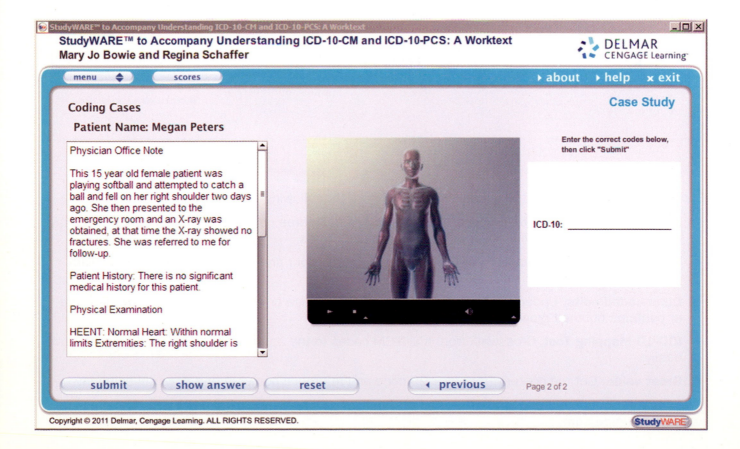

EncoderPro.com 59-Day Free Trial

With the purchase of this textbook you receive free 59-day access to *EncoderPro.com—Expert*, the powerful online medical coding solution from Ingenix®. With *EncoderPro.com*, you can simultaneously search across all three code sets.

How to Access the Free Trial

Information on how to access your 59-day trial of *EncoderPro.com* is included on the printed tear-out card bound into this textbook. Your unique user access code is also printed on the card. Be sure to check with your instructor before beginning your free trial because it will expire 59 days after your initial login.

Features and Benefits of EncoderPro.com

EncoderPro.com is the essential code lookup software for CPT®, ICD-9-CM, and HCPCS code sets from Ingenix®. It gives users fast searching capabilities across all code sets. EncoderPro can greatly reduce the time it takes to build or review a claim, and it helps improve overall coding accuracy.

During your free trial period to *EncoderPro.com—Expert*, the following tools will be available to you:

- **Powerful Ingenix CodeLogic™ search engine.** Search all three code sets simultaneously using lay terms, acronyms, abbreviations, and even misspelled words.

- **Lay descriptions for thousands of CPT® codes.** Enhance your understanding of procedures with easy-to-understand descriptions.

- **Color-coded edits.** Understand whether a code carries an age or sex edit, is covered by Medicare, or contains bundled procedures.

- **ICD-10 Mapping Tool.** Crosswalk from ICD-9-CM codes to the appropriate ICD-10 code quickly and easily.

- **Great value.** Get the content from over 20 code and reference books in one powerful solution.

For more information about *EncoderPro.com* or to become a subscriber beyond the free trial, email us at **esales@cengage.com**.

Acknowledgments

A special thank-you is extended to the reviewers who have provided recommendations to enhance the content of this work.

Mary M. Cantwell, RHIT, CPC, CPC-H, CPC-P, CPC-I, RMC
Professor, Health Information Management
Metro Community College
Omaha, Nebraska

Melanie Endicott, MBA/HCM, RHIA, CCS, CCS-P
HIM Program Director
Spokane Community College
Spokane, Washington

Rashmi Gaonkar, MS
Senior Instructor/Subject Specialist
ASA Institute
Brooklyn, New York

Betty Haar
Program Director
Kirkwood Community College
Cedar Rapids, Iowa

Pat King, MA, RHIA
MIS System Program Coordinator and Adjunct Faculty
Baker College of Cass City
Cass City, Michigan

Kathleen O'Gorman, BS, CPC
Lead Instructor, Health Claims Program
Branford Hall Career Institute
Southington, Connecticut

Angela P. Rein, RMA, AS, BSHM, CPC, MAHS, CPC-H
Medical Billing and Coding Department Chairperson
Sanford-Brown College
Collinsville, Illinois

Danielle Robel, MBA, BA, medical assistant
Adjunct Professor, School of Health Sciences
Kaplan University
Fort Lauderdale, Florida

Technical Reviewer

A special thank-you to Patricia ("Patti") Griffin, who reviewed this book and provided content insight. The timeliness of your work was greatly appreciated.

Patricia J. Griffin, AAS, RHIT, HIC
United Methodist Homes
Elizabeth Church Campus
Binghamton, New York

About the Authors

Mary Jo Bowie, MS, BS, AAS, RHIA, RHIT

Mary Jo has worked in the health information field for over 30 years as a consultant, HIM department director, and college instructor. As consultant and owner of Health Information Professional Services in Binghamton, New York, she has consulted nationally in various levels of care, including inpatient hospital settings, ambulatory care settings, skilled nursing facilities, physician offices, and clinics. She is an active member of the American Health Information Management Association. She has held the following positions in the New York Health Information Management Association: education director and a member of the board of directors, and Ambulatory Care Coding Guidelines Committee chairperson. At the collegiate level, teaching both in the classroom and in an Internet-based format, she has taught numerous health information technology and coding and reimbursement courses. Mary Jo also conducts professional coding workshops for coders as well as for physicians and clinical staff.

Regina Schaffer, AAS, RHIT, CPC

Regina has worked in the health information field for over 13 years as a consultant, HIM technician, coding and reimbursement educator, and technical institute and college instructor. Regina has audited, educated, and consulted in various specialties as she currently works in a multispecialty organization that employs over 135 providers. As part of her job in this organization, Regina develops and conducts professional coding workshops for coders as well as for physicians and clinical staff. Regina is regularly asked to speak on various aspects of coding in the Binghamton–Johnson City–Endicott region of New York State. She is a member in good standing of AHIMA and the AAPC and currently sits on the board of the Johnson City Chapter of AAPC. Regina has been teaching for the last four years at a business and technical institute in the Binghamton area, most recently at the local community college.

Introduction to Coding and Coding Professions

Chapter Outline

Objectives

Key Terms

Introduction

Professional Coding

History of Coding

Health Insurance Portability and
   Accountability Act of 1996

Professional Coding Associations

Employment Opportunities for Coders

Internet Links

Summary

Chapter Review

Objectives

At the conclusion of this chapter, the learner should be able to:

1. Describe the purpose of coding.
2. Explain the development of the ICD classification system.
3. Identify professional coding certifications and organizations.
4. Discuss the standards mandated by the Health Insurance Portability and Accountability Act of 1996.

Key Terms

Accrediting Bureau of Health Education Schools (ABHES)

Administrative Simplification

American Academy of Professional Coders (AAPC)

American Association of Medical Assistants (AAMA)

American Health Information Management Association (AHIMA)

American Medical Technologists (AMT)

Centers for Medicare and Medicaid Services (CMS)

Certified Coding Associate (CCA)

Certified Coding Specialist (CCS)

Certified Coding Specialist, Physician-Based (CCS-P)

Certified in Healthcare Privacy (CHP)

Certified in Healthcare Privacy and Security (CHPS)

Certified in Healthcare Security (CHS)

Certified Medical Assistant (CMA)

Certified Professional Coder (CPC)

Certified Professional Coder, Hospital-Based (CPC-H)

coding

Commission on Accreditation of Allied

Health Education Programs (CAAHEP)

Health Insurance Portability and Accountability Act of 1996 (HIPAA), Public Law 104-191

ICD-10-CM

ICD-10 Procedure Coding System, ICD-10-PCS

International Classification of Diseases, Tenth Revision, Clinical Modification

International Classification of Diseases, Tenth Revision (ICD-10)

morbidity

mortality

National Center for Health Statistics (NCHS)

Registered Health Information Administrator (RHIA)

Registered Health Information Technician (RHIT)

Registered Medical Assistant (RMA)

World Health Organization (WHO)

Introduction

Medical **coding** is the assignment of numeric or alphanumeric digits and characters to specific diagnostic and procedural phrases. This coding, like any other language, needs to be translated to be understood, and each combination of numbers or of numbers and letters represents a diagnostic or procedural phrase.

> **EXAMPLE:** The diagnostic phrase "appendicitis" is translated into diagnostic code K37 in the ICD-10-CM coding system. The procedural phrase "open appendectomy" is translated into procedure code ODTJ0ZZ in ICD-10-PCS.

By using ICD-10-CM and ICD-10-PCS codes, health-care professionals can effectively collect, process, and analyze diagnostic and procedural information.

Professional Coding

Coding is the language used by insurance companies and health-care providers to describe what brought a person to a facility for treatment and what services were performed. The ability of health-care professionals to communicate and translate these codes is vital to the care and treatment rendered to the patient. These codes are also communicated to the insurance company, which is required to make payment for the patient's care. All involved parties must be able to understand and fluently "speak" the coding language to convey the essence of the patient's visit and treatment.

In the chapters that follow, the student will gain a greater knowledge of the language of coding, specifically ICD-10-CM and ICD-10-PCS. By the completion of this book, the student will have the knowledge base needed to become fluent in the language of ICD-10-CM and ICD-10-PCS coding, which is an ever increasingly used tool in the health-care industry.

History of Coding

ICD-10-CM, an abbreviation for the **International Classification of Diseases, Tenth Revision, Clinical Modification**, is an arrangement of classes or groups of diagnoses and procedures by systematic division. ICD-10-CM is based on the official version of the **International Classification of Diseases, Tenth Revision (ICD-10)**, which was developed by the **World Health Organization (WHO)** in Geneva, Switzerland. In 1948, the WHO assumed responsibility for preparing and publishing the revisions to ICD every 10 years. Thus, with every 10-year revision, the name of the current ICD changes.

> **EXAMPLE:** ICD-8 was revised to become ICD-9; ICD-9 was revised to become ICD-10.

The ICD classification system was designed to compile and present statistical data on **morbidity** (the rate or frequency of disease) and **mortality** (the rate or frequency of deaths). Hospitals first used this form of classification to track, store, and retrieve statistical information. However, a more efficient basis for the storage and retrieval of diagnostic data was needed. In 1950, the Veterans Administration and the U.S. Public Health Service began independent studies of the use of the ICD for hospital indexing purposes. By 1956, the American Hospital Association and the American Association of Medical Record

Librarians (now the American Health Information Management Association) felt that the ICD form of classification provided an efficient and useful vehicle for indexing hospital records.

With hospital indexing in mind, the WHO international conference published its eighth revision of the ICD in 1966. Health-care professionals in some countries found that ICD-8 lacked the detail needed for diagnostic indexing. In the United States, consultants were asked to study ICD-8 for its applicability to various users. In 1968, the Advisory Committee to the Central Office on ICD published the International Classification of Diseases, Eighth Revision, adapted for use in the United States. It became known as ICDA-8 and was used for coding diagnostic data for both morbidity and mortality statistics in the United States.

In 1979, ICD-9-CM replaced earlier, less specific versions of the classification system. The ICD-9-CM streamlined the other versions of ICD classification into a single system that was intended for use primarily in U.S. hospitals. The ICD-9-CM provided a more complete classification system for morbidity data to be used for indexing and reviewing patient records and medical care.

In 1992, the WHO published ICD-10, which is currently being used in many countries. In 1997 the National Center for Health Statistics (NCHS) began testing the ICD-10 system for implementation in the United States, where two agencies are responsible for the annual updates to the ICD-CM codes.

- The **National Center for Health Statistics (NCHS)** is responsible for maintaining the diagnostic codes in volumes 1 and 2 of the ICD-CM manuals.

- The **Centers for Medicare and Medicaid Services (CMS)** is responsible for maintaining the procedure codes of ICD-CM, found in volume 3.

As the NCHS was testing ICD-10-CM, the draft and the preliminary crosswalk between ICD-9-CM and ICD-10-CM were made available on the NCHS Web site for public review and comment. In the summer of 2003, the American Hospital Association and the American Health Information Management Association conducted a field test for ICD-10-CM and reported the findings. Modifications were then made to the tenth revision.

In 2001 the Centers for Medicare and Medicaid Services funded a project to design a replacement system for the procedural codes of ICD-9-CM. The contract to redesign the procedural codes was awarded to 3M Health Information System. The new system is known as **ICD-10 Procedure Coding System, ICD-10-PCS**.

ICD-10-CM and ICD-10-PCS, when compared to ICD-9-CM, has the addition of information relevant to:

- Ambulatory and managed-care encounters.
- Expanded injury codes.
- More combination diagnosis/symptom codes to reduce the number of codes needed to fully describe a condition.
- Expanded use of sixth and seventh characters.
- Laterality and greater specificity in code assignment.

On August 22, 2008, the U.S. Department of Health and Human Services (HHS) published a proposed rule to adopt ICD-10-CM and ICD-10-PCS to replace ICD-9-CM. On January 16, 2009, the final rule on adoption of ICD-10-CM and ICD-10-PCS was published with an implementation date of October 1, 2013. So the transition to ICD-10-CM and ICD-10-PCS has begun.

This system will become the key storyteller to the insurance companies, explaining what brought the patient into the office or facility (by means of a diagnostic code), as well as what services the facility provided (by means of a procedural code). Because coding plays such a critical role in the reimbursement for services rendered, *correct coding practices are essential.*

Health Insurance Portability and Accountability Act of 1996

The **Health Insurance Portability and Accountability Act of 1996 (HIPAA), Public Law 104-191**, was passed by Congress to improve the portability and continuity of health-care coverage. The **Administrative Simplification** aspect of this legislation developed standards for the electronic exchange of health-care data for administrative and financial transactions. The final rule on transactions and code sets mandated the use of standardized code sets for the electronic submission of health-care data.

HIPAA mandated that ICD-9-CM diagnostic codes are reported for diagnoses for all levels of care, including all hospital services, clinic services, long-term care, and physician offices. ICD-9-CM procedural codes are reported for inpatient hospital services. Health-care providers must now use ICD-9-CM codes to accurately report diagnoses and services provided on submitted insurance claims. The codes are used to determine not only payment but also the medical necessity of care, which is defined by Medicare as "the determination that a service or procedure rendered is reasonable and necessary for the diagnosis or treatment of an illness or injury." Thus, coders perform a vital role in the health-care system.

ICD-10-CM and ICD-10-PCS codes will replace ICD-9-CM for use by inpatient facilities starting on October 1, 2013. Also on that date, ambulatory services and physician services will start using ICD-10-CM codes for diagnosis and will continue to use CPT codes for procedures.

Professional Coding Associations

To assist and promote correct coding and reimbursement, several organizations educate, train, and credential coders. Credentialing ensures the proper training and education of coders. As the transition is made from ICD-9-CM to ICD-10-CM and ICD-10-PCS, many of the following professional organizations will be offering educational materials to assist in the transition.

American Health Information Management Association (AHIMA)

The **American Health Information Management Association (AHIMA)** represents health information professionals who manage, organize, process, and manipulate patient data. Health information professionals have knowledge of electronic and paper medical record systems, as well as of coding, reimbursement, and research methodologies. The information that these professionals manage directly impacts patient care and financial decisions made in the health-care industry. Members of AHIMA feel that the quality of patient care is directly related to the effectiveness of the information available.

Health-care providers, insurance companies, and institutional administrators depend on the accuracy and quality of that information. For this reason, AHIMA members are trained to provide a level of service that maintains the quality and accuracy of the medical information they come into contact with.

AHIMA offers a number of certifications and credentials to ensure that its members meet the level of proficiency needed to provide educated professionals to manage health-care information. The members receive the following certifications or credentials through a combination of education, experience, and performance on national certification examinations:

- CCA—Certified Coding Associate
- CCS—Certified Coding Specialist
- CCS-P—Certified Coding Specialist, Physician-Based
- CHP—Certified in Healthcare Privacy
- CHPS—Certified Healthcare Privacy and Security
- CHS—Certified in Healthcare Security
- RHIA—Registered Health Information Administrator
- RHIT—Registered Health Information Technician

Once the certifications have been earned, continuing education credits are required to maintain them. These credits can be obtained through conferences, seminars, classes, or other avenues of career development that AHIMA publishes and makes available to its members.

American Academy of Professional Coders (AAPC)

The **American Academy of Professional Coders (AAPC)** was founded to elevate the standards of medical coding. The AAPC provides networking opportunities through local chapter memberships and conferences. It also provides ongoing educational opportunities for members. Whereas AHIMA deals with all aspects of health information, AAPC focuses on coding and reimbursement.

Like AHIMA, AAPC offers certifications for professional proficiency. The **Certified Professional Coder (CPC)** certification is available for coders in physician offices and clinics, and the **Certified Professional Coder, Hospital-Based (CPC-H)** is available for coders in the hospital setting. Two additional certifications are for individuals who have not yet met the work experience requirements of the CPC and CPC-H certifications:

- The Certified Professional Coder Apprentice (CPC-A)
- The Certified Professional Coder, Hospital Apprentice (CPC-H-A)

Continuing education credits are also required on a biannual basis to maintain AAPC certification.

American Association of Medical Assistants (AAMA)

The **American Association of Medical Assistants (AAMA)** represents individuals trained in performing routine administrative and clinical jobs, including coding, that keep medical offices and clinics running efficiently and smoothly. Credentialing is voluntary in most states; a medical assistant is not required to be certified or registered. However, the AAMA offers the national credential of **Certified Medical Assistant (CMA)** certification for medical assistants. The **Commission on Accreditation of Allied Health Education Programs (CAAHEP)** collaborates with the Curriculum Review Board of the AAMA Endowment to accredit medical assisting programs in both public and private postsecondary institutions throughout the United States.

This accreditation prepares candidates for entry in the medical assisting field. Students who have graduated from a medical assisting program accredited by the CAAHEP or the **Accrediting Bureau of Health Education Schools (ABHES)** are eligible to take the CMA examination, which tests candidates on tasks performed in the workplace. Recertification is required every five years, either by continuing education or by examination.

American Medical Technologists (AMT)

The **American Medical Technologists (AMT)** offers professional credentials such as **Registered Medical Assistant (RMA)**. These professionals perform the same tasks as those of a CMA but are credentialed by AMT. Students who have completed a college-level program approved by the U.S. Department of Education may voluntarily take the examination that credentials them as RMAs.

Employment Opportunities for Coders

Regardless of the credentialing path that an individual takes, career opportunities are numerous. Coders work in all aspects of health care, including hospitals, physician offices, clinics, long-term care facilities, insurance companies, and billing agencies. With the evolution of the electronic health record, more coders will be needed to review the generated information for its accuracy and compliance. The Bureau of Labor Statistics calculates that the number of coding jobs in the United States will grow faster through 2015 than the average of all occupations. As the population of the United States ages, more individuals will use health-care services and at a greater rate, thus increasing the need for additional services and for coded health-care data.

Internet Links

To obtain information about ICD-10-CM visit *www.cdc.gov/nchs/about/otheract/icd9/abticd10.htm*

To view the ICD-10-CM files visit *www.cdc.gov/nchs/about/otheract/icd9/icd10cm.htm*

To obtain information on the AAMA, visit *www.aama-ntl.org*

To obtain information on the AAPC, visit *www.aapc.com*

To obtain information on the AHIMA, visit *www.ahima.org*

To obtain information on AMT, visit *www.amt1.com*

To obtain information on career statistics and opportunities, visit the Bureau of Labor Statistics at *www.bls.gov*

Summary

- Coding is the assignment of numeric or alphanumeric digits and characters to diagnostic and procedural phrases.
- ICD-10-CM and ICD-10-PCS will be implemented in the United States to code diagnoses and procedures on October 1, 2013.
- The National Center for Health Statistics coordinates the modifications to disease classifications.
- The Centers for Medicare and Medicaid Services coordinates the procedural classification updates.
- The American Health Information Management Association offers the following credentials: Certified Coding Associate; Certified Coding Specialist; Certified Coding Specialist, Physician-Based; Certified in Healthcare Privacy; Certified in Healthcare Privacy and Security; Certified in Healthcare Security; Registered Health Information Administrator; and Registered Health Information Technician.
- The American Academy of Professional Coders offers the following credentials: Certified Professional Coder; Certified Professional Coder, Hospital-Based; Certified Professional Coder Apprentice; and Certified Professional Coder, Hospital Apprentice.
- The American Association of Medical Assistants offers the Certified Medical Assistant credential.
- The American Medical Technologists offers professional credentials such as a Registered Medical Assistant.

Chapter Review

True/False: Indicate whether each statement is true (T) or false (F).

1. _____ The CPC credential is offered by the American Health Information Management Association.

2. _____ AHIMA requires credentialed professionals to obtain continuing education credits to maintain their credentials.

3. _____ CMAs must be licensed to practice in the United States.

4. _____ The final rule on transactions and code sets mandated the use of ICD-9-CM for the electronic submission of health-care data.

5. _____ The Centers for Medicare and Medicaid Services coordinates the procedural classification updates.

Fill-in-the-Blank: Enter the appropriate term(s) to complete each statement.

6. The rate or frequency of a disease is known as _____.

7. ICD-9 was developed by the _____.

8. ICD-10-CM is an abbreviation for the International Classification of Diseases, Tenth Revision, _____.

9. Modifications of the ICD-10-CM disease classification is coordinated by _____.

10. Public Law 104-191, known as _____, was passed by Congress to improve the portability and continuity of health care coverage.

Short Answer: Define each abbreviation and acronym.

11. AHIMA

_____
_____
_____

12. RHIA

_____
_____
_____

13. CPC-H

_____
_____
_____

14. AMT

_____
_____
_____

15. CPC

_____
_____
_____

16. AAMA

_____
_____
_____

17. RMA

_____
_____
_____

18. CMA

_____
_____
_____

19. CCS

_____
_____
_____

20. CCS-P

_____
_____
_____

An Overview of ICD-10-CM

Chapter Outline

Objectives

At the conclusion of this chapter, the learner should be able to:

1. List the chapters in ICD-10-CM.
2. State the chapter titles.
3. Identify the codes that correspond to the chapters.

Key Terms

Index to Diseases and Injuries

Index to External Causes of Injury

Tabular List of Diseases and Injuries (Tabular)

Reminder

As you work through this chapter and the remaining chapters, you will need to have a copy of the ICD-10-CM coding book to reference.

Introduction

The ICD-10-CM coding system allows health-care providers and facilities to answer the question "what brought the patient to my office/facility?" This information is needed for statistical purposes, reimbursement, and continuity of patient care. To accurately convey this information, the coder must become familiar with all aspects of the ICD-10-CM coding book. This chapter presents an overview of ICD-10-CM.

ICD-10-CM Coding Book Format

The ICD-10-CM 2009 draft was released by the U.S. government for morbidity coding. ICD-10-CM is compatible with ICD-10, which is used for cause of death coding in the United States. ICD-10-CM has a greater number of codes than ICD-9-CM and has been expanded to include health-related conditions and to provide greater specificity in code assignment.

ICD-10-CM has two parts:

- The Index
- The Tabular List of Diseases and Injuries

The Index to Diseases and Injuries is an alphabetic listing of terms and corresponding codes. The two sections of the index are:

- **Index to Diseases and Injuries**
- **Index to External Causes of Injury**

There are also a Neoplasm Table and a Table of Drugs and Chemicals found in the Index.

The **Tabular List of Diseases and Injuries** is an alphanumerical list of codes, commonly referred to as the "*Tabular*." The Tabular is divided into chapters based on body system (anatomical site) or condition (etiology). The specific organization of the chapters is discussed throughout this book and overviewed in the next section.

ICD-10-CM Tabular List of Diseases and Injuries

The Tabular List of Diseases and Injuries is an alphanumerical list of the diseases and injuries found in ICD-10-CM. The Tabular consists of the following chapters:

1. Certain Infectious and Parasitic Diseases
2. Neoplasms
3. Diseases of the Blood and Blood-Forming Organs and Certain Disorders Involving the Immune Mechanism
4. Endocrine, Nutritional, and Metabolic Diseases
5. Mental and Behavioral Disorders
6. Diseases of the Nervous System
7. Diseases of the Eye and Adnexa
8. Diseases of the Ear and Mastoid Process
9. Diseases of the Circulatory System
10. Diseases of the Respiratory System
11. Diseases of the Digestive System

12. Diseases of the Skin and Subcutaneous Tissue

13. Diseases of the Musculoskeletal System and Connective Tissue

14. Diseases of the Genitourinary System

15. Pregnancy, Childbirth, and the Puerperium

16. Certain Conditions Originating in the Perinatal Period

17. Congenital Malformations, Deformations, and Chromosomal Abnormalities

18. Symptoms, Signs, and Abnormal Clinical and Laboratory Findings, not elsewhere classified

19. Injury, Poisoning, and Certain Other Consequences of External Causes

20. External Causes of Morbidity

21. Factors Influencing Health Status and Contact with Health Services

Exercise 2.1 – Identifying Chapters

For each chapter title, indicate whether the chapter is organized by etiology or by anatomical site.

1. Congenital Malformations, Deformations, and Chromosomal Abnormalities _____

2. Diseases of the Circulatory System _____

3. Diseases of the Digestive System _____

4. Endocrine, Nutritional, and Metabolic Diseases _____

5. Certain Infectious and Parasitic Diseases _____

6. Diseases of Skin and Subcutaneous Tissue _____

7. Mental and Behavioral Disorders _____

8. Diseases of the Nervous System _____

9. Diseases of the Genitourinary System _____

10. Diseases of the Respiratory System _____

Chapters of the Tabular List of Diseases and Injuries

The Tabular contains the following chapters.

Chapter 1—Certain Infectious and Parasitic Diseases (Code Range A00–B99)

This chapter includes diseases generally recognized as communicable or transmissible.

EXAMPLE: Using the Tabular section of your ICD-10-CM book, locate the start of chapter 1. Here you will find the code listing for infectious and parasitic diseases. Reference the following codes to familiarize yourself with this chapter.

```
Diagnostic Code        Diagnostic Description
A01.00                 Typhoid fever, unspecified
A06.0                  Acute amebic dysentery
A59.09                 Other urogenital trichomoniasis
B36.2                  White piedra
B86                    Scabies
```

Chapter 2—Neoplasms (Code Range C00–D49)

This chapter contains code assignments for malignant, benign, carcinoma in situ, and neoplasms of uncertain and unspecified behavior.

EXAMPLE: Using the Tabular section of your ICD-10-CM book, locate the start of chapter 2. Here you will find the code listing for neoplasms. Reference the following codes to familiarize yourself with this chapter.

```
Diagnostic Code        Diagnostic Description
C02.4                  Malignant neoplasm of lingual tonsil
C46.9                  Kaposi's sarcoma, unspecified
C94.02                 Acute erythoid leukemia, not in remission
D37.1                  Neoplasm of uncertain behavior of stomach
D38.4                  Neoplasm of uncertain behavior of thymus
```

Chapter 3—Diseases of the Blood and Blood-Forming Organs and Certain Disorders Involving the Immune Mechanism (Code Range D50–D89)

Contained within this chapter are:

- Types of anemias.
- Coagulation defects.
- Hemorrhagic conditions.
- Diseases of the white blood cells and other components of the blood.
- Some diseases of the spleen and lymphatic system.

EXAMPLE: Using the Tabular section of your ICD-10-CM book, locate the start of chapter 3. Here you will find the code listing for diseases of the blood and blood-forming organs. Reference the following codes to familiarize yourself with this chapter.

```
Diagnostic Code        Diagnostic Description
D56.0                  Alpha thalassemia
D67                    Hereditary factor IX deficiency
D73.0                  Hyposplenism
D73.4                  Cyst of spleen
D86.0                  Sarcoidosis of lung
```

Chapter 4—Endocrine, Nutritional, and Metabolic Diseases (Code range E00–E90)

In this chapter are:

- Disorders and diseases of the thyroid and other endocrine glands.
- Nutritional deficiencies.
- Metabolic disorders.
- Disorders of the immune mechanism and immunity deficiencies.

EXAMPLE: Using the Tabular section of your ICD-10-CM book, locate the start of chapter 4. Here you will find the code listing for diseases of the endocrine system, as well as nutritional and metabolic diseases. Reference the following codes to familiarize yourself with this chapter.

Diagnostic Code	Diagnostic Description
E04.0	Nontoxic diffuse goiter
E30.0	Delayed puberty
E55.0	Rickets, active
E61.2	Magnesium deficiency
E67.3	Hypervitaminosis D

Chapter 5—Mental and Behavioral Disorders (Code Range F01–F99)

This chapter contains:

- Mental disorders, including psychotic, personality, neurotic, and nonpsychotic disorders.
- Chemical dependencies, such as alcoholism and drug dependence.
- Mental retardation and developmental disorders.
- Psychopathic symptoms that are not part of an organic illness.

EXAMPLE: Using the Tabular section of your ICD-10-CM book, locate the start of chapter 5. Here you will find the code listing for mental and behavioral disorders. Reference the following codes to familiarize yourself with this chapter.

Diagnostic Code	Diagnostic Description
F01.50	Vascular dementia without behavioral disturbance
F20.0	Paranoid schizophrenia
F41.9	Anxiety disorder
F60.6	Avoidant personality disorder
F84.0	Autistic disorder

Chapter 6—Diseases of the Nervous System (Code Range G00–G99)

This chapter contains diseases of the central and peripheral nervous systems that include the brain, spinal cord, meninges, and nerves.

EXAMPLE: Using the Tabular section of your ICD-10-CM book, locate the start of chapter 6. Here you will find the code listing for diseases of the nervous system. Reference the following codes to familiarize yourself with this chapter.

Diagnostic Code	Diagnostic Description
G00.0	Hemophilus meningitis
G35	Multiple sclerosis
G43.011	Migraine without aura, intractable, with status migrainosus
G80.2	Spastic hemiplegic cerebral palsy
G92	Toxic encephalopathy

Chapter 7—Diseases of the Eye and Adnexa (Code Range H00–H59)

This chapter includes diseases of the eye and adnexa.

EXAMPLE: Using the Tabular section of your ICD-10-CM book, locate the start of chapter 7. Here you will find the code listing for diseases of the eye and adnexa. Reference the following codes to familiarize yourself with this chapter.

```
Diagnostic Code        Diagnostic Description
H04.131                Lacrimal cyst right lacrimal gland
H11.151                Pinguecula, right eye
H16.149                Punctate keratitis, unspecified eye
H17.9                  Unspecified corneal scar and opacity
H27.00                 Aphakia, unspecified eye
```

Chapter 8—Diseases of the Ear and Mastoid Process (Code Range H60–H95)

This chapter includes diseases of the ear and mastoid process.

EXAMPLE: Using the Tabular section of your ICD-10-CM book, locate the start of chapter 8. Here you will find the code listing for diseases of the ear and mastoid process. Reference the following codes to familiarize yourself with this chapter.

```
Diagnostic Code        Diagnostic Description
H61.21                 Impacted cerumen, right ear
H65.22                 Chronic serous otitis media, left ear
H81.311                Aural vertigo, right ear
H83.02                 Labyrinthitis, left ear
H92.09                 Otalgia, unspecified ear
```

Chapter 9—Diseases of the Circulatory System (Code Range I00–I99)

The circulatory system includes the heart, arteries, veins, and lymphatic system. Therefore, this chapter contains:

- Cardiac disorders.

- Arterial, venous, and some lymphatic diseases.

EXAMPLE: Using the Tabular section of your ICD-10-CM book, locate the start of chapter 9. Here you will find the code listing for diseases of the heart, arteries, arterioles, capillaries, veins, and lymphatic system. Reference the following codes to familiarize yourself with this chapter.

```
Diagnostic Code        Diagnostic Description
I05.0                  Rheumatic mitral stenosis
I38                    Endocarditis, valve unspecified
I51.0                  Cardiac septal defect, acquired
I82.0                  Budd-Chiari syndrome
I89.1                  Lymphangitis
```

Chapter 10—Diseases of the Respiratory System (Code Range J00–J99)

In this chapter are diseases of the:

- Pharynx.

- Larynx.

- Trachea.

- Bronchus.

- Vocal cords.

- Sinuses.

- Nose.

- Tonsils and adenoids.

- Parts of the lung.

  EXAMPLE: Using the Tabular section of your ICD-10-CM book, locate the start of chapter 10. Here you will find the code listing for diseases of the respiratory system. Reference the following codes to familiarize yourself with this chapter.

Diagnostic Code	Diagnostic Description
J12.89	Other viral pneumonia
J35.1	Hypertrophy of tonsils
J43.1	Panlobular emphysema
J86.0	Pyothorax with fistula
J94.0	Chylous effusion

Chapter 11—Diseases of the Digestive System (Code Range K00–K94)

This chapter deals with diseases of the:

- Oral cavity.

- Salivary glands.

- Jaws.

- Esophagus.

- Stomach.

- Duodenum.

- Appendix.

- Abdominal cavity.

- Small and large intestines.

- Peritoneum.

- Anus.

- Liver.

- Gallbladder.

- Biliary tract.

- Pancreas.

  EXAMPLE: Using the Tabular section of your ICD-10-CM book, locate the start of chapter 11. Here you will find the code listing for diseases of the digestive system. Reference the following codes to familiarize yourself with this chapter.

Diagnostic Code	Diagnostic Description
K11.9	Disease of salivary gland, unspecified
K22.0	Achalasis of cardia
K59.00	Constipation, unspecified
K65.0	Generalized (acute) peritonitis
K81.0	Acute cholecystitis

Chapter 12—Diseases of the Skin and Subcutaneous Tissue (Code Range L00–L99)

This chapter includes:

- Inflammatory and infectious conditions of the skin and subcutaneous tissue.

- Diseases of the nail, hair and hair follicles, sweat, and sebaceous glands.

  EXAMPLE: Using the Tabular section of your ICD-10-CM book, locate the start of chapter 12. Here you will find the code listing for diseases of the subcutaneous tissue and skin. Reference the following codes to familiarize yourself with this chapter.

Diagnostic Code	Diagnostic Description
L03.012	Cellulitis of left finger
L56.0	Drug phototoxic response
L85.0	Acquired ichthyosis
L89.514	Pressure ulcer of right ankle, stage IV
L94.1	Linear scleroderma

Chapter 13—Diseases of the Musculoskeletal System and Connective Tissue (Code Range M00–M99)

This chapter includes diseases of the:

- Bones.

- Joints.

- Bursa.

- Muscles.

- Ligaments.

- Tendons.

- Soft tissues.

  EXAMPLE: Using the Tabular section of your ICD-9-CM book, locate the start of chapter 13. Here you will find the code listing for diseases of the musculoskeletal system and connective tissue. Reference the following codes to familiarize yourself with this chapter.

Diagnostic Code	Diagnostic Description
M06.9	Rheumatoid arthritis, unspecified
M21.531	Acquired clawfoot, right foot
M24.232	Disorder of ligament, left wrist
M24.569	Contracture, unspecified knee
M91.0	Juvenile osteochondrosis of pelvis

Chapter 14—Diseases of the Genitourinary System (Code Range N00–N99)

Coded from this chapter are diseases of the:

- Kidney.

- Ureter.

- Urinary bladder.

- Urethra.

- Male genital organs.

- Male and female breast, and female genital organs (not related to pregnancy, childbirth, and the postpartum period).

    EXAMPLE: Using the Tabular section of your ICD-10-CM book, locate the start of chapter 14. Here you will find the code listing for diseases of the genitourinary system. Reference the following codes to familiarize yourself with this chapter.

Diagnostic Code	Diagnostic Description
N17.0	Acute renal failure with tubular necrosis
N34.1	Nonspecific urethritis
N48.1	Balanitis
N75.0	Cyst of Bartholin's gland
N89.0	Mild vaginal dysplasia

Chapter 15—Pregnancy, Childbirth, and the Puerperium (Code Range O00–O9A)

This chapter includes:

- Ectopic and molar pregnancies.

- Spontaneous abortions.

- Legally and illegally induced abortions.

- Complications of pregnancy, abortions, labor and delivery, and the postpartum period.

    EXAMPLE: Using the Tabular section of your ICD-10-CM book, locate the start of chapter 15. Here you will find the code listing for complications of pregnancy, childbirth, and the puerperium. Reference the following codes to familiarize yourself with this chapter.

Diagnostic Code	Diagnostic Description
O02.9	Abnormal product of conception, unspecified
O23.02	Infections of kidney in pregnancy, second trimester
O92.4	Hypogalactia
O99.011	Anemia complicating pregnancy, first trimester
O9A.53	Psychological abuse complicating the puerperium

Chapter 16—Certain Conditions Originating in the Perinatal Period (Code Range P00–P96)

This chapter includes conditions that have their origin in the perinatal period, a period of time before birth through the first 28 days after birth.

    EXAMPLE: Using the Tabular section of your ICD-10-CM book, locate the start of chapter 16. Here you will find the code listing for conditions originating in the perinatal period. Reference the following codes to familiarize yourself with this chapter.

Diagnostic Code	Diagnostic Description
P03.82	Meconium passage during delivery
P15.5	Birth injury to external genitalia
P28.3	Primary sleep apnea of newborn
P76.0	Meconium plug syndrome
P93.0	Grey baby syndrome

Chapter 17—Congenital Malformations, Deformations, and Chromosomal Abnormalities (Code Range Q00–Q99)

This chapter contains any congenital anomaly or malformation regardless of the body system involved. A congenital anomaly is an anomaly present at or existing from the time of birth.

> **EXAMPLE:** Using the Tabular section of your ICD-10-CM book, locate the start of chapter 17. Here you will find the code listing for congenital anomalies. Reference the following codes to familiarize yourself with this chapter.

Diagnostic Code	Diagnostic Description
Q01.0	Frontal encephalocele
Q06.0	Amyelia
Q21.3	Tetralogy of Fallot
Q36.0	Cleft lip, bilateral
Q52.0	Congenital absence of vagina

Chapter 18—Symptoms, Signs, and Abnormal Clinical and Laboratory Findings, Not Elsewhere Classified (Code Range R00–R99)

This chapter includes symptoms, signs, abnormal results of laboratory tests and investigative procedures, as well as ill-defined conditions.

> **EXAMPLE:** Using the Tabular section of your ICD-10-CM book, locate the start of chapter 18. Here you will find the code listing for symptoms, signs, and ill defined conditions. Reference the following codes to familiarize yourself with this chapter.

Diagnostic Code	Diagnostic Description
R10.0	Acute abdomen
R25.0	Abnormal head movements
R43.0	Anosmia
R57.0	Cardiogenic shock
R94.2	Abnormal results of pulmonary function studies

Chapter 19—Injury and Poisoning and Certain Other Consequences of External Causes (Code Range S00–T98)

This chapter includes:

- Fractures, dislocations, sprains, and strains of joints and muscles.
- Intracranial injuries.
- Internal injuries to the chest, abdomen, and pelvis.
- Open wounds.
- Superficial injuries.
- Contusions.
- Burns.
- Poisonings by drugs and by medicinal and biological substances.
- The late effects of previous conditions.

EXAMPLE: Using the Tabular section of your ICD-10-CM book, locate the start of chapter 19. Here you will find the code listing for injuries and poisonings. Reference the following codes to familiarize yourself with this chapter.

Diagnostic Code	Diagnostic Description
S00.211A	Abrasion of right eyelid and periocular area, initial encounter
S09.91xA	Unspecified injury to ear, initial encounter
S68.721A	Partial traumatic transmetacarpal amputation of right hand, initial encounter
S76.212D	Strain of left adductor muscle, fascia and tendon of thigh, subsequent encounter
S81.841A	Puncture wound with foreign body, right lower leg, initial encounter

Chapter 20—External Causes of Morbidity (Code Range V01–Y99)

This chapter includes the classification of environmental events and circumstances as the cause of injury and other adverse effects. These codes are intended to be secondary codes to accompany those from other chapters.

EXAMPLE: Using the Tabular section of your ICD-10-CM book, locate the start of chapter 20. Here you will find the code listings for external causes of morbidity. Reference the following codes to familiarize yourself with this chapter.

Diagnostic Code	Diagnostic Description
V00.131A	Fall from skateboard, initial encounter
Y35.211A	Legal intervention involving injury by tear gas, law enforcement official injured, initial encounter
W00.0xxA	Fall on same level due to ice and snow, initial encounter
W20.1xxA	Struck by object due to collapse of building, initial encounter
W17.0xxA	Fall into well, initial encounter

Chapter 21—Factors Influencing Health Status and Contact with Health Services (Z00–Z99)

This chapter codes reasons for encounters when a person may or may not be sick and when some circumstance or problem influences the person's health status but is not in itself a current illness or injury.

EXAMPLE: Using the Tabular section of your ICD-10-CM book, locate the start of chapter 21. Here you will find the code listing for factors influencing health status and contact with health services. Reference the following codes to familiarize yourself with this chapter.

Diagnostic Code	Diagnostic Description
Z00.00	Encounter for general adult medical examination without abnormal findings
Z01.110	Encounter for hearing examination following failed hearing screening
Z04.42	Encounter for examination and observation following alleged child rape
Z17.0	Estrogen receptor positive status
Z20.3	Contact with and (suspected) exposure to rabies

Internet Links

The National Center for Health Statistics (NCHS) maintains information about ICD-10-CM. For a wealth of information, explore *www.cdc.gov/nchs/about/otheract/icd9/abticd10.htm*

Summary

- ICD-10-CM consists of an Index to Diseases and Injuries and a Tabular Listing of Diseases and Injuries.
- The Tabular List of Diseases and Injuries is divided into 21 chapters.
- The Index to Diseases and Injuries contains a Neoplasm Table and Table of Drugs and Chemicals.

Chapter Review

For each of the following ICD-10-CM Tabular chapters, list the related code range.

Chapter	Code Range
1. Neoplasms	_____
2. Endocrine, Nutritional, and Metabolic Diseases	_____
3. Diseases of the Circulatory System	_____
4. Diseases of the Digestive System	_____
5. Congenital Malformations, Deformations, and Chromosomal Abnormalities	_____
6. Diseases of the Nervous System	_____
7. External Causes of Morbidity	_____
8. Diseases of the Skin and Subcutaneous Tissue	_____
9. Pregnancy, Childbirth, and the Puerperium	_____
10. Mental and Behavioral Disorders	_____
11. Certain Infectious and Parasitic Diseases	_____
12. Diseases of the Blood and Blood-Forming Organs and Certain Disorders Involving the Immune Mechanism	_____
13. Diseases of the Eye and Adnexa	_____
14. Diseases of the Ear and Mastoid Process	_____
15. Diseases of the Respiratory System	_____
16. Diseases of the Musculoskeletal System and Connective Tissue	_____
17. Diseases of the Genitourinary System	_____
18. Certain Conditions Originating in the Perinatal Period	_____
19. Symptoms, Signs, and Abnormal Clinical and Laboratory Findings	_____
20. Injury, Poisoning, and Certain Other Consequences of External Causes	_____

CHAPTER 3

ICD-10-CM Coding Conventions

Chapter Outline

Objectives

Key Terms

Introduction

Convention Types

Coding Guidelines

Comparing ICD-9-CM to ICD-10-CM

Summary

Chapter Review

Objectives

At the conclusion of this chapter, the learner should be able to:

1. Describe the conventions used in ICD-10-CM.
2. Differentiate among abbreviations, symbols, and instructional notes.
3. Identify the difference between type 1 and type 2 Excludes notes.
4. Define the abbreviations NOS and NEC.

Key Terms

brackets

Code Also

code first

colon

conventions

Excludes

Excludes 1

Excludes 2

In diseases classified elsewhere

Includes

instructional notes

NEC (not elsewhere classified)

nonessential modifiers

NOS (not otherwise specified)

parentheses

point dash

See

See also

Use additional code

Reminder

As you work through this chapter, you will need to have a copy of the ICD-10-CM coding book to reference.

Introduction

This chapter highlights concepts that must be followed for coding to be accurate. Appendix A, Section 1, A, of your textbook also lists the ICD-10-CM Official Guidelines for Coding and Reporting that are relevant to this chapter.

Stop! When you see a stop sign while driving, you must stop and then proceed with caution. Similarly, ICD-10-CM uses the equivalent of "traffic signs" to guide coders: instructional notes, punctuation marks, abbreviations, and symbols, all of which are called **conventions**. To code accurately, a coder must understand what these conventions mean. You must follow these "traffic signs" to ensure accurate coding.

Convention Types

Conventions are used in both the Tabular List and the Alphabetic Index of ICD-10-CM. Four types of conventions are used in ICD-10-CM to provide guidance to the coder:

- Instructional notes
- Punctuation marks
- Abbreviations
- Symbols

Some of the conventions are used in one volume and not in the other; other conventions are used in both the Tabular and Alphabetic volumes.

Instructional Notes

Instructional notes appear in both the Tabular List and Alphabetic Index of ICD-10-CM.

Includes Note

The **Includes** note is used to define and/or give examples of the content of a category of ICD-10-CM or of a block of category codes.

The location of the Includes note determines the category or block of category codes that the note governs.

When an Includes note appears in the Tabular List immediately *under a three-digit code title*, the note applies to the three-digit category. The word *Includes* is followed by examples of diagnostic terms that are included in that category.

> **EXAMPLE:** The category code A02, Other salmonella infections, appears as follows in ICD-10-CM:

```
A02 Other salmonella infections
Includes:    infection or foodborne intoxication due to any Salmonella species
                    other than S. typhi and S. paratyphi
```

The Includes note signifies that infections or foodborne intoxication due to any Salmonella species other than S. *typhi* and S. *paratyphi* are included in this category.

When the Includes note appears *after the start of a chapter or block title*, the note governs the entire chapter or block of category codes.

> **EXAMPLE:** The block of category codes A15–A19, Tuberculosis, appears as follows in the Tabular List of ICD-10-CM:

```
TUBERCULOSIS (A15-A19)
Includes:    infections due to Mycobacterium tuberculosis and
                Mycobacterium bovis
Excludes:    congenital tuberculosis (P37.0)
             pneumoconiosis associated with tuberculosis, any type in
                A15 (J65)
             sequelae of tuberculosis (B90.-)
             silicotuberculosis (J65)
```

When the Includes note appears at this level, the block of category codes is (as below) governed by the note. Therefore, in this example, code block A15–A19 is governed by the notes that follow the block title.

At times the word *Includes* is not listed before the list of terms in the code; just the diagnostic terms are listed. This is explained by the coding guideline on the right.

ICD-10-CM Official Guidelines

Inclusion terms

List of terms is included under some codes. These terms are the conditions for which that code number is to be used. The terms may be synonyms of the code title, or, in the case of "other specified" codes, the terms are a list of the various conditions assigned to the code. The inclusion terms are not necessarily exhaustive. Additional terms found only in the Index may also be assigned to a code.

Exercise 3.1 – Identifying Inclusion Notes

For each of the following items, list the diagnoses that are included as described by the inclusion note. The first one is completed for you.

1. category code A06   <u>infection due to *Entamoeba histolytica*</u>

2. code A04.9   _____

3. code N18.6   _____

4. category code R51   _____

5. code R48.8   _____

6. category code F30   _____

Excludes Instructional Notes

The **Excludes** notes are used to signify that the conditions listed are not assigned to the category or block of category codes. There are two types of Excludes notes in ICD-10-CM.

Excludes 1 Note

The **Excludes 1** note is easy to understand and apply. This note means that the diagnostic terms listed are *not* coded to the category or subcategory; therefore, the two conditions are mutually exclusive. The Official Coding Guidelines for Coding and Reporting define the Excludes 1 note as shown on the right.

Category I00 is an example of the use of the Excludes 1 note. The following appears for code I00.

> **ICD-10-CM Official Guidelines**
>
> *Excludes 1*
>
> *A type 1 Excludes note is a pure excludes note. It means "NOT CODED HERE!" An Excludes 1 note indicates that the code excluded should never be used at the same time as the code above the Excludes 1 note. An Excludes 1 is used when two conditions cannot occur together, such as a congenital form versus an acquired form of the same condition.*

EXAMPLE:

```
I00 Rheumatic fever without heart involvement
Includes:   arthritis, rheumatic, acute or subacute
Excludes 1: rheumatic fever with heart involvement (I01.0-I01.9)
```

Reading the category title and the diagnostic description following the Excludes 1 note, you can see that the two are mutually exclusive because rheumatic fever would occur with or without heart involvement.

Excludes 2 Note

The **Excludes 2** note is used to signify that the diagnostic terms listed after the note are *not* part of the condition(s) represented by the code or code block. This note also indicates that at times the assignment of more than one code should occur to fully represent the diagnostic statement being coded and to accurately record the patient's condition.

The Official Coding Guidelines define the Excludes 2 note as shown on the right.

> **ICD-10-CM Official Guidelines**
>
> *Excludes 2*
>
> *A type 2 Excludes note represents "Not included here." An Excludes 2 note indicates that the condition excluded is not part of the condition represented by the code, but a patient may have both conditions at the same time. When an Excludes 2 note appears under a code, it is acceptable to use both the code and the excluded code together, when appropriate.*

An example of the use of the Excludes 2 note appears for code C02.0. The code appears as follows in ICD-10-CM.

EXAMPLE:

```
C02.0 Malignant neoplasm of dorsal surface of tongue
      Malignant neoplasm of anterior two-thirds of tongue, dorsal surface
      Excludes 2: malignant neoplasm of dorsal surface of base of tongue (C01)
```

The Excludes 2 note means that code C02.0 does not code a malignant neoplasm of the dorsal surface of base of tongue. Code C01 is the appropriate code. Both code C02.0, malignant neoplasm of dorsal surface of tongue, and code C01, malignant neoplasm of base of tongue, would be selected if the patient had a neoplasm in both sites.

See Instructional Note

The **See** note is used in the Alphabetical Index of ICD-10-CM and instructs the coder to cross-reference the term or diagnosis that follows the notation.

EXAMPLE: In the Alphabetic Index the following appears for the entry of Thromboarteritis:

EXAMPLE:

```
Thromboarteritis—see Arteritis
```

This notation instructs the coder to cross-reference to the term Arteritis in the Alphabetic Index to obtain the correct code.

See Also Instructional Note

Another cross-reference note used in ICD-10-CM, the **See Also** note refers the coder to another location in the alphabetic index when the initial listing does not contain all the necessary information to accurately select a code.

EXAMPLE: When coding a diagnosis of altitude hypoxia, the coder first references the term *hypoxia* in the Alphabetic Index. Here the coder finds the following:

```
Hypoxia (see also Anoxia) R09.01
            cerebral, during a procedure NEC G97.81
                postprocedural NEC G97.82
            intrauterine P84
            myocardial—see Insufficiency, coronary
            newborn P84
            sleep related G47.34
```

Since the modifying term *altitude* does not appear in the entries under the main term of *hypoxia*, the coder references the term *anoxia* in the Alphabetic Index. The following appears at the start of the entry for Anoxia:

```
Anoxia (pathological) R09.01
            altitude T70.20
            cerebral G93.1
             complicating
                anesthesia (general) (local) or other sedation T88.59
                in labor and delivery O74.3
```

Since the modifying term *altitude* appears, the coder selects T70.20 for the diagnostic statement of altitude hypoxia.

Use Additional Code and Code First Instructional Notes

The Use Additional Code and the Code First notes appear in the Tabular section of ICD-10-CM and must always be followed. These notes are used to signal that, when there is an underlying etiology and multiple body system manifestation due the underlying etiology, two codes are needed. The **Use Additional Code** note instructs the coder to use an additional code to identify the manifestation that is present. The **Code First** note instructs the coder to select a code to represent the etiology that caused the manifestation. The two codes must appear in the correct order. The code that represents the etiology is sequenced first, followed by the code that represents the manifestation.

EXAMPLE: In coding the diagnostic statement of encephalitis in poliovirus, the coder references first the Alphabetic Index and then the Tabular List. In the Tabular List, the coder finds the following entry for the start of G05—Encephalitis, myelitis and encephalomyelitis in diseases classified elsewhere.

```
G05 Encephalitis, myelitis and encephalomyelitis in diseases classified elsewhere
            Code first underlying disease, such as:
                poliovirus (A80.-)
                suppurative otitis media (H66.01–H66.4)
                trichinellosis (B75)
```

The phrase "Code first underlying disease" signals to the coder that two codes are needed: code G05 and a code for the poliovirus from the A80.– subcategory, with the A80.– code listed first.

In addition to the notes found in the Tabular, the coding for an etiology and manifestation has a unique Alphabetic entry structure. This is explained by the Official Coding Guideline on the right.

In Diseases Classified Elsewhere: Note

A third note applies to the etiology/manifestation conventions, **In Diseases Classified Elsewhere**. The Official Coding Guidelines for Coding and Reporting explain the use of this note as follows:

> ### ICD-10-CM Official Guidelines
>
> *In addition to the notes in the Tabular, these conditions also have a specific Index entry structure. In the Index both conditions are listed together with the etiology code first followed by the manifestation codes in brackets. The code in brackets is always to be sequenced second.*

> ### ICD-10-CM Official Guidelines
>
> *In most cases the manifestation codes will have in the code title, "in diseases classified elsewhere." Codes with this title are a component of the etiology/manifestation convention. The code title indicates that it is a manifestation code. "In diseases classified elsewhere" codes are never permitted to be used as first listed or principal diagnosis codes. They must be used in conjunction with an underlying condition code and they must be listed following the underlying condition. See category F02, Dementia in other diseases classified elsewhere, for an example of this convention. There are manifestation codes that do not have "in diseases classified elsewhere" in the title. For such codes a "use additional code" note will still be present and the rules for sequencing apply.*

Code Also Instructional Note

The **Code Also** note is used in ICD-10-CM to instruct the coder that two codes may be needed to fully code a diagnostic phrase. The note, however, does not provide sequencing direction. Code F80.4 provides an example of the Code Also note:

```
F80.4 Speech and language development delay due to hearing loss
      Code also type of hearing loss (H90.-, H91.-)
```

Therefore, when both codes are assigned, the coder must determine the proper sequencing of the codes based on the case.

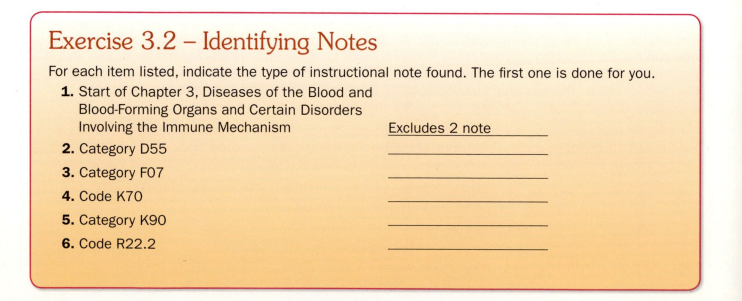

Exercise 3.2 – Identifying Notes

For each item listed, indicate the type of instructional note found. The first one is done for you.

1. Start of Chapter 3, Diseases of the Blood and Blood-Forming Organs and Certain Disorders Involving the Immune Mechanism   Excludes 2 note _____

2. Category D55   _____

3. Category F07   _____

4. Code K70   _____

5. Category K90   _____

6. Code R22.2   _____

Punctuation Marks

Coders must understand the meaning of the punctuation marks used in the code book as ICD-10-CM defines them. Their definitions are unique to the coding system.

Parentheses: ( )

Parentheses are used in both the Tabular List and Alphabetic Index. Parentheses are used around terms providing additional information about the main diagnostic term. The terms found within the parentheses are referred to as **nonessential modifiers**. The terms do not affect the code assignment for the diagnostic statement being coded.

> **EXAMPLE:** In the Alphabetical Index, the term *dermatitis* is found as follows at the start of the entry:

```
Dermatitis (eczematous) L30.9
   ab igne L59.0
   acarine B88.0
   actinic (due to sun) L57.8
```

The parentheses are used around the nonessential modifying term of *eczematous*. If a coder is coding dermatitis or eczematous dermatitis, then code L30.9 is assigned.

Brackets: [ ]

Brackets are used in the Tabular Listing and in the Alphabetic Index.

In the Tabular List, the brackets enclose synonyms, alternative wording, abbreviations, or explanatory phrases. The presence or absence of the phrase in the bracket does not affect code assignment.

> **EXAMPLE:** Category Code B01 appears in the Tabular List as follows:

```
B01 Varicella [chickenpox]
```

Chickenpox is enclosed in brackets to provide an alternative word for *varicella*. Therefore this category would be used to code the diagnoses chickenpox and varicella. Brackets are used in the Index to identify manifestation codes.

Colon: :

The **colon** is used in the Tabular listing after a term that is modified by one or more of the terms following the colon. The term to the left of the colon must be modified by a term to the right to be included in the code being considered.

> **EXAMPLE:** Code D77 appears in the Tabular as follows:

```
D77 Other disorders of blood and blood-forming organs in diseases classified
    elsewhere
            Code first underlying disease, such as:
                amyloidosis (E85.-)
                congenital early syphilis (A50.0)
                echinococcosis (B67.0-B67.9)
                malaria (B50.0-B54)
                schistosomiasis [bilharziasis] (B65.0-B65.9)
                vitamin C deficiency (E54)
    Excludes 1: rupture of spleen due to Plasmodium vivax malaria (B51.0)
                splenitis, splenomegaly in:
                late syphilis (A52.79)
                tuberculosis (A18.65)
```

The use of the colon after the phrase "splenitis, splenomegaly in" means that the phrase must be followed by "late syphilis" or "tuberculosis." If the diagnosis does not specify the terms to the right of the colon, the diagnosis is not coded to the code listed.

Abbreviations

Two abbreviations are consistently used in ICD-10-CM, NEC and NOS.

NEC: Not Elsewhere Classifiable

NEC means **not elsewhere classifiable**. This abbreviation is used in both the Tabular List and Alphabetic Index.

- In the Alphabetic Index, NEC represents "other specified" when a specific code is not available for a condition the Index directs the coder to the "other specified" code in the Tabular.

- In the Tabular List, NEC still means "not elsewhere classifiable" and can be read as "other specified." When a specific code is not available in the Tabular List for the condition being coded, the NEC entry under a code identifies it as the "other specified:" code.

NOS: Not Otherwise Specified

NOS is the abbreviation for **not otherwise specified**. The note is used in the Tabular List and interpreted to mean "unspecified." NOS codes are not specific and should be used only after the coder has clarified with the physician that a more specific diagnosis is not available. The coder should also reference the medical record to see if it contains documentation that can further specify the diagnosis.

EXAMPLE: The physician makes a diagnosis of sinusitis, orders a series of sinus X-rays, and records sinusitis on the coding form. The coder then references sinusitis in the alphabetical index and Tabular and records code J32.9. However, at the time of coding, the X-ray is complete and records that frontal sinusitis is present.

The coder should then select code J32.1, which identifies frontal sinusitis. If there was no further documentation or findings—in this case, no X-rays taken—to expand on the original diagnosis of sinusitis, then code J32.9 is correct. The entry in the Tabular appears as follows:

```
J32.9 Chronic Sinusitis, unspecified
        Sinusitis (chronic) NOS
```

The abbreviation *NOS* should signal to the coder to try to clarify the diagnosis more specifically prior to assigning the code.

Symbols

Symbols are used in ICD-10-CM to give direction to the coder.

Point Dash: . –

The **point dash** symbol (. –) tells the coder that the code contains a list of options at a level of specificity past the three-character category.

EXAMPLE: In the Tabular List, at the start of the code block for mycoses, the following appears:

```
MYCOSES (B35-B49)
Excludes 2: hypersensitivity pneumonitis due to organic dust (J67.-)
             Mycosis fungoides (C84.0-)
```

The point dash after J67 and the .0– after code C84 indicate that the codes are defined to a level of specificity higher than the three-character and four-character levels.

Coding Guidelines

The following ICD-10-CM Official Guidelines for Coding and Reporting apply to the conventions discussed in this chapter.

ICD-10-CM Official Guidelines

Section I. Conventions, general coding guidelines and chapter specific guidelines

The conventions, general guidelines and chapter-specific guidelines are applicable to all health care settings unless otherwise indicated. The conventions and instructions of the classification take precedence over guidelines.

A. Conventions for the ICD-10-CM The conventions for the ICD-10-CM are the general rules for use of the classification independent of the guidelines. These conventions are incorporated with the Index and Tabular of ICD-10-CM as instructional notes.

1. The Alphabetic Index and Tabular List

The ICD-10-CM is divided into the Index, an alphabetical list of terms and their corresponding code, and the Tabular List, a chronological list of codes divided into chapters based on body system or condition. The Index is divided into two parts, the Index to Diseases and Injury, and the Index to External Causes of Injury. Within the Index of Diseases and Injury there is a Neoplasm Table and a Table of Drugs and Chemicals.

See Section I.C2. General guidelines

See Section I.C.19. Adverse effects, poisoning, underdosing and toxic effects

2. Format and Structure:

The ICD-10-CM Tabular List contains categories, subcategories and codes.

Characters for categories, subcategories and codes may be either a letter or a number. All categories are 3 characters. A three-character category that has no further subdivision is equivalent to a code. Subcategories are either 4 or 5 characters. Codes may be 4, 5, 6 or 7 characters. That is, each level of subdivision after a category is a subcategory. The final level of subdivision is a code. All codes in the Tabular List of the official version of the ICD-10-CM are in bold. Codes that have applicable 7th characters are still referred to as codes, not subcategories. A code that has an applicable 7th character is considered invalid without the 7th character.

The ICD-10-CM uses an indented format for ease in reference

3. Use of codes for reporting purposes

For reporting purposes only codes are permissible, not categories or subcategories, and any applicable 7th character is required.

4. Placeholder character

The ICD-10-CM utilizes a placeholder character "X". The "X" is used as a 5th character placeholder at certain 6 character codes to allow for future expansion. An example of this is at the poisoning, adverse effect and underdosing codes, categories T36–T50. Where a placeholder exists, the X must be used in order for the code to be considered a valid code.

5. 7th Characters

Certain ICD-10-CM categories have applicable 7th characters. The applicable 7th character is required for all codes within the category, or as the notes in the Tabular List instruct. The 7th character must always be the 7th character in the data field. If a code that requires a 7th character is not 6 characters, a placeholder X must be used to fill in the empty characters.

6. Abbreviations

a. Index abbreviations

NEC "Not elsewhere classifiable"

This abbreviation in the Index represents "other specified". When a specific code is not available for a condition the Index directs the coder to the "other specified" code in the Tabular.

(continued)

b. Tabular abbreviations

NEC "Not elsewhere classifiable"

This abbreviation in the Tabular represents "other specified". When a specific code is not available for a condition the Tabular includes an NEC entry under a code to identify the code as the "other specified" code.

NOS "Not otherwise specified"

This abbreviation is the equivalent of unspecified.

7. Punctuation

[ ] Brackets are used in the tabular list to enclose synonyms, alternative wording or explanatory phrases. Brackets are used in the Index to identify manifestation codes.

( ) Parentheses are used in both the Index and Tabular to enclose supplementary words that may be present or absent in the statement of a disease or procedure without affecting the code number to which it is assigned. The terms within the parentheses are referred to as nonessential modifiers.

: Colons are used in the Tabular List after an incomplete term which needs one or more of the modifiers following the colon to make it assignable to a given category.

8. Use of "and"

When the term "and" is used in a narrative statement it represents and/or.

9. Other and Unspecified codes

a. "Other" codes

Codes titled "other" or "other specified" are for use when the information in the medical record provides detail for which a specific code does not exist. Index entries with NEC in the line designate "other" codes in the Tabular. These Index entries represent specific disease entities for which no specific code exists so the term is included within an "other" code.

b. "Unspecified" codes

Codes (usually a code with a 4th digit 9 or 5th digit 0 for diagnosis codes) titled "unspecified" are for use when the information in the medical record is insufficient to assign a more specific code. For those categories for which an unspecified code is not provided, the "other specified" code may represent both other and unspecified.

10. Includes Notes

This note appears immediately under a three-digit code title to further define, or give examples of, the content of the category.

11. Inclusion terms

List of terms is included under some codes. These terms are the conditions for which that code number is to be used. The terms may be synonyms of the code title, or, in the case of "other specified" codes, the terms are a list of the various conditions assigned to that code. The inclusion terms are not necessarily exhaustive. Additional terms found only in the Index may also be assigned to a code.

12. Excludes Notes

The ICD-10-CM has two types of excludes notes. Each type of note has a different definition for use but they are all similar in that they indicate that codes excluded from each other are independent of each other.

a. Excludes 1

A type 1 Excludes note is a pure excludes note. It means "NOT CODED HERE!" An Excludes 1 note indicates that the code excluded should never be used at the same time as the code above the Excludes 1 note. An Excludes 1 is used when two conditions cannot occur together, such as a congenital form versus an acquired form of the same condition.

b. Excludes 2

A type 2 excludes note represents "Not included here". An Excludes 2 note indicates that the condition excluded is not part of the condition represented by the code, but a patient may have both conditions at the same time. When an Excludes 2 note appears under a code, it is acceptable to use both the code and the excluded code together, when appropriate.

13. Etiology/manifestation convention ("code first", "use additional code" and "in diseases classified elsewhere" notes)
Certain conditions have both an underlying etiology and multiple body system manifestations due to the underlying etiology. For such conditions, the ICD-10-CM has a coding convention that requires the underlying condition be sequenced first followed by the manifestation. Wherever such a combination exists, there is a "use additional code" note at the etiology code, and a "code first" note at the manifestation code. These instructional notes indicate the proper sequencing order of the codes, etiology followed by manifestation.

In most cases the manifestation codes will have in the code title, "in diseases classified elsewhere." Codes with this title are a component of the etiology/manifestation convention. The code title indicates that it is a manifestation code. "In diseases classified elsewhere" codes are never permitted to be used as first listed or principal diagnosis codes. They must be used in conjunction with an underlying condition code and they must be listed following the underlying condition. See category F02, Dementia in other diseases classified elsewhere, for an example of this convention.

There are manifestation codes that do not have "in diseases classified elsewhere" in the title. For such codes a "use additional code" note will still be present and the rules for sequencing apply.

In addition to the notes in the Tabular, these conditions also have a specific Index entry structure. In the Index both conditions are listed together with the etiology code first followed by the manifestation codes in brackets. The code in brackets is always to be sequenced second.

An example of the etiology/manifestation convention is dementia in Parkinson's disease. In the index, code G20 is listed first, followed by code F02.80 or F02.81 in brackets. Code G20 presents the underlying etiology, Parkinson's disease, and must be sequenced first, whereas codes F02.80 and F02.81 represent the manifestation of dementia in diseases classified elsewhere, with or without behavioral disturbance.

"Code first" and "Use additional code" notes are also used as sequencing rules in the classification for certain codes that are not part of an etiology/manifestation combination.

See section I.B.7. Multiple coding for a single condition.

14. "And"

The word "and" should be interpreted to mean either "and" or "or" when it appears in a title.

15. "With"

The word "with" in the Alphabetic Index is sequenced immediately following the main term, not in alphabetical order.

16. "See" and "See Also"

The "see" instruction following a main term in the Index indicates that another term should be referenced. It is necessary to go to the main term referenced with the "see" note to locate the correct code.

A "see also" instruction following a main term in the index instructs that there is another main term that may also be referenced that may provide additional index entries that may be useful. It is not necessary to follow the "see also" note when the original main term provides the necessary code.

17. "Code also note"

A "code also" note instructs that two codes may be required to fully describe a condition, but this note does not provide sequencing direction.

18. Default codes

A code listed next to a main term in the ICD-10-CM Index is referred to as a default code. The default code represents that condition that is most commonly associated with the main term, or is the unspecified code for the condition. If a condition is documented in a medical record (for example, appendicitis) without any additional information, such as acute or chronic, the default code should be assigned.

19. Syndromes

Follow the Alphabetic Index guidance when coding syndromes. In the absence of index guidance, assign codes for the documented manifestations of the syndrome.

Comparing ICD-9-CM to ICD-10-CM

Table 3-1 compares the coding conventions used in ICD-9-CM to ICD-10-CM.

Table 3-1 Comparison of Coding Conventions in ICD-9-CM and ICD-10-CM

Convention	Used in ICD-9-CM	Used in ICD-10-CM	Comments
Brackets	Yes	Yes	ICD-9-CM contained squared and italicized brackets; ICD-10-CM contains only one type of bracket.
Code Also	No	Yes	ICD-10-CM uses this convention to instruct coder to add a code.
Code First	Yes	Yes	Both ICD-9-CM and ICD-10-CM contain this convention with the same meaning.
Colon	Yes	Yes	This has same meaning in both ICD-9-CM and ICD-10-CM.
Excludes	Yes	Yes	ICD-9-CM had one type of Excludes note; ICD-10-CM has two types of Excludes notes.
Includes	Yes	Yes	This has same meaning in both ICD-9-CM and ICD-10-CM.
In diseases classified elsewhere	Yes	Yes	This has same meaning in both ICD-9-CM and ICD-10-CM.
Parentheses	Yes	Yes	These have same meaning in both ICD-9-CM and ICD-10-CM.
Point Dash	No	Yes	This has unique meaning in ICD-10-CM.
See	Yes	Yes	This has same meaning in both ICD-9-CM and ICD-10-CM.
See Also	Yes	Yes	This has same meaning in both ICD-9-CM and ICD-10-CM.
Use Additional Code	Yes	Yes	This has same meaning in both ICD-9-CM and ICD-10-CM.

Internet Links

To review information about ICD-10-CM, reference *www.cdc.gov/nchs/icd/icd10cm.htm#10update*

Summary

- ICD-10-CM uses a group of instructional notes, punctuation marks, abbreviations, and symbols to guide coders.
- The Includes notes found in ICD-10-CM give examples of the content of a section of the code book.
- Two types of Excludes notes are found in ICD-10-CM.
- *NEC* means not elsewhere classifiable.
- *NOS* means not otherwise specified.
- Brackets are used to enclose synonyms, alterative wording, or explanatory phrases.
- Parentheses are used to enclose nonessential modifiers.
- Colons are used after an incomplete term to identify one or more modifiers.
- Code First and Use Additional Code notes are used to identify the sequencing of codes.
- Coders should read all instructional notes that appear in the Alphabetic Index and the Tabular List and use them as a guide when selecting codes.

Chapter Review

True/False: Indicate whether each statement is true (T) or false (F).

1. _____ *NEC* means "not elsewhere coded."

2. _____ Terms that appear in parentheses must appear in the diagnostic statement being coded.

3. _____ *NOS* means "not otherwise specified."

4. _____ The placement of an Includes note signifies the section of the code book that the note governs.

5. _____ The See Also notation refers the coder to another location in the Tabular List.

6. _____ At times, two codes are used to code a diagnostic statement.

7. _____ The point dash symbol signifies that a code is not further specified.

8. _____ The abbreviation *NEC* is used only in the Alphabetic Index.

9. _____ A type 2 Excludes note represents Not Coded Here.

10. _____ There are two types of Includes notes in ICD-10-CM.

Short Answer: Briefly respond to the following:

11. Differentiate between the abbreviation NOS and NEC.

12. Explain why coders must reference both the Alphabetic Index and Tabular List.

13. Compare and contrast the uses of the two types of Excludes notes.

14. Give an example of a code that contains an instructional note. List the instructional note.

15. List the purpose of the See instruction.

CHAPTER

4

Steps in Diagnostic Code Selection

Chapter Outline

Objectives
Key Terms
Introduction
ICD-10-CM Documentation Essentials

Steps in Coding
Summary
Chapter Review

Objectives

At the conclusion of this chapter, the learner should be able to:

1. Describe the medical documentation that must be present to select an ICD-10-CM code.
2. Identify the ICD-10-CM Official Guidelines for Coding and Reporting that impact the steps a coder follows when selecting diagnostic codes.
3. Identify and select main terms that are referenced in the Alphabetic Index.
4. Summarize the steps in coding.

Key Terms

granularity   laterality

Introduction

This chapter discusses the location of main terms in the Alphabetic Index of ICD-10-CM and the steps involved in the selection of diagnostic codes using ICD-10-CM.

> **Reminder**
>
> *As you work through this chapter, you will need to have a copy of the ICD-10-CM coding book to reference.*

ICD-10-CM Documentation Essentials

Equally important to understanding the conventions that ICD-10-CM uses to accurately assign codes is having specific written diagnoses and conditions to code. If the diagnoses and conditions are not specifically recorded or if they are recorded in more than more one location in the record, the coder must review the complete record to select all the diagnoses and conditions to be coded. Even if the diagnoses and conditions are located on only one form in the record, coders should still review the whole record to obtain all the relevant information.

- For *inpatient* records, diagnoses are typically recorded on a face sheet.

- In the *outpatient* setting, various forms are used to record the diagnosis and conditions treated.

- In a *physician office*, an encounter form or a problem list is used to record the diagnoses.

When reviewing the record, the coder should note any diagnoses based on findings from procedures or tests that had been ordered and whose results were not available at the time of the patient encounter. The test results could change the diagnosis, and therefore the coder should wait for the results of a test to determine the most accurate diagnosis to code. However, in some settings, such as a physician's office, coders do not wait for all test results. Organizations establish coding policies to address this issue.

Granularity and Laterality

For coders to select accurate codes using ICD-10-CM, medical documentation must be detailed. The increased number of codes in ICD-10-CM, compared to ICD-9-CM, makes for a greater level of detail, known as **granularity**. Because of the increase in the granularity, diagnoses can be recorded and retrieved in a more detailed and efficient manner; thus, the reporting of diagnoses and statistics retrieved will be of greater use to the health-care industry.

However, for the coder to be able to select codes at the highest level of detail, providers must document diseases to the level required by ICD-10-CM.

> **EXAMPLE:** In ICD-10-CM, the codes for a fracture of the femur are differentiated at the fifth-digit level between unspecified fracture of unspecified femur (S72.90), unspecified fracture of right femur (S72.91), and unspecified fracture of left femur (S72.92).

This level of specificity provides **laterality** in code assignment. In other words, for bilateral sites ICD-10-CM indicates the specific site, in this example the right or left femur.

Currently most providers clearly define whether the left or right femur was fractured, but in other cases when ICD-10-CM requires laterality providers will have to be educated. Let's look at the Alphabetic Index (Figure 4-1) and Tabular List (Figure 4-2) entries for bursitis. Note in the Alphabetic Index (Figure 4-1) that the term *bursitis* is further divided by means of many modifying terms. When coding the diagnostic phrase "bursitis of the right hand," the coder references the term *bursitis* and then the modifying term of *hand*. Here the coder sees that code M70.1– appears in the Alphabetic Index. Then, referring to the Tabular List entry (Figure 4-2), the coder notes that the code is further divided into the following codes:

- M70.10– bursitis, unspecified hand

- M70.11– bursitis, right hand

- M70.12– bursitis, left hand

Not until the coder references the Tabular List are the codes differentiated by laterality. After referencing the Tabular List, the coder selects M70.11.

Documentation plays an important role in the coding process. Coders have to query providers for more specific information when it is missing and has an impact on code selection. Increased dialogue between coders and providers is essential.

- - - third degree T23.371
- - second degree T23.279
- - third degree T23.379
Burnett's syndrome E83.52
Burning
- feet syndrome E53.9
- sensation R20.8
- tongue K14.6
Burn-out (state) Z73.0
Burns' disease or osteochondrosis - see Osteochondrosis, juvenile, ulna
Bursa - see condition
Bursitis M71.9
- Achilles - see Tendinitis, Achilles
- adhesive - see Bursitis, specified NEC
- ankle - see Enthesopathy, lower limb, ankle, specified type NEC
- calcaneal - see Enthesopathy, foot, specified type NEC
- collateral ligament, tibial - see Bursitis, tibial collateral
- due to use, overuse, pressure - see also Disorder, soft tissue, due to use, specified type NEC
- - specified NEC - see Disorder, soft tissue, due to use, specified NEC
- Duplay's M75.0
- elbow NEC M70.3-
- - olecranon M70.2-
- finger - see Disorder, soft tissue, due to use, specified type NEC, hand
- foot - see Enthesopathy, foot, specified type NEC
- gonococcal A54.49
- gouty - see Gout, idiopathic
- hand M70.1-
- hip NEC M70.7-
- - trochanteric M70.6-
- infective NEC M71.10
- - abscess - see Abscess, bursa
- - ankle M71.17-
- - elbow M71.12-
- - foot M71.17-
- - hand M71.14-
- - hip M71.15-
- - knee M71.16-
- - multiple sites M71.19
- - shoulder M71.11-
- - specified site NEC M71.18
- - wrist M71.13-
- ischial - see Bursitis, hip
- knee NEC M70.5-
- - prepatellar M70.4-
- occupational NEC - see also Disorder, soft tissue, due to, use
- olecranon - see Bursitis, elbow, olecranon
- pharyngeal J39.1
- popliteal - see Bursitis, knee
- prepatellar M70.4-
- radiohumeral M77.8
- rheumatoid M06.20
- - ankle M06.27-
- - elbow M06.22-
- - foot joint M06.27-
- - hand joint M06.24-
- - hip M06.25-

Figure 4-1a ICD-10-CM Alphabetic Index pages for bursitis.

- - knee M06.26-
- - multiple site M06.29
- - shoulder M06.21-
- - vertebra M06.28
- - wrist M06.23-
- scapulohumeral - see Bursitis, shoulder
- semimembranous muscle (knee) - see Bursitis, knee
- shoulder M75.5-
- - adhesive - see Capsulitis, adhesive
- specified NEC M71.50
- - ankle M71.57-
- - due to use, overuse or pressure - see Disorder, soft tissue, due to, use
- - elbow M71.52-
- - foot M71.57-
- - hand M71.54-
- - hip M71.55-
- - knee M71.56-
- - shoulder - see Bursitis, shoulder
- - specified site NEC M71.58
- - tibial collateral M76.4-
- - wrist M71.53-
- subacromial - see Bursitis, shoulder
- subcoracoid - see Bursitis, shoulder
- subdeltoid - see Bursitis, shoulder
- syphilitic A52.78
- Thornwaldt, Tornwaldt J39.2
- tibial collateral - see Bursitis, tibial collateral
- toe - see Enthesopathy, foot, specified type NEC
- trochanteric (area) - see Bursitis, hip, trochanteric
- wrist - see Bursitis, hand
Bursopathy M71.9
- specified type NEC M71.80
- - ankle M71.87-
- - elbow M71.82-
- - foot M71.87-
- - hand M71.84-
- - hip M71.85-
- - knee M71.86-
- - multiple sites M71.89
- - shoulder M71.81-
- - specified site NEC M71.88
- - wrist M71.83-
Burst stitches or sutures (complication of surgery) T81.31
- external operation wound T81.31
- internal operation wound T81.32
Buruli ulcer A31.1
Bury's disease L95.1
Buschke's
- disease B45.3
- scleredema - see Sclerosis, systemic
Busse-Buschke disease B45.3
Buttock - see condition
Button
- Biskra B55.1
- Delhi B55.1
- oriental B55.1

Figure 4-1b ICD-10-CM Alphabetic Index pages for bursitis.

M67.95   Unspecified disorder of synovium and tendon, thigh

M67.951 Unspecified disorder of synovium and tendon, right thigh

M67.952 Unspecified disorder of synovium and tendon, left thigh

M67.959 Unspecified disorder of synovium and tendon, unspecified thigh

M67.96   Unspecified disorder of synovium and tendon, lower leg

M67.961 Unspecified disorder of synovium and tendon, right lower leg

M67.962 Unspecified disorder of synovium and tendon, left lower leg

M67.969 Unspecified disorder of synovium and tendon, unspecified lower leg

M67.97   Unspecified disorder of synovium and tendon, ankle and foot

M67.971 Unspecified disorder of synovium and tendon, right ankle and foot

M67.972 Unspecified disorder of synovium and tendon, left ankle and foot

M67.979 Unspecified disorder of synovium and tendon, unspecified ankle and foot

M67.98   Unspecified disorder of synovium and tendon, other site

M67.99   Unspecified disorder of synovium and tendon, multiple sites

Other soft tissue disorders (M70-M79)

M70 Soft tissue disorders related to use, overuse and pressure
     Includes: soft tissue disorders of occupational origin
     Excludes1:bursitis NOS (M71.9-)
     Excludes2:bursitis of shoulder (M75.5)
          enthesopathies (M76-M77)
     Use additional external cause code to identify activity causing disorder (Y93)
     M70.0   Crepitant synovitis (acute) (chronic) of hand and wrist

Figure 4-2a ICD-10-CM Tabular List pages for bursitis.

M70.03   Crepitant synovitis (acute) (chronic), wrist
     M70.031 Crepitant synovitis (acute) (chronic), right wrist
     M70.032 Crepitant synovitis (acute) (chronic), left wrist
     M70.039 Crepitant synovitis (acute) (chronic), unspecified wrist
M70.04   Crepitant synovitis (acute) (chronic), hand
     M70.041 Crepitant synovitis (acute) (chronic), right hand
     M70.042 Crepitant synovitis (acute) (chronic), left hand
     M70.049 Crepitant synovitis (acute) (chronic), unspecified hand

M70.1   **Bursitis of hand**
  M70.10   **Bursitis, unspecified hand**
  M70.11   **Bursitis, right hand**
  M70.12   **Bursitis, left hand**

M70.2   **Olecranon bursitis**
  M70.20   **Olecranon bursitis, unspecified elbow**
  M70.21   **Olecranon bursitis, right elbow**
  M70.22   **Olecranon bursitis, left elbow**

M70.3   **Other bursitis of elbow**
  M70.30   **Other bursitis of elbow, unspecified elbow**
  M70.31   **Other bursitis of elbow, right elbow**
  M70.32   **Other bursitis of elbow, left elbow**

M70.4   **Prepatellar bursitis**
  M70.40   **Prepatellar bursitis, unspecified knee**
  M70.41   **Prepatellar bursitis, right knee**
  M70.42   **Prepatellar bursitis, left knee**

M70.5   **Other bursitis of knee**
  M70.50   **Other bursitis of knee, unspecified knee**
  M70.51   **Other bursitis of knee, right knee**
  M70.52   **Other bursitis of knee, left knee**

M70.6   **Trochanteric bursitis**
Trochanteric tendinitis
  M70.60   **Trochanteric bursitis, unspecified hip**
  M70.61   **Trochanteric bursitis, right hip**
  M70.62   **Trochanteric bursitis, left hip**

M70.7   **Other bursitis of hip**

Figure 4-2b ICD-10-CM Tabular List pages for bursitis.

When the ICD-10-CM codes are used at their greatest level of granularity, they demonstrate the full degree of the patient's illness. Therefore, the processing of medical claims is enhanced because there is less need for payers to query providers for additional diagnostic information. Also, because patients' records have more accurate and detailed descriptions of the medical conditions and diseases treated, the quality of care is enhanced.

Steps in Coding

For accurate coding to occur, the coder should follow the following steps:

1. Locate the Main Term in the Alphabetic Index

To locate a main term in the Alphabetic Index, the coder must identify the term in the diagnostic phrase being coded. The main term is the condition that is present.

> **EXAMPLE:** When coding the diagnostic phrase "chronic allergic sinusitis due to pollen," the main term to be located in the Alphabetic Index is *sinusitis*. (This example is used to illustrate the steps in coding.)

Remember that, in the Alphabetic Index, for diagnoses the primary arrangement of the terms is by condition.

2. Scan the Main Term Entry for Any Instructional Notations

After locating the main term in the Alphabetic Index, a coder should review the main term entry in the Alphabetic Index for any instructional notations. If a notation is present, follow it.

> **EXAMPLE:** No notations appear with the diagnosis of sinusitis.

3. In the Diagnostic Phrase Being Coded, Identify Any Terms That Modify the Main Term

Terms that serve as modifiers in this example are *chronic* and *allergic*.

> **EXAMPLE:** Following the main term of *sinusitis*, the term *allergic* appears as a subterm, indented under the main term.

4. Follow Any Cross-Reference Notes

Cross-references appear in the form of instructional notes such as See.

> **EXAMPLE:** Next to the term *allergic*, the instructional note of ("See Rhinitis, allergic") appears. The coder should follow this instruction. The coder should now reference "Rhinitis, allergic" in the Alphabetic Index. The entry of "Rhinitis, allergic" is further divided. The entry lists pollen as the allergen; therefore the coder should select the code J30.1.

5. Always Verify the Code in the Tabular List

After selecting a code from the Alphabetic List, the coder must always verify the code in the Tabular List. Additional instructional notations can appear in the Tabular that are not present in the Alphabetic List.

6. Follow Any Instructional Terms

After turning to the Tabular list, scan for any instructional terms that may be present. Coders should scan the following areas:

- *The start of the chapter*—Here instructional notes appear that govern the entire chapter.

  EXAMPLE: In the case of sinusitis, the coder scans the start of chapter 10, Diseases of the Respiratory System. Here numerous notes appear that provide instruction to the coder. The notes for chapter 10 do not impact the case in the example.

- *The beginning of the block range*—Instructional notations that govern the section range would appear here.

  EXAMPLE: The block range is titled "Other Diseases of the Upper Respiratory Tract (J30–J39)." No instructional notations appear at this level.

- *At the beginning of the category*—

  EXAMPLE: The following appears:

  ```
  J30 Vasomotor and allergic rhinitis
      Includes: spasmodic rhinorrhea
      Excludes 1: allergic rhinitis with asthma (bronchial) (J45.909)
          rhinitis NOS (J31.0)
  ```

  The presence of the notes does not impact this case.

7. Select the Code

After completing these steps, the coder can now select the code but should scan the code selected to ensure that the most specific one has been selected.

  EXAMPLE: The descriptions listed support selecting code J30.1. This is the most specific level that can be coded.

Summary

- The Alphabetic Index and the Tabular List must both be used when assigning codes.
- All instructional notations that appear in the Alphabetic Index and the Tabular List should be read and used as a guide when selecting codes because they can have an impact on code assignment.
- ICD-10-CM codes are very detailed, and medical documentation needs to be specific to justify the selection of codes.
- ICD-10-CM codes indicate laterality.
- The steps in coding need to be followed for accurate code selection.

Chapter Review

True/False: Indicate whether each statement is true (T) or false (F).

1. _____ There were more codes in ICD-9-CM than there are in ICD-10-CM.

2. _____ The Tabular Listing of ICD-10-CM provides great detail in code assignment, and therefore the coder does not have to reference the Alphabetic Index to assign codes.

3. _____ The instructional notes in the Alphabetic Index take precedence over the instructional notes in the Tabular List.

4. _____ Medical documentation should be detailed to support the granularity of the codes present in ICD-10-CM.

5. _____ The coder must follow the See note in the Alphabetic Index to review additional entries in the Index.

Short Answer: For each diagnostic statement, identify the main term that would be used in the Alphabetic Index of ICD-10-CM.

6. unstable angina

_____
_____
_____

7. congestive heart failure

_____
_____
_____

8. acute punctured eardrum

_____
_____
_____

9. fracture of mandible

_____
_____
_____

10. benign lesion of lip

_____
_____
_____

11. ulcerative chronic tonsillitis

_____
_____
_____

12. chronic left quadrant abdominal pain

_____
_____
_____

13. gastritis due to diet deficiency

_____
_____
_____

14. primary neoplasm of stomach

_____
_____
_____

15. abscess of vas deferens

_____

_____

_____

16. sepsis following immunization

_____

_____

_____

17. streptococcal peritonitis

_____

_____

_____

18. ileo-jejunal ulceration

_____

_____

_____

19. ulcer with gangrene

_____

_____

_____

20. dermatitis due to allergy

_____

_____

_____

21. abdominal wall gangrene

_____

_____

_____

22. congenital coronary fistula

_____

_____

_____

23. bilateral conductive and sensorineural deafness

_____

_____

_____

24. lateral condyle, lower end, fracture

_____

_____

_____

25. pelvic phlebitis following molar pregnancy

_____

_____

_____

Essay: Briefly respond to the following.

26. List the steps in coding.

_____
_____
_____
_____
_____
_____
_____
_____
_____
_____
_____
_____
_____
_____
_____
_____
_____
_____
_____
_____

27. Explain why it is important to use both the Alphabetic Index and Tabular List for code assignment.

_____
_____
_____
_____
_____
_____
_____
_____
_____
_____

Diagnostic Coding Guidelines

Chapter Outline

Objectives

At the conclusion of this chapter, the learner should be able to:

1. List the Cooperating Parties for ICD-10-CM.
2. Explain the purpose of the ICD-10-CM Official Guidelines for Coding and Reporting.
3. Identify the four sections of the ICD-10-CM Official Guidelines for Coding and Reporting.
4. Differentiate and explain the guidelines for inpatient versus outpatient and physician office visits.
5. Summarize the guidelines for the sequencing of diagnostic codes.

Key Terms

combination code	late effect	principal diagnosis	secondary diagnoses

> **Reminder**
>
> *As you work through this chapter, you will need to reference the ICD-10-CM Official Guidelines for Coding and Reporting. These guidelines can be found in Appendix A of this book.*

Introduction

To ensure accurate diagnostic and procedural information, ICD-10-CM will be used to capture information for third-party reimbursement, continuity of patient care, health-care statistics, and other reporting functions.

To assist coders in consistently using ICD-10-CM, the Official Guidelines for Coding and Reporting were developed by the Centers for Medicare and Medicaid Services and the National Center for Health Statistics.

The Cooperating Parties for ICD-10-CM, which have cooperatively approved the ICD-10-CM Official Guidelines for Coding and Reporting, are the following organizations:

- American Hospital Association (AHA)
- American Health Information Management Association (AHIMA)
- Centers for Medicare and Medicaid Services (CMS)
- National Center for Health Statistics (NCHS)

The guidelines are used as a set of rules to guide in the selection of ICD-10-CM codes. They are organized into four sections with one appendix, as follows:

- *Section I—Conventions, General Coding Guidelines, and Chapter-Specific Guidelines*. In this section the guidelines address the structure and conventions of ICD-10-CM and provide general guidelines that apply to the entire classification, as well as chapter-specific guidelines.
- *Section II—Selection of Principal Diagnosis*. This section includes guidelines for the selection of the principal diagnosis for non-outpatient settings. Non-outpatient settings include acute care, short-term care, long-term care, and psychiatric hospitals, home health agencies, rehab facilities, nursing homes, and the like.
- *Section III—Reporting Additional Diagnoses*. In this section the guidelines cover the reporting of additional diagnoses that affect patient care in non-outpatient settings.
- *Section IV—Diagnostic Coding and Reporting Guidelines for Outpatient Services*. This section outlines the guidelines for outpatient coding and reporting. These guidelines for outpatient diagnoses have been approved for use by hospitals and providers in coding and reporting hospital-based outpatient services and provider-based office visits.

Section I—ICD-10-CM Conventions, General Coding Guidelines, and Chapter-Specific Guidelines

Section I provides guidelines for conventions as well as general coding guidelines and chapter-specific guidelines. The general coding guidelines are reviewed in this chapter, and the chapter-specific guidelines are reviewed in the remaining chapters of this book. The chapter-specific guidelines are sequenced in the same order as the chapters appear in the ICD-10-CM Tabular List.

> **EXAMPLE:** In the ICD-10-CM Tabular List, chapter 1 is titled "Certain Infectious and Parasitic Diseases," and the first subsection in the chapter-specific guidelines is C1, titled "Chapter 1: Certain Infectious and Parasitic Diseases (A00–B99)."

Numerous guidelines have been used in the development of this textbook and appear in the highlighted Coding Guideline areas. However, coders need to read and become familiar with *all* of the Official Guidelines to enhance their coding accuracy. In fact, new coding students should read the Official Guidelines from front to back numerous times! The guidelines can be compared to the directions for baking. If you don't follow the directions when baking, your cake will not turn out as it should. If you don't follow the coding guidelines, you will not select the proper codes. Coding is also like baking in that the more you bake, the better baker you become. The more you code, the better coder you become!

General Coding Guidelines

The following general coding guidelines apply to the selection of ICD-10-CM diagnostic codes.

The first guidelines describe locating a code in ICD-10-CM, the level of detail in coding, and the codes from A00.0 through T888.9, Z00–Z99.8.

ICD-10-CM Official Coding Guidelines

1. Locating a code in the ICD-10-CM

To select a code in the classification that corresponds to a diagnosis or reason for visit documented in a medical record, first locate the term in the Index, and then verify the code in the Tabular List. Read and be guided by instructional notations that appear in both the Index and the Tabular List.

It is essential to use both the Index and Tabular List when locating and assigning a code. The Index does not always provide the full code. Selection of the full code, including laterality and any applicable 7th character can only be done in the Tabular list. A dash (–) at the end of an Index entry indicates that additional characters are required. Even if a dash is not included at the Index entry, it is necessary to refer to the Tabular list to verify that no 7th character is required.

2. Level of Detail in Coding

Diagnosis codes are to be used and reported at their highest number of digits available.

ICD-10-CM diagnosis codes are composed of codes with 3, 4, 5, 6 or 7 digits. Codes with three digits are included in ICD-10-CM as the heading of a category of codes that may be further subdivided by the use of fourth and/or fifth digits, which provide greater detail.

A three-digit code is to be used only if it is not further subdivided. A code is invalid if it has not been coded to the full number of characters required for that code, including the 7th character, if applicable.

3. Code or codes from A00.0 through T88.9, Z00–Z99.8

The appropriate code or codes from A00.0 through T88.9, Z00–Z99.8 must be used to identify diagnoses, symptoms, conditions, problems, complaints or other reason(s) for the encounter/visit.

Codes That Describe Symptoms and Signs

Codes that describe symptoms and signs, such as pain and fever, are acceptable for coding when a definitive diagnosis has not been established. For example, when a patient presents in a physician office for abdominal pain and the cause has not been confirmed, the abdominal pain is coded.

Conditions That Are an Integral Part of a Disease Process

When a definitive diagnosis is recorded, along with signs and symptoms, the coder should code the definitive diagnosis only if the signs and symptoms are integral to the disease process. Symptoms such as cough and fever are not recorded for a patient who has been diagnosed with a respiratory infection.

Conditions That Are Not an Integral Part of a Disease Process

If signs and symptoms exist that are not routinely associated with a disease process, the signs and

ICD-10-CM Official Coding Guidelines

4. Signs and symptoms

Codes that describe symptoms and signs, as opposed to diagnoses, are acceptable for reporting purposes when a related definitive diagnosis has not been established (confirmed) by the provider. Chapter 18 of ICD-10-CM, Symptoms, Signs, and Abnormal Clinical and Laboratory Findings, Not Elsewhere Classified (codes R00.0–R99) contains many, but not all codes for symptoms.

ICD-10-CM Official Coding Guidelines

5. Conditions that are an integral part of a disease process

Signs and symptoms that are associated routinely with a disease process should not be assigned as additional codes, unless otherwise instructed by the classification.

symptoms should be coded. If a patient presents for a sprained ankle and is also experiencing vomiting, both the ankle sprain and the symptom of vomiting are recorded.

Multiple Coding for a Single Condition

Some conventions instruct coders to assign multiple codes to a single condition. These conventions include the instruction notations of Use Additional Code and Code First Underlying Condition.

ICD-10-CM Official Coding Guidelines

6. Conditions that are not an integral part of a disease process

Additional signs and symptoms that may not be associated routinely with a disease process should be coded when present.

ICD-10-CM Official Coding Guidelines

7. Multiple coding for a single condition

In addition to the etiology/manifestation convention that requires two codes to fully describe a single condition that affects multiple body systems, there are other single conditions that also require more than one code. "Use additional code" notes are found in the Tabular at codes that are not part of an etiology/manifestation pair where a secondary code is useful to fully describe a condition. The sequencing rule is the same as the etiology/manifestation pair, "use additional code" indicates that a secondary code should be added.

For example, for bacterial infections that are not included in chapter 1, a secondary code from category B95, Streptococcus, Staphylococcus, and Enterococcus, as the cause of diseases classified elsewhere, or B96, Other bacterial agents as the cause of diseases classified elsewhere, may be required to identify the bacterial organism causing the infection. A "use additional code" note will normally be found at the infectious disease code, indicating a need for the organism code to be added as a secondary code.

"Code first" notes are also under certain codes that are not specifically manifestation codes but may be due to an underlying cause. When there is a "code first" note and an underlying condition is present, the underlying condition should be sequenced first.

"Code, if applicable, any causal condition first", notes indicate that this code may be assigned as a principal diagnosis when the causal condition is unknown or not applicable. If a causal condition is known, then the code for that condition should be sequenced as the principal or first-listed diagnosis.

Multiple codes may be needed for late effects, complication codes and obstetric codes to more fully describe a condition. See the specific guidelines for these conditions for further instruction.

Acute and Chronic Conditions

This guideline instructs the coder to use multiple codes in the following situation.

ICD-10-CM Official Coding Guidelines

8. Acute and Chronic Conditions

If the same condition is described as both acute (subacute) and chronic, and separate subentries exist in the Alphabetic Index at the same indentation level, code both and sequence the acute (subacute) code first.

Combination Code

A combination code is defined in the guidelines as follows:

ICD-10-CM Official Coding Guidelines

9. Combination Code

*A **combination code** is a single code used to classify:*

Two diagnoses, or

A diagnosis with an associated secondary process (manifestation)

A diagnosis with an associated complication

Combination codes are identified by referring to subterm entries in the Alphabetic Index and by reading the inclusion and exclusion notes in the Tabular List.

Assign only the combination code when that code fully identifies the diagnostic conditions involved or when the Alphabetic Index so directs. Multiple coding should not be used when the classification provides a combination code that clearly identifies all of the elements documented in the diagnosis. When the combination code lacks necessary specificity in describing the manifestation or complication, an additional code should be used as a secondary code.

Late Effects

The following guideline needs to be followed when coding late effects:

ICD-10-CM Official Coding Guidelines

10. Late Effects (Sequela)

*A **late effect** is the residual effect (condition produced) after the acute phase of an illness or injury has terminated. There is no time limit on when a late effect code can be used. The residual may be apparent early, such as in cerebral infarction, or it may occur months or years later, such as that due to a previous injury. Coding of late effects generally requires two codes sequenced in the following order: The condition or nature of the late effect is sequenced first. The late effect code is sequenced second.*

An exception to the above guidelines are those instances where the code for late effect is followed by a manifestation code identified in the Tabular List and title, or the late effect code has been expanded (at the fourth, fifth or sixth character levels) to include the manifestation(s). The code for the acute phase of an illness or injury that led to the late effect is never used with a code for the late effect.

See Section I.C.9. Sequelae of cerebrovascular disease

See Section I.C.15. Sequelae of complication of pregnancy, childbirth and the puerperium

See Section I.C.19. Code extensions

Impending or Threatened Conditions

To accurately code a diagnosis that is modified by the terms *impending* or *threatened*, the coder must answer the question "did the condition actually occur?"

- If the condition occurred, then code the diagnosis as confirmed.
- If the condition did not occur, reference the Alphabetic Index to determine whether the condition has a subentry term for *impending* or *threatened*. Also reference main term entries for *impending* and *threatened*.

ICD-10-CM Official Coding Guidelines

11. Impending or Threatened Condition

Code any condition described at the time of discharge as "impending" or "threatened" as follows:

If it did occur, code as confirmed diagnosis.

If it did not occur, reference the Alphabetic Index to determine if the condition has a subentry term for "impending" or "threatened" and also reference main term entries for "Impending" and for "Threatened."

If the subterms are listed, assign the given code.

If the subterms are not listed, code the existing underlying condition(s) and not the condition described as impending or threatened.

Reporting Same Diagnosis Code More Than Once

The guidelines give the following direction when reporting the same diagnosis code more than once:

ICD-10-CM Official Coding Guidelines

12. Reporting Same Diagnosis Code More Than Once

Each unique ICD-10-CM diagnosis code may be reported only once for an encounter. This applies to bilateral conditions when there are no distinct codes identifying laterality or two different conditions classified to the same ICD-10-CM diagnosis code.

Laterality

The guidelines give the following direction when reporting the laterality of a condition:

ICD-10-CM Official Coding Guidelines

13. For bilateral sites, the final character of the codes in the ICD-10-CM indicates laterality. An unspecified side code is also provided should the side not be identified in the medical record. If no bilateral code is provided and the condition is bilateral, assign separate codes for both the left and right side.

Chapter-Specific Coding Guidelines

The Official ICD-10-CM Guidelines for Coding and Reporting outline the chapter-specific coding guidelines in Section I, C. These guidelines are for specific diagnoses and complications found in ICD-9-CM, and they are discussed throughout the remaining chapters of this book.

Exercise 5.1 – Section I

State whether each statement is true (T) or false (F). based on Section I of the ICD-10-CM Official Guidelines for Coding and Reporting.

1. A three-digit code is to be used only if it is not further subdivided. _____

2. If the same condition is described as both acute and chronic and if separate subentries exist in the Alphabetic Index at the same indentation level, code both, with the acute code first. _____

3. The Index provides the full code. _____

4. Each unique ICD-10-CM diagnosis code may be reported only once for an encounter. _____

5. For bilateral sites, the final character of the codes in the ICD-10-CM indicates laterality. _____

Section II—Selection of Principal Diagnosis

Section II of the guidelines is used to provide consistency in selecting the **principal diagnosis**, which is defined in the Uniform Hospital Discharge Data Set (UHDDS) as "that condition established after study to be chiefly responsible for occasioning the admission of the patient to the hospital for care." Hospitals use the UHDDS definitions to report inpatient data elements in a consistent, standardized manner. To review the definitions and the data elements that the definitions apply to, review the July 31, 1985, *Federal Register* (Vol. 50, No. 147, pp. 31038–40).

> **Note:**
>
> *The guidelines in this section are for all non-outpatient settings (acute care; short-term care, long-term care, and psychiatric hospitals; home health agencies; rehab facilities; nursing homes; and the like).*

The guidelines for coding and reporting outpatient services, which include hospital-based outpatient services and physician office visits, are outlined in Section IV of the ICD-10-CM Official Guidelines for Coding and Reporting.

Codes for Symptoms, Signs, and Ill-Defined Conditions

Codes from chapter 18 of ICD-10-CM, "Symptoms, Signs, and Abnormal Clinical and Laboratory Findings, Not Elsewhere Classified (Codes R00.0-R99)," are not to be used as a principal diagnosis when a related definitive diagnosis has been established.

> **EXAMPLE:** A patient is admitted because of severe abdominal pain. After diagnostic testing, it is determined that the patient has a gastric ulcer. The gastric ulcer is the principal diagnosis.

Two or More Interrelated Conditions, Each Potentially Meeting the Definition for Principal Diagnosis

The guidelines listed at the right state:

> **EXAMPLE:** Tom Pick is admitted due to severe vomiting, nausea, and abdominal pain. After study, it is determined that he has a gastric ulcer and diverticulitis. Treatment was directed equally at both diagnoses, and the physician documents that both conditions prompted the admission. Either condition could be listed as the principal diagnosis.

> ### ICD-10-CM Official Coding Guidelines
>
> *When two or more interrelated conditions (such as diseases in the same ICD-10-CM chapter or manifestations characteristically associated with a certain disease) potentially meeting the definition of principal diagnosis, either condition may be sequenced first, unless the circumstances of the admission, the therapy provided, the Tabular List or the Alphabetic Index indicate otherwise.*

Two or More Comparative or Contrasting Conditions

At times physicians record comparative or contrasting diagnoses by using the terms *either* or *or*. The coding guidelines listed at the right state:

> ### ICD-10-CM Official Coding Guidelines
>
> *In those rare instances when two or more contrasting or comparative diagnoses are documented as "either/or" (or similar terminology), they are coded as if the diagnoses were confirmed and the diagnoses are sequenced according to the circumstances of the admission. If no further determination can be made as to which diagnosis should be principal, either diagnosis may be sequenced first.*

Symptoms Followed by Contrasting or Comparative Diagnoses

At the time of discharge, physicians may not be able to distinguish a definitive diagnosis and may record a symptom, followed by contrasting or comparative diagnoses. The guidelines instruct coders how to code symptoms followed by contrasting or comparative diagnoses.

Original Treatment Plan Not Carried Out

When treatment is not carried out, the coder must still answer the question "what diagnosis, after study, occasioned the admission to the hospital?" The principal diagnosis remains the same even if the treatment is not carried out.

> **EXAMPLE:** Denny Sams is an 80-year-old man with a past history of gastric ulcer. He is admitted because of severe abdominal pain and back pain. After diagnostic study, it is determined that he has kidney stones, and lithotripsy is planned. Before the lithotripsy, he is discharged at his request because he feels he needs to go home to care for his wife. The procedure is not performed.

In this example the kidney stones are the reason for the admission and are therefore reported as the principal diagnosis.

The coding guidelines instruct coders how to sequence codes when the original treatment plan is not carried out.

Complications of Surgery and Other Medical Care

Complications may result after surgery or from other medical care. In these cases, the complication is considered the principal diagnosis. The coding guidelines give direction in the coding of complications of surgery and other medical care.

Uncertain Diagnosis

At times a physician does not have sufficient knowledge to make a definitive diagnosis at the time of discharge. In these cases, the physician commonly records the diagnosis as questionable or suspected. The relevant guideline applies only to the selection of a principal diagnosis for inpatient admissions to short-term, acute, or long-term care, and psychiatric hospitals. The guidelines give direction in the coding of an uncertain diagnosis.

This guideline is not used for outpatient hospital records or physician office records. These settings are discussed later in this chapter under diagnostic coding and reporting guidelines for outpatient services.

ICD-10-CM Official Coding Guidelines

A symptom(s) followed by contrasting/comparative diagnoses

When a symptom(s) is followed by contrasting/comparative diagnoses, the symptom code is sequenced first. All the contrasting/comparative diagnoses should be coded as additional diagnoses.

ICD-10-CM Official Coding Guidelines

F. Original treatment plan not carried out

Sequence as the principal diagnosis the condition, which after study occasioned the admission to the hospital, even though treatment may not have been carried out due to unforeseen circumstances.

ICD-10-CM Official Coding Guidelines

G. Complications of surgery and other medical care

When the admission is for treatment of a complication resulting from surgery or other medical care, the complication code is sequenced as the principal diagnosis. If the complication is classified to the T80–T88 series and the code lacks the necessary specificity in describing the complication, an additional code for the specific complication should be assigned.

ICD-10-CM Official Coding Guidelines

H. Uncertain Diagnosis

If the diagnosis documented at the time of discharge is qualified as "probable", "suspected", "likely", "questionable", "possible", or "still to be ruled out", or other similar terms indicating uncertainty, code the condition as if it existed or was established. The bases for these guidelines are the diagnostic workup, arrangements for further workup or observation, and initial therapeutic approach that correspond most closely with the established diagnosis.

Note: This guideline is applicable only to inpatient admissions to short-term, acute, long-term care and psychiatric hospitals.

Admission from Observation Unit or Outpatient Surgery

The following guidelines are used when coding an admission from an observation unit or outpatient surgery. At times patients are admitted as inpatients following medical observation, for postoperative observation following outpatient surgery, or for continuing inpatient care following outpatient surgery.

ICD-10-CM Official Coding Guidelines

1. Admission Following Medical Observation

When a patient is admitted to an observation unit for a medical condition, which either worsens or does not improve, and is subsequently admitted as an inpatient of the same hospital for this same medical condition, the principal diagnosis would be the medical condition which led to the hospital admission.

2. Admission Following Post-Operative Observation

When a patient is admitted to an observation unit to monitor a condition (or complication) that develops following outpatient surgery, and then is subsequently admitted as an inpatient of the same hospital, hospitals should apply the Uniform Hospital Discharge Data Set (UHDDS) definition of principal diagnosis as "that condition established after study to be chiefly responsible for occasioning the admission of the patient to the hospital for care."

J. Admission from Outpatient Surgery

When a patient receives surgery in the hospital's outpatient surgery department and is subsequently admitted for continuing inpatient care at the same hospital, the following guidelines should be followed in selecting the principal diagnosis for the inpatient admission:

- *If the reason for the inpatient admission is a complication, assign the complication as the principal diagnosis.*

- *If no complication, or other condition, is documented as the reason for the inpatient admission, assign the reason for the outpatient surgery as the principal diagnosis.*

- *If the reason for the inpatient admission is another condition unrelated to the surgery, assign the unrelated condition as the principal diagnosis.*

EXAMPLE: Tom Smith is placed in observation due to extreme renal colic. He is admitted because it is determined that he has kidney stones that are not going to pass. Surgery was completed to remove the kidney stones. The principal diagnosis for the admission is the kidney stones.

Exercise 5.2 – Section II

State whether each statement is true (T) or false (F) based on the ICD-10-CM Official Guidelines for Coding and Reporting

1. When a symptom(s) is followed by contrasting/comparative diagnoses, the symptom code is sequenced first. _____

2. When the admission is for treatment of a complication resulting from surgery or other medical care, the complication code is sequenced as the secondary diagnosis. _____

3. If the diagnosis documented at the time of discharge is qualified with such terms as "probable," suspected," "likely," "questionable," "possible," "still to be ruled out," or other phrases indicating uncertainty, code the condition as if it existed or is established. _____

(continued)

4. When a patient is admitted to an observation unit for a medical condition, which either worsens or does not improve, and is subsequently admitted as an inpatient of the same hospital for the same medical condition, the principal diagnosis is the medical condition that led to the hospital admission. _____

5. Codes for symptoms, signs, and ill-defined conditions from chapter 18 are not to be used as principal diagnosis when a related definitive diagnosis has been established. _____

Section III—Reporting Additional Diagnoses

In addition to the principal diagnosis, additional diagnoses are coded and reported. UHDDS defines other diagnoses, commonly called **secondary diagnoses**, as "all conditions that coexist at the time of admission, that develop subsequently, or that affect the treatment received and/or length of stay. Diagnoses that relate to an earlier episode which have no bearing on the current hospital stay are to be excluded." This definition is used to standardize reporting for inpatients in such facilities as:

- Acute care, short-term care, long-term care, and psychiatric hospitals
- Home health agencies.
- Rehab facilities.
- Nursing homes.

The guidelines state the following:

ICD-10-CM Official Coding Guidelines

The following guidelines are to be applied in designating "other diagnoses" when neither the Alphabetic Index nor the Tabular List in ICD-10-CM provide direction. The listing of the diagnoses in the patient record is the responsibility of the attending provider.

A. Previous conditions

If the provider has included a diagnosis in the final diagnostic statement, such as the discharge summary or the face sheet, it should ordinarily be coded. Some providers include in the diagnostic statement resolved conditions or diagnoses and status-post procedures from previous admission that have no bearing on the current stay. Such conditions are not to be reported and are coded only if required by hospital policy.

However, history codes (categories Z80–Z87) may be used as secondary codes if the historical condition or family history has an impact on current care or influences treatment.

B. Abnormal findings

Abnormal findings (laboratory, x-ray, pathologic, and other diagnostic results) are not coded and reported unless the provider indicates their clinical significance. If the findings are outside the normal range and the attending provider has ordered other tests to evaluate the condition or prescribed treatment, it is appropriate to ask the provider whether the abnormal finding should be added.

Please note: This differs from the coding practices in the outpatient setting for coding encounters for diagnostic tests that have been interpreted by a provider.

C. Uncertain Diagnosis

If the diagnosis documented at the time of discharge is qualified as "probable", "suspected", "likely", "questionable", "possible", or "still to be ruled out" or other similar terms indicating uncertainty, code the condition as if it existed or was established. The bases for these guidelines are the diagnostic workup, arrangements for further workup or observation, and initial therapeutic approach that correspond most closely with the established diagnosis.

Note: This guideline is applicable only to inpatient admissions to short-term, acute, long-term care and psychiatric hospitals.

Section IV—Diagnostic Coding and Reporting Guidelines for Outpatient Services

Section IV of the ICD-10-CM Official Guidelines for Coding and Reporting is approved for use by hospitals and by providers for reporting hospital-based outpatient services and provider-based office visits.

In the outpatient or office setting, the definition of principal diagnosis does not apply. In the outpatient setting, the term *first-listed diagnosis* is used. The following guidelines are used in reporting outpatient services:

> **Note:**
>
> *The guidelines in other sections can differ at times from the guidelines for outpatient and provider-based office visits.*

ICD-10-CM Official Coding Guidelines

A. Selection of first-listed condition

In the outpatient setting, the term first-listed diagnosis is used in lieu of principal diagnosis.

In determining the first-listed diagnosis the coding conventions of ICD-10-CM, as well as the general and disease specific guidelines take precedence over the outpatient guidelines.

Diagnoses often are not established at the time of the initial encounter/visit. It may take two or more visits before the diagnosis is confirmed.

The most critical rule involves beginning the search for the correct code assignment through the Alphabetic Index. Never begin searching initially in the Tabular List as this will lead to coding errors.

1. Outpatient Surgery

When a patient presents for outpatient surgery (same day surgery), code the reason for the surgery as the first-listed diagnosis (reason for the encounter), even if the surgery is not performed due to a contraindication.

2. Observation Stay

When a patient is admitted for observation for a medical condition, assign a code for the medical condition as the first-listed diagnosis.

When a patient presents for outpatient surgery and develops complications requiring admission to observation, code the reason for the surgery as the first reported diagnosis (reason for the encounter), followed by codes for the complications as secondary diagnoses.

B. Codes from A00.0 through T88.9, Z00–Z99

The appropriate code(s) from A00.0 through T88.9, Z00–Z99 must be used to identify diagnoses, symptoms, conditions, problems, complaints, or other reason(s) for the encounter/visit.

C. Accurate reporting of ICD-10-CM diagnosis codes

For accurate reporting of ICD-10-CM diagnosis codes, the documentation should describe the patient's condition, using terminology which includes specific diagnoses as well as symptoms, problems, or reasons for the encounter. There are ICD-10-CM codes to describe all of these.

D. Codes that describe symptoms and signs

Codes that describe symptoms and signs, as opposed to diagnoses, are acceptable for reporting purposes when a diagnosis has not been established (confirmed) by the provider. Chapter 18 of ICD-10-CM, Symptoms, Signs, and Abnormal Clinical and Laboratory Findings Not Elsewhere Classified (codes R00–R99) contain many, but not all codes for symptoms.

E. Encounters for circumstances other than a disease or injury

ICD-10-CM provides codes to deal with encounters for circumstances other than a disease or injury. The Factors Influencing Health Status and Contact with Health Services codes (Z00–99) is provided to deal with occasions when circumstances other than a disease or injury are recorded as diagnosis or problems.

(continued)

See Section I.C.21. Factors influencing health status and contact with health services.

F. Level of Detail in Coding

1. ICD-10-CM codes with 3, 4, or 5 digits

ICD-10-CM is composed of codes with either 3, 4, 5, 6 or 7 digits. Codes with three digits are included in ICD-10-CM as the heading of a category of codes that may be further subdivided by the use of fourth, fifth digits, sixth or seventh digits which provide greater specificity.

2. Use of full number of digits required for a code

A three-digit code is to be used only if it is not further subdivided. A code is invalid if it has not been coded to the full number of characters required for that code, including the 7th character extension, if applicable.

G. ICD-10-CM code for the diagnosis, condition, problem, or other reason for encounter/visit

List first the ICD-10-CM code for the diagnosis, condition, problem, or other reason for encounter/visit shown in the medical record to be chiefly responsible for the services provided. List additional codes that describe any coexisting conditions. In some cases the first-listed diagnosis may be a symptom when a diagnosis has not been established (confirmed) by the physician.

H. Uncertain diagnosis

Do not code diagnoses documented as "probable", "suspected," "questionable," "rule out," or "working diagnosis" or other similar terms indicating uncertainty. Rather, code the condition(s) to the highest degree of certainty for that encounter/visit, such as symptoms, signs, abnormal test results, or other reason for the visit.

Please note: This differs from the coding practices used by short-term, acute care, long-term care and psychiatric hospitals.

I. Chronic diseases

Chronic diseases treated on an ongoing basis may be coded and reported as many times as the patient receives treatment and care for the condition(s)

J. Code all documented conditions that coexist

Code all documented conditions that coexist at the time of the encounter/visit, and require or affect patient care treatment or management. Do not code conditions that were previously treated and no longer exist. However, history codes (categories Z80–Z87) may be used as secondary codes if the historical condition or family history has an impact on current care or influences treatment.

K. Patients receiving diagnostic services only

For patients receiving diagnostic services only during an encounter/visit, sequence first the diagnosis, condition, problem, or other reason for encounter/visit shown in the medical record to be chiefly responsible for the outpatient services provided during the encounter/visit. Codes for other diagnoses (e.g., chronic conditions) may be sequenced as additional diagnoses.

For encounters for routine laboratory/radiology testing in the absence of any signs, symptoms, or associated diagnosis, assign Z01.89, Encounter for other specified special examinations. If routine testing is performed during the same encounter as a test to evaluate a sign, symptom, or diagnosis, it is appropriate to assign both the V code and the code describing the reason for the non-routine test.

For outpatient encounters for diagnostic tests that have been interpreted by a physician, and the final report is available at the time of coding, code any confirmed or definitive diagnosis(es) documented in the interpretation. Do not code related signs and symptoms as additional diagnoses.

Please note: This differs from the coding practice in the hospital inpatient setting regarding abnormal findings on test results.

L. Patients receiving therapeutic services only

For patients receiving therapeutic services only during an encounter/visit, sequence first the diagnosis, condition, problem, or other reason for encounter/visit shown in the medical record to be chiefly responsible for the outpatient services provided during the encounter/visit. Codes for other diagnoses (e.g., chronic conditions) may be sequenced as additional diagnoses.

The only exception to this rule is that when the primary reason for the admission/encounter is chemotherapy or radiation therapy, the appropriate Z code for the service is listed first, and the diagnosis or problem for which the service is being performed listed second.

M. Patients receiving preoperative evaluations only

For patients receiving preoperative evaluations only, sequence first a code from subcategory Z01.81, Encounter for pre-procedural examinations, to describe the pre-op consultations. Assign a code for the condition to describe the reason for the surgery as an additional diagnosis. Code also any findings related to the pre-op evaluation.

N. Ambulatory surgery

For ambulatory surgery, code the diagnosis for which the surgery was performed. If the postoperative diagnosis is known to be different from the preoperative diagnosis at the time the diagnosis is confirmed, select the postoperative diagnosis for coding, since it is the most definitive.

O. Routine outpatient prenatal visits

See Section I.C.15. Routine outpatient prenatal visits.

P. Encounters for general medical examinations with abnormal findings

The subcategories for encounters for general medical examinations, Z00.0–, provide codes for with and without abnormal findings. Should a general medical examination result in an abnormal finding, the code for general medical examination with abnormal finding should be assigned as the first listed diagnosis. A secondary code for the abnormal finding should also be coded.

Q. Encounters for routine health screenings

See Section I.C.21. Factors influencing health status and contact with health services, Screening.

Exercise 5.3 – Sections III and IV

State whether each statement is true (T) or false (F) based on the ICD-10-CM Official Guidelines for Coding and Reporting.

1. In the coding of secondary diagnoses, if the provider has included a diagnosis in the final diagnostic statement, such as the discharge summary or the face sheet, that diagnosis should ordinarily be coded. _____

2. Abnormal findings (laboratory, X-ray, pathologic, and other diagnostic results) are coded and reported. _____

3. When a general medical examination results in an abnormal finding, the code for general medical examination with abnormal finding should be assigned as the first listed diagnosis. _____

4. For patients receiving preoperative evaluations only, sequence first a code from subcategory Z01.81, Encounter for pre-procedural examinations, to describe the preop consultations. _____

5. For ambulatory surgery, code the diagnosis for which the surgery was performed. _____

Internet Links

The ICD-10-CM Official Guidelines for Coding and Reporting can be found online at **www.cdc.gov/nchs/ icd/icd10cm.htm**. Click on the link at the bottom of the page titled "Guidelines."

Summary

- The ICD-10-CM Official Guidelines for Coding and Reporting were developed to provide coding consistency.

- The Cooperating Parties for ICD-10-CM are the American Hospital Association, American Health Information Association, Centers for Medicare and Medicaid Services, and the National Center for Health Statistics.

- The ICD-10-CM Official Guidelines for Coding and Reporting have four sections.

- Section I contains the ICD-10-CM Conventions, General Coding Guidelines, and Chapter-Specific Guidelines.

- Section II describes the Selection of Principal Diagnosis(es) for inpatient, short-term, acute care, and long-term care hospital records.

- Section III describes the Reporting of Additional Diagnoses for inpatient, short-term, acute care, and long-term care hospital records.

- Section IV describes the Diagnostic Coding and Reporting Guidelines for outpatient services.

Chapter Review

True/False: Indicate whether each statement is true (T) or false (F).

1. _____ The ICD-10-CM Official Guidelines for Coding and Reporting were developed by the American Health Information Management Association.

2. _____ For outpatient and physician office visits, the code that is listed first for coding and reporting purposes is the reason for the encounter.

3. _____ Codes that describe symptoms and signs are acceptable for coding when a definitive diagnosis has not been established in a physician office.

4. _____ If signs and symptoms exist that are not routinely associated with a disease process, the signs and symptoms should not be coded.

5. _____ Late effect codes should be used only within six months after the initial injury or disease.

6. _____ The principal diagnosis is defined as "that condition established after study to be chiefly responsible for occasioning the outpatient visit of the patient to the hospital for care."

7. _____ If the diagnosis documented at the time of discharge is qualified as "probable" or "suspected," do not code the condition.

8. _____ Codes from chapter 18 of ICD-10-CM, "Symptoms, Signs, and Abnormal Clinical and Laboratory Findings, Not Elsewhere Classified," are not to be used as a principal diagnosis when a related definitive diagnosis has been established.

9. _____ A patient is admitted because of severe abdominal pain. After diagnostic testing, it is determined that the patient has appendicitis. The abdominal pain is the principal diagnosis.

10. _____ In a physician's office, a chronic disease treated on an ongoing basis may be coded and reported as many times as the patient receives treatment and care for the condition.

Fill-in-the-Blank: Enter the appropriate term(s) to complete each statement.

11. A _____ is the residual effect (condition produced) after the acute phase of an illness or injury has terminated.

12. For ambulatory surgery, if the postoperative diagnosis is known to be different from the preoperative diagnosis at the time the diagnosis is confirmed, select the _____ diagnosis for coding.

13. In the _____ setting, the definition of principal diagnosis does not apply.

14. All conditions that coexist at the time of admission, that devlop subsequently, or affect the treatment received and/or length of stay are known as the _____.

15. Rule-out conditions are not coded in the _____ setting.

16. In the outpatient setting, do not code conditions that were previously _____ and no longer exist.

17. Abnormal findings are not coded and reported for unless the _____ indicates their clinical significance.

18. In the outpatient setting, the term _____ is used in lieu of *principal diagnosis*.

19. In most cases when coding late effects, two codes are required, with the _____ sequenced first, followed by the late effect code.

20. Each unique ICD-10-CM code may be reported _____ for an encounter.

Short Answer: Briefly answer each of the following.

21. Discuss how to code a diagnosis recorded as "suspected" in both an inpatient and an outpatient record.
    _____
    _____
    _____

22. List the Cooperating Parties that developed the ICD-10-CM Official Coding Guidelines.
    _____
    _____
    _____

23. List the sections of the ICD-10-CM Official Guidelines for Coding and Reporting.
    _____
    _____
    _____

CHAPTER 6

Infectious and Parasitic Diseases

Chapter Outline

Objectives

At the conclusion of this chapter, the learner should be able to:

1. Identify infectious and parasitic diseases.
2. Explain single-code, combination-code, and dual-code assignment.
3. Discuss ICD-9-CM versus ICD-10-CM coding guidelines and coding assignments for infectious and parasitic diseases.
4. Summarize the coding of symptomatic and asymptomatic cases of HIV.
5. List the types of hepatitis and the code for each.
6. Accurately code infectious and parasitic diseases.
7. Select and code diagnoses from case studies.

Key Terms

acariasis

acquired
   immunodeficiency
   syndrome (AIDS)

arthropods

bacteria

candidiasis

combination-code
   assignment

culture and sensitivity
   (C&S)

dual-code assignment

Escherichia coli (E. coli)

fungi

Reminder

As you work through this chapter, you will need to have a copy of the ICD-10-CM coding book to reference.

helminths	molds	pediculosis	single-code assignment
host	moniliasis	protozoa	spirochetal
human immunodeficiency virus (HIV)	parasite	septicemia	viruses
	parasitic diseases	sepsis	yeast infection
infectious diseases	pathogen	severe sepsis	tuberculosis

Introduction

Certain infectious and parasitic diseases are found in Chapter 1 of ICD-10-CM. The code range is A00–B99. **Infectious diseases** are diseases that occur when a **pathogen**, a micro-organism that can cause disease in humans, invades the body and causes disease. A **parasite** lives within another organism, known as a **host**, and can cause diseases known as **parasitic diseases**. In this relationship, the parasite benefits and the host is harmed.

An easy reference to the diseases discussed in this chapter can be found at the start of chapter 1 in the Tabular List. The following table notes the blocks found in chapter 1.

Block Title	Category Codes
Intestinal infectious diseases	A00–A09
Tuberculosis	A15–A19
Certain zoonotic bacterial diseases	A20–A28
Other bacterial diseases	A30–A49
Infections with a predominantly sexual mode of transmission	A50–A64
Other spirochetal diseases	A65–A69
Other diseases caused by chlamydiae	A70–A74
Rickettsioses	A75–A79
Viral infections of the central nervous system	A80–A89
Arthropod-borne viral fevers and viral hemorrhagic fevers	A90–A99
Viral infections characterized by skin and mucous membrane lesions	B00–B09
Other human herpes viruses	B10
Viral hepatitis	B15–B19
Human immunodeficiency virus [HIV] disease	B20
Other viral diseases	B25–B34
Mycoses	B35–B49
Protozoal diseases	B50–B64
Helminthiases	B65–B83
Pediculosis, acariasis, and other infestations	B85–B89
Sequelae of infectious and parasitic diseases	B90–B94
Bacterial, viral, and other infectious agents	B95–B97
Other infectious diseases	B99

Several instructional notations are also at the start of the chapter, and they need to be referenced prior to code assignment.

The various blocks in chapter 1 identify the types of organisms that cause infections. In ICD-10-CM the organisms are classified into the following groups:

* Bacteria
* Fungi
* Parasites
* Viruses

Bacteria

Bacteria are one-celled organisms named according to their shapes and arrangements. (See Figure 6-1.)

> **EXAMPLE:** Diplococci bacteria are round, spherical, or coffee bean-shaped bacteria that occur in pairs. (See Figure 6-2.)

Bacteria can live inside or outside the body. Outside the body, bacteria can be found on most surfaces such as countertops, faucet handles, and doorknobs.

Singular Name of Bacterial Shape	Plural Form	Description
Coccus	Cocci	Spherical or round
Bacillus	Bacilli	Straight rod
Spirillum	Spirilla	Spiral, corkscrew, or slightly curved

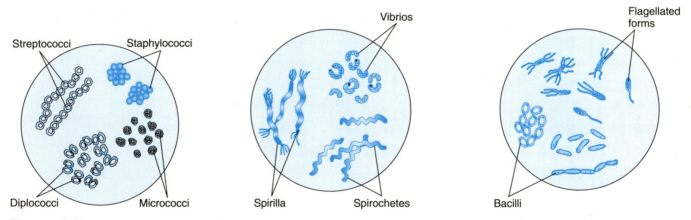

Figure 6-1   Forms of cocci, bacilli, and spirilla. (From Bowie MJ, Schaffer RM. *Nursing Assistant: Approach*, 9th ed. Clifton Park, NY: Delmar, Cengage Learning, 2003.)

Arrangement	Medical Word Part
Single	There is no specific medical term.
Pairs	**diplo-**
Chains	**strepto-**
Clusters	**staphylo-**

Figure 6-2   Arrangements of bacteria.

Inside the body, some common bacterial infection sites are the bloodstream, the skin, and the gastrointestinal, respiratory, and urinary tracts. Some organisms are commonly found in the human body and do not cause disease in one body site but can cause disease in another site.

The bacterial organism enters a cell and begins poisoning the cell by producing toxins that cause disease. Because a specific organism can cause disease in different body sites, a coder must note the type of organism and body site when coding.

> **EXAMPLE:** *Escherichia coli*, also known as *E. coli*, is a rod-shaped bacillus found in the large intestine of humans, where it is normally nonpathogenic. However, when *E. coli* is found outside the intestine, it can cause disease in the urinary tract or infections in pressure ulcers.

To accurately diagnose a specific bacterial infection that is affecting a patient, a physician orders a **culture and sensitivity** test, also known as a **C&S**. The *culture* identifies the type of organism causing the infection, and the *sensitivity* identifies the antibiotic that should be used to treat the infection. The coder has to reference the culture and sensitivity report to identify the specific bacteria causing the infection and the sensitivity identifying the antibiotic to be used. Common bacterial infections include:

Name of Infection	Common Pathogen
Pseudomembraneous colitis	*Clostridium difficile*
Salmonella food poisoning	*Salmonella*
Urinary tract infection	*E. coli*
	Pseudomonas aeruginosa
Tuberculosis	*Mycobacterium tuberculosis*
Impetigo	*Streptococci A*
Strep throat	*Streptococcus*

Fungi

Fungi are microscopic plant life that lack chlorophyll and must have a source of matter for nutrition because they cannot manufacture their own food. The two common forms of fungal infections that affect humans are molds and yeast. **Yeast infections** are caused by unicellular fungi that reproduce by budding; **molds** are caused by long filament-shaped fungi. Yeasts and molds that infect human tissues are known as opportunistic parasites; they cause opportunistic infections when a patient has a weakened immune system. Opportunistic infections commonly occur in the following types of individuals:

- Patients with chronic conditions, such as AIDS, diabetes, and cancer

- Infants and newborns

- Patients who are postsurgery

- Patients who have taken antibiotics

- Steroid users

Common Yeast and Molds That Affect Humans

Name of Infection	Common Pathogen
Athlete's foot	*Tinea pedis*
Thrush	*Candida aibicans*
Ringworm	*Tinea capitis*
Chicago disease	*Blastomyces dermatitidis*

Parasites

Parasites are organisms that feed on other organisms to nourish themselves. Specific parasitic organisms are:

* **Protozoa**—one-celled organisms that live on living matter and are classified by the way they move.

* **Helminths**—organisms such as flatworms, roundworms, and flukes.

* **Arthropods**—organisms such as insects, ticks, spiders, and mites.

Parasitic infections are found in the intestinal tract, bloodstream, lymph nodes, central nervous system, and skin. Some parasitic infections multiply in the bloodstream and move into the tissue of body organs, such as the liver and spleen. Figure 6-3 shows malarial parasites in red blood cells. Other parasites, such as tapeworms, attach to body structures and cause disorders. A tapeworm uses hooks and suckers to attach to the intestinal wall of its host, causing weight loss (Figure 6-4).

Common Parasitic Infections

Name of Infection	Common Pathogen
African sleeping sickness	Trypanosoma gambiense
Chagas' disease	Trypanosoma cruzi
Malaria	Plasmodium falciparum
	Plasmodium vivax
	Plasmodium malariae
	Plasmodium ovale
Pinworm	Enterobius vermicularis
Head lice	Pediculus
Scabies	Sarcoptes

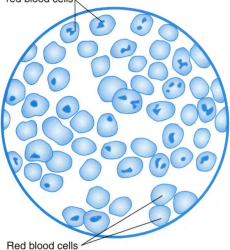

Malarial parasites in red blood cells

Red blood cells (not yet invaded)

Figure 6-3 Malarial parasites in red blood cells. (From Grover-Lakomia LL, Fong E. *Microbiology for Health Careers*, 6th ed. Clifton Park, NY: Delmar, Cengage Learning, 1991, p. 181.)

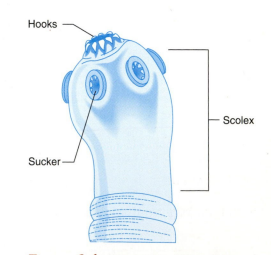

Hooks

Scolex

Sucker

Figure 6-4 Tapeworm. (From Grover-Lakomia LL, Fong E. *Microbiology for Health Careers*, 6th ed. Clifton Park, NY: Delmar, Cengage Learning, 1991, p. 181.)

Viruses are the smallest of infectious pathogens. They penetrate cells and release their DNA or RNA into the cell nucleus, causing damage to the cell. Viruses are completely dependent on the nutrients inside the cells for reproduction and metabolism, and they vary in their effects from a common cold to viral hepatitis and acquired immunodeficiency syndrome (AIDS).

Common Viral Infections

Name of Disease	Name of Pathogen
Shingles	*Herpes zoster*
Chickenpox	*Varicella*
AIDS	Human immunodeficiency virus
Genital herpes	*Herpes simplex*
German measles	RNA virus
West Nile fever	*Flavivirus*

Exercise 6.1 – Code Assignments and Instructional Notations

For each of the conditions listed, identify any instructional notations and then assign an ICD-10-CM code. The first one is done for you.

Condition	Instructional Notation	Code Assignment
1. Shingles	Includes shingles, zona	B02.9
2. German measles		
3. Hutchinson's teeth		
4. Scarlet fever with otitis media		
5. Amebic lung abscess		

Coding of Infectious and Parasitic Diseases

Infectious and parasitic diseases are coded in ICD-10-CM in one of three ways: single-code assignment, combination-code assignment, or dual-code assignment.

Single-Code Assignment

Single-code assignment occurs when only one code is needed to code the diagnostic statement. The blocks noted at the beginning of the chapter help the coder identify the available categories. The condition is referenced and the code selection is made.

EXAMPLE: Millie presents with an acute case of scarlet fever. To code this condition, the coder references the terms *fever* or *scarlet fever* in the Alphabetic Index. Assume the coder references the term *scarlet fever* in the alphabetic index. The coder finds:

```
Scarlatina (anginosa)(malignant) (ulcerosa) A38.9
        myocarditis (acute) A38.1
            old-see Myocarditis
        otitis media A38.0
```

Scarlet fever (albuminuria) (angina) A38.9

Schamberg's disease (progressive pigmentary dermatosis) L81.7

After referencing the index, the coder now verifies the code in the Tabular List. Code A38.9 appears in the Tabular List:

```
A38     Scarlet fever
        Includes        scarlatina
        Excludes 2      streptococcal sore throat (J02.0)
        A38.0 Scarlet fever with otitis media
        A38.1 Scarlet fever with myocarditis
        A38.8 Scarlet fever with other complications
        A38.9 Scarlet fever, uncomplicated
                Scarlet fever NOS
```

Referencing the Tabular Listing verifies the correct code assignment of A38.9.

Combination-Code Assignment

Combination-code assignment occurs when a single code is used to identify the organism and the condition caused by the organism. Here, only one code is need to code the diagnostic statement.

> **EXAMPLE:** Patient presents with lesions and fatigue. The patient is subsequently diagnosed with herpes simplex meningitis. To code this diagnostic statement, the coder references the term *meningitis* in the Alphabetic Index. The entry appears in the Alphabetic Index as shown:

```
Meningitis
        in (due to)
                bacterial disease NEC A48.8 [G01]
                Chagas' disease [chronic] B57.41
                chickenpox B01.0
                coccidioidmycosis B38.4
                Diplococcus pneumonia G00.1
                enterovirus A87.0
                herpes (simplex) virus B00.3
                    zoster B02.1
                infectious mononucleosis B27.92
```

After referencing the Alphabetic Index, the coder notes the code B00.3. The coder needs to verify the code in the Tabular List. Only one code, B00.3, is needed to code the herpes simplex organism and the manifestation of the meningitis.

Dual-Code Assignment

Dual-code assignment occurs when two codes are needed to code a diagnostic statement. In these cases, the infectious and parasitic disease codes are sequenced before the code from another ICD-10-CM chapter. Due to the level of specificity of ICD-10-CM coding, there are fewer dual-assignment codes than there were with ICD-9-CM.

> **EXAMPLE:** A patient is diagnosed with late syphilitic anemia. To code this diagnostic statement, the coder references the term *anemia* and the subterm *syphilitic* in the Alphabetic Index:

```
Anemia
        Syphyilitic (acquired) (late) A52.79 [D63.8]
```

In the Alphabetic Index, two codes are listed: A52.79 and D63.8. Code A52.79 identifies the syphilis, and the D63.8 identifies the anemia. The D63.8 is found in the second code position within brackets. The brackets signal the coder that the D63.8 should be reported in the second position on the claim form.

A Codes

The A codes include the various blocks as outlined at the start of chapter. The various blocks are now discussed in greater detail.

Intestinal Infectious Diseases (Category Codes A00–A09)

This range of codes includes infections that include cholera, shigellosis, and other bacterial intestinal infections. Also found here are codes for food poisoning, cyclosporiasis, and viral intestinal infections.

Disease Highlight—Infectious Intestinal Diseases

Signs and Symptoms:

> Nausea
>
> Vomiting
>
> Anorexia
>
> Abdominal pain
>
> Fever
>
> Muscular aches
>
> Malaise

Clinical Testing:

> Blood and stool cultures to identify the type of infectious organisms

Treatment:

> Patients are given an antiemetric drug to reduce the vomiting.
>
> Antimotility drugs are used to relieve the abdominal pain.
>
> To replace lost fluids, patients are encouraged to increase fluid intake.
>
> In severe cases, patients are given IV replacement therapy.

Tuberculosis (Category Codes A15–A19)

Tuberculosis is an infection caused by *Mycobacterium tuberculosis* that spreads throughout the body via lymph and blood vessels and that most commonly localizes in the lungs. At the start of the A15–A19 coding section of ICD-10-CM, an Includes note states that infections due to *Mycobacterium tuberculosis* and *Mycobacterium bovis* are coded from this section. An *Excludes 1* note excludes from this code block:

- Congenital tuberculosis (P37.0).

- Pneumoconiosis associated with tuberculosis, any type in A15 (J65).

- Sequelae of tuberculosis (B90.–).

- Silicotuberculosis (J65).

An understanding of the symptoms of tuberculosis is important. Symptoms of the disease are:

- Fatigue and weakness.
- Loss of appetite and weight.
- Coughing.
- Hemoptysis.
- Night sweats.
- Increased temperature late in the day and evening.

Clinical tests used to diagnosis tuberculosis include:

- Chest X-rays.
- Mantoux skin test.
- Sputum culture.

The tuberculosis codes are broken down by site, such as category A15. A15, Respiratory tuberculosis, further breaks down to identify tuberculosis of the lungs, the lymph nodes, the larynx, and the bronchus. Coders must be able to identify the site of the disease for accurate coding.

Certain Zoonotic Bacterial Diseases (Category Codes A20–A28)

This section includes zoonotic bacterial diseases that are transmitted to humans after contact with infected animals, insects, fleas, ticks, or their discharges or products. Common symptoms of diseases in this range include fever, chills, headache, sweating, body aches, weakness, and fatigue. Blood specimens are used for diagnosis. Diseases in this section include:

- Anthrax
- Bubonic plague
- Glanders and melioidosis
- Leptospirosis

Other Bacterial Diseases (Category Codes A30–A49)

This range of codes classifies a wide range of bacterial diseases. Some of them are:

- Meningococcal meningitis.
- Whooping cough.
- Diphtheria.

Septic infections are also coded to this category. Physicians commonly use the terms *septicemia* and *sepsis* synonymously; however, current medical practice makes a distinction between these terms and related conditions. The distinction is that **septicemia** is defined as bacteremia with sepsis.

Sepsis is a life-threatening bacterial infection that causes blood clots to form, which block blood flow to vital organs. For a diagnosis of sepsis, assign the appropriate code for the underlying systemic infection. If the type of infection or causal organism is not further specified, assign code A41.9, Sepsis, unspecified. ICD-10-CM guides the coder to R78.81 for septicemia, even though most providers use the term *sepsis* and *septicemia* interchangeably. The coder should review the medical documentation and query the provider to make the distinction.

Severe sepsis is a septic infection with associated acute organ dysfunction or failure. One or more organs may be affected, and coding

> **Note:**
>
> *Additional coding for the associated acute organ dysfunction is also required.*

accurately requires a minimum of two codes: first a code for the underlying systemic infection, followed by a code from subcategory R65.2, Severe sepsis. If the causal organism is not documented, assign code A41.9, Sepsis, unspecified, for the infection.

Whenever possible, identify the causal organism. If the patient is diagnosed with sepsis and an acute organ dysfunction, the documentation must clearly identify the relationship between the organ dysfunction and the sepsis. If the relationship is not clearly identified, then R65.2, Severe sepsis, is not assigned. If the documentation does not identify a causal relationship code, then A41.9, Sepsis, unspecified, is the correct code to assign.

EXAMPLE: Mr. Bahji is admitted to the hospital with low blood pressure. After admission testing is performed, it is determined that he has sepsis. The kidneys have begun to shut down, but Dr. Smyth is not ready to consider this as related to the sepsis infection because Mr. Bahji was having urinary problems prior to admission.

The diagnosis code A41.9 is used because the diagnosis documented is "sepsis" and not "severe sepsis." The kidney problem is not being associated with the sepsis at this time; so the additional code of R65.2 for the severe sepsis does not apply.

Infections with a Predominantly Sexual Mode of Transmission (Category Codes A50–A64)

The Excludes 1 notation at the start of this subcategory acts as a guide to coding for human immunodeficiency virus (HIV) disease, Reiter's disease, and nonspecific and nongonococcal urethritis. These conditions are found in other categories of the code book.

This block of codes, A50–A64, does include such conditions as early and late congenital syphilitic pneumonia, gonococcal infections, and other sexually transmitted diseases. Careful attention to the documentation is necessary to properly assign a code from this section because the selection of codes from this range of codes is very specific. Only diagnoses that are clearly documented should be coded from this section.

Other Spirochetal Diseases (Category Codes A65–A69)

Spirochetal is a term for a gram-negative bacteria made up of spiral-shaped cells. This code set contains codes for nonvenereal syphilis, yaws, and Lyme disease. The Excludes 2 note at the beginning of the code set excludes leptospirosis and syphilis, which are located in other areas of the chapter.

Other Diseases Caused by Chlamydiae (Category Codes A70–A74)

Chlamydiae is a type of bacteria that live inside host cells. This bacterium is usually dormant but at some point may become active in the disease process.

Rickettsioses (Category Codes A75–A79)

Rickettsioses is a bacterial infection that might also be referred to as typhus or a form of spotted fever. Also found in this code set are codes for trench fever and ehrlichiosis.

Viral Infections of the Central Nervous System (Category Codes A80–A89)

Viral infections found in this set of codes include:

- Poliomyelitis.
- Rabies.
- Encephalitis.
- Viral meningitis.

It is very important that the coder review the code descriptions found in the Tabular List because they involve many Include and Exclude notations.

Exercise 6.2 – Bacterial, Parasitic, and Infectious Diseases

Using an ICD-10-CM code book, assign codes to the following diagnostic statements.

1. campylobacter enteritis _____

2. acute amebic dysentery _____

3. meningitis due to anthrax _____

4. Kyasanur Forest disease _____

5. necrotizing ulcerative stomatitis _____

6. urban rabies _____

7. enteroviral meningitis _____

8. Pasteurellosis _____

9. respiratory tuberculosis _____

10. anthrax sepsis _____

B Codes

B codes are used to report:

- Viral infections characterized by skin and mucous membrane lesions.

- Human herpes viruses.

- Viral hepatitis.

- Human immunodeficiency virus disease.

- Other viral diseases.

- Mycoses.

- Protozoal diseases.

- Helminthiases.

- Pediculosis, acariasis, and other infestations.

- Sequelae of infectious and parasitic diseases.

Code	Description
B00–B09 Viral infections characterized by skin and mucous membrane lesions	Some viral infections that have been more commonly heard about are found in this range of codes. Some of the herpes simplex viral infections are found here: varicella, measles, and rubella. Viral warts are also located in this code set. Verruca simplex and verruca vulgaris are coded to the B07 code. These conditions are commonly seen in family practice, pediatrics, and internal medicine areas.

B10 Other human herpes viruses	Coders need to read the Excludes 2 note under the category heading for B10. Documentation needs to be carefully reviewed prior to code assignment.
B15–B19 Viral hepatitis	Viral hepatitis is found in this section of ICD-10-CM. The coder has to identify the type of hepatitis present and any complications. The various types of hepatitis are:
	Hepatitis A (HAV)
	Hepatitis B (HBV)
	Hepatitis C (HCV)
	Hepatitis D (HDV-delta)
	Hepatitis E (HEV)

Disease Highlight—Viral Hepatitis (Category Codes B15–B19)

Signs and Symptoms:

- Nausea
- Vomiting
- Fever
- Anorexia
- Malaise
- Enlarged and tender liver
- Jaundice

Clinical Testing:

- White blood cell count in the normal to low range
- Abnormal liver tests showing that especially markedly elevated aminotransferases are present early in the course of the disease
- Biopsy of the liver showing hepatocellular necrosis and mononuclear infiltrates
- Mild proteinuria and bilirubinuria

Treatment:

- Antiviral drug therapy
- Bed rest
- A gradual return to normal activity without overexertion

Human Immunodeficiency Virus (HIV) Disease (Category Code B20)

Human immunodeficiency virus (HIV) is the virus that leads to **AIDS**, or **acquired immunodeficiency syndrome**. AIDS is a condition in which the body's immune system deteriorates.

The ICD-10-CM Official Guidelines for Coding and Reporting give the coder guidance on the reporting of cases that involve HIV. Reference the guidelines, found in Appendix A of this textbook, for the following topics:

- Coding of only confirmed cases
- Selection and sequencing of HIV codes

- Patient admitted for HIV-related condition
- Patient with HIV disease admitted for unrelated condition
- Coding for a newly diagnosed patient
- Asymptomatic HIV
- Patients with inconclusive HIV serology
- Previously diagnosed HIV-related illness
- HIV in pregnancy, childbirth, and the puerperium
- Encounters for testing for HIV

Other Viral Diseases (Category Codes B25–B34)

This section contains codes for mumps, mononucleosis, and viral conjunctivitis. The detail of the codes requires that the coder identify the site that the condition is impacting. For example, for mumps the code book is differentiated as follows:

- Mumps orchitis, B26.0
- Mumps meningitis, B26.1
- Mumps encephalitis, B26.2
- Mumps pancreatitis, B26.3
- Mumps with other complications, B26.81 to B26.89
- Mumps without complications, B26.9

When coding mononucleosis, the coder needs to identify the type of mononucleosis and complications.

Disease Highlight—Infectious Mononucleosis

Signs and Symptoms:
- Enlarged lymph nodes
- Fever
- Sore throat
- Malaise
- Anorexia
- Myalgia
- Splenomegaly

Clinical Testing:
- Elevated WBC and atypical lymphocytes
- A positive monospot test
- Abormal liver function tests

Treatment:
- Steroid therapy is common.
- Symptomatic treatment includes over-the-counter pain relievers and throat gargles using warm saline.

Mycoses (Category Codes B35–B49)

This section includes fungal infections that affect various body sites. An instructional notation at the start of the section excludes hypersensitivity pneumonitis due to organic dust and mycosis fungoides. In this code range, a coder finds codes for *tinea pedis* and *tinea coporis*.

Candidiasis and **moniliasis** infections are fungal infections caused by the fungus *Candida*, which can affect various sites. Common sites are:

- Mouth (commonly called thrush), B37.0
- Vulva and vagina (commonly called candidial or monilial vulvovaginitis), B37.3
- Skin and nails (commonly called candidial onychia), B37.2

Additional B codes

The additional B codes are found in ICD-10-CM.

Code	Description
B50–B64 Protozoal disease	This code range includes plasmodium malaria, other specified forms of malaria, leishmaniasis, African trypanosomiasis, Chagas' disease, and toxoplasmosis.
B65–B83 Helminthiasis	This code range is where the coder would locate echinococcosis, filariasis, trichinellosis, and other intestinal helminthiases. The documentation in the medical record is needed to assign the proper code from this code range.
B85–B89 Pediculosis, acariasis, and other infestations	**Pediculosis**, also known as lice, is coded to this code range, as are scabies, myiasis, and acariasis. **Acariasis** is an infestation with mites or acariads.
B90–B94 Sequelae of infectious and parasitic diseases	This code range is used to indicate conditions in categories A00–B89 as the cause of sequelae that are classified elsewhere. Also included are residuals of diseases classifiable to the same categories (A00–B89) if there is documented evidence that the disease no longer exists.
B95–B97 Bacterial and viral infectious agents and B99 other infectious diseases	Streptococcus, staphylococcus, and enterococcus are coded to this code range if they are the cause of diseases. Retrovirus is also coded to this code range.

Exercise 6.3 – Selecting Codes

Assign a diagnosis code for each diagnostic phrase.

1. candidial pyelonephritis _____
2. acute gonococcal vulvovaginitis _____
3. latent early syphilis _____
4. acute pulmonary blastomycosis _____
5. fluke infection _____
6. herpes simplex iridocyclitis _____
7. acute hepatitis E _____
8. candidial stomatitis _____
9. syphilitic meningitis, late congenital _____
10. *tinea cruris* _____

Comparing ICD-9-CM to ICD-10-CM

The number of codes for Infectious and parasitic diseases has increased in ICD-10-CM when compared to ICD-9-CM. The following conditions have expanded codes:

- *Typhoid fever*—Codes now differentiate the manifestation of the typhoid fever.
- *Amebic infections*—Codes now reflect specific sites.
- *Intestinal infections*—Additional category codes identify the specific types of infection.

The descriptions of codes for tuberculosis have changed in ICD-10-CM. Additionally in ICD-10-CM many of the codes throughout the chapter have been expanded to reflect manifestations of the diseases coded in chapter 1 of ICD-10-CM.

The following conditions have been changed in ICD-10-CM to include additional categories or changes in terminology:

- Sepsis
- Smallpox
- Malaria
- Infectious mononucleosis
- Hepatitis
- Leprosy
- Poliomyelitis

Internet Links

A comprehensive infectious disease syllabus can be found at *www.atsu.edu/kcom*

Categories of acquired immunity can be found at *www.wisc-online.com*

For information on infectious and parasitic diseases, search the Centers for Disease Control and Prevention Web site at *www.cdc.gov* and the National Institutes of Health Web site at *www.nih.gov*

For recent research on infectious diseases from the National Foundation on Infectious Diseases, go to *www.nfid.org*

For more information regarding parasitic diseases, reference the Karolinska Institute Web site at *www.mic.ki.se/Diseases*

Summary

- ICD-10-CM chapter 1 includes infectious and parasitic diseases.
- Organisms are classified into the following groups: bacteria, fungi, parasites, and viruses.
- Opportunistic infections occur when a patient has a weakened immune system.
- Single-code assignment, combination-code assignment, and dual-code assignment are used in chapter 1.

- An underlying condition/infection code is sequenced first, followed by the manifestation code.
- Septicemia occurs when there is a systematic infection with the presence of organisms or their toxins in the blood.
- Coding HIV depends on the place of service.
- If a patient is admitted for an HIV-related condition, the principal diagnosis should be code B20, followed by additional diagnosis codes for all reported HIV-related conditions.
- Asymptomatic HIV cases are coded to code Z21.
- Viral hepatitis includes hepatitis A, B, C, D, and E.

Chapter Review

True/False: Indicate whether each statement is true (T) or false (F).

1. _____ The terms *cocci*, *bacilli*, and *spirilla* describe fungal shapes.

2. _____ To describe clusters of bacteria, the medical word part *staphylo-* is used.

3. _____ A culture and sensitivity test is used to identify parasitic infections.

4. _____ Yeast infections are caused by fungi.

5. _____ Dual-code assignment is mandatory for all bacterial infections.

Fill-in-the-Blank: Enter the appropriate term(s) to complete each statement.

6. In dual-code assignment, two codes appear in the Alphabetic Index. This is to signal to the coder that the code in the brackets should be listed as the _____ code.

7. Clinical tests used to diagnosis tuberculosis include chest X-rays _____ and sputum cultures.

8. Two forms of fungal infections that affect humans are yeasts and _____.

9. Thrush is a common candidiasis infection of the _____.

10. Athlete's foot is caused by the pathogen _____.

Coding Assignments

Instructions: Using an ICD-10-CM coding book, select the code for each diagnostic statement.

1. botulism _____

2. gonococcal keratitis _____

3. scarlet fever _____

4. amebic balanitis _____

5. herpes simplex meningitis   _____

6. frambesioma   _____

7. warts, viral   _____

8. congential syphilis   _____

9. hyperkeratosis of pinta   _____

10. scabies   _____

11. internal hirudiniasis   _____

12. syphilitic bursitis   _____

13. malaria   _____

14. foot and mouth disease   _____

15. conjunctivitis, viral   _____

16. chronic viral hepatitis   _____

17. West Nile virus   _____

18. rubella   _____

19. shingles   _____

20. genital herpes   _____

21. mumps without mention of complications   _____

22. tuberculosis of bronchus   _____

23. tetanus neonatorum   _____

24. shigellosis due to *Shigella sonnei*   _____

25. oxyurasis   _____

Case Studies

Instructions: Review each case study and select the correct ICD-9-CM diagnostic code.

CASE 1

S: Fifty-year-old male presents today with severe abdominal pain, nausea, and vomiting, persistent over the last 24 hours. Diarrhea has developed, and abdominal cramping is also present. Pt states he cannot keep anything down. Upon questioning, he states he attended a neighborhood clambake and ate at least a dozen raw clams. No OTC medications were tried because pt cannot keep anything down.

O: Pleasant, alert gentleman who appears in mild discomfort. **Vital signs:** Temp—99, pulse—70, resp—22, BP—120/75. **Skin:** Warm and clammy.

  HEENT: Unremarkable except for dryness around conjunctiva and the mouth. Patient appears slightly dehydrated.

  Neck: No JVD; no thyromegaly or bruits.

  Lungs: Clear to auscultation and percussion.

  Heart: No murmurs.

  Extremities: No edema.

A: Food poisoning due to *salmonella*

P: Will order a suppository to help with the nausea. Stressed the importance of forcing fluids once the suppository has had time to work. Patient will call in the morning if not better. If he is improving, he will follow up as needed.

ICD-10-CM Code Assignment: _____

CASE 2

S: Nineteen-year-old woman presents today with slight fever, cough, and fatigue x 4 days. OTC medications were tried with little relief. No other family members are symptomatic. No nausea or vomiting, no shortness of breath.

O: **Vital Signs:** Temp—98.7, BP—100/72; Skin: warm and dry; **HEENT:** TM's normal; throat is slightly red; **Neck:** normal; **Lungs:** clear; **Heart:** RRR.

A: Viral Infection

P: I explained to patient that I feel this is a viral infection and could have come on in a variety of different ways. I suggested Advil for comfort and plenty of fluids. Patient requested an antibiotic. I explained that since this was viral in nature, an antibiotic would not be effective. She said she would try the Advil and notify us if she is not improved in 7–10 days.

ICD-10-CM Code Assignment: _____

CASE 3

S: This is a 29-year-old female who presents today with fever and nausea for 3 days. Patient has tried over-the-counter cold and flu medicine with no results. No other family members are ill at this time. Temp has been running anywhere from 99 to 102. When asked about any other symptoms, patient states that she "feels like my heart is racing sometimes." Patient has not voided in 2 days.

O: **Respirations:** 31; **Pulse:** 100; **BP:** 150/90. She is alert, oriented, and in no acute distress.

  Lungs: Clear, no rhonci or wheezing.

  HEENT: WNL.

  Skin: Clammy to touch.

(continued)

Heart: RRR with no murmurs.

Abdomen: Soft and nontender.

Extremities: Ankle edema +12.

A: Staphylococcus septicemia

P: Patient is admitted to hospital and will follow staphylococcus septicemia protocol.

ICD-10-CM Code Assignment: _____

CASE 4

Dr. Malik had just returned from a trip to overseas. He was providing free medical care to the people of a small village in a very desolate region of central Africa. Upon his return, he suddenly developed a severe headache, pain in his joints and back, and an extremely high fever. After extensive testing, combined with the fact that he had just returned from overseas, it was determined that Dr. Malik had contracted African tick typhus.

ICD-10-CM Code Assignment: _____

CASE 5

Kaley presented today with an unsightly sore on the lower lip and onto the skin. The patient said this is extremely painful and occurs usually around the time of her period. After a brief examination, Dr. Snyder diagnoses Kaley with herpes simplex, at which time he prescribes medication that will help relieve her symptoms.

ICD-10-CM Code Assignment: _____

Neoplasms

Chapter Outline

Objectives

At the conclusion of this chapter, the learner should be able to:

1. Identify the groups of neoplasms classified in ICD-10-CM.

2. Discuss the coding guidelines that relate to neoplasms.

3. Identify the differences between the ICD-9-CM and the ICD-10-CM codes.

4. Select and code diagnoses from case studies.

Key Terms

benign tumors

biopsy

ca in situ (CIS)

cancer

cancerous growths

carcinoma

carcinoma in situ (CIS)

encapsulated

in situ neoplasms

leukemia

lipoma

lymphoma

malignant neoplasms

malignant primary

malignant secondary

melanoma

metastasize

morphology

neoplasms

neoplasms of uncertain
   behavior

neoplasms of
   unspecified behavior

noninfiltrating
   carcinoma

noninvasive carcinoma

nonmalignant tumors

preinvasive carcinoma

sarcoma

transitional cell
   carcinoma

tumors

Reminder

As you work through this chapter, you will need to have a copy of the ICD-10-CM coding book for reference.

Introduction

Chapter 2 of ICD-10-CM contains diagnostic codes for neoplasms. ICD-10 classifies neoplasms into the following broad groups:

- C00–C96, Malignant neoplasms
- C00–C75, Malignant neoplasms, stated or presumed to be primary (of specified sites), and certain specified histologies, except neuroendocrine, and of lymphoid, hematopoietic, and related tissue
- C00–C14, Malignant neoplasms of lip, oral cavity, and pharynx
- C15–C26, Malignant neoplasms of digestive organs
- C30–C39, Malignant neoplasms of respiratory and intrathoracic organs
- C40–C41, Malignant neoplasms of bone and articular cartilage
- C43–C44, Melanoma and other malignant neoplasms of skin
- C45–C49, Malignant neoplasms of mesothelial and soft tissue
- C50, Malignant neoplasms of breast
- C51–C58, Malignant neoplasms of female genital organs
- C60–C63, Malignant neoplasms of male genital organs
- C64–C68, Malignant neoplasms of urinary tract
- C69–C72, Malignant neoplasms of eye, brain, and other parts of central nervous system
- C73–C75, Malignant neoplasms of thyroid and other endocrine glands
- C76–C80, Malignant neoplasms of ill-defined, secondary, and unspecified sites
- C81–C96, Malignant neoplasms of lymphoid, hematopoietic, and related tissue
- D00–D09 In situ neoplasms
- D10–D36, Benign neoplasms, except benign neuroendocrine tumors
- D37–D48, Neoplasms of uncertain behavior, polycythemia vera, and myelodysplastic syndromes
- D49, Neoplasms of unspecified behavior

Neoplasms, or **tumors**, are defined as an uncontrolled abnormal growth of cells and are characterized as malignant or benign. **Malignant neoplasms**, called **cancerous growths**, are life-threatening, whereas **benign** or **nonmalignant tumors** are usually not life-threatening.

Introduction to the Body System

To understand the organization of codes in ICD-10-CM, the coder must realize that neoplasms are described according to the form and structure of the neoplastic growth of the cell, known as the **morphology**, and the anatomical site. Neoplastic conditions are located in the Alphabetic Index by referring to the morphological term or to the Neoplasm Table. Coders must be familiar with the medical terms used to characterize neoplasms before attempting to locate the terms in ICD-10-CM.

Malignant Versus Benign Neoplasms

Malignant neoplasms, also called **cancer**, grow relatively rapidly and may **metastasize**, or spread, to other body parts. The malignant cells multiply excessively and can invade or infiltrate normal tissue, making the condition life-threatening if untreated. The cancerous cells interfere with normal cell growth (Figure 7-1) and draw nutrients away from body tissue. Compared with normal tissue, cancerous cells appear disorderly and do not look like the tissue of origin. Patients with malignant conditions may experience:

- Anorexia.
- Abnormal bleeding or bruising.
- Difficulty swallowing.
- Indigestion.
- Malaise.
- Fever.
- Sores that do not heal or that change to the appearance of a wart or mole.
- Bladder and bowel habit changes.
- Mass growth in the breast or other body site.
- Persistent cough.
- Weight loss.

To determine whether a patient has a tumor, various laboratory tests and procedures [such as endoscopies, magnetic resonance imaging (MRI), computed tomography (CT) scans, X-rays, and ultrasound] are used. A **biopsy**, or the removal of tissues for pathological examination, is completed to differentiate between malignant and benign tumors.

Benign neoplasms:

- Usually grow slowly
- Typically are **encapsulated** (surrounded by a capsule)
- Do not metastasize

Under a microscope, benign neoplastic cells appear similar to the tissue of origin. **Benign tumors** do not cause death unless they are located in vital organs. For example, if a patient has a benign tumor located in the spinal cord or brain, removal may be complicated because of the location of the tumor thus causing death.

Both benign and malignant neoplasms are named and classified by the tissue of origin. Neoplasms are typically named by adding the suffix -*oma* to the name of the body part, such as in **lipoma**, a benign neoplasm of adipose tissue. Malignant tumors are called:

- **Carcinoma**—Cancer of the epithelial cells of connective tissue.
- **Lymphoma**—Cancer of the lymph nodes and immune system.
- **Leukemia**—Cancer of the blood-forming organs.
- **Melanoma**—Cancer of melanin-producing cells.
- **Sarcoma**—Cancer of supportive tissue such as blood vessels, bones, cartilage, and muscles.

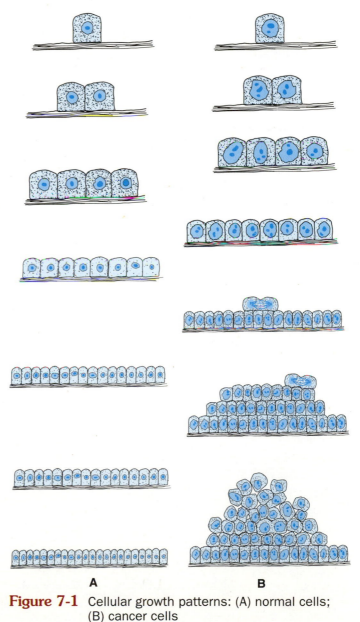

A   B

Figure 7-1   Cellular growth patterns: (A) normal cells; (B) cancer cells

Disease Highlight—Basal Cell Carcinoma of Skin

Basal cell carcinoma of the skin is the most common form of skin cancer. The cancer forms at the skin's epidermal layer. The types of basal cell carcinoma are sclerosing, noduloulcerative, and superficial. The most common cause of basal cell carcinoma is prolonged sun exposure, but it can also be a result of radiation exposure, immunosuppression, or even arsenic ingestion.

Signs and Symptoms:

- In the noduloulcerative type of basal cell carcinoma—Small, smooth, pinkish, or translucent lesions form in the early stages; ulcerations and tumors spread and become infected in later stages

- Sclerosing basal cell carcinoma—Waxy looking and has yellowish plaques without any distinct border

- Superficial types of basal cell carcinoma—Irregularly shaped lesions, most often found on the chest and back, sometimes a scaly look with atrophic areas in the centers

Clinical Testing:

- Biopsy and examination

Treatment:

- Excision

- Chemotherapy

- Radiotherapy

- Cryotherapy

Common benign and malignant neoplasms are listed in Table 7-1.

Table 7-1   Benign and Malignant Neoplasms

Tissue of Origin	Benign Neoplasms	Malignant Neoplasms
Adipose	Lipoma	Liposarcoma
Blood vessel	Hemangioma	Hemangiosarcoma
Bone	Osteoma	Osteogenic sarcoma Osteosarcoma
Bone marrow		Ewing sarcoma Multiple myeloma Leukemia
Breast		Carcinoma of breast
Cartilage	Chondroma	Chondrosarcoma
Cervix		Epidermoid carcinoma of the cervix
Colon		Carcinoma of colon
Esophagus		Esophageal adenocarcinoma
Fibrous	Fibroma	Fibrosarcoma

Ganglion cells	Ganglioneuroma	Neuroblastoma
Kidney		Hypernephroma Wilm's tumor
Lung		Adenocarcinoma of the lung Oat cell carcinoma
Meninges	Meningioma	Malignant meningioma
Muscle tissue, smooth	Leiomyoma	Leiomyosarcoma
Muscle tissue, striated	Rhabdomyoma	Rhabdomyosarcoma
Nerve tissue	Neuroma Neurinoma Neurofibroma	Neurogenic sarcoma
Ovaries		Cystadenocarcinoma of the ovaries
Penis		Carcinoma of penis
Skin		Basal cell carcinoma
Stomach		Gastric adenocarcinoma Melanoma Squamous cell carcinoma
Testes		Seminona
Uterus	Fibroid	Adenocarcinoma of the uterus

Exercise 7.1 – Identifying Neoplasms

For each of the terms listed, determine whether the neoplasm is benign (B) or malignant (M).

1. choriocarcinoma _____

2. reticulosarcoma _____

3. uterine leiomyoma _____

4. adenomatous polyp _____

5. giant-cell sarcoma _____

6. juxtacortical chondroma _____

7. fibromyxosarcoma of connective tissue _____

8. osteofibroma _____

9. psammocarcinoma _____

10. angiomyolipoma _____

11. squamous cell carcinoma _____

12. Wilm's tumor _____

13. leukemia _____

14. Kaposi's sarcoma _____

15. uterine fibroid _____

Coding of Neoplasms

ICD-10-CM groups neoplasms into the following behavior groups:

- Malignant neoplasms, C00–C96—A malignant neoplasm that grows rapidly, can spread to other organs, and can be life-threatening if not treated

- **In situ neoplasms**, also known as **carcinoma in situ**, **ca in situ**, or **CIS**, D00–D09—Neoplastic cells undergoing malignant changes that are confined to the original epithelium site without invading surrounding tissues. Common sites of in situ neoplasms include the breast, bladder, cervix, and vulva. Ca in situ is also referred to as **transitional cell carcinoma**, **noninfiltrating carcinoma**, **noninvasive carcinoma**, and **preinvasive carcinoma**.

- Benign neoplasms, D10–D36—Characterized by slow growth, not spreading, and typically not life-threatening

- **Neoplasms of uncertain behavior**, D37–D48—Neoplasms in which the cells are not histologically confirmed even after pathological investigation. The cells exhibit characteristics of both benign and malignant behavior, and further study is needed to arrive at a definitive diagnosis. To specify the purpose of this code range, the following note appears in the Tabular List after the heading D37–D48 (Figure 7-2).

NEOPLASMS OF UNCERTAIN BEHAVIOR (D37–D48)

Note: Categories D37–D48 classify by site neoplasms of uncertain behavior, i.e., histologic confirmation whether the neoplasm is malignant or benign cannot be made.

Such neoplasms are assigned behavior code /1 in the classification of the morphology of neoplsms.

Excludes 1: neoplasms of unspecified behavior (D49-)

Figure 7-2 Neoplasms of uncertain behavior

- **Neoplasms of unspecified behavior**, D49—Neoplasms in which the morphology and behavior of the neoplasm is not specified in the patient's record. To specify the purpose of this category, a note is included in the Tabular List after the category heading D49, Neoplasms of unspecified behavior (Figure 7-3).

D49   Neoplasms of unspecified behavior

Note: Category D49 classifies by site neoplasms of unspecified morphology and behavior. The term "mass", unless otherwise stated, is not to be regarded as a neoplastic growth.

Includes: "growth" NOS
                 neoplasm NOS
                 new growth NOS
                 tumor NOS

Excludes 1: neoplasms of uncertain behavior (D37-D48)

Figure 7-3 Neoplasms of unspecified behavior

Neoplasm Table

In the Alphabetic Index, codes for neoplasms are located by referencing the name of the neoplasm and using the Neoplasm Table. The Neoplasm Table is organized alphabetically by anatomical structure. Once you locate the anatomical site, the table lists codes for malignant, benign, uncertain, and unspecified behaviors.

Malignant neoplasms are organized in three columns in the table: primary, secondary, and ca in situ.

- *Ca in situ* is used when the pathological report or diagnostic statement records "ca in situ."

- The column for **malignant primary** is used when the neoplasm originated from the site being coded.

- The column for **malignant secondary** is used when the neoplasm metastasized or spread to the site being coded.

At the start of the Neoplasm Table are the notes shown in Figure 7-4.

Notes- 1. The list below gives the code numbers for neoplasms by anatomical site. For each site there are six possible code numbers according to whether the neoplasm in question is malignant, benign, in situ, of uncertain behavior, or of unspecified nature. The description of the neoplasm will often indicate which of the six columns is appropriate; e.g. malignant melanoma of skin, benign fibroadenoma of breast, carcinoma in situ of cervix uteri.

Where such descriptors are not present, the remainder of the Index should be consulted where guidance is given to the appropriate column for each morphological (histological) variety listed; e.g. Mesonephroma- see Neoplasm, malignant; Embryoma- see also Neoplasm, uncertain behavior; Disease, Bowen's- see Neoplasm, skin, in situ. However, the guidance in the Index can be overridden if one of the descriptors mentioned above is present; e.g. malignant adenoma of colon is coded to C18.9 and not to D12.6 as the adjective "malignant" overrides the Index entry "Adenoma- see also Neoplasm, benign."

2. Sites marked with the sign * (e.g., face NEC*) should be classified to malignant neoplasm of skin of these sites if the variety of neoplasm is a squamous cell carcinoma or an epidermoid carcinoma and to benign neoplasm of skin of these sites if the variety of neoplasm is a papilloma (any type).

Figure 7-4 Notes at the start of the Neoplasm Table

EXAMPLE: To code the term *basal cell* carcinoma of the *chin*, the coder first references the term *carcinoma* in the Alphabetic Index and then *basal cell*. The entry appears as shown in Figure 7-5.

The Alphabetic Index instructs the coder to reference "Neoplasm, skin, malignant." This refers the coder to the Neoplasm Table. The coder must follow that instruction to locate the proper type of neoplasm. In this case, the neoplasm is malignant.

The table groups neoplasms as shown in the Alphabetic Index under the term *Neoplasm*.

The table lists anatomical sites and then subterms for some sites. To code basal cell carcinoma of the chin, the coder searches the table for the anatomical site of skin and then the subterm *chin*.

Columns to the right of the terms list the codes for each type of neoplasm. The appropriate code is then selected from the columns.

Sequencing of Codes

When coding for the treatment of neoplasms, a coder must read the patient's record to determine the reason for the visit or admission. The record governs the sequencing of the codes.

Malignancy as Principal Diagnosis

If the focus of the patient's visit is to treat the neoplasm, then the neoplasm is sequenced as the principal diagnosis, unless the treatment is solely for the purpose of radiotherapy, immunotherapy, or chemotherapy. (The specific guidelines for coding encounters or admissions involving radiotherapy or chemotherapy are discussed later in this chapter.) If a patient with cancer is seen for an acute or chronic condition and the treatment is focused on that condition, then the acute or chronic condition becomes the principal diagnosis.

Carcinoma (M8010/3) - see also Neoplasm, by site, malignant

with —

apocrine metaplasia (M8573/3)

cartilaginous (ans osseous) metaplasia (M8571/3)

osseous (and cartilaginous) metaplasia (M8571/3)

productive fibrosis (M8141/3)

spindle cell metaplasia (M8572/3)

squamous metaplasia (M8570/3)

acidophil (M8280/3)

specified site - see Neoplasm, malignant

unspecified site C75. 1

acinar (cell) (M8550/3)

acinic cell (M8550/3)

adenocystic (M8200/3)

adenoid

cystic (M8200/3)

squamous cell (M8075/3)

adenosquamous (M8560/3)

adnexal (skin) (M8390/3) - see Neoplasm, skin, malignant

adrenal cortical (M8370/3) C74.0-

alveolar (M8251/3) - see Neoplasm, lung, malignant

cell (M8250/3) - see Neoplasm, lung, malignant

ameloblastic (M9270/3) C41.1

upper jaw (bone) C41.0

anaplastic type (M8021/3)

apocrine (M8401/3)

breast - see Neoplasm, breast, malignant

specified site NEC - see Neoplasm, skin, malignant

unspecified site C44.9

basal cell (pigmented) (M8090/3) - see also Neoplasm, skin, malignant

fibro-epithelial (M8093/3) - see Neoplasm, skin, malignant

morphea (M8092/3) - see Neoplasm, skin, malignant

multicentric (M8091/3) - see Neoplasm, skin, malignant

basaloid (M8123/3)

Figure 7-5 Alphabetical Listing for carcinoma

Exercise 7.2 – Coding for Neoplasms

For each diagnostic statement listed, select the appropriate code.

1. subependymal glioma D43.2 _____

2. malignant neoplasm of skin of breast _____

3. ca of lung _____

4. ceruminous adenocarcinoma _____

5. metastatic carcinoma to lung _____

6. liposarcoma of the left shoulder _____

7. pheochromocytoma (benign) of the adrenal gland _____

8. metastatic tumor to the common bile duct _____

9. amelobastic odontoma _____

10. fibromyoma of the uterus _____

11. neoplasm, benign, of left lacrimal gland and duct _____

12. malignant neoplasm of retroperitoneum _____

13. tonsillar fossa neoplasm malignant _____

14. bronchial carcinoma (right lower lobe) _____

15. benign neoplasm of brain _____

EXAMPLE: On May 1, Sally Jones is admitted to Hill Top Hospital with a blood sugar level of 375. The following diagnoses are on the face sheet at admission: carcinoma of the breast, uncontrolled insulin-dependent diabetes, and hypertension. She is admitted to control the diabetes. For this admission, the diabetes is the principal diagnosis.

The same patient is admitted on September 1 for a mastectomy due to carcinoma of the breast. Although her medical condition also includes insulin-dependent diabetes and hypertension, on this admission the principal diagnosis is the carcinoma of the breast.

> **ICD-10-CM Official Coding Guidelines**
>
> If the treatment is directed at the malignancy, designate the malignancy as the principal diagnosis. (See Appendix A, Section I, C2, a.)

Eradication of Malignancy and Follow-Up Examinations

Cancer patients are monitored on a regular basis to monitor them for recurrence or metastasis. Code selection is based on the status of the patient at the time of the encounter.

Treatment Followed by Recurrence

When a patient is treated for a malignancy, whether it is with chemotherapy, radiation, or surgery, and there is evidence that the cancer has recurred, the primary malignancy is the principal diagnosis.

Excised Malignancy Followed by Recurrence

When a previously excised malignancy recurs, the code for the malignancy is used for the principal diagnosis.

Follow-Up Visit with No Recurrence

Follow-up Z code category Z08, Encounter for follow-up examination after completed treatment for malignant neoplasm, is used when a patient is seen for follow-up after undergoing surgery, chemotherapy, radiation, or other treatment and when no evidence of a recurrence or metastasis exists. The follow-up Z codes are used to explain the continuing surveillance of the patient. This code implies that the neoplastic condition has been fully treated and no longer exists. The follow-up code explains the repeated visits. The Tabular entry for Z08 is shown in Figure 7-6.

Z08 Encounter for follow-up examination after completed treatment for malignant neoplasm

Includes: medical surveillance following completed treatment

Use additional code to identify any acquired absence of organs (Z90.-)

Use additional code to identify the personal history of malignant neoplasm (Z85.-)

Excludes1: aftercare following medical care (Z43-Z49, Z51)

Figure 7-6 Tabular entry for Z08

Two Primary Sites

In some malignant cancer cases, two primary sites are present. The coder must determine whether the treatment is directed at one site or at both.

- When the treatment is directed at one site, that site should be designated as the principal diagnosis.
- When the treatment is directed at both sites, either site can be designated as the principal diagnosis.

EXAMPLE: Tom Top has a diagnosis of primary carcinoma of the esophagus and primary carcinoma of the stomach. On February 1, he was admitted for partial removal of carcinogenic esophageal tissue. There was no treatment for the carcinoma of the stomach. In this case the principal diagnosis is the primary carcinoma of the esophagus (C15.9). On May 1, he was admitted for removal of the tissue of the esophagus and stomach due to carcinoma. Because the treatment was directed at two primary sites, either site can be used as the principal diagnosis (C15.9 or C16.9).

Primary and Secondary Malignancies

When a patient has both primary and secondary malignancies, the coder must determine the focus of treatment to ensure correct code sequencing. Patients with primary and secondary malignancies can be admitted or seen to:

- Address the primary malignancy only.
- Address the secondary malignancy only.
- Address both the primary and secondary malignancies.
- Address the secondary site when a primary site has been excised or eradicated.

Primary Malignancy Only

When the primary malignancy is the only condition treated, designate the primary malignancy as the principal diagnosis.

Secondary Malignancy Only

When treatment is directed only at the secondary, or metastatic malignancy, the secondary site is designated as the principal diagnosis, unless the admission is for radiotherapy or chemotherapy. An additional code is assigned for the primary site.

EXAMPLE: Bob Pint is admitted for removal of a metastatic tumor of the spinal cord that has metastasized from the lung. The secondary malignant tumor of the spinal cord is the principal diagnosis, and the primary malignant cancer of the lung is used as an additional code.

ICD-10-CM Official Coding Guidelines

When a patient is admitted because of a primary neoplasm with metastasis and treatment is directed toward the secondary site only, the secondary neoplasm is designated as the principal diagnosis even though the primary malignancy is still present. (See Appendix A, Section I, C2, b.)

Primary and Secondary Malignancy

When the treatment is directed equally at both primary and secondary malignancies, the primary malignancy is sequenced as the principal diagnosis and the secondary malignancy is sequenced as an additional code.

EXAMPLE: Nate Newman was admitted to the hospital for surgery on a malignant tumor of the pancreas and a malignant tumor of the spleen, which had been discovered with the latest CT scan done before admission. The tumor of the spleen is believed to have metastasized from the pancreas, but this will be confirmed when the pathology report comes back after surgery.

In this case, the pancreatic tumor has already been diagnosed, making it the primary malignancy. The tumor in the spleen is a new tumor that is going to be removed during the same surgery and is coded as a secondary diagnosis.

Secondary Sites with Excision or Eradication of Primary Site

A patient may undergo treatment for a primary site that could include excision, chemotherapy, and radiation therapy. After such treatment, the site may show no evidence of any existing primary malignancy, and therefore further treatment is not directed at the primary site. Treatment may then be directed at the secondary site. The secondary site is then used as the principal diagnosis, and the former primary site is assigned a code from category Z85, Personal history of a primary and secondary malignant neoplasm. The start of category Z85 appears in the Tabular Listing as shown in Figure 7-7.

Z85   Personal history of primary and secondary malignant neoplasm

Code first any follow-up examination after treatment of malignant neoplasm (Z08).
Use additional code to identify:

  alcohol use and dependence (F10.0-)
  exposure to environmental tobacco smoke (Z58.7)
  history of tobacco use (Z87.82)
  occupational exposure to environmental tobacco smoke (Z57.31)
  tobacco dependence (F17.-)
  tobacco use (Z72.0)

Excludes 2: personal history of benign neoplasm (Z86.01-)
          personal history of carcinoma-in-situ (Z86.00-)

Figure 7-7 Tabular Listing for Z85

EXAMPLE: Steve Smith was treated for carcinoma of the gallbladder with metastasis to the lungs. In January he underwent removal of the gallbladder, and currently there is no evidence of the carcinoma in the biliary area. He is now being admitted for removal of his left lung due to cancer. The secondary site of the lung cancer is coded and sequenced first, and the previous primary site is coded to Z85.09, Personal history of malignant neoplasm of other digestive organs.

Coders should be cautious when looking up "personal history of a malignant neoplasm" in the Alphabetic Index. Be sure to pay particular attention to the indentations because there is also a category for family history of malignant neoplasms.

ICD-10-CM Official Coding Guidelines

When a primary malignancy has been previously excised or eradicated from its site and there is no further treatment directed to that site, and there is no evidence of any existing primary malignancy, a code from category Z85, Personal history of primary and secondary malignant neoplasm, should be used to indicate the former site of the malignancy. Any mention of extension, invasion, or metastasis to another site is coded as a secondary malignant neoplasm to that site. The secondary site may be the principal or first-listed with the Z85 code used as a secondary code. (See Appendix A, Section I, C2, d.)

Figures 7-8 and 7-9 compare the two Alphabetic Listing entries for family and personal history of malignant neoplasms.

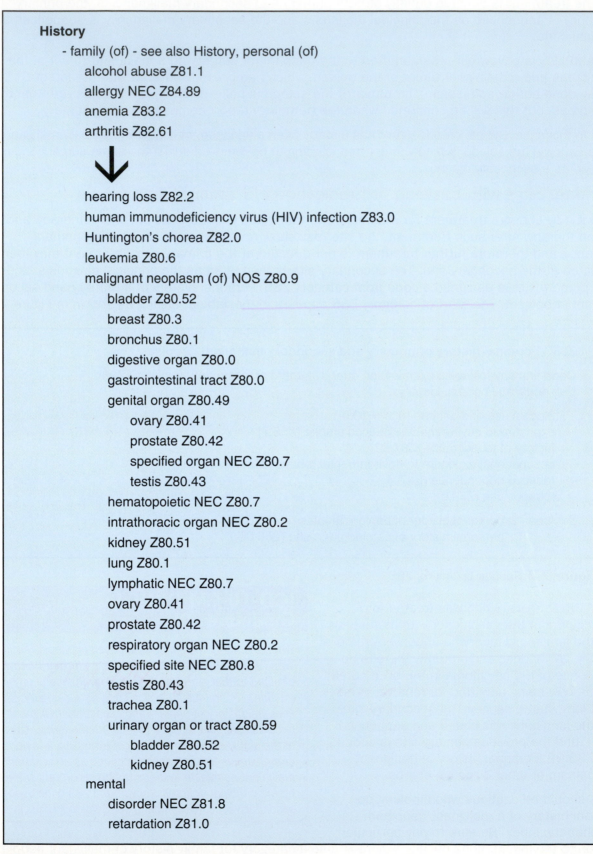

History

- family (of) - see also History, personal (of)

   alcohol abuse Z81.1

   allergy NEC Z84.89

   anemia Z83.2

   arthritis Z82.61

   hearing loss Z82.2

   human immunodeficiency virus (HIV) infection Z83.0

   Huntington's chorea Z82.0

   leukemia Z80.6

   malignant neoplasm (of) NOS Z80.9

      bladder Z80.52

      breast Z80.3

      bronchus Z80.1

      digestive organ Z80.0

      gastrointestinal tract Z80.0

      genital organ Z80.49

         ovary Z80.41

         prostate Z80.42

         specified organ NEC Z80.7

         testis Z80.43

      hematopoietic NEC Z80.7

      intrathoracic organ NEC Z80.2

      kidney Z80.51

      lung Z80.1

      lymphatic NEC Z80.7

      ovary Z80.41

      prostate Z80.42

      respiratory organ NEC Z80.2

      specified site NEC Z80.8

      testis Z80.43

      trachea Z80.1

      urinary organ or tract Z80.59

         bladder Z80.52

         kidney Z80.51

   mental

      disorder NEC Z81.8

      retardation Z81.0

Figure 7-8 Alphabetical Listing for family history

History-continued
    personal (of)
        injury NEC Z91.69
        irradiation Z92.3
        kidney stones Z87.43
        leukemia Z85.6
        lymphoma (non-Hodgkin's) Z85.72
        malignant neoplasm (of) Z85.9
            bone Z85.822
                secondary Z85.863
            brain Z85.831
                secondary Z85.862
            breast Z85.3
            bronchus Z85.11
            digestive organ Z85.00
                anus Z85.04
                colon Z85.03
                esophagus Z85.01
                large intestine Z85.03
                lip Z85.819
                liver Z85.05
                    secondary Z85.861
            oral cavity Z85.819
                specified site NEC Z85.818
                tongue Z85.810

Figure 7-9 Alphabetical Entry for personal history of malignant neoplasm

Malignancy in Two or More Noncontiguous Sites

The following coding guideline should be followed when a patient has a malignancy in two or more noncontiguous sites.

ICD-10-CM Official Coding Guidelines

Malignancy in two or more noncontiguous sites

A patient may have more than one malignant tumor in the same organ. These tumors may represent different primaries or metastatic disease, depending on the site. Should the documentation be unclear, the provider should be queried as to the status of each tumor so that the correct codes can be assigned. (See Appendix A, Section I, C2, i)

Unspecified Disseminated Malignant Neoplasm

In cases when a patient has advanced metastatic disease and no know primary or secondary sties are specified the following coding guideline should be followed:

ICD-10-CM Official Coding Guidelines

Disseminated malignant neoplasm, unspecified

Code C80.0, Disseminated malignant neoplasm, unspecified, is for use only in those cases where the patient has advanced metastatic disease and no known primary or secondary sites are specified. It should not be used in place of assigning codes for the primary site and all known secondary sites. (See Appendix A, Section I, C2, j)

Malignant Neoplasm Without Specification of Site

When the medical record of the patient does not designate the site of a malignant neoplasm, the following guideline gives direction to the coder.

ICD-10-CM Official Coding Guidelines

Malignant Neoplasm Without Specification of Site

Code C80.1, Malignant neoplasm, unspecified, equates to Cancer, unspecified. This code should only be used when no determination can be made as to the primary site of a malignancy. This code should rarely be used in the inpatient setting. (See Appendix A, Section 1C, 2 k)

Additional Coding Guidelines for Sequencing of Neoplasm Codes

The following coding guidelines also appear in the Official ICD-10-CM Coding Guidelines for the sequencing of neoplasm codes and should be referenced before coding assignment is completed.

ICD-10-CM Official Coding Guidelines

Sequencing of neoplasm codes

1) Encounter for treatment of primary malignancy

If the reason for the encounter is for treatment of a primary malignancy, assign the malignancy as the principal/first listed diagnosis. The primary site is to be sequenced first, followed by any metastatic sites.

2) Encounter for treatment of secondary malignancy

When an encounter is for a primary malignancy with metastasis and treatment is directed toward the metastatic (secondary) site(s) only, the metastatic site(s) is designated as the principal/first listed diagnosis. The primary malignancy is coded as an additional code.

3) Malignant neoplasm in a pregnant patient

Codes from chapter 15, Pregnancy, childbirth, and the puerperium, are always sequenced first on a medical record. A code from subcategory O94.1-, Malignant neoplasm complicating pregnancy, childbirth, and the puerperium, should be used first, followed by the appropriate code from Chapter 2 to indicate the type of neoplasm.

The exception to this guideline is anemia. When the admission/encounter is for management of an anemia associated with the malignancy, and the treatment is only for anemia, the appropriate code for the malignancy is sequenced as the principal or first-listed diagnosis, followed by code D63.0, Anemia in neoplastic disease.

4) Encounter for complication associated with a neoplasm

When an encounter is for management of a complication associated with a neoplasm, such as dehydration, and the treatment is only for the complication, the complication is coded first, followed by the appropriate code(s) for the neoplasm. The exception to this guideline is anemia. When the admission/encounter is for management of an anemia associated with the malignancy, and the treatment is only for anemia, the appropriate code for the malignancy is sequenced as the principal or first-listed diagnosis followed by code D63.0, Anemia in neoplastic disease.

5) Complication from surgical procedure for treatment of a neoplasm

When an encounter is for treatment of a complication resulting from a surgical procedure performed for the treatment of the neoplasm, designate the complication as the principal/first listed diagnosis. See guideline regarding the coding of a current malignancy versus personal history to determine if the code for the neoplasm should also be assigned.

6) Pathologic fracture due to a neoplasm

When an encounter is for a pathological fracture due to a neoplasm, if the focus of treatment is the fracture, a code from subcategory M84.5, Pathological fracture in neoplastic disease, should be sequenced first, followed by the code for the neoplasm. If the focus of treatment is the neoplasm with an associated pathological fracture, the neoplasm code should be sequenced first, followed by a code from M84.5 for the pathological fracture. The "code also" note at M84.5 provides this sequencing instruction. (See Appendix A, Section I, C2, I 1–6)

Complications Associated with Neoplasms

Numerous complications are associated with malignant neoplasms and their treatment. Patients commonly seek health care that is directed at the treatment of the complications, not at the treatment of the neoplasm.

Anemia

Cancer patients can experience anemia, a deficiency of the red blood cells, caused by the malignancy or chemotherapy. When encounters or admissions occur for the management of the anemia, the following coding guidelines should be followed:

> **EXAMPLE:** Patty Pink is diagnosed with carcinoma of the breast and is undergoing chemotherapy. She has developed anemia from the chemotherapy and is being admitted for its management. Because she is being admitted for treatment of the anemia, the diagnosis for the cancer of the breast is listed first followed by the D63.0 code for anemia in neoplastic disease.

ICD-10-CM Official Coding Guidelines

1. Anemia associated with malignancy

When the admission/encounter is for management of an anemia associated with the malignancy and the treatment is only for anemia, the appropriate anemia code for the malignancy is sequenced as the principal or first-listed diagnosis (followed by code D63.0, Anemia in neoplastic disease).

2. Anemia associated with chemotherapy, immunotherapy and radiation therapy

When the admission/encounter is for management of an anemia associated with an adverse effect of chemotherapy, immunotherapy or radiotherapy and the only treatment is for the anemia, the appropriate adverse effect should be sequenced first, followed by the appropriate codes for the anemia and neoplasm. (See Appendix A, Section I, C2, c, 1–2.)

Dehydration

Dehydration, the excess loss of fluids, is also a complication that can occur due to vomiting and diarrhea caused by the malignancy, chemotherapy, or radiation therapy. When a patient has experienced dehydration, an encounter or admission may be necessary to rehydrate the patient.

> **EXAMPLE:** Sally Smith has been undergoing radiation therapy for leukemia on an outpatient basis. She has experienced diarrhea and vomiting, and she is now dehydrated. Her physician is admitting her to Sunny Hill Hospital to receive intravenous rehydration. In this case the dehydration is sequenced as the principal diagnosis, followed by a code for the leukemia.

ICD-10-CM Official Coding Guidelines

When the admission/encounter is for management of dehydration due to the malignancy or the therapy or a combination of both, and only the dehydration is being treated (intravenous rehydration), the dehydration is sequenced first, followed by the code(s) for the malignancy. (See Appendix A, Section I, C2, c, 3.)

Surgical Procedure Performed for Treatment of a Malignancy

Sometimes a malignancy requires surgical intervention. A complication that results from the surgery is coded as the primary diagnosis when an admission or encounter is needed.

EXAMPLE: Amanda Pan had surgery on a malignant tumor of the small intestine. One month after the surgery, Amanda developed an infection that required treatment with antibiotics as an inpatient. The infection is designated as the principal diagnosis.

ICD-10-CM Official Coding Guidelines

When the admission/encounter is for treatment of a complication resulting from a surgical procedure, designate the complication as the principal or first-listed diagnosis if treatment is directed at resolving the complication. (See Appendix A, Section I, C2, c, 4.)

Pain

As the malignancy progresses and as treatment occurs, cancer patients sometimes experience pain that can result in depression, anxiety, difficulty sleeping, and loss of appetite. Narcotic medications may be necessary to control the pain. If a patient seeks medical care or is admitted for control of the pain, the malignancy code is designated as the principal diagnosis. The following coding guideline should be followed when assigning codes:

ICD-10-CM Official Coding Guidelines

Neoplasm Related Pain

Code G89.3 is assigned to pain documented as being related, associated or due to cancer, primary or secondary malignancy, or tumor. This code is assigned regardless of whether the pain is acute or chronic.

This code may be assigned as the principal or first-listed code when the stated reason for the admission/encounter is documented as pain control/pain management. The underlying neoplasm should be reported as an additional diagnosis.

When the reason for the admission/encounter is management of the neoplasm and the pain associated with the neoplasm is also documented, code G89.3 may be assigned as an additional diagnosis. It is not necessary to assign an additional code for the site of the pain. (See Appendix A, Section I, C6, b, 5)

Admissions/Encounters Involving Surgery, Chemotherapy, Immunotherapy, and Radiation Therapy

After a patient has been diagnosed with a malignant condition, treatment options can include surgery, chemotherapy, immunotherapy, radiation therapy, or a combination of treatments. A coder must identify the treatment occurring during the current encounter or admission.

Surgery Followed by Chemotherapy or Radiation

In some cases a patient will undergo surgery to remove the cancerous tissue and then undergo chemotherapy or radiation.

EXAMPLE: Sally Pink, who was diagnosed with carcinoma of the breast, is admitted for a total mastectomy followed by radiation therapy. In this case the carcinoma of the breast is the principal diagnosis.

ICD-10-CM Official Coding Guidelines

When an episode of care involves the surgical removal of a neoplasm, primary or secondary site, followed by adjunct chemotherapy or radiation treatment during the same episode of care, the neoplasm code should be assigned as principal or first-listed diagnosis, using codes in the C00–D49 series or where appropriate in the C83–C90 series. (See Appendix A, Section I, C2, e, 1.)

Encounter or Admission Solely for Administration of Chemotherapy or Radiation

The Official Coding Guidelines provide instructions in selecting codes for encounters or admissions solely for the administration of chemotherapy, immunotherapy, and radiation therapy.

ICD-10-CM Official Coding Guidelines

Patient admission/encounter solely for administration of chemotherapy, Immunotherapy and radiation therapy

If a patient admission/encounter is solely for the administration of chemotherapy, immunotherapy or radiation therapy assign code Z51.0, Encounter for antineoplastic radiation therapy, or Z51.11, Encounter for antineoplastic chemotherapy, or Z51.12, Encounter for antineoplastic immunotherapy as the first-listed or principal diagnosis. If a patient receives more than one of these therapies during the same admission more than one of these codes may be assigned, in any sequence.

The malignancy for which the therapy is being administered should be assigned as a secondary diagnosis. (See Appendix A, Section I, C2, e, 2)

EXAMPLE: Mary Ann Jones is admitted for chemotherapy for plasma cell leukemia. The principal diagnostic code listed first is Z51.11, Encounter for antineoplastic chemotherapy. A code for the plasma cell leukemia is also assigned as an additional code.

EXAMPLE: Mary Ann Jones's physician decides not only to have her receive chemotherapy but also to follow up the treatment with radiation therapy. Codes Z51.0, Encounter for antineoplastic radiation therapy, or Z51.11, Encounter for antineoplastic chemotherapy, should be used. Either can be sequenced first.

Radiation Therapy, Chemotherapy, or Immunotherapy Followed by Complications

It is common for patients to experience nausea, vomiting, and dehydration after chemotherapy, immunotherapy, or radiation therapy. When a patient is admitted for the purpose of chemotherapy, immunotherapy, or radiation and subsequently develops a complication, the following coding guideline offers coding guidance.

ICD-10-CM Official Coding Guidelines

Patient admitted for radiation therapy, chemotherapy or immunotherapy and develops complications

When a patient is admitted for the purpose of radiotherapy, immunotherapy or chemotherapy and develops complications such as uncontrolled nausea and vomiting or dehydration, the principal or first-listed diagnosis is Z51.0, Encounter for antineoplastic radiation therapy, or Z51.11, Encounter for antineoplastic chemotherapy, or Z51.12, Encounter for antineoplastic immunotherapy followed by any codes for the complications. (See Appendix A, Section I, C2, e, 3)

EXAMPLE: Sally Jones is admitted for radiation therapy for blast cell leukemia. Immediately after the treatment, she develops nausea and excessive vomiting, for which she is treated. Code Z51.0, Encounter for antineoplastic radiation therapy, is sequenced first, followed by R11.0, Nausea and vomiting.

Admission or Encounter to Determine Extent of Malignancy or to Perform a Procedure

At times patients are seen for a paracentesis, which is a surgical puncture of the abdominal cavity for the aspiration of fluid, or for a thoracentesis, which is a surgical procedure for the aspiration of fluid from the chest wall or to determine the extent of a malignancy. In these cases, the primary malignancy or metastatic site is the primary diagnosis, even if radiation or chemotherapy is administered.

When an admission or encounter occurs to determine the extent of malignancy or to perform a procedure, the following guideline should be followed:

ICD-10-CM Official Coding Guidelines

When the reason for the admission/encounter is to determine the extent of the malignancy, or for a procedure such as paracentesis or thoracentesis, the primary malignancy or appropriate metastatic site is designated as the principal or first-listed diagnosis, even though chemotherapy or radiotherapy is administered. (See Appendix A, Section I, C2, f.)

Comparing ICD-9-CM to ICD-10-CM

The ICD-10-CM chapter on Neoplasms has many more additions, deletions, and combination codes, compared to the ICD-9-CM chapter. Categories and subcategories have been renamed or expanded. The coder should be guided by the Alphabetic Index.

Code Description	ICD-9-CM	ICD-10-CM
Malignant neoplasm of breast	Female, category 174 Male, category 175	C50 is used for both female and male.
Hodgkin's disease	Category 201 is used to identify the various types.	Category 81 is used with differentiation as to the type of Hodgkin's disease. Terminology is similar to ICD-9-CM.
Leukemia	Categories 204–208 are used with the types differentiated at the fourth-digit level.	Categories 91 to 95 are used to differentiate the various types of leukemia. The terminology is similar to that of ICD-9-CM.
Malignant neoplasm of esophagus	Category 150 is used to report malignant neoplasm of the esophagus. Specific codes are present for the cervical, thoracic, and abdominal esophagus.	C15 is used to report a malignant neoplasm of the esophagus. Cervical, thoracic, and abdominal esophagus is not differentiated in ICD-10-CM.
Benign neoplasm of major salivary glands	Code 210.2 is used to report a benign neoplasm of a major salivary gland that includes parotid, sublingual, or submandibular glands.	In ICD-10-CM the coding of a benign neoplasm of the major salivary glands is further divided into separate codes at the fourth-character level. This is an example of the specificity of ICD-10-CM.

Internet Links

For a complete list of approved cancer drugs, go to **www.fda.gov/cder/cancer**

For information on cancer, visit the American Cancer Society Web site at **www.cancer.org**

For information on cancer research, visit **www.cancer.gov/cancerinfo/literature**

For information on types of cancer, treatments, and other information about the disease, visit **www.CancerCenter.com**

To watch free videos on cancer topics, visit **www.healthline.com/video/cancer**

Summary

- ICD-10-CM codes neoplastic conditions to code range C00–D49.
- Neoplasms are classified as malignant, benign, cancer in situ, of uncertain behavior, and unspecified.
- A biopsy is completed to determine whether a neoplasm is malignant or benign.
- Carcinoma in situ is defined as neoplastic cells undergoing malignant changes that are confined to the original epithelium site without invading surrounding tissues.
- Neoplasms of uncertain behavior include cases in which the neoplasm exhibits characteristics of both benign and malignant behavior.
- Neoplasms of unspecified behavior include cases in which the behavior or morphology of the neoplasm is not specified in the patient's medical record.
- In the Alphabetic Index, codes for neoplasms are located by referencing the name of the neoplasm and by using the Neoplasm Table.
- Sequencing of codes for neoplasms depends on the reason for the encounter or admission.

Chapter Review

True/False: Indicate whether each statement is true (T) or false (F).

1. _____ There is no differentiation between malignant and benign neoplasm in ICD-10-CM.

2. _____ Lipoma and chondroma are malignant neoplasms.

3. _____ Carcinoma of the breast is malignant.

4. _____ Code block D10–D36 reports benign neoplasms.

5. _____ In the Neoplasm Table, benign neoplasms are divided into primary and secondary sites.

6. _____ When a patient is seen for chemotherapy, the neoplasm is sequenced as the principal diagnosis.

7. _____ If treatment is directed at a malignancy and the patient is also treated for an acute condition, the malignancy is designated as the principal diagnosis.

8. _____ When an encounter is for management of a complication associated with a neoplasm, such as dehydration, and the treatment is only for the complication, the complication is coded first, followed by the appropriate code(s) for the neoplasm.

9. _____ Narcotic medications are used to control the pain of cancer patients.

10. _____ When an encounter is for treatment of a complication resulting from a surgical procedure performed for the treatment of the neoplasm, designate the complication as the principal/first-listed diagnosis.

Coding Assignments

Instructions: Using an ICD-10-CM code book, assign the proper diagnosis code to the following diagnostic statements.

1. carcinoma of mouth   _____

2. adenocarcinoma of adrenal cortical   _____

3. left kidney lipoma   _____

4. leiomyoma of uterus   _____

5. neoplasm of anterior wall of urinary bladder, malignant   _____

6. plasma cell leukemia   _____

7. B cell lymphoma; intrapelvic lymph nodes   _____

8. acute promyelocytic leukemia   _____

9. secondary malignant neoplasm of skin of the chin   _____

10. carcinoma of uterine cervix   _____

11. carcinoma of bone   _____

12. carcinoma in situ of bladder   _____

13. primary neoplasm of ovary   _____

14. secondary cancer of islet cells of pancreas   _____

15. cancer of prostate gland   _____

16. neoplasm of uncertain behavior of renal pelvis   _____

17. basal cell carcinoma of skin on scalp   _____

18. plasma cell tumor   _____

19. Wilm's nephroblastoma   _____

20. benign neoplasm of abdomen   _____

21. benign neoplasm of the bursa of the shoulder   _____

22. CIS of the rectosigmoid junction   _____

23. malignant neoplasm of the adrenal gland (left side) with metastasis to the kidney and renal pelvis   _____

24. metastatic cancer from the bladder dome to the ureter   _____

25. cancer of the stomach (fundus)   _____

Case Studies

Instructions: Review each case study and select the correct ICD-10-CM diagnostic code.

CASE 1

Physician Office Note

4/25/XX Weight: 154 pounds, decrease from 2 weeks ago; weight then was 160.

CHIEF COMPLAINT: loss of weight, here for follow-up from breast biopsy.

Sally was seen 2 weeks ago, and I palpated a mass in her left breast. She was sent for a biopsy. She is here today for follow-up.

BREAST: Mass present in left breast; right breast has no masses present.

ABDOMEN: Normal, no masses or tenderness.

Patient is anxious about results of biopsy.

Pathology report reviewed with patient that confirmed cancer of central portion, left breast. Patient was referred to Dr. Smith at West Oncology.

ICD-10-CM Code Assignment: _____

CASE 2

Inpatient Discharge Summary

HISTORY OF PRESENT ILLNESS: The patient is a 76-year-old with a known history of cancer of the lung with metastasis to the brain.

Cancer of lung was resected 6 months ago. The patient was admitted because his daughter noticed him getting weaker and because he was not eating or drinking well for the last 2 days. He has undergone chemotherapy and radiation in the past 5 months, and he has asked for the treatment to be stopped.

Upon examination at the time of admission, he was dehydrated and weak due to lack of eating.

HOSPITAL COURSE: Patient requested that he receive care only for his dehydration. He was given IV hydration and refused all other treatment.

MEDICATIONS AT DISCHARGE: Patient was discharged on Vicodin for pain management, 1 every 4 hours as needed for pain.

DISCHARGE DIAGNOSES: Dehydration, metastatic cancer to the brain; history of lung cancer

ICD-10-CM Code Assignment: _____

CASE 3

Oncology Clinic Note

Patient is seen today to receive his first chemotherapy treatment for his diagnosis of acute lymphoid leukemia.

EXAM:

VITALS: Temperature 98.9, B/P 125/80. Pulse: regular.

LUNGS: Normal

ABDOMEN: Soft, no masses noted.

HEENT: Normal

HEART: Normal rate and rhythm

Chemotherapy schedule was reviewed, and side effects of treatment were discussed. Chemotherapy given; patient tolerated treatment well.

ICD-10-CM Code Assignment: _____

(continued)

CASE 4

Clinic Visit

Ellen is a 65-year-old female who presents today with severe headaches and blurred vision. She said these symptoms have been going on for approximately 2 weeks. She says that the pain is 10 out of 10 and that nothing seems to help relieve it. She has a history of breast cancer, which has been in remission for one year. A CT scan of the head and neck reveals a tumor in the temporal lobe of the brain.

A biopsy was performed and confirmed this to be a metastasis from the breast tumor.

ICD-10-CM Code Assignment: _____

CASE 5

Clinic Visit

A 52-year-old female presented with a 1-year history of epiphora. During this year, the tears were not bloodstained but very much a nuisance to the patient. CT revealed a small tumor connected to the right lacrimal sac and duct. Incisional biopsy revealed a benign tumor of the right lacrimal sac. The patient was treated by removing the tumor.

ICD-10-CM Code Assignment: _____

CASE 6

Emergency Department Visit

A 59-year-old male presented to the ED with dyspnea on exertion, fevers, and cough. A routine chest X-ray was completed to rule out pneumonia. The X-ray revealed a mass in the left lung. The patient was instructed to follow up with Dr. Ram in oncology.

Diagnosis: Probable neoplastic lung disease

ICD-10-CM Code Assignment: _____

CASE 7

Inpatient Admission

A 40-year-old female was admitted with severe abdominal pain. She has a history of cervical cancer that was excised four years ago. An MRI showed possible metastasis to the left ovary, which was confirmed during this admission as ovarian carcinoma, malignant secondary site.

ICD-10-CM Code Assignment: _____

CASE 8

Inpatient Admission

This 89-year-old female patient was transferred from a nursing home due to a suspected urinary bladder mass, after she underwent a series of diagnostic tests that concluded that she has malignant primary adenocarcinoma of the posterior wall of the urinary bladder. She has requested no treatment and was discharged to hospice care.

ICD-10-CM Code Assignment: _____

Diseases of the Blood and Blood-Forming Organs

Chapter Outline

Objectives

At the conclusion of this chapter, the learner should be able to:

1. List the three types of blood cells.
2. Identify diseases of the blood and blood-forming organs.
3. Explain the various types of anemia and the codes for each.
4. Accurately code diseases of the blood and blood-forming organs.
5. Identify the differences between the ICD-9-CM codes and the ICD-10-CM codes.
6. Select and code diagnoses from case studies.

Key Terms

agammaglobulinemia	aplastic anemia	eosinophilia	hemoglobin (Hgb)
agranulocytes	beta thalassemia	erythrocytes	hemolytic anemia
alpha thalassemia	coagulation	folate	hereditary factor VIII
anemia	constitutional aplastic anemia	folate deficient anemia	idiopathic aplastic anemia
angiohemophilia		granulocytes	

Reminder

As you work through this chapter, you will need to have a copy of the ICD-10-CM coding book to reference.

immune system	pernicious anemia	red blood cells (RBC)	thrombocytopenia
leukocytes	plasma	sickle-cell anemia	thrombophilia
lupus	platelets	sickle-cell trait	transcobalamin II
methemoglobinemia	polymorphonuclear neutrophils	sideropenic dysphagia	vitamin B_{12} deficiency anemia
myelophthisis		spleen	
neutropenia	pure red cell aplasia	thalassemia	Von Willebrand's disease
pancytopenia	purpura	thrombocytes	white blood cells (WBC)

Introduction

Chapter 3 of ICD-10-CM contains diagnoses codes for nutritional anemias, hemolytic anemias, aplastic anemias, bone marrow failure syndromes, coagulation defects, purpura and other hemorrhagic conditions, and other types of disorders of the blood and blood-forming organs such as the spleen. This chapter also contains disorders involving the immune mechanisms, such as deficiency of immunoglobulin A, G, and M.

Introduction to the Body System

Blood performs many functions in the body. The blood transports oxygen from the lungs to the cells and then moves waste from the cells to organs that dispose of the waste. Blood transports various nutrients throughout the body. Different fluids and electrolyte balance are maintained by the flow of the blood through the body. The interior of the body is also protected from infection by ability of the blood to clot, thereby keeping out infection and also preventing death due to excessive blood loss.

Blood Composition

The liquid portion of the blood, without its cellular elements, is known as **plasma**. The cellular elements in blood are erythrocytes (red blood cells), leukocytes (white blood cells), and thrombocytes (platelets). Red bone marrow produces three types of blood cells, which all originate from a stem cell. The stem cells become a red blood cell, the white blood cell, or platelets.

Erythrocytes, also known as **red blood cells (RBC)**, form in the bone marrow. These red blood cells are disc-shaped and contain hemoglobin. **Hemoglobin (Hgb)** absorbs oxygen and transports it to the tissues of the body.

Leukocytes, also known as **white blood cells (WBC)**, work to protect the body from disease. Leukocytes contain no hemoglobin and are less numerous than RBCs. These cells have an irregular ball-like shape. Leukocytes are classified into two major groups: **granulocytes** (cells with a granular appearance) and **agranulocytes** (cells that are not granular). The various types of granulocytes and agranulocytes are as follows:

Type of Leukocyte	Specific Type of Granulocyte or Agranulocyte
Granulocyte	Neutrophils
	Eosinophils
	Basophils
Agranulocytes	Lymphocytes
	Monocytes

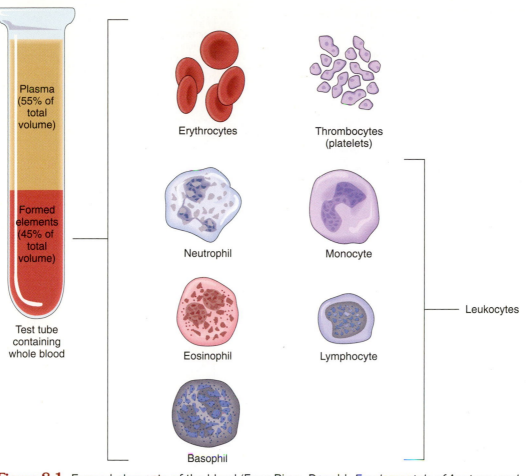

Figure 8-1 Formed elements of the blood (From Rizzo, Donald. *Fundamentals of Anatomy and Physiology*, 2nd ed. Clifton Park, NY: Delmar, 2003, Cengage Learning, p. 298.)

Thrombocytes, also called **platelets**, are ovoid-shaped structures that initiate blood clotting, or **coagulation**. A so-called platelet plug is formed by the body to stop bleeding when a cut or injury occurs. The platelet plug slows or stops bleeding, which in the worst case keeps the person from bleeding to death. Figure 8-1 illustrates the formed elements of the blood.

Coders should understand the components of blood and the terminology associated with it to be able to review blood test reports and accurately substantiate the diagnosis code assigned. The reports provide the medical documentation to justify the medical necessity of the tests. Figure 8-2 provides a listing of normal ranges for white blood cell tests.

Exercise 8.1 – Blood Components

Match the term in the first column with the description in the second column.

_____ **1.** granulocyte   **a.** protects the body from disease

_____ **2.** plasma   **b.** ovoid-shaped cell, also called a platelet

_____ **3.** bone marrow   **c.** neutrophil, for example

_____ **4.** thrombocyte   **d.** liquid portion of blood without cellular elements

_____ **5.** white blood cell   **e.** where a RBC is formed

Blood Test	Definition of Test	Normal Range		Examples of Diseases Indicated by Abnormal Value
White blood cell count, also known as leukocyte count or WBC	Identifies the number of white blood cells found in a cubic millimeter of blood (mm^3).	Adults and children	5000–10,000/mm^3	Leukocytosis Leukopenia
		Children 2 years or younger	6200–17,000/mm^3	
		Newborns	9000–30,000/mm^3	
Differential white blood cell count, also known as Differential leukocyte count, or (diff)	Identifies the percentage of each type of white cell relative to the total number of leukocytes.	Neutrophils	55–70%	Neutrophilia Neutropenia Measles Mumps Hepatitis Lymphocytosis Monocytosis Asthma Allergies
		Monocytes	2–8%	
		Lymphocytes	20–40%	
		Basophils	0.5–1%	
		Eosinophils	1–4%	
Red blood cell count, also known as erythrocyte count or RBC	Identifies the number of red blood cells found in a cubic millimeter of blood (mm^3).	Men	4.7–6.1 million/mm^3	Anemia Erythrocytosis Rheumatic fever
		Women	4.2–5.4 million/mm^3	
		Infants and children	3.8–5.5 million/mm^3	
		Newborns	4.8–7.1 million/mm^3	
Hematocrit (Hct) also known as packed cell volume (PCV)	Determines the percentage of red blood cells in whole blood.	Men	42–52%	Anemia
		Women	37–47% (in pregnancy: >33%)	
		Children	30–42%	
		Newborns	44–64%	
Hemoglobin (Hgb)	Evaluates the oxygen-carrying capacity of the red blood cells by determining the grams of hemoglobin per deciliter of blood.	Men	14–18 g/dl	Anemias Hyperthyroidism Lymphoma
		Women	12–16 g/dl (in pregnancy: >11 g/dl)	
		Children	11–16 g/dl	
		Newborns	14–24 g/dl	
Mean corpuscular volume (MCV)	Describes the average size of an individual red blood cell in cubic microns.	Adults and children	80–95 um^3	Iron deficiency Anemia Thalassemia Pernicious anemia
		Newborns	96–108 um^3	
Mean corpuscular hemoglobin (MCH)	Identifies the average weight of hemoglobin in an average red blood cell reported in picograms (pg).	Adults and children	27–31 pg	Macrocytic and Microcytic anemia
		Newborns	32–38 pg	
Mean corpuscular hemoglobin concentration (MCHC)	Measures the average concentration or percentage of hemoglobin within each red blood cell.	Adults and children	32–36%	Hypochromic Anemia Spherocytosis
		Newborns	32–33%	
Erythrocyte sedimentation rate (ESR, sed rate)	Measures the rate at which red blood cells settle out of unclotted blood in an hour. Expressed as millimeters per hour (mm/hr).	Men <50 yrs	0–10 mm/hr	Polycythemia vera Sickle cell anemia
		Men >50 yrs	0–13 mm/hr	
		Women <50 yrs	0–13 mm/hr	
		Women >50 yrs	0–20 mm/hr	
		Children	0–10 mm/hr	
Platelet count	Measures the number of platelets per cubic millimeter of blood (mm^3).	Adults and children	150,000– 400,00/mm^3	Thrombocytosis Thrombopenia
Mean platelet volume (MPV)	Measures the relative size of platelets expressed in micrometers.	Adults and children	2–4 um diameter	Systematic lupus Erythematosus Anemia

Figure 8-2 Normal ranges for blood tests

Coding of Diseases of the Blood and Blood-Forming Organs

This chapter of ICD-10-CM begins with an Excludes 2 instructional note. This instructional note means that the conditions noted are not part of the conditions represented in the chapter. If the patient has the condition noted in the Excludes 2 notation in addition to another condition coded to chapter 3 of ICD-10-CM, both codes can be assigned provided there is not another instructional note at the code site.

> **EXAMPLE:** Mrs. Barton was diagnosed with vitamin B_{12} deficiency due to malabsorption with proteinuria. She also is a type II diabetic.

In our example, code D51.1 would reflect the vitamin B_{12} deficiency anemia with malabsorption with proteinuria. The Excludes 2 note at the beginning of chapter 3 contains "endocrine, nutritional and metabolic diseases (E00-E90)." Code E11.69 is also assigned to indicate the type II diabetes.

Anemia

ICD-10-CM breaks the conditions of anemia down into nutritional, hemolytic, and aplastic, among other types. **Anemia** is a condition marked by a decrease in red blood cells, hemoglobin, hematocrit, or a combination thereof. There are numerous causes and types of anemia. When anemia is coded, identifying the type of anemia is important. The correct code assignment is based on the documentation in the medical record.

Nutritional Anemias (D50–D53)

Nutritional anemias are conditions caused by decreased or nonexistent supplies of nutrients in the blood. Category D50 begins this section of chapter 3 in ICD-10-CM.

Code	Description
D50.0	Iron deficiency anemia is considered a chronic condition due to blood loss. The term *posthermorrhagic anemia* also codes to this subcategory.
D50.1	**Sideropenic dysphagia** is a type of iron-deficiency anemia that becomes so severe that the patient has difficulty swallowing in addition to the other symptoms of anemia. Also known as Plummer-Vinson syndrome.
D50.8	Should the provider document that the patient is iron deficient due to lack of iron in the diet, this is the code assignment.
D50.9	This code is reported for other iron-deficiency anemias and is assigned when a more specific code cannot be used.

Vitamin B_{12} deficiency anemia was expanded upon in ICD-10-CM and is coded with category code D51. This type of anemia is due to insufficient dietary intake of vitamin B_{12} or the inability of the body to absorb the vitamin B_{12} appropriately.

Disease Highlight—Pernicious Anemia

Pernicious anemia is an autoimmune disorder in which the stomach is unable to produce the intrinsic factor, which is needed to absorb vitamin B_{12}. This type of anemia can be caused by gastritis, gastric surgery, or endocrine or metabolic disorders.

Signs and Symptoms:

- Anorexia
- Gastrointestinal symptoms that include diarrhea or intermittent constipation
- Nonlocalized abdominal pain
- Atrophic gastritis
- Fatigue
- Shortness of breath
- Pallor
- Positive Babinski's reflex

Clinical Testing:

Pernicious anemia is confirmed by a positive Schilling test. Additional laboratory testing would show:

- Increased MCV.
- Increased serum LDH.
- Increased bilirubin.
- Decreased WBC and platelet count.
- Decrease in vitamin B_{12} serum.
- Abnormal bone marrow.

Treatment:

Since intrinsic factor is not being produced, the patient's body inadequately absorbs vitamin B_{12}. Therefore the patient receives monthly injections of vitamin B_{12} for his or her lifetime.

Other types of vitamin B_{12} deficient anemias can be summarized as follows:

Code	Description
D51.0	Vitamin B_{12} deficiency occurs when there is a lack of the protein necessary for the B_{12} to bond within the cell.
D51.1	The deficiency is stated as being selective vitamin B_{12} malabsorption with proteinuria.
D51.2	**Transcobalamin II** deficiency is a very rare autosomal recessive disease. Transcobalamin II is necessary to transport vitamin B_{12}.
D51.3–D51.9	This range of codes is used for other vitamin B_{12} deficiencies, such as dietary vitamin B_{12} deficiency anemia, vegan anemia, and unspecified vitamin B_{12} anemia.

Folate deficient and other nutritional deficiency anemias are coded to the D52 and D53 categories. **Folate deficient anemia** is the result of insufficient amounts of folic acid, which is needed for proper cell reproduction and growth. **Folate** itself is a salt of the folic acid. Medical record documentation should be referenced for the specific type of nutritional anemia that needs to be reported. Providers should be

Exercise 8.2 – Assigning Codes

Using an ICD-10-CM code book, assign the proper code for each diagnosis:

Diagnosis	*Code*
1. Kelly-Paterson syndrome	_____
2. folic acid deficiency anemia	_____
3. anemia associated with copper deficiency	_____
4. Addison anemia	_____
5. megaloblastic anemia	_____

encouraged to document as much detail as possible so that a proper code assignment can be made. Documentation should include whether the folate deficiency anemia is caused by a dietary deficiency, drug-induced folate deficiency, or other folate deficiency.

Hemolytic Anemias (Category Codes D55–D59)

Hemolytic anemia occurs when red blood cells are broken down at a faster rate than bone marrow can produce them, leading to an abnormal reduction of red blood cells. This disease can be acquired or hereditary.

Category D55 is used to report anemia in enzyme disorders such as glucose-6-phosphate dehydrogenase deficiency (G6PD), glycolytic enzyme disorders, and nucleotide metabolism disorders.

Category D56 is used to report thalassemia disorders. **Thalassemia** is a condition in which the red blood cells are not formed or are not functioning properly and the globulin gene arrangement is affected. Due to the different types of thalassemia, the malfunction of the cells varies. Codes from the category D56 can be summarized as follows:

Code	Description
D56.0	**Alpha thalassemia** is a condition in which there is a deficiency in the alpha protein being produced. There are four types of alpha thalassemia. The coder must read the diagnostic statement and the code description to be sure the correct code is assigned.
D56.1	**Beta thalassemia** is a condition in which there is a lack of the beta protein being produced. There are three types of beta thalassemia, and verification of the code description is necessary before a code assignment is made.
D56.2	Delta-beta thalassemia, as well as homozygous delta-beta thalassemia, is reported using this code.
D56.3	This code is used to report thalassemia minor, alpha thalassemia trait, beta thalassemia minor, and delta-beta thalassemia minor.
D56.4	Hereditary persistence of fetal hemoglobin (HPFH) is reported with this code.
D56.8	Other thalassemias, including Hb-Bart disease. This code is used to report other thalassemias that are given a specific code within ICD-10-CM.
D56.9	Thalassemia, unspecified. Mediterranean anemia and thalassemia mixed with other hemoglobinopathy are reported using this code.

Exercise 8.3 – Code Block D55–D56

Complete the statements.

1. There are _____ types of beta thalassemia.

2. Cooley's anemia is reported using ICD-10-CM code _____.

3. _____ occurs when red blood cells are broken down at a faster rate than bone marrow can produce them.

4. The D56 category of codes excludes _____.

5. Alpha thalassemia trait is reported using ICD-10-CM code _____.

Sickle-cell disorders are coded to category D57. Sickle-cell anemia and sickle-cell trait are inherited conditions. **Sickle-cell trait** is an asymptomatic condition in which the patient receives the genetic trait from only one parent. **Sickle-cell anemia** occurs when a patient receives the genetic trait from both parents, thus developing an abnormal type of hemoglobin in the red blood cell that causes decreased oxygenation in the tissues. When a patient is in crisis—that is, experiencing painful symptoms—an additional code for the type of crisis may be needed if the category does not contain a combination code reflecting what is going on with the patient at the encounter, such as fever.

Category D58, Other hereditary hemolytic anemias, and D59, Acquired hemolytic anemias, contain the remaining codes used to report the different types of hemolytic anemias. Autoimmune and nonautoimmune hemolytic anemias are also included in these subsections.

Exercise 8.4 – Category D57–D59

Answer the following questions using the ICD-10-CM coding book.

1. Code D58.8, Other specified hereditary hemolytic anemias, includes what condition?

_____

2. When coding hemoglobinuria due to hemolysis from other external causes, code _____ is used to report the condition.

3. Would Evans syndrome be coded to D59.1?_____

4. Code D59.0, Drug-induced autoimmune hemolytic anemia, instructs the coder to

_____.

5. Paroxysmal nocturnal hemoglobinuria codes to _____.

Aplastic and Other Anemias and Other Bone Marrow Failure Syndromes (Category Codes D60–D64)

Aplastic anemia is caused by the failure of bone marrow to produce blood components. ICD-10-CM refers to acquired and constitutional aplastic anemias. **Constitutional aplastic anemia** is the same as congenital or hereditary anemia. ICD-10-CM offers more specific reportable diagnosis codes for aplastic anemia conditions. Code range D60–D64 is summarized as follows:

Codes	Descriptions
D60.0	Chronic acquired **pure red cell aplasia**. Pure red cell aplasia is a condition in which precursors to the red blood cells are affected in the bone marrow and eventually cease to be produced. White cells are not affected.
D60.1	This code is used to report transient acquired pure red cell aplasia.
D60.8	Other acquired pure red cell aplasias are reported using this code.
D60.9	This code is used to report acquired pure red cell aplasia in which the documentation does not specify the type of aplasia.
D61.01	This code is used to report constitutional (pure) red blood cell aplasia.
D61.09	Other constitutional aplastic anemias including Fanconi's anemia and pancytopenia with malformations are reported using code D61.09.
D61.1	Drug-induced aplastic anemia. This code requires that the drug be identified and coded first. An instructional note appears under the code that instructs the coder to code first (T36–T50) to identify the drug.
D61.2	Aplastic anemia due to other external agents is reported using this code. The coder must also follow the note that instructs the coder to code first (T51–T65) to identify the cause of the anemia.
D61.3	**Idiopathic aplastic anemia** is a condition in which the bone marrow is not able to produce cells properly for unknown reasons.
D61.8	Other specified aplastic anemias and other bone marrow failure syndromes are reported with the following codes.
D61.81	**Pancytopenia** is a condition in which there is a decrease in the number of platelets, white blood cells, and red blood cells.
D61.82	**Myelophthisis** is a severe form of anemia in which certain bone marrow material shows up in the peripheral blood.
D61.89	Other specified aplastic anemias and other bone marrow failure syndromes are reported with this code.
D61.9	Aplastic anemia in which the documentation is unspecified is assigned this code.
D62	This code is used to report acute posthemorrhagic anemia and is one of the few three-digit codes in ICD-10-CM.
D63.0	Anemia in neoplastic disease is assigned this code. The coder is instructed to code first the neoplasm (C00–D49).
D63.1	This code is used to report anemia in chronic kidney disease.
D63.8	Anemia in other chronic diseases classified elsewhere is reported with this code.
D64	This category is used to report other types of anemia.

Coagulation Defects, Purpura, and Other Hemorrhagic Conditions (Category Codes D65–D69)

Coagulation defects occur when there is a deficiency in one or more of the blood clotting factors, resulting in prolonged clotting time and possibly serious bleeding. The normal stages of blood clotting are summarized in Figure 8-3. A coagulation defect occurs when there is a disruption in the process because of heredity or acquired conditions.

Code	Description
D65	Disseminated intravascular coagulation (defibrination syndrome) is reported with this code. It should be noted that there are extensive Includes and Excludes 1 notes for this code.
D66	**Hereditary factor VIII** deficiency is a form of hemophilia. The hereditary factor diseases noted in this block of codes involve clotting factor problems.
D67	Hereditary factor IX deficiency includes Christmas disease, factor IX deficiency, hemophilia B, and plasma thromboplastin component deficiency. These conditions are reported via this code.

(continued)

D68.0	**Von Willebrand's disease** is the most common of the hereditary bleeding disorders. The Von Willebrand factor is missing from the blood or is not working properly. This factor is essential in the clotting process.
D68.1	Hereditary factor XI deficiency, hemophilia C, and Rosenthal's disease are reported with this code.
D68.2	Hereditary deficiency of other clotting factors are reported with this code. The coder should note the extensive list of diseases included in the ICD-10-CM book under the heading for this code.
D68.3	Hemorrhagic disorder due to circulating anticoagulants is divided as follows:
D68.31	Hemorrhagic disorder due to intrinsic circulating anticoagulants is reported with this code. This code includes hemorrhagic disorders due to intrinsic increase in antithrombin, anti-VIIIa, anti-IXa, anti-Xa, anti-XIa, and hyperheparinemia.
D68.32	This code is used to report a hemorrhagic disorder due to extrinsic circulating anticoagulants. The coder must first code any administered anticoagulant from the T45.5-series of codes.
D68.4	This code reports acquired coagulation factor deficiency, including deficiencies of coagulation factors due to liver disease and lack of vitamin K. This code does not, however, include a vitamin K deficiency in a newborn. The coder has to reference code P53 for this condition.
D68.5	Primary thrombophilia is a condition that can be genetic (primary) or acquired. **Thrombophilia** is a condition in which the patient is predisposed to develop thromboses. ICD-10-CM reports the following codes for the various types of primary thrombophilia:
D68.51	Activated protein C resistance
D68.52	Prothrombin gene mutation
D68.59	Other primary thrombophilia such as antithrombin III deficiency, hypercoagulable state, protein C deficiency, and protein S deficiency are reported using this code.
D68.61	Anticardiolipin syndrome is reported with this code.
D68.62	Lupus anticoagulant syndrome is reported by using this code. **Lupus** is a disease in which the body produces too many antibodies, which begin to turn against the patient's own body attacking body organs, joints, and muscles.
D68.69	Other thrombophilia for which ICD-10-CM does not provide a specific code is assigned D68.69.
D68.8	Other specified coagulation defects for which ICD-10-CM does not report a specify code are assigned D68.8.
D68.9	Coagulation defect, unspecified, is coded with D68.9.
D69	Purpura and other hemorrhagic conditions are reported using this category of codes. **Purpura** is the accumulation of blood under the skin that forms multiple pinpoint hemorrhages. The following codes are used:
D69.0	Allergic purpura
D69.1	Qualitative platelet defects
D69.2	Other nonthrombocytopenic purpura
D69.3	Immune thrombocytopenic purpura is reported by using this code. **Thrombocytopenia** is an abnormal decrease in platelet count that causes purpural hemorrhages.
D69.4	Other primary thrombocytopenia is reported with this range of codes as follows:
D69.41	Evans syndrome
D69.42	Congenital and hereditary thrombocytopenia purpura
D69.49	Other primary thrombocytopenia
D69.5	Secondary thrombocytopenia is reported using this code.
D69.6	If the documentation does not specify the type of thrombocytopenia, this code is used for thrombocytopenia, unspecified.
D69.8	Other specified hemorrhagic conditions that include capillary fragility and vascular pseudo hemophilia are reported with this code.
D69.9	An unspecified hemorrhagic condition is reported with this code.

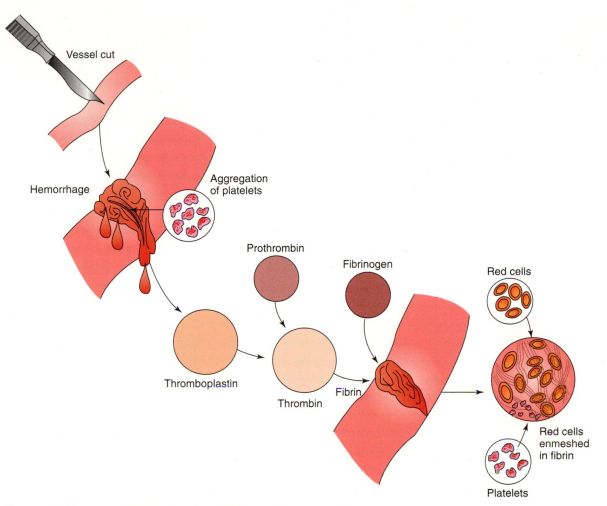

Figure 8-3 Normal stages of blood clotting (From Rizzo, Donald. *Fundamentals of Anatomy and Physiology*, 2nd ed. Clifton Park, NY: Delmar, 2003, Cengage Learning, p. 306.)

One disease that is coded within this block of codes is Von Willebrand's disease, code D68.0.

Disease Highlight—Von Willebrand's Disease

Von Willebrand's disease, also known as **angiohemophilia**, is the most common of the inherited bleeding disorders. This disease is caused by a deficiency in clotting factor and platelet function and is categorized as a hereditary autosomal dominant disorder.

Signs and Symptoms:

Patients with Von Willebrand's disease have an increase in mucosal bleeding that includes:

- Epistaxis.
- Gingival bleeding.
- Monorrhagia.
- Gastrointestinal bleeding.

Other symptoms include an increase in the amount of bleeding following surgery, injury, and dental procedures.

(continued)

Clinical Testing:

Laboratory tests show prolonged bleeding time and a decrease in the vW factor level in plasma.

Treatment:

- Patients diagnosed with Von Willebrand's disease are to avoid using aspirin because it exacerbates bleeding.

- Patients who have lost a significant amount of blood will have a transfusion of plasma cryoprecipitate.

- Antifibrinolytic agents are administered to patients during surgery and dental procedures to decrease bleeding.

- Desmopressin acetate is also given to patients to control the disease.

Exercise 8.5 – Coding Exercise: Anemia and Coagulation Coding

Use an ICD-10-CM coding book to code the following diagnoses:

Diagnosis	Code
1. idiopathic aplastic anemia	_____
2. leukoerythroblastic anemia	_____
3. sideroblastic anemia	_____
4. angiohemophilia	_____
5. primary thrombophilia	_____

Other Disorders of the Blood and Blood-Forming Organs (Category Codes D70–D77)

This category of codes encompasses more blood disorders, mainly genetic blood disorders and disorders of the white blood cells.

Neutropenia is an abnormal decrease of granular leukocytes in the blood and is coded to this category of codes. Additional codes are required for any associated fever and mucositis. Transient neonatal neutropenia is not included in this series of codes.

The following box lists the codes associated with these disorders and explains some of the conditions.

Code	Description
D70	Neutropenia is further defined in ICD-10-CM as follows:
D70.0	Congenital agranulocytosis
D70.1	When assigning agranulocytosis secondarily to cancer chemotherapy, the coder is instructed to code any underlying neoplasms along with the identifying drugs used.
D70.2	Other drug-induced agranulocytosis is reported using this code along with the appropriate T code (T36–T50) to identify the drug used.

D70.3	Neutropenia due to infection
D70.4	Cyclic neutropenia
D70.8	Other neutropenia
D70.9	Neutropenia, unspecified
D71	Functional disorders of **polymorphonuclear neutrophils** are reported using this code. Polymorphonuclear neutrophils are white blood cells found in the peripheral blood and are the most numerous of the white blood cells.
D72	Other disorders of white blood cells are reported with this category which is differentiated as follows:
D72.0	Genetic anomalies of leukocytes
D72.1	**Eosinophilia** is a condition in which the eosinophil white blood cell is found in excess in the blood or body tissues.
D72.8	Other specified disorders of white blood cells are differentiated more specifically in ICD-10-CM by use of the following codes:
D72.81	Decreased white blood cell count. The coder needs to read the note that appears at this level governing codes D72.810–D72.819.
D72.810	Lymphocytopenia
D72.818	Other decreased white blood cell count
D72.819	Decreased white blood cell count, unspecified
D72.82	Elevated white blood cell count. The coder needs to read the note that governs codes D72.820–D72.829.
D72.820	Lymphocytosis (symptomatic)
D72.821	Monocytosis (symptomatic)
D72.822	Plasmacytosis
D72.823	Leukemoid reaction
D72.824	Basophilia
D72.825	Bandemia
D72.828	Other elevated white blood cell count
D72.829	Elevated white blood cell count, unspecified
D72.9	Disorder of white blood cells, unspecified, as well as abnormal leukocyte differential, is assigned this code.
D73	Diseases of the spleen are coded to this category. The **spleen** is located in the upper left quadrant of the abdomen. The spleen forms lymphocytes and monocytes and also stores erythrocytes. This category is reported using the following codes:
D73.0	Hyposplenism
D73.1	Hypersplenism
D73.2	Chronic congestive splenomegaly
D73.3	Abscess of spleen
D73.4	Cyst of spleen
D73.5	This code is used to report infarction of the spleen, nontraumatic splenic rupture, and torsion of the spleen.
D73.8	Other diseases of the spleen are further differentiated as follows:
D73.81	Neutropenic splenomegaly
D73.89	Other diseases of spleen
D73.9	Disease of the spleen, unspecified, is reported with this code.
D74	**Methemoglobinemia** is a disorder of the hemoglobin in which oxygen is not transported by the cells. The codes are further divided:

(continued)

D74.0	Congenital methemoglobinemia
D74.8	Other methemoglobinemias include the acquired methemoglobinemia conditions.
D74.9	Methemoglobinemia, unspecified
D75	Other and unspecified diseases of blood and blood-forming organs are reported with codes from the D75 category and are differentiated as follows:
D75.0	This code for familial erythrocytosis includes benign and familial polycythemia.
D75.1	Secondary polycythemia
D75.8	Other specified diseases of blood and blood-forming organs. This is further divided:
D75.81	Myelofibrosis
D75.82	Heparin-induced thrombocytopenia (HIT)
D75.89	Other specified diseases of blood and blood-forming organs
D75.9	Disease of blood and blood-forming organs, unspecified, is reported with this code.
D76	Certain diseases involving lymphoreticular tissue and the reticulohistocytic system are reported with the specific codes that follow:
D76.1	Hemophagocytic lymphohistiocytosis
D76.2	For hemophagocytic syndrome, infection-associated, this code is reported. The coder is instructed that an additional code is needed to identify the infectious agent or disease.
D76.3	Other histiocytosis syndromes include xanthogranuloma, reticulohistiocytoma, and sinus histiocytosis with massive lymphadenopathy.
D77	Other disorders of the blood and blood-forming organs in diseases classified elsewhere are reported with this code.

Exercise 8.6 – Other Disorders of the Blood and Blood-Forming Organs

Using an ICD-10-CM coding book, code the diagnoses.

Diagnosis	Code
1. congenital neutropenia	_____
2. cyclic neutropenia	_____
3. hyposplenism	_____
4. nontraumatic splenic rupture	_____
5. leukopenia	_____

Intraoperative and Postprocedural Complications of the Spleen (Category Code D78)

This code category includes accidental punctures and lacerations of the spleen during a procedure as well as postprocedural hemorrhaging. The specific codes for these conditions are as follows:

Code	Description
D78	This category reports intraoperative and postprocedural complications of the spleen, and the codes are differentiated as follows:
D78.0	Intraoperative hemorrhage and hematoma of the spleen complicating a procedure are further divided and reported using the following codes:
D78.01	Intraoperative hemorrhage and hematoma of spleen complicating a procedure on the spleen
D78.02	Intraoperative hemorrhage and hematoma of spleen complicating other procedure
D78.1	Accidental puncture and laceration of spleen during a procedure is reported using:
D78.11	Accidental puncture and laceration of spleen during a procedure on the spleen
D78.12	Accidental puncture and laceration of spleen during other procedure
D78.2	Postprocedural hemorrhage and hematoma of spleen following a procedure is reported with one of the following codes:
D78.21	Postprocedural hemorrhage and hematoma of spleen following a procedure on the spleen
D78.22	Postprocedural hemorrhage and hematoma of spleen following other procedure
D78.8	Other intraoperative and postprocedural complications of spleen are reported by using:
D78.81	Other intraoperative complications of spleen
D78.89	Other postprocedural complications of spleen

Certain Disorders Involving the Immune Mechanism (Category Codes D80–D89)

The **immune system** is the body's defense mechanism against disease and other foreign agents. This category of codes includes defects in the complement system and immunodeficiency disorders, except for HIV. Also excluded from this block of codes are some systemic autoimmune diseases and functional disorders of polymorphonuclear neutrophils (discussed earlier in the chapter). The following list contains the codes found in these categories:

Code	Description
D80	Immunodeficiency with predominantly antibody defects are reported using codes that are differentiated as follows:
D80.0	Hereditary hypogammaglobulinemia, such as autosomal recessive agammaglobulinemia. **Agammaglobulinemia** is a hereditary disorder in which the immunoglobulin or immune proteins are extremely low, leaving the person open to frequent infections.
D80.1	Nonfamilial hypogammaglobulinemia
D80.2	Selective deficiency of immunoglobulin A [IgA]
D80.3	Selective deficiency of immunoglobulin G [IgG] subclasses
D80.4	Selective deficiency of immunoglobulin M [IgM]
D80.5	Immunodeficiency with increased immunoglobulin M [IgM]
D80.6	Antibody deficiency with near-normal immunoglobulins or with hyperimmunoglobulinemia
D80.7	Transient hypogammaglobulinemia of infancy
D80.8	Other immunodeficiencies with predominantly antibody defects
D80.9	Immunodeficiency with predominantly antibody defects, unspecified
D81	Combined immunodeficiencies are reported with the specific codes that follow. Coders should note the Excludes 1 note at this level.
D81.0	Severe combined immunodeficiency [SCID] with reticular dysgenesis

(continued)

D81.1	Severe combined immunodeficiency [SCID] with low T- and B-cell numbers
D81.2	Severe combined immunodeficiency [SCID] with low or normal B-cell numbers
D81.3	Adenosine deaminase [ADA] deficiency
D81.4	Nezelf's syndrome
D81.5	Purine nucleoside phosphorylase [PNP] deficiency
D81.6	Major histocompatibility complex class I deficiency
D81.7	Major histocompatibility complex class II deficiency
D81.8	Other combined immunodeficiencies are coded with increased granularity as follows:
D81.81	Biotin-dependent carboxylase deficiency disorders are specified as follows in ICD-10-CM. Providers may have to be queried to differentiate the deficiency so that a specific code can be assigned.
D81.810	Biotinidase deficiency
D81.818	Other biotin-dependent carboxylase deficiency
D81.819	Biotin-dependent carboxylase deficiency, unspecified
D81.89	Other combined immunodeficiencies not given a specific code in ICD-10-CM are reported with this code.
D81.9	Combined immunodeficiency, unspecified, including severe combined immunodeficiency disorder, is reported with this code.
D82	Immunodeficiency associated with other major defects is reported with codes from this category as follows:
D82.0	Wiskott-Aldrich syndrome
D82.1	DiGeorge's syndrome
D82.2	Immunodeficiency with short-limbed stature
D82.3	Immunodeficiency following hereditary defective response to Epstein-Barr virus
D82.4	Hyperimmunoglobulin E [IgE] syndrome
D82.8	Immunodeficiency associated with other specified major defects
D82.9	Immunodeficiency associated with major defect, unspecified
D83	This category is used to report common variable immunodeficiencies. Documentation is essential when selecting codes because the codes are very specific as to the cell abnormalities. The diseases are reported as follows:
D83.0	Common variable immunodeficiency with predominant abnormalities of B-cell numbers and function
D83.1	Common variable immunodeficiency with predominant immunoregulatory T-cell disorders
D83.2	Common variable immunodeficiency with autoantibodies to B- or T-cells
D83.8	Other common variable immunodeficiencies
D83.9	Common variable immunodeficiency, unspecified
D84	Other immunodeficiencies are coded using this category, which is differentiated as follows:
D84.0	Lymphocyte function antigen-1 [LFA-1] defect
D84.1	Defects in the complement system
D84.8	Other specified immunodeficiencies
D84.9	Immunodeficiency, unspecified
D86	Category D86 is used to report various forms of sarcoidosis. The following codes identify the sites of the sarcoidosis:
D86.0	Sarcoidosis of lung
D86.1	Sarcoidosis of lymph nodes
D86.2	Sarcoidosis of lung with sarcoidosis of lymph nodes
D86.3	Sarcoidosis of skin

D86.8	Sarcoidosis of other sites are further differentiated within ICD-10-CM as follows:
D86.81	Sarcoid meningitis
D86.82	Multiple cranial nerve palsies in sarcoidosis
D86.83	Sarcoid iridocyclitis
D86.84	Sarcoid pyelonephritis
D86.85	Sarcoid myocarditis
D86.86	Sarcoid arthropathy
D86.87	Sarcoid myositis
D86.89	Sarcoidosis of other sites
D86.9	Sarcoidosis, unspecified, is reported with this code. Prior to the assignment of this code, the provider should be queried to determine whether more specific information is available.
D89	Other disorders involving the immune mechanism, not elsewhere classified, is reported with this category, with the codes divided as follows:
D89.0	Polyclonal hypergammaglobulinemia
D89.1	Cryoglobulinemia
D89.2	Hypergammaglobulinemia, unspecified
D89.8	Other specified disorders involving the immune mechanism, not elsewhere classified
D89.9	Disorders involving the immune mechanism, unspecified

Comparing ICD-9-CM to ICD-10-CM

The following table presents changes in codes from ICD-9-CM to ICD-10-CM.

Code Description	ICD-9-CM	ICD-10-CM
Anemia—chronic due to blood loss	280.0	D50.0
Vitamin B$_{12}$ deficiency	281.0–218.1	D51.1, D51.3, D51.8
Sickle-cell trait	282.5	D57.3
Sickle-cell anemia	282.60	D57.1
Aplastic anemia	284.01, 284.09	D61.01, D61.09
Coagulation defects—Von Willebrand's disease	286.4	D68.0
Allergic purpura	287.0	D69.0
Thrombocytopenia	287.5	D69.6
Neutropenia	288.00	D70.9
Diseases of the spleen	289.59	D73.4, D73.5, D73.89

Internet Links

To learn about various types of anemia, visit *www.mayoclinic.com* and type in the key term *anemia*.

For a comprehensive review of blood coagulation, visit *http://tollefsen.wustl.edu* or *www.thrombin.com/ BloodCoagulation.phtml*

To learn about neutropenia, visit *www.neutropenia.ca/about/index.html*

Summary

- ICD-10-CM recognizes far more specific conditions of the blood and blood-forming organs than were found in ICD-9-CM.

- Erythrocytes are red blood cells; leukocytes are white blood cells.

- Leukocytes are divided into two groups: granulocytes and agranulocytes.

- Thrombocytes function in the initiation of blood clotting.

- Anemia occurs when there is a decrease in red blood cells, hemoglobin, and/or hematocrit.

- Sickle-cell trait and sickle-cell anemia are separately identifiable conditions that are classified with different codes.

- Aplastic anemia can be congenital or acquired.

- Coagulation defects cause prolonged clotting time and can result in serious bleeding, which can lead to death.

Chapter Review

True/False: Indicate whether each statement is true (T) or false (F).

1. _____ Different fluids and electrolyte balance are maintained by the flow of the blood through the body.

2. _____ Monocytes, basophils, and eosinophils are all types of granulocytes.

3. _____ A platelet plug slows or stops bleeding.

4. _____ Transcobalamin II deficiency is a common recessive disease.

5. _____ Thalassemia is a condition in which the white blood cells are not formed or functioning properly and the globulin gene arrangement is affected.

Multiple Choice: Select the best answer that completes the statement or answers the question.

6. Of the following, which is not a function of blood?
   a. transportation of nutrients
   b. transportation of bone marrow
   c. transportation of waste

7. The bone marrow is where _____ is/are formed.
   a. red blood cells
   b. hemoglobin
   c. plasma

8. Which of the following statements is *not* true of white blood cells?
   a. WBCs are less numerous than RBCs.
   b. WBCs contain hemoglobin and have an irregular ball-like shape.
   c. WBCs are classified into two major groups: granulocytes and agranulocytes.

9. A marked decrease in red blood cells, hemoglobin, and/or hematocrit could result in a diagnosis of:
   a. anemia.
   b. anaphylactic shock.
   c. phagocytosis.

10. A type of iron-deficiency anemia that becomes so severe the patient has difficulty swallowing, in addition to other symptoms of anemia, is known as:
    a. aplastic anemia.
    b. vitamin B$_{12}$ anemia.
    c. sideropenic dysphagia.

Coding Assignments

Instructions: Using an ICD-10-CM code book, assign the proper diagnosis code to the following diagnostic statements.

1. sarcoidosis of the skin _____

2. hypergammaglobulinemia _____

3. DiGeorge's syndrome _____

4. biotin-dependent carboxylase deficiency _____

5. selective deficiency of IgA _____

6. cryoglobulinemia _____

7. sarcoid myositis _____

8. LFA-1 defect _____

9. Common variable immunodeficiency with predominant immunoregulatory T cell disorder _____

10. postprocedural complication of the spleen _____

11. microangiopathic hemolytic anemia _____

12. IgE syndrome _____

13. Wiskott-Aldrich syndrome _____

14. Nezelf's syndrome _____

15. iridocyclitis in sarcoidosis _____

16. polycythemia acquired _____

17. cyst of the spleen _____

18. intraoperative hemorrhage of the spleen, complicating a procedure _____

19. myelofibrosis _____

20. plasmacytosis _____

Case Studies

Instructions: Review each case study and select the correct ICD-10-CM diagnostic code.

CASE 1

Discharge Summary

PATIENT NAME: Polly Patch

AGE: 72 years old

Polly was admitted from home because she passed out from dizziness. Her daughter called my office, and I admitted her to the medical unit because this is the third time in 2 weeks that she passed out.

On initial examination she was conscious and alert and appeared pale. Physical findings can be found on the history and physical dated 02/13/XX.

CBC, chest x-ray, and EKG were ordered.

CBC revealed a low platelet count of 53,000, supporting a diagnosis of thrombocytopenia. Chest x-ray and EKG were normal.

The rest of her 2-day admission was uneventful, and she was discharged home. She was instructed to follow up in my office in 2 weeks or to call my office if her symptoms increase.

ICD-10-CM Code Assignment: _____

CASE 2

Hospital Note: 3/4/xx

Bob was admitted on Monday with a diagnosis of anemia associated with a primary malignancy of the prostate. Today I ordered a blood transfusion due to his low blood count. CBC is to be repeated after the transfusion. I instructed the charge nurse to call me with the results.

ICD-10-CM Code Assignment: _____

CASE 3

Postsurgical Note

Mary is now 1-day postop for a right breast mass excision. During the surgery she lost a significant amount of blood due to uncontrolled bleeding. A CBC was ordered that showed an abnormally low hematocrit and hemoglobin confirming anemia due to blood loss. She was given a transfusion and has tolerated the transfusion well.

ICD-10-CM Code Assignment: _____

Endocrine, Nutritional, and Metabolic Diseases

Chapter Outline

Objectives

At the conclusion of this chapter, the learner should be able to:

1. Understand how hormones influence functions within the body.
2. Distinguish between the different types of diabetes and select ICD-10-CM codes for the various types of diabetes.
3. Apply the ICD-10-CM coding guidelines to the coding of diabetes and endocrine, nutritional, and metabolic diseases.
4. Accurately code endocrine, nutritional, and metabolic diseases.
5. Identify the differences between the ICD-9-CM codes and the ICD-10-CM codes.
6. Select and code diagnoses from case studies.

Key Terms

adult onset diabetes	endocrine system	hormones	hyperthyroidism
Cushing's syndrome	glucose	hyperparathyroidism	hypothyroidism
diabetes mellitus	goiter	hypoparathyroidism	insulin

Reminder

As you work through this chapter, you will need to have a copy of the ICD-10-CM coding book to reference.

insulin-dependent diabetes mellitus (IDDM)	metabolism	pancreas	thyrotoxic storm
	noninsulin-dependent diabetes mellitus (NIDDM)	thyroid gland	type 1 diabetes mellitus
juvenile diabetes, IDDM		thyrotoxic crisis	type 2 diabetes mellitus

Introduction

Chapter 4 of ICD-10-CM, "Endocrine, Nutritional, and Metabolic Diseases," classifies conditions that affect the endocrine system, as well as nutritional and metabolic diseases. A common disease coded to this chapter is **diabetes mellitus**, which is a chronic disorder resulting from a problem with the pancreas. The **pancreas** is located under the stomach in the upper abdomen and performs various physiological functions. One of these functions is secreting digestive hormones into the gastrointestinal tract to aid in digestion. The other function is to regulate insulin in the body. **Insulin** is used in the body to process glucose. If the pancreas does not regulate the insulin properly or does not produce insulin at all, glucose levels are thrown out of control. **Glucose** is needed for the cells to properly supply energy for the body's metabolic functions.

Nutritional and metabolic disorders, with the exception of anemias caused by nutritional deficiencies, are also classified to this chapter. Anemias caused by nutritional deficiencies are classified to chapter 3 of ICD-10-CM, "Diseases of the Blood and Blood-Forming Organs and Certain Disorders Involving the Immune Mechanism." The nutritional and metabolic disorders classified to chapter 4 of ICD-10-CM are caused by deficiencies of vitamins, minerals, and proteins, as well as other conditions such as obesity, malnutrition, and carbohydrate and lipid imbalances.

> **Note:**
>
> *Some endocrine and metabolic disturbances—such as conditions that affect pregnancy and neonates and certain types of anemia resulting from nutritional deficiencies—are coded to other chapters in ICD-10-CM. Coders should read the Excludes: notes throughout chapter 4 to become familiar with the conditions excluded from this chapter.*

Introduction to the Body System

The **endocrine system** (*endo-* means "within," *-crin* means "secrete") consists of several different internal groups of glands and structures that produce or secrete hormones. Figure 9-1 illustrates the structures of the endocrine system. **Hormones** are chemical substances produced by the body to keep organs and tissues functioning properly. Each hormone has a specific function, as summarized in Figure 9-2.

When chemical changes occur in the body, hormone release may be either increased or decreased, provided that the organ producing the hormone is functioning properly. When endocrine body structures do not function properly, hormones are not released.

> **EXAMPLE:** The **thyroid gland** secretes hormones that regulate growth and metabolism. A condition known as **hypothyroidism** occurs when the thyroid is not as active as it should be, creating a deficiency of thyroid hormone secretion. An underactive thyroid, left undiagnosed, can cause conditions such as depression, sensitivity to cold, and fatigue. Medications can be prescribed to stimulate or replace the needed hormones to get the thyroid hormones back in balance.

Coding of Endocrine, Nutritional, and Metabolic Diseases

Chapter 4 of ICD-10-CM is organized into the following blocks:

- E00–E07, Disorders of thyroid gland
- E08–E13, Diabetes mellitus

- E15–E16, Other disorders of glucose regulation and pancreatic internal secretion
- E20–E35, Disorders of other endocrine glands
- E36–, Intraoperative complications of endocrine system
- E40–E46, Malnutrition
- E50–E64, Other nutritional deficiencies
- E65–E68, Overweight, obesity, and other hyperalimentation
- E70–E88, Metabolic disorders
- E89–, Postprocedural endocrine and metabolic complications and disorders, not elsewhere classified

At the start of the chapter 4 of ICD-10-CM, a notation appears that governs the entire chapter, as shown in Figure 9-3. Coders need to understand this notation and be guided by these instructions.

Disorders of the Thyroid Gland (Category Codes E00–E07)

ICD-10-CM classifies disorders of the thyroid gland to category codes E00–E07. The primary function of the thyroid gland is to regulate the body's **metabolism**, which is the rate at which the body uses energy and at which body functions occur.

Common conditions that are classified to this code range are different types of goiters. When hormone secretions fall within normal limits but the thyroid itself becomes enlarged, this condition is known as a **goiter**. A lack of iodine can cause goiters. Categories E01 and E04 contain codes for various types of goiters.

Other conditions affecting the thyroid are hypothyroidism, which is an underactive thyroid, and **hyperthyroidism**, which occurs when the thyroid oversecretes hormones, causing excessive amounts of thyroid hormones in the blood. Hyperthyroidism can cause weight loss, nervousness, tachycardia, and goiters. In some extreme cases of hyperthyroidism, known as **thyrotoxic crisis** or **thyrotoxic storm**, the symptoms of hyperthyroidism are so severe that they put the patient in a life-threatening situation or crisis.

ICD-10-CM category E02 classifies subclinical iodine-deficiency hypothyroidism, and category E03 is used for other types of hypothyroidism. Hyperthyroidism, or thyrotoxicosis, is classified to category E05. Fourth digits identify whether a goiter, toxic nodule or nodules, factitia, or ectopic thyroid tissue are present. Fifth digits indicate whether thyrotoxic crisis or storm is present.

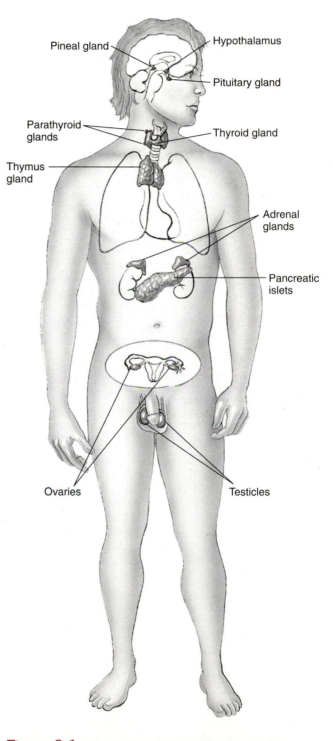

Figure 9-1 Structures of the endocrine system

Hormone	Functions
Aldosterone	Aids in regulating the levels of salt and water in the body.
Androgens	Influence sex-related characteristics.
Adrenocorticotropic hormone (ACTH)	Stimulates the growth and secretions of the adrenal cortex.
Antidiuretic hormone (ADH)	Helps control blood pressure by reducing the amount of water that is excreted.
Calcitonin	Works with the parathyroid hormone to regulate calcium levels in the blood and tissues.
Cortisol	Regulates the metabolism of carbohydrates, fats, and proteins in the body. Also has an anti-inflammatory action.
Epinephrine	Stimulates the sympathetic nervous system.
Estrogen	Develops and maintains the female secondary sex characteristics and regulates the menstrual cycle.
Follicle-stimulating hormone (FSH)	In the female, stimulates the secretion of estrogen and the growth of ova (eggs). In the male, stimulates the production of sperm.
Glucagon	Increases the level of glucose in the bloodstream.
Growth hormone (GH)	Regulates the growth of bone, muscle, and other body tissues.
Human chorionic gonadotropin (HCG)	Stimulates the secretion of the hormones required to maintain the pregnancy.
Insulin (In)	Regulates the transport of glucose to body cells and stimulates the conversion of excess glucose to glycogen for storage.
Lactogenic hormone (LTH)	Stimulates and maintains the secretion of breast milk.
Luteinizing hormone (LH)	In the female, stimulates ovulation. In the male, stimulates testosterone secretion.
Melatonin	Influences the sleep-wakefulness cycles.
Norepinephrine	Stimulates the sympathetic nervous system.
Oxytocin (OXT)	Stimulates uterine contractions during childbirth. Causes milk to flow from the mammary glands after birth.
Parathyroid hormone (PTH)	Works with calcitonin to regulate calcium levels in the blood and tissues.
Progesterone	Completes preparation of the uterus for possible pregnancy.
Testosterone	Stimulates the development of male secondary sex characteristics.
Thymosin	Plays an important role in the immune system.
Thyroid hormones (T_4 and T_3)	Regulates the rate of metabolism.
Thyroid-stimulating hormone (TSH)	Stimulates the secretion of hormones by the thyroid gland.

Figure 9-2 Hormones and their functions

> **Chapter 4—Endocrine, nutritional, and metabolic diseases (E00-E90)**
>
> All neoplasms, whether functionally active or not, are classified in Chapter 2. Appropriate codes in this chapter (i.e. E05.8, E07.0, E16-E31, E34.-) may be used as additional codes to indicate either functional activity by neoplasms and ectopic endocrine tissue or hyperfunction and hypofunction of endocrine glands associated with neoplasms and other conditions classified elsewhere.
>
> Excludes 1: transitory endocrine and metabolic disorders specific to fetus and newborn (P70-P74)

Figure 9-3 Start of chapter 4 of ICD-10-CM

Other common conditions classified to this code range are different types of thyroiditis, an inflammation of the thyroid gland. This is classified to category E06, which is summarized as follows:

Code	Description
E06.0	Acute thyroiditis, abscess of the thyroid, pyogenic thyroiditis, and suppurative thyroiditis are assigned this code. An additional code is needed to identify the infectious agent that is present.
E06.1	Subacute thyroiditis, which includes granulomatous thyroiditis, giant-cell thyroiditis, and viral thyroiditis, are coded in this subcategory range.
E06.2	Chronic thyroiditis with transient thyrotoxicosis
E06.3	Autoimmune thyroiditis, Hashimoto's thyroiditis, hashitoxicosis (transient), lymphadenoid goiter, lymphocytic thyroiditis, and struma lymphomatosa are classified in this subcategory.
E06.4	Drug-induced thyroiditis is classified with this code. The code book instructs coders to "Code First (T36–T50) to identify drug" that caused the thyroiditis.
E06.5	Other chronic forms of thyroiditis are coded here: chronic fibrous thyroiditis, chronic thyroiditis NOS, ligneous thyroiditis, and Riedel thyroiditis.
E06.9	The last code in this range is used to code unspecified thyroiditis.

Disease Highlight—Hypothyroidism

Hypothyroidism occurs when there is a decrease in the production of the thyroid hormone secondary to the dysfunction of the thyroid gland. The causes of the decreased function may relate to:

- Surgery.
- Inflammatory conditions.
- Irradiation therapy.
- Chronic autoimmune thyroid diseases.

Signs and Symptoms:

In the early stages of hypothyroidism, the patient presents with:

- Fatigue.
- Weakness.
- Muscle cramps.
- Constipation.
- Arthralgias.

(continued)

- Headache.
- Thinning of nails and hair.

In the later stages the patient may have:

- Slow speech.
- Thickening of the tongue.
- Puffiness of the face and eyelids.
- Decreased sense of smell and taste.
- Dyspnea.
- Pitting edema.
- Hypoventilation.
- Hypoxia.
- Hypothermia.
- Hyponatremia.
- Hypotension.

Clinical Testing:

The following results of lab testing indicate hypothyroidism:

- An increase in serum cholesterol and prolactin
- Elevated liver enzymes and creatine
- An increase in TSH
- Low to normal serum T4 levels

Treatment:

Patients are treated with medication, the most common of which is Levothyroxine.

Disease Highlight—Hyperthyroidism

Hyperthyroidism, also known as hyperactivity of the thyroid, occurs when the thyroid gland secretes excessive amounts of thyroxine.

Signs and Symptoms:

- Enlarged thyroid gland
- Accelerated metabolic processes of the body
- Tachycardia
- Nervousness
- Excessive excitability
- Increased appetite with weight loss
- Tremors
- Fatigue
- Heat intolerance

- Diarrhea
- Moist skin
- Extreme thirst

Clinical Testing:

- Serum T3, T4, thyroid resin uptake, and free thyroxine index are elevated.
- TSI levels are usually high.
- Serum ANA and anti-double-stranded DNA antibodies are usually elevated.
- Thyroid radioactive iodine uptake and scan are often performed.
- MRI, CT scanning, and ultrasound are performed to visualize ophthalmopathy.

Treatment:

Depending on the intensity of the hyperthyroidism, the following treatment options are considered:

- Medications, such as propylthiouracil or methimazole
- Radioactive iodine to destroy the overfunctioning of the thyroid tissue
- Thyroid surgery to remove part or all of the thyroid gland (When removal of the entire thyroid gland occurs, hormonal supplements are needed for the rest of the patient's life.)
- Radiation of the thyroid

Exercise 9.1 – Coding Disorders of the Thyroid Gland

Select the appropriate ICD-10-CM code for each diagnostic statement.

Diagnosis	*Code*
1. multinodular goiter	_____
2. congenital hypothyroidism	_____
3. acquired atrophy of thyroid	_____
4. congenital atrophy of thyroid	_____
5. cyst of thyroid	_____
6. pyogenic thyroiditis	_____
7. Hashimoto's disease	_____
8. chronic lymphocytic thyroiditis	_____
9. Iatrogenic hypothyroidism	_____
10. thyrotoxicosis with thyrotoxic crisis	_____
11. mixed type endemic cretinism	_____
12. Riedel thyroiditis	_____
13. cystic goiter	_____
14. chronic thyroiditis	_____
15. myxedema	_____

Diabetes Mellitus E08–E13

Codes for diabetes mellitus, a complex metabolic disease characterized by hyperglycemia, caused by defects in insulin secretion, insulin action, or both, are classified to code range E08–E13 except for gestational diabetes. Various types of diabetes are identified by the severity of the disorder in the pancreas and the onset of the disease. In ICD-10-CM, the diabetes codes are organized as follows:

- Category E08–, Diabetes mellitus due to underlying condition
- Category E09–, Drug- or chemical-induced diabetes mellitus
- Category E10–, Type 1 diabetes mellitus
- Category E11–, Type 2 diabetes mellitus
- Category E13–, Other specified diabetes mellitus

E08 Diabetes mellitus due to underlying condition

Code first the underlying condition, such as:

      Congenital rubella (P35.0)

      Cushing's syndrome (E24.-)

      Cystic fibrosis (E84.-)

      Malignant neoplasm (C00-C96)

      Malnutrition (E40-E46)

      Pancreatitis and other diseases of the pancreas (K85-K86.-)

Use additional code of identify any insulin use (Z79.4)

Excludes 1:   drug or chemical induced diabetes mellitus (E09.-)

            gestational diabetes (O24.4-)

            neonatal diabetes mellitus (P70.2)

            type 1 diabetes mellitus (E10.-)

            type 2 diabetes mellitus (E11.-)

Figure 9-4 Start of Category E08

Coders need to be familiar with the notations that appear under the headings for the various categories. For example, the instructional note shown in Figure 9-4 appears for category E08. This notation instructs the coder to code first the underlying condition and then the diabetes code from this category. An additional code is also needed to identify any insulin use. Read the start of all of the diabetes mellitus category codes to become familiar with the notations that appear.

Fourth-digit characters for these categories are used to define specified complications. Fifth digits are used to classify the specific manifestation of the disease, such as neuropathy, retinopathy, skin ulcerations, peripheral angiopathy, and the like. To provide additional information on manifestations, sixth characters are used. The coder has to read the medical record to determine the manifestations of diabetes. If the information is not documented, the coder has to query the providers so that the code selected will most accurately reflect the patient's diagnostic condition. Providers should be educated on the terminology used for the diabetes codes in relation to their documentation and proper code assignment.

Types of Diabetes Mellitus

When the pancreas does not secrete insulin at all or secretes an insufficient amount, the patients might be diagnosed as having **type 1 diabetes mellitus**. The onset for type 1 diabetes is generally between puberty and adulthood, but it can also occur at birth; thus the term **juvenile diabetes, IDDM** (as well as juvenile type, juvenile onset, or ketosis-prone diabetes) is used to describe this type of diabetes. Symptoms of the disease are increased hunger, frequent urination, and thirst. The person with type 1 diabetes takes injections of insulin to replace the insulin not being produced by the pancreas. These insulin injections are necessary to keep the person alive. Blood sugars need to be monitored very carefully to prevent serious or even life-threatening conditions.

The other type of diabetes is **type 2 diabetes mellitus,** or **adult onset diabetes.** Type 2 diabetes results from the body's inability either to produce sufficient amounts of insulin or to process the insulin it does produce. This type of diabetes usually develops later on in life and is far more common than type 1 diabetes. The symptoms of type 2 diabetes are the same as those of type 1. Whereas patients with type 1 diabetes require injections of insulin to maintain control of their diabetes, type 2 diabetes is controlled by diet, exercise, and oral medications. If the oral medications are not successful in bringing insulin levels under control, then insulin injections may be necessary.

Providers rarely write out the insulin dependency of a patient; the abbreviations *IDDM* or *NIDDM* are used instead. These two abbreviations stand for **insulin-dependent diabetes mellitus** and **noninsulin-dependent diabetes mellitus**, respectively. The coder may see "type 2 NIDDM" or "type 2 IDDM" on the note to distinguish the use of insulin or not. Type 2 diabetics can be either insulin-dependent or non-insulin-dependent, and clarification is needed before the encounter is coded. Type 1 diabetes is always insulin-dependent.

When selecting codes for diabetes, following ICD-10-CM Coding Guidelines need to be followed:

ICD-10-CM Official Guidelines

Diabetes mellitus

The diabetes mellitus codes are combination codes that include the type of DM, the body system affected, and the complications affecting that body system. As many codes within a particular category as are necessary to describe all of the complications of the disease may be used. They should be sequenced based on the reason for a particular encounter. Assign as many codes from categories E08–E13 as needed to identify all of the associated conditions that the patient has.

1) Type of diabetes

The age of a patient is not the sole determining factor, though most type 1 diabetics develop the condition before reaching puberty. For this reason type 1 diabetes mellitus is also referred to as juvenile diabetes.

2) Type of diabetes mellitus not documented

If the type of diabetes mellitus is not documented in the medical record the default is E11.-, Type 2 diabetes mellitus.

3) Diabetes mellitus and the use of insulin

If the documentation in a medical record does not indicate the type of diabetes but does indicate that the patient uses insulin, code E11, Type 2 diabetes mellitus, should be assigned for type 2 patients who routinely use insulin, code Z79.4, Long-term (current) use of insulin, should also be assigned to indicate that the patient uses insulin. Code Z79.4 should not be assigned if insulin is given temporarily to bring a type 2 patient's blood sugar under control during an encounter.

4) Diabetes mellitus in pregnancy and gestational diabetes

See Section I.C.15. Diabetes mellitus in pregnancy.

See Section I.C.15. Gestational (pregnancy induced) diabetes

5) Complications due to insulin pump malfunction

(a) Underdose of insulin due to insulin pump failure

An underdose of insulin due to an insulin pump failure should be assigned to a code from subcategory T85.6, Mechanical complication of other specified internal and external prosthetic devices, implants and grafts, that specifies the type of pump malfunction, as the principal or first listed code, followed by code T38.3x6–, Underdosing of insulin

(continued)

and oral hypoglycemic [antidiabetic] drugs. Additional codes for the type of diabetes mellitus and any associated complications due to the underdosing should also be assigned.

(b) Overdose of insulin due to insulin pump failure

The principal or first listed code for an encounter due to an insulin pump malfunction resulting in an overdose of insulin, should also be T85.6–, Mechanical complication of other specified internal and external prosthetic devices, implants and grafts, followed by code T38.3x1–, Poisoning by insulin and oral hypoglycemic [antidiabetic] drugs, accidental (unintentional). (Section 1, C, 4a, 5)

6. Secondary Diabetes Mellitus

Secondary diabetes mellitus is always caused by another condition or event (e.g., cystic fibrosis, malignant neoplasm or pancreas, pancreatectomy, adverse effect of drug, or poisoning). (Section 1,C, 6)

Exercise 9.2 – Coding of Diabetes

Enter the appropriate term(s) to complete each statement.

1. A condition that occurs when the thyroid is not as active as it should be is referred to as _____.

2. A chronic disorder that results from a problem with the pancreas not secreting insulin properly is called _____.

3. The thyroid gland secretes hormones that regulate _____.

4. Diabetes mellitus falls into the _____ block of codes.

5. The type of diabetes that is always insulin dependent is type _____.

6. Code _____ is used to code type 2 diabetes with periodontal disease.

7. To code type 1 diabetes with ketoacidosis with coma, the coder should select code _____.

8. Type 2 DM with moderate nonproliferative diabetic retinopathy with macular edema is coded with code _____.

9. Type 1 DM with diabetic peripheral angiopathy with gangrene is coded with code _____.

10. Type 2 DM with diabetic neuropathy is coded with _____.

Other Disorders of Glucose Regulation and Pancreatic Internal Secretion (Category Codes E15–E16)

This block of codes includes codes for the following conditions:

- *Nondiabetic hypoglycemic coma (E15)*—This includes drug induced insulin coma in nondiabetics, hyperinsulinism with hypoglycemic coma and hypoglycemic coma.

- *Other disorders of pancreatic internal secretion (E16)*—Fourth digits differentiate the codes for drug-induced hypoglycemia without coma, other hypoglycemia, increased secretion of glucagon, increased secretion of gastrin, and other specified disorders of pancreatic internal secretion.

Disorders of Other Endocrine Glands (Category Codes E20–E35)

Category codes that are found in this section of ICD-10-CM include:

- E20, Hypoparathyroidism—This includes idiopathic, pseudo hypothyroidism, and other forms. **Hypoparathyroidism** is defined as an abnormal insufficient secretion of parathyroid hormone by the parathyroid glands caused by primary parathyroid dysfunction or by an elevated serum calcium level.

- E21, Hyperparathyroidism and other disorders of parathyroid gland—This category is divided into primary, secondary, and other types of hyperparathyroidism as well as disorders of the parathyroid. **Hyperparathyroidism** is defined as an abnormal condition of the parathyroid glands in which there is an excessive secretion of parathyroid hormone.

- E22, Hyperfunction of pituitary gland—This category includes acromegaly and pituitary gigantism as well as hyperprolactinemia.

- E23, Hypofunction and other disorders of the pituitary gland—Hypopituitarism, diabetes insipidus, and other hypothalamic dysfunction are classified to this range.

- E24, Cushing's syndrome—Various forms of Cushing's syndrome are coded using category E24. **Cushing's syndrome** results from the excessive and chronic production of cortisol by the adrenal cortex or by the administration of glucocorticoids in large doses for a period of several weeks or longer.

- E25, Adrenogenital disorders—This category includes both female and male adrenogenital disorders.

- E26, Hyperaldosteronism—The fourth digits differentiate primary, secondary, and other forms of hyperaldosteronism.

- E27, Other disorders of the adrenal gland—Some of the diseases classified here include adrenocortical overactivity, Addisonian crisis, drug-induced and other adrenocortical insufficiencies, as well as adrenal medullary hyperfunction.

- E28, Ovarian dysfunction—Included in this category are codes for primary ovarian failure, polycystic ovarian syndrome, and other ovarian dysfunctions.

- E29, Testicular dysfunction—Hyperfunction and hypofunction testicular diseases are classified to this category.

- E30, Disorders of puberty, not elsewhere classified—Delayed, precocious, and other disorders of puberty are coded here.

- E31, Polyglandular dysfunction—This category codes diseases that involve dysfunction of multiple glands such as Schmidt's syndrome and multiple endocrine neoplasia syndromes.

- E32, Disease of the thymus—This category is differentiated by the fourth-digit level to indicate persistent hyperplasia of the thymus, abscess of thymus, and other diseases of the thymus.

- E34, Other endocrine disorders—This category classifies other endocrine disorders and syndromes.

- E35, Disorders of endocrine glands in diseases classified elsewhere—A notation appears after the heading of this category to instruct the coder to "Code first underlying disease."

- E36, Intraoperative complications of endocrine system—This category codes complications of the endocrine system, such as an intraoperative hematoma, that occurs during a procedure. The fourth and fifth digits identify the type of complication.

Malnutrition (Category Codes E40–E46)

This block of codes is used to code malnutrition and includes the following categories:

- E40, Kwashiorkor
- E41, Nutritional marasmus

- E42, Marasmic kwashiorkor
- E43, Unspecified severe protein-calorie malnutrition
- E44, Protein-calorie malnutrition of moderate and mild degree
- E45, Retarded development following protein-calorie malnutrition
- E46, Unspecified protein-calorie malnutrition

Other Nutritional Deficiencies (Category Codes E50–E64) and Overweight, Obesity, and Other Hyperalimentation (Category Codes E65–E68)

Nutritional deficiencies are commonly seen as a result of poverty, substance abuse, and the so-called diet craze. Malnourished patients commonly have vitamin deficiencies, but these deficiencies can also be found in patients who exhibit problems such as malabsorption of nutrients. Although malabsorption typically is found in infants, children, and the elderly, the condition can be found in anyone.

ICD-10-CM classifies nutritional deficiencies to codes E50–E64, differentiating by type.

Codes E65–E68 are used to classify overweight, obesity, and other hyperalimentation. Category E66 differentiates the type of obesity as obesity due to excess calories, drug-induced obesity, morbid obesity, and other and unspecified obesity.

Metabolic Disorders (Category Codes E70–E90)

Conditions classified in the E70–E90 block of codes include disorders of metabolism and postprocedural endocrine and metabolic complications and disorders. The coder should review the numerous notations that are found throughout this section.

Comparing ICD-9-CM to ICD-10-CM

One of the most expansive changes in ICD-10-CM involves the codes for diabetes mellitus. ICD-10-CM has added a new category for drug- or chemical-induced diabetes mellitus. This was not found in ICD-9-CM. All of the diabetes codes have been expanded to define the manifestation of the disease; thus an additional code is not required to identify the manifestation. Many of the codes that fall in the E70–E90 range, Metabolic Disorders, are expanded to the sixth-character level.

Code Description	ICD-9-CM	ICD-10-CM
Diabetes mellitus	Category 250	Categories E08–E13 provide greater detail about the cause.
Hypoparathyroidism	Code 252.1	E20, Hypoparathroidism, is expanded to include various forms of hypoparathyroidism.
Hypothyroidism, acquired	Category 244, codes are delineated by cause of hypothyroidism.	E03.9, Unspecified hypothyroidism.
Hypothyroidism, postsurgical	244.0	E89.0
Hyperthyroidism, thyrotoxicosis	Category 242, Thyrotoxicosis with or without goiter	Category E05, Thyrotoxicosis, [hyperthyroidism] The coding of hyperthyroidism in ICD-10-CM identifies the type of goiter, ectopic thyroid tissue present. Thyrotoxic crisis or storm is also identified.

Internet Links

Visit *http://yourtotalhealth.ivillage.com/diabetes-heart-blood-vessel* to learn about diabetes and the endocrine system.

Additional information about the endocrine system can be found at *www.endocrinweb.com* and *www.ndei.org*

Educational information about the endocrine system is also found at *http://www.nrdc.org/health/effects/qendoc.asp*

The National Institute of Diabetes and Digestive and Kidney Disease has a Web site that contains a wealth of information at *www.endocrine.niddk.nih.gov*

To research information about metabolic syndrome, visit *http://www.metabolicyndrome.com/*

Summary

- The endocrine system is comprised of structures that produce or secrete hormones.
- Hormones keep organs and tissues functioning properly.
- The thyroid gland secretes hormones that regulate growth and metabolism.
- Diabetes is a chronic condition that can affect the proper functioning of organs and systems in the body.
- ICD-10-CM uses categories E08–E13 to classify the various types of diabetes.
- Documentation is key to coding diabetes and reflecting the manifestations of the disease.
- Nutritional deficiencies and other metabolic and immunity disorders are also coded from chapter 4 of ICD-10-CM.

Chapter Review

True/False: Indicate whether each statement is true (T) or false (F).

1. _____ When the pancreas does not secrete insulin, these patients typically have type 2 diabetes.

2. _____ Hypothyroidism is a thyroid that is not as active as it should be.

3. _____ Type 2 diabetes is also known as adult onset diabetes.

4. _____ Ketoacidosis is most commonly found in type 2 diabetics.

5. _____ Gestational diabetes develops during childhood.

Fill-in-the-Blanks: Enter the appropriate term(s) to complete the phrase.

6. Hyperthyroidism, also known as hyperactivity of the thyroid, occurs when the thyroid gland secretes excessive amounts of _____.

7. Hyperthyroidism with extreme crisis is also known as _____ or _____.

8. When hormone selections fall within normal limits but the thyroid itself becomes enlarged, this is known as a(n) _____ .

9. Type 1 diabetes is also referred to as juvenile type, juvenile onset, or _____ diabetes.

10. Patients with hypothyroidism are often treated with the medication _____.

Multiple Choice: Select the best answer that completes the statement or answers the question.

11. Which code is assigned for thyroiditis?
    a. E06
    b. E06.0
    c. E06.9
    d. E07

12. To code a disorder of the hypersecretion of intestinal hormones, the coder should reference the term _____ in the alphabetic index.
    a. disorder
    b. hormones
    c. hypersecretion
    d. intestinal

13. Severe malnutrition with nutritional edema with dyspigmentation of skin and hair is coded using code(s):
    a. E40.
    b. E40 and E41.
    c. E41.
    d. E46.

14. Sam Somo is diagnosed with a deficiency of vitamin E and vitamin K. This is coded as:
    a. E56.0.
    b. E56.1.
    c. E56.0, E56.1.
    d. E56.8.

15. Which of the following diagnoses is *not* coded to E72.3?
    a. hydroxylysinemia
    b. ornithinemia type1
    c. glutaric aciduria
    d. hyperlysinemia

Coding Assignments

Instructions: Using an ICD-10-CM code book, assign the proper diagnosis code to the following diagnostic statements.

1. hyperthyroidism _____

2. fructose intolerance _____

3. hyperlipidemia NOS _____

4. morbid obesity _____

5. Wilson's disease with Kayser-Fleischer ring, right eye _____

6. hypoglycemia _____

7. vitamin D–resistant rickets _____

8. type 1 diabetes _____

9. type 2 diabetes with hyperosmolarity _____

10. type 2 diabetes with retinopathy _____

11. simple nontoxic goiter _____

12. cystathioninemia _____

13. mild-degree of malnutrition _____

14. type 1 diabetic, under good control, with gangrene of the right great toe _____

15. type 2 diabetic, with hyperosmolarity   _____

16. nondiabetic insulin coma   _____

17. vitamin B$_{12}$ deficiency   _____

18. galactosemia   _____

19. vitamin A deficiencies with night blindness   _____

20. hypophosphatasia   _____

21. multinodular nontoxic goiter   _____

22. ovarian hyperfunction   _____

23. acquired iodine deficient hypothyroidism   _____

24. nutritional dwarfism   _____

25. hypopotassemia   _____

Case Studies

Instructions: Review each case study and select the correct ICD-10-CM diagnostic code.

CASE 1

Physician Office Visit

This 39-year-old female recently underwent GYN surgery and now is experiencing sleeplessness, headache, and lack of concentration. Her physical exam is negative. Diagnostic workup concludes ovarian failure. I am referring her to a specialist. Diagnosis: symptomatic postprocedural ovarian failure.

ICD-10-CM Code Assignment: _____

CASE 2

Clinic Visit

Patient presents today with symptoms of excessive thirst and frequent urination, which has been going on for approximately 1 month. Patient states that these symptoms are affecting her sleep, and she is concerned that there might be something wrong. Patient denies any shortness of breath, nausea, or stomach cramping. Patient does state that mother had type 2 diabetes, and she is fearful since the symptoms are similar. Patient states that she was borderline diabetic during her pregnancy.

WEIGHT: 198 lb Temp: 98.7 BP: 110/70

HEART: No murmurs, RRR

LUNGS: Normal

SKIN: Warm and dry

EXTREMITIES: No edema

(continued)

We did a finger stick, which indicated an elevated blood sugar level of 201. A HgA1C was ordered, which came back at a level 9. With these results and the symptoms involved, diabetes is the diagnosis here. We will try and control her diabetes with diet, exercise, and Glucophage. She will be set up for diabetic education as soon as possible.

ICD-10-CM Code Assignment: _____

CASE 3

S: This patient is a 68-year-old female presenting with severe muscle cramps most evenings. Sometimes the cramping wakes her out of a sound sleep. This has been going on for several months and doesn't seem to be getting better.

O: Pleasant older female, well nourished, and in no acute distress. Weight is 175 lb; blood pressure is 176/72; temperature, 98.4; pulse, 72; and respiration, 18. Skin: Normal and dry to touch; no rashes. Heart: No murmurs. Lungs: Clear. Extremities: No edema, clubbing, or cyanosis.

LAB RESULTS: Hemoglobin, 11.6; hematocrit, 35.3; potassium is 5.6, which is slightly elevated.

A & P: Hyperkalemia. I gave the patient a form that lists foods high in potassium content. I asked her to limit her intake of these foods as much as possible. If this approach works and the cramping lessens, we can avoid medication. She is willing to try this for 2 weeks. If she has not improved over that time, we will explore other options.

ICD-10-CM Code Assignment: _____

CASE 4

This patient presents today with a history of thyroid problems 6 years prior to today's visit. Today she is complaining of some tingling in the hands and feet, some lethargy, and some anxiety. We ran some lab tests, which showed low serum and urinary calcium, as well as low urinary phosphate with increase in the serum phosphate. Parathyroid hormone levels were almost absent. It was determined that the patient has hypoparathyroidism.

ICD-10-CM Code Assignment: _____

CASE 5

A 2-month-old male presents with chronic, severe diarrhea and fatigue. His growth is stunted. His family is concerned because he has been treated for several different disorders, none of which have been the problem. After extensive lab testing over the last week, we found very low-density lipoprotein levels. We now have a definite diagnosis of Andersen's disease and will begin vitamin E therapy.

ICD-10-CM Code Assignment: _____

CASE 6

Patient presents today as a follow-up for her type 2 DM with Charcot's joints. There is no change in her medical, family, or social history. On exam there are no abnormal findings in the cardiac, abdominal, or respiratory systems. Her knees are swollen with instability. Pain is moderate at this time. She is instructed to continue on her current medications with no changes. She is to follow up with me in four months.

ICD-10-CM Code Assignment: _____

Mental and Behavioral Disorders

Chapter Outline

Objectives

At the conclusion of this chapter, the learner should be able to:

1. Define mental health disorders and conditions.
2. Discuss the sequencing of codes for drug and alcohol abuse and dependence.
3. Summarize how the coding for this specialty is different from the other specialties and why the coding is challenging.
4. Identify the differences between the ICD-9-CM codes and the ICD-10-CM codes.
5. Select and code diagnoses from case studies.

Key Terms

alcohol abuse
alcohol dependence
alcoholism
anxiolytics
bed wetting
conversion disorders

delusional disorders
dementia
Diagnostic and
  Statistical Manual
  of Mental Disorders,
  Fourth Revision
  (DSM-IV)

dissociative disorders
developmental
  dyspraxia
drug abuse
drug dependence
encopresis

enuresis
factitious disorder
hallucinogens
hypnotics
impulse disorders
inhalants

Reminder

As you work through this chapter, you will need to have a copy of the ICD-10-CM coding book to reference.

kleptomania

mental retardation

mild mental retardation

moderate mental
retardation

nicotine

nocturnal enuresis

obsessive-compulsive
disorder

paraphilias

pica

polysubstance drug use

profound mental
retardation

pyromania

rumination disorder of
infancy

schizophrenia

sedatives

severe mental
retardation

somatoform disorders

tic disorder

trichotillomania

Introduction

Chapter 5 of ICD-10-CM, "Mental and Behavioral Disorders," classifies disorders of psychological development. It includes mental disorders that are due to known physiological conditions and substance use, along with other psychotic and nonpsychotic mental disorders.

Introduction to the Body System

Mental disorders are disorders that affect the ability of a person to function in a healthy, socially acceptable way and are classified to chapter 5 of ICD-10-CM. Persons with the same mental disorder are not always affected the same way. The severity may be different, or a person's reaction to treatment may differ from those of other patients. Because psychiatric terminology changes frequently, coders need to have reference materials. For the most current definitions of psychiatric conditions, coders should reference http://allpsych.com.

Psychiatric disorders diagnosed by psychiatrists most commonly are recorded according to a nomenclature established by the American Psychiatric Association, the **Diagnostic and Statistical Manual of Mental Disorders, Fourth Revision (DSM-IV)**. Although most psychiatrists use the terminology from DSM-IV, the ICD-10-CM codes are used to report mental disorders to third-party payers. To learn more about the *Diagnostic and Statistical Manual of Mental Disorders*, visit http://www.psych.org/MainMenu/Research/DSMIV.aspx. DSM-IV is being revised, with DSM-V tentatively slated for release in 2012.

Exercise 10.1 – Defining Psychiatric Terms

Define the following psychiatric terms by using the preceding Web site or a medical dictionary:

1. anxiety   _____

2. depression   _____

3. panic attack   _____

4. hallucination   _____

5. personality disorder   _____

6. paranoid reaction   _____

7. schizophrenia   _____

8. dementia   _____

9. attention deficit disorder _____

10. dissociative amnesia   _____

Coding of Mental and Behavioral Disorders

Chapter 5, "Mental and Behavioral Disorders," in the ICD-10-CM coding book is divided into the following blocks of codes:

- F01–F09, Mental disorders due to known physiological conditions
- F10–F19, Mental and behavioral disorders due to psychoactive substance use
- F20–F29, Schizophrenia, schizotypal and delusional, and other non-mood psychotic disorders
- F30–F39, Mood [affective] disorders
- F40–F48, Anxiety, dissociative, stress-related, somatoform, and other nonpsychotic mental disorders
- F50–F59, Behavioral syndromes associated with physiological disturbances and physical factors
- F60–F69, Disorders of adult personality and behavior
- F70–F79, Mental retardation
- F80–F89, Pervasive and specific developmental disorders
- F90–F98, Behavioral and emotional disorders with onset usually occurring in childhood and adolescence
- F99, Unspecified mental disorder

Mental Disorders Due to Known Physiological Conditions (Category Codes F01–F09)

The F01–F09 range of codes includes mental disorders that have an etiology in cerebral disease, brain injury, or other cause that has led to cerebral dysfunction. This etiology can lead to forms of dementia. **Dementia** is a loss of brain function that impacts memory, language, judgment, and the ability to think logically. This range of codes can best be summarized by reading the following notation that appears under the code block heading.

Mental disorders due to known physiological conditions (F01-F09)
This block comprises a range of mental disorders grouped together on the basis of their having in common a demonstrable etiology in cerebral disease, brain injury, or other insult leading to cerebral dysfunction. The dysfunction may be primary, as in diseases, injuries, and insults that affect the brain directly and selectively; or secondary, as in systemic diseases and disorders that attack the brain only as one of the multiple organs or systems of the body that are involved.

Codes that are included in this range are the following:

Category Code	Description
F01	This category is used to classify vascular dementia and includes arteriosclerotic dementia. A notation also appears in the Tabular Listing that instructs the coder to "Code first the underlying physiological condition or sequelae of cerebrovascular disease."
F02	Dementia in other diseases classified elsewhere is classified to category F02. A notation appears at the category level that instructs the coder to "Code first the underlying physiological condition, such as:" Alzheimer's, cerebral lipidosis, epilepsy and recurrent seizures, to name a few that are listed. This indicates to the coder that if a patient's dementia is caused by an underlying physiological condition, the physiological condition must be listed first. For example, if a patient has Alzheimer's dementia, the proper code sequence is G30.9, Alzheimer's disease, unspecified, and then F02.80, Dementia in other diseases classified elsewhere, without behavioral disturbance.

(continued)

F03	F03, used to classify unspecified dementia, is an example of a three-character code. Examples of diagnoses that are classified to F03 include: • Presenile dementia. • Presenile psychosis. • Primary degenerative dementia. • Senile dementia. • Senile dementia, depressed or paranoid type. • Senile psychosis.
F04	Amnestic disorders due to known physiological conditions are classified to category F04. This includes nonalcoholic Korsakov's psychosis or syndrome. The underlying physiological condition that caused the amnestic disorder should also be coded and listed first, as instructed by the coding notation.
F05	Delirium due to a known physiological condition is classified to F05. This code is used for: • Acute or subacute brain syndrome. • Acute or subacute confusional state (nonalcoholic). • Acute or subacute infective psychosis. • Acute or subacute organic reaction. • Acute or subacute psycho-organic syndrome. • Delirium of mixed etiology. • Delirium superimposed on dementia. • Sundowning.
F06	Other mental disorders due to known physiological condition is classified to category F06. This category is differentiated at the fourth-character level to indicate catatonic, psychotic, mood, anxiety, and other specified mental disorders.
F07	F07 codes personality and behavioral disorders due to known physiological conditions. Fourth and fifth digits are used to define the specific disorders.
F09	Code F09, Unspecified mental disorder due to known physiological condition, is used to code: • Organic brain syndrome NOS. • Organic mental disorder NOS. • Organic psychosis NOS. • Symptomatic psychosis NOS. Coders should heed the notation to "Code first the underlying physiological condition."

Mental and Behavioral Disorders due to Psychoactive Substance Use (Category Codes F10–F19)

Mental disorders related to the excessive use of substances are classified to the F10–F19 codes. The codes in this section identify the drug of choice and the level of abuse or dependence. Common addictive drugs are listed in Figure 10-1.

Alcohol abuse is defined as drinking alcohol to excess but not having a physical dependence on the alcohol. **Alcohol dependence**, also known as **alcoholism**, occurs when a person has become dependent on alcohol and is unable to stop drinking even though the alcoholism has negative effects on the person's health, social relationships, and normal daily activities, such as work. **Drug abuse** is defined as taking drugs to excess but not having a dependence on them. **Drug dependence** occurs when a chronic use of drugs creates a compulsion to take the drug in order to experience the effects from the drug.

When selecting codes from the F10–F19 code range, the coder must first carefully read the medical documentation in the patient's record to select the fifth and sixth digits used in this code range. The F10–F19 categories are organized as follows:

Opiates
Buprenex (buprenorphine)
Darvon, Darvocet (propoxyphene)
Demerol (meperidine)
Dilaudid (hydromorphone)
Fentanyl
Heroin
Immodium (loperamide)
Lomotil (diphenoxylate)
Lorcet (hydrocodone)
MS Contin/morphine
Methadone (Dolophine, Dolobid),
        LAAM (levomethadyl)
Nubain (nalbuphine)
Nyquil, cough syrups (dextromethorphan)
OxyContin (oxycodone)
Percocet, Percodan
Stadol (butorphanol)
Talwin (pentazocine)
Ultram (trammodol)
Vicodin (hydrocodone)

Benzodiazipines
Ambien (zoldipem)
Ativan (lorazepam)
Dalmane (flurazepam)
Halcion (triazolam)
Klonopin (clonazepam)
Librium (chlordiazepoxide)
Restoril (temazepam)
Serax (oxazepam)
Tranzene (chlorazepate)
Valium (diazepam)
Versed (midlazolam)
Xanax (alprazolam)

Barbituates
Amytal (amobarbital)
Fiorinal (butalbital)
Nembutal (pentobarbital)
Phenobarbital
Seconal (secobarbital)

Hallucinogens
Ecstasy (methylenedioxymethamphetamine
        or MDMA)
Ketamine
LSD (lysergic acid diethylamide)
Marijuana
Mescaline
MDA (methylenedioxyamphetamine)
Mushrooms
PCP (phtencyclidine)
Peyote
XTC

Stimulants
Amphetamine diet pills
Cocaine
Dexadrine
Ephedrine
Methamphetamine
Pseudoephedrine
Ritalin (methylphenidate)

Inhalants
Anesthetic gases
Diprivan (propofol)
Gasoline/paint thinner
Poppers, snappers (nitrous oxide)
Propellant

Others
Benadryl (diphenhydramine)
Chloral hydrate
Flexeril (cyclobenzaprine)
Miltown (meprobamate)
Placidyl (ethchlorvynol)
Skelaxin (methaxalone)
Soma (carisoprodol)

Figure 10-1 Common addictive drugs

Category Code	Description
F10	Alcohol-related disorders are classified to category F10. The category is further divided into F10.1, Alcohol abuse; F10.2, Alcohol dependence; and F10.9, Alcohol use, unspecified. Each of these subcategories is then divided into fifth and at times sixth digits, which further specify disorders and conditions accompanying the abuse or dependence. To select the most detailed codes, the coder must read the medical records to determine whether the patient is exhibiting other disorders such as delirium, psychotic disorders with delusions or hallucinations, anxiety disorders, and the like. One of the common code sets utilized is the F10.230–F10.239 range, Alcohol dependence with withdrawal. These codes are used when a patient has been diagnosed as having a dependence on alcohol and is experiencing withdrawal.
F11	Opioid-related disorders are coded using the F11 category. The category is divided to indicate abuse, dependence, or unspecified use. Fifth and sixth digits are used to identify intoxication, mood disorders, and other disturbances that the patient may be experiencing due to the use of opioids.
F12	Cannabis-related disorders are coded using the F12 category. This category includes disorders related to the use of marijuana. The fifth and six digits are organized in the same manner as the F10 and F11 categories. ICD-10-CM follows the same pattern for the fifth and sixth digits for all of the F10–F19 codes.

(continued)

F13	Sedative-, hypnotic-, or anxiolytic-related disorders are coded using the F13 category. **Sedatives** are drugs that induce a relaxed state and calm or tranquilize a patient. **Hypnotics** are sleep-inducing agents. **Anxiolytics** relieve anxiety.
F14	Cocaine-related disorders are coded using the F14 category. ICD-10-CM provides a separate category for cocaine-related disorders, even though cocaine is actually a stimulant.
F15	Stimulant-related disorders, other than cocaine, are coded using the F15 category. This category includes amphetamine-related disorders and caffeine-related disorders.
F16	Hallucinogen-related disorders are coded using the F16 category. **Hallucinogens** are substances that induce a perception of something being present that has no external cause. The patient may have a perception of a visual image or a sound that is not present.
F17	Nicotine dependence is coded using the F17 category. **Nicotine** is a poisonous alkaloid found in tobacco.
F18	Inhalant-related disorders are coded using the F18 category. **Inhalants** are substances that are inhaled for their euphoric effect. Common inhalants are glue, paint, and paint thinner.
F19	Other psychoactive-substance-related disorders are coded using the F19 category This category includes **polysubstance drug use**, which is the indiscriminate use of multiple drugs.

Schizophrenia, Schizotypal, Delusional, and Other Non-Mood Psychotic Disorders (Category Codes F20–F29)

The F20–F29 range of codes is used for the following disorders:

Category Code	Description
F20	Schizophrenia is classified to F20. **Schizophrenia** is a psychotic disorder characterized by disruptive behavior, hallucinations, delusions, and disorganized speech. ICD-10-CM differentiates the types of schizophrenia at the fourth-digit level to include paranoid schizophrenia, disorganized schizophrenia, catatonic schizophrenia, undifferentiated schizophrenia, residual schizophrenia, and other forms. Coders need to become familiar with the various terms used to describe the types of schizophrenia that are listed in the code book under each fourth-digit level.
F21	Schizotypal disorder is classified to F21 and includes: • Borderline schizophrenia. • Latent schizophrenia. • Latent schizophrenic reaction. • Prepsychotic schizophrenia. • Prodromal schizophrenia. • Pseudoneurotic schizophrenia. • Pseudopsychopathic schizophrenia. • Schizotypal personality disorder.
F22	Category F22 is used to classify delusional disorders. **Delusional disorders** include the feeling of paranoia in which the patient has a constant distrust and suspicion of others.
F23	Brief psychotic disorder is the title of category F23, and it includes paranoid reactions and psychogenic paranoid psychosis.
F24	F24 classifies shared psychotic disorder and includes folie à deux, induced paranoid disorder, and induced psychotic disorders.
F25	Schizoaffective disorders are classified to F25. This category is defined at the fourth-digit level to identify the various types of schizoaffective disorders that include bipolar type, depressive type, and other forms.
F28	Other psychotic disorders not due to a substance or known physiological condition are classified to this category. A diagnosis of chronic hallucinatory psychosis is coded here.
F29	The last category in this range of codes is unspecified psychosis not due to a substance or known physiological condition. The diagnosis of psychosis is coded here.

Mood [Affective] Disorders (Category Codes F30–F39)

Mood disorders, also known as affective disorders, are characterized by abnormal emotional states. This range of codes is differentiated as follows:

- F30, Manic episode—Fourth and fifth digits are used to identify the presence or absence of psychotic symptoms and the severity of the symptoms if they are present.

- F31, Bipolar disorder—Numerous fourth and fifth digits are used to classify the various forms of bipolar disorder. The coder needs to identify whether the patient is having a current episode of bipolar disorder or is in partial remission.

- F32, Major depressive disorder, single episode—The coder should note the numerous diagnoses listed as an Includes: note for this category. The coder also needs to read the patient's record to determine whether the disorder is a single or recurrent episode and the severity of the episode. Providers may have to be queried to get the level of detail needed for code selection.

- F33, Major depressive disorder, recurrent—The coder should consult the Includes note that appears under the F33 category heading. The severity of the depressive disorder also needs to be determined for code selection: mild, moderate, severe, and associated psychotic symptoms.

- F34, Persistent mood [affective] disorders—This category includes cyclothymic disorders such as affective personality disorder, cycloid personality, cyclothymia, and cyclothymic personality, which are classified to F34.0. Dysthymic disorders are classified to F34.1 and include depressive neurosis, depressive personality disorder dysthymia, neurotic depression, and persistent anxiety depression. F34.8 classifies other persistent mood [affective] disorders, and F34.9 classifies persistent mood [affective] disorder, unspecified.

- F39, Unspecified mood [affective] disorder—This code includes affective psychosis.

Anxiety, Dissociate, Stress-Related, Somatoform, and Other Nonpsychotic Mental Disorders (Category Codes F40–F48)

The F40–F48 range of codes classifies anxiety, dissociate, stress-related, somatoform, and other nonpsychotic mental disorders. The categories include:

- F40, Phobic anxiety disorder—Common phobias classified here include agoraphobia, social phobias, and isolated phobias such as claustrophobia, acrophobia, fear of flying, and the like.

- F41, Other anxiety disorder—Panic disorder, generalized and other mixed anxiety disorders are classified at the fourth-digit levels in this category. F41.9, Anxiety, is a commonly used code in this category.

- F42, Obsessive-compulsive disorder—**Obsessive-compulsive disorder** is a psychoneurotic disorder. The patient has obsessions or compulsions and suffers extreme anxiety or depression that can interfere with the patient's ability to function occupationally, interpersonally, or socially.

- F43, Reaction to severe stress, and adjustment disorders—This category includes codes for combat fatigue, grief reaction, post-traumatic stress disorder, and other reactions to stress.

- F44, Dissociative and conversion disorders—**Dissociative disorders** are characterized by emotional conflicts; the patient represses his or her emotions in such a manner that a separation in the personality occurs. The result can be a confusion in identity or an altered state of consciousness. **Conversion disorders** occur when a patient represses emotional conflicts, and sensory, motor, or visceral symptoms occur. The symptoms can include involuntary muscle movements, blindness, paralysis, aphonia, hallucinations, and choking sensations to name a few. ICD-10-CM uses the fourth- and fifth-digit levels to identify the disorder and the symptoms that occur.

- F45, Somatoform disorders—**Somatoform disorders** are characterized by symptoms that suggest a physical illness or disease but for which there is no organic cause or physiologic dysfunction.

- F48, Other nonpsychotic mental disorders—The last category in this range of codes includes codes for neurosis, Dhat syndrome, neurasthenia, occupational neurosis, psychasthenia, and other nonpsychotic mental disorders.

Behavioral Syndromes Associated with Physiological Disturbances and Physical Factors (Category Codes F50–F59)

Categories F50–F59 classifies behavioral syndromes associated with physiological disturbances and physical factors, including the following categories:

- F50, Eating disorders—Anorexia and bulimia nervosa are classified here.

- F51, Sleep disorders not due to substance or known physiological condition.

- F52, Sexual dysfunction not due to a substance or known physiological condition.

- F53, Puerperal psychosis—This includes postpartum depression.

- F54, Psychological and behavioral factors associated with disorders or diseases classified elsewhere—An instructional notation tells the coder to "Code first the associated physical disorder, such as . . . ." Two codes are needed. Please see the code book for the specific notation.

- F55, Abuse of nonpsychoactive substances—This category classifies the abuse of substances such as antacids, herbal or folk remedies, laxatives, steroids, hormones, vitamins, and other substances.

- F59, Unspecified behavioral syndromes associated with physiological disturbances and physical factors—This includes psychogenic physiological dysfunction.

Disorders of Adult Personality and Behavior (Category Codes F60–F69)

Disorders of adult personality and behavior are classified to F60–F69. This range includes the following categories:

- F60, Specific personality disorders—Paranoid personality disorder, schizoid personality disorder, antisocial personality disorder, borderline personality disorder, histrionic personality disorder, obsessive-compulsive personality disorder, avoidant personality disorder, dependent personality disorder, and other personality disorders are differentiated at the fourth-digit levels for this category.

- F63, Impulse disorder—**Impulse disorders** are characterized by a sudden desire or urge to act without consideration of consequences that may result. Fourth digits identify pathological gambling, **pyromania** (fire setting), **kleptomania** (pathological stealing), **trichotillomania** (hair plucking), and other impulse disorders.

- F64, Gender identity disorders—This includes dual role transvestism and transsexualism. Coders need to read the instructional notations for this category for proper code assignment.

- F65, Paraphilias—**Paraphilias** are sexual perversions or deviations. Fourth digits are used to differentiate the types of paraphilias.

- F66, Other sexual disorders—These are classified to category F66 and include sexual maturation disorder and sexual relationship disorder.

- F68, Other disorders of adult personality and behavior—Code F68.1 classifies **factitious disorders**, which are characterized by disease symptoms that have been caused by the patient's deliberate actions to gain attention.

- F69, Unspecified disorder of adult personality and behavior—This category is used for disorders that are not specified by the provider as to the specific disorder.

Mental Retardation (Category Codes F70–F79)

Mental retardation is a condition in which the mind of the patient never fully develops. The coding in this section is based on the person's current level of functioning. Mental retardation is classified and defined in ICD-10-CM as follows:

- **Mild mental retardation**—Code F70, an IQ of 50–55 to approximately 70, also referred to as mild mental subnormality

- **Moderate mental retardation**—Code F71, an IQ of 35–40 to 50–55, also referred to as moderate mental subnormality

- **Severe mental retardation**—Code F72, an IQ of 20–25 to 35–40, also referred to as severe mental subnormality

- **Profound mental retardation**—Code F73, an IQ below 20–25, also referred to as profound mental subnormality

- Other mental retardation—Code F78

- Unspecified mental retardation—Code F79, used when the medical documentation states that the patient is mentally retarded but the level of functioning is not recorded, includes mental deficiency and mental subnormality

Disease Highlight—Mental Retardation

Mental retardation is a genetic or acquired condition in which there is decreased intelligence. The genetic causes of mental retardation are:

- Down's syndrome.
- Hypothyroidism.
- Phenylketonuria.

Acquired causes include:

- Birth injuries.
- Anoxia.
- Head trauma.
- Poor nutrition.
- Premature birth.
- Prenatal maternal rubella or syphilis.
- Blood type incompatibility.

Signs and Symptoms:

Children with mental retardation show signs of decreased mental functioning compared to other children of the same age.

Clinical Testing:

IQ testing and observation of a child's functional levels confirm the diagnosis.

Treatment:

Treatment of patients with mental retardation varies depending on their functioning level. Severely retarded persons are institutionalized because they are unable to care for themselves without assistance. Mildly retarded persons are able to live fairly normal lives and to find employment with little psychological and social assistance.

Pervasive and Specific Developmental Disorders (Category Codes F80–F89)

This code range is used to classify developmental disorders according to the following categories:

Category Code	Description
F80	Specific developmental disorders of speech and language are classified to the F80 category. The category is further divided to identify the types of disorder: • Phonological disorders (F80.0) • Expressive language disorder (F80.1) • Mixed receptive-expressive language disorder (F80.2) • Acquired aphasia with epilepsy (F80.3) • Speech and language development delay due to hearing loss (F80.4) • Other developmental disorders of speech or language (F80.8) • Developmental disorder of speech or language, unspecified (F80.9) Code F80.4 contains an instructional notation for the coder to "Code also type of hearing loss (H90.-, H91.-)."
F81	Specific developmental disorders of scholastic skills are coded to the F81 category and are divided at the fourth-digit level to identify the specific delay. This category lists various terms used to describe the scholastic skills delay such as developmental dyslexia, specific reading retardation, developmental arithmetical disorder, and specific spelling disorder.
F82	F82 identifies specific developmental disorder of motor function and includes clumsy child syndrome, developmental coordination disorder, and developmental dyspraxia. **Developmental dyspraxia** is defined as an impaired ability to perform coordinated movements in the absence of any defect in sensory or motor functions.
F84	At the start of this category, Pervasive developmental disorders, an instructional notation tells the coder to "Use additional code to identify any associated medical condition and mental retardation." This category is used to code: • F84.0, Autistic disorder. • F84.2, Rett's syndrome. • F84.3, Other childhood disintegrative disorder. (The code book lists various diagnoses that are coded here. An instructional notation also appears to "Use additional code to identify any associated neurological condition.") • F84.5, Asperger's syndrome. • F84.8, Other pervasive developmental disorders. • F84.9, Pervasive developmental disorder, unspecified.
F88	Other disorders of psychological development are classified to category F88.
F89	F89 is used to classify an unspecified disorder of psychological development and developmental disorder.

Behavioral and Emotional Disorders with Onset Usually Occurring in Childhood and Adolescence (Category Codes F90–F98)

Although the title for the F90–F98 range of codes leads the reader to believe that these codes are assigned only for disorders that occur in childhood and adolescence, coders should follow the notation that appears under the heading for this range of codes:

Behavioral and emotional disorders with onset usually occurring in childhood and adolescence (F90–F98)
Note: Codes within categories F90–F98 may be used regardless of the age of a patient. These disorders generally have onset within the childhood or adolescent years, but may continue throughout life or not be diagnosed until adulthood.

This range of codes is differentiated as follows:

- F90, Attention-deficit hyperactivity disorders—This category includes attention deficit disorder with hyperactivity and attention deficit syndrome with hyperactivity. Fourth digits are used to differentiate inattentive type, hyperactive, combined, other, or unspecified types of this disorder.

- F91, Conduct disorders—When selecting codes from this category, coders need to carefully read the Excludes: notes at the category level. Coders should also become familiar with the diagnoses listed at the F91.1, F91.2, and F91.9 codes; the listed diagnoses are included to provide further definition to the code descriptions.

- F93, Emotional disorders with onset specific to childhood—Separation anxiety disorders of childhood and other childhood emotional disorders are classified to this category.

- F94, Disorders of social functioning with onset specific to childhood and adolescence—This category is divided into the following fourth-digit codes:

  - F94.0, Selective mutism
  - F94.1, Reactive attachment disorder of childhood
  - F94.2, Disinhibited attachment disorder of childhood
  - F94.8, Other childhood disorders of social functioning
  - F94.9, Childhood disorder of social functioning, unspecified

- F95, Tic disorder—A **tic disorder** is defined is a repetitive involuntary muscle spasm that is usually psychogenic and can increase due to stress or anxiety. Fourth digits are used to identify the types of tic disorders, such as transient tic disorder, chronic motor or vocal tic disorder, and Tourette's disorder.

- F98, Other behavioral and emotional disorders with onset usually occurring in childhood and adolescence—This category is used to code the following:

  - F98.0, Enuresis not due to a substance or known physiological condition—**Enuresis** is incontinence of urine. **Nocturnal enuresis**, also known as **bed wetting**, is incontinence of urine that occurs at night. Note that this category is for enuresis with no known physiological cause or not due to a substance.

  - F98.1, Encopresis not due to a substance or known psychological condition—**Encopresis** is the involuntary passage of feces. An instructional notation for this code tells the coder to "Use additional code to identify the cause of any coexisting constipation."

  - F98.2, Other feeding disorders of infancy and childhood—This category includes **rumination disorder of infancy**, which is when a person regurgitates and chews previously swallowed food, and other feeding disorders.

  - F98.3, Pica of infancy and childhood—**Pica** occurs when a person has an abnormal craving and eating of substances that are not normally eaten by humans. Common ingested substances are chalk, paper, and ashes.

  - F98.4, Stereotyped movement disorders—This category also includes stereotype and habit disorders.

  - F98.5, Stuttering and stammering.

  - F98.8, Other specified behavioral and emotional disorders with onset usually occurring in childhood and adolescence—This category includes cluttering, excessive masturbation, nail biting, nose picking, and thumb sucking.

Unspecified Mental Disorder (Category Code F99)

The last category in this chapter, F99, is for mental disorders that are not specified elsewhere or that are listed in the patient's record as mental illness not otherwise specified.

Comparing ICD-9-CM to ICD-10-CM

A number of mental and behavioral disorder codes have been expanded in ICD-10-CM. Alcohol- and substance-related abuse and dependence have been expanded in ICD-10-CM. Mood affective disorders, anxiety, dissociative, stress-related, somatoform, and other nonpsychotic mental disorders have been expanded at the fourth- and fifth-character levels.

Diagnostic Description	ICD-9-CM Code	ICD-10-CM Code
Alcohol abuse and dependence	Category 303 is used to code alcohol dependence, 304 used to code drug dependence, and 305 to code nondependent abuse of drugs including alcohol.	Categories F10–F 19 are used to report alcohol/drug abuse and dependence. Fifth and sixth digits provide greater specificity for associated disorders.
Mental retardation	Category codes 317–319 report the various degrees of mental retardation.	Category codes F70–F79 are used to report mental retardation. An instructional notation appears that directs the coder to code first any associated physical or developmental disorder. In ICD-9-CM the coder does not list the disorders first.

Internet Links

To learn about addictions, Alzheimer's, depression, stress, personality disorders, and other psychiatric conditions, go to *www.apa.org*, the home page of the American Psychological Association.

To learn more about the diagnosis and treatment of mental and emotional illness and substance use disorders, go to the *www.psych.org*, the home page of the American Psychiatric Association.

For information on current treatment, research, and prevention of drug abuse, go to *www.drugabuse.gov*, the home page of the National Institute on Drug Abuse.

The American Academy of Addiction Psychiatry provides information about the treatment of addiction and research on the etiology, prevention, and identification of addictions at *www.aaap.org*

The Alcohol Medical Scholars Program provides information on the identification and care of individuals with alcohol use disorders and other substance-related problems at *www.alcoholmedicalscholars.org*

To learn more about the treatment of mental disorders, visit *www.mentalhealth.org* and *http://psychcentral.com/disorders*

Summary

- Chapter 5 of ICD-10-CM classifies mental disorders.
- Provider documentation must be reviewed, and it must be used to justify the codes selected for mental disorders.
- ICD-10-CM and DSM-IV are both used to classify mental disorders.
- Dementia is a form of psychosis.
- Fourth, fifth, and sixth digits or characters are frequently used with chapter 5 of ICD-10-CM; therefore, coders need to thoroughly review provider documentation before selecting codes.
- Alcohol abuse and alcohol dependence are classified separately in ICD-10-CM.
- Drug abuse and drug dependence are classified separately in ICD-10-CM.

- Abuse occurs when there is excess use of a substance; dependence occurs when person has become dependent on a substance and is unable to stop using the substance.

- Any diagnoses that fall in chapter 5 must be clearly supported by provider documentation for code selection.

- Mental retardation is classified in ICD-10-CM by a person's functional level and is described as mild, moderate, severe, profound, or unspecified.

Chapter Review

True/False: Indicate whether each statement is true (T) or false (F).

1. _____ DSM-IV is the preferred nomenclature of mental disorders for third-party reimbursement.

2. _____ Alcohol abuse and dependence are classified to different codes in ICD-10-CM.

3. _____ Mild retardation is diagnosed when a person has an IQ of 30.

4. _____ Mental disorders are always congenital.

5. _____ Ginger Gin is admitted to New Days Drug and Alcohol Treatment Facility with the following diagnoses: gastritis due to alcoholism, continuous alcohol dependence. The code for the alcohol dependence should be sequenced first when payment for services is billed.

Fill-in-the-Blank: Enter the appropriate term(s) to complete each statement.

6. A slowly progressive decrease in mental abilities that includes lack of judgment, decreased memory, and a decrease in the ability to pay attention is known as _____.

7. A chronic use of drugs that creates a compulsion to take the drug in order to experience the effects from the drug is known as _____.

8. Psychiatric disorders diagnosed most commonly by psychiatrists are recorded by using _____.

9. Mood disorders, also known as _____ disorders, are characterized by abnormal emotional states.

10. A person with an IQ of 30 would be diagnosed as having _____ mental retardation.

Multiple Choice: Select the best answer that completes the statement or answers the question.

11. Which code is used for the diagnosis of infantile autism?
   - a. F84
   - b. F84.0
   - c. F84.5
   - d. F84.9

12. Which of the following diagnoses would *not* be coded to F60.0?
   - a. expansive paranoid personality disorder
   - b. fanatic personality disorder
   - c. inadequate personality disorder
   - d. sensitive paranoid personality disorder

13. Category F53 is used to code:
   - a. aversion sexual disorder.
   - b. hypoactive sexual disorder.
   - c. nymphomania.
   - d. puerperal psychosis.

14. Which of the following diagnoses are coded with F51.01?
   a. adjustment insomnia
   b. paradoxical insomnia
   c. primary insomnia
   d. unspecified insomnia

15. Code F03 includes all of the following diagnoses *except*:
   a. presenile dementia.
   b. presenile psychosis.
   c. senile dementia.
   d. senility.

Coding Assignments

Instructions: Using an ICD-10-CM code book, assign the proper diagnosis code to the following diagnostic statements.

1. presenile dementia with depressive features   _____

2. obsessive-compulsive disorder   _____

3. anxiety   _____

4. borderline personality disorder   _____

5. social phobia   _____

6. narcissistic personality disorder   _____

7. mental retardation, IQ of 29   _____

8. premature ejaculation   _____

9. heroin dependence   _____

10. passive personality disorder   _____

11. acute stress reaction   _____

12. anorexia nervosa   _____

13. psychogenic dysuria   _____

14. neurotic depression   _____

15. marijuana abuse, current   _____

16. alcoholic paranoia   _____

17. alcohol withdrawal syndrome   _____

18. hyperorexia nervosa   _____

19. alcoholic dementia   _____

20. chronic paranoid schizophrenia   _____

21. senile dementia with depressive features _____

22. vascular dementia _____

23. organic psychosis _____

24. psychogenic confusion _____

25. hypomanic type psychosis _____

Case Studies

Instructions: Review each case study and select the correct ICD-10-CM diagnostic code.

CASE 1

PATIENT: Tom Smith DATE OF SERVICE: 9/10/XX

BLOOD PRESSURE: 140/90 WEIGHT: 164 PULSE: Rapid TEMPERATURE: 100

Tom was seen today at the request of his wife for what she suspects is a recurrence of his cocaine dependence.

On physical examination, the following was noted:

EARS, EYES, NOSE, AND THROAT: Pupils are dilated.

HEART: Heart rate is increased; blood pressure is 140/90.

ABDOMEN: Soft, nontender, no abnormal masses

PSYCHIATRIC: Oriented to time and place. Patient is very talkative and admits to not eating for the last 36 hours with no sleep for the last 48 hours. The lack of sleep is cocaine induced. Patient admits to using cocaine over the last month and recent days.

Referral made for inpatient treatment.

ICD-10-CM Code Assignment: _____

CASE 2

Nursing Facility Note of 2/7/XX

Sally Andover was admitted on 2/5/XX because of her medical conditions and her inability to care for herself at home. She was mildly cooperative throughout the exam; however, her dementia makes her obviously confused, and she has a diagnosis of senile dementia. Her medications were reviewed. Her full medical history and physical was completed 2/5/XX by Dr. Jones.

HEENT: Normal

LUNGS: Clear

ABDOMEN: Soft, nontender; active bowel sound; no masses noted

HEART: Regular rhythm without murmurs, pulses normal

TEMPERATURE: 98.8 BLOOD PRESSURE: 125/85 PULSE: Regular

Medication orders written.

ICD-10-CM Code Assignment: _____

CASE 3

Psychiatric Office Note

Terry was seen today experiencing symptoms of mania, speech disturbances, and lack of sleep for 3 days due to his bipolar disorder. Patient states that he has not been taking his medications. I discussed with

(*continued*)

the patient the importance of taking his medications and instructed him to regularly take them. Current issues that create stress for the patient were discussed, including marital distress and financial issues. Patient was instructed to follow up at 1 month due to this current manic bipolar episode.

ICD-10-CM Code Assignment: _____

CASE 4

Emergency Department Note

PATIENT: Samantha Hill DATE OF SERVICE: 12/31/XX

AGE: 23

Samantha was brought in by ambulance. She was at a New Year's Eve's Party, and she has been drinking alcohol for 4 hours and passed out. According to her friend who accompanied her to the ER, Mary does not have an alcohol addiction and has no known medical conditions.

Physical Exam

Pupils are dilated.

HEART: Heart rate is decreased.

ABDOMEN: No abnormal findings

Patient has limited response to questions. While she was in the emergency room, she started to vomit. She was observed for 7 hours and then sent home. She was advised to seek counseling for possible alcohol addiction.

ICD-10-CM Code Assignment: _____

CASE 5

Physician's Office Note

NAME: John Nown DATE OF SERVICE: 3/1/XX

BLOOD PRESSURE: 130/83 WEIGHT: 168 TEMPERATURE: 98.6

John is being seen today at his request because he has felt tired and has lost his appetite for the last 3 weeks since his wife died. He has no other complaints at this time.

He said he wants to make sure that he has no physical problems. Reviewing his record, I noted that all of his immunizations are current and that he is not due for any additional preventative medicine testing at this time.

Physical Exam:

HEENT: Within normal limits

HEART: Normal R&R, no murmurs

ABDOMEN: Soft and nontender, no masses; active bowel sounds

EXTREMITIES: Within normal limits

Patient is oriented to time, person, and surroundings with no confusion. Patient expressed that he is sad because of the loss of his wife. I told the patient that his tiredness is most likely due to the loss of his wife and that there are no abnormal physical findings at this time.

DIAGNOSIS: Adjustment disorder with depressed mood.

PLAN: Patient refused antidepressive medications and said he would seek counseling if he felt he needed it. He was instructed to call the office if he experienced any other symptoms and said he wanted to follow up with me in 3 weeks.

ICD-10-CM Code Assignment: _____

Diseases of the Nervous System

Chapter Outline

Objectives

At the conclusion of this chapter, the learner should be able to:

1. Identify the major structures of the nervous system.
2. Explain conditions that involve the nervous system.
3. Identify the differences between the ICD-9-CM codes and the ICD-10-CM codes.
4. Select and code diagnoses from case studies.

Key Terms

Alzheimer's disease

autonomic nervous system

central nervous system (CNS)

cerebral palsy

encephalitis

encephalomyelitis

epilepsy

grand mal

hemiparesis

hemiplegia

meningitis

multiple sclerosis

myelitis

nervous system

Parkinson's disease

peripheral nervous system (PNS)

petit mal

Reminder

As you work through this chapter, you will need to have a copy of the ICD-10-CM coding book to reference.

Introduction

Chapter 6 of ICD-10-CM, entitled Diseases of the Nervous System, classifies conditions that impact the nervous system. Categories G00 through G99 are used within this chapter of ICD-10-CM.

Introduction to the Body System

The **nervous system** controls all bodily activities and is divided into two main parts. The **central nervous system (CNS)** is the part of the nervous system made up of the brain and spinal cord. The **peripheral nervous system (PNS)** is the part of the nervous system that directly branches off the central nervous system. The 12 pairs of cranial nerves and 31 pairs of spinal nerves make up this system. Included in the peripheral nervous system is what is known as the **autonomic nervous system**. The autonomic nervous system regulates the activities of the cardiac muscle, smooth muscle, and glands. Ultimately, the brain controls all bodily activities. If the brain dies, the body dies. Figure 11-1 illustrates the organization of the central nervous system and the peripheral nervous system.

Coding of Diseases of the Nervous System

Chapter 6 of ICD-10-CM is organized into the following blocks:

- G00–G09, Inflammatory diseases of the central nervous system
- G10–G14, Systemic atrophies primarily affecting the central nervous system
- G20–G26, Extrapyramidal and movement disorders
- G30–G32, Other degenerative diseases of the nervous system
- G35–G37, Demyelinating diseases of the central nervous system
- G40–G47, Episodic and paroxysmal disorders
- G50–G59, Nerve, nerve root, and plexus disorders
- G60–G64, Polyneuropathies and other disorders of the peripheral nervous system
- G70–G73, Diseases of myoneural junction and muscle
- G80–G83, Cerebral palsy and other paralytic syndromes
- G89–G99, Other disorders of the nervous system

Inflammatory Diseases of the Central Nervous System (Category Codes G00–G09)

The first block in this chapter classifies inflammatory diseases of the central nervous system. A diagnosis that is commonly coded to this block is meningitis. **Meningitis** is an inflammation of the membranes, or the meninges, of

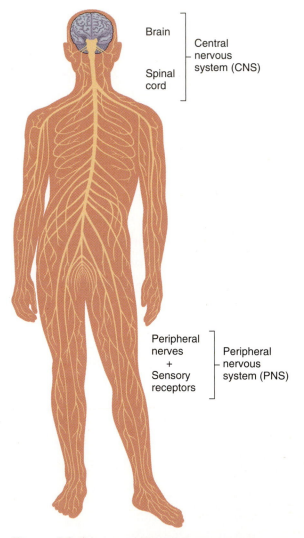

Figure 11-1 Central and peripheral nervous systems (From Ehrlich A, Schroeder CI. *Medical Terminology for Health Professions*, 4th ed. Clifton Park, NY: Delmar, Cengage Learning, 2001.)

the spinal cord or brain. Meningitis can be bacterial, nonbacterial, viral, or aseptic. ICD-10-CM classifies meningitis according to the type of organism or cause.

Other conditions that code to these categories of the nervous system include **encephalitis**, an inflammation of the brain; **myelitis**, an inflammation of the spinal cord; and **encephalomyelitis**, an inflammation of both the brain and the spinal cord. The G00–G09 block is summarized as follows:

Category Code	Description
G00	This category is used to code bacterial meningitis, not elsewhere classified, and is differentiated at the fourth-character level to identify the type of meningitis, such as hemophilus, pneumococcal, streptococcal, staphylococcal, and other forms. To identify the type of bacterial meningitis present, reference the laboratory reports.
G01	G01 is used to code meningitis in bacterial diseases classified elsewhere. This category contains an instructional notation stating "Code first underlying disease."
G02	Meningitis in other infectious and parasitic diseases classified elsewhere is coded here. As in G01, an instructional notation appears to "Code first underlying disease."
G03	Meningitis due to other and unspecified causes is classified with this category and is differentiated at the fourth-character level according to the following types of meningitis: nonpyogenic, chronic, benign recurrent. and other causes. Meningitis, unspecified is coded to G03.9.
G04	The title for this category is "encephalitis, myelitis, and encephalomyelitis." Fourth and fifth characters are used to identify the various forms of the conditions. There are several Includes and Excludes notations that need to be referred prior to code selection.
G05	This category reports encephalitis, myelitis, and encephalomyelitis in diseases classified elsewhere. This category contains an instructional notation to "Code first underlying disease." The lengthy Excludes 1 note should be reviewed.
G06	"Intracranial and intraspinal abscess and granuloma" is the title of this category. Additional codes should be added to identify infectious agents present, as instructed by the notation.
G07	Intracranial and intraspinal abscess and granuloma in diseases classified elsewhere are included in this category. A "Code first underlying disease" note appears in the code book for this category as well as an Excludes 1 note.
G08	Intracranial and intraspinal phlebitis and thrombophlebitis are assigned this code. This code is used for various forms of septic conditions of the venous sinuses and veins.
G09	Sequelae of inflammatory diseases of central nervous system are assigned this code. This category contains the following note to explain the purpose of this code: Category G09 is to be used to indicate conditions whose primary classification is to G00-G08 as the cause of sequelae, themselves classifiable elsewhere. The "sequelae" include conditions specified as residuals. Code first condition resulting from (sequela) of inflammatory diseases of central nervous system.

Systemic Atrophies Primarily Affecting the Central Nervous System (Category Codes G10–G14)

This block of codes contains the following categories:

- G10, Huntington's disease
- G11, Hereditary ataxia
- G12, Spinal muscular atrophy and related syndromes
- G13, Systematic atrophies primarily affecting central nervous system in diseases classified elsewhere
- G14, Postpolio syndrome

This block of codes includes some congenital disorders such as code G11.0, Congenital nonprogressive ataxia. Coders must carefully read the diagnostic statement and match it with one of the many diagnostic descriptions in this block. For example, code G12.1 has many diagnostic descriptions following the heading.

Extrapyramidal and Movement Disorders (Category Codes G20–G26)

This block of codes includes codes for Parkinson's disease and other degenerative diseases of basal ganglia, dystonia, and other movement disorders.

Parkinson's disease, a progressive disease characterized by a mask-like facial expression, weakened muscles, tremors, and involuntary movement, is classified by this section of ICD-10-CM to category codes G20–G21. With Parkinson's disease, the coder must identify any other associated conditions that may exist because these can affect code assignment.

Exercise 11.1 – Coding from Category Codes G00–G26

For each diagnostic statement select the correct ICD-10-CM code.

1. congenital nonprogressive ataxia   _____

2. genetic torsion dystonia   _____

3. tropical spastic paraplegia   _____

4. late-onset cerebellar ataxia   _____

5. drug-induced tics   _____

6. spasmodic torticollis   _____

7. progressive bulbar palsy   _____

8. chronic meningitis   _____

9. myelitis   _____

10. motor neuron disease   _____

Other Degenerative Diseases of the Nervous System (Category Codes G30–G32)

Alzheimer's disease, a disease in which brain structure changes lead to memory loss, personality changes, and ultimately impaired ability to function, is coded to category G30. Category G31 is used to report other degenerative diseases of the nervous system such as frontotemporal dementia, senile degeneration of the brain, and mild cognitive impairment. Category G32 reports other degenerative disorders of the nervous system in diseases classified elsewhere.

Demyelinating Diseases of the Central Nervous System (Category Codes G35–G37)

This block of codes has only three categories:

- G35, Multiple sclerosis
- G36, Other acute disseminated demyelination
- G37, Other demyelinating diseases of central nervous system

Multiple sclerosis is a demyelinating disorder in which patches of hardened tissue form in the brain or spinal cord and cause partial or complete paralysis and muscle tremors.

Disease Highlight—Multiple Sclerosis

Multiple sclerosis (MS) is a chronic disease that attacks the central nervous system. The patient's own body attacks the myelin fibers, causing scarring or sclerosis. This sclerosis interrupts the nerve impulses traveling to and from the brain and spinal cord. There is no clear conclusive clinical evidence of any type of pathogenesis that would cause MS.

Signs and Symptoms:

The symptoms of MS vary from person to person and include:

- Numbness in the limbs.
- Visual disturbances.
- Muscle weakness.
- Emotional problems, such as mood swings and depression.
- Urinary problems, such as incontinence, urgency, or frequency.

Clinical Testing:

MS is difficult to diagnose. Testing may include:

- Electrophoresis.
- Computed tomography (CT) and magnetic resonance imaging (MRI) scans.
- Lumbar puncture.
- Electroencephalography (EEG).

Treatment:

Patients with MS receive symptomatic treatment, such as physical therapy and steroid treatment, to relieve the symptoms.

Episodic and Paroxysmal Disorders (Category Codes G40–G47)

One of the most common disorders assigned in this code block is epilepsy and recurrent seizures. G40 is used to report these disorders. This category is very detailed in the description of the codes, and coders may have to query providers to assign codes when diagnostic statements are not detailed.

Epilepsy is a transient disturbance of cerebral function that is recurrent and characterized by episodes of seizures. The most severe seizure is the **grand mal**. Less severe seizures are identified as **petit mal**. The seizure may involve convulsions, abnormal behavior, and loss of consciousness. Because seizures can occur in other diseases or conditions, the coder should not assume that epilepsy is present unless the provider specifically documents the cause as the patient's epilepsy. A diagnosis of epilepsy carries serious legal consequences, such as loss of a driver's license or the inability to obtain insurance; so extreme care needs to be taken when assigning this diagnosis.

G43 is used to report migraine and is differentiated to indicate the various types of migraine, such as migraine with aura, status migrainosus, hemiplegic migraine, menstrual migraine, persistent migraine, and chronic migraine.

Other headache syndromes are coded to category code G44. Cluster, vascular, post-traumatic, and drug-induced are some of the differentiations.

G45 reports transient cerebral ischemic attacks and related syndromes, and G46 reports vascular syndromes of the brain in cerebrovascular diseases. Category G47 is used to report sleep disorders such as insomnia, hypersomnia, sleep apnea, narcolepsy, and parasomnia.

Nerve, Nerve Root, and Plexus Disorders (Category Codes G50–G59)

This block of codes is used to report various nerve disorders. The categories are differentiated according to the nerve involved. Coders must identify the nerve involvement for proper code assignment.

Polyneuropathies and Other Disorders of the Peripheral Nervous System (Category Codes G60–G64)

Hereditary and idiopathic neuropathies are classified with category code G60.

An extensive list of diagnoses fall into this category as evidenced by the diagnoses listed after the category heading. Codes G61–G65 report other types of polyneuropathies.

Diseases of Myoneural Junction and Muscle (Category Code G70–G73)

This category includes code G71.0, Muscular dystrophy, and G71.1, Myotonic disorders. The G71.1 codes are further differentiated by the type of myotonic condition, such as congenital, drug induced, and other forms.

Cerebral Palsy and Other Paralytic Syndromes (Category Codes G80–G83)

This block of codes is divided as follows:

- G80, Cerebral palsy
- G81, Hemiplegia and hemiparesis
- G82, Paraplegia (paraparesis) and quadriplegia (quadriparesis)
- G83, Other paralytic syndromes

Cerebral palsy, a disorder in which the motor function of the brain is impaired, is present at birth, and is chronic and nonprogressive. The disorder is coded in this section. **Hemiplegia** is a condition in which one side of the body is paralyzed due to brain hemorrhage, cerebral thrombosis, embolism, or a tumor of the cerebrum. **Hemiparesis** is a synonym for hemiplegia.

This block of codes is governed by the following coding guideline:

ICD-10-CM Official Coding Guidelines

Dominant/nondominant side

Codes from category G81, Hemiplegia and hemiparesis, and subcategories, G83.1, Monoplegia of lower limb, G83.2, Monoplegia of upper limb, and G83.3, Monoplegia, unspecified, identify whether the dominant or nondominant side is affected. Should this information not be available in the record and the classification system does not indicate a default, the default should be dominant. For ambidextrous patients, the default should also be dominant.

Other Disorders of the Nervous System (Category Codes G89–G99)

This block of codes includes codes for pain. The following coding guidelines should be followed when selecting codes from this block.

ICD-10-CM Official Coding Guidelines

Pain—Category G89

1) General coding information

Codes in category G89, Pain, not elsewhere classified, may be used in conjunction with codes from other categories and chapters to provide more detail about acute or chronic pain and neoplasm-related pain, unless otherwise indicated below.

If the pain is not specified as acute or chronic, post-thoracotomy, postprocedural, or neoplasm-related, do not assign codes from category G89.

A code from category G89 should not be assigned if the underlying (definitive) diagnosis is known, unless the reason for the encounter is pain control/management and not management of the underlying condition.

When an admission or encounter is for a procedure aimed at treating the underlying condition (e.g., spinal fusion, kyphoplasty), a code for the underlying condition (e.g., vertebral fracture, spinal stenosis) should be assigned as the principal diagnosis. No code from category G89 should be assigned.

(a) Category G89 Codes as Principal or First-Listed Diagnosis

Category G89 codes are acceptable as principal diagnosis or the first-listed code:

- *When pain control or pain management is the reason for the admission/encounter (e.g., a patient with displaced intervertebral disc, nerve impingement and severe back pain presents for injection of steroid into the spinal canal). The underlying cause of the pain should be reported as an additional diagnosis, if known.*

- *When a patient is admitted for the insertion of a neurostimulator for pain control, assign the appropriate pain code as the principal or first listed diagnosis. When an admission or encounter is for a procedure aimed at treating the underlying condition and a neurostimulator is inserted for pain control during the same admission/encounter, a code for the underlying condition should be assigned as the principal diagnosis and the appropriate pain code should be assigned as a secondary diagnosis.*

(b) Use of Category G89 Codes in Conjunction with Site Specific Pain Codes

   (i) Assigning Category G89 and Site-Specific Pain Codes

Codes from category G89 may be used in conjunction with codes that identify the site of pain (including codes from chapter 18) if the category G89 code provides additional information. For example, if the code describes the site of the pain, but does not fully describe whether the pain is acute or chronic, then both codes should be assigned.

   (ii) Sequencing of Category G89 Codes with Site-Specific Pain Codes

The sequencing of category G89 codes with site-specific pain codes (including chapter 18 codes) is dependent on the circumstances of the encounter/admission as follows:

- *If the encounter is for pain control or pain management, assign the code from category G89 followed by the code identifying the specific site of pain (e.g., encounter for pain management for acute neck pain from trauma is assigned code G89.11, Acute pain due to trauma, followed by code M54.2, Cervicalgia, to identify the site of pain).*

- *If the encounter is for any other reason except pain control or pain management, and a related definitive diagnosis has not been established (confirmed) by the provider, assign the code for the specific site of pain first, followed by the appropriate code from category G89.*

2) Pain due to devices, implants, and grafts

See Section I.C.19. Pain due to medical devices

(continued)

3) Postoperative Pain

The provider's documentation should be used to guide the coding of postoperative pain, as well as Section III. Reporting Additional Diagnoses and Section IV. Diagnostic Coding and Reporting in the Outpatient Setting.

The default for post-thoracotomy and other postoperative pain not specified as acute or chronic is the code for the acute form.

Routine or expected postoperative pain immediately after surgery should not be coded.

(a) Postoperative pain not associated with specific postoperative complication

Postoperative pain not associated with a specific postoperative complication is assigned to the appropriate postoperative pain code in category G89.

(b) Postoperative pain associated with specific postoperative complication

Postoperative pain associated with a specific postoperative complication (such as painful wire sutures) is assigned to the appropriate code(s) found in Chapter 19, Injury, poisoning, and certain other consequences of external causes. If appropriate, use additional code(s) from category G89 to identify acute or chronic pain (G89.18 or G89.28).

4) Chronic pain

Chronic pain is classified to subcategory G89.2. There is no time frame defining when pain becomes chronic pain. The provider's documentation should be used to guide use of these codes.

5) Neoplasm Related Pain

Code G89.3 is assigned to pain documented as being related, associated or due to cancer, primary or secondary malignancy, or tumor. This code is assigned regardless of whether the pain is acute or chronic.

This code may be assigned as the principal or first-listed code when the stated reason for the admission/encounter is documented as pain control/pain management. The underlying neoplasm should be reported as an additional diagnosis.

When the reason for the admission/encounter is management of the neoplasm and the pain associated with the neoplasm is also documented, code G89.3 may be assigned as an additional diagnosis. It is not necessary to assign an additional code for the site of the pain.

See Section I.C.2 for instructions on the sequencing of neoplasms for all other stated reasons for the admission/ encounter (except for pain control/pain management).

6) Chronic pain syndrome

Central pain syndrome (G89.0) and chronic pain syndrome (G89.4) are different than the term "chronic pain," and therefore codes should only be used when the provider has specifically documented this condition.

See Section I.C.5. Pain disorders related to psychological factors

Comparing ICD-9-CM to ICD-10-CM

The major change in this chapter involves the movement out of this chapter of codes for disorders of the eye and adnexa and for diseases of the ear and mastoid process. Two new chapters are added in ICD-10-CM: chapter 7, "Diseases of the Eye and Adnexa," and chapter 8, "Diseases of the Ear and Mastoid Process."

Internet Links

To learn more about Parkinson's disease, visit **www.apdaparkinson.com** and **www.pdf.org**

Visit **www.biausa.org** and **www.neuroexam.com** to learn about neurological disorders

and **www.epilepsyfoundation.org** to learn about epilepsy.

Summary

- The nervous system controls all bodily activity.
- The nervous system is comprised of the central nervous system and the peripheral nervous system.
- Nervous system codes are found in categories G00–G83.
- Meningitis is an inflammation of the meninges.
- Some congenital nervous system disorders are coded in this chapter.

Chapter Review

True/False: Indicate whether each statement is true (T) or false (F).

1. _____ Parkinson's disease is a congenital disease.

2. _____ The autonomic nervous system is part of the central nervous system.

3. _____ Myelitis is an inflammation of the spinal cord.

4. _____ Encephalomyelitis is an inflammation of the spinal cord and meningitis.

5. _____ Multiple sclerosis is a disease in which brain structure changes lead to memory loss, personality changes, and impaired ability to function.

Fill-in-the-Blank: Enter the appropriate term(s) to complete each statement.

6. Numbness in the limbs, visual disturbances, muscle weakness, and urinary problems can all be symptoms of _____.

7. PNS stands for _____.

8. The most severe seizure is a _____ seizure.

9. A chronic and nonprogressive disorder that is present at birth and that impacts the motor function of the brain is _____.

10. Hemiparesis is a synonym for _____.

Coding Assignments

Instructions: Using an ICD-10-CM code book, assign the proper diagnosis code to the following diagnostic statements.

Diagnosis	Code
1. communicating hydrocephalus	_____
2. Alpers' disease	_____
3. multiple sclerosis	_____
4. intractable epilepsy	_____
5. transient global amnesia	_____
6. intractable menstrual migraine	_____

7. anterior cerebral artery syndrome _____

8. REM sleep behavior disorder _____

9. lesion of sciatic nerve, left side _____

10. carpal tunnel syndrome _____

11. facial palsy _____

12. atypical facial pain _____

13. spastic diplegic cerebral palsy _____

14. hydrocephalus _____

15. central pain syndrome _____

16. cerebral edema _____

17. postviral fatigue syndrome _____

18. paralysis of both lower limbs _____

19. cerebral palsy _____

20. Horner's syndrome _____

Case Studies

Instructions: Review each case study and select the correct ICD-10-CM diagnostic code.

CASE 1

Clinic Note

This 57-year-old female patient comes to the clinic today for her annual physical.

HEENT: Normal

LUNGS: Clear

ABDOMEN: Soft, nontender

RECTAL EXAM: Refused

NEUROLOGICAL: Congenital spastic paralysis, left leg

There are no physical findings that need to be addressed at this time. I have reviewed her care plan, and she should continue per her care plan at the residential home where she resides.

ICD-10-CM Code Assignment: _____

CASE 2

Sleep Clinic Note

This patient returns today following sleep testing completed last week. The testing revealed abnormal sleep patterns. I discussed with the patient if she is experiencing any stress or anxiety. She denies both. She also stated that she does not want to take any sleep-aid medications at this time. I referred her to the educator at this clinic to discuss treatment options other than medications. She should return in one month.

DIAGNOSIS: Delayed sleep phase syndrome

ICD-10-CM Code Assignment: _____

CASE 3

Office Note

This 49-year-old secretary is being seen today for pain that is present in her right hand. She has had a series of imaging that showed no fractures or other abnormalities.

Upon exam she has weakness and pain, and she complains of disturbances of sensations in her right hand.

DIAGNOSIS: carpal tunnel syndrome

ICD-10-CM Code Assignment: _____

CASE 4

This 39-year-old male presents today because of pain in his right leg that occurs at night. He describes this as a cramping feeling. He states that he has not injured his leg in the past or in the recurrent days.

EXAM:

HEENT: Normal

LUNGS: Clear

EXTREMITIES: Normal to touch and neurological testing

I instructed him to heat his leg prior to going to bed and offered to give him a referral to PT at this time. He stated he wanted to try the at-home treatment first. Since this is only occurring at night when sleeping, I feel that this is sleep-related leg cramps.

ICD-10-CM Code Assignment: _____

CASE 5

Inpatient Drug and Alcohol Facility Progress Note

I was called by the nurse to see this newly admitted patient. He is having drug-induced tremor. At this time we have not determined his drug of choice. He will be placed in the detox unit to be monitored for 48 hours.

ICD-10-CM Code Assignment: _____

Disorders of the Eye and Adnexa

Chapter Outline

Objectives

At the conclusion of this chapter, the learner should be able to:

1. Identify the major structures of the eye and adnexa.
2. Explain the disorders that impact the eye and adnexa.
3. Accurately code disorders of the eye and adnexa.
4. Select and code diagnoses from case studies.

Key Terms

adnexa	ciliary body	hordeolum	pterygium
anterior chamber	conjunctiva	iris	pupil
aqueous humor	cornea	lacrimal duct	retina
blepharitis	dacryoadenitis	lacrimal gland	sclera
blepharochalasis	entropion	lagophthalmos	suspensory ligaments
canthus	epiphora	lens	trichiasis
cataracts	eyelashes	optic disc	vitreous humor
chalazion	eyelids, upper and lower	optic nerve	
choroids	glaucoma	posterior chamber	

> **Reminder**
>
> *As you work through this chapter, you will need to have a copy of the ICD-10-CM coding book to reference.*

Introduction

Chapter 7 of ICD-10-CM classifies diseases of the eye and adnexa. It excludes certain conditions that originate in the perinatal period, certain infectious and parasitic diseases, congenital malformations, diabetes related eye conditions, injuries, and neoplasms that impact the eye and adnexa. Coders should reference the Excludes note that appears at the start of the chapter. Chapter 7 of ICD-10-CM contains the following blocks of codes:

- H00–H05 Disorders of eyelid, lacrimal system, and orbit
- H10–H11, Disorders of conjunctiva
- H15–H22, Disorders of sclera, cornea, iris, and ciliary body
- H25–H28, Disorders of lens
- H30–H36, Disorders of choroid and retina
- H40–H42, Glaucoma
- H43–H44, Disorders of vitreous body and globe
- H46–H47, Disorders of optic nerve and visual pathways
- H49–H52, Disorders of ocular muscles, binocular movement, accommodation, and refraction
- H53–H54, Visual disturbances and blindness
- H55–H57, Other disorders of eye and adnexa
- H59, Intraoperative and postprocedural complications and disorders of eye and adnexa, not elsewhere classified

Introduction to the Body System

When coding disorders of the eye, the coder must understand the anatomy of the eye or have detailed diagrams and well documented provider notes to assist with the coding. Figures 12-1 and 12-2 illustrate the complexity of the eye anatomy. **Adnexa** is a term for the accessory or appendage of an organ. Figure 12-3 diagrams the adnexa of the eyes.

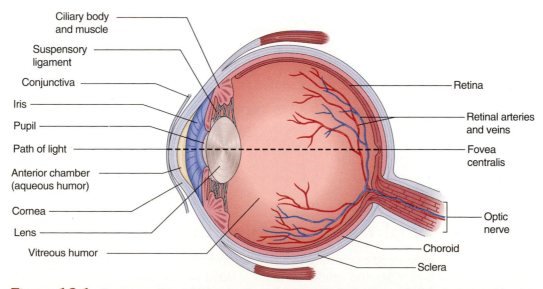

Figure 12-1 Cross section of the structures of the eyeball (From Ehrlich A, Schroeder Cl. *Medical Terminology for Health Professions*, 4th ed. Clifton Park, NY: Delmar, Cengage Learning, 2001.)

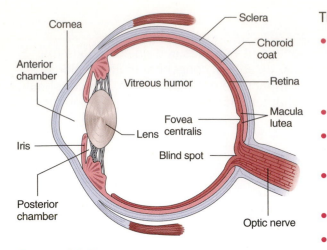

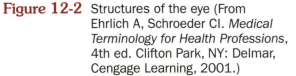

Figure 12-2 Structures of the eye (From Ehrlich A, Schroeder Cl. *Medical Terminology for Health Professions*, 4th ed. Clifton Park, NY: Delmar, Cengage Learning, 2001.)

The parts of the eye are as follows:

- **Sclera**—The white portion of the eye that is a fibrous membrane, that serves as a protective covering for the eye, and that maintains the shape of the eyeball

- **Iris**—The colored portion of the eye

- **Pupil**—The center of the iris that controls the amount of light entering the eye

- **Conjunctiva**—The colorless mucous membrane that lines the anterior part of the eye

- **Lacrimal gland**—The gland that produces tears

- **Lacrimal duct**—The duct that drains the tears from the eye though the eye and that is located at the inner edge of the eye, which is known as the **canthus**

- **Upper and lower eyelids**—The lids that protect the eyes and help to keep the surface of the eyeball lubricated

- **Eyelashes**—Hairs that are located along the edge of the eyelids to protect the eye from foreign materials

- **Cornea**—A transparent nonvascular structure located on the anterior portion of the sclera

- **Choroids**—The layer just beneath the sclera containing capillaries that provide the blood supply and nutrients to the eye

- **Lens**—Posterior to the iris, a colorless structure that allows the eye to focus on images

- **Ciliary body**—The muscles responsible for adjusting the lens

- **Suspensory ligaments**—Attached to the ciliary body, the ligaments that attach to the lens and hold it in place

- **Retina**—The nerve cell layer of the eye that changes light rays into nerve impulses

- **Optic nerve**—The nerve that transmits impulses to the brain from the eye

- **Optic disc**—The blind spot on the optic nerve that is the point of entry for the artery supplying blood to the retina

- **Aqueous humor**—The fluid that fills the two cavities of the interior of the eye

- **Anterior chamber**—A chamber located in front of the lens

- **Posterior chamber**—A chamber located behind the lens

- **Vitreous humor**—The clear, jelly-like fluid that fills the posterior chamber of the eye and helps to shape the eye

Coding Disorders of the Eye and Adnexa

Chapter 7 of ICD-10-CM is organized according to the anatomical structures of the eye and adnexa. When selecting codes, the coder should read the medical documentation to determine whether the condition or disorder is impacting one or both eyes because many codes delineate the eye or eyes affected.

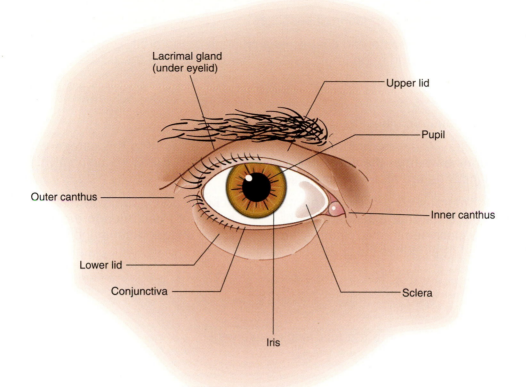

Figure 12-3   Major structures and adnexa of the right eye (From Ehrlich A, Schroeder Cl. *Medical Terminology for Health Professions*, 4th ed. Clifton Park, NY: Delmar, Cengage Learning, 2001.)

Disorders of Eyelid, Lacrimal System, and Orbit (Category Codes H00–H05)

This block of codes classifies disorders of the eyelid, lacrimal system, and orbit. It includes the following categories:

- H00, Hordeolum and chalazion—**Hordeolum**, commonly known as a sty, and **chalazion**, a small tumor of the eyelid caused by the retention of secretions of the meibomian gland, are classified to this category.

- H01, Other inflammation of eyelid—This category classifies **blepharitis**, an inflammation of the eyelids, and noninfectious dermatoses of the eyelid.

- H02, Other disorders of eyelid—This category is used to report the various forms of **entropion**, the turning inward of the border of the eyelid against the eyeball, and **trichiasis**, the turning inward of the eyelashes that often causes the eyeball to become irritated. Also coded to this category is **lagophthalmos**, the inability to close the eyelids completely, and **blepharochalasis**, atrophy of the intercellular tissue that causes a relaxation of the skin of the eyelid.

- H04, Disorders of lacrimal system—Coded to this category are:

  o **Dacryoadenitis**—Inflammation of the lacrimal gland.

  o **Epiphora**—Tearing of the eyes.

- ○ Acute, chronic and unspecified inflammation of the lacrimal system.
- ○ Stenosis and insufficiency of lacrimal passages.
- H05, Disorders of orbit—Acute and chronic inflammation of the orbit, exophthalmic conditions, deformities of the orbit, and enophthalmos and other disorders of the orbit are classified here.

Disorders of Conjunctiva (Category Codes H10–H11)

Many common conditions are classified to this range of codes:

- H10, Conjunctivitis—The various forms of conjunctivitis are coded to this category. The coder needs to determine whether the condition is acute or chronic. Blepharoconjunctivitis and other forms of conjunctivitis are also classified here.
- H11, Other disorders of conjunctiva—This category includes **pterygium**, which is a thick patch of hypertrophied tissue that extends from the nasal border of the cornea to the inner canthus of the eye. Also classified in this category are conjunctival degenerations and deposits, scars, hemorrhage, and other conjunctival vascular disorders.

Disorders of Sclera, Cornea, Iris, and Ciliary Body (Category Code H15–H22)

This range of codes is divided into the following categories:

- H15, Disorders of sclera
- H16, Keratitis
- H17, Corneal scars and opacities
- H18, Other disorders of cornea
- H20, Iridocyclitis
- H21, Other disorders of iris and ciliary body
- H22, Disorders of iris and ciliary body in diseases classified elsewhere

Disorders of Lens (Category Codes H25–H28)

Cataracts, the abnormal loss of transparency of the lens of the eye, are classified to this block of codes. The types of cataracts and other disorders of the lens are classified as follows:

- H25, Age-related cataract
- H26, Other cataract
- H27, Other disorders of lens
- H28, Cataract in diseases classified elsewhere

It is important for coders to note the numerous instructional notations that appear throughout the categories for the cataract codes.

Disorders of Choroid and Retina (Category Codes H30–H36)

This range of codes includes chorioretinal inflammation, chorioretinal scars, choroidal degeneration, choroidal hemorrhage and rupture, and choroidal detachment. Also classified to this range are retinal detachments and breaks, H33. Code H34 classifies the various types of retinal vascular occlusions. Code H35 classifies other retinal disorders, such as background retinopathy and retinal vascular changes, retinopathy of prematurity, degeneration of macular and posterior pole, peripheral retinal degeneration, and hereditary retinal dystrophy.

Exercise 12.1 – Coding Diseases of the Eye

For each diagnostic statement, assign an ICD-10-CM code:

1. hemorrhagic detachment of retinal pigment epithelium, left eye _____

2. bilateral cyst of ora serrata _____

3. subluxation of lens of right eye _____

4. cataract with neovascularization, left eye _____

5. aphakia _____

Glaucoma (Category Codes H40–H42)

Glaucoma, an eye disease marked by increased pressure in the eyeball that may result in damage to the optic disk and the gradual loss of vision, is reported using category codes H40–H42. The codes are differentiated according to the types of glaucoma and whether the diseases is impacting one or both eyes. Some of the codes, such as H40.3 and H40.4, contain instructional notations directing the coder to "Code also underlying condition." H40.5 instructs the coder to "Code also underlying eye disorder," and H40.6 instructs the coder to "Code first (T36–T50) to identify drug."

Disorders of Vitreous Body and Globe (Category Codes H43–H44)

H43–H44 categories are used to report disorders of the vitreous body and globe. The H43 category codes vitreous prolapse, hemorrhage, deposits, opacities, and other disorders of the vitreous body. Code H44 reports disorders of the globe that include purulent endophthalmitis, degenerative myopia, hypotony of the eye, degenerative conditions of the globe, and other disorders. Retained foreign body particles are also coded to H44 category codes.

Disorders of Optic Nerve and Visual Pathways (Category Codes H46–H47)

Optic neuritis is reported using category code H46. Code H47 reports other disorders of optic nerve and visual pathways. The H47.4, H47.5, and H47.6 series of codes has an instructional notation stating "Code also underlying condition."

Disorders of Ocular Muscles, Binocular Movement, Accommodation, and Refraction (Category Codes H49–H52)

This block of codes is divided into the following categories:

- H49, Paralytic strabismus—This category is differentiated according to the nerve involved in the palsy. The H49.0 codes involve the third nerve, H49.1 codes involve the fourth nerve, and H49.2 codes involve the sixth nerve.

- H50, Other strabismus—This category reports esotropia, exotropia, vertical strabismus, intermittent heterotropia, other and unspecified heterotropia.

- H51, Other disorders of binocular movement—Disorders reported here include convergence insufficiency and excess and internuclear ophthalmoplegia.

- H52, Disorders of refraction and accommodation—Myopia, hypermetropia, astigmatism, anisometropia, presbyopia, and other disorders of accommodation are classified to this category.

Visual Disturbances and Blindness (Category Codes H53–H54)

This category reports visual disturbance and blindness. Legal blindness, as defined in the United States, is classified by severity. In the ICD-10-CM code book under the code H54.8, a table lists the classification of the severity of visual impairment. The notation directly above the table assists the coder in selecting codes for the terms *low vision* and *blindness*.

Other Disorders of Eye and Adnexa (Category Codes H55–H59)

The last block of codes found in chapter 7 of ICD-10-CM reports other disorders of the eye and adnexa and includes the following:

- H55, Nystagmus and other irregular eye movements

- H57, Other disorders of eye and adnexa, such as anomalies of papillary function and ocular pain

- H59, Intraoperative and postprocedural complications and disorders of eye and adnexa, not elsewhere classified, including complications following cataract surgery and other procedures

Comparing ICD-9-CM to ICD-10-CM

In ICD-10-CM, an entirely new chapter has been added for diseases of the eye and adnexa. Previously in ICD-9-CM, these diseases were found in chapter 6. Despite having their own chapter in ICD-10-CM, the code descriptions have not changed greatly. Many of the codes now have fourth, fifth, or sixth characters to provide detail regarding anatomy and laterality. Another change is that in ICD-10-CM, the term *age-related cataract* has replaced *senile cataract*.

Internet Links

To learn about glaucoma, visit **www.glaucoma.org**

To learn about cataracts, visit **http://www.nei.nih.gov/health/cataract/cataract_facts.asp**

To learn about the eye, visit **www.medicinenet.com**

Summary

- Chapter 7 of ICD-10-CM classifies diseases of the eye and adnexa.

- A cataract is the abnormal loss of transparency of the eye's lens.

- Glaucoma is an eye disease marked by increased pressure in the eyeball that may result in damage to the optic disk and the gradual loss of vision.

- Legal blindness, as defined in the United States, is classified by severity.

Chapter Review

True/False: Indicate whether each statement is true (T) or false (F).

1. _____ The transparent nonvascular structure located on the anterior portion of the sclera is the cornea.

2. _____ The structure that is posterior to the iris and is a colorless structure that allows the eye to focus on images is the lens.

3. _____ Epiphora is an inflammation of the lacrimal gland.

4. _____ Category code H04 reports disorders of the eyelid.

5. _____ Amyloid pterygium of the right eye is reported with code H11.011.

Fill-in-the-Blank: Enter the appropriate term(s) to complete each statement.

6. The layer just beneath the sclera that contains capillaries that provide the blood supply and nutrients to the eye is the _____.

7. The muscles that are responsible for adjusting the lens are the _____.

8. Tearing of the eyes is _____.

9. To report conjunctival granuloma of both eyes, use code _____.

10. Posterior cyclitis would be classified to code _____.

Coding Assignments

Instructions: Using an ICD-10-CM code book, assign the proper diagnosis code to the following diagnostic statements.

Diagnosis	Code
1. acute atopic conjunctivitis	_____
2. angular blepharoconjunctivitis	_____
3. macular keratitis	_____
4. left eye photokeratitis	_____
5. perforated corneal ulceration of right eye	_____
6. scleral ectasia, bilateral	_____
7. conjunctival hyperemia, both eyes	_____
8. Mooren's corneal ulcer left eye	_____
9. left eye ghost vessels	_____
10. diffuse interstitial keratitis	_____
11. descemetocele, right eye	_____
12. band keratopathy	_____
13. bilateral degeneration of ciliary body	_____
14. pupillary occlusion	_____
15. iris atrophy right eye	_____
16. bilateral choroidal rupture	_____

17. diffuse secondary atrophy of choroid   _____

18. serous choroidal detachment, left eye   _____

19. partial retinal artery occlusion   _____

20. parasitic cyst of retina, right eye   _____

Case Studies

Instructions: Review each case study and select the correct ICD-10-CM diagnostic code.

CASE 1

Office Note

This 7-year-old male presents today with redness in both eyes. Upon examination, the conjunctiva are swollen. He is experiencing no other symptoms.
Dx: acute conjunctivitis

Eye ointment given. Instructed to return in 10 days.

ICD-10-CM Code Assignment: _____

CASE 2

ER Visit Note

This 37-year-old male was working in the yard and an object hit his eyelid. Because the object is deeply embedded in the skin, I am asking for a consultation from Dr. Ferrar. The object is retained in the lower right eyelid. The patient was sent to Dr. Ferrar's office.

ICD-10-CM Code Assignment: _____

CASE 3

Office Visit Note

This 54-year-old man works on a dairy farm and two weeks ago he "got something in my eye." Exam of the eyes reveals that there are no foreign objects in the eyes at this time. The left eye is red and there is an abscess of the right upper eyelid. The patient was given antibiotics, drops, and patient education material. He was instructed to follow up with me if the eye becomes worse or in 10 days.

ICD-10-CM Code Assignment: _____

CHAPTER 13

Diseases of the Ear and Mastoid Process

Chapter Outline

Objectives
Key Terms
Introduction
Introduction to the Body System
Coding Diseases of the Ear and
  Mastoid Process

Comparing ICD-9-CM to ICD-10-CM
Internet Links
Summary
Chapter Review
Coding Assignments
Case Studies

Objectives

At the conclusion of this chapter, the learner should be able to:

1. Identify diseases of the ear and mastoid process.
2. Discuss the anatomy of the ear.
3. Accurately code diseases of the ear and mastoid process.
4. Select and code diagnoses from case studies.

Key Terms

auditory ossicles
auditory tube
auricle
bony labyrinth
cerumen
ceruminous glands
cilia
cochlea
cochlear duct
ear lobe

endolymph
eustachian tube
external auditory canal
external auditory
  meatus
external ear
incus
labyrinth
malleus
membranous labyrinth

middle ear
organ of Corti
otalgia
otitis externa
otorrhagia
otorrhea
otosclerosis
oval window
perilymph
pharyngotympanic tube

pinna
saccule
semicircular canals
semicircular ducts
stapes
tympanic cavity
tympanic membrane
utricle
vestibule

Reminder

As you work through this chapter, you will need to have a copy of the ICD-10-CM coding book to reference.

Introduction

Chapter 8 of ICD-10-CM, "Diseases of the Ear and Mastoid Process," contains the following blocks of codes:

- H60–H62, Diseases of external ear
- H65–H75, Diseases of middle ear and mastoid
- H80–H83, Diseases of inner ear
- H90–H94, Other disorders of ear
- H95, Intraoperative and postprocedural complications and disorders of ear and mastoid process, not elsewhere classified

Introduction to the Body System

The ear is considered part of the nervous system and has the following functions:

- It allows hearing to occur by picking up sound waves and sending them to the brain.
- It helps to maintain a person's balance.

The ear is divided into three regions: the external ear, the middle ear, and the inner ear. Figure 13-1 illustrates the regions of the ear.

The outermost part of the ear, known as the **external ear**, is the visible part of the ear and is not within the structure of the skull. The external ear consists of the auricle and the external auditory meatus. The **auricle**, also known as the **pinna**, is a flexible cartilaginous flap that has a bottom portion known as the **ear lobe**. The auricle allows sound waves to enter the ear canal, which is known as the **external auditory canal** or the **external auditory meatus**. Along the external auditory canal, tiny hairs called **cilia** aid in transmitting the sound waves inward to other auditory structures. Also within the external auditory canal are sweat glands, called **ceruminous glands**, that secrete a honey-colored, thick, waxy substance known as earwax, or **cerumen**. Cerumen helps to protect and lubricate the ear. In combination with the cilia, the cerumen helps to protect the eardrum from foreign objects.

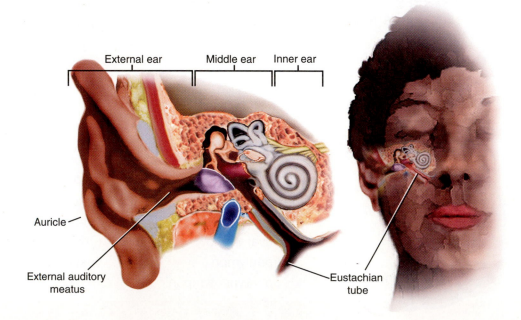

Figure 13-1 External, middle, and inner ear

The **tympanic membrane**, commonly called the eardrum, separates the external ear from the middle ear. The tympanic membrane is a thin, semitransparent membrane, silvery gray in color. The membrane transmits sound vibrations to the inner ear through the **auditory ossicles**.

The **middle ear**, also known as the **tympanic cavity**, is found within the temporal bone and houses the auditory ossicles and the eustachian tube. The auditory ossicles consist of three small bones that transmit and amplify sound waves. The bones are named according to their shapes:

- **Malleus**—Shaped like a hammer
- **Incus**—Shaped like an anvil
- **Stapes**—Shaped like a stirrup

The **eustachian tube**, also known as the **auditory tube** or **pharyngotympanic tube**, connects the bony structures of the middle ear to the pharynx. The purpose of the eustachian tube is to equalize air pressure in the middle ear.

The middle ear is separated from the inner ear by the **oval window**. In the inner ear, also known as the **labyrinth**, are bony structures and membranous structures. The bony structures, called the **bony labyrinth**, consist of the:

- **Vestibule**—The central portion of the inner ear, this structure contains the **utricle** and the **saccule**, which are membranous sacs that aid in maintaining balance.
- **Semicircular canals**—Located behind the vestibule are three bony structures, filled with fluid, that also help to maintain balance. The **semicircular ducts** are also found in this area and aid in balance.
- **Cochlea**—This snail-shaped, bony structure contains **endolymph** and **perilymph**, which are auditory fluids that transmit sound. The **organ of Corti**, also found in the cochlea, is the true organ of hearing. The **cochlear duct**, a membranous structure, is found in this area of the ear and aids in the hearing process.

Membranous labyrinth is a term used to describe the utricle, saccule, semicircular ducts, and cochlear ducts because these structures are all membranous structures.

Figure 13-2 illustrates the numerous structures found in the ear, and Figure 13-3 illustrates the inner ear structures in greater detail.

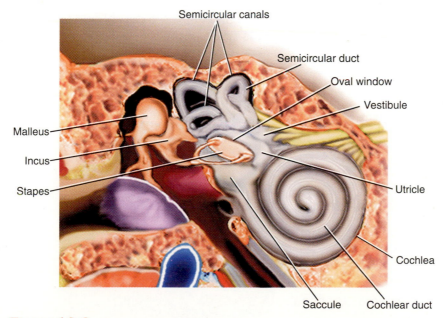

Figure 13-2 Structures of the ear

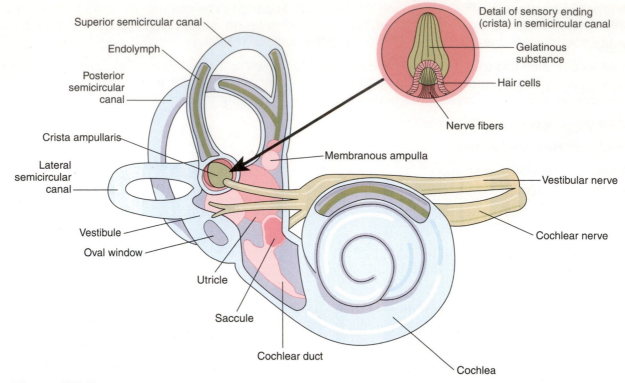

Figure 13-3   Inner ear structures

Coding Diseases of the Ear and Mastoid Process

Codes for diseases of the ear and mastoid process are organized according to the anatomy of the ear.

Diseases of the External Ear (Category Codes H60–H62)

Category code H60 applies to **otitis externa**, an inflammation of the external auditory canal. This category is differentiated according to the various types of otitis:

- Abscess of external ear
- Cellulitis of external ear
- Malignant otitis externa
- Infective otitis externa
- Cholesteatoma of external ear
- Acute noninfective otitis externa

Category code H61 is used to report other disorders of the external ear, including:

- Chondritis and perichondritis of the external ear.
- Noninfective disorders of the pinna.
- Impacted cerumen.
- Acquired stenosis of the external ear canal.
- Exostosis of the external ear.

Category code H62 reports disorders of the external ear in diseases classified elsewhere. Instructional notations direct the coder to "Code first underlying disease, such as erysipelas (A46) or impetigo (L01.0)."

Diseases of the Middle Ear and Mastoid Process (Category Codes H65–H75)

The diseases classified to this block of codes, H65–H75, include the following:

Category	Description
H65, Nonsuppurative Otitis media	This category of codes is differentiated according to whether the otitis media is acute, subacute, chronic, or unspecified. The codes are then further differentiated to indicate whether the condition is impacting the left or right ear or is a bilateral condition and whether the otitis is recurrent. The coder must carefully read the medical documentation to capture all the elements reflected in these codes.
H66, Suppurative and unspecified otitis media	This category contains an Includes note stating that suppurative and unspecified otitis media with myringitis is also coded to this category.
H67, Otitis media in diseases classified elsewhere	An instructional notation tells the coder to code first the underlying disease that is associated with the otitis media.
H68, Eustachian salpingitis and obstruction	Conditions that are classified here include eustachian salpingitis and obstructions of the eustachian tube.
H69, Other and unspecified disorders of eustachian tube	Patulous eustachian tube and other specified disorders of the eustachian tube that are not listed elsewhere are coded with this category.
H70, Mastoiditis and related conditions	The codes in this category are differentiated by acute or chronic mastoiditis, petrositis, and other mastoiditis, and related conditions.
H71, Cholesteatoma of middle ear	These codes are differentiated according to the anatomical structure impacted by the cholesteatoma and whether the condition is impacting the left or right ear or is bilateral.
H72, Perforation of tympanic membrane	This category includes persistent post-traumatic perforation of the eardrum and postinflammatory perforation of the eardrum. An instructional notation appears that instructs the coder to "Code first any associated otitis media (H65.-, H66.1-, H66.2-, H66.3-, H66.4-, H66.9-, H67.-)."
H73, Other disorders of tympanic membrane	Included in this category are acute, chronic, and unspecified myringitis; other specified disorders of the tympanic membrane; and unspecified disorders of the tympanic membrane.
H74, Other disorders of middle ear mastoid	Diseases classified in this category include tympanosclerosis, adhesive middle ear disease, discontinuity and dislocation of ear ossicles, polyp of middle ear, and other and unspecified disorders of the middle ear and mastoid.
H75, Other disorders of middle ear and mastoid in diseases classified elsewhere	This category includes mastoiditis in infectious and parasitic diseases and other specified disorders of the middle ear and mastoid in diseases classified elsewhere.

Exercise 13.1 – Coding Diseases from Code Range H60–H75

Using an ICD-10-CM code book, select the diagnostic code for each diagnosis.

1. chronic perichondritis of right external ear   _____

2. bilateral abscess of external ear   _____

3. acute contact otitis externa, right ear   _____

4. bilateral impacted cerumen   _____

5. chondritis of left external ear   _____

6. chronic allergic otitis media   _____

7. recurrent, right ear acute serous otitis media   _____

8. bilateral chronic eustachian tube salpingitis   _____

9. right ear diffuse cholesteatosis   _____

10. left ear attic perforation of tympanic membrane   _____

Diseases of Inner Ear (Category Codes H80–H83)

This category is used to report diseases of the inner ear. The categories that are present include:

- H80, Otosclerosis—**Otosclerosis** is the growth of spongy bone in the inner ear. The growth can progress, causing the obstruction of the oval or round window and progressive deafness. This category is differentiated according to the site of the otosclerosis and the ear involved.

- H81, Disorders of vestibular function—Included in this category of codes is Ménière's disease, benign paroxysmal vertigo, vestibular neuronitis, other peripheral vertigo, and other vestibular disorders.

- H82, Vertiginous syndromes in diseases classified elsewhere—An instructional notation directs the coder to "Code first underlying disease."

- H83, Other diseases of inner ear—This category is used to code labyrinthitis, labyrinthine fistula, labyrinthine dysfunction, noise effects on the inner ear, and other diseases.

Other Disorders of Ear (Category Codes H90–H95)

The last block of codes in this chapter of ICD-10-CM consists of the following categories:

- H90, Conductive and sensorineural hearing loss—This category is differentiated to identify the type of hearing loss and whether the hearing loss is unilateral or bilateral. The types of hearing loss include conductive, sensorineural, and mixed.

- H91, Other and unspecified hearing loss—This category is used to report other and unspecified hearing loss, including ototoxic, presbycusis, sudden idiopathic, congenital deafness, and other specified and unspecified forms of hearing loss.

- H92, Otalgia and effusion of ear—A number of common disorders are coded to this category:

  - **Otalgia**—Earache
  - **Otorrhea**—Discharge from the external ear
  - **Otorrhagia**—Hemorrhage from the ear

- H93, Other disorders of ear, not elsewhere classified—Degenerative and vascular disorders of the ear, tinnitus, other abnormal auditory perceptions, disorders of acoustic nerve, and other specified disorders of the ear are categorized here.

- H94, Other disorders of ear in diseases classified elsewhere—Coders are instructed to "Code first underlying disease, such as parasitic disease (B65-B89)" for this category. Reference the headings of H94.0 and H94.8 to review the instructional notations.

- H95, Intraoperative and postprocedural complications and disorders of ear and mastoid process, not elsewhere classified—This category is used to report complications in the ear and mastoid process that occurred during a procedure or postprocedure.

Comparing ICD-9-CM to ICD-10-CM

Although this chapter is new, it has similarities to ICD-9-CM. Many of the codes have been expanded to include more detail. For example, otitis media codes have been expanded to denote left and right ear or bilateral conditions. The ICD-10-CM chapter also contains a new section for intraoperative and postprocedural complications (H95). Numerous instructional notations are added to codes that instruct the coder to code first underlying diseases.

Internet Links

To learn more about the diseases of the ear and mastoid process, visit the following sites for information:

http://www.noah–Health.org/en/ear/

http://www.hearingcentral.com/hearingdiseasesanddisorders.asp

http://www.nlm.nih.gov/medlineplus/eardisorders.html

Summary

- Chapter 8 of ICD-10-CM is "Diseases of the Ear and Mastoid Process."
- The ear is considered part of the nervous system.
- The ear is divided into three regions: external ear, middle ear, and inner ear.
- Codes for diseases of the ear and mastoid process are organized according to ear anatomy.
- Coders must be able to identify the ear or ears impacted by the disorder to correctly assign codes for chapter 8 of ICD-10-CM.

Chapter Review

True/False: Indicate whether each statement is true (T) or false (F).

1. _____ The auricle is also known as the external auditory canal.

2. _____ The cochlea is a snail-shaped, bony structure that contains endolymph and perilymph.

3. _____ Category H83 classifies labyrinthitis.

4. _____ Aural vertigo is classified to category H80.

5. _____ Code H66.0 is used to classify acute suppurative otitis externa.

Fill-in-the-Blank: Enter the appropriate term(s) to complete each statement.

6. The canals located behind the vestibule that are three bony structures and that are filled with fluid are known as the _____.

7. Category H65 is used to report _____.

8. Bilateral sensorineural hearing loss is coded to _____.

9. Right ear ototoxic hearing loss is coded to _____.

10. Bilateral acute eczematoid otitis externa is coded to _____.

Coding Assignments

Instructions: Using an ICD-10-CM code book, assign the proper diagnosis code to the following diagnostic statements.

Diagnosis   *Code*

1. congenital auditory imperception   _____

2. right ear otalgia   _____

3. bilateral labyrinthitis   _____

4. left ear aural vertigo   _____

5. bilateral multiple perforations of tympanic membrane   _____

6. exostosis of right external ear canal   _____

7. acquired stenosis of external ear canal, both ears   _____

8. hematoma of pinna, left ear   _____

9. acute chemical otitis externa, both ears   _____

10. chronic serous otitis media, left ear   _____

11. bilateral Ménière's disease   _____

12. bilateral acoustic nerve disorder   _____

13. otorrhagia, bilateral   _____

14. presbycusis   _____

15. right ear auditory recruitment   _____

16. chronic inflammation of postmastoidectomy cavity, left side   _____

17. right ear osseous obstruction of eustachian tube   _____

18. chronic mucoid otitis media, bilateral   _____

19. left ear chronic allergic otitis media   _____

20. bilateral chondritis of pinna   _____

Case Studies

Instructions: Review each case study and select the correct ICD-10-CM diagnostic code.

CASE 1

Emergency Department Note

This 9-year-old male patient was brought to the ER by his mother. His left external ear is warm to touch, and it appears red and swollen. He has a fever of 100 for the past two days. Upon otoscopic exam, the middle and inner ear are reviewed with no findings. There is definitely cellulitis of the external auditory canal. Antibiotics were given, and the patient was instructed to return to his doctor in seven days or to call if the symptoms worsen.

ICD-10-CM Code Assignment: _____

CASE 2

Office Note

This 19-year-old female has been complaining of ear pain for three days and feeling tired.

EXAM

EYES: Appear normal

NOSE: No findings

CERVICAL LYMPH NODES: Unremarkable

EARS: The right ear shows otitis media is present.

Antibiotics and drops given. Instructed to return in 10 days.

ICD-10-CM Code Assignment: _____

CASE 3

Audiology Note

This 54-year-old male patient is being seen by me today to review the results of previous hearing tests and to determine a course of action of the hearing loss. Diagnostic testing reveals a bilateral conductive hearing loss. The outcome of the testing was discussed with the patient and the patient will follow up with the audiology department to further discuss treatment options.

ICD-10-CM Code Assignment: _____

CASE 4

Office Note

This is the third time in a four-month period this year that this patient has been seen for myringitis. The patient was also seen last year three times for the same condition. Treatment options have not controlled the myringitis. I have referred the patient to Dr. Payal in the audiology department for further treatment for the chronic myringitis of the left ear.

ICD-10-CM Code Assignment: _____

CASE 5

Hospital Discharge Note

This 31-year-old male is being discharged today following correction of an deformity of the right pinna that he acquired during a automobile accident. His stay was uneventful, the surgery corrected the deformity, and there were no complications. He is instructed to follow the discharge orders that were given to him and follow up in my office in one week.

ICD-10-CM Code Assignment: _____

14

Diseases of the Circulatory System

Chapter Outline

Objectives

At the conclusion of this chapter, the learner should be able to:

1. Identify diseases of the circulatory system.
2. Discuss ICD-10-CM coding guidelines for diseases of the circulatory system.
3. List the types of hypertension and the codes for each.
4. Accurately code diseases of the circulatory system.
5. Select and code diagnoses from case studies.

Key Terms

angina pectoris

arteries

cardiomyopathy

cerebral hemorrhage

cerebrovascular
accident (CVA)

cerebrovascular disease

diastolic blood
pressure

endocarditis

healed myocardial
infarction

heart

heart attack

heart failure

hemorrhoids

hypertension

hypotension

ischemic heart disease

lymphadenitis

myocardial infarction (MI)

myocarditis

occlusion

occlusion of cerebral and
precerebral arteries

old myocardial infarction

pericarditis

pericardium

phlebitis

portal vein thrombosis

secondary hypertension

stenosis

stroke

systolic blood pressure

thrombolytic therapy

thrombophlebitis

transient hypertension

unstable angina

varicose veins

veins

> **Reminder**
>
> *As you work through this chapter, you will need to have a copy of the ICD-10-CM coding book to reference.*

Introduction

Chapter 9 of ICD-10-CM, "Diseases of the Circulatory System," contains codes for diseases of the circulatory system, except circulatory conditions that occur during pregnancy, childbirth, and the puerperium or conditions that are determined to be a congenital anomaly. Circulatory disorders that occur during the obstetrical period are coded to chapter 15 of ICD-10-CM, "Pregnancy, Childbirth, and the Puerperium." Circulatory congenital anomalies are coded to chapter 17 of ICD-9-CM, "Congenital Malformations, Deformations, and Chromosomal Abnormalities."

EXAMPLE: Hypertensive diseases code to I10–I15 excluding hypertensive diseases that complicate pregnancy, childbirth, or the puerperium, which code to O10–O11, O13–O16, or neonatal hypertension that codes to P29.2. The diagnosis of essential hypertension codes to I10, whereas a diagnosis of preexisting essential hypertension complicating childbirth codes to O10.02, as found in chapter 15 of ICD-10-CM, "Pregnancy, Childbirth, and the Puerperium."

Chapter 9 of ICD-10-CM contains the following blocks:

- I00–I02, Acute rheumatic fever
- I05–I09, Chronic rheumatic heart diseases
- I10–I15, Hypertensive diseases
- I20–I25, Ischemic heart diseases
- I26–I28, Pulmonary heart disease and diseases of pulmonary circulation
- I30–I52, Other forms of heart disease
- I60–I69, Cerebrovascular diseases
- I70–I79, Diseases of arteries, arterioles, and capillaries
- I80–I89, Diseases of veins, lymphatic vessels, and lymph nodes, not elsewhere classified
- I95–I99, Other and unspecified disorders of the circulatory system

Introduction to the Body System

The body structures found in this chapter of ICD-10-CM are also referred to as the *cardiovascular system* or *circulatory system*. This system consists of the following organs and body structures:

- **Arteries**—Carry oxygen-rich blood from the heart to the body (with the exception of the pulmonary artery, which carries deoxygenated blood from the heart to the lungs).
- **Veins**—Carry deoxygenated blood from the body back to the heart (with the exception of the pulmonary vein, which carries oxygenated blood back to the heart).
- **Heart**—A muscular organ, located between the lungs and to the left of the midline of the body, that pumps blood throughout the body.

The blood vessels of the body are considered the longest system of the body. The heart is considered one of the strongest organs of the body, pumping an average of 4,000 gallons of blood a day for an adult. Coders must be able to identify the various arteries, veins, and specific parts and structures of the heart.

EXAMPLE: A patient has been diagnosed with left posterior tibial artery occlusion due to stenosis. To accurately code this diagnosis, the coder must be able to identify that this artery is found in the lower extremities. To select a code, the term *occlusion* is located in the Alphabetic Index, which is further divided into anatomical structures. Figure 14-1 illustrates the index entry. To locate the correct code, the coder references the entry of occlusion, then artery, then lower extremities due to stenosis or stricture. Here code I77.1 appears in the alphabetic index.

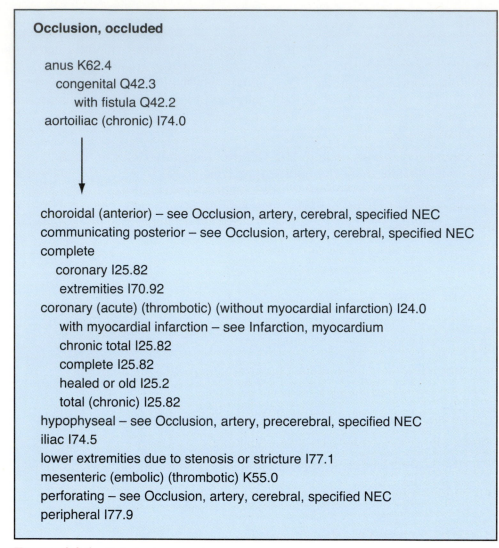

Occlusion, occluded

anus K62.4
  congenital Q42.3
    with fistula Q42.2
  aortoiliac (chronic) I74.0

choroidal (anterior) – see Occlusion, artery, cerebral, specified NEC
communicating posterior – see Occlusion, artery, cerebral, specified NEC
complete
  coronary I25.82
  extremities I70.92
coronary (acute) (thrombotic) (without myocardial infarction) I24.0
  with myocardial infarction – see Infarction, myocardium
  chronic total I25.82
  complete I25.82
  healed or old I25.2
  total (chronic) I25.82
hypophyseal – see Occlusion, artery, precerebral, specified NEC
iliac I74.5
lower extremities due to stenosis or stricture I77.1
mesenteric (embolic) (thrombotic) K55.0
perforating – see Occlusion, artery, cerebral, specified NEC
peripheral I77.9

Figure 14-1 Alphabetic entry for occlusion

Because not all arteries and veins have separate entries in the Alphabetical Index, the coder has to understand arterial circulation (Figure 14-2), venous circulation (Figure 14-3), and heart pulmonary circulation (Figure 14-4) to make a correct code selection.

Exercise 14.1 – Identifying Arteries and Veins

For each of the arteries and veins listed, state where the structure is located using the following legend: abdominal cavity (A), lower extremities (L), thoracic (T), and upper extremities (U). (Reference Figures 14-2, 14-3, and 14-4.)

1. right femoral artery   _____

2. left renal vein   _____

3. left great saphenous vein   _____

4. right ulnar artery   _____

5. arch of aorta

_____

6. left ovarian vein

_____

7. pulmonary artery

_____

8. superior palmar arch

_____

9. peroneal artery

_____

10. hepatic artery

_____

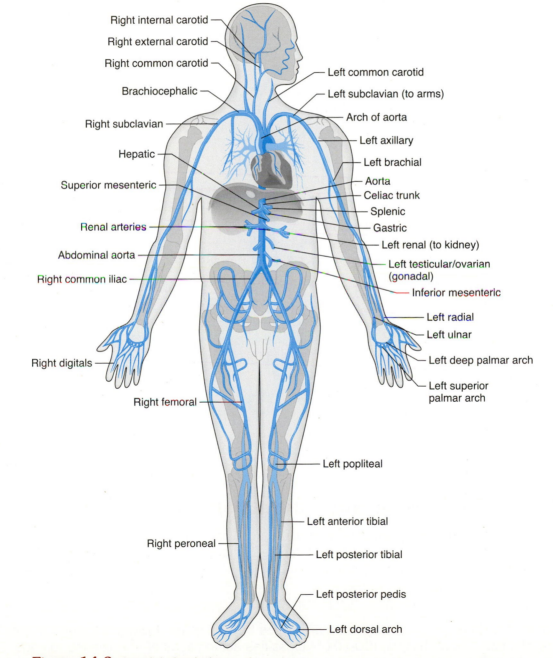

Right internal carotid
Right external carotid
Right common carotid
Brachiocephalic
Right subclavian
Hepatic
Superior mesenteric
Renal arteries
Abdominal aorta
Right common iliac
Right digitals
Right femoral
Right peroneal

Left common carotid
Left subclavian (to arms)
Arch of aorta
Left axillary
Left brachial
Aorta
Celiac trunk
Splenic
Gastric
Left renal (to kidney)
Left testicular/ovarian (gonadal)
Inferior mesenteric
Left radial
Left ulnar
Left deep palmar arch
Left superior palmar arch
Left popliteal
Left anterior tibial
Left posterior tibial
Left posterior pedis
Left dorsal arch

Figure 14-2 Arterial circulation

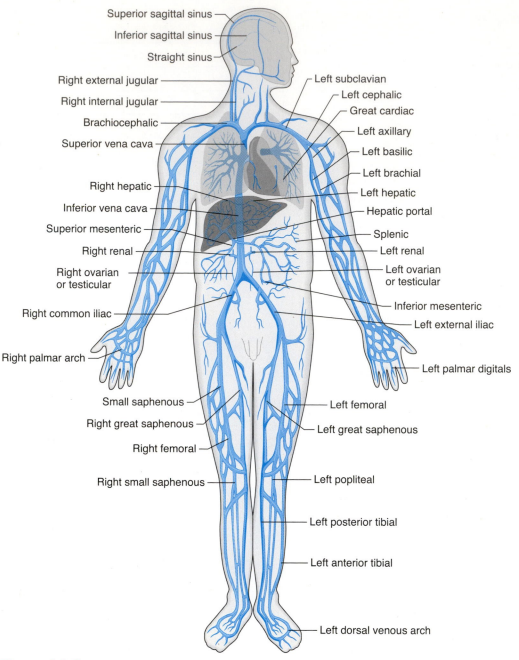

Figure 14-3 Venous circulation

Coding of Diseases of the Circulatory System

Many circulatory system disorders are interrelated. A cardiovascular disease can affect many vessels throughout the entire cardiovascular system and damage organs. Circulatory system disorders can be caused by infections as well as by physiological factors.

Acute and Chronic Rheumatic Fever (Category Codes I00–I09)

Acute rheumatic fever develops, usually in children ages 5 to 15 years, following a group A hemolytic *Streptococci* infection of the pharynx. ICD-10-CM classifies acute cases of the disease to codes I00–I02 and chronic rheumatic heart disease to codes I05–I09. Symptoms of acute rheumatic fever include abdominal pain, fever, joint pain, skin changes, chorea (involuntary movements of the face, tongue, and upper extremities), and lesions of the heart, blood vessels, and connective tissue. Chronic rheumatic

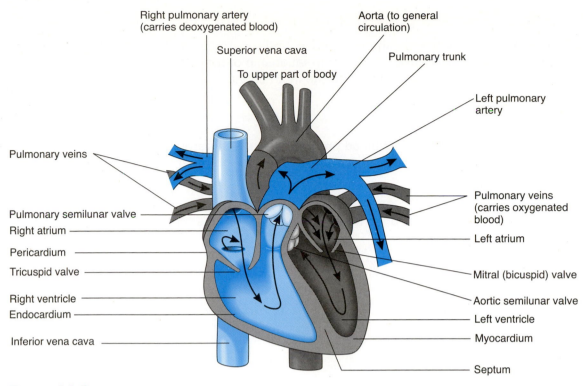

Figure 14-4 Heart pulmonary circulation

heart disease results from an attack or attacks of rheumatic fever that cause damage to the heart, particularly the aortic and mitral valves.

Chronic rheumatic heart disease can impact the mitral, aortic, tricuspid, or multiple valves. Category codes I05–I08 differentiate the valves that are impacted when chronic rheumatic heart disease has occurred. For accurate coding, the coder must be able to identify the valves involved.

Exercise 14.2 – Coding Acute and Chronic Rheumatic Heart Diseases

Select the appropriate ICD-9-CM code for the following diagnoses.

1. rheumatic aortic stenosis with insufficiency _____
2. acute rheumatic endocarditis _____
3. rheumatic aortic and mitral valve insufficiency _____
4. rheumatic chorea with heart involvement _____
5. rheumatic tricuspid stenosis _____
6. mitral valve insufficiency and stenosis, rheumatic _____
7. rheumatic mitral valve insufficiency _____
8. rheumatic aortic valve insufficiency _____
9. aortic valve insufficiency and stenosis, rheumatic _____
10. chronic rheumatic myopericarditis _____

Hypertensive Diseases (Category Codes I10–I15)

Codes for hypertension, hypertensive heart disease, and hypertensive chronic kidney disease are coded to category codes I10–I15. Because of the interrelationship of hypertension and other hypertensive conditions, coders must pay close attention to the instructional notations found in both the Alphabetic Index and the Tabular List.

Hypertension

Hypertension is an increase in **systolic blood pressure** (the pressure on the arterial walls during the heart muscle contraction), in **diastolic blood pressure** (the pressure on the arterial walls during relaxation of the heart muscle), or in both.

At times physicians may describe hypertension as "controlled" or "uncontrolled." There is no way to differentiate between controlled and uncontrolled states of hypertension within the ICD-10-CM coding system; so follow these guidelines.

ICD-10-CM Official Coding Guidelines

Hypertension, Controlled—

This diagnostic statement usually refers to an existing state of hypertension under control by therapy. Assign code I10.

Hypertension, Uncontrolled—

Uncontrolled hypertension may refer to untreated hypertension or hypertension not responding to current therapeutic regimen. In either case, assign code I10.

(See Appendix A, Section I, C9, a, 8-9)

EXAMPLE: Tim Long was seen by Dr. Hardy for uncontrolled hypertension, and his medications were adjusted. The appropriate code to assign is I10.

Before assigning a code for hypertension, medical documentation must be available clearly stating that the patient has hypertension rather than an elevated blood pressure reading. ICD-10-CM code R03.0 is used when a patient has elevated blood pressure but the physician has not made a diagnosis of hypertension. Some physicians refer to elevated blood pressure as **transient hypertension**.

Secondary Hypertension

Secondary hypertension is defined as high arterial blood pressure due to another disease such as central nervous system disorders, renal disorders, and endocrine and vascular diseases. Secondary hypertension is coded to category code I15, which is divided as follows:

- I15.0, Renovascular hypertension
- I15.1, Hypertension secondary to other renal disorders
- I15.2, Hypertension secondary to endocrine disorders
- I15.8, Other secondary hypertension
- I15.9, Secondary hypertension, unspecified

Note:

At the start of this category, an instructional notation directs the coder to "Code also underlying condition." Thus the following coding guideline needs to be followed:

ICD-10-CM Official Coding Guidelines

Hypertension, Secondary

Secondary hypertension is due to an underlying condition. Two codes are required: one to identify the underlying etiology and one from category I15 to identify the hypertension. Sequencing of codes is determined by the reason for admission/encounter. (See Appendix Section I, C9, a, 6.)

EXAMPLE: Gale Carerro is admitted to Sunny Valley Hospital to address her secondary malignant hypertension that is caused by adult polycystic kidney disease. Because she was admitted to treat the secondary malignant hypertension, this is sequenced first. The appropriate codes to assign are I15.1 and Q61.2.

Coding Guidelines for Hypertension

Coders need to be familiar with the following coding guidelines that impact the coding of hypertension and other conditions associated with hypertension.

ICD-10-CM Official Coding Guidelines

Hypertension

1) Hypertension with Heart Disease

Heart conditions classified to I50.– or I51.4–I51.9, are assigned to, a code from category I11, Hypertensive heart disease, when a causal relationship is stated (due to hypertension) or implied (hypertensive). Use an additional code from category I50, Heart failure, to identify the type of heart failure in those patients with heart failure.

The same heart conditions (I50.–, I51.4–I51.9) with hypertension, but without a stated causal relationship, are coded separately. Sequence according to the circumstances of the admission/encounter.

2) Hypertensive Chronic Kidney Disease

Assign codes from category I12, Hypertensive chronic kidney disease, when both hypertension and a condition classifiable to category N18, Chronic kidney disease (CKD), are present. Unlike hypertension with heart disease, ICD-10-CM presumes a cause-and-effect relationship and classifies chronic kidney disease with hypertension as hypertensive chronic kidney disease.

The appropriate code from category N18 should be used as a secondary code with a code from category I12 to identify the stage of chronic kidney disease.

See Section I.C.14, Chronic kidney disease.

If a patient has hypertensive chronic kidney disease and acute renal failure, an additional code for the acute renal failure is required.

3) Hypertensive Heart and Chronic Kidney Disease

Assign codes from combination category I13, Hypertensive heart and chronic kidney disease, when both hypertensive kidney disease and hypertensive heart disease are stated in the diagnosis. Assume a relationship between the hypertension and the chronic kidney disease, whether or not the condition is so designated. If heart failure is present, assign an additional code from category I50 to identify the type of heart failure.

The appropriate code from category N18, Chronic kidney disease, should be used as a secondary code with a code from category I13 to identify the stage of chronic kidney disease.

See Section I.C.14. Chronic kidney disease.

The codes in category I13, Hypertensive heart and chronic kidney disease, are combination codes that include hypertension, heart disease, and chronic kidney disease. The Includes note at I13 specifies that the conditions included at I11 and I12 are included together in I13. If a patient has hypertension, heart disease and chronic kidney disease then a code from I13 should be used, not individual codes for hypertension, heart disease, and chronic kidney disease, or codes from I11 or I12.

For patients with both acute renal failure and chronic kidney disease an additional code for acute renal failure is required.

4) Hypertensive Cerebrovascular Disease

For hypertensive cerebrovascular disease, first assign the appropriate code from categories I60–I69, followed by the appropriate hypertension code.

(continued)

5) Hypertensive Retinopathy

Code H35.0, Hypertensive retinopathy, should be used with code I10, Essential (primary) hypertension, to include the systemic hypertension. The sequencing is based on the reason for the encounter.

(See Appendix A, Section I, C9, a, 1-5)

Exercise 14.3 – Coding of Hypertension

Select the appropriate ICD-10-CM diagnostic codes for each diagnosis.

1. essential hypertension _____
2. hypertension due to primary malignant neoplasm of brain _____
3. uncontrolled malignant hypertension _____
4. hypertension, benign _____
5. hypertensive chronic kidney disease, stage 3 _____
6. hypertensive renal disease, stage 2 _____
7. elevated blood pressure _____
8. hypertensive heart disease without heart failure _____
9. systemic hypertension _____
10. arterial hypertension _____

Ischemic Heart Diseases (Category Codes I20–I25)

Ischemic heart disease occurs when there is an inadequate supply of blood to the heart, which is caused by a blockage, also called an **occlusion**, or constriction of an arterial blood vessel. The vessels commonly become blocked or constricted because of the presence of fatty deposits on the walls of the arteries. Ischemic heart disease is also referred to as:

- Arteriosclerotic coronary artery disease (ACAD).
- Arteriosclerotic heart disease (ASHD).
- Atherosclerosis.
- Coronary artery disease (CAD).
- Coronary arteriosclerosis.
- Coronary heart disease.
- Coronary ischemia.

Note:

An instructional notation in the Tabular listing of ICD-10-CM, after the heading of Ischemic Heart Disease, tells the coder to "Use additional code to identify presence of hypertension (I10–I15)."

Angina Pectoris (Category Code I20)

Angina pectoris, which is assigned to ICD-10-CM category code I20, is defined as severe chest pain caused by an insufficient amount of blood reaching the heart. It is relieved rapidly by rest or nitrates. Factors that usually bring on an angina attack include exertion, heavy eating, and stress.

Unstable angina, which is assigned to ICD-10-CM code I20.0, is an accelerating, or crescendo, pattern of chest pain that occurs at rest or during mild exertion, typically lasting longer than does angina

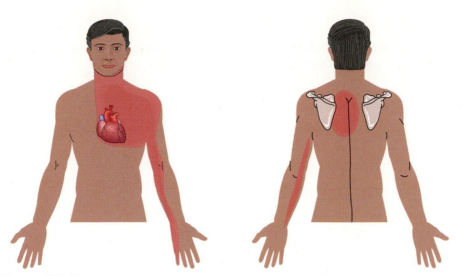

Figure 14-5 Most common patterns of angina (From Neighbors M & Tannehill-Jones R. *Human Diseases*, 2nd ed. Clifton Park, NY: Delmar, Cengage Learning, p. 141.)

pectoris, and that is not responsive to medications. Unstable angina can progress to infarction or may heal and return to a stable condition. This code is assigned only when there is no documentation of infarction. Diseases that code to I20.0 are accelerated angina, crescendo angina, de novo effort angina, intermediate coronary syndrome, preinfarction syndrome, and worsening effort angina. Figure 14-5 illustrates the most common patterns of angina. Patients typically complain of tightness in the chest that radiates to the left arm, neck, and jaw.

The following note appears after the category heading I20, Angina pectoris. It directs coders to use additional codes with category I20.

Use additional code to identify:
exposure to environmental tobacco smoke (Z77.22)
history of tobacco use (Z87.891)
occupational exposure to environmental tobacco smoke (Z57.31)
tobacco dependence (F17.-)
tobacco use (Z72.0)

Coding guidelines that apply to this range of codes include the following:

ICD-10-CM Official Coding Guidelines

Atherosclerotic coronary artery disease and angina

ICD-10-CM has combination codes for atherosclerotic heart disease with angina pectoris. The subcategories for these codes are I25.11, Atherosclerotic heart disease of native coronary artery with angina pectoris, and I25.7, Atherosclerosis of coronary artery bypass graft(s) and coronary artery of transplanted heart with angina pectoris.

When using one of these combination codes it is not necessary to use an additional code for angina pectoris. A causal relationship can be assumed in a patient with both atherosclerosis and angina pectoris, unless the documentation indicates the angina is due to something other than the atherosclerosis.

If a patient with coronary artery disease is admitted due to an acute myocardial infarction (AMI), the AMI should be sequenced before the coronary artery disease.

See Section I.C.9. Acute myocardial infarction (AMI)

(See Appendix a, Section I, C 9,b)

Myocardial Infarction

An acute **myocardial infarction (MI)**, commonly called a **heart attack**, occurs when there is inadequate blood supply to a section or sections of the heart.

Disease Highlight—Myocardial Infarction

A myocardial infarction (MI) occurs when there is a decrease in the blood flow through one of the coronary arteries, causing a decrease in the amount of oxygen supplied to the heart tissue. The decreased blood flow causes myocardial ischemia and necrosis.

Sign and Symptoms:

- Severe chest pain that typically radiates down the left arm and up to the neck and jaw
- Sweating
- Nausea
- Vomiting
- Shortness of breath
- Weakness
- Dysrhythmias

Clinical Testing:

- Electrocardiography—An ST segment elevation or depression, symmetric inversion of T waves, and evolving Q waves
- Blood tests—Elevation of cardiac enzymes in the blood
- Cardiac imaging studies—Appearance of segmental wall motion abnormality
- Chest X-ray—Possible signs of congestive heart failure, which may develop behind other clinical findings

Treatment:

If the patient is currently having an MI:

- Place the patient in a lying position. If cardiac arrest occurs, cardiopulmonary resuscitation should be administered.
- Medical treatment is directed at pain management and the administration of oxygen.
- If the patient is experiencing arrhythmias, medications are administered.
- **Thrombolytic therapy**, the intravenous administration of thrombolytic agents, is often completed to open the coronary artery occlusion and to restore blood flow to the cardiac tissue.

Following the management of the acute MI:

- Patients may undergo cardiac catheterization to evaluate the heart.
- Angioplasty and/or coronary artery bypass surgery may be indicated depending on the clinical findings.
- Cardiac rehabilitation and patient education are also part of the treatment regimen.

In ICD-10-CM, myocardial infarctions are coded to categories I21–I22. Category I21 is used to code a myocardial infarction specified as acute or with a stated duration of four weeks (28 days) or less from onset. This category also includes:

- Cardiac infarction.
- Coronary (artery) embolism.
- Coronary (artery) occlusion.
- Coronary (artery) rupture.
- Coronary (artery) thrombosis.
- Infarction of heart, myocardium, or ventricle

Coders are instructed, via an instructional notation that appears after the heading for category I21, to use an additional code to identify:

- Body mass index (BMI), if known (Z68.–).
- Exposure to environmental tobacco smoke (Z77.22).
- History of tobacco use (Z87.891).
- Occupational exposure to environmental tobacco smoke (Z57.31).
- Status postadministration of tPA (rtPA) in a different facility within the last 24 hours prior to admission to current facility (Z92.82).
- Tobacco dependence (F17.–).
- Tobacco use (Z72.0).

Category I22 is used to report an acute myocardial infarction occurring within four weeks (28 days) of a previous acute myocardial infarction, regardless of site. This category also includes:

- Cardiac infarction.
- Coronary (artery) embolism.
- Coronary (artery) occlusion.
- Coronary (artery) rupture.
- Coronary (artery) thrombosis.
- Infarction of heart, myocardium, or ventricle.
- Recurrent myocardial infarction.
- Reinfarction of myocardium.
- Rupture of heart, myocardium, or ventricle.

As with category I21, the following instructional notation appears after the heading of category I22:

Use an additional code to identify:
• body mass index (BMI), if known (Z68.–)
• exposure to environmental tobacco smoke (Z77.22)
• history of tobacco use (Z87.891)
• occupational exposure to environmental tobacco smoke (Z57.31)
• tobacco dependence (F17.–)
• tobacco use (Z72.0)

Category I22 also contains the following note that must be followed when selecting codes:

The following coding guidelines are to be followed when assigning codes for myocardial infarctions:

> **Note:**
>
> *A code from category I22 must be used in conjunction with a code from category I21. The I22 code should be sequenced first, if it is the reason for encounter, or, it should be sequenced after the I21 code if the subsequent MI occurs during the encounter for the initial MI.*

ICD-10-CM Official Coding Guidelines

Acute myocardial infarction (AMI)

1) ST elevation myocardial infarction (STEMI) and non ST elevation myocardial infarction (NSTEMI)

The ICD-10-CM codes for acute myocardial infarction (AMI) identify the site, such as anterolateral wall or true posterior wall. Subcategories I21.0–I21.2 and code I21.4 are used for ST elevation myocardial infarction (STEMI). Code I21.4, Non-ST elevation (NSTEMI) myocardial infarction, is used for non ST elevation myocardial infarction (NSTEMI) and nontransmural MIs.

2) Acute myocardial infarction, unspecified

Code I21.3, ST elevation (STEMI) myocardial infarction of unspecified site, is the default for the unspecified term acute myocardial infarction. If only STEMI or transmural MI without the site is documented, query the provider as to the site, or assign code I21.3.

3) AMI documented as nontransmural or subendocardial but site provided

If an AMI is documented as nontransmural or subendocardial, but the site is provided, it is still coded as a subendocardial AMI. If NSTEMI evolves to STEMI, assign the STEMI code. If STEMI converts to NSTEMI due to thrombolytic therapy, it is still coded as STEMI.

See Section I.C.21.3 for information on coding status post administration of tPA in a different facility within the last 24 hours.

4) Subsequent acute myocardial infarction

A code from category I22, Subsequent ST elevation (STEMI) and non ST elevation (NSTEMI) myocardial infarction, is to be used when a patient who has suffered an AMI has a new AMI within the 4 week time frame of the initial AMI. A code from category I22 must be used in conjunction with a code from category I21.

The sequencing of the I22 and I21 codes depends on the circumstances of the encounter. Should a patient who is in the hospital due to an AMI have a subsequent AMI while still in the hospital, code I21 would be sequenced first as the reason for admission, with code I22 sequenced as a secondary code. Should a patient have a subsequent AMI after discharge for care of an initial AMI, and the reason for admission is the subsequent AMI, the I22 code should be sequenced first followed by the I21. An I21 code must accompany an I22 code to identify the site of the initial AMI, and to indicate that the patient is still within the 4 week time frame of healing from the initial AMI.

The guidelines for assigning the correct I22 code are the same as for the initial AMI.

(See Appendix A, Section I, C9, e, 1-4)

Old Myocardial Infarction

Code I25.2 is assigned for an **old myocardial infarction**, sometimes referred to as a **healed myocardial infarction**. This code is used when a past MI is diagnosed by electrocardiogram (EKG) or other investigation and the patient is not presenting with any symptoms. The code is not assigned when current symptoms or ischemic heart disease is present. It actually records a history of an MI and is most commonly used when a past MI has been diagnosed after a diagnostic study or EKG has been completed. The coder must determine from the medical documentation that no symptoms are present before this code is assigned.

EXAMPLE: Don Duckster presented to the physician's office for a follow-up visit six months after an EKG showed a slight MI. The patient complained of no symptoms. Code I25.2 is appropriately assigned for this visit.

Pulmonary Heart Disease and Diseases of Pulmonary Circulation (Category Codes I26–I28)

Category I26 reports pulmonary embolisms and includes pulmonary (artery or vein):

- Infarction.
- Thromboembolism.
- Thrombosis.

Category code I27 reports other pulmonary heart diseases such as primary pulmonary hypertension, kyphoscoliotic heart disease, and other specified pulmonary diseases.

Category code I28 reports other diseases of pulmonary vessels such as arteriovenous fistula of pulmonary vessels, aneurysm of pulmonary artery, and other diseases of pulmonary vessels.

Other Forms of Heart Disease (Category Codes I30–I52)

This range of codes classifies other forms of heart disease:

- **Pericarditis**—code I30—Inflammation of the outer layers of the heart, known as the **pericardium**
- Other diseases of pericardium—category code I31—This includes other types of pericarditis, hemopericardium, and other diseases.
- Pericarditis in diseases classified elsewhere—category code I32
- Acute and subacute **endocarditis**—category code I33—Inflammation of the inner layer of the heart
- Nonrheumatic mitral valve disorders—category code I34
- Nonrheumatic aortic valve disorders—category code I35
- Nonrheumatic tricuspid valve disorders—category code I36
- Nonrheumatic pulmonary valve disorders—category code I37
- Endocarditis, valve unspecified—category code I38
- Endocarditis and heart valve disorders in diseases classified elsewhere—category code I39
- Acute myocarditis—category code I40
- **Myocarditis** in diseases classified elsewhere—category code I41— Inflammation of the heart muscle
- **Cardiomyopathy**—category codes I42–I43—Diseases of the heart muscle
- Atrioventricular and left bundle-branch block—category code I44
- Other conduction disorders—category code I45
- Cardiac arrest—category code I46
- Paroxysmal tachycardia—category code I47
- Atrial fibrillation and flutter—category code I48
- Other cardiac arrhythmias—category code I49
- **Heart failure**—category code I50—A decreased ability of the heart to pump a sufficient amount of blood to the body's tissue. Code I50.9 is used to report congestive heart failure NOS. Figure 14-6 illustrates signs of congestive heart failure.
- Complications and ill-defined descriptions of heart disease—category code I51
- Other heart disorders in diseases classified elsewhere—category code I52

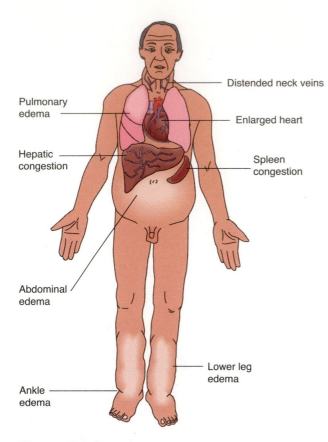

Pulmonary edema

Hepatic congestion

Abdominal edema

Ankle edema

Distended neck veins

Enlarged heart

Spleen congestion

Lower leg edema

Figure 14-6 Signs of congestive heart failure (From Marianne Neighbors & Ruth Tannehill-Jones. *Human Diseases*, 2nd ed, Clifton Park, NY: Delmar, Cengage Learning, p. 143.)

When selecting codes in this section of the code book, the coder must be able to identify modifying terms associated with the main diagnostic term. For example, myocarditis has numerous causes. The coder needs to reference the main term *myocarditis* and then search for any modifying terms such as *bacterial*. This leads the coder to the correct form of myocarditis.

Cerebrovascular Diseases (Category Codes I60–I69)

ICD-10-CM category codes I60–I69 are used to code various forms of cerebrovascular diseases. **Cerebrovascular disease** includes abnormal nontraumatic conditions that affect the cerebral arteries:

- **Cerebral hemorrhage**—Bleeding within the brain or layers of brain lining

- **Cerebrovascular accident (CVA)**—The disruption in the normal blood supply to the brain, commonly called a **stroke**

- **Occlusion of cerebral and precerebral arteries**—The blocking of the artery

- **Stenosis** of the cerebral arteries—The narrowing of the cerebral arteries that supply blood to the brain

The categories are as follows:

- I60, Nontraumatic subarachnoid hemorrhage

- I61, Nontraumatic intracerebral hemorrhage

- I62, Other and unspecified nontraumatic intracranial hemorrhage

- I63, Cerebral infarction

- I65, Occlusion and stenosis of precerebral arteries, not resulting in cerebral infarction

- I66, Occlusion and stenosis of cerebral arteries, not resulting in cerebral infarction

- I67, Other cerebrovascular diseases

- I68, Cerebrovascular disorders in diseases classified elsewhere

- I69, Sequelae of cerebrovascular disease

> **Note:**
>
> *Many of the codes are differentiated by the side of the body that the disease occurs on. For example, I63.0 series of codes differentiate between right versus left vertebral artery. The coder must glean the details for code assignment from the medical documentation of the case.*

Disease of Arteries, Arterioles, and Capillaries (Category Codes I70–I79)

Coders should reference a diagram of the body's arteries when coding in this section. Many of the codes require identification of the specific diseased artery. Coders must also identify whether the disease is affecting the patient's own arteries or grafted or transplanted arteries.

EXAMPLE: Atherosclerosis, category code I70, is divided to identify atherosclerosis of the native arteries of the extremities and bypass grafts of the extremities. The I70.2 codes identify atherosclerosis of native arteries of the extremities, and the I70.3 codes identify atherosclerosis of unspecified type of bypass grafts of the extremities.

The detail in the I70–I79 code range is great. For accurate coding, coders need to thoroughly read the diagnosis being coded and match it with the descriptions in the code book.

Diseases of Veins and Lymphatic Vessels and Lymph Nodes, Not Elsewhere Classified (Category Codes I80–I89)

Code range I80–I89 includes numerous commonly treated conditions. The category codes found in this section of the code book are:

- I80, **Phlebitis**, inflammation of a vein, and **thrombophlebitis**, inflammation of a vein with the formation of a thrombus.

- I81, **Portal vein thrombosis**, the formation of a blood clot in the main vein of the liver.

- I82, Other venous embolism and thrombosis. An instructional notation appears in the code book in regard to reporting embolisms and thrombosis that are complicating abortion, ectopic or molar pregnancy, pregnancy, childbirth, and the puerperium.
  Codes I82.40–I82.499 describe embolism and thrombosis of deep veins of the lower extremities with codes to identify left versus right and the specific vein involved.

- I83, **Varicose veins** of the lower extremities—Dilated superficial veins of the legs.

- I84, **Hemorrhoids**—Enlarged veins in or near the anus.

- I85, Esophageal varices. For this category an instructional notation requires using an additional code to identify alcohol abuse and dependence.

- I86, Varicose veins of other sites—Varicose veins of the sublingual, scrotal, pelvic, gastric, vulval, and other specified areas are classified to this code range.

- I87, Other disorders of veins—This category includes the following disorders: postphlebitic syndrome, compression of vein, venous insufficiency, and chronic venous hypertension.

- I88, Nonspecific lymphadenitis—**Lymphadenitis** is the inflammation of the lymph nodes.

- I89, Other noninfective disorders of lymphatic vessels and lymph nodes.

Other and Unspecified Disorders of the Circulatory System (Category Codes I95–I99)

The last code block of this chapter is I95–I99:

- I95, **Hypotension**—Low blood pressure

- I96, Gangrene, not elsewhere classified—Includes gangrenous cellulitis

- I97, Intraoperative and postprocedural complications and disorders of circulatory system, not elsewhere classified

- I99, Other and unspecified disorders of circulatory system—Codes from this category are not specific. The coder should query the provider to determine whether more specific information is available before assigning codes.

Comparing ICD-9-CM to ICD-10-CM

A number of diseases are now coded into ICD-10-CM chapter 9, "Diseases of the Circulatory System," that were previously in other chapters in ICD-9-CM. These include gangrene (I96) and Binswanger's disease (I67.3).

Expansions have been made for rheumatic tricuspid valve diseases. Previously, code 397.0 would have been used, and now five codes delineate the manifestations of the valve diseases (I07.0 to I07.9).

Added in ICD-10-CM is code I97, Intraoperative and postprocedural complications of disorders of the circulatory system. The late effects of cerebrovascular diseases has now been expanded by the use of section I69.

Hypertension in ICD-9-CM was classified as malignant, benign, and unspecified; however, in ICD-10-CM these terms are no longer used as a classification axis.

Internet Links

For general cardiology information, visit *http://www.cardio–info.com*

To learn more about peripheral vascular disease, visit *http://www.footcare4u.com*

To better understand the various forms of heart disease, visit *http://www.medicinenet.com* and search the term *heart disease*.

Summary

- ICD-10-CM chapter 7 covers diseases of the circulatory system.
- The primary structures of the circulatory system are arteries, veins, and the heart.
- Cardiovascular disease can affect many vessels throughout the body.
- Secondary hypertension is high arterial blood pressure due to another disease.
- Hypertensive heart disease includes heart diseases caused by hypertension.
- Hypertensive renal disease includes renal diseases caused by hypertension.
- Cerebrovascular disease includes abnormal nontraumatic conditions that affect the cerebral arteries.
- Chronic ischemic heart disease is also referred to as arteriosclerotic heart disease.
- Cerebrovascular disease includes abnormal nontraumatic conditions that affect the cerebral arteries.

Chapter Review

True/False: Indicate whether each statement is true (T) or false (F).

1. _____ Angina pectoris and unstable angina are classified to the same code.

2. _____ Veins carry deoxygenated blood from the body back to the heart with one exception, the pulmonary vein.

3. _____ Rheumatic tricuspid stenosis is assigned code I07.9.

4. _____ Diastolic blood pressure is the pressure on the arterial walls during heart muscle contraction.

5. _____ Benign hypertension is mildly elevated blood pressure that remains stable over many years.

Fill-in-the-Blank: Enter the appropriate term(s) to complete each statement.

6. Uncontrolled hypertension may refer to _____ hypertension or hypertension not responding to current _____ .

7. Hypertensive cardiomegaly and hypertensive heart failure are types of _____ disease.

8. Stenosis of the cerebral arteries is caused by a _____ of the cerebral arteries that supply blood to the brain.

9. Circulatory system disorders can be caused by infections as well as _____ factors.

10. An acute _____ is commonly called a heart attack.

Coding Assignments

Instructions: Using an ICD-10-CM code book, assign the proper diagnosis code to the following diagnostic statements.

Diagnosis   *Code*

1. benign essential hypertension   _____

2. moderate arterial hypertension   _____

3. Raynaud's syndrome with gangrene   _____

4. dissection of carotid artery   _____

5. rheumatic aortic regurgitation   _____

6. unstable angina   _____

7. angina pectoris with essential hypertension _____

8. spasm-induced angina   _____

9. congestive heart failure   _____

10. peripheral venous insufficiency   _____

11. alcoholic cardiomyopathy   _____

12. cardiac arrest   _____

13. Dressler's syndrome   _____

14. atrial septal defect following acute MI _____

15. acute pericarditis   _____

16. atrial flutter   _____

17. cardiomegaly   _____

18. aortic aneurysm   _____

19. chronic ischemic heart disease   _____

20. acute myocardial infarction   _____

21. obstructive hypertrophic cardiomyopathy   _____

22. extrasystolic arrhythmia   _____

23. aneurysm of renal artery   _____

24. arterial stricture   _____

25. bleeding external hemorrhoids   _____

26. phlebosclerosis   _____

27. subacute lymphangitis   _____

28. atheroembolism of left lower extremity   _____

29. endomyocardial fibrosis   _____

30. idiopathic pulmonary arteriosclerosis   _____

Case Studies

Instructions: Review each case study and select the correct ICD-10-CM diagnostic code.

CASE 1

Physician Office Note

VITAL SIGNS: Temperature 100.2; Blood pressure 130/80; Weight 175 pounds

Bridgit presents today with a chief complaint of pain in her left leg that has been present on and off for the last week. She has previously experienced phlebitis in her left leg.

EXAM:

HEENT: Normal

CHEST: Clear

EXTREMITIES: There is edema in her left leg. An area on her calf is tender to palpation. She states that the pain is also unbearable when I touch it.

Because of her previous phlebitis, I sent her to the X-ray department for a STAT venogram that revealed thrombophlebitis of the left tibial vein.

Patient was given heparin, and a prescription was written for antibiotics. The left leg was immobilized, and she was instructed to return to me in 3 days.

ICD-10-CM Code Assignment: _____

CASE 2

DISCHARGE SUMMARY:

Admitted 2/03/XX

Discharged 2/7/XX

Admitting Diagnosis:

Unstable angina

Atrial fibrillation

HISTORY: This 69-year-old man was admitted through the ER with chest pain that began while he was eating his lunch. After lunch he went to do his grocery shopping, and he began to develop discomfort in his chest as well as in his jaw. He drove himself to the ER. The ER physician admitted the patient due to unstable angina.

Vital signs at time of admission: BP 140/60, heart rate 110 to 120

HEART: Patient complains of chest pain.

All other physical findings were within normal limits.

HOSPITAL COURSE:

Cardiac enzymes—CPK of 105, Troponin—4.7 with a relative index of 5.4

Digoxin level was 1.8.

All other lab values were normal.

EKG was positive for a new anterior wall infarction.

The patient was maintained on Imdur 30 mg daily and metoprolol 50 mg in the morning and evening.

The patient stabilized and was instructed to see me in 7 days.

Discharge Diagnosis:

Acute anterolateral transmural Q wave infarction

Hypertension

ICD-10-CM Code Assignment: _____

CASE 3

Skilled Nursing Facility Physician Monthly Progress Note

4/22/XX

This patient was admitted in January of 2003 with a primary diagnosis of ischemic heart disease, history of bladder cancer, and uncontrolled malignant hypertension. Patient continues to be stable. On exam he appears comfortable and still has some coughing spells during my physical examination.

Vital signs include a weight of 223.8 lb. Compared to last 3 months, it varies from 222 to 225. No weight gain or weight loss.

BLOOD PRESSURE: 160/90, which is not under control; pulse—70 per minute; regular, respirations—24.

LUNGS: Still occasional rhonchi but no wheeze

HEART: Regular rhythm with no change in systolic murmur

Abdomen is soft. Bowel sounds are active.

EXTREMITIES: No pedal edema; no clubbing or cyanosis

Medications, including Advil, Cytotec, Ascriptin, Tylenol, Tenormin, Pulmoaid therapy, Senna laxative, Artificial Tears, Analgesic Balm, Casadex, Mycolog, to be continued, along with the standing orders.

I will see the patient in 30 days or at the request of the charge nurse.

ICD-10-CM Code Assignment: _____

CASE 4

Physician's Office Note

Mr. Cafferty presents today with some ascites and complaint of exertional dyspnea. When queried about any other symptoms, he stated that at night he sometimes wakes up coughing, which in his words is described as "real dry." He has a history of congestive heart failure and microvascular spasms.

On physical examination, mild ascites, tachycardia, and peripheral edema are noted. Previous diagnostic testing was reviewed, which confirmed cardiomyopathy.

ICD-10-CM Code Assignment: _____

(continued)

CASE 5

Physician's Office Note

VITAL SIGNS: Temperature 98.8; blood pressure 120/70; weight 185 pounds

This 42-year-old male presents today with shortness of breath, fatigue, ankle edema, and anxiety. He states that these symptoms have begun to increase in severity, and he is concerned.

Chest X-ray and EKG confirmed congestive heart failure.

ICD-10-CM Code Assignment: _____

Diseases of the Respiratory System

Chapter Outline

Objectives

At the conclusion of this chapter, the learner should be able to:

1. Identify the major structures of the respiratory system.
2. Explain the diseases and conditions that impact the respiratory system.
3. Understand the terminology associated with the respiratory system.
4. Summarize coding guidelines for diseases of the respiratory system.
5. Assign diagnostic codes for conditions and diseases of the respiratory system.
6. Select and assign diagnostic code from case studies.

Key Terms

acute bronchitis	chronic sinusitis	pharyngitis	trachea
aspiration pneumonia	emphysema	pharynx	vocal cords
bronchi	influenza	pneumonia	
bronchitis	larynx	respiratory system	
chronic bronchitis	lungs	tonsils	

Reminder

As you work through this chapter, you will need to have a copy of the ICD-10-CM coding book to reference.

Introduction

Chapter 10 of ICD-10-CM, "Diseases of the Respiratory System" (category codes J00–J99), classifies conditions such acute respiratory infections, diseases of the upper respiratory tract, acute respiratory failure, asthma, pneumonia, influenza, and chronic obstructive pulmonary disease.

The following blocks of codes are present in this chapter:

- J00–J06, Acute upper respiratory infections
- J09–J18, Influenza and pneumonia
- J20–J22, Other acute lower respiratory infections
- J30–J39, Other diseases of upper respiratory tract
- J40–J47, Chronic lower respiratory diseases
- J60–J70, Lung diseases due to external agents
- J80–J84, Other respiratory diseases principally affecting the interstitium
- J85–J86, Suppurative and necrotic conditions of the lower respiratory tract
- J90–J94, Other diseases of the pleura
- J95, Intraoperative and postprocedural complications and disorders of respiratory system, not elsewhere classified
- J96–J99, Other diseases of the respiratory system

Introduction to the Body System

The respiratory system begins its function when air enters the body through the nose or mouth. The **respiratory system** is comprised of structures that exchange oxygen and carbon dioxide in the body.

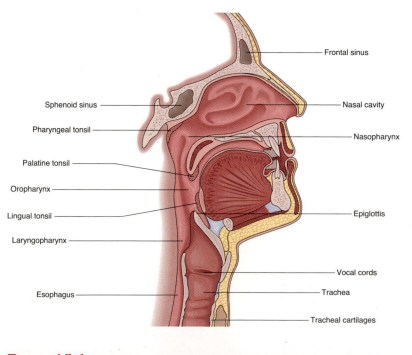

Figure 15-1   Structures of the respiratory system (From Ehrlich A, Schroeder CL. Medical Terminology for Health Professionals, 4th ed. Clifton Park, NY: Delmar, Cengage Learning, 2001.)

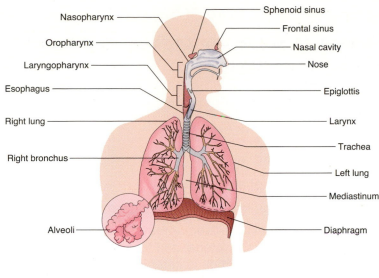

Respiratory System

Figure 15-2 Structures of the upper respiratory system (From Ehrlich A, Schroeder CL. Medical Terminology for Health Professionals, 4th ed. Clifton Park, NY: Delmar, Cengage Learning, 2001.)

The main organs of the respiratory system are the **lungs**, where this gas exchange occurs. The lungs also work as a purification or filtering system for the air the body takes in. Two lobes, one on the right and one on the left, hold the bronchi. The **bronchi** are formed when the **trachea**, or windpipe, branches off in the chest. Figure 15-1 illustrates the structures of the respiratory system.

The larynx and pharynx are also part of the respiratory system. The **larynx** is made up of cartilage and ligaments that compose the vocal cords, or the voice box. When air passes through the **vocal cords**, sound or speech is produced. The **pharynx** is also known as the "throat." This structure connects the mouth and nose to the larynx. Once air has passed from the nose or mouth through the pharynx, the air then moves into the trachea. Figure 15-2 illustrates the structures of the upper respiratory system.

Coding Diseases of the Respiratory System

Categories J00–J99 report diseases of the respiratory system. Instructional notations appear after the chapter heading that state:

Note: When a respiratory condition is described as occurring in more than one site and is not specifically indexed, it should be classified to the lower anatomic site (e.g. tracheobronchitis to bronchitis in J40).
Use additional code, where applicable, to identify:
exposure to environmental tobacco smoke (Z77.22)
exposure to tobacco smoke in the perinatal period (P96.81)
history of tobacco use (Z87.891)
occupational exposure to environmental tobacco smoke (Z57.31)
tobacco dependence (F17.–)
tobacco use (Z72.0)

These instructions must be followed for proper code selection. Coders should also keep in mind that provider documentation is key in the diagnostic coding for respiratory disease. Laboratory results, on their own, are not enough to assign a diagnosis code in this chapter. The coder must also reference provider diagnostic statements for code selection.

Acute Upper Respiratory Infections (Category Codes J00–J06)

This subcategory of codes contains some of the more common diagnoses codes used by a primary care office:

- J00, Acute nasopharyngitis [common cold]
- J01, Acute sinusitis
- J02, Acute pharyngitis
- J03, Acute tonsillitis
- J04, Acute laryngitis and tracheitis
- J05, Acute obstructive laryngitis [croup] and epiglottitis
- J06, Acute upper respiratory infections in multiple and unspecified sites

Acute **pharyngitis**, or what is commonly called a "sore throat," is coded to category code J02. There are many causes of pharyngitis, such as a virus, bacteria, and tobacco abuse. The code J02 is for acute pharyngitis and should not be used if the condition is chronic, which codes to J31.2. If the pharyngitis is due to an infection, codes from the "Certain Infectious and Parasitic Diseases" chapter should be reported to identify the cause of the infection. A notation appears after code J02.8 that directs the coder to "Use additional code (B95–B97) to identify infections."

EXAMPLE:

Patient 1

An 8-year-old girl presents today with a runny nose, cough, and sore throat. A rapid strep test is done, which comes back negative.

DX: Cold and sore throat

Code assignment: J00 and J02.9

Patient 2

An 10-year-old boy presents today with a runny nose, cough, and sore throat. A rapid strep test is done, which comes back positive.

DX: Strep throat

Code assignment: J02.0

When coding in this section, be sure your documentation supports an acute condition. If there is any question, consult the provider for clarification.

Influenza and Pneumonia (Category Codes J09–J18)

This category of codes includes influenza and pneumonia. Some forms of pneumonia are not coded to this section, and the listing appears as an Excludes 1 note under the heading for this block of codes, as follows:

Excludes 1:	allergic or eosinophilic pneumonia (J82)
	aspiration pneumonia NOS (J69.0)
	meconium pneumonia (P24.01)
	neonatal aspiration pneumonia (P24.–)
	pneumonia due to solids and liquids (J69–)
	pneumonia with abscess of lung (J85.1)
	congenital pneumonia (P23.9)
	lipid pneumonia (J69.1)
	rheumatic pneumonia (I00)
	ventilator associated pneumonia (J95.851)

This block of codes has many instructional notations that instruct coders to code first any associated conditions and to use additional codes to identify the presence of a virus.

The following category codes are present in this block of codes:

- J09, Influenza due to certain identified influenza viruses
- J10, Influenza due to other influenza virus
- J12, Viral pneumonia, not elsewhere classified
- J13, Pneumonia due to *Streptococcus pneumoniae*
- J14, Pneumonia due to *Hemophilus influenzae*
- J15, Bacterial pneumonia, not elsewhere classified
- J16, Pneumonia due to other infectious organisms, not elsewhere classified
- J17, Pneumonia in diseases classified elsewhere
- J18, Pneumonia, unspecified organism

Influenza, a highly contagious respiratory disease that is caused by various viruses, is coded in ICD-10-CM to category codes J09–J10. The following coding guideline needs to be referenced when coding from categories J09–J10.

ICD-10-CM Official Coding Guidelines

Influenza due to certain identified influenza viruses

Code only confirmed cases of avian influenza (code J09.0-, Influenza due to identified avian influenza virus) or novel H1N1 or swine flu, code J09.1-. This is an exception to the hospital inpatient guideline Section II, H. (Uncertain Diagnosis).

In this context, "confirmation" does not require documentation of positive laboratory testing specific for avian or novel H1N1 (H1N1 or swine flu) influenza. However, coding should be based on the provider's diagnostic statement that the patient has avian influenza.

If the provider records "suspected or possible or probable avian influenza," the appropriate influenza code from category J10, Influenza due to other influenza virus, should be assigned. A code from category J09, Influenza due to certain identified influenza viruses, should not be assigned.

Pneumonia is a condition in which liquid, known as "exudate," and pus infiltrate the lung and cause an inflammation. Bacteria, viruses, inhaled irritants, or fungi can cause pneumonia. There are many types of pneumonia, so it is very important to verify the type of pneumonia documented in the medical record. ICD-10-CM classifies pneumonia by the organism or irritant causing the pneumonia.

At times a provider documents the term *lobar pneumonia*. When there is mention of pneumonia in a lobe of the lung, it is lobar pneumonia only if documented by the provider as such. If you reference the term *lobar pneumonia* in the Alphabetic Index of ICD-10-CM, you will note that numerous entries under the term *lobar*. Therefore coders may have to clarify with the provider as to the type of lobar pneumonia that is present. Lobar pneumonia is usually caused by *Streptococcus pneumoniae*, and it is coded to J13.

Other Acute Lower Respiratory Infections (Category Codes J20–J22)

This range of codes is divided into the following categories:

- J20, Acute bronchitis
- J21, Acute bronchiolitis
- J22, Unspecified acute lower respiratory infection

Bronchitis, an inflammation of the bronchus, can be diagnosed as both acute and chronic. ICD-10-CM provides separate codes for the acute and chronic manifestations of bronchitis. The J20 codes are used for acute bronchitis. **Acute bronchitis** is an inflammation of the bronchus that lasts for a short period of time and is typically caused by a spreading of an inflammation from the nasopharynx. Symptoms of acute bronchitis include fever, cough, and substernal pain.

Chronic bronchitis is a prolonged inflammation of the bronchus, lasting for more than three months and occurring for two consecutive years. Chronic bronchitis can occur because of exposure to bronchial irritants such as cigarette smoking. Symptoms of chronic bronchitis include a severe, persistent cough and large amounts of discolored sputum. Chronic bronchitis is classified to category codes J40–J42.

Other Diseases of Upper Respiratory Tract (Category Codes J30–J39)

This block of codes reports other diseases of the upper respiratory tract.

This section of the chapter contains many of the codes needed to code the chronic inflammatory diseases of the upper respiratory tract (see Figure 15–2). This section also classifies conditions that affect the accessory structures of the respiratory system such as the sinus cavities, tonsils and adenoids, larynx and vocal cords.

One of the more common conditions coded to this section is **chronic sinusitis**, category code J32, which is a prolonged inflammation of one or more of the sinus cavities. Chronic sinusitis can be a result of exposure to something the patient may be allergic to or an infective agent. Acute sinusitis is coded to the J01 codes.

Chronic diseases of the tonsils are coded to this section. The **tonsils** protect the entrance to the respiratory system from invading organisms. Abscess of the tonsils is coded to J36, Peritonsillar abscess. Acute tonsillitis is coded to J03.90. Other chronic conditions found here are chronic laryngitis, J37.0, and chronic rhinitis, J31.0.

> **Note:**
>
> *Coders must reference the many instructional notations throughout this entire block when selecting codes.*

Exercise 15.1 – Coding Category Codes J00–J39

Select the appropriate ICD-9-CM code for the diagnosis listed.

1. bacterial pneumonia   _____
2. pneumonia due to *Mycoplasma pneumoniae*   _____
3. *E. coli* pneumonia   _____
4. common cold   _____
5. acute tonsillitis   _____
6. acute laryngopharyngitis   _____
7. pneumonia due to *Hemophilus influenzae*   _____
8. chronic maxillary sinusitis   _____
9. hypertrophy of tonsils   _____
10. allergic rhinitis   _____

Chronic Lower Respiratory Diseases (Category Codes J40–J47)

This category of codes is divided as follows:

- J40, Bronchitis, not specified as acute or chronic
- J41, Simple and mucopurulent chronic bronchitis
- J42, Unspecified chronic bronchitis
- J43, Emphysema
- J44, Other chronic obstructive pulmonary disease
- J45, Asthma
- J47, Bronchiectasis

Emphysema, a loss of lung function due to progressive decrease in the number of alveoli in the bronchus of the lung, is coded to category code J43. Asthma is a stricture of the airway that causes difficulty breathing. Asthma is usually an allergic disorder in which wheezing and coughing are common indicators. The J45 category, Asthma, is further divided to indicate the type of asthma: mild intermittent, mild persistent, moderate persistent, etc.

The following coding guideline should also be noted when coding from categories J44 to J45.

ICD-10-CM Official Coding Guidelines

Acute exacerbation of chronic obstructive bronchitis and asthma

The codes in categories J44 and J45 distinguish between uncomplicated cases and those in acute exacerbation. An acute exacerbation is a worsening or a decompensation of a chronic condition. An acute exacerbation is not equivalent to an infection superimposed on a chronic condition, though an exacerbation may be triggered by an infection.

Lung Diseases due to External Agents (Category Codes J60–J70)

This block of codes is used to code lung diseases that are due to external agents such as solids, liquids, chemicals, gases, fumes, and vapors. This block includes such diseases as black lung disease, asbestosis, pneumoconiosis, any airway disease due to organic dust, and pneumonitis due to solids and liquids.

A common condition that is coded to J69.0 is aspiration pneumonia. **Aspiration pneumonia** occurs when a solid or liquid is inhaled into the lung. Aspiration pneumonia can be caused by the inhalation of food, gastric secretions, milk, vomit, among other things.

Other Respiratory Diseases Principally Affecting the Interstitium (Category Codes J80–J84)

This block of codes contains the following categories:

- J80, Acute respiratory distress syndrome
- J81, Pulmonary edema
- J82, Pulmonary eosinophilia, not elsewhere classified
- J84, Other interstitial pulmonary diseases

Pulmonary edema, category J81, contains an instructional notation that instructs the coder to:

Use additional code to identify:
exposure to environmental tobacco smoke (Z77.22)
history of tobacco use (Z87.891)
occupational exposure to environmental tobacco smoke (Z57.31)
tobacco dependence (F17.–)
tobacco use (Z72.0)

An Excludes 1 note reads:

Excludes 1:	chemical (acute) pulmonary edema (J68.1)
	hypostatic pneumonia (J18.2)
	passive pneumonia (J18.2)
	pulmonary edema due to external agents (J60–J70)
	pulmonary edema with heart disease NOS (I50.1)
	pulmonary edema with heart failure (I50.1)

Coders need to be guided by these notations when selecting codes for acute and chronic pulmonary edema.

Suppurative and Necrotic Conditions of the Lower Respiratory Tract (Category Codes J85–J86)

This block of codes reports abscess of the lung and mediastinum with category J85 and pyothorax with category J86. Category J86 is differentiated to identify the presence of fistula.

Other Diseases of the Pleura (Category Codes J90–J94) and Intraoperative and Postprocedural Complications and Disorders of Respiratory System, Not Elsewhere Classified (Category Code J95)

This block of codes is divided as follows:

- J90, Pleural effusion, not elsewhere classified
- J91, Pleural effusion in condition classified elsewhere
- J92, Pleural plaque
- J93, Pneumothorax
- J94, Other pleural conditions
- J95, Intraoperative and postprocedural complications and disorders of respiratory system, not elsewhere classified

Other Diseases of the Respiratory System (Category Codes J96–J99)

This block of codes has three categories:

- J96, Respiratory failure, not elsewhere classified
- J98, Other respiratory disorders
- J99, Respiratory disorders in diseases classified elsewhere

The following coding guideline governs these codes:

ICD-10-CM Official Coding Guidelines

Acute Respiratory Failure

1) Acute respiratory failure as principal diagnosis

Code J96.0, Acute respiratory failure, or code J96.2, Acute and chronic respiratory failure, may be assigned as a principal diagnosis when it is the condition established after study to be chiefly responsible for occasioning the admission to the hospital, and the selection is supported by the Alphabetic Index and Tabular List. However, chapter-specific coding guidelines (such as obstetrics, poisoning, HIV, newborn) that provide sequencing direction take precedence.

2) Acute respiratory failure as secondary diagnosis

Respiratory failure may be listed as a secondary diagnosis if it occurs after admission, or if it is present on admission, but does not meet the definition of principal diagnosis.

3) Sequencing of acute respiratory failure and another acute condition

When a patient is admitted with respiratory failure and another acute condition, (e.g., myocardial infarction, cerebrovascular accident, aspiration pneumonia), the principal diagnosis will not be the same in every situation. This applies whether the other acute condition is a respiratory or nonrespiratory condition. Selection of the principal diagnosis will be dependent on the circumstances of admission. If both the respiratory failure and the other acute condition are equally responsible for occasioning the admission to the hospital, and there are no chapter-specific sequencing rules, the guideline regarding two or more diagnoses that equally meet the definition for principal diagnosis (Section II, C.) may be applied in these situations.

If the documentation is not clear as to whether acute respiratory failure and another condition are equally responsible for occasioning the admission, query the provider for clarification.

Comparing ICD-9-CM to ICD-10-CM

Compared with the ICD-9-CM respiratory chapter, the ICD-10-CM chapter contains numerous changes. There has been expansion to:

- Reflect manifestations of influenza.
- Indicate the organism causing tonsillitis.
- Add a new subcategory to report acute recurrent sinusitis with expansion to the fifth-character level.
- Identify the organism causing pharyngitis.
- Further define asthma as mild, moderate, or severe.

Coders should note that ICD-10-CM has an increased number of instructional notations throughout the chapter, compared to the corresponding ICD-9-CM respiratory chapter. Coders need to pay attention to these notations, which may signal the need for additional codes.

Internet Links

To learn more about diseases of the respiratory system, visit **www.lungusa.org** and **www.emphysema.net**

The Pulmonary Education and Research Foundation also provides current information at **www.perf2ndwind.org**

For additional illustrations of the respiratory system and information about diseases of the respiratory system, visit ***http://users.rcn.com/jkimball.ma.ultranet/BiologyPages/P/Pulmonary.html***

Summary

- The respiratory system works as a purifying system, filtering air and carrying oxygen to the blood cells and carrying carbon dioxide out of the body.

- The lungs are the main organ of the respiratory system.

- The larynx is where the vocal cords are located.

- The trachea branches off into each lung; the branches are called bronchi.

- Respiratory conditions are commonly identified as acute, chronic, or both acute and chronic.

- ICD-10-CM classifies pneumonia by the organism or irritant causing the pneumonia.

- ICD-10-CM provides separate codes for the acute and chronic manifestations of bronchitis.

- Acute and chronic sinusitis is classified to different category codes in ICD-10-CM.

- The ICD-10-CM Official Guidelines for Coding and Reporting give instructions for coding acute exacerbation of chronic obstructive bronchitis and asthma, acute respiratory failure, and influenza due to avian influenza virus.

Chapter Review

True/False: Indicate whether each statement is true (T) or false (F).

1. _____ The bronchi are located in the lungs.

2. _____ The respiratory system begins its function when air enters the body.

3. _____ When air passes through the pharynx, sound is produced.

4. _____ Code J02.9 is used for acute pharyngitis.

5. _____ The code for maxillary sinusitis is J32.0.

Fill-in-the-Blank: Enter the appropriate term(s) to complete each statement.

6. Acute respiratory failure is coded to _____.

7. An inflammation of the bronchus that lasts for a short time and suddenly occurs is called _____.

8. The vocal cords are located in the _____.

9. Chronic bronchitis is a bronchial infection that lasts longer than _____.

10. Acute _____ is commonly called a sore throat.

Coding Assignments

Instructions: Using an ICD-10-CM code book, assign the proper diagnosis code to the following diagnostic statements.

Diagnosis	Code
1. acute tonsillitis	_____
2. edema of pharynx	_____

3. chronic ethmoidal sinusitis   _____

4. acute tracheitis without obstruction   _____

5. farmer's lung   _____

6. acute and chronic respiratory failure   _____

7. chronic pulmonary insufficiency following surgery   _____

8. chronic laryngitis   _____

9. allergic rhinitis due to dog hair   _____

10. chronic tonsillitis and adenoiditis   _____

11. COPD   _____

12. parapharyngeal abscess   _____

13. acute bronchitis due to rhinovirus   _____

14. hypertrophy of nasal turbinates   _____

15. acute epiglottitis with obstruction   _____

16. acute and chronic obstructive bronchitis   _____

17. hay fever with asthma   _____

18. necrotic pneumonia   _____

19. spontaneous tension pneumothorax   _____

20. interstitial pneumonia   _____

21. Löffler's syndrome   _____

22. hypostatic bronchopneumonia   _____

23. postprocedural respiratory failure   _____

24. Maltworker's lung   _____

25. smokers' cough   _____

Case Studies

Instructions: Review each case study and select the correct ICD-10-CM diagnostic code.

CASE 1

CHIEF COMPLAINT: This 71-old-year male, whom I have treated for a number of years, returns today with a persistent cough.

HISTORY OF THE PRESENT ILLNESS: The patient has a 4-month history of a cough. He also experienced this last year.

PAST MEDICAL HISTORY: Acute bronchitis and pneumonia

SOCIAL HISTORY: Patient is a 2-pack-a-day smoker. Denies alcohol use.

ALLERGIES: NKA

EXAM: BP 125/80, pulse 72, respirations 22

HEENT: No findings.

LUNGS: Bilateral wheezing and scattered rales. Sputum is discolored. Abdomen: no findings.

Chest X-ray ordered. Sputum C&S.

I feel that the patient has progressed to a chronic state of bronchitis due to his cigarette smoking. Patient to follow up in 2 weeks. Medications ordered as per med sheet.

ICD-10-CM Code Assignment: _____

CASE 2

CHIEF COMPLAINT: A 36-year-old male patient presents with headache and pressure in his head.

VITAL SIGNS: Temperature 100.3, BP 130/70

HEENT: Pain over the eyes in the frontal area of the forehead. Palpation increases pain. Throat appears red. There is a discolored discharge from his nose.

LUNGS: Clear

ABDOMEN: Normal findings

Patient has responded to Z-pac in the past for acute recurrent frontal sinusitis; therefore, this was ordered.

ICD-10-CM Code Assignment: _____

CASE 3

Katy presented to the ED at 5:00 a.m. very flushed with difficulty breathing, chest tightness, and tachycardia. She was examined by the ED physician, who ordered a pulmonary function test, arterial blood gases, chest X-ray, and ECG. Katy was diagnosed with an acute exacerbation of asthma. She was given two nebulizer treatments, which helped. After 12 hours observation, she was sent home.

ICD-10-CM Code Assignment: _____

CASE 4

This 72-year-old male presents today with productive cough, fever, chills, dyspnea, and chest pain. He was given a complete examination, which included a chest X-ray, EKG, and blood and sputum cultures.

The cultures came back with a positive for pneumonia infection due to streptococcus, group A. We have begun antibiotic therapy and will have him set up with 1 liter of O_2 at night if he needs it.

ICD-10-CM Code Assignment: _____

CASE 5

Mary, age 14, presented to our office today with complaints of tearing, sneezing, headache, and problems "catching her breath." When asked whether she noted any changes in her routine, body lotions, or laundry soap, she said no. She did say that she is spending more time outside. Her mother said she noticed this same thing happening last spring as well. We did a blood chemistry as well as some allergy sensitivity testing. Mary was diagnosed with allergic rhinitis. She was started on antihistamine therapy.

ICD-10-CM Code Assignment: _____

Diseases of the Digestive System

Chapter Outline

Objectives

At the conclusion of this chapter, the learner should be able to:

1. Identify the various anatomical structures of the digestive system.
2. Explain different conditions that are related to the digestive system.
3. Discuss the specific coding related to the different conditions encountered in the digestive system.
4. Assign diagnostic codes to diagnoses for the digestive system.
5. Select and code diagnoses from case studies.

Key Terms

accessory organs
alimentary canal
appendicitis
appendix
bile
cecum

cholecystitis
cholelithiasis
colitis
Crohn's disease
direct inguinal hernia
diverticula

diverticulitis
diverticulosis
duodenal ulcer
duodenum
enteritis
esophagitis

esophagus
gallbladder
gastric ulcer
gastroesophageal reflux
  disease (GERD)
gastrointestinal (GI) tract

Reminder

As you work through this chapter, you will need to have a copy of the ICD-10-CM coding book to reference.

gastrojejunal ulcer	ileum	pancreas	pulpitis
geographic tongue	indirect inguinal hernia	peptic ulcer	regional enteritis
hepatic	inguinal hernia	periapical abscess	stomach
hernia	jejunum	peritonitis	ulcerative colitis
hiatal hernia	liver	pulp	

Introduction

Chapter 11 of ICD-10-CM, "Diseases of the Digestive System," classifies conditions of the digestive system, which is also known as the **gastrointestinal (GI) tract**. The category codes found in this chapter include:

- K00–K14, Diseases of oral cavity and salivary glands.
- K20–K31, Diseases of esophagus, stomach, and duodenum.
- K35–K38, Diseases of appendix.
- K40–K46, Hernia.
- K50–K52, Noninfective enteritis and colitis.
- K55–K63, Other diseases of intestines.
- K65–K68, Diseases of peritoneum and retroperitoneum.
- K70–K77, Diseases of liver.
- K80–K87, Disorders of gallbladder, biliary tract, and pancreas.
- K90–K94, Other diseases of the digestive system.

Introduction to the Body System

The digestive system is also referred to as the **alimentary canal** (*aliment-* means "nourishment" and *-ary* means "pertaining to"; thus *alimentary* means "pertaining to nourishment"). The oral cavity (mouth), the pharynx (throat), esophagus, stomach, small intestine, large intestine, rectum, and the anus are the major organs of the digestive system. Figure 16-1 illustrates the major organs and anatomical structures of this system.

The digestive process begins when food is taken into the mouth for nourishment and is broken down for digestion, absorption, or nutrients. The process ends with the elimination of waste. The breakdown of food begins with chewing and continues as chemicals in the body further break food down and assist in the absorption and elimination process.

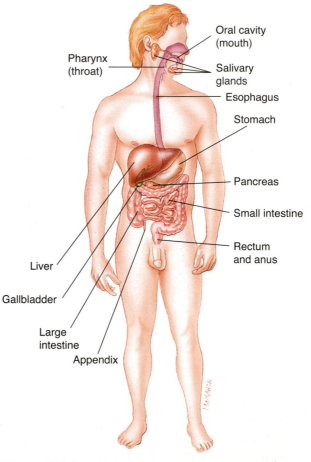

Figure 16-1   Major and accessory structures of the digestive system (From Ehrlich A, Schroeder CL. *Medical Terminology for Health Professionals*, 4th ed. Clifton Park, NY: Delmar, Cengage Learning, 2001, p. 166.)

Coding Diseases of the Digestive System

This chapter of ICD-10-CM is organized according to the anatomical order of the digestive tract, starting with the mouth through the intestines to the rectum and anus. This helps the coder determine the correct areas of the chapter for code selection. Disorders of the liver, gallbladder, and pancreas also code to this section because they are considered **accessory organs**, or secondary organs, of the digestive system.

Diseases of the Oral Cavity and Salivary Glands (Category Codes K00–K14)

These categories of codes classify disorders of the oral cavity, such as tooth development anomalies, disturbances of tooth formation, dental caries, and other periodontal diseases.

When coding disorders of the oral cavity, the coder should refer to a diagram of the mouth and teeth. Figures 16-2 and 16-3 illustrate the structures of the tooth and oral cavity.

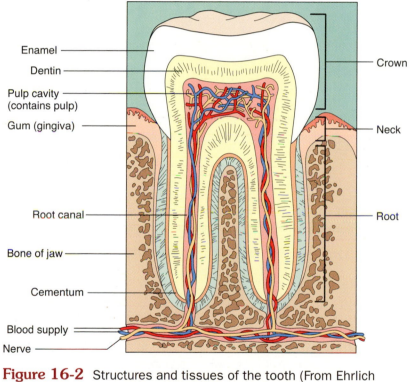

Figure 16-2 Structures and tissues of the tooth (From Ehrlich A, Schroeder CL. *Medical Terminology for Health Professionals*, 4th ed. Clifton Park, NY: Delmar, Cengage Learning, 2001, p. 168.)

Diseases of the enamel, hard tissue of the teeth, and center of the teeth, known as **pulp**, are classified to this section of the book. **Pulpitis**, code K04.0, is an abscess of the pulp, usually of bacterial origin. Another condition that is encountered in this category of codes is **periapical abscess**, which is an infection of the pulp and surrounding tissue.

Other conditions coded to this section of the chapter are gingivitis, diseases of the jaw and salivary glands, and diseases and conditions of the tongue, such as geographic tongue. **Geographic tongue**, K14.1, is a condition in which irregularly shaped patches are present on the tongue and resemble landforms on a map. The cause is unknown, but the condition usually goes away on its own or, in some cases, with a topical steroid.

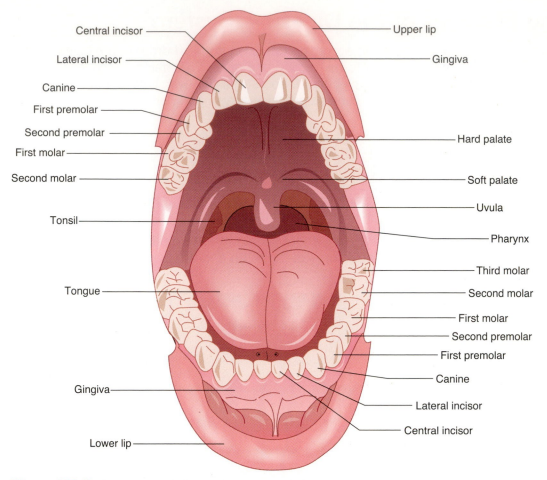

Figure 16-3 Structures of the oral cavity (From Ehrlich A, Schroeder CL. *Medical Terminology for Health Professionals*, 4th ed. Clifton Park, NY: Delmar, Cengage Learning, 2001, p. 167.)

Disease of Esophagus, Stomach, and Duodenum (Category Codes K20–K31)

The **esophagus** connects the throat to the stomach. When food and water pass through the oral cavity, they travel down the esophagus to the stomach. When a person has an upset stomach and vomits, the reverse occurs. **Esophagitis** is an inflammation of the esophagus due to the reflux of acid and pepsin from the stomach into the esophagus. **Gastroesophageal reflux disease (GERD)** is a common condition that primary care providers treat.

The esophagus connects to the **stomach**, a pouch-like structure. The stomach connects to the **duodenum**, where the small intestine begins. Figure 16-4 illustrates the stomach and its structures as well as its relation to the esophagus and the duodenum.

The duodenum extends to the **jejunum**, which is the middle portion of the small intestine. The jejunum connects the duodenum to the **ileum**, which is the last part of the small intestine. The ileum connects to the **cecum**, which is the beginning of the large intestine. Coders must know where certain structures stop and start so that they assign the correct codes.

Coding of Gastrointestinal Ulcers

Ulcerations of the gastrointestinal (GI) tract occur when there is erosion of the mucous membrane.

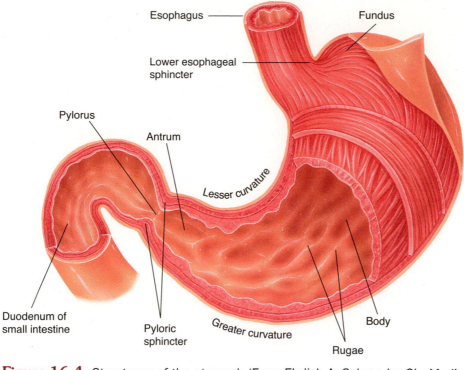

Esophagus

Fundus

Lower esophageal
sphincter

Pylorus

Antrum

Lesser curvature

Duodenum of
small intestine

Pyloric
sphincter

Greater curvature

Body

Rugae

Figure 16-4   Structures of the stomach (From Ehrlich A, Schroeder CL. *Medical Terminology for Health Professionals*, 4th ed. Clifton Park, NY: Delmar, Cengage Learning, 2001, p. 169.)

Disease Highlight—Gastrointestinal Ulcers

Gastrointestinal ulcers occur throughout the gastrointestinal tract and include gastric, duodenal, peptic, and gastrojejunal ulcers. All ulcers involve the destruction of tissue occurring in areas that are exposed to acid and/or pepsin. The mucous membrane penetrates through the muscularis mucosa and becomes inflamed. The etiology of ulcers is unclear, but contributing factors include the reflux of bile or hyperacidity in the stomach, the extended use of anti-inflammatory drugs such as aspirin, the heavy intake of steroids and alcohol, smoking, and the presence of *Helicobacter pylori* bacteria.

Signs and Symptoms:

Patients with gastrointestinal ulcers complain of burning pain in the stomach or epigastric region, which may or may not subside with food intake or use of antacids. Patients also experience:

- Weight loss.

- Nausea.

- Vomiting.

- Anemia.

Clinical Testing:

Ulcers are diagnosed by means of:

- Upper GI and barium studies (endoscopy), which shows the ulceration.

(*continued*)

- Lab tests that review the patient's hemoglobin, hematocrit, and serum gastric and amylase levels. Hemoglobin and hematocrit are decreased in patients with bleeding from the ulcer. Serum gastrin and serum amylase levels are increased.

- Stool sample, which can be positive for occult blood.

Treatment:

Treatment for patients with ulcers is directed at decreasing the acidity of the ulcer site, thereby promoting the healing of the mucosa.

- Elimination of contributing factors is essential.

- Antacids and dietary restrictions neutralize the gastric acids.

- If *Helicobacter pylori* is present, patients are given antibiotics.

- Patients are encouraged to eat nutritious and regular meals.

- Anticholinergic drugs are prescribed to reduce the secretion of acid.

- Surgical intervention is necessary in severe cases when patient have a hemorrhage, perforation, obstruction, or severe pain from the ulcer site.

ICD-10-CM classifies ulcers according to the site of the ulcer by using the following category codes:

- **Gastric ulcer**, category code K25—An ulcer that occurs in the stomach

- **Duodenal ulcer**, category code K26—An ulcer that occurs in the upper part of the small intestine

- **Peptic ulcer** (site unspecified), category code K27—An ulcer that occurs in an unspecified site of the GI tract

- **Gastrojejunal ulcer**, category code K28—An ulcer that occurs in the stomach and jejunum

  EXAMPLE: An 82-year-old man presents today for persistent pain in the stomach. The patient states that he suffers from indigestion, nausea, and darker-than-normal stools. Lab results indicate that the patient is anemic and that the guaiac is positive. When the stomach area is palpated, pain is noted around the lower stomach area. After endoscopic examination, the patient is confirmed to have an acute gastrojejunal ulcer, which has not yet begun to hemorrhage. No obstructions are noted, and, because we have not encountered hemorrhaging, medication is prescribed at this time for treatment.

Because the confirmed diagnosis of acute gastrojejunal ulcer is given, the code assigned is K28.3, Acute gastrojejunal ulcer without mention of hemorrhage or perforation. The K25–K28 category codes are differentiated by whether the ulcer is acute, chronic, or unspecified and whether hemorrhage and/or perforation are present.

Diseases of Appendix (Category Codes K35–K38)

The **appendix** is a wormlike structure that is found, in most people, at the blind end of the cecum. When the appendix becomes inflamed or infected, a condition known as **appendicitis**, the patient may experience pain and the white blood cell count becomes elevated. The appendix does not serve any known purpose in the digestive system, but it is the most common nonobstetrical problem encountered during pregnancy. Figure 16-5 illustrates the location of the appendix.

In the case of appendicitis, the coder must determine whether any other complications are associated with the appendicitis, such as generalized peritonitis or peritoneal abscess. The coder should also note whether the term is modified by the terms *acute, chronic,* or *recurrent*. These complications and terms all affect code assignment.

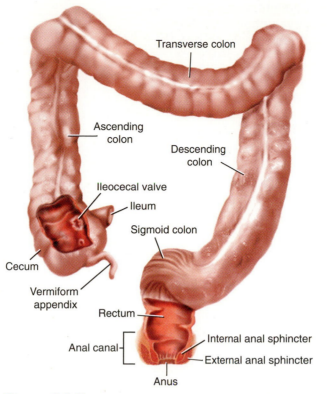

Figure 16-5 Large intestine and location of appendix

EXAMPLE: The diagnostic statement of appendicitis codes to K37, Unspecified appendicitis. Chronic appendicitis and recurrent appendicitis code to K36. Acute appendicitis codes to category K35 with differentiation to indicate the following:

- K35.2, Acute appendicitis with generalized peritonitis

- K35.3, Acute appendicitis with localized peritonitis

- K35.80, Acute appendicitis, unspecified

- K35.89, Other acute appendicitis

Hernia (Category Codes K40–K46)

A **hernia** is simply a protrusion or bulge through the tissue that normally contains the structure. There are several different types of hernias.

An **inguinal hernia** occurs when a part of the intestine passes through a weak point or tear in the wall that holds the abdominal organs. Sometimes the doctor's note refers to a "**direct inguinal hernia**," which is a protrusion in the groin area. An **indirect inguinal hernia** is a protrusion that has moved to the scrotum. These types of hernias code to the K40 category and require additional digits to indicate whether the hernia is unilateral or bilateral, whether it is recurrent, and whether gangrene or an obstruction is present.

EXAMPLE: A 23-year-old man presents with a bulging in the scrotal area on the right side. The patient experiences sharp pain on the right when urinating. Over the last week, patient has noticed pain in the area at the end of his workday. The patient has not experienced this before and is quite concerned. Upon examination, it was determined that the patient is suffering from an indirect inguinal hernia. We will refer him to a surgeon for further evaluation.

Code assignment in our example is K40.90. The K40.90, Unilateral inguinal hernia, without obstruction or gangrene, not specified as recurrent, is chosen based on the information given in the note. There is no mention of obstruction or gangrene, which may change with the surgeon's evaluation. With the information given, the hernia appears to be on only the right side and is not recurrent.

Other types of hernias are a femoral hernia, umbilical hernia, ventral hernia, diaphragmatic hernia, and hiatal hernia. Hiatal hernias are common and are coded to category K44. A **hiatal hernia** is the sliding of part of the stomach into the chest cavity. (See Figure 16-6.) The coder needs to indicate whether the hernia is with obstruction, with gangrene, or without obstruction and gangrene.

Noninfective Enteritis and Colitis (Category Code K50–K52)

Noninfectious enteritis and colitis are classified to category codes K50–K52. **Enteritis** is an inflammation of the intestines, and **colitis** is an inflammation of the colon. Conditions that are classified to this section include Crohn's disease and ulcerative colitis. **Crohn's disease** (K50), also known as **regional enteritis**, is a form of inflammatory bowel disease that can cause the thickening and scarring of the abdominal wall; most commonly found in the large intestine, it can attack anywhere in the GI tract. Fourth characters are used to identify the specific site affected. Additional fifth and sixth characters are also assigned.

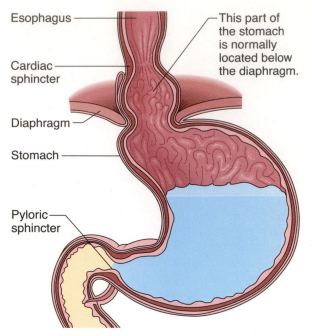

Figure 16-6 Hiatal hernia (From Neighbors M, Tannehill-Jones R. *Human Diseases*, 2nd ed. Clifton Park, NY: Delmar, Cengage Learning, 2001, p. 191.)

> **EXAMPLE:** Mark presented with diarrhea, which has been going on for the last week, along with abdominal pain, fever, and noticeable weight loss. The physician ordered a barium enema and small bowel X-ray. The results of these tests confirmed a diagnosis of Crohn's disease of the small intestine.

Crohn's disease of the small intestine is classified to subcategory K50.0, Crohn's disease of the large intestine is classified to subcategory K50.1, Crohn's disease of both small and large intestine is classified to subcategory K50.8, and Crohn's disease, unspecified, is classified to subcategory K50.9. Additional characters are used with all of these subcategories to indicate whether rectal bleeding, intestinal obstruction, fistula, abscess, or some other complication is present. **Ulcerative colitis** affects the colon by causing frequent diarrhea. The colon becomes inflamed, and ulcers develop in the lining of the intestine. Ulcerative colitis is classified to category code K51 with additional characters to identify the site affected.

To accurately code Crohn's disease and ulcerative colitis, the coder needs to identify the site by reviewing the patient's medical record. If the site cannot be determined from review of the medical documentation, query the provider.

Other Diseases of the Intestines (Category Codes K55–K63)

Common conditions that are classified to this section of the code book are diverticulosis and diverticulitis. **Diverticula** are abnormal pouches or sacs in the lining of the intestine that cause a condition known as **diverticulosis**. If these sacs become inflamed, the patient is diagnosed with **diverticulitis**. A note at the beginning of the K57.0, K57.2, K57.4, and K57.8 subcategories indicates that diverticulitis with peritonitis is included in these subcategories. **Peritonitis** is an inflammation of the lining of the abdominal cavity.

When coding diverticulosis or diverticulitis, coders must determine the site of the condition: either the small intestine or large intestine. Coders must also determine whether the condition occurs with or without bleeding and whether perforation and an abscess is present.

Category K58 is used to report irritable bowel syndrome, irritable colon, and spastic colon. Category K59 is used to report other functional intestinal disorders such as constipation, functional diarrhea, neurogenic bowel, anal spasm, and other functional intestinal disorders.

Diseases of Peritoneum and Retroperitoneum (Category Codes K65–K68)

This block of codes is used to report the following:

- K65, Peritonitis
- K66, Other disorders of the peritoneum
- K67, Disorders of peritoneum in infectious diseases classified elsewhere
- K68, Disorders of retroperitoneum

> **Note:**
>
> *Coders need to become familiar with the numerous instructional notations and Excludes 1 notes in this section.*

Disease of Liver (Category Codes K70–K77)

This block of codes includes codes for diseases of the liver. The liver is considered one of the accessory organs of the digestive system. (See Figure 16-7.) The **liver** filters red blood cells, produces glycogen, and secretes **bile**, which breaks down fat. A coder may encounter the term **hepatic**, which means pertaining to the liver.

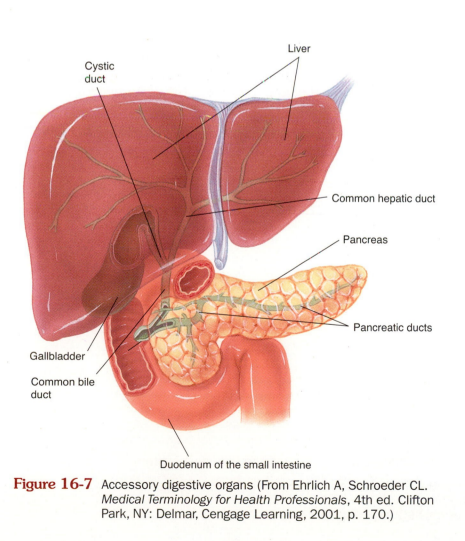

Figure 16-7 Accessory digestive organs (From Ehrlich A, Schroeder CL. *Medical Terminology for Health Professionals*, 4th ed. Clifton Park, NY: Delmar, Cengage Learning, 2001, p. 170.)

The category codes for this block are:

- K70, Alcoholic liver disease. (An additional code is used to identify alcohol abuse and dependence.)
- K71, Toxic liver disease.
- K72, Hepatic failure, not elsewhere classified.
- K73, Chronic hepatitis, not elsewhere classified.
- K74, Fibrosis and cirrhosis of liver.
- K75, Other inflammatory liver diseases.
- K76, Other diseases of liver.
- K77, Liver disorders in diseases classified elsewhere.

Disorders of Gall Bladder, Biliary Tract, and Pancreas (Category Codes K80–K87)

The **gallbladder** is found under the liver and is connected to the liver via the cystic duct. The purpose of the gallbladder is to store bile secreted by the liver until the bile is needed in digestion. The **pancreas** is located behind the stomach and is connected to the gallbladder and the liver by the common bile duct. This organ has a function in both the digestive system and the endocrine system. The pancreas secretes juices necessary for digestion but also regulates blood sugar levels through the release of the hormone insulin.

Cholecystitis and Cholelithiasis

Cholecystitis, a sudden and severe onset of inflammation of the gallbladder, and **cholelithiasis**, the formation or presence of gallstones, are classified to this section of the code book. Cholecystitis and cholelithiasis can occur with or without the other condition. The coder must therefore review the medical documentation carefully to identify the clinical picture of the patient.

Cholelithiasis is classified to category code K80, with additional digits used to identify the location of the gallstones and whether cholecystitis is present or not. Digits are also used to identify an obstruction. Cholecystitis is classified to category code K81.

Category K82 reports other diseases of gallbladder, and category K83 reports other diseases of the biliary tract. Acute pancreatitis is reported with category code K85, other diseases of the pancreas are reported with K86, and K87 reports disorders of the gallbladder, biliary tract, and pancreas in diseases classified elsewhere.

Other Diseases of the Digestive System (Category Codes K90–K94)

The last block of codes reports other diseases of the digestive system. This includes the following category codes:

- K90, Intestinal malabsorption
- K91, Intraoperative and postprocedural complications and disorders of digestive system, not elsewhere classified
- K92, Other diseases of digestive system
- K94, Complications of artificial openings of the digestive system

The K94 category codes differentiate colostomy, enterostomy, gastrostomy, and esophagostomy complications.

Comparing ICD-9-CM to ICD-10-CM

As we have seen in other chapters of ICD-10-CM, the chapter 11 codes are expanded in ICD-10-CM. Section K91, Intraoperative and postprocedural complications and disorders of the digestive system, has been added. The expansion and addition of codes has occurred as follows:

- Category K42, Umbilical hernia, now includes fourth characters that indicate whether an obstruction or/and gangrene is present.

- Changes in category titles and the use of fourth-character levels have impacted the coding of abscess of anal and rectal regions, K61.

- Diseases of the liver, K70–K77, has been added.

- Disorders of the gallbladder, biliary tract, and pancreas have been added, K80–K87.

- Crohn's disease has been expanded at the fourth-, fifth-, and sixth-character levels to specify the site of the disease, indicating whether a complication is present and identifying specific complications.

- Irritable bowel syndrome, K58, includes fourth characters to indicate whether the disease is with or without diarrhea.

- Specific categories have been created for embedded and impacted teeth (K01), dyspepsia (K30), and chronic hepatitis (K73).

- The coding of ulcers has been refined.

- Hernias (K40–K46) are classified according to type with fourth and sometimes fifth characters indicating an obstruction, gangrene, laterality, and recurrence.

- Cholelithiasis (K80) is expanded at the fourth-character level in ICD-10-CM to identify whether cholangitis or cholecystitis is present.

Internet Links

To learn more about diseases and conditions of the digestive system, visit
http://www.gastro.org, *http://www.jr2.ox.ac.uk*, and *http://www.saem.org*

The Cleveland Clinic has a Web site that can be found at *http://my.clevelandclinic.org*. Search on the names of diseases of the gastrointestinal system. This site has abundant information on gastrointestinal disorders.

Additional information can also be found at *www.iffgd.org*. This site is maintained by the International Foundation for Functional Gastrointestinal Disorders.

Summary

- The digestive process begins when food is taken into the mouth for nourishment and finishes its work with the elimination of waste.

- The *alimentary canal* and the *gastrointestinal tract* are terms used to describe the digestive system.

- Diseases of the oral cavity, including the teeth, are included in chapter 11 of ICD-10-CM.

- Accessory organs, such as the appendix, liver, gallbladder, and pancreas, are also classified to chapter 11 off ICD-10-CM.

- Appendicitis can be accompanied by peritonitis or peritoneal abscess.

- Hernias are classified in ICD-10-CM according to the site of the hernia.
- Noninfectious enteritis and colitis are classified to chapter 11 of ICD-10-CM.
- Diverticula are abnormal sacs in the lining of the intestine.
- Diverticulitis occurs when there is an inflammation of the diverticula.

Chapter Review

True/False: Indicate whether the statement is true (T) or false (F).

1. _____ Food is broken down for nourishment by the digestive tract.

2. _____ Cholelithiasis means kidney stones.

3. _____ The pancreas is not an accessory organ.

4. _____ Irregularly shaped patches that appear on the tongue are known as mapped tongue.

5. _____ The stomach is a pouch-like structure that connects to the esophagus on one end and to the ileum on the other.

Fill-in-the-Blank: Enter the appropriate term(s) to complete each statement.

6. An infection of the pulp and the surrounding tissue in the mouth is called _____.

7. An inflammation of the esophagus due to acid reflux is known as _____.

8. The _____ secretes bile, which breaks down fat.

9. The _____ has functions in both the digestive and endocrine system.

10. Hernias are classified in ICD-10-CM according to _____.

Coding Assignments

Instructions: Using an ICD-10-CM code book, assign the proper diagnosis code to the following diagnostic statements.

Diagnosis	Code
1. chronic pulpitis	_____
2. reflux esophagitis	_____
3. odontogenesis imperfecta	_____
4. recurrent bilateral femoral hernia	_____
5. hematemesis	_____
6. denture hyperplasia	_____
7. phlebitis of portal vein	_____
8. stenosis of cystic duct	_____
9. sliding hiatal hernia	_____

10. GERD   _____

11. gastric diverticulum   _____

12. umbilical hernia   _____

13. dental pulp degeneration   _____

14. granulomatous colitis   _____

15. dentinal dysplasia   _____

16. pyloric stenosis   _____

17. fecalith of appendix   _____

18. Barrett's esophagus   _____

19. hypertophic gastritis with hemorrhage   _____

20. biliary cirrhosis   _____

21. IBS with diarrhea   _____

22. calculus of gallbladder and bile duct with acute
    cholecystitis with obstruction   _____

23. hepatic infarction   _____

24. fistula of bile duct   _____

25. pancreatic steatorrhea   _____

Case Studies

Instructions: Review each case study and select the correct ICD-10-CM diagnostic code.

CASE 1

CHIEF COMPLAINT: Abdominal pain

HISTORY: This is a 70-year-old man who had a diagnostic sigmoidoscopy done 3 days ago for rectal bleeding. He is having some abdominal pain. He has noted some nausea and pain when he eats solid food. He says he feels better if he has only liquids, and once he has a bowel movement he feels better.

When asked if he knew the results of his sigmoidoscopy, he replied that the doctor had told him he had some diverticula. He denies any diarrhea but said there is some constipation. He also denies chest pain or shortness of breath. He has had some coughing, but no other symptoms are noted. All other reviews of systems are noted as normal.

PAST MEDICAL HISTORY: Positive for diverticulosis. No known allergies, no diabetes. Patient had thyroidectomy 25 years ago.

EXAM:

HEENT: Normal

MOUTH: Partially edentulous; gums look healthy.

(continued)

HEART: Regular sinus rate and rhythm; heart sounds are good.

LUNGS: Clear to auscultation and percussion.

ABDOMEN: Soft; slight tenderness on palpation in lower left quadrant; no organomegaly; no masses palpable; bowel sounds good.

GENITALIA: Normal male.

RECTAL: Good sphincter tone; guaiac testing shows occult blood; blood is noted upon visual exam.

EXTREMITIES: No edema, ulceration, or discoloration; pedal pulses are normal.

NEUROLOGICAL: Normal

IMPRESSION: Diverticulitis with hemorrhage

PLAN: We will begin antibiotic therapy with Flagyl.

ICD-10-CM Code Assignment: _____

CASE 2

This is a 25-year-old female with a history of ulcerative colitis who presents today with diarrhea and bleeding. She was hospitalized last June with a similar problem and had been on IV steroids and then oral steroids prior to discharge. She has been off the steroids now for approximately 2 months and had been doing fairly well. She now is having abdominal cramping and loose stools, which have become bloody. She noted that over the last 48 hours, her bowel movements have increased dramatically, which is why she has presented to the ER. She has been drinking and eating very bland foods, as well as avoiding dairy products. Nothing seems to help.

PHYSICAL EXAM: This is a 25-year-old female who appears slightly dehydrated and in mild distress.

Temp: 98.1; respiratory rate: 20; pulse: 110 and regular; BP: 100/70

HEENT: Normal; oral cavity is moist without lesions.

NECK: Supple, no thyromegaly or lymphadenopathy

CHEST: Clear to auscultation and percussion

HEART: No murmurs, rubs, or gallops

ABDOMEN: Nondistended. Normal bowel sounds. Some epigastric tenderness with deep palpation, without radiation. Has some right lower quadrant discomfort without rebound or guarding associated.

RECTAL: Some internal hemorrhoids noted. Stool is light brown and not bloody at this time.

IMPRESSION and PLAN: Exacerbation of ulcerative colitis with rectal bleeding. Admit patient at this time. Would like to start IV rehydration and also intravenous steroids. Will observe stool count, consistency, and whether there is blood in the stool. Amylase, creatinine, BUN, WBC, Hgb, and MCV ordered.

ICD-10-CM Code Assignment: _____

CASE 3

Skilled Nursing Facility Monthly Progress Note

This resident was admitted in May of this year with the primary diagnoses of diabetes mellitus and chronic gastritis. The patient has been complaining of heartburn and is occasionally irritated by banana and some cereals. She denies any nausea or vomiting, but she thinks that every time she eats there is fullness in the stomach.

PHYSICAL EXAMINATION:

She is alert, conscious, not in any acute pain or distress. Fasting blood sugar is 86; BP 120/74; P, 80 per minute and regular; R, 20; and temp, 95.7. Her weight is 110.

Abdomen is soft. Bowel sounds are positive; it is not distended, and there is tenderness.

HEART: regular rhythm with no change in the systolic murmur.

Lung is clear to auscultation.

MEDICATIONS INCLUDE: See medication list for her current medications. Start Maalox 15cc 3 times a day for chronic gastritis. I will reevaluate her if she needs additional medication for her gastritis.

ICD-10-CM Code Assignment: _____

CASE 4

ED Summary Note

Sylvia presented to the ED with abdominal distention and pain, along with nausea, and reported an earlier bout of vomiting. Upon examination, no bowel sounds were noted, but an increase in white cell count was noted. Barium studies showed a twisting of the intestine. A surgical consult was requested for Sylvia.

ICD-10-CM Code Assignment: _____

CASE 5

ED Summary Note

Kyle presented to the ED with abdominal distention and tenderness, a fever of 102°, and a complaint of nausea. Kyle has a history of perforated peptic ulcer. Physical exam was performed, along with arterial blood gases (which showed lowered potassium and carbon dioxide), urinalysis, and lab tests, all of which confirm the diagnosis of generalized acute peritonitis.

ICD-10-CM Code Assignment: _____

Diseases of the Skin and Subcutaneous Tissue

Chapter Outline

Objectives

At the conclusion of this chapter, the learner should be able to:

1. Identify and name the layers of the skin.
2. Explain the conditions classified in this chapter.
3. Code diagnoses of diseases of the skin and subcutaneous tissue.
4. Select and code diagnoses and procedures from case studies.

Key Terms

abscess	decubitus ulcers	hives	pressure ulcers
alopecia	dermatitis	integumentary	sebaceous glands
bedsores	dermis	melanocytes	subcutaneous
carbuncles	epidermis	melanoma	ulcers
cellulitis	hair	nails	urticaria
cutane	hirsutism	pressure sores	

Reminder

As you work through this chapter, you will need to have a copy of the ICD-10-CM coding book to reference.

Introduction

Diseases of the skin and subcutaneous tissue, category code range L00–L99, are classified in chapter 12 of ICD-9-CM, "Diseases of the Skin and Subcutaneous Tissue." The following blocks of codes are in this chapter:

- L00–L08, Infections of the skin and subcutaneous tissue

- L10–L14, Bullous disorders

- L20–L30, Dermatitis and eczema

- L40–L45, Papulosquamous disorders

- L49–L54, Urticaria and erythema

- L55–L59, Radiation-related disorders of the skin and subcutaneous tissue

- L60–L75, Disorders of skin appendages

- L76, Intraoperative and postprocedural complications of skin and subcutaneous tissue

- L80–L99, Other disorders of the skin and subcutaneous tissue

Introduction to the Body System

The coding in this chapter classifies disorders and diseases of the integumentary system, or the skin. **Integumentary** means "covering" or "outer layer." The integumentary system acts as a shield for the body and is considered the largest body system. The functions of the integumentary system include the protection of deeper tissue by retaining fluid in the body and the regulation of body temperature by controlling heat loss. This natural shield also works as a factor in the immune system by blocking bacteria and other foreign materials from entering the body. Receptors for touch are located on the skin. Because the skin is porous, it protects the body from ultraviolet radiation from the sun while letting the ultraviolet light in so that the body can produce vitamin D. The skin also temporarily stores the fat, glucose, water, and salts that are absorbed by the blood and used by various organs of the body.

The skin is specialized tissue made up of three layers. The **epidermis** is the outermost layer of the skin. Epithelial tissues make up the epidermis. There are no blood vessels or connective tissue within the epidermis; so this layer of skin depends on the lower layers for nourishment.

The color of the skin is determined by the amount of melanin pigment contained in **melanocytes**, or cells that produce dark pigment. When these cells exhibit abnormal behavior, a person might be diagnosed with melanoma. **Melanoma** is a fast-growing cancer of the skin, usually identified as a mole that has changed in some way.

The **dermis** is the thick layer of tissue located directly below the epidermis. This is the layer of skin that enables a person to recognize touch, pain, pressure, and temperature changes. This layer of skin contains blood and lymph vessels, so it is more sensitive and self-sufficient than the epidermis.

The layer of skin that connects to the muscle surface is called the **subcutaneous** layer. **Cutane** means "skin," so *subcutaneous* means "below the skin." Fat cells are found in this layer of skin. Figure 17-1 illustrates the three layers of skin and some of the structures they contain.

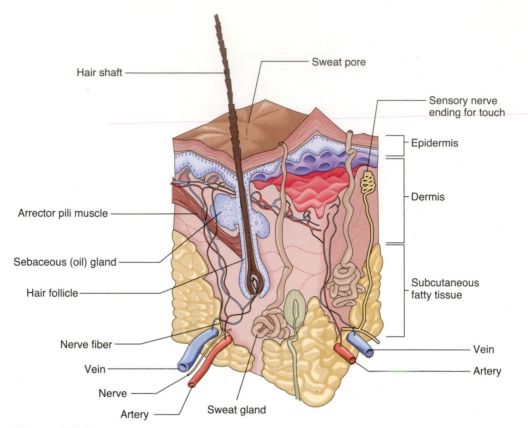

Figure 17-1 Cross section of the skin (From Scott AS, Fong E. *Body Structures and Functions*, 9th ed. Clifton Park, NY: Delmar, Cengage Learning, 1998, p. 58.)

Coding of Diseases of the Skin and Subcutaneous Tissue

Coding for this chapter includes diseases and disorders not only of the skin but also of the nails, sweat glands, hair, and hair follicles. Figure 17-2 illustrates various diseases of the skin.

Infections of Skin and Subcutaneous Tissue (Category Codes L00–L08)

The first section of this chapter classifies disorders such as cellulitis, carbuncles, and furuncles, which may be caused by bacterial organisms. The following notation appears right after the heading for this block of codes.

> Use additional code (B95–B97) to identify infectious agent.

Therefore two codes may be needed to code diagnostic statements.

Category code L00 reports staphylococcal scalded skin syndrome, and category code L01 reports impetigo. Cutaneous abscess, furuncle, and carbuncle are reported using category code L02.

Carbuncles occur when furuncles cluster and form a pus-filled sac. Additional characters are used in the L02 category to identify the anatomic site of the abscess, furuncle, or carbuncle.

NONPALPABLE

Macule:
Localized changes in skin color of less than 1 cm in diameter
Example: Freckle

Patch:
Localized changes in skin color of greater than 1 cm in diameter
Examples: Vitiligo, stage 1 of pressure ulcer

PALPABLE

Papule:
Solid, elevated lesion less than 0.5 cm in diameter
Examples: Warts, elevated nevus

Plaque:
Solid, elevated lesion greater than 0.5 cm in diameter
Example: Psoriasis

Nodules:
Solid and elevated, but extending deeper than papules into the dermis or subcutaneous tissues, 0.5–2.0 cm
Examples: Lipoma, erythema nodosum, cyst

Wheal:
Localized edema in the epidermis causing irregular elevation that may be red or pale
Examples: Insect bite, hives

FLUID-FILLED CAVITIES WITHIN THE SKIN

Vesicle:
Accumulation of fluid between the upper layers of the skin; elevated mass containing serous fluid; less than 0.5 cm
Examples: Herpes simplex, herpes zoster, chickenpox

Bulla:
Same as a vesicle only greater than 0.5 cm
Examples: Contact dermatitis, large second degree burns, bulbous impetigo, pemphigus

Pustule:
Vesicles or bullae that become filled with pus, usually described as less than 0.5 cm in diameter
Examples: Acne, impetigo, furuncles, carbuncles, folliculitis

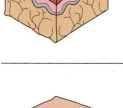

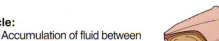

Figure 17-2 Disorders of the skin (From Sormunen C. *Terminology for Allied Health Professions*, 5th ed. Clifton Park, NY: Delmar, Cengage Learning, 2003, p. 103.)

EXAMPLE:

> S: Patient presents with a "bump on my neck" that is beginning to hurt. Patient cannot recall any injury to the area. Patient has started with a low-grade fever of 99.3 and has noticed an increase in the pain over the last day or two.

> O: Upon examination, a large red lump is located at the base of the posterior side of the neck. The lump is fluctuating and causes pain upon touch.

> A & P: Carbuncle of the neck. At this time we will start antibiotics and warm compresses. If this does not relieve some of the pain and some improvement is not noticed in the next 5 days, he will return and we will look at other options.

The code for this example is L02.13, Carbuncle of neck.

Categories L03 classify cellulitis and acute lymphangitis. **Cellulitis** is another type of infection that develops within the layers of the skin that can be a result of an ulcer, laceration, or wound. In some cases, two codes are necessary when coding a patient encounter for cellulitis. Reference to provider documentation is necessary for determining the need for two codes and also their sequencing. If cellulitis is noticed when a patient is being treated for an open wound or a burn, the open wound or burn is coded first with an additional code for the cellulitis. If the cellulitis is what brought the patient in after treatment has already been rendered for another condition, such as a burn or open wound, the cellulitis is coded first with the burn or open wound second. The open wound is coded as complicated in either case because complication indicates infection. Also, if cellulitis is associated with an open wound that has been repaired, the documentation should reflect whether the cellulitis is a postoperative infection. These issues are discussed further in Chapter 24 of this textbook when injuries are discussed.

This section of the chapter also classifies abscesses. An **abscess** is a localized collection of pus and indicates tissue destruction. As with cellulitis, if an organism is identified as the cause of the abscess, this finding should be coded in addition to the code for the abscess.

Documentation is critical for these categories of the chapter. The coder needs to reference the provider note to accurately code the condition, the sequencing, and the site of the cellulitis or abscess.

Exercise 17.1 – Coding Category Codes L00–L08

For each diagnostic statement, select the appropriate ICD-10-CM code(s).

1. carbuncle of face _____
2. pyoderma _____
3. acute lymphangitis of trunk _____
4. cutaneous abscess of right lower limb _____
5. acute lymphangitis of right axilla _____
6. acute lymphadenitis of face _____
7. cellulitis of toes _____
8. furuncle of right hand _____
9. cellulitis of neck _____
10. furuncle of the right axilla _____

Bullous Disorders (Category Codes L10–L14)

This block of codes is divided into the following categories:

- L10, Pemphigus
- L11, Other acantholytic disorders

- L12, Pemphigoid
- L13, Other bullous disorders
- L14, Bullous disorders in diseases classified elsewhere

Each category is further divided into various types of the disorders.

Dermatitis and Eczema (Category Codes L20–L30)

This section of the chapter contains codes for common conditions such as cradle cap, dermatitis, eczema, and erythematosquamous dermatosis. **Dermatitis** is an inflammation of the upper layer of the skin and is classified to this section of the chapter. Various types of dermatitis exist; therefore, if a provider documents a specific type of dermatitis, a coder must select a code to identify the type, such as category code L20, Atopic dermatitis or category code L21, Seborrheic dermatitis.

Another type of dermatitis coded to this section of the chapter is dermatitis due to medication. A distinction is made here between drugs ingested and drugs or plants that come into contact with the skin topically. Category L27, Dermatitis due to substances taken internally, is used if the coder sees the diagnosis of drug eruption, dermatitis medicamentosa, or medication properly administered with an allergic reaction or adverse side effect. A reaction to medication ingested is when a patient ingests the proper medication prescribed by a medical professional at the proper dosage. A notation appears after the heading for L27 that instructs the coder to "Code first (T36–T65) to identify drug or substance."

EXAMPLE:

S: A 21-month-old male presents today with low-grade fever, hives, and slight swelling in the joints of the lower extremities. Mother notes that child was started on Amoxicillin, 500 mg, for an ear infection. Child started medication 1 day ago. Review was made with mom on the dosage. Child was given proper dosage but now appears to have had an allergic reaction.

O: Upon examination, child is alert and in no acute distress. He is a bit lethargic but is not crying or fussy. He allows examination of ears: TMs red, some fluid. Rest of HEENT is unremarkable. Skin is warm to touch, and it should be noted that child has low-grade temp of 99.8. He is showing a localized skin eruption on the trunk, and it is now moving to the extremities. Joints of the upper extremities are fine, but the lower extremities are showing signs of slight swelling. As for rest of exam, heart and lungs are normal. No other problems noted in either of these areas.

A: Allergic reaction to Amoxicillin

P: Will start child on Benadryl and change the antibiotic to Ceclor for the ear infection. If he is not exhibiting signs of reduced hives and disappearance of joint swelling in 24 hours or if temperature spikes and reaction starts to become worse, mom will bring child back here, if during regular office hours, or to the Emergency Room, if after hours.

This example clearly describes an allergic reaction to Amoxicillin. The documentation supports that the medication was given properly. The coding for this example is L27.1 and T36.0x5.

Papulosquamous Disorders (Category Codes L40–L45) and Urticaria and Erythema (Category Codes L49–L54)

These two blocks of codes are used to report the following disorders:

- L40, Psoriasis
- L41, Parapsoriasis
- L42, Pityriasis rosea
- L43, Lichen planus
- L44, Other papulosquamous disorders
- L45, Papulosquamous disorders in diseases classified elsewhere
- L49, Exfoliation due to erythematous conditions according to extent of body surface involved

- L50, Urticaria
- L51, Erythema multiforme
- L52, Erythema nodosum
- L53, Other erythematous conditions
- L54, Erythema in diseases classified elsewhere

The L50 category, Urticaria, is used to report **urticaria**, commonly known as **hives**. Fourth digits are needed to specify the type of urticaria: allergic, idiopathic, urticaria due to cold and heat, dermatographic, vibratory, cholinergic, contact, and other forms.

Disease Highlight—Urticaria

Urticaria is a skin disorder in which there are raised edematous areas of skin accompanied by intense itching. Urticaria may be an indication of an allergic reaction to foods, inhaled allergens, drugs, or an insect bite. Nonallergic reactions can be caused by an infection or some type of external physical stimuli.

Signs and Symptoms:

The patient presents with lesions that have very distinct dermal wheals accompanied by erythematous areas surrounding the lesions. In the areas of the wheals there is severe itching.

Clinical Testing:

The following tests may be performed to confirm or rule out an inflammatory process:

- Allergy testing
- Urinalysis
- Sedimentation rate
- CBC

Treatment:

Patients are given antihistamines and instructed to avoid the allergen if the urticaria is caused by an allergic reaction. Topical ointments may also be given.

Radiation-Related Disorders of the Skin and Subcutaneous Tissue (Category Codes L55–L59)

This block of codes is divided as follows:

- L55, Sunburn
- L56, Other acute skin changes due to ultraviolet radiation
- L57, Skin changes due to chronic exposure to nonionizing radiation
- L58, Radiodermatitis
- L59, Other disorders of skin and subcutaneous tissue related to radiation

Sunburn, category L55, is divided according to the degree of the burn. L56 includes drug phototoxic response and photoallergic response. An instructional notation appears to "Use additional code to identify the source of the ultraviolet radiation (W89, X32)." Under codes K56.0 and K56.1 are instructional notations to "Code first (T36–T50) to identify drug."

Disorders of Skin Appendages (Category Codes L60–L75)

This block of codes includes disorders that impact the nails, hair, and skin. Disorders of nails are coded to this section because **nails** are hardened cells of the epidermis. Some of the conditions a coder sees are ingrown nail, code L60.0, and onycholysis, code L60.1.

Conditions involving the hair are coded to this section because hair follicles extend out of the dermis. **Hair** is a form of protection used by the body to keep foreign material from entering through the skin. Some of the conditions a coder might have to code from this section are **hirsutism**, excessive hair growth, coded to L68.0, and **alopecia**, the loss of hair, codes to codes within category L63.

The **sebaceous glands** are located in the skin and produce an oily secretion that conditions the skin. Oversecretion of the sebaceous glands can cause acne. Acne is coded to the L70 category of codes, with fourth digits used to identify the type of acne.

Intraoperative and Postprocedural Complications of Skin and Subcutaneous Tissue (Category Code L76)

This next block contains only one category, L76. This category is further differentiated according to the type of skin complication. Complications include hemorrhage, hematoma, puncture, and lacerations.

Other Diseases of the Skin and Subcutaneous Tissue (Category Codes L80–L99)

This block of codes contain the following categories:

- L80, Vitiligo
- L81, Other disorders of pigmentation
- L82, Seborrheic keratosis
- L83, Acanthosis nigricans
- L84, Corns and callosities
- L85, Other epidermal thickening
- L86, Keratoderma in diseases classified elsewhere
- L87, Transepidermal elimination disorders
- L88, Pyoderma gangrenosum
- L89, Pressure ulcer
- L90, Atrophic disorders of skin
- L91, Hypertrophic disorders of skin
- L92, Granulomatous disorders of skin and subcutaneous tissue
- L93, Lupus erythematosus
- L94, Other localized connective tissue disorders
- L95, Vasculitis limited to skin, not elsewhere classified
- L97, Nonpressure chronic ulcer of lower limb, not elsewhere classified
- L98, Other disorders of skin and subcutaneous tissue, not elsewhere classified
- L99, Other disorders of skin and subcutaneous tissue in diseases classified elsewhere

The L89 category of the chapter also contains codes for pressure ulcers. **Ulcers** are erosions of the skin in which the tissue becomes inflamed and then is lost. Ulcers not only appear on the skin but can be found within the body. A **decubitus ulcer** is a result of continuous pressure in an area that eventually limits or stops circulation and oxygen flow to an area. Decubitus ulcers are also called **pressure ulcers**, **bedsores**, or **pressure sores**.

Ulcers are staged as one through four depending on their severity. The staging affects the coding assignment. ICD-10-CM defines the stages of ulceration as follows:

- Stage I, limited to erythema
- Stage II, abrasion, blister, partial thickness skin loss involving epidermis and dermis
- Stage III, full thickness skin loss involving damage or necrosis of subcutaneous tissue extending to the underlying fascia
- Stage IV, necrosis of muscle, bone, and supporting structures (i.e., the tendon or joint capsule)

The ICD-10-CM Official Guidelines for Coding give the following direction for coding pressure ulcers:

ICD-10-CM Official Coding Guidelines

a. Pressure ulcer stage codes

1) Pressure ulcer stages

Codes from category L89, Pressure ulcer, are combination codes that identify the site of the pressure ulcer as well as the stage of the ulcer.

The ICD-10-CM classifies pressure ulcer stages based on severity, which is designated by stages 1–4, unspecified stage and unstageable.

Assign as many codes from category L89 as needed to identify all the pressure ulcers the patient has, if applicable.

2) Unstageable pressure ulcers

Assignment of the code for unstageable pressure ulcer (L89.–0) should be based on the clinical documentation. These codes are used for pressure ulcers whose stage cannot be clinically determined (e.g., the ulcer is covered by eschar or has been treated with a skin or muscle graft) and pressure ulcers that are documented as deep tissue injury but not documented as due to trauma. This code should not be confused with the codes for unspecified stage (L89.–9). When there is no documentation regarding the stage of the pressure ulcer, assign the appropriate code for unspecified stage (L89.–9).

3) Documented pressure ulcer stage

Assignment of the pressure ulcer stage code should be guided by clinical documentation of the stage or documentation of the terms found in the index. For clinical terms describing the stage that are not found in the index, and there is no documentation of the stage, the provider should be queried.

4) Patients admitted with pressure ulcers documented as healed

No code is assigned if the documentation states that the pressure ulcer is completely healed.

5) Patients admitted with pressure ulcers documented as healing

Pressure ulcers described as healing should be assigned the appropriate pressure ulcer stage code based on the documentation in the medical record. If the documentation does not provide information about the stage of the healing pressure ulcer, assign the appropriate code for unspecified stage.

If the documentation is unclear as to whether the patient has a current (new) pressure ulcer or if the patient is being treated for a healing pressure ulcer, query the provider.

6) Patient admitted with pressure ulcer evolving into another stage during the admission

If a patient is admitted with a pressure ulcer at one stage and it progresses to a higher stage, assign the code for the highest stage reported for that site.

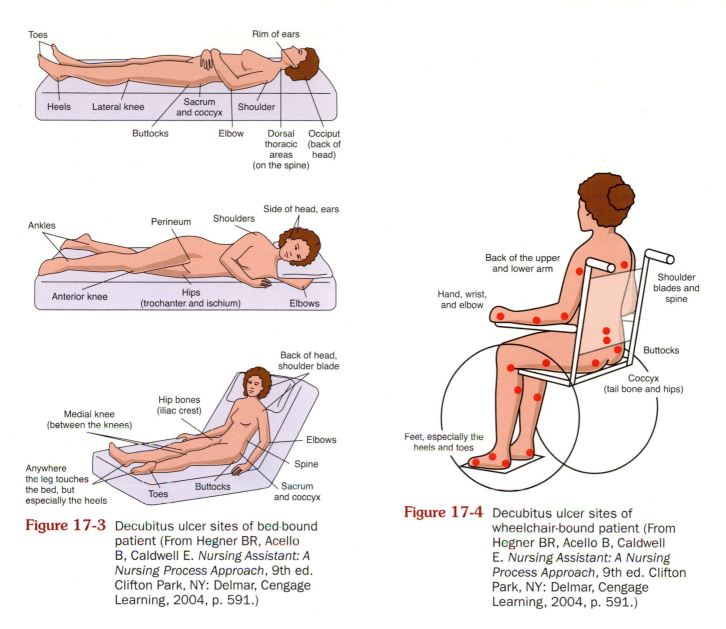

Figure 17-3 Decubitus ulcer sites of bed-bound patient (From Hegner BR, Acello B, Caldwell E. *Nursing Assistant: A Nursing Process Approach*, 9th ed. Clifton Park, NY: Delmar, Cengage Learning, 2004, p. 591.)

Figure 17-4 Decubitus ulcer sites of wheelchair-bound patient (From Hegner BR, Acello B, Caldwell E. *Nursing Assistant: A Nursing Process Approach*, 9th ed. Clifton Park, NY: Delmar, Cengage Learning, 2004, p. 591.)

When selecting codes for pressure ulcers, the coder must be able to identify the site of the ulceration and the stage. If the stage is not recorded, the coder should query the provider or assign the code to indicate that the stage is unspecified.

Patients who are confined to bed or in a wheelchair are at risk for developing decubitus ulcers. Figures 17-3 and 17-4 illustrate common sites of decubitus ulcers for patients confined to bed or a wheelchair.

A notation appears after the category heading that reads, "Code first any associated gangrene (I96)."

EXAMPLE: Debbie Diabetic presents with a heel pressure ulcer. The ulcer has developed gangrene on the wound. I have referred her to the Wound Care Center for treatment today. She will return in approximately 1 week.

The codes for our example are L89.609 for the ulcer and I96 for the gangrene. As with all coding, the medical documentation must be used as a guide in the selection and the sequencing of the codes.

Comparing ICD-9-CM to ICD-10-CM

Compared the ICD-9-CM chapter, ICD-10-CM's "Diseases of the Skin and Subcutaneous Tissue" contains many changes. In ICD-9-CM there were only three sections of codes; in ICD-10-CM there are nine code blocks. With this increase has come numerous title changes and expansions of codes. ICD-10-CM additions, expansions, and changes include:

- The addition of L76, Intraoperative and postprocedural complications of skin and subcutaneous tissue.

- Expansion of the specificity of codes at the fourth-, fifth-, and sixth-character levels to further define pemphigus, alopecia, erythrasma, ainhum, to name a few.

- Carbuncles and furuncles that occur on the trunk have been expanded to further classify the site of the disorder: abdominal wall, back, chest wall, groin, perineum, umbilicus, and unspecified.

- Pressure ulcers are expanded to indicate the site of the ulceration and stage.

- Category L40, Psoriasis, has been expanded to identify the manifestation of the disorder by identifying: psoriasis vulgaris, generalized pustular psoriasis, acrodermatitis continua, and so on.

- L01, Impetigo, now defines specific types.

Internet Links

To learn more about disorders of the skin and subcutaneous system, visit *http://www.medicinenet.com/atopic_dermatitis/article.htm* and *www.emedicine.com*

To learn more about decubitus ulcers, visit: *http://en.wikipedia.org/wiki/Decubitus_ulcer*

Summary

- This chapter codes diseases of the skin, hair, nails, and sebaceous glands.

- The skin is also known as the integumentary system and is made up of three layers: the epidermis, the dermis, and the subcutaneous layers.

- Conditions of the integumentary system include melanoma, furuncles, carbuncles, cellulitis, abscesses, and dermatitis.

- Conditions of the nails are coded to this chapter.

- Codes for skin ulcers are found in this chapter.

Chapter Review

True/False: Indicate whether each statement is true (T) or false (F).

1. _____ Pressure ulcers are also known as bedsores.

2. _____ Patient presents with an open wound of the leg area. During the examination, it is noted that the patient has cellulitis. The wound is coded first, then the cellulitis.

3. _____ The dermis layer is located below the subcutaneous layer of skin.

4. _____ Sclerodactyly is coded with code L94.3.

5. _____ An inflammation of the upper layer of the skin is called alopecia.

Fill-in-the-Blank: Enter the appropriate term(s) to complete each statement.

6. Another name for bedsore or pressure ulcer is _____.

7. The outermost layer of the skin is called the _____.

8. Corns are coded to _____.

9. The subcutaneous layer connects the bottom layer of the skin to the top surface of _____.

10. Another name for skin is _____.

Coding Assignments

Instructions: Using an ICD-10-CM code book, assign the proper diagnosis code to the following diagnostic statements.

Diagnosis	*Code*
1. seborrheic infantile dermatitis	_____
2. cellulitis of cheek	_____
3. stage 2 decubitus ulcer, buttock	_____
4. hidradenitis	_____
5. paronychia of right toe	_____
6. pyogenic granuloma	_____
7. impetigo	_____
8. vitiligo	_____
9. acne varioliformis	_____
10. vegetans dermatitis	_____
11. ingrown toenail	_____
12. carbuncle of left lower leg	_____
13. ulcer of ankle	_____
14. pilonidal cyst with abscess	_____
15. cheloid	_____
16. sunburn	_____
17. acne vulgaris	_____
18. subcutaneous calcification	_____
19. urticaria due to cold and heat	_____
20. stage 3 bedsore of left hip	_____
21. xerosis cutis	_____
22. cicatrix	_____

23. lichen nitidus   _____

24. septic dermatitis   _____

25. benign mucous membrane pemphigus   _____

Case Studies

Instructions: Review each case study and select the correct ICD-10-CM diagnostic code.

CASE 1

S: A 15-year-old male presents with acne. Patient says that he has had continual breakouts over the last 6 months, which appear, to the patient, to be getting worse. He tries not to touch his face and washes it three and four times a day.

O: Examination reveals a well nourished, well developed 15-year-old male with acne lesions on the face. There are also a few lesions on the chest and back. The rest of the skin exam is unremarkable.

A: Acne

P: I explained to patient that washing the face too much is just as harmful as not washing enough.

Patient will wash once in the morning and then again before bed with a mild soap, followed by Differin q.h.s., and will start doxycycline once a day, 100 mg p.o. q.d. He will return in 1 month for follow-up.

ICD-10-CM Code Assignment: _____

CASE 2

Skilled Nursing Facility Note

VITAL SIGNS: See nurse's vital signs sheet.

This patient was admitted in March and she is wheelchair bound.

EXAM:

HEENT: Within normal limits

ABDOMEN: Soft, no masses

HEART: Normal

SKIN: There is skin breakdown in the sacrum area, which shows some necrotic tissue in the ulcerative area. It shows some granulation, and there is drainage at this time. Stage 4 decubitus present.

PLAN: I have instructed the nurses to treat with Sorbsan, packing twice a day and using a dry sterile dressing.

ICD-10-CM Code Assignment: _____

CASE 3

Physician Office Note

Patient presents with a complaint of pain in left hand and has been running a low-grade fever.

EXAM:

EXTREMITIES: Right arm and hand within normal limits. Left hand and thumb are sore to touch. The nail around the thumb is swollen, and the cuticle is edematous and red. The cuticle lifts away from the base, and there is pus present. Paronychia of thumb present.

Antibiotics ordered as per med sheet. Patient encouraged to wash hands frequently.

Patient instructed to follow up in 10 days or if symptoms worsen.

ICD-10-CM Code Assignment: _____

CASE 4

Physician Office Note

Tim is a 5-year-old male who presents today with a red area on his right finger. Mom noticed this spot about 3 weeks ago and said that it has gotten darker than when it first appeared.

The child is having no problems eating or drinking. Upon examination, it is noted that there is a considerable amount of inflammation on the right second finger. This spot is tender. No other spots, lesions, or abnormalities are noted. The diagnosis for this child is cellulitis of right finger.

ICD-10-CM Code Assignment: _____

CASE 5

Physician Office Note

Tess presented today with a complaint of burning and itching around her abdominal scar. The scar is a result of an automobile accident she was in approximately 3 years ago. Upon examination, the scar is approximately 15 cm in length and appears to be elevated and slightly irregular in shape. I believe this to be a keloid and will administer a steroid injection at the site to relieve the symptoms. Tess will return to the office in 2 weeks for follow-up or sooner if necessary.

ICD-10-CM Code Assignment: _____

Diseases of the Musculoskeletal System and Connective Tissue

Chapter Outline

Objectives

At the conclusion of this chapter, the learner should be able to:

1. Identify the anatomical structures of the musculoskeletal system.
2. Explain the conditions and disorders that affect the musculoskeletal system.
3. Discuss specific coding guidelines related to the conditions encountered in the musculoskeletal system.
4. Explain the coding guidelines for coding acute fractures versus aftercare.
5. Select and code diagnoses from case studies.

Key Terms

ankylosing spondylitis	bursa	degenerative joint disease	infectious arthropathies
ankylosis	bursitis		joints
aporosity	cartilage	dorsopathies	ligaments
arthritis	Colles' fracture	Dowager's hump	malunion fracture
bones	compression fractures of the spine	fascia	muscles
		herniated disc	

> **Reminder**
>
> *As you work through this chapter, you will need to have a copy of the ICD-10-CM coding book to reference.*

myelopathy

myositis

nonunion fracture

osteoarthritis (OA)

osteoporosis

pathologic fracture

rheumatism

rheumatoid arthritis (RA)

spondylitis

stress fracture

synovia

tendons

Introduction

This chapter of ICD-10-CM classifies musculoskeletal disorders and conditions that occur as a disease process. Injuries that affect the musculoskeletal system, such as a fracture, are classified to chapter 19 of ICD-10-CM, "Injury, Poisoning and Certain Other Consequences of External Causes," with the exception of stress fractures, pathologic fractures, and malunion of a fracture; these are classified to this chapter of ICD-10-CM. This chapter contains the following blocks of codes:

- M00–M02, Infectious arthropathies
- M05–M14, Inflammatory polyarthropathies
- M15–M19, Osteoarthritis
- M20–M25, Other joint disorders
- M26–M27, Dentofacial anomalies (including malocclusion) and other disorders of jaw
- M30–M36, Systemic connective tissue disorders
- M40–M43, Deforming dorsopathies
- M45–M49, Spondylopathies
- M50–M54, Other dorsopathies
- M60–M63, Disorders of muscles
- M65–M67, Disorders of synovium and tendon
- M70–M79, Other soft tissue disorders
- M80–M85, Disorders of bone density and structure
- M86–M90, Other osteopathies
- M91–M94, Chondropathies
- M95, Other disorders of the musculoskeletal system and connective tissue
- M96, Intraoperative and postprocedural complications and disorders of musculoskeletal system, not elsewhere classified
- M99, Biomechanical lesions, not elsewhere classified

Introduction to the Body System

When coding diseases of the musculoskeletal system and connective tissue, the coder must have good reference materials, a sound understanding of anatomy and physiology, and specific enough documentation from the provider to guide the coder in making the correct code assignment.

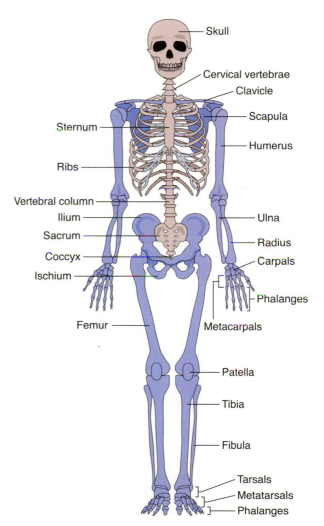

Figure 18-1 Anterior view of the human skeleton (From Ehrlich A, Schroeder CL. *Medical Terminology for Health Professionals*, 4th ed. Clifton Park, NY: Delmar, Cengage Learning, 2001, p. 49.)

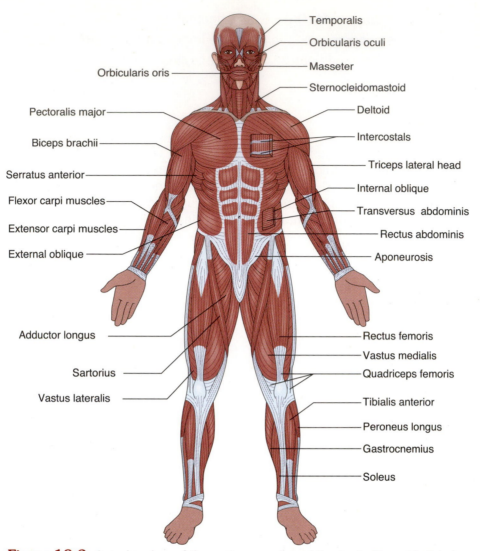

Temporalis
Orbicularis oculi
Orbicularis oris
Masseter
Sternocleidomastoid
Pectoralis major
Deltoid
Biceps brachii
Intercostals
Serratus anterior
Triceps lateral head
Flexor carpi muscles
Internal oblique
Extensor carpi muscles
Transversus abdominis
External oblique
Rectus abdominis
Aponeurosis
Adductor longus
Rectus femoris
Vastus medialis
Sartorius
Quadriceps femoris
Vastus lateralis
Tibialis anterior
Peroneus longus
Gastrocnemius
Soleus

Figure 18-2   Anterior view of the major muscles of the body (From Ehrlich A, Schroeder CL. *Medical Terminology for Health Professionals*, 4th ed. Clifton Park, NY: Delmar, Cengage Learning, 2001, p. 78.)

This chapter of the coding book classifies diseases of the musculoskeletal system. *Musculoskeletal* refers to the **muscles**, which hold the body erect and allow movement, and the **bones**, which are connective tissue that protect the internal organs and form the framework of the body. For correct code assignments to be made from this chapter, coders must understand the terms associated with the musculoskeletal system.

- **Cartilage** is smooth, nonvascular connective tissue that comprises the more flexible parts of the skeleton, such as the outer ear.

- **Joints** allow for bending and rotating movements.

- **Ligaments** are bands of connective tissue that connect the joints.

- **Tendons** connect muscle to bone.

- **Synovia** is the fluid that acts as a lubricant for the joints, tendon sheath, or bursa.

- The **bursa** is the synovial-filled sac that works as a cushion to assist in movement.

- **Fascia** is the connective tissue that not only covers but supports and separates muscles.

Figures 18-1, 18-2, and 18-3 illustrate the anatomical features of the musculoskeletal system.

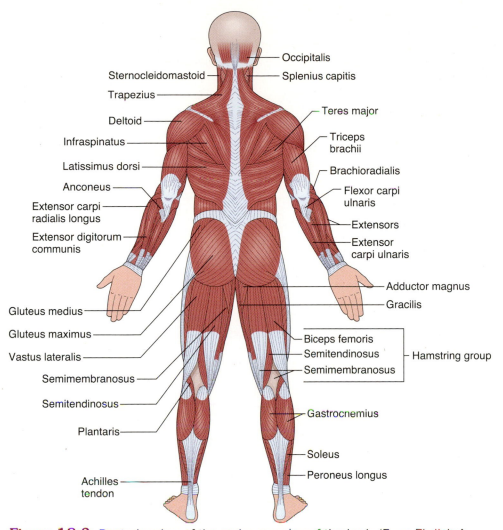

Figure 18-3 Posterior view of the major muscles of the body (From Ehrlich A, Schroeder CL. *Medical Terminology for Health Professionals*, 4th ed. Clifton Park, NY: Delmar, Cengage Learning, 2001, p. 78.)

Coding of Diseases of the Musculoskeletal System and Connective Tissue

The Official Guidelines for Coding and Reporting state the following concerning chapter 13 of ICD-10-CM:

ICD-10-CM Official Coding Guidelines

Site and laterality

a) Most of the codes within chapter 13 have site and laterality designations. The site represents either the bone, joint, or the muscle involved. For some conditions where more than one bone, joint, or muscle is usually involved, such as osteoarthritis, there is a "multiple sites" code available. For categories where no multiple site code is provided and more than one bone, joint, or muscle is involved, multiple codes should be used to indicate the different sites involved.

(continued)

1) Bone versus joint

For certain conditions, the bone may be affected at the upper or lower end, (e.g., avascular necrosis of bone, M87, Osteoporosis, M80, M81). Though the portion of the bone affected may be at the joint, the site designation will be the bone, not the joint.

b) Acute traumatic versus chronic or recurrent musculoskeletal conditions

Many musculoskeletal conditions are a result of previous injury or trauma to a site, or are recurrent conditions. Bone, joint, or muscle conditions that are the result of a healed injury are usually found in chapter 13. Recurrent bone, joint, or muscle conditions are also usually found in chapter 13. Any current, acute injury should be coded to the appropriate injury code from chapter 19. Chronic or recurrent conditions should generally be coded with a code from chapter 13. If it is difficult to determine from the documentation in the record which code is best to describe a condition, query the provider.

Keep these guidelines in mind when coding in this chapter.

Infectious Arthropathies (Category Codes M00–M02)

Infectious arthropathies are disorders of the joints that are caused by an infectious agent. The tabular list of ICD-10-CM explains this block of codes as follows:

This block comprises arthropathies due to microbiological agents. Distinction is made between the following types of etiological relationship:
a) direct infection of joint, where organisms invade synovial tissue and microbial antigen is present in the joint;
b) indirect infection, which may be of two types: a reactive arthropathy, where microbial infection of the body is established but neither organisms nor antigens can be identified in the joint, and a postinfective arthropathy, where microbial antigen is present but recovery of an organism is inconstant and evidence of local multiplication is lacking.

Coders have to identify the type of arthropathy present because ICD-10-CM differentiates the categories as follows: M00, Pyogenic arthritis; M01, Direct infections of joint in infectious and parasitic diseases classified elsewhere; and M02, Postinfective and reactive arthropathies.

Inflammatory Polyarthropathies (Category Codes M05–M14)

This block of codes includes the following categories:

- M05, Rheumatoid arthritis with rheumatoid factor
- M06, Other rheumatoid arthritis
- M07, Enteropathic arthropathies
- M08, Juvenile arthritis
- M1a, Chronic gout
- M10, Gout
- M11, Other crystal arthropathies
- M12, Other and unspecified arthropathy
- M13, Other arthritis
- M14, Arthropathies in other diseases classified elsewhere

Arthritis, an inflammation of a joint, is a common condition coded to this block of the musculoskeletal chapter. Another common condition coded to this block is **rheumatism**, which is a general term for the deterioration and inflammation of connective tissues, including muscles, tendons, synovium, and bursa.

One of the most painful types of arthritis is **rheumatoid arthritis (RA)**, which is a disease of the autoimmune system in which the synovial membranes are inflamed and thickened. Rheumatoid arthritis can affect children or adults, and it can affect one site or many sites throughout the body. Rheumatoid arthritis may also be referenced as "progressive arthritis" and "proliferative arthritis." Medical documentation needs to specify the site or sites affected so that the appropriate code can be assigned. Because joint swelling and pain are considered an integral part of the condition, they should not be coded separately when a definitive diagnosis of rheumatoid arthritis is given.

Osteoarthritis (Category Codes M15–M19)

This block of codes reports the following categories:

- M15, Polyosteoarthritis
- M16, Osteoarthritis of hip
- M17, Osteoarthritis of knee
- M18, Osteoarthritis of first carpometacarpal joint
- M19, Other and unspecified osteoarthritis

The most common form of arthritis is known as **osteoarthritis (OA)**. Osteoarthritis is also referred to as "degenerative arthritis" because it causes the degeneration of the articular cartilage. Osteoarthritis also causes enlargement of the bone. It occurs almost always in older patients. The term **degenerative joint disease** is frequently used to describe this type of osteoarthritis.

Other Joint Disorders (Category Codes M20–M25)

The block of codes includes the following:

- M20, Acquired deformities of fingers and toes
- M21, Other acquired deformities of limbs
- M22, Disorder of patella
- M23, Internal derangement of knee
- M24, Other specific derangements
- M25, Other joint disorders, not elsewhere classified

This block of codes is very detailed as to the type of deformity or disorder present. Coders must reference the medical documentation to ensure proper code assignment.

Dentofacial Anomalies [Including Malocclusion] and Other Disorders of Jaw (Category Codes M26–M27)

The anomalies classified to categories M26–M27 include those of the jaw, jaw-cranial base, dental arch, tooth position, malocclusion, dentofacial function, and temporomandibular joint disorders. Other diseases of the jaw, such as developmental disorders and inflammatory jaw conditions, are also classified here.

Systemic Connective Tissue Disorders (Category Codes M30–M36)

This block of codes reports systemic connective tissue disorders that include:

- Autoimmune disease NOS.
- Collagen (vascular) disease NOS.
- Systemic autoimmune disease.
- Systemic collagen (vascular) disease.

When reporting code M36.2, Hemophilic arthropathy, the coder should be aware of the following instructional notation:

Code first underlying disease, such as:
factor VIII deficiency (D66)
with vascular defect (D68.0)
factor IX deficiency (D67)
hemophilia (classical) (D66)
hemophilia B (D67)
hemophilia C (D68.1)

This signals to the coder that two codes are needed to fully code the disease.

Exercise 18.1 – Coding for Categories M00–M36

For each diagnostic statement, select the appropriate ICD-10-CM diagnostic code.

Diagnosis	Code
1. enteropathic arthropathy left ankle and foot	_____
2. right shoulder juvenile arthritis	_____
3. gout due to renal impairment, right wrist	_____
4. Charcot's joint, left knee	_____
5. mallet finger of left finger	_____

Deforming Dorsopathies (Category Codes M40–M54)

Dorsopathies, which are disorders of the back, are reported using the following ranges of codes:

- M40–M43, Deforming dorsopathies
- M45–M49, Spondylopathies
- M50–M54, Other dorsopathies

One of the conditions encountered in this section is **ankylosing spondylitis,** a form of rheumatoid arthritis. It is a chronic inflammation of the spine and sacroiliac joints, which leads to stiffening of the spine. **Ankylosis** is the complete fusion of the vertebrae. **Spondylitis** is an inflammation of the vertebrae. Ankylosing spondylitis is also referred to as Marie-Strümpell or Bekhterev's disease. The cause is unknown, but it is progressive and affects mainly the small joints of the spine. This condition is classified to category code M45.

Category code M46 reports other inflammatory spondylopathies, and category code M47 reports spondylosis.

The term **myelopathy** refers to any disorder of the spinal cord. Back disorders that involve herniation of the intervertebral disc or spondylitis need the distinction of "with myelopathy" or "without myelopathy."

A **herniated disc** is a result of the rupture of the nucleus pulposus, or the material in the center of the disc. The rupture causes the nucleus pulposus to move outward, placing pressure on the spinal cord. Because back pain is an integral part of a herniated disc, it is not coded separately. Sciatica is another symptom and is not coded separately. Herniated discs are classified to intervertebral disc displacement codes and are classified by the site of the displacement, such as M51.2 codes, Other thoracic, thoracolumbar and lumbosacral intervertebral disc displacement, and M50.2 codes, Other cervical disc displacement.

Soft Tissue Disorders (Category Codes M60–M79)

Soft tissue disorders are grouped into the following blocks of codes:

- M60–M63, Disorders of muscles
- M65–M67, Disorders of synovium and tendon
- M70–M79, Other soft tissue disorders

Myositis, an inflammation of the muscle, is coded using category code M60. The various types of myositis are differentiated. Muscle wasting and atrophy, commonly seen in the elderly, is reported using the M62.5 codes.

Synovitis and tenosynovitis is reported using category M65. Codes M65.30- to M65.35-, Trigger finger, are commonly reported.

Bursitis, an inflammation of the bursa, is reported with codes from category M71. The type of bursitis needs to be determined for proper code selection. Fibromyalgia is reported with code M79.7.

Osteopathies and Chondropathies (Category Codes M80–M94)

Osteopathies and chondropathies are divided into the following blocks of codes:

- M80–M85, Disorders of bone density and structure
- M86–M90, Other osteopathies
- M91–M94, Chondropathies

One of the most common diseases reported to this section of the code book is osteoporosis, M80–M81. **Osteoporosis** is a reduction in bone mass that is responsible for different conditions that can affect a person's health. The more severe condition that affects patients with osteoporosis is fractures.

Disease Highlight—Osteoporosis

Osteoporosis is a bone disorder, related to metabolism, in which bone mass is lost due to decreased bone formation and increased bone resorption. The disease causes aporosity, or a Swiss cheese appearance, of the bones, creating a decrease in bone mass. The numerous causes of osteoporosis include:

- Malnutrition.
- Decreased calcium absorption.
- Inadequate calcium intake.
- Estrogen deficiency.
- As a side effect of some chronic diseases.

Signs and Symptoms:

Osteoporosis is a slowly developing disease that may take decades before symptoms present. Compression fractures of the spine and pathologic wrist fractures commonly present as an early sign of osteoporosis.

(continued)

As the disease progresses, the patient may have:

- Kyphosis (see Figure 18-4).

- Pain in the back and trunk area.

- A decrease in the size of the chest and abdominal cavity.

- A loss of height.

- The appearance of **Dowager's hump**, an abnormal curvature in the upper thoracic spine. (Figure 18-5 illustrates the loss in height and the appearance of Dowager's hump in a patient with osteoporosis.)

As the disease advances, the patient's risk of fracturing a bone increases. Common fracture sites include the distal radius and proximal femur. Figure 18-4 illustrates these fracture sites.

Clinical Testing:

Osteoporosis is diagnosed by:

- Taking bone mass measurements, bone biopsy, and X-rays.

- Completing blood testing to determine the serum calcium, phosphorus, and alkaline phosphatase levels.

Treatment:

Because osteoporosis is irreversible, there is no treatment to reverse the bone mass loss.

- Patients are encouraged to take calcium and vitamin D and to complete a daily exercise routine.

- Reducing risk factors, such as decreasing caffeine and alcohol consumption and not smoking, is also encouraged.

- Physical therapy, estrogen therapy, and the surgical correction of pathological fractures are also treatment options for some patients.

- The drug alendronate (Fosamax) is often prescribed in an effort to increase bone mass.

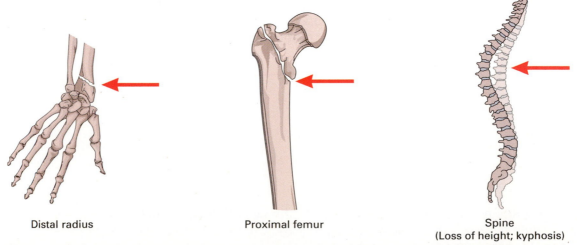

Distal radius   Proximal femur   Spine
                                                          (Loss of height; kyphosis)

Figure 18-4   Fracture and related osteoporosis (From Neighbors M, Tannehill-Jones, R. *Human Disease*, 2nd ed. Clifton Park, NY: Delmar, Cengage Learning, 2001, p. 91.)

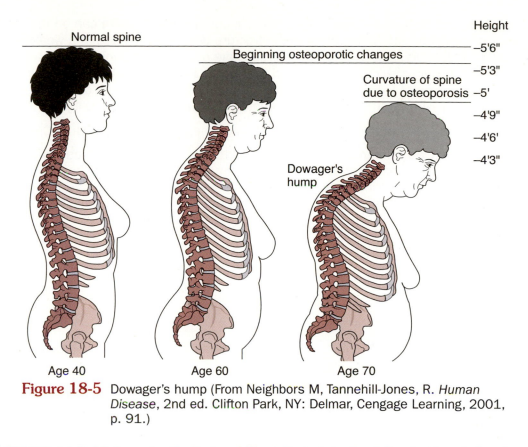

Figure 18-5 Dowager's hump (From Neighbors M, Tannehill-Jones, R. *Human Disease*, 2nd ed. Clifton Park, NY: Delmar, Cengage Learning, 2001, p. 91.)

The ICD-10-CM Official Guidelines for Coding and Reporting state the following in relation to coding osteoporosis.

ICD-10-CM Official Coding Guidelines

Osteoporosis

c) Osteoporosis is a systemic condition, meaning that all bones of the musculoskeletal system are affected. Therefore, site is not a component of the codes under category M81, Osteoporosis without current pathological fracture. The site codes under category M80, Osteoporosis with current pathological fracture, identify the site of the fracture, not the osteoporosis.

1) Osteoporosis without pathological fracture

Category M81, Osteoporosis without current pathological fracture, is for use for patients with osteoporosis who do not currently have a pathologic fracture due to the osteoporosis, even if they have had a fracture in the past. For patients with a history of osteoporosis fractures, status code Z87.31, Personal history of osteoporosis fracture, should follow the code from M81.

2) Osteoporosis with current pathological fracture

Category M80, Osteoporosis with current pathological fracture, is for patients who have a current pathologic fracture at the time of an encounter. The codes under M80 identify the site of the fracture. A code from category M80, not a traumatic fracture code, should be used for any patient with known osteoporosis who suffers a fracture, even if the patient had a minor fall or trauma, if that fall or trauma would not usually break a normal, healthy bone.

Three types of fractures are commonly associated with osteoporosis. (1) Pathologic or **compression fractures of the spine** occur when the vertebrae in the spine become weak and collapse under low stress. (2) **Colles' fracture** is a wrist fracture that typically occurs when a person tries to break a fall by extending the arm. (3) The last type, and the most dangerous, is a hip fracture. The hip fracture can be caused by a fall or, in some cases, can occur spontaneously. Loss of mobility or even death can be the result of this type of fracture. Coders must determine whether the fracture occurred because of a weakened diseased bone or as a result of an injury. Fractures that occur because of a traumatic injury, such as a child who falls and breaks an arm while playing, are classified to chapter 19 of ICD-10-CM, "Injury, Poisoning and Certain Other Consequences of External Causes." For correct code assignment, coders must read the medical record to identify whether the fracture is pathologic or due to a traumatic injury.

The following types of fractures are coded to this section of chapter 13 of the ICD-10-CM code book:

- **M84.4–M86.6, Pathologic fractures**—A pathologic fracture is a break of a diseased bone that occurs from a minor stress or injury that would not normally occur in healthy bone. Pathologic fractures can also occur spontaneously. Note that a seventh character is added to this group. The following instructional notation appears at the start of M84.4, M84.5, and M84.6:

The appropriate 7th character is to be added to each code from subcategory M84.4, M84.5, M84.6:
A   initial encounter for fracture
D   subsequent encounter for fracture with routine healing
G   subsequent encounter for fracture with delayed healing
K   subsequent encounter for fracture with nonunion
P   subsequent encounter for fracture with malunion
S   sequela

- **M84.3, Stress fractures**—Stress fractures occur when repetitive force is applied to a bone over a period of time. Another term used for stress fractures is "fatigue fracture," "march fracture," and "stress reaction." Individuals who run or exercise frequently may develop stress fractures. Stress fractures are not always visualized by X-ray initially when they are suspected.

Two terms that are also associated with fractures is **malunion fracture** and **nonunion fracture**. A malunion occurs when the fracture site is misaligned. A nonunion occurs when the fracture fragments fail to unite.

The ICD-9-CM Official Guidelines for Coding and Reporting gives coders directions for the coding of pathologic fractures.

ICD-10-CM Official Coding Guidelines

Coding of Pathologic Fractures

7th character A is for use as long as the patient is receiving active treatment for the fracture. Examples of active treatment are: surgical treatment, emergency department encounter, evaluation and treatment by a new physician. 7th character, D is to be used for encounters after the patient has completed active treatment. The other 7th characters, listed under each subcategory in the Tabular List, are to be used for subsequent encounters for treatment of problems associated with the healing, such as malunions and nonunions, and sequelae.

Care for complications of surgical treatment for fracture repairs during the healing or recovery phase should be coded with the appropriate complication codes.

See Section I.C.19. Coding of traumatic fractures.

Other Disorders of the Musculoskeletal System and Connective Tissue (Category Code M95)

This code category includes other acquired deformities of musculoskeletal system and connective tissue. The codes are differentiated according to the site.

Intraoperative and Postprocedural Complications and Disorders of Musculoskeletal System, Not Elsewhere Classified (Category Code M96) and Biomechanical Lesions, Not Elsewhere Classified (Category Code M99)

These categories report complications and biomechanical lesions that are not classified elsewhere in chapter 13.

Comparing ICD-9-CM to ICD-10-CM

Many of the ICD-9-CM category and subcategory titles have been changed in ICD-10-CM. Also, codes have been reassigned from other chapters to the new musculoskeletal and connective tissue chapter. The additions, deletions, and new codes include the following:

- Gout is now classified to M10. It was previously in chapter 3 of ICD-9-CM, "Endocrine, Nutritional, and Metabolic Diseases."

- Osteomalacia is now classified to M83. It was previously in chapter 3 of ICD-9-CM.

- Dislocation of the knee is now classified to M22. It was previously in chapter 17 of ICD-9-CM, "Injury and Poisoning."

- The following new categories have been added in ICD-10-CM: hydroxyapatite deposition disease, adult osteomalacia, pathological fracture of bone in neoplastic disease, and subacute osteomyelitis.

- Intraoperative and postprocedural complications and disorders of musculoskeletal system, M96, has been added.

- Most of the codes have been expanded to include laterality codes.

- Osteoporosis codes have been expanded to identify additional types and the sites of the osteoporosis.

- Extensions have been added to codes to indicate initial or subsequent encounters and fractures with routine healing, delayed healing, nonunion, malunion, and sequela.

Internet Links

The learn more about the musculoskeletal system, visit *http://www.aaos.org*

To learn about rheumatoid arthritis visit *http://www.rheumatoidarthritis.com*

To view a video on osteoporosis visit *http://www.answers.com/topic/musculoskeletal-system-2*

Summary

- Chapter 13 of ICD-10-CM classifies musculoskeletal disorders and conditions that occur as a disease process.

- Stress fractures, pathologic fractures, and malunion of a fracture are coded with chapter 13 of ICD-10-CM.

- Most of the codes in chapter 13 of ICD-10-CM have site and laterality designations.

- Bone, joint, or muscle conditions that are the result of a healed injury are found in chapter 13 of ICD-10-CM.

- Osteoporosis with or without a current pathological fractures is reported with category codes M80 and M81.

Chapter Review

True/False: Indicate whether each statement is true (T) or false (F).

1. _____ All fractures are coded to chapter 13 of ICD-10-CM, "Diseases of the Musculoskeletal System and Connective Tissue."

2. _____ A compression fracture can occur when a person tries to break a fall by extending an arm.

3. _____ All congenital disorders of the back are classified to chapter 13 of ICD-10-CM.

4. _____ Coxa plana, right hip is coded to code M91.21.

5. _____ Aneurysmal bone cyst is coded to code M85.51.

Fill-in-the-Blank: Enter the appropriate term(s) to complete each statement.

6. Tendons connect muscle to _____.

7. _____ is an inflammation of a joint.

8. _____ separates and covers the muscles.

9. Disorders of bone density and structure are classified to block _____.

10. _____ acts as a lubricant for joints.

Coding Assignments

Instructions: Using an ICD-10-CM code book, assign the proper diagnosis code to the following diagnostic statements.

Diagnosis	Code
1. cauliflower ear, left ear	_____
2. coccygodynia	_____
3. kyphosis due to radiation	_____
4. hypertrophy of right humerus	_____
5. senile osteoporosis	_____
6. pathological fracture of left humerus, subsequent encounter with nonunion	_____
7. pain in limb	_____
8. polymyositis	_____
9. spinal stenosis, thoracolumbar region	_____
10. joint mice, right knee	_____
11. Felty's syndrome left shoulder	_____
12. rheumatoid arthritis	_____

13. acute osteomyelitis of shoulder   _____

14. low back pain   _____

15. Baker's cyst, left knee   _____

16. mandibular hyperplasia   _____

17. effusion of right elbow   _____

18. cervical spondylosis   _____

19. osteoporosis   _____

20. contracture of left hand   _____

21. pneumococcal arthritis, left hip   _____

22. cavus deformity of foot, acquired   _____

23. flexion deformity, left shoulder   _____

24. displacement of cervical intervertebral disc
    without myelopathy   _____

25. bunion   _____

Case Studies

Instructions: Review each case study and select the correct ICD-10-CM diagnostic code.

CASE 1

Physician Office Visit

VITAL SIGNS: B/P 125/80 Temperature 98.9 Weight 164 pounds

Sally is here today to follow up on her blood sugar levels.

HEENT: Normal, no pathological changes due to diabetes

ABDOMEN: Soft, tender. No masses, spleen normal.

CHEST/HEART: Within normal limits

EXTREMITIES: Feet were examined and revealed joint inflammation due to Charcot's arthritis. The arthritis is a result of the advancing diabetes. Patient was instructed to avoid wearing tight footwear and to file calluses that are present on feet with an emery board. Patient was advised to schedule an appointment with Dr. Town, a podiatrist, for ongoing care.

Diabetes is controlled at this time. Follow up in 1 month.

ICD-10-CM Code Assignment: _____

CASE 2

Emergency Room Visit

This 16-year-old female was running at track practice today and started to experience foot pain. This has occurred in the past when she runs, but today the pain is at an increased level.

(continued)

VITAL SIGNS: Temperature 98.6, B/P 120/75, weight 124 pounds

EXAM:

HEENT: Within normal limits

HEART: Normal

ABDOMEN: Normal, with no complaints

EXTREMITIES: Left foot pain present, and pain increases to touch in the metatarsal area.

X-ray ordered.

X-RAY RESULTS: Negative

Clinical diagnosis of stress reaction of metatarsals.

Referred to orthopedics.

ICD-10-CM Code Assignment: _____

CASE 3

Skilled Nursing Facility Note

Mary was admitted in June with a diagnosis of dementia and osteoporosis. She is seen today at the request of the charge nurse because she is complaining of pain in her right midthigh area. She has not fallen or injured herself.

EXAM:

EXTREMITIES: When the patient's right leg is moved, she complains of pain in her thigh. She does not complain of pain in her left leg.

Onsite X-ray was ordered, which showed a fracture of the shaft of the femur.

Patient was sent to hospital for treatment.

CLINICAL IMPRESSION: Fracture due to postmenopausal osteoporosis.

ICD-10-CM Code Assignment: _____

CASE 4

Physician Office Visit

Mark presents today for follow-up of a torn meniscus. The injury occurred while skiing 2 years ago. He was going downhill, fell, and twisted his right knee during this fall. He was in a wheelchair for 2 weeks and then moved to crutches and physical therapy. He is now walking and performing activities of daily living without assistance. The diagnosis given for today's visit is old bucket handle tear of medial meniscus of the right knee.

ICD-10-CM Code Assignment: _____

CASE 5

Physician Office Visit

Mrs. Kennedy presents today with "terrible pain in my knees." It has been 6 months since I have seen her. We discussed the medications she is taking, which are limited to Advil or Tylenol. Examination reveals decreased range of motion and a slight change in gait. It was decided to run a few lab tests and also take some X-rays, which confirmed the diagnosis of osteoarthritis of the knee, bilaterally. We decided that glucosamine plus chondroitin sulfate, which are OTC medications, could be tried at this time prior to anything stronger. If she experiences no relief in the next 3 to 4 weeks, we will explore other options.

ICD-10-CM Code Assignment: _____

Diseases of the Genitourinary System

Chapter Outline

Objectives

At the conclusion of this chapter, the learner should be able to:

1. Identify the anatomical structures of the urinary system.
2. Identify the anatomical structures of the male and female genital tracts.
3. Explain the conditions related to the genitourinary system.
4. Discuss specific coding guidelines related to the conditions encountered in the genitourinary system.
5. Select and code diagnoses from case studies.

Key Terms

acute kidney failure

benign prostatic
   hypertrophy (BPH)

calculus

chronic kidney disease
   (CKD)

chronic renal failure

complete prolapse

cystitis

dysplasia

endometriosis

end-stage renal disease
   (ESRD)

female genital prolapse

female genitalia

Reminder

As you work through this chapter, you will need to have a copy of the ICD-10-CM coding book to reference.

glomerulonephritis	nephrons	premenopausal	urinary bladder
incomplete prolapse	nephropathy	prostate gland	urinary system
kidneys	nephrosis	renal colic	urinary tract infection (UTI)
male genitalia	ovarian cysts	ureters	urine
menopause	penis	urethra	voiding
micturate	perimenopausal	urethral stricture	
nephritis	postmenopausal	urethritis	

Introduction

Chapter 14 of ICD-10-CM, "Diseases of the Genitourinary System," classifies conditions of the urinary system and of the male and female genital tracts except for certain genitourinary transmissible infections, neoplasms, and conditions associated with pregnancy, childbirth, and the puerperium. This chapter contains the following blocks:

- N00–N08, Glomerular diseases
- N10–N16, Renal tubulo-interstitial diseases
- N17–N19, Acute kidney failure and chronic kidney disease
- N20–N23, Urolithiasis
- N25–N29, Other disorders of kidney and ureter
- N30–N39, Other diseases of the urinary system
- N40–N51, Diseases of male genital organs
- N60–N64, Disorders of breast
- N70–N77, Inflammatory diseases of female pelvic organs
- N80–N98, Noninflammatory disorders of female genital tract
- N99, Intraoperative and postprocedural complications and disorders of genitourinary system, not elsewhere classified

Introduction to the Body System

The urinary system is comprised of the kidneys, ureter, bladder, and urethra. The main function of the **urinary system** is to maintain a balance of the contents of the fluids within the body. Urea is removed from the bloodstream and then, along with other excess fluids and waste products, is converted to **urine**, which is expelled from the body by way of the bladder. Figure 19-1 illustrates the structures of the urinary system.

The kidneys are the primary organs of the urinary system. A person usually has two kidneys, which are located against the dorsal wall of the abdominal cavity and lie on either side of the vertebral column. The **kidneys** filter blood constantly to remove waste and work to filter the blood, reabsorb waste, and secrete urine. The **nephrons**, microscopic units of the kidneys, are the structures that actually form urine.

Urine is moved from the kidney to the bladder by way of the **ureters**. The ureters are very narrow tubes, which can easily be damaged in certain types of surgery. They must function properly for the urinary system to function properly.

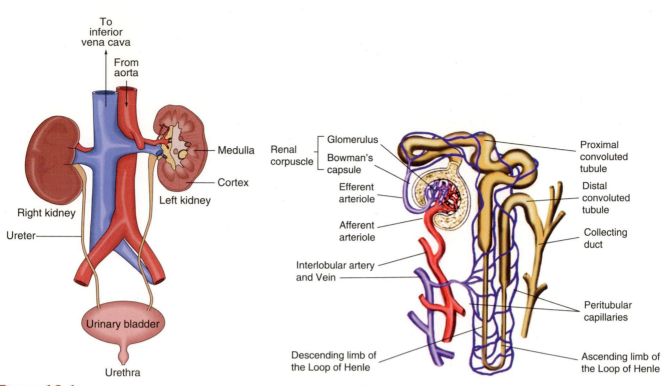

Figure 19-1   Structures and blood flow of the kidneys (From Ehrlich A, Schroeder CL. *Medical Terminology for Health Professionals*, 4th ed. Clifton Park, NY: Delmar, Cengage Learning, 2001, p. 189.)

The ureters connect to the **urinary bladder**, which holds urine until it moves to the urethra. The **urethra** is a small tube extending from the bladder to outside the body. When the bladder fills, pressure is exerted on the urethra, causing the urge to urinate. The coder may note the terms **micturate** or **voiding**, which are synonymous terms for urination. Coders must be very careful to identify the proper body part and the spelling of *urethra* and *ureter*. The spellings of these structures are very close, so paying attention to the specific terminology used in the medical record when locating a code is critical.

The **male genitalia** are made up of the scrotum, testicles, and the penis. The function of these organs is primarily for reproduction, but they also function as part of the urinary system; hence they are included in this chapter.

In the male, the urethra passes through the penis to outside the body. The **penis** functions in both the urinary and reproductive systems. The ureters move urine from the kidneys to the bladder. The urethra moves the urine from the urinary bladder to outside the body. In the reproductive function, semen moves through the vas deferens to the urethra from the ejaculatory duct.

The prostate gland, also part of the male genitalia, is located under the bladder and on the upper end of the urethra. The **prostate gland** secretes a fluid that is part of the semen and also aids in the motility of the sperm. Figure 19-2 illustrates a cross section of the male genitalia and its relation to the urethra and the urinary bladder.

The primary function of the **female genitalia** is the same as that of the male genitalia—reproduction—but because of its proximity to the urinary system, it is included in this chapter.

The female genitalia are made up of the uterus, vagina, ovaries, fallopian tubes, cervix, perineum, clitoris, labia, and mammary glands, or breasts. Figure 19-3 illustrates a cross section of the female genitalia and its relation to the urinary system.

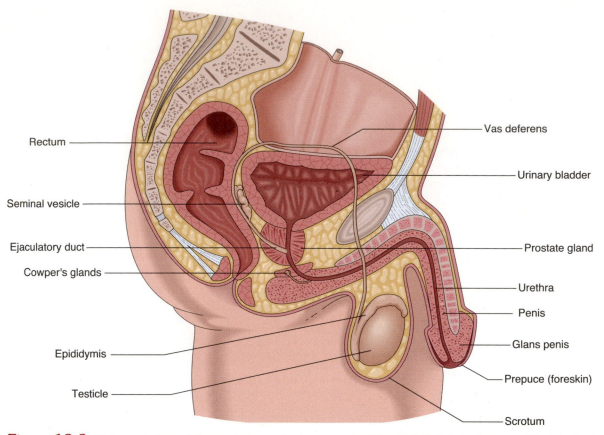

Figure 19-2 Cross section of the male reproductive organs (From Ehrlich A, Schroeder CL. *Medical Terminology for Health Professionals*, 4th ed. Clifton Park, NY: Delmar, Cengage Learning, 2001, p. 296.)

Coding Diseases of the Genitourinary System

This chapter of ICD-10-CM includes genitourinary diseases for both males and females.

Glomerular Diseases (Category Codes N00–N08)

This block of codes includes the following categories:

- N00, Acute nephritic syndrome
- N01, Rapidly progressive nephritic syndrome
- N02, Recurrent and persistent hematuria
- N03, Chronic nephritic syndrome
- N04, Nephrotic syndrome
- N05, Unspecified nephritic syndrome
- N06, Isolated proteinuria with specified morphological lesion
- N07, Hereditary nephropathy, not elsewhere classified
- N08, Glomerular disorders in diseases classified elsewhere

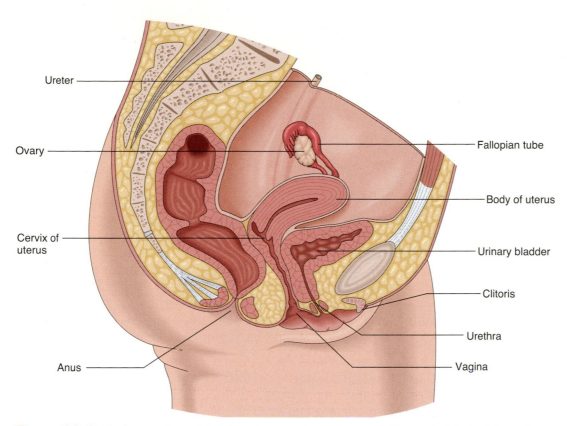

Figure 19-3 Cross section of the female reproductive organs (From Ehrlich A, Schroeder CL. *Medical Terminology for Health Professionals*, 4th ed. Clifton Park, NY: Delmar, Cengage Learning, 2001, p. 301.)

This block of codes reports **nephritis**, an inflammation of the kidneys. **Nephrosis** refers to a disease or disorder of the kidney. The coder may also encounter the term **nephropathy**, which is a synonymous term for nephrosis.

Some conditions that are classified to this section of the code book have separate codes for the acute and chronic manifestations of the disease. One such condition is **glomerulonephritis**, an inflammation of the glomeruli of the kidney. Acute glomerulonephritis is classified to category N00, Acute nephritic syndrome, whereas chronic glomerulonephritis is classified to category N03. These two codes are not usually billed together in the same episode of care. If the chronic glomerulonephritis is exacerbated, the condition causing the exacerbation is coded along with a code from the N03 category.

> **EXAMPLE:** Polly Patient came in for a follow-up of her chronic glomerulonephritis. She has been feeling a little tired and she thought she should communicate this to me.

For this example the correct code to use is N03.9.

Renal Tubulo-Interstitial Diseases (Category Codes N10–N16)

This block of codes also codes various forms of nephritis. The blocks are arranged as follows:

- N10, Acute tubulo-interstitial nephritis
- N11, Chronic tubulo-interstitial nephritis
- N12, Tubulo-interstitial nephritis, not specified as acute or chronic

- N13, Obstructive and reflux uropathy
- N14, Drug and heavy-metal-induced tubulo-interstitial nephritis and tubular conditions
- N15, Other renal tubulo-interstitial diseases
- N16, Renal tubulo-interstitial disorders in diseases classified elsewhere

> **Note:**
>
> *To code to categories N10–N12, the coder needs to review the documentation to determine whether the condition is acute or chronic. If the documentation does not state "acute" or "chronic," the physician should be queried. If the determination cannot be made, then category code N12 should be used.*

Acute Kidney Failure and Chronic Kidney Disease (Category Codes N17–N19)

This block of codes is used to report acute kidney failure and chronic kidney diseases. Two serious conditions encountered in this section of the chapter are acute and chronic renal failure. For **acute kidney failure**, use codes in the N17 category when the renal function is interrupted suddenly. The cause can be any number of reasons, and the renal function usually returns with treatment. Causes of acute renal failure include blockage of urine flow caused by stones, tumors, or an enlarged prostate; embolism; congestive heart failure; surgical shock; hemorrhagic shock; and dehydration. In the event that renal function does not return, the condition may progress to chronic renal insufficiency or failure and ultimately to death. Under the heading for category N17, an instructional notation states "Code also associated underlying condition," thus instructing the coder to use two codes when necessary.

Chronic renal failure, also known as **chronic kidney disease (CKD)** is a progressive disease in which renal function deteriorates, causing multisystem problems. As the disease progresses, other organs are affected until the patient advances to the late stages of chronic renal failure, which is then considered **end-stage renal disease (ESRD)**. Patients with chronic renal failure may be on dialysis or awaiting a kidney transplant. Chronic kidney disease code determination is based on the stage of the disease. The diagnosis code category for chronic kidney disease is N18, and fourth digits are used to indicate the stage.

- Stage 1 involves some kidney damage with a glomerular filtration rate (GFR) slightly greater than 90, which is considered a normal GFR.
- Stage 2 has a GFR of 60–89 with mild or minor kidney damage.
- Stage 3 involves more damage to the kidney with a GFR of 30–59.
- Stage 4 has a GFR of 15–29 with severe kidney damage.
- Stage 5 involves severe kidney damage with a GFR less than 15.
- At stage 5, the patient is on dialysis or awaiting a transplant.

Category N18 contains instructional notations that appear in the Tabular List as follows:

N18 Chronic kidney disease (CKD)
Code first any associated:
diabetic chronic kidney disease (E08.22, E09.22, E10.22,
E11.22, E13.22)
hypertensive chronic kidney disease (I12.-, I13.-)
Use additional code to identify kidney transplant status, if
applicable, (Z94.0)

Review of medical documentation is essential when coding for chronic renal failure/chronic kidney disease. The coder may encounter such phrases as "chronic renal insufficiency," "chronic renal failure," "chronic renal disease," and "chronic renal uremia," all of which are coded to N18.9 because the terms do not indicate the stage of the disease.

Laboratory tests are generally an indication of chronic renal failure. Elevated serum creatinine or blood urea nitrogen (BUN) values may indicate this condition. Clinical manifestations such as anemia, hypocalcemia, and renal osteodystrophy may be documented. Unless the provider has documented specifically that the patient has ESRD, renal failure, chronic renal failure, or renal insufficiency, clarification must be made before a code is assigned. Coders may assign only a diagnosis that can be supported by medical documentation, so they must be in communication with the provider for clarification of the diagnosis before assigning a code.

The ICD-10-CM Official Guidelines for Coding and Reporting on the coding of chronic kidney disease are as follows:

ICD-10-CM Official Coding Guidelines

Chronic kidney disease

1) Stages of chronic kidney disease (CKD)

The ICD-10-CM classifies CKD based on severity. The severity of CKD is designated by stages I–V. Stage II, code N18.2, equates to mild CKD; stage III, code N18.3, equates to moderate CKD; and stage IV, code N18.4, equates to severe CKD. Code N18.6, End stage renal disease (ESRD), is assigned when the provider has documented end-stage renal disease (ESRD).

If both a stage of CKD and ESRD are documented, assign code N18.6 only.

2) Chronic kidney disease and kidney transplant status

Patients who have undergone kidney transplant may still have some form of chronic kidney disease (CKD), because the kidney transplant may not fully restore kidney function. Therefore, the presence of CKD alone does not constitute a transplant complication. Assign the appropriate N18 code for the patient's stage of CKD and code Z94.0, Kidney transplant status. If a transplant complication such as failure or rejection or other transplant complication is documented, see section I.C.19.g for information on coding complications of a kidney transplant. If the documentation is unclear as to whether the patient has a complication of the transplant, query the provider.

3) Chronic kidney disease with other conditions

Patients with CKD may also suffer from other serious conditions, most commonly diabetes mellitus and hypertension. The sequencing of the CKD code in relationship to codes for other contributing conditions is based on the conventions in the Tabular List.

See I.C.9. Hypertensive chronic kidney disease.

See I.C.19. Chronic kidney disease and kidney transplant complications.

Urolithiasis (Category Codes N20–N23)

This block of codes is used to report some very common situations:

- N20, Calculus of kidney and ureter—A **calculus** is a stone. In this case, a kidney stone is in the kidney and or ureter.

- N21, Calculus of lower urinary tract

- N22, Calculus of urinary tract in diseases classified elsewhere

- N23, Unspecified renal colic—**Renal colic** is an acute pain caused by the passage of a kidney stone from the kidney through the ureter.

Other Disorders of Kidney and Ureter (Category Codes N25–N29)

This block includes the following categories:

- N25, Disorders resulting from impaired renal tubular function
- N26, Unspecified contracted kidney
- N27, Small kidney of unknown cause
- N28, Other disorders of kidney and ureter, not elsewhere classified
- N29, Other disorders of kidney and ureter in diseases classified elsewhere

The N28.0 code classifies some common disorders that include renal artery embolism, renal artery obstruction, renal artery occlusion, renal artery thrombosis, and renal infarct.

Other Diseases of the Urinary System (Category Codes N30–N39)

This block of codes includes:

- N30, Cystitis—**Cystitis** is an inflammation of the bladder.
- N31, Neuromuscular dysfunction of bladder, not elsewhere classified—This category includes neuropathic conditions that affect the bladder function.
- N32, Other disorders of the bladder—This includes various obstructions, fistula, diverticulum of the bladder, and other specified bladder disorders.
- N33, Bladder disorders in diseases classified elsewhere
- N34, Urethritis and urethral syndrome—**Urethritis** is an inflammation of the urethra.
- N35, **Urethral stricture**—the narrowing of the urethra
- N36, Other disorders of the urethra
- N37, Urethral disorders in diseases classified elsewhere
- N39, Other disorders of urinary system

A commonly seen condition that is classified to this block of ICD-10-CM is the **urinary tract infection (UTI)**, which is an abnormal presence of microorganisms in the urine. UTIs, unspecified, are classified to code N39.0, Urinary tract infection, site not specified. The following notation appears in the Tabular List for subcategory code N39.0, which coders must use when coding UTIs.

> Use additional code (B95–B97), to identify infectious agent.

The Excludes 1 notation should also be referenced because it lists UTIs that are excluded from this code.

Urinary tract infections can occur in various sites throughout the urinary tract. Figure 19-4 identifies various UTI sites. When a specific infection site is identified, ICD-10-CM assigns codes from the following categories:

- N10–N11, Pyelitis or pyelonephritis
- N30, Cystitis
- N34, Urethritis

In reviewing these categories, the coder may need to determine whether the condition is acute or chronic, with or without hematuria, and whether the infectious agent can be identified. All of these factors may have an impact on code assignment.

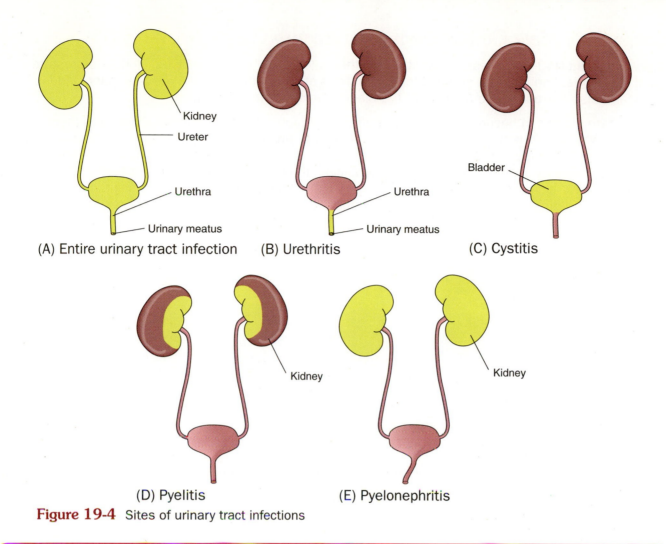

(A) Entire urinary tract infection   (B) Urethritis   (C) Cystitis

(D) Pyelitis   (E) Pyelonephritis

Figure 19-4 Sites of urinary tract infections

Exercise 19.1 – Code Selection for Category Codes N00–N39

For each diagnostic statement, select the appropriate ICD-10-CM diagnostic code.

Diagnosis   *Code*

1. urethral fistula   _____

2. renal failure   _____

3. ureteric stone   _____

4. pyonephrosis   _____

5. acute cortical necrosis   _____

6. vesicorectal fistula   _____

7. uremia   _____

8. abscess of urethral gland   _____

9. renal osteodystrophy   _____

10. nonvenereal urethritis   _____

Diseases of Male Genital Organs (Category Codes N40–N51)

Category codes N40–N51 classify conditions of the male genital organs, which include the prostate gland and penis. The prostate gland is located in front of the rectum and under the urinary bladder. This gland also surrounds the opening of the bladder leading into the urethra.

The prostate gland can become enlarged and affect a person's ability to urinate. Physicians must determine why a male is unable to urinate. The inability to urinate can be caused by hyperplasia, an enlargement of the prostate, and by prostatic cancer. Both conditions can cause urinary obstruction and are typically why patients seek care. The physician, through diagnostic testing, determines whether the patient has a neoplastic condition or hyperplasia. Neoplastic conditions are classified in ICD-10-CM to chapter 2, "Neoplasms." Hyperplasia and inflammatory diseases of the prostate are classified to category codes N40 and N41.

Benign prostatic hypertrophy (BPH) is an abnormal enlargement of the prostate, a common condition that affects men over 60 years of age. BPH is classified in ICD-10-CM to category code N40. Fourth digits are used in this category to identify the whether the condition exists with or without lower urinary tract symptoms.

Category N41 is used to code inflammatory disease of the prostate. Fourth digits are used to indicate acute or chronic prostatitis, abscess of prostate, prostatocystitis, granulomatous prostatitis, or prostatitis in diseases classified elsewhere. The following notation also appears in the Tabular List for category N41:

Use additional code B95–B97, to identify infectious agent

Therefore, coders have to identify whether a specific organism has been identified as the cause of the prostatitis. Be aware of this instructional notation.

The remaining codes found in this block classify disorders of the testes, penis, and seminal vesicles. Male erectile dysfunction, N52, uses fourth and fifth digits to identify the cause of the dysfunction.

Disorders of Breast (Category Codes N60–N65)

This block of codes classifies disorders of the breast. The codes are used for both males and females. Disorders of the breast are coded to different chapters within ICD-10-CM. Neoplastic conditions are classified to chapter 2, "Neoplasms," and other disorders of the breast that occur during pregnancy or during the postpartum period are classified to chapter 15, "Pregnancy, Childbirth, and the Puerperium." The remaining disorders of the breast are classified to category code N60, Benign mammary dysplasias; category code N61, Inflammatory disorders of breast; category code N62, Hypertrophy of breast; N63, Unspecified lump in breast; and N64, Other disorders of breast.

Review of the medical record is essential when you are coding disorders of the breast. If you have any questions about the cause of the disorders, query the provider. When a provider documents terms such as "breast lump," "cyst," or "growth," clarification is needed to determine whether the condition is of neoplastic origin. Biopsies of breast tissue are completed to determine whether the growth is neoplastic, and coders need to reference pathology reports before assigning codes for neoplastic conditions. When a provider records "mass in breast," "lump," "cyst," or "growth," use code N63, Unspecified lump in breast, until further diagnostic testing reveals the cause of the mass.

Other common non-neoplastic disorders of the breast that are classified to these codes are:

- N60.01–N60.09, Cyst of breast—A single encapsulated fluid-filled sac of the breast
- N60.11–N60.19, Fibrocystic disease of the breast—The presence of a single cyst or multiple cysts of the breast

Inflammatory Diseases of Female Pelvic Organs (Category Codes N70–N77)

This block of codes is used to report the following categories:

- N70, Salpingitis and oophoritis
- N71, Inflammatory disease of uterus, except cervix
- N72, Inflammatory disease of cervix uteri
- N73, Other female pelvic inflammatory diseases
- N74, Female pelvic inflammatory disorders in diseases classified elsewhere
- N75, Diseases of Bartholin's gland
- N76, Other inflammation of the vagina and vulva
- N77, Vulvovaginal ulceration and inflammation in diseases classified elsewhere

At the start of categories N70 and N76, instructional notations instruct the coder to "Use additional code (B95–B97), to identify infectious agent," signaling that two codes may be needed for some diagnostic phrases. Category N74 also includes a notation to "Code first underlying disease." Coders need to become familiar with the numerous notations and listings of Includes notes in this block.

Noninflammatory Disorders of the Female Genital Tract (Category Codes N80–N98)

The following disorders of the female genital tract are classified in this ICD-10-CM chapter according to the following blocks:

- N80, **Endometriosis**—This is an abnormal growth of the endometrium outside the uterus.

- N81, **Female genital prolapse**—This is the downward displacement of the genital organs. Coders must also identify whether the prolapse is diagnosed as a **complete prolapse**, when the entire uterus descends and protrudes beyond the introitus and the vagina becomes inverted, or as an **incomplete prolapse**, when the uterus descends into the introitus.

- N82, Fistulae involving female genital tract—This includes vesicovaginal fistula, uterovesical fistula, cervicovesical fistula, and other specified types of fistula.

- N83, Noninflammatory disorders of the ovary, fallopian tube, and broad ligament—This category includes **ovarian cysts**, encapsulated sacs of the ovary that are filled with a semisolid or liquid material.

- N84, Polyp of female genital tract—This category includes polyps of the corpus uteri, cervix uteri, vagina, vulva, and other parts of the female genital tract.

- N85, Other noninflammatory disorders of uterus, except cervix—This includes hypertrophy of uterus, subinvolution of the uterus, and other malpositions of uterus.

- N86, Erosion and ectropion of cervix uteri

- N87, Dysplasia of cervix uteri

- N88, Other inflammatory disorders of cervix uteri

- N89, Other noninflammatory disorders of vagina—This category includes **dysplasia**, the abnormal development or growth of cells.

- N90, Other noninflammatory disorders of the vulva and perineum

- N91, Absent, scanty, and rare menstruation

- N92, Excessive, frequent, and irregular menstruation

- N93, Other abnormal uterine and vaginal bleeding
- N94, Pain and other conditions associated with female genital organs and menstrual cycle
- N95, Menopausal and other perimenopausal disorders—This category includes menopausal and perimenopausal disorders. **Menopause** refers to the time of a woman's life when her menstrual cycle ceases. A woman may experience problems that are **premenopausal** (the time period right before menopause), **perimenopausal** (when symptoms of menopause begin, such as hot flashes), menopausal (which is marked by a woman's not having a period for one year), and **postmenopausal** (when a woman has not had a period for at least one year until the time she celebrates her 100th birthday).
- N96, Habitual aborter
- N97, Female infertility
- N98, Complications associated with artificial fertilization

Intraoperative and Postprocedural Complications and Disorders of Genitourinary System, Not Elsewhere Classified (Category Code N99)

This category classifies intraoperative and postprocedural complications and disorders of the genitourinary system. The category is further differentiated to include the specific complication.

Comparing ICD-9-CM to ICD-10-CM

In ICD-10-CM, the following category titles are changed:

- Urethritis, not sexually transmitted and urethral syndrome, is now changed to urethritis and urethral syndrome.
- Hydrocele is now changed to hydrocele and spermatocele.
- The title "Other disorders of the female genital tract" is changed to noninflammatory disorders of female genital tract.

Other changes in ICD-10-CM are:

- The addition of category N99, Intraoperative and postprocedural complications and disorders of genitourinary system.
- Expansion of fourth or fifth characters for recurrent and persistent hematuria.
- Category N70, Salpingitis and oophoritis, is expanded to identify acute, chronic, and unspecified conditions.
- Laterality is now identified for N60, Benign mammary dysplasia.
- Stages of dysplasia of vagina are identified in category N89.

Internet Links

To learn more about the genitourinary systems, visit the *Digital Urology Journal* at *http://www.becomehealthynow.com/category/bodygenito/*

To take an online quiz about the anatomy of the genitourinary system, visit *http://www.getbodysmart.com/ap/urinarysystem/menu/menu.html*

To learn more about the male and female reproductive systems, visit *http://www.malehealthcenter.com* and *http://www.healthywomen.org*

Summary

- The urinary system and the genital system are so closely connected that in some cases the function of one depends on the ability of the other to work properly.

- Not classified in chapter 15 of ICD-10-CM, "Diseases of the Genitourinary System," are certain genitourinary transmissible infections, neoplasms, and conditions associated with pregnancy, childbirth, and the puerperium.

- The late stage of chronic renal failure is considered end-stage renal disease.

- The coder needs to be cautious in this chapter because of the many notes for coding underlying disease and for additional codes to identify organisms.

- Noninflammatory disorders of the female genital tracts are classified to chapter 15 of ICD-10-CM.

Chapter Review

True/False: Indicate whether the statement is true (T) or false (F).

1. _____ The urethra is a narrow tube connecting the kidney to the bladder.

2. _____ The mammary glands are located in the breasts.

3. _____ The prostate gland is part of the male urinary system.

4. _____ Nephrosis refers to a disease or disorder of the kidney.

5. _____ If renal failure is confirmed as being acute, codes from the N20 category are used.

Fill-in-the-Blank: Enter the appropriate term(s) to complete each statement.

6. The _____ holds urine until it is expelled from the body.

7. _____ is a progressive disease in which renal function deteriorates.

8. _____ is synonymous with nephropathy.

9. _____ marks the end of a woman's menstrual cycle.

10. The _____ filters blood to remove waste, and the _____ actually form urine.

Coding Assignments

Instructions: Using an ICD-10-CM code book, assign the proper diagnosis code to the following diagnostic statements.

Diagnosis   *Code*

1. atrophy of kidney   _____

2. galactorrhea not associated with childbirth   _____

3. bilateral small kidneys   _____

4. paralysis of the bladder   _____

5. chronic renal failure   _____

6. postmenopausal bleeding _____

7. dysplasia of the cervix, uteri _____

8. acute renal failure with acute cortical necrosis _____

9. hyperplasia of prostate with urinary obstruction _____

10. prolapsed urethral mucosa _____

11. renal tubular necrosis _____

12. benign prostatic hypertrophy _____

13. UTI _____

14. weakening of pubocervical tissue _____

15. ureterolithiasis _____

16. renal cortical necrosis NOS _____

17. chronic interstitial cystitis _____

18. Peyronie's disease _____

19. acute salpingo-oophoritis _____

20. overactive bladder _____

21. fibrosclerosis of breast _____

22. atrophy of the spermatic cord _____

23. azoospermia _____

24. abscess of the epididymis _____

25. glomerulitis _____

Case Studies

Instructions: Review each case study and select the correct ICD-10-CM diagnostic code.

CASE 1

Physician Office Note

This 50-year-old patient was seen today in follow-up for renal insufficiency.

HISTORY OF THE PRESENT ILLNESS: The patient had a renal biopsy that showed focal and segmental glomerular sclerosis. He was placed on Vasotec but developed hyperkalemia, and then the Vasotec was stopped.

ALLERGIES: NKA

PHYSICAL EXAM:

BP 170/90, Pulse 88, Respirations 19

HEENT: Fundi are unremarkable. PERRLA

NECK: No JVD, adenopathy, or goiter

LUNGS: Clear

CARDIAC: Regular rate and rhythm without murmurs, rubs, or gallops

ABDOMEN: Soft, nontender, no masses

LABORATORY DATA: His most recent data completed on August 1, 200X, showed his sedimentation rate at 50, potassium at 5.3, BUN 75, creatinine 3.8, potassium down to 5.1, and calcium 9.6 with an albumin of 3.2. WBC is 16.4, hemoglobin 9.1, and platelets 530.

DIAGNOSTIC IMPRESSION: Chronic nephritic syndrome with focal and segmental sclerosis

MEDICATIONS ORDERED: Diovan 80 mg daily

Instructed him to follow a low-potassium diet and follow up with me in 1 month.

ICD-10-CM Code Assignment: _____

CASE 2

Discharge Summary

PERTINENT HISTORY: The patient is a 31-year-old white female admitted from my office because of increasing abdominal pain. The patient is gravida II, para II. The pain has been present for the last 6 months, occurring more severely the day before the onset of menses. The pain radiated down her back, vagina, and her lower abdomen.

HOSPITAL COURSE:

Pelvis exam revealed generalized tenderness. A laparoscopy revealed endometriosis of pelvic peritoneum. The patient was counseled as to available treatment options, which include hormonal therapy, surgical resection, or electrocautery. After pain management, she was discharged in 1 day. She wishes to discuss the treatment options with her husband.

DISCHARGE INSTRUCTIONS TO PATIENT: Patient was instructed to see me in my office in 3 days.

ICD-10-CM Code Assignment: _____

CASE 3

Skilled Nursing Facility Progress Note

VITAL SIGNS: B/P 120/80, Weight 165 pounds, Temperature 100.1

This 84-year-old man was seen today at the request of the charge nurse. The patient is experiencing urinary retention. No other complaints were noted by patient.

EXAM:

HEENT: Normal

CHEST: Lungs are clear.

HEART: Normal sinus rhythm. No murmurs noted.

ABDOMEN: Soft, nontender. No masses noted.

RECTAL: Smooth enlarged prostate, no other findings noted.

Because of the enlarged prostate I ordered a PSA to rule out prostate cancer since the patient has not had a previous PSA completed. The following tests were also ordered: urinalysis and urine culture.

Patient will be seen again when results are received.

ICD-10-CM Code Assignment: _____

(continued)

CASE 4

ED Summary Note

Eric presented to the ED with severe flank pain, hematuria, and a palpable flank mass. He said the pain was 10 on the pain scale. He had a dull pain for most of the day, but pain escalated over the last hour. Dr. Smith ordered a renal scan and ultrasound. Eric was diagnosed with hydronephrosis. He was sent home on pain medications and antibiotic therapy.

ICD-10-CM Code Assignment: _____

CASE 5

Physician Office Visit

Mrs. Vinton presents with complaint of painful urination. She states she has pain and burning when urinating. She also notes that she feels urgency and has recently started with low back pain over the last 24 hours. A urinalysis was positive for pyuria, the culture showing 150,000 organisms/mL. She was diagnosed with cystitis. She was started on antibiotics.

ICD-10-CM Code Assignment: _____

Pregnancy, Childbirth, and the Puerperium

Chapter Outline

Objectives

At the conclusion of this chapter, the learner should be able to:

1. Identify the stages of pregnancy.
2. Explain the complications encountered during pregnancy and how they affect code assignment.
3. Discuss specific coding guidelines related to coding for "Pregnancy, Childbirth, and the Puerperium."
4. Summarize the use of the final character indicating the trimester of pregnancy.
5. List the different types of abortions and explain how the code assignments are affected.
6. Select and code diagnoses from case studies.

Key Terms

abruptio placentae	complete placenta previa	embryo	legally induced abortion
antepartum		fetus	missed abortion
childbirth	ectopic pregnancy	labor and delivery	molar pregnancy

---

Reminder

As you work through this chapter, you will need to have a copy of the ICD-10-CM coding book to reference.

obstetrical care   placenta previa   puerperium
partial placenta previa   postpartum   uterus

Introduction

Chapter 15 of ICD-10-CM, "Pregnancy, Childbirth, and the Puerperium," classifies conditions that occur during pregnancy, childbirth, and six weeks after delivery. This chapter also codes normal deliveries. **Obstetrical care**, medical care that occurs during pregnancy and delivery, is divided into the antepartum period, labor and delivery, and the postpartum period. The blocks of codes found in this chapter are as follows:

- O00–O08, Pregnancy with abortive outcome
- O09, Supervision of high-risk pregnancy
- O10–O16, Edema, proteinuria, and hypertensive disorders in pregnancy, childbirth, and the puerperium
- O20–O29, Other maternal disorders predominantly related to pregnancy
- O30–O48, Maternal care related to the fetus and amniotic cavity and possible delivery problems
- O60–O77, Complications of labor and delivery
- O80–O82, Encounter for delivery
- O85–O92, Complications predominantly related to the puerperium
- O94–O9A, Other obstetric conditions, not elsewhere classified

Introduction to the Body System

To code from this section correctly, coders need to understand the terminology associated with the different stages of maternity and delivery care. Through the eighth week of pregnancy, the developing child is known as an **embryo**. From the ninth week until birth, the developing child is referred to as a **fetus**. When a fetus has reached the point at which it is capable of living outside the uterus, childbirth occurs. Figure 20-1 illustrates the position of a fetus at term. The **uterus** sits above the cervix and is the part of the female anatomy that houses the fetus until birth. Pregnancy, in most cases, takes 40 weeks. In some instances, conditions or problems alter the length of time a woman is pregnant.

Antepartum encompasses the time before childbirth. **Childbirth** refers to the delivery of one or more infants and is referred to as **labor and delivery**. The term **puerperium** relates to the postpartum period, which begins immediately after delivery and lasts for six weeks. **Postpartum** means after childbirth.

The ICD-10-CM Official Guidelines for Coding and Reporting define the postpartum and peripartum periods in the guidelines as follows.

ICD-10-CM Official Coding Guidelines

1) Peripartum and Postpartum periods

The postpartum period begins immediately after delivery and continues for six weeks following delivery. The peripartum period is defined as the last month of pregnancy to five months postpartum.

2) Peripartum and postpartum complication

A postpartum complication is any complication occurring within the six-week period.

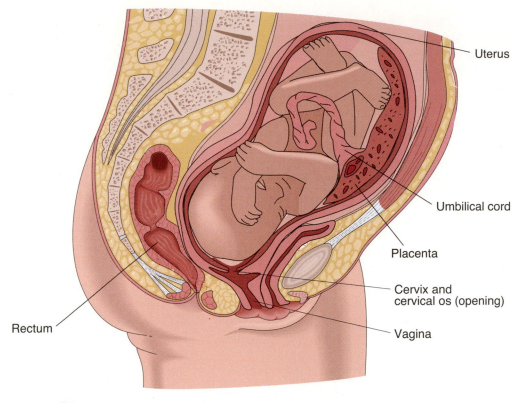

Figure 20-1 Position of a fetus at term (From Lindh WQ. *Delmar's Comprehensive Medical Assisting: Administrative and Clinical Competencies*, 2nd ed. Clifton Park, NY: Delmar, Cengage Learning, 2002, p. 461.)

Coding for Pregnancy, Childbirth, and the Puerperium

Chapter 15 of ICD-10-CM, "Pregnancy, Childbirth and the Puerperium," is governed by numerous coding guidelines. For proper code selection, you must understand and follow the guidelines.

The codes from this chapter are used only in the mother's record. These codes are never used in the medical record of the newborn. The following guidelines are the general rules for obstetric cases.

ICD-10-CM Official Coding Guidelines

1) Codes from chapter 15 and sequencing priority

Obstetric cases require codes from chapter 15, codes in the range O00–O9A, Pregnancy, Childbirth, and the Puerperium. Chapter 15 codes have sequencing priority over codes from other chapters. Additional codes from other chapters may be used in conjunction with chapter 15 codes to further specify conditions. Should the provider document that the pregnancy is incidental to the encounter, then code Z33.1, Pregnant state, incidental, should be used in place of any chapter 15 codes. It is the provider's responsibility to state that the condition being treated is not affecting the pregnancy.

2) Chapter 15 codes used only on the maternal record

Chapter 15 codes are to be used only on the maternal record, never on the record of the newborn.

3) Final character for trimester

(*continued*)

The majority of codes in Chapter 15 have a final character indicating the trimester of pregnancy. The timeframes for the trimesters are indicated at the beginning of the chapter. If trimester is not a component of a code it is because the condition always occurs in a specific trimester, or the concept of trimester of pregnancy is not applicable. Certain codes have characters for only certain trimesters because the condition does not occur in all trimesters, but it may occur in more than just one.

Assignment of the final character for trimester should be based on the trimester for the current admission/encounter. This applies to the assignment of trimester for pre-existing conditions as well as those that develop during or are due to the pregnancy.

Whenever delivery occurs during the current admission, and there is an "in childbirth" option for the obstetric complication being coded, the "in childbirth" code should be assigned.

4) Selection of trimester for extended inpatient admissions that encompass more than one trimesters

In instances when a patient is admitted to a hospital for complications of pregnancy during one trimester and remains in the hospital into a subsequent trimester, the trimester character for the antepartum complication code should be assigned on the basis of the trimester when the complication developed, not the trimester of discharge. If the condition developed prior to the current admission/encounter or represents a pre-existing condition, the trimester character for the trimester at the time of the admission/encounter should be assigned.

5) Unspecified trimester

Each category that includes codes for trimester has a code for "unspecified trimester." The "unspecified trimester" code should rarely be used, such as when the documentation in the record is insufficient to determine the trimester and it is not possible to obtain clarification.

Any conditions encountered during a pregnancy or postpartum period are coded to this chapter as a complication unless the provider documents that such a condition is incidental to the pregnancy. The documentation must clearly state that the visit was not directly related to the pregnancy. In this case, a Z33.1, Pregnant state, incidental, should be used instead of codes from this chapter.

> **EXAMPLE:** A female presents with sinus pressure and pain for the past 3 days; no OTC medications were tried because she is pregnant for approximately 24 weeks. The diagnosis is acute sinusitis. Although the decision for medication is affected by the pregnancy, the visit is for a condition not directly related to it. The code assignment is J01.90 as the primary diagnosis for the acute sinusitis, along with the Z33.1 as the second code.

Pregnancy with Abortive Outcome (Category Codes O00–O08) and Supervision of High-Risk Pregnancy (Category Code O09)

This block of codes is divided into the following categories:

- O00, Ectopic pregnancy
- O01, Hydatidiform mole
- O02, Other abnormal products of conception
- O03, Spontaneous abortion
- O04, Complications following (induced) termination of pregnancy
- O07, Failed attempted termination of pregnancy
- O08, Complications following ectopic and molar pregnancy
- O09, Supervision of high-risk pregnancy

Category O00, Ectopic pregnancy, and code O02.0, Blighted ovum and nonhydatidiform mole, classify ectopic and molar pregnancy. An **ectopic pregnancy** is one that occurs outside the uterus. Abdominal, tubal, and ovarian pregnancies are all included in this section. If a blighted ovum in the

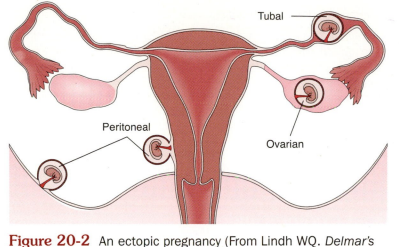

Figure 20-2 An ectopic pregnancy (From Lindh WQ. *Delmar's Comprehensive Medical Assisting: Administrative and Clinical Competencies*, 2nd ed. Clifton Park, NY: Delmar, Cengage Learning, 2002, p. 463.)

uterus develops into a mole or benign tumor, this is considered a **molar pregnancy**. The products of conception have not yet developed into a fetus in these cases. When the current episode of care is for an ectopic or molar pregnancy, a code from this series is the primary diagnosis. A code from the O08 category can be used secondarily to describe the complication. Figure 20-2 illustrates an ectopic pregnancy.

Code O02.1 is used for a missed abortion. A **missed abortion** is one in which a fetus has died before the completion of 22 weeks' gestation with the retention of the dead fetus or products of conception up to four weeks after demise. This period of completion varies legally from state to state and in some states may be as few as 19 weeks. The coder needs to be aware of state and local laws regarding this criterion in order to make the correct code assignment. Abnormal products of conception, which include carneous mole, hydatidiform mole, and blighted ovum, are reported by using category O01, Hydatidiform mole or category O02, Other abnormal products of conception.

Category O03 reports spontaneous abortions. A spontaneous abortion is the complete or incomplete expulsion of products of conception before a pregnancy goes beyond 22 weeks' gestation. The O03 category is differentiated according to the types of complications.

Category O04 reports complications following (induced) termination of pregnancy. An abortion that is induced by medical personnel working within the law is considered a **legally induced abortion**. The legally induced abortion can be elective or for therapeutic reasons such as when the mother's health is in danger.

The following coding guidelines are used for coding abortions.

ICD-10-CM Official Coding Guidelines

Abortions

1) Abortion with Liveborn Fetus

When an attempted termination of pregnancy results in a liveborn fetus assign a code from subcategory O60.1, Preterm labor with preterm delivery, and a code from category Z37, Outcome of Delivery. The procedure code for the attempted termination of pregnancy should also be assigned.

(continued)

2) Retained Products of Conception following an abortion

Subsequent encounters for retained products of conception following a spontaneous abortion or elective termination of pregnancy are assigned the appropriate code from category O03, Spontaneous abortion, or code Z33.2, Encounter for elective termination of pregnancy. This advice is appropriate even when the patient was discharged previously with a discharge diagnosis of complete abortion.

Category O08 reports complications following an ectopic or molar pregnancy. Sepsis following ectopic or molar pregnancy is reported with code O08.82. The following guideline applies to this code and to other chapter 15 codes for sepsis that complicates abortion, pregnancy, childbirth, and the puerperium.

ICD-10-CM Official Coding Guidelines

j. Sepsis and septic shock complicating abortion, pregnancy, childbirth, and the puerperium

When assigning a chapter 15 code for sepsis complicating abortion, pregnancy, childbirth, and the puerperium, a code for the specific type of infection should be assigned as an additional diagnosis. If severe sepsis is present, a code from subcategory R65.2, Severe sepsis, and code(s) for associated organ dysfunction(s) should also be assigned as additional diagnoses.

k. Puerperal sepsis

Code O85, Puerperal sepsis, should be assigned with a secondary code to identify the causal organism (e.g., for a bacterial infection, assign a code from category B95-B96, Bacterial infections in conditions classified elsewhere). A code from category A40, Streptococcal sepsis, or A41, Other sepsis, should not be used for puerperal sepsis. If applicable, use additional codes to identify severe sepsis (R65.2-) and any associated acute organ dysfunction.

Category O09, Supervision of high-risk pregnancy, is used when a provider is managing the care for a woman who is a high-risk pregnancy. The pregnancy can be high risk due to:

- A history of infertility.
- A history of ectopic or molar pregnancy.
- Other poor reproductive or obstetric history.

The following coding guideline applies:

ICD-10-CM Official Coding Guidelines

Prenatal outpatient visits for high-risk patients

For routine prenatal outpatient visits for patients with high-risk pregnancies, a code from category O09, Supervision of high-risk pregnancy, should be used as the first-listed diagnosis. Secondary chapter 15 codes may be used in conjunction with these codes if appropriate.

Edema, Proteinuria, and Hypertensive Disorders in Pregnancy, Childbirth, and the Puerperium (Category Codes O10–O16)

This block of codes reports edema, proteinuria, and hypertensive disorders complicating pregnancy, childbirth, and the puerperium:

- O10, Preexisting hypertension
- O11, Preexisting hypertension disorder with superimposed proteinuria
- O12, Gestational [pregnancy-induced] edema and proteinuria without hypertension

- O13, Gestational [pregnancy-induced] hypertension without significant proteinuria
- O14, Gestational [pregnancy-induced] hypertension with significant proteinuria
- O15, Eclampsia
- O16, Unspecified maternal hypertension

The following guidelines apply to this section:

ICD-10-CM Official Coding Guidelines

c. Pre-existing conditions versus conditions due to the pregnancy

Certain categories in chapter 15 distinguish between conditions of the mother that existed prior to pregnancy (pre-existing) and those that are a direct result of pregnancy. When assigning codes from Chapter 15, it is important to assess if a condition was pre-existing prior to pregnancy or developed during or due to the pregnancy in order to assign the correct code.

Categories that do not distinguish between pre-existing and pregnancy-related conditions may be used for either. It is acceptable to use codes specifically for the puerperium with codes complicating pregnancy and childbirth if a condition arises postpartum during the delivery encounter.

d. Pre-existing hypertension in pregnancy

Category O10, Pre-existing hypertension complicating pregnancy, childbirth, and the puerperium, includes codes for hypertensive heart and hypertensive chronic kidney disease. When assigning one of the O10 codes that includes hypertensive heart disease or hypertensive chronic kidney disease, it is necessary to add a secondary code from the appropriate hypertension category to specify the type of heart failure or chronic kidney disease.

See Section I.C.9. Hypertension.

Other Maternal Disorders Predominantly Related to Pregnancy (Category Codes O20–O29)

This block of codes report the following:

- O20, Hemorrhage in early pregnancy
- O21, Excessive vomiting in pregnancy
- O22, Venous complications in pregnancy
- O23, Infections of genitourinary tract in pregnancy
- O24, Diabetes mellitus in pregnancy, childbirth, and the puerperium
- O25, Malnutrition in pregnancy, childbirth, and the puerperium
- O26, Maternal care for other conditions predominantly related to pregnancy
- O28, Abnormal findings on antenatal screening of mother
- O29, Complications of anesthesia during pregnancy

This block of codes reports many types of disorders, including:

- O20.0, Threatened abortion.
- O21.0–O21.1, Hyperemesis.
- O26.20–O26.23, Pregnancy care of habitual aborter.

A complication that should be noted is gestational diabetes (category code O24). The following guidelines apply to diabetes mellitus in pregnancy and gestational diabetes.

ICD-10-CM Official Coding Guidelines

Diabetes mellitus in pregnancy

Diabetes mellitus is a significant complicating factor in pregnancy. Pregnant women who are diabetic should be assigned a code O24, Diabetes mellitus in pregnancy, childbirth, and the puerperium, first, followed by the appropriate diabetes code(s) (E08–E13) from Chapter 4.

h. Long term use of insulin

Code Z79.4, Long-term (current) use of insulin, should also be assigned if the diabetes mellitus is being treated with insulin.

i. Gestational (pregnancy induced) diabetes

Gestational (pregnancy induced) diabetes can occur during the second and third trimester of pregnancy in women who were not diabetic prior to pregnancy. Gestational diabetes can cause complications in the pregnancy similar to those of pre-existing diabetes mellitus. It also puts the woman at greater risk of developing diabetes after the pregnancy. Codes for gestational diabetes are in subcategory O24.4, Gestational diabetes mellitus. No other code from category O24, Diabetes mellitus in pregnancy, childbirth, and the puerperium, should be used with a code from O24.4.

The codes under subcategory O24.4 include diet controlled and insulin controlled. If a patient with gestational diabetes is treated with both diet and insulin, only the code for insulin-controlled is required.

Code Z79.4, Long-term (current) use of insulin, should not be assigned with codes from subcategory O24.4.

An abnormal glucose tolerance in pregnancy is assigned a code from subcategory O99.81, Abnormal glucose complicating pregnancy, childbirth, and the puerperium.

Maternal Care Related to the Fetus and Amniotic Cavity and Possible Delivery Problems (Category Codes O30–O48)

This block contains the following categories:

- O30, Multiple gestation
- O31, Complications specific to multiple gestation
- O32, Maternal care for malpresentation of fetus
- O33, Maternal care for disproportion
- O34, Maternal care for abnormality of pelvic organs
- O35, Maternal care for known or suspected fetal abnormality and damage
- O36, Maternal care for other fetal problems
- O40, Polyhydramnios
- O41, Other disorders of amniotic fluid and membranes
- O42, Premature rupture of membranes
- O43, Placental disorders
- O44, Placenta previa
- O45, Premature separation of placenta (abruptio placentae)
- O46, Antepartum hemorrhage, not elsewhere classified
- O47, False labor
- O48, Late pregnancy

Category O35, Maternal care for known or suspected fetal abnormality and damage, and category O36, Maternal care for other fetal problems, are governed by the following coding guideline.

ICD-10-CM Official Coding Guidelines

1) Codes from categories O35 and O36

Codes from categories O35, Maternal care for known or suspected fetal abnormality and damage, and O36, Maternal care for other fetal problems, are assigned only when the fetal condition is actually responsible for modifying the management of the mother, i.e., by requiring diagnostic studies, additional observation, special care, or termination of pregnancy. The fact that the fetal condition exists does not justify assigning a code from this series to the mother's record.

2) In utero surgery

In cases when surgery is performed on the fetus, a diagnosis code from category O35, Maternal care for known or suspected fetal abnormality and damage, should be assigned identifying the fetal condition. Assign the appropriate procedure code for the procedure performed.

No code from chapter 16, the perinatal codes, should be used on the mother's record to identify fetal conditions. Surgery performed in utero on a fetus is still to be coded as an obstetric encounter.

Two conditions that can complicate pregnancies are O45, Abruptio placentae, and O44, Placenta previa.

Disease Highlight—Abruptio Placentae

When there is a premature sudden separation of the placenta from the uterus prior to or during labor, the patient is said to have **abruptio placentae**. The abrupt separation can be caused by trauma, chronic hypertension, convulsions, and multiple births. See Figure 20-3.

Signs and Symptoms:

The presenting signs and symptoms are determined by the amount of separation of the placenta. When a partial separation occurs, the patient may be asymptomatic. When a complete separation occurs:

- The patient needs to seek medical care quickly because a complete separation can lead to maternal and fetal death.
- The mother may experience severe abdominal pain with vaginal bleeding.
- Shock can also occur.
- Fetal heart tones and fetal activity decrease due to the lack of oxygen and nutrition being supplied to the fetus.

Clinical Testing:

Because of the urgency of the condition, diagnosis is made based on clinical history and observation. At times a uterine ultrasound is completed.

Treatment:

If the placenta separation is partial, the patient is placed on bed rest and may be hospitalized to monitor the mother and fetus.

(continued)

If the placenta separation is complete:

- The patient is prepared for delivery.
- Continuous fetal monitoring is started to determine fetal distress.
- Often a cesarean section is performed.
- If the mother has lost a significant amount of blood, she is given units of blood.

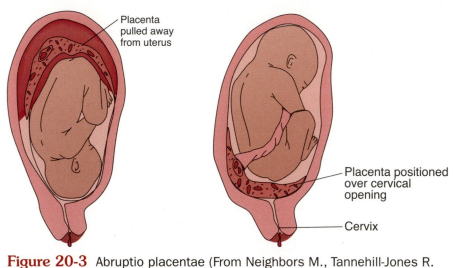

Figure 20-3 Abruptio placentae (From Neighbors M., Tannehill-Jones R. *Human Diseases*, 2nd ed. Clifton Park, NY: Delmar, Cengage Learning, 2002, p. 323.)

Placenta previa is another complication that occurs during pregnancy.

Disease Highlight—Placenta Previa

Placenta previa is the abnormal positioning of the placenta in the lower uterus so that the cervical os is partially or completely covered.

- A **complete placenta previa** occurs when the placenta entirely covers the cervical os.
- A **partial placenta previa** occurs when the placenta covers part of the cervical os.

Risk factors include:

- Maternal age greater than 35.
- Large or abnormal placenta formation.
- Multiparity.
- Previous uterine surgery.
- Smoking.

Signs and Symptoms:

The patient has spotting during the first and second trimester. During the third trimester, the patient may have bright red vaginal bleeding and uterine cramping. If the bleeding is severe, the patient may experience shock, which can be life threatening.

Clinical Testing:

Pelvic ultrasound is completed to visualize the placenta.

Treatment:

The treatment is determined by the extent of the placenta previa.

- Medications may be administered to prevent premature labor and to stop contractions.

- If there is minimal bleeding, the patient is placed on bed rest and observed.

- If the bleeding is severe or if the fetus is in distress, an emergency cesarean section is performed.

Blood transfusions may also be necessary.

Exercise 20.1 – Coding for Categories O00–O48

For each diagnostic statement, select the appropriate ICD10-CM diagnostic code.

Diagnosis   *Code*

1. false labor   _____

2. pregnancy of triplets in the third trimester   _____

3. malnutrition in the first trimester of pregnancy   _____

4. ovarian pregnancy   _____

5. missed abortion   _____

6. acute renal failure following induced termination of pregnancy _____

7. fat embolism following molar pregnancy   _____

8. hemorrhoids in second trimester pregnancy   _____

9. mild hyperemesis gravidarum   _____

10. polyhydramnios   _____

Complications of Labor and Delivery (Category Codes O60–O77)

Complications that occur during labor and delivery are classified to category codes O60–O77. These include preterm labor, failed induction of labor, abnormalities of forces of labor, long labor, obstructed labor, complication of intrapartum hemorrhage, abnormality of fetal acid-base balance, umbilical cord complications, perineal laceration during labor, obstetric trauma, postpartum hemorrhage, retained placenta, and other complications during labor and delivery.

Coders should carefully read the medical documentation to determine the type of complication that occurred during labor and delivery.

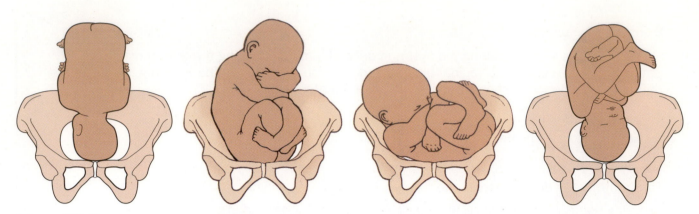

Figure 20-4   Delivery positions: (A) occiput anterior (normal); (B) breech; (C) transverse; (D) occiput posterior (From Sormunen C. *Terminology for Allied Health Professions*, 5th ed. Clifton Park, NY: Delmar, Cengage Learning, 2002, p. 420.)

Use category O64, Obstructed labor due to malposition and malpresentation of fetus, to report labor obstructed by abnormal positions and presentation of the newborn. Figure 20-4 illustrates various delivery positions.

Encounter for Delivery (Category Codes O80 and O82)

Two category codes are used to code deliveries: O80, Encounter for full-term uncomplicated delivery, and O82, Encounter for cesarean delivery without indication. These categories are defined in the tabular listing as follows:

O80 Encounter for full-term uncomplicated delivery
Delivery requiring minimal or no assistance, with or without episiotomy, without fetal manipulation [e.g., rotation version] or instrumentation [forceps] of a spontaneous, cephalic, vaginal, full-term, single, live-born infant. This code is for use as a single diagnosis code and is not to be used with any other code from chapter 15. This code must be accompanied by a delivery code from the appropriate procedure classification. Use additional code to indicate outcome of delivery (Z37.0)
O82 Encounter for cesarean delivery without indication
This code must be accompanied by a delivery code from the appropriate procedure classification. Use additional code to indicate outcome of delivery (Z37.0)

Figure 20-5 illustrates the presentation of a fetus during normal delivery.

Code O80, Normal delivery, is governed by the following coding guidelines.

ICD-10-CM Official Coding Guidelines

Normal Delivery, Code O80

1) Encounter for full term uncomplicated delivery

Code O80 should be assigned when a woman is admitted for a full-term normal delivery and delivers a single, healthy infant without any complications antepartum, during the delivery, or postpartum during the delivery episode. Code O80 is always a principal diagnosis. It is not to be used if any other code from chapter 15 is needed to describe a current complication of the antenatal, delivery, or perinatal period. Additional codes from other chapters may be used with code O80 if they are not related to or are in any way complicating the pregnancy.

2) Uncomplicated delivery with resolved antepartum complication

Code O80 may be used if the patient had a complication at some point during the pregnancy, but the complication is not present at the time of the admission for delivery.

3) Outcome of delivery for O80

Z37.0, Single live birth, is the only outcome of delivery code appropriate for use with O80.

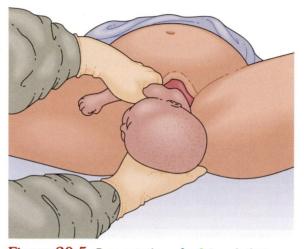
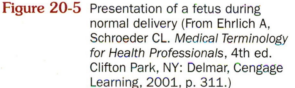

Figure 20-5 Presentation of a fetus during normal delivery (From Ehrlich A, Schroeder CL. *Medical Terminology for Health Professionals*, 4th ed. Clifton Park, NY: Delmar, Cengage Learning, 2001, p. 311.)

Delivery cases are also governed by these additional guidelines.

ICD-10-CM Official Coding Guidelines

4) When a delivery occurs

When a delivery occurs, the principal diagnosis should correspond to the main circumstances or complication of the delivery. In cases of cesarean delivery, the selection of the principal diagnosis should be the condition established after study that was responsible for the patient's admission. If the patient was admitted with a condition that resulted in the performance of a cesarean procedure, that condition should be selected as the principal diagnosis. If the reason for the admission/encounter was unrelated to the condition resulting in the cesarean delivery, the condition related to the reason for the admission/encounter should be selected as the principal diagnosis, even if a cesarean was performed.

5) Outcome of delivery

A code from category Z37, Outcome of delivery, should be included on every maternal record when a delivery has occurred. These codes are not to be used on subsequent records or on the newborn record.

At times a pregnant patient presents for care because of a complication but no delivery occurs. In such cases, here is the coding guideline.

ICD-10-CM Official Coding Guidelines

3) Episodes when no delivery occurs

In episodes when no delivery occurs, the principal diagnosis should correspond to the principal complication of the pregnancy which necessitated the encounter. Should more than one complication exist, all of which are treated or monitored, any of the complications codes may be sequenced first.

Complications Predominately Related to the Puerperium (Category Codes O85–O92)

Category codes O85–O92 report complications predominately relating to the puerperium: puerperal sepsis, other puerperal infections, obstetric embolism, complications of anesthesia during the puerperium, infections of breast associated with pregnancy, and other disorders of lactation.

Code O90.3 is governed by the following coding guideline.

ICD-10-CM Official Coding Guidelines

Pregnancy associated cardiomyopathy

Pregnancy associated cardiomyopathy, code O90.3, is unique in that it may be diagnosed in the third trimester of pregnancy but may continue to progress months after delivery. For this reason, it is referred to as peripartum cardiomyopathy. Code O90.3 is only for use when the cardiomyopathy develops as a result of pregnancy in a woman who did not have pre-existing heart disease.

Other Obstetric Conditions, Not Elsewhere Classified (Category Codes O94–O9A)

Category codes O94–O9A report other obstetric conditions that are not classified elsewhere in this chapter.

Category O94, Sequelae of complications of pregnancy, childbirth, and the puerperium, is governed by the following guidelines.

ICD-10-CM Official Coding Guidelines

Code O94, Sequelae of complication of pregnancy, childbirth, and the puerperium

1) Code O94

Code O94, Sequelae of complication of pregnancy, childbirth, and the puerperium, is for use in those cases when an initial complication of a pregnancy develops a sequelae requiring care or treatment at a future date.

2) After the initial postpartum period

This code may be used at any time after the initial postpartum period.

3) Sequencing of Code O94

This code, like all late effect codes, is to be sequenced following the code describing the sequelae of the complication.

Code assignment for patients admitted because of an HIV-related illness should follow the following coding guideline.

ICD-10-CM Official Coding Guidelines

HIV Infection in Pregnancy, Childbirth, and the Puerperium

During pregnancy, childbirth, or the puerperium, a patient admitted because of an HIV-related illness should receive a principal diagnosis from subcategory O98.7–, Human immunodeficiency [HIV] disease complicating pregnancy, childbirth, and the puerperium, followed by the code(s) for the HIV-related illness(es).

Patients with asymptomatic HIV infection status admitted during pregnancy, childbirth, or the puerperium should receive codes of O98.7– and Z21, Asymptomatic human immunodeficiency virus [HIV] infection status.

The following coding guidelines govern alcohol and tobacco use complicating pregnancy, childbirth, and the puerperium.

ICD-10-CM Official Coding Guidelines

Alcohol and tobacco use during pregnancy, childbirth, and the puerperium

1) Alcohol use during pregnancy, childbirth, and the puerperium

Codes under subcategory O99.31, Alcohol use complicating pregnancy, childbirth, and the puerperium, should be assigned for any pregnancy case when a mother uses alcohol during the pregnancy or postpartum. A secondary code from category F10, Alcohol related disorders, should also be assigned.

2) Tobacco use during pregnancy, childbirth, and the puerperium

Codes under subcategory O99.33, Smoking (tobacco) complicating pregnancy, childbirth, and the puerperium, should be assigned for any pregnancy case when a mother uses any type of tobacco product during the pregnancy or postpartum. A secondary code from category F17, Nicotine dependence, or code Z72.0, Tobacco use, should also be assigned.

Another coding guideline applies to injuries, poisonings, and certain other consequences of external causes of pregnancy, childbirths, and the puerperium.

ICD-10-CM Official Coding Guidelines

Poisoning, toxic effects, adverse effects, and underdosing in a pregnant patient

A code from subcategory O9A.2, Injury, poisoning, and certain other consequences of external causes complicating pregnancy, childbirth, and the puerperium, should be sequenced first, followed by the appropriate poisoning, toxic effect, adverse effect, or underdosing code, and then the additional code(s) that specifies the condition caused by the poisoning, toxic effect, adverse effect, or underdosing.

See Section I.C.19. Adverse effects, poisoning, underdosing, and toxic effects.

Coders need to be familiar with these guidelines for proper code selection.

Additional Coding Guidelines

Two additional coding guidelines apply to this chapter of ICD-10-CM.

ICD-10-CM Official Coding Guidelines

3) Pregnancy-related complications after 6 week period

Chapter 15 codes may also be used to describe pregnancy-related complications after the peripartum or postpartum period if the provider documents that a condition is pregnancy related.

(continued)

4) Admission for routine postpartum care following delivery outside hospital

When the mother delivers outside the hospital prior to admission and is admitted for routine postpartum care and no complications are noted, code Z39.0, Encounter for care and examination of mother immediately after delivery, should be assigned as the principal diagnosis.

Comparing ICD-9-CM to ICD-10-CM

Many of the ICD-9-CM codes have been expanded in the ICD-10-CM to identify additional information about disorders related to pregnancy and childbirth. The changes include:

- O03, Spontaneous abortion, now identifies whether the abortion was complete or incomplete or complicated.

- O09, Supervision of high-risk pregnancy, identifies the trimester in which the treatment occurred.

- O10, Preexisting hypertensive heart disease complicating pregnancy, childbirth, and the puerperium, has been expanded at the fourth-character level to indicate the nature of the hypertension; at the fifth-character level to indicate whether the hypertension complicates, pregnancy, childbirth, or the puerperium; and at the sixth-character level to indicate the trimester.

- Many of the codes in ICD-10-CM identify the trimester in which the condition is present.

- Category O30, Multiple gestations, is expanded to identify specific complications.

- Category O42, Premature rupture of membranes, is expanded to identify the length of time between the rupture and the onset of delivery, the weeks of gestation at the time of the membrane rupture, and the trimester.

Internet Links

To learn more about pregnancy, childbirth, and the puerperium, visit Dr. Donnica's Women's Health site at *http://www.drdonnica.com* and the National Women's Health Resource Center at *http://www.healthywomen.org*

For information on labor and delivery, visit *http://www.babies.sutterhealth.org* and *http://www.nlm.nih.gov/medlineplus/childbirth.html*

Summary

- Understanding terminology is extremely important in assigning the correct codes.

- The codes in chapter 15 of ICD-10-CM apply to the medical record or encounter of the mother.

- Any conditions encountered during a pregnancy or postpartum period are coded to this chapter as a complication unless the provider documents that such a condition is incidental to the pregnancy.

Chapter Review

True/False: Indicate whether each statement is true (T) or false (F).

1. _____ Through the tenth week of pregnancy, the developing child is known as an embryo.

2. _____ The second trimester is from 14 to 20 weeks.

3. _____ The phrase "unspecified episode of care" is used only if there is absolutely no other information available.

4. _____ A spontaneous abortion is coded to O03.

5. _____ Codes from this chapter should appear only on the mother's encounter.

Fill-in-the-Blanks: Enter the appropriate term(s) to complete each statement.

6. A blighted ovum that has developed into a benign tumor is called a _____.

7. A pregnancy that occurs outside the uterus is called an _____.

8. A developing child from nine weeks until birth is known as a _____.

9. An encounter for cesarean delivery without indication is reported with code _____.

10. The time before childbirth is called _____.

11. Through eight weeks of pregnancy, the developing child is known as a(n) _____.

12. The puerperium, or postpartum period, lasts up to _____ weeks after delivery.

13. A premature sudden separation of the placenta from the uterus prior to or during labor is called _____.

14. The only outcome of delivery code assigned with code O80 is _____.

15. During pregnancy, childbirth, or the puerperium, a patient admitted because of an HIV-related illness should be coded with a principal diagnosis from subcategory _____.

Coding Assignments

Instructions: Using an ICD-10-CM code book, assign the proper diagnosis code to the following diagnostic statements.

Diagnosis	Code
1. postpartum fibrinolysis	_____
2. severe pre-eclampsia second trimester	_____
3. antepartum hemorrhage first trimester	_____
4. vomiting complicating pregnancy	_____
5. low-lying placenta (during pregnancy, no hemorrhage)	_____
6. tubal pregnancy	_____
7. termination of pregnancy complicated by renal failure	_____
8. miscarriage at 10 weeks' gestation	_____
9. cervical pregnancy	_____
10. uterine fibroid found during last ultrasound before delivery	_____

11. twin pregnancy, second trimester   _____

12. cervical incompetence, Shirodkar suture needed to hold
     pregnancy   _____

13. premature rupture of membranes   _____

14. threatened abortion at 15 weeks' gestation, no delivery   _____

15. obstruction of delivery during labor caused by prolapsed
     arm of fetus   _____

16. pelvic peritonitis following incomplete spontaneous
     abortion   _____

17. delivery with retained placenta with manual removal of
     retained placenta   _____

18. contraction ring dystocia   _____

19. postpartum hemorrhage   _____

20. false labor at 38 weeks   _____

21. hydatidiform mole   _____

22. pelvic peritonitis following an ectopic pregnancy   _____

23. syphilis during pregnancy   _____

24. liver disorders in childbirth   _____

25. antepartum anemia complicating pregnancy   _____

Case Studies

Instructions: Review each case study and select the correct ICD-10-CM diagnostic code.

CASE 1

Physician Office Note of 2/04/XX

WEIGHT: 150 pounds. This is a weight gain of 7 pounds since her last visit 3 weeks ago. Blood pressure: 140/80. Lab: Urinalysis reveals protein present.

Patient is complaining of increased headaches and dizziness.

VAGINAL EXAM: Normal

HEENT: Face appears swollen.

EXTREMITIES: Edema of hands and feet

Patient symptoms indicates mild pre-eclampsia during her third trimester. Patient advised to decrease salt intake and to follow up in 2 weeks.

ICD-10-CM Code Assignment: _____

CASE 2

Discharge Summary

ADMISSION DATE: 5/6/XX, Discharge date: 5/8/XX

HISTORY:

This patient is gravida 2, para 1 and was seen in my office for all of her prenatal visits. Her prenatal course was uneventful. She was admitted with a history of contractions every 3 to 5 minutes. Cervix was 100% effaced and 9 cm dilated.

HOSPITAL COURSE:

At the time of admission, patient received IV and was placed on a fetal monitor. Her water broke at 2 a.m. After 3 hours the patient delivered a baby boy with apgar scores of 8 at 1 minute and 10 at 5 minutes. Postpartum care was uneventful. The patient was discharged 2 days later.

INSTRUCTIONS TO PATIENT: Diet as tolerated. Tylenol every 4 hours for pain. She is to follow up in my office in 2 weeks.

ICD-10-CM Code Assignment: _____

CASE 3

Physician Office Note

This patient presents today in the eighth month of her pregnancy. She complains of increased fatigue over the last month, edema of both legs, shortness of breath, and difficulty breathing when lying down.

I have monitored her closely for the last 2 months. Last week I sent her for an EKG, chest X-ray, and coronary angiography. Today I am reviewing the results with her.

EXAM: Reveals an obese, gravida 1, para 0, 29-year-old woman.

HEENT: Normocephalic, palpebrale conjunctiva, pinkish, PERRLA

NECK: Supple. No mass noted.

HEART: Tachycardia present. Slight murmur.

LUNGS: There is congestion in both lungs.

ABDOMEN: Protuberant, soft, and nontender. Liver and spleen not palpable. Uterus enlarged to gestational size. Fetal heart tones are noted to be normal.

PELVIC: External genitalia, normal. Vagina, clear. Membranes, intact.

EXTREMITIES: There is edema in both legs.

Review of diagnostic testing: EKG, chest X-ray, and coronary angiography results support a diagnosis of peripartum cardiomyopathy.

I discussed with the patient the need for medications to improve her heart function, decrease edema, and prevent the formation of blood clots that can occur with the diagnosis of peripartum cardiomyopathy.

Medications were ordered as per medication record.

INSTRUCTIONS TO PATIENT: I explained to the patient the need to take her medications as prescribed. She is to follow up with me in 5 days.

ICD-10-CM Code Assignment: _____

CASE 4

Discharge Note

Linda presented to the hospital in active labor. She was admitted, and a fetal monitor was used, which showed a very unstable fetal heart rate of 100–125. After physical examination, it was determined that she was fully dilated but the baby was in breech position. Linda was instructed to begin pushing, at which time the fetal heart rate dropped. It was decided that an attempt would be made to turn the baby, but this attempt was unsuccessful. At this point, an emergency cesarean delivery was successfully performed.

ICD-10-CM Code Assignment: _____

(continued)

CASE 5

Physician Office Visit

This 27-year-old female, who is 12 weeks pregnant, is experiencing increased thirst, increased urination, increased fatigue, and bouts of nausea. An in-office blood sugar reading was 245, so a glucose tolerance test was ordered. The results confirmed gestational diabetes. Insulin is not necessary at this time.

ICD-10-CM Code Assignment: _____

Certain Conditions Originating in the Perinatal Period

Chapter Outline

Objectives

At the conclusion of this chapter, the learner should be able to:

1. Understand how perinatal conditions of the mother affect the fetus or newborn.
2. Describe conditions that may affect the fetus or newborn.
3. Define various perinatal conditions.
4. Discuss the specific coding guidelines that relate to conditions originating in the perinatal period.
5. Select and code diagnoses from case studies.

Key Terms

omphalitis   perinatal period

> **Reminder**
>
> *As you work through this chapter, you will need to have a copy of the ICD-10-CM coding book to reference.*

Introduction

The time just before the birth of the child up to 28 days after birth is considered the **perinatal period**. The codes in chapter 16 of ICD-10-CM are organized into the following blocks of codes:

- P00–P04, Newborn affected by maternal factors and by complications of pregnancy, labor, and delivery
- P05–P08, Disorders of newborn related to length of gestation and fetal growth
- P09, Abnormal findings on neonatal screening
- P10–P15, Birth trauma
- P19–P29, Respiratory and cardiovascular disorders specific to the perinatal period
- P35–P39, Infections specific to the perinatal period
- P50–P61, Hemorrhagic and hematological disorders of newborn
- P70–P74, Transitory endocrine and metabolic disorders specific to newborn
- P76–P78, Digestive system disorders of newborn
- P80–P83, Conditions involving the integument and temperature regulation of newborn
- P84, Other problems with newborn
- P90–P96, Other disorders originating in the perinatal period

Coding Guidelines for Certain Conditions Originating in the Perinatal Period

The ICD-10-CM Official Coding Guidelines state the following.

ICD-10-CM Official Coding Guidelines

For coding and reporting purposes the perinatal period is defined as before birth through the 28th day following birth. The following guidelines are provided for reporting purposes.

a. General Perinatal Rules

1) Use of Chapter 16 Codes

Codes in this chapter are never for use on the maternal record. Codes from Chapter 15, the obstetric chapter, are never permitted on the newborn record. Chapter 16 codes may be used throughout the life of the patient if the condition is still present.

2) Principal Diagnosis for Birth Record

When coding the birth episode in a newborn record, assign a code from category Z38, Liveborn according to place of birth and type of delivery, as the principal diagnosis. A code from category Z38 is assigned only once, to a newborn at the time of birth. If a newborn is transferred to another institution, a code from category Z38 should not be used at the receiving hospital.

A code from category Z38 is used only on the newborn record, not on the mother's record.

3) Use of Codes from other Chapters with Codes from Chapter 16

Codes from other chapters may be used with codes from chapter 16 if the codes from the other chapters provide more specific detail. Codes for signs and symptoms may be assigned when a definitive diagnosis has not been established. If the reason for the encounter is a perinatal condition, the code from chapter 16 should be sequenced first.

4) Use of Chapter 16 Codes after the Perinatal Period

Should a condition originate in the perinatal period, and continue throughout the life of the patient, the perinatal code should continue to be used regardless of the patient's age.

5) Birth process or community acquired conditions

If a newborn has a condition that may be either due to the birth process or community acquired and the documentation does not indicate which it is, the default is due to the birth process and the code from chapter 16 should be used. If the condition is community-acquired, a code from chapter 16 should not be assigned.

6) Code all clinically significant conditions

All clinically significant conditions noted on routine newborn examination should be coded. A condition is clinically significant if it requires:

- *clinical evaluation; or*
- *therapeutic treatment; or*
- *diagnostic procedures; or*
- *extended length of hospital stay; or*
- *increased nursing care and/or monitoring; or*
- *has implications for future health care needs*

Note: The perinatal guidelines listed above are the same as the general coding guidelines for "additional diagnoses", except for the final point regarding implications for future health care needs. Codes should be assigned for conditions that have been specified by the provider as having implications for future health care needs.

Newborn Affected by Maternal Factors and by Complications of Pregnancy, Labor, and Delivery (Category Codes P00–P04)

This block of codes is explained by the note that appears at the start of the block.

When assigning codes from this section, coder must carefully read the recorded medical information to determine the proper code assignment. The descriptions for these codes are very detailed.

The Official Coding Guidelines state the following with regard to categories P00–P04.

Note:

These codes are for use when the listed maternal conditions are specified as the cause of confirmed morbidity or potential morbidity which have their origin in the perinatal period (before birth through the first 28 days after birth). Codes from these categories are also for use for newborns who are suspected of having an abnormal condition resulting from exposure from the mother or the birth process, but without signs or symptoms, and, which after examination and observation, is found not to exist. These codes may be used even if treatment is begun for a suspected condition that is ruled out.

ICD-10-CM Official Coding Guidelines

b. Observation and Evaluation of Newborns for Suspected Conditions not Found

Assign a code from categories P00–P04 to identify those instances when a healthy newborn is evaluated for a suspected condition that is determined after study not to be present. Do not use a code from categories P00–P04 when the patient has identified signs or symptoms of a suspected problem; in such cases, code the sign or symptom.

Disorders of Newborn Related to Length of Gestation and Fetal Growth (Category Codes P05–P08)

This block of codes includes the following categories:

- P05, Disorders of newborn related to slow fetal growth and fetal malnutrition

- P07, Disorders of newborn related to short gestation and low birth weight, not elsewhere classified. Be aware of the note and the Includes notations that appear in the Tabular section at the start of category P07.

- P08, Disorders of newborn related to long gestation and high birth weight. Be aware of the note and the Includes notations that appear in the code book at the start of category P08.

A situation that can affect newborns is prematurity and/or fetal growth retardation. The Official Coding Guidelines give the following direction to coders in this situation.

ICD-10-CM Official Coding Guidelines

d. Prematurity and Fetal Growth Retardation

Providers utilize different criteria in determining prematurity. A code for prematurity should not be assigned unless it is documented. Assignment of codes in categories P05, Disorders of newborn related to slow fetal growth and fetal malnutrition, and P07, Disorders of newborn related to short gestation and low birth weight, not elsewhere classified, should be based on the recorded birth weight and estimated gestational age. Codes from category P05 should not be assigned with codes from category P07.

When both birth weight and gestational age are available, two codes from category P07 should be assigned, with the code for birth weight sequenced before the code for gestational age.

e. Low birth weight and immaturity status

Codes from subcategory Z91.7, Low birth weight and immaturity status, are for use as personal status codes for a child or adult who was premature or had a low birth weight as a newborn and this is affecting the patient's current health status.

Abnormal Findings on Neonatal Screening (Category Code P09)

The title of this category makes it self-explanatory in that it records abnormal findings on neonatal screenings. A notation appears after the category heading instructing the coder to "Use additional code to identify signs, symptoms, and conditions associated with the screening."

Birth Trauma (Category Codes P10–P15)

These codes report injuries that occurred during birth:

- P10, Intracranical laceration and hemorrhage due to birth injury

- P11, Other birth injuries to central nervous system

- P12, Birth injury to scalp

- P13, Birth injury to skeleton

- P14, Birth Injury to peripheral nervous system

- P15, Other birth injuries

ICD-10-CM Official Coding Guidelines

c. Coding Additional Perinatal Diagnoses

1) Assigning codes for conditions that require treatment

Assign codes for conditions that require treatment or further investigation, prolong the length of stay, or require resource utilization.

2) Codes for conditions specified as having implications for future health care needs

Assign codes for conditions that have been specified by the provider as having implications for future health care needs.

Note: This guideline should not be used for adult patients.

To assign these codes, you must have supporting documentation that the injury is a birth trauma.

The following two coding guidelines apply to the entire chapter.

Respiratory and Cardiovascular Disorders Specific to the Perinatal Period (Category Codes, P19–P29)

This block of codes is used to report metabolic acidemia in the newborn, respiratory distress of the newborn, congenital pneumonia, neonatal aspiration, interstitial emphysema, pulmonary hemorrhage, chronic respiratory disease, and other respiratory and cardiovascular disorders that originated in the perinatal period.

Infections Specific to the Perinatal Period (Category Codes P35–P39)

Category codes P35–P39 include infections acquired in utero, during birth via the umbilicus, or during the first 28 days after birth:

- P35, Congenital viral diseases
- P36, Bacterial sepsis of newborn
- P37, Other congenital infectious and parasitic diseases
- P38, **Omphalitis** of newborn (an inflammation of the navel)
- P39, Other infections specific to the perinatal period

Category P36, Bacterial sepsis of newborn, is governed by the following guideline.

ICD-10-CM Official Coding Guidelines

f. Bacterial Sepsis of Newborn

*Category P36, Bacterial sepsis of newborn, includes congenital sepsis. If a perinate is documented as having sepsis without documentation of congenital or community acquired, the default is congenital and a code from category P36 should be assigned. If the P36 code includes the causal organism, an additional code from category B95, Streptococcus, Staphylococcus, and Enterococcus as the cause of diseases classified elsewhere, or B96, Other bacterial agents as the cause of diseases classified elsewhere, should **not** be assigned. If the P36 code does not include the causal organism, assign an additional code from category B96. If applicable, use additional codes to identify severe sepsis (R65.2–) and any associated acute organ dysfunction.*

Exercise 21.1 – Coding for Categories P00–P39

For each diagnostic statement listed, select the appropriate ICD-10-CM diagnostic code.

Diagnosis   *Code*

1. Newborn suspected to be affected by prolapsed cord   _____

2. fracture of skull due to birth injury   _____

3. meconium aspiration   _____

4. neonatal candidiasis   _____

5. exceptionally large newborn, 4600 grams   _____

6. subconjunctival hemorrhage due to birth injury   _____

7. congenital malaria   _____

8. neonatal aspiration of blood   _____

9. congenital rubella pneumonitis   _____

10. idiopathic tachypnea of newborn   _____

Hemorrhagic and Hematologic Disorders of Newborn (Category Codes P50–P61)

The block of codes in this section of the code book includes the following categories:

- P50, Newborn affected by intrauterine (fetal) blood loss
- P51, Umbilical hemorrhage of newborn
- P52, Intracranial nontraumatic hemorrhage of newborn
- P53, Hemorrhagic disease of newborn
- P54, Other neonatal hemorrhage
- P55, Hemolytic disease of newborn
- P56, Hydrops fetalis due to hemolytic disease
- P57, Kernicterus
- P58, Neonatal jaundice due to other excessive hemolysis
- P59, Neonatal jaundice from other and unspecified causes
- P60, Disseminated intravascular coagulation of newborn
- P61, Other perinatal hematological disorders

Coders need to pay attention to the numerous notations and code descriptions in this block of codes. For example, code P54.5 lists a number of diagnoses that are coded here as well as an important Excludes 2 notation.

Transitory Endocrine and Metabolic Disorders Specific to Newborn (Category Codes P70–P74)

This block of codes includes transitory endocrine and metabolic disturbances caused by the infant's response to maternal endocrine and metabolic factors or its adjustment to extrauterine environment.

Digestive System Disorders of Newborn (Category Codes P76–P78)

Three categories in this block of codes are used to report an intestinal obstruction of the newborn, necrotizing enterocolitis of the newborn, and other perinatal digestive system disorders.

Conditions Involving the Integument and Temperature Regulation of Newborn (Category Codes P80–P83) and Other Problems with Newborns (Category Code P84)

Hypothermia of the newborn, disturbances of temperature regulation, and conditions of integument specific to the newborn are reported using category codes P80–P83.

Category P84 reports the following problems with a newborn:

- Acidosis
- Anoxia NOS
- Asphyxia NOS
- Hypercapnia
- Hypoxemia
- Hypoxia
- Mixed metabolic and respiratory acidosis

Other Disorders Originating in the Perinatal Period (Category Codes P90–P96)

The last block of codes in this chapter reports other disorders originating in the perinatal period:

- P90, Convulsions of newborn
- P91, Other disturbances of cerebral status of newborn
- P92, Feeding problems of newborn
- P93, Reactions and intoxication due to drugs administered to newborn
- P94, Disorders of muscle tone of newborn
- P95, Stillbirth
- P96, Other conditions originating in the perinatal period

Category P95 is governed by the following coding guideline:

ICD-10-CM Official Coding Guidelines

g. Stillbirth

Code P95, Stillbirth, is only for use in institutions that maintain separate records for stillbirths. No other code should be used with P95. Code P95 should not be used on the mother's record.

Comparing ICD-9-CM to ICD-10-CM

For conditions originating in the perinatal period, the following changes have been made in the ICD-10-CM codes:

- Slow fetal growth and fetal malnutrition, category P05, identifies newborns light for gestational age (P05.0) and newborns small for gestational age (P05.1), with further expansion at the fifth-character level.

- Category P07, Disorders of newborn related to short gestation and low birth weight, is expanded at the fourth- and fifth-character levels to identify specific conditions of the preterm newborns.

- Codes, P10–P15, identify various types of birth traumas.

- The following codes have been expanded in ICD-10-CM: congenital pneumonia, interstitial emphysema, and related conditions originating in the perinatal period; pulmonary hemorrhage; fetal blood loss; gastrointestinal hemorrhage; and perinatal jaundice.

Many of the ICD-10-CM codes are very specific when describing conditions originating in the perinatal period. Providers therefore have to be instructed to provide the detail necessary to select the appropriate codes.

Internet Links

To learn more about conditions that arise in the perinatal period, go to the following Web sites:

- U.S. Department of Health and Human Services at *http://www.hhs.gov*

- Neonatal Resuscitation Program at *http://www.aap.org*

Summary

- The codes from chapter 16 of ICD-10-CM classify conditions that affect the fetus or newborn.

- These codes are used on the chart of the newborn *only*; they *never* appear in the mother's medical record.

- Congenital conditions that are not detected until later in life should be coded from this section.

- Numerous coding guidelines apply to this chapter of ICD-10-CM.

- When coding from chapter 16 of ICD-10-CM, the coder must determine that the condition being coded originated in the perinatal period.

Chapter Review

True/False: Indicate whether each statement is true (T) or false (F).

1. _____ Code P95 reports stillbirth.

2. _____ Codes from this chapter can be found in the record of either the mother or the newborn.

3. _____ Low birth weight may be referred to as "fetal immaturity."

4. _____ Code P83.9 would be used to report congenital hydrocele.

5. _____ Acidosis of the newborn would be reported with code P70.

Fill-in-the-Blank: Enter the appropriate term(s) to complete each statement.

6. The perinatal period extends from birth up to _____.

7. Code _____ reports massive umbilical hemorrhage of the newborn.

8. Code P29.0 reports _____.

9. Respiratory failure of the newborn is reported with code _____.

10. Congenital tuberculosis is coded with code _____.

Coding Assignments

Instructions: Using an ICD-10-CM code book, assign the proper diagnosis code to the following diagnostic statements.

Diagnosis   *Code*

1. maternal hypertension affecting the fetus   _____

2. neonatal bradycardia   _____

3. dehydration of newborn   _____

4. post-term infant, 41 weeks   _____

5. neonatal peritonitis   _____

6. premature baby, birth weight of 1,900 grams   _____

7. fetal malnutrition, 6 days old, 1,300 grams   _____

8. meconium peritonitis   _____

9. congenital hypertonia   _____

10. cold injury syndrome of the newborn   _____

11. transitory neonatal hypoglycemia   _____

12. neonatal thyrotoxicosis   _____

13. CNS dysfunction in newborn due to birth injury   _____

14. polycythemia neonatorum   _____

15. neonatal tachycardia   _____

16. stillbirth   _____

17. mild birth asphyxia   _____

18. pulmonary hemorrhage originating in the perinatal period   _____

19. bronchopulmonary dysplasia originating in the perinatal period   _____

20. neonatal moniliasis   _____

21. neonatal bruising   _____

22. placenta previa affecting the fetus   _____

23. neonatal hypertension   _____

24. acidosis of newborn   _____

25. birth injury to brachial plexus   _____

Case Studies

Instructions: Review each case study and select the correct ICD-10-CM diagnostic code.

CASE 1

Inpatient Physician's Progress Note

12/20/XX Two-day-old infant examined today to follow up after the results of diagnostic tests.

BLOOD GAS: Study indicates reduced oxygen tension and ineffective gas exchange.

CHEST X-RAY: Presence of infiltrate

Infant continues to exhibit signs of infant respiratory distress syndrome, type 2.

ORDERS: Continue titrated oxygen and aerosol infusion of Survanta.

ICD-10-CM Code Assignment: _____

CASE 2

Inpatient Physician's Progress Note

2/3/XX Five-hour-old neonate is jaundiced, and delivering physician has just determined that the child is Rh-positive and mother is Rh-negative. The mother just moved to the area, and it cannot be determined from history whether the mother had screening for Rh incompatibility prior to delivery.

EXAM:

ABDOMEN: Liver and spleen are enlarged.

CHEST: Lungs are clear.

PLAN: Phototherapy and albumin infusion standard protocol as per written orders.

IMPRESSION: Hemolytic disease of the newborn due to Rh isoimmunization.

ICD-10-CM Code Assignment: _____

CASE 3

Discharge Summary

The patient was discharged in stable condition on 1/20/XX. She is to continue on breast milk and can be supplemented with Similac with iron.

This patient is the product of a full-term gestation. The Apgars were 9 and 10. Birth weight was 6 pounds 10 ounces. Physical examination shortly after birth was negative. The infant's temperature was elevated, and urinalysis revealed a urinary tract infection. The plan was to observe the patient. Antibiotic therapy was started.

She had no difficulty nursing and ate well while she was in the hospital. She had no problems with her bowel movements. On the day of discharge, the patient's weight was down 3 ounces from birth. She will be seen in my office in 7 days.

ICD-10-CM Code Assignment: _____

CASE 4

Hospital Visit Note

The patient is a female, born 36 hours ago and now experiencing convulsions. The product of a normal delivery with birth weight of 7 pounds 2 ounces. Her vital signs are normal at this time. The nursing staff contacted this physician immediately upon noting the convulsions, which they said lasted several seconds. An EEG and ECG have been ordered, along with a complete blood workup. The baby will be monitored closely until all test results are back.

ICD-10-CM Code Assignment: _____

CASE 5

Hospital Visit Note

The patient is a newborn infant male, born 2 hours ago to a mother who was experiencing severe hypertension prior to her pregnancy. The mother was being monitored closely for this condition during her current pregnancy because she had difficulty during her last one. It appears now that this baby boy is experiencing some respiratory distress due to the maternal hypertension. Pulse ox reading was 70, and his respirations were elevated. His vital signs at this time are all within normal limits since we started the oxygen. His pulse ox reading is now at 98. He will be monitored until such time as there is no need for the oxygen and his vital signs remain normal.

ICD-10-CM Code Assignment: _____

CHAPTER 22

Congenital Malformations, Deformations, and Chromosomal Abnormalities

Chapter Outline

Objectives

At the conclusion of this chapter, the learner should be able to:

1. Define the terms *congenital anomaly* and *deformity*.
2. Explain the conditions classified to chapter 17 of ICD-10-CM.
3. Discuss the organization of chapter 17 of ICD-10-CM.
4. Differentiate between congenital and acquired conditions.
5. Discuss the coding guidelines that relate to congenital anomalies.
6. Select and code diagnoses from case studies.

Key Terms

acquired conditions	cleft palate	hydrocephalus	valgus deformities of feet
anomaly	congenital anomaly	polycystic kidney disease	varus deformities of feet
birth defect	deformity	spina bifida	Volkmann's deformity
cleft lip	harelip	teratogens	

> **Reminder**
>
> *As you work through this chapter, you will need to have a copy of the ICD-10-CM coding book to reference.*

Introduction

Congenital anomalies, category codes Q00–Q99, are classified in chapter 17 of ICD-10-CM. This chapter is organized according to anatomical site. The blocks found in this chapter are:

- Q00–Q07, Congenital malformations of the nervous system.
- Q10–Q18, Congenital malformations of eye, ear, face, and neck.
- Q20–Q28, Congenital malformations of the circulatory system.
- Q30–Q34, Congenital malformations of the respiratory system.
- Q35–Q37, Cleft lip and cleft palate.
- Q38–Q45, Other congenital malformations of the digestive system.
- Q50–Q56, Congenital malformations of genital organs.
- Q60–Q64, Congenital malformations of the urinary system.
- Q65–Q79, Congenital malformations and deformations of the musculoskeletal system.
- Q80–Q89, Other congenital malformations.
- Q90–Q99, Chromosomal abnormalities, not elsewhere classified.

Introduction to the Body System

To understand the conditions that are classified to this chapter of ICD-10-CM, coders need to understand its terminology. A **congenital anomaly** is a disorder that exists at the time of birth and may be a result of genetic factors, agents causing defects in the embryo, or both. Agents that cause defects in an embryo are called **teratogens**. ICD-10-CM makes a clear distinction between an anomaly and a deformity. A **deformity** is a problem in the structure or form, which may or may not be disfiguring. An example of this is **Volkmann's deformity**, which is a congenital dislocation of the tibiotarsal. An **anomaly**, or **birth defect**, is a deviation from what is normal in the development of a structure or organ. An example of an anomaly is spina bifida cystica. **Spina bifida** is a congenital condition in which the spinal canal fails to close around the spinal cord.

Coding Congenital Malformations, Deformations, and Chromosomal Abnormalities

When selecting codes for congenital anomalies and defects, coders must closely review the Alphabetic Index. Many conditions are identified in ICD-10-CM as both congenital and acquired. **Acquired conditions** occur during a person's life. ICD-10-CM makes a distinction in the Alphabetic Index between congenital and acquired conditions, with the terms *acquired* or *congenital* in parentheses for some conditions. The terms in parentheses act as modifiers for the condition being coded because they further describe it.

> **EXAMPLE:** Holly presented to the emergency room with extreme pain in the right wrist joint. Holly is 10 years old. Upon examination, it was noted that the joint was somewhat deformed in that it was indented in the middle of the joint. Patient cannot flex the wrist. Mom noted that the wrist has been like this since birth. Until she has finished growing, surgery is not an option. The condition will be treated with ibuprofen and ice until the patient can be seen by primary care. Clinical Impression: congenital deformity of the right wrist

When coding the diagnostic statement "deformity of the joint," the coder finds the following in the Alphabetic Index:

Deformity
wrist (joint)(acquired)—see also Deformity, limb, forearm
congenital Q68.8
contraction—see Contraction, Joint, wrist

In the Alphabetic Index, both acquired and congenital categories are listed, with the term *acquired* appearing in parentheses and the term *congenital* appearing as an indentation. The coder has to be able to read the documentation when confronted with this type of situation in order to assign the correct code. If this is not possible based on the available information, then the coder needs to get clarification from the provider. For this example, code Q68.8 is the correct code assignment.

When selecting codes for this chapter of ICD-10-CM, coders need to be familiar with the following coding guidelines.

ICD-10-CM Official Coding Guidelines

Chapter 17: Congenital malformations, deformations, and chromosomal abnormalities (Q00–Q99)

Assign an appropriate code(s) from categories Q00–Q99, Congenital malformations, deformations, and chromosomal abnormalities when a malformation/deformation/or chromosomal abnormality is documented. A malformation/deformation/or chromosomal abnormality may be the principal/first listed diagnosis on a record or a secondary diagnosis.

When a malformation/deformation/or chromosomal abnormality does not have a unique code assignment, assign additional code(s) for any manifestations that may be present.

When the code assignment specifically identifies the malformation/deformation/or chromosomal abnormality, manifestations that are an inherent component of the anomaly should not be coded separately. Additional codes should be assigned for manifestations that are not an inherent component.

Codes from chapter 17 may be used throughout the life of the patient. If a congenital malformation or deformity has been corrected, a personal history code should be used to identify the history of the malformation or deformity. Although present at birth, malformation/deformation/or chromosomal abnormality may not be identified until later in life. Whenever the condition is diagnosed by the physician, it is appropriate to assign a code from codes Q00–Q99.

For the birth admission, the appropriate code from category Z38, Liveborn infants, according to place of birth and type of delivery, should be sequenced as the principal diagnosis, followed by any congenital anomaly codes, Q00–Q89. (Section I, 17)

Congenital Malformations of the Nervous System (Category Codes Q00–Q07)

Block Q00–Q07 is divided into the following categories:

- Q00, Anencephaly and similar malformations
- Q01, Encephalocele
- Q02, Microcephaly
- Q03, Congenital hydrocephalus
- Q04, Other congenital malformations of brain
- Q05, Spina bifida

Note:

The codes in this chapter are not assigned by age. Some congenital conditions do not manifest themselves until later in life even though they may have been present at birth. Also, a condition that occurs during the birthing process is considered a perinatal condition; a condition that is due to birth injury is coded to chapter 16, "Conditions in the Perinatal Period."

- Q06, Other congenital malformations of spinal cord
- Q07, Other congenital malformations of nervous system

Spina bifida is classified to category code Q05, except for spina bifida occulta, which is classified to code Q76.0. Figure 22-1 illustrates the different types of spina bifida. **Hydrocephalus**, an accumulation of fluid in the cranial meninges, is also found in the Q05 category when associated with spina bifida.

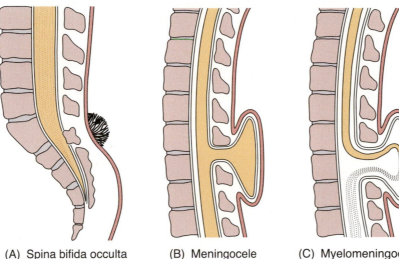

(A) Spina bifida occulta   (B) Meningocele   (C) Myelomeningocele

Figure 22-1 Types of spina bifida (From Neighbors M., Tannehill-Jones R. *Human Diseases*, 2nd ed. Clifton Park, NY: Delmar, Cengage Learning, 2002, p. 374.)

Congenital Malformations of Eye, Ear, Face, and Neck (Category Codes Q10–Q18)

This block of codes includes congenital malformations of the eye, ear, face, and neck and is classified to the following categories:

- Q10, Congenital malformations of eyelid, lacrimal apparatus, and orbit
- Q11, Anophthalmos, microphthalmos, and macrophthalmos
- Q12, Congenital lens malformations
- Q13, Congenital malformations of anterior segment of eye
- Q14, Congenital malformations of posterior segment of eye
- Q15, Other congenital malformations of eye
- Q16, Congenital malformations of ear causing impairment of hearing
- Q17, Other congenital malformations of ear
- Q18, Other congenital malformations of face and neck

As evidenced by their titles, the categories in this section are organized according to the specific sites and types of malformation. For many of the codes, numerous diagnostic descriptions and instructional notations are given. Careful attention to documentation is necessary for proper code assignment.

Congenital Malformations of the Circulatory System (Category Codes Q20–Q28)

Congenital anomalies of the cardiovascular system involve the heart and other structures of the circulatory system. The category codes are organized according to the anatomical structures affected by the anomaly. The terminology is the most challenging aspect of coding in this part of the code book. Because of the complexity of some of the conditions encountered in this part of the chapter, coders must research any questions regarding terminology, site, or abbreviations. Once a coder is familiar with the provider's documentation on these types of anomalies, code assignments become easier. Coders also need to identify that the cardiac condition being coded is congenital.

> **EXAMPLE:** Stenosis of the mitral valve can be congenital or acquired. Congenital stenosis of the mitral valve is coded to Q23.2, and mitral valve stenosis is coded to I05.0. Reading the documentation in the medical record and querying the provider are key in determining the proper code assignment.

Congenital Malformations of the Respiratory System (Category Codes Q30–Q34)

Congenital malformations of the respiratory system affect the nose, larynx, trachea, bronchus, lung, and pleura:

- Q30, Congenital malformations of nose
- Q31, Congenital malformations of larynx
- Q32, Congenital malformations of trachea and bronchus
- Q33, Congenital malformations of lung
- Q34, Other congenital malformations of the respiratory system

Many congenital malformations, such as malformation of the lungs, bronchus, or trachea, are located in this section. Keep in mind, though, that some of these anomalies or deformities may not present right away but are diagnosed later in life. If they are determined to be congenital, they are still coded from this section.

Cleft Lip and Cleft Palate (Category Codes Q35–Q37)

This block of codes reports Q35, Cleft palate; Q36, Cleft lip; and Q37, Cleft palate with cleft lip. An instructional notation after the block heading reads, "Use additional code to identify associated malformations of the nose (Q30.2)."

A **cleft palate** is a congenital groove or opening of the palate that involves the hard palate, soft palate, or both, as well as the upper lip. A **cleft lip**, also referred to as **harelip**, is a congenital defect that results in a deep groove or opening of the lip running upward to the nose.

Other Congenital Malformations of the Digestive System (Category Codes Q38–Q45)

Congenital malformations of the tongue, mouth, pharynx, esophagus, upper alimentary tract, small and large intestines, gallbladder, bile ducts, and liver are reported with category codes Q38–Q45.

The categories are differentiated by anatomical site and then by the specific malformation.

Exercise 22.1 – Congenital Malformations

Match the code in column 1 with the description in column 2.

Column 1   *Column 2*

_____ **1.** Q01.8   **a.** schizencephaly

_____ **2.** Q04.6   **b.** macrostomia

_____ **3.** Q06.4   **c.** congenital tricuspid stenosis

_____ **4.** Q13.5   **d.** encephalocele of other sites

_____ **5.** Q13.1   **e.** blue sclera

_____ **6.** Q18.4   **f.** hydroachis

_____ **7.** Q24.2   **g.** cor triatriatum

_____ **8.** Q22.4   **h.** aniridia

Congenital Malformations of Genital Organs (Category Codes Q50–Q56)

Categories Q50–Q56 include malformations of both male and female genital organs. These codes are organized by anatomical site and then by the specific malformation.

Congenital Malformations of the Urinary System (Category Codes Q60–Q64)

Five categories are used to report congenital malformations of the urinary system:

- Q60, Renal agenesis and other reduction defects of kidney
- Q61, Cystic kidney disease
- Q62, Congenital obstructive defects of renal pelvis and congenital malformations of ureter
- Q63, Other congenital malformations of kidney
- Q64, Other congenital malformations of the urinary system

Category code Q61 reports the various forms of cystic kidney disease. **Polycystic kidney disease**, a slowly progressive disorder in which the normal tissue of the kidneys is replaced with multiple grape-like cysts, is reported from this range of codes.

Disease Highlight—Polycystic Kidney Disease

Polycystic kidney disease is an inherited disorder in which the kidneys gradually lose the ability to function due to the grape-like clusters of cysts that form. The fluid-filled cysts cause a gradual inability of the kidneys to function because the renal tissue becomes compressed and eventually stops working. Figure 22-2 illustrates a polycystic kidney.

(continued)

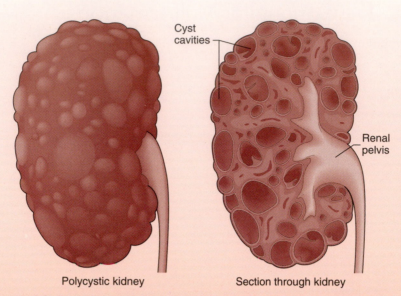

Figure 22-2 Polycystic kidney (From Neighbors M., Tannehill-Jones R. *Human Diseases,* 2nd ed. Clifton Park, NY: Delmar, Cengage Learning, 2002, p. 230.)

Signs and Symptoms:

As the disease progresses, renal tissue is destroyed and hypertension typically develops. Lumbar pain, blood in the urine, and frequent urinary tract infections occur. In some cases renal failure occurs.

Clinical Testing:

- A family history of polycystic kidney disease determines whether a patient is at risk.
- An intravenous pyelogram confirms the diagnosis.
- Urine tests, ultrasound, CT scans, and lab tests would be used to check creatinine levels and also confirm the diagnosis.

Treatment:

- There is no cure for the disease, but treatment of symptoms and surgical intervention may be necessary.
- If the kidney fails, dialysis is necessary.
- A kidney transplant is needed for end-stage management of the disease.
- Treatment is also directed by managing the hypertension and urinary tract infections.

Congenital Malformations and Deformations of the Musculoskeletal System (Category Codes Q65–Q79)

Category codes Q65–Q79 report musculoskeletal deformities of the hip, feet, head, face, fingers, knee, skull, limbs, ribs, spine, and chest.

Category Q66 is used to report congenital deformities of the feet, including clubfoot, or talipes varus. **Varus deformities of feet** is the congenital turning inward of the feet, and **valgus deformities of feet** is the congenital outward turning of the feet. Figure 22-3 illustrates a talipes varus deformity of the feet.

Other Congenital Malformations (Category Codes Q80–Q89) and Chromosomal Abnormalities, Not Elsewhere Classified (Category Codes Q90–Q99)

Category codes Q80–Q89 include such conditions as:

- Malformations of the skin.
- Malformations of the breast.
- Malformations of the hair.
- Fetal alcohol syndrome.
- Malformations affecting facial appearance.
- Congenital absence of spleen.
- Malformations of glands.

Chromosomal abnormalities reported with categories Q90–Q99 include:

- Down syndrome.
- Trisomy 18 and trisomy 13.
- Autosomal abnormalities.
- Rearrangements and structural markers.
- Turner's syndrome.
- Fragile X chromosome.

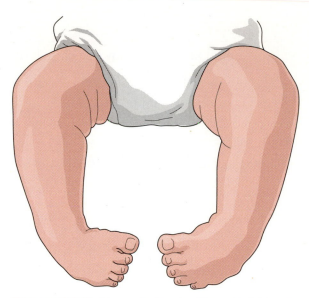

Figure 22-3 Varus deformity (From Neighbors M., Tannehill-Jones R. *Human Diseases*, 2nd ed. Clifton Park, NY: Delmar, Cengage Learning, 2002, p. 58.)

Comparing ICD-9-CM to ICD-10-CM

ICD-10-CM contains an increased number of codes for congenital conditions and chromosomal abnormalities. The following have been expanded:

- Encephalocele
- Other congenital malformations of brain
- Congenital malformations of the nose
- Congenial malformations of the larynx
- Cleft palate
- Congenital malformations of the esophagus
- Hypospadias
- Congenital malformations of the breast

Laterality has also been added to codes. For example, reduction defects of upper and lower limbs now identify right versus left or unspecified side.

Internet Links

To learn more about congenital anomalies, visit the National Institutes of Health at *http://www.health.nih.gov* and the National Library of Medicine at *http://www.nlm.nih.gov*

Summary

- Congenital anomalies may be a result of genetic factors, teratogens, or both.
- The anomalies can be present at birth and obvious, or they may not be identified until later in life.
- Documentation is critical, and the coder must be clear on the diagnoses to be certain of the code assignment.
- ICD-9-CM classifies anomalies to congenital and acquired states; therefore, for accurate coding to occur, medical documentation must clearly identify whether the anomaly is congenital.

Chapter Review

True/False: Indicate whether each statement is true (T) or false (F).

1. _____ The agents causing defects in an embryo are called teratogens.

2. _____ The codes in this chapter are assigned by age.

3. _____ The first block of codes in the chapter deals with anomalies of the nervous system.

4. _____ Anomalies of the eye are coded to the specific site of the defect.

5. _____ Spina bifida is a congenital condition in which the spinal canal fails to close around the spinal cord.

Fill-in-the-Blank: Enter the appropriate term(s) to complete each statement.

6. A _____ is a disorder that exists at the time of birth.

7. Code Q01.0 reports _____.

8. A birth defect is also known as a(n) _____.

9. _____ is a condition in which there is an accumulation of fluid in the cranial meninges.

10. A _____ is a problem in the structure or form that may or may not be disfiguring.

Coding Assignments

Instructions: Using an ICD-10-CM code book, assign the proper diagnosis code to the following diagnostic statements.

Diagnosis	Code
1. congenital hydrocephalus	_____
2. macrocheilia	_____
3. unspecified anomaly of the ear with impairment of hearing	_____
4. congenital deformity of the auricle of the heart	_____
5. Arnold-Chiari syndrome	_____
6. congenital brachial cleft cyst	_____
7. Klippel-Feil syndrome	_____

8. complete transposition of great vessels, congenital _____

9. congenital upper-limb vessel anomaly _____

10. hydromyelia _____

11. congenital renal dysplasia _____

12. exstrophy of urinary bladder _____

13. microcephalus _____

14. trisomies due to extra rings _____

15. congenital deformity of lip _____

16. congenital clubnail _____

17. tuberous sclerosis _____

18. macrotia _____

19. Meckel's diverticulum _____

20. congenital coronary artery anomaly _____

21. fragile x syndrome _____

22. velo-cardio-facial syndrome _____

23. scrotal transposition _____

24. embryonal nuclear cataract _____

25. hemicephaly _____

Case Studies

Instructions: Review each case study and select the correct ICD-10-CM diagnostic code.

CASE 1

Inpatient Orthopedic Consultation

Mary is a 3-year-old female child I am seeing at the request of Dr. Sharp. She is presently admitted to remove a cystic hygroma on her neck. I was asked to see her because she has severe congenital spastic quadriplegia with more involvement on the left than on the right. She was born 4 weeks premature and spent 5 weeks in the NICU and was diagnosed with congenital adduction contracture of the left hip. Her development has been extremely delayed due to cerebral palsy.

EXAM:

Generalized spastic quadriplegia. Increased tone on her left side than on her right. There is a significant adduction contracture of her left hip, with abduction to 10 degrees.

IMPRESSION:

Congenital adduction contracture of left hip.

(continued)

RECOMMENDATIONS: The spasticity in her hip adductors may cause her hip to dislocate, and an X-ray was ordered. She was scheduled for an adductor tenotomy to prevent her hip from dislocating.

ICD-10-CM Code Assignment: _____

CASE 2

Office Visit

Samantha returns today for follow-up of her elbow and knee flexion contractures.

EXAM:

UPPER EXTREMITIES: Rigid bilateral 37 degree elbow flexion contractures.

PELVIC JOINTS: She has no contractures of her hips.

LOWER EXTREMITIES: Rigid bilateral 40-degree knee flexion contractures

ANKLES: There are no contractures of her ankles.

X-RAYS REVIEWED: AP pelvis, AP and lateral knee, and AP and lateral elbow X-rays show no significant findings. The findings are consistent with multiplex, congenital arthrogryposis involving the elbows and knees.

RECOMMENDATIONS:

Measurements have been taken to have elbow and knee night splints made. She was scheduled for fitting and a 1-month follow-up visit.

ICD-10-CM Code Assignment: _____

CASE 3

Ambulatory Surgery Discharge Note

This is a 7-year-old female who presented with a problem swallowing. The mother states that she took the child to her pediatrician for evaluation when she started having problems eating and holding food down. The pediatric office sent over results of CT scans of the neck, chest, and trunk as well as lab test results. Upon review of the CT scans, it is noted that a slight mass is present on the esophagus that has probably been present since birth. Today a surgical removal of the mass and path examination was completed. The postoperative diagnosis of esophageal cyst (congenital) was made.

ICD-10-CM Code Assignment: _____

CASE 4

Physician Office Note

This is a 5-year-old male who presents today with a complaint of abdominal pain. His mother has noted a history of complaints of abdominal pain in the past. He is now experiencing vomiting since last night around 1 a.m. and is quite lethargic and in mild distress. Examination reveals the abdomen is distended and tender. An abdominopelvic CT scan reveals a stricture in the small bowel. This appears to have been present since birth, but due to the child's growth it has now become a problem. He will be admitted to the hospital for surgical correction.

ICD-10-CM Code Assignment: _____

CASE 5

Pediatric Office Note

Theresa Louise presents today for a 2-week checkup after a normal vaginal delivery. Mom says baby is eating well and is alert, responds appropriately when she hears noise, and is overall healthy. Upon examination there is a slight murmur when listening to the heart. We performed an EKG and chest X-ray.

There appears to be a small ventricular septal defect, which would have been present at birth. We will not do anything further at this time but monitor this condition to see if it corrects itself over this coming year.

ICD-10-CM Code Assignment: _____

Symptoms, Signs, and Abnormal Clinical Laboratory Findings

Chapter Outline

Objectives

At the conclusion of this chapter, the learner should be able to:

1. Identify terms used in locating codes for symptoms, signs, and ill-defined conditions found in chapter 18 of ICD-10-CM.
2. Explain terms found in documentation that would lead a coder to chapter 18 of ICD-10-CM.
3. Describe and understand the conditions classified to chapter 18 of ICD-10-CM.
4. Discuss the specific coding guidelines that relate to "Symptoms, Signs, and Abnormal Clinical and Laboratory Findings, Not Elsewhere Classified."
5. Select and code signs, symptoms, and ill-defined conditions from case studies.

Key Terms

altered states of consciousness	coma	mortality	symptom
	morbidity	sign	syncope

Reminder

As you work through this chapter, you will need to have a copy of the ICD-10-CM coding book to reference.

Introduction

Chapter 18 of ICD-10-CM, "Symptoms, Signs, and Abnormal Clinical and Laboratory Findings, Not Elsewhere Classified," allow the coder to locate codes for the abnormal results of laboratory or other investigative procedures, as well as for signs and symptoms for conditions that do not have a specific diagnosis code found elsewhere in ICD-10-CM. The codes for symptoms that affect only one body system are classified to the relevant chapters of ICD-10-CM, whereas symptoms that affect multiple systems or more than one disease are found in chapter 18.

The code blocks found in this code range are:

- R00–R09, Symptoms and signs involving the circulatory and respiratory systems.
- R10–R19, Symptoms and signs involving the digestive system and abdomen.
- R20–R23, Symptoms and signs involving the skin and subcutaneous tissue.
- R25–R29, Symptoms and signs involving the nervous and musculoskeletal systems.
- R30–R39, Symptoms and signs involving the urinary system.
- R40–R46, Symptoms and signs involving cognition, perception, emotional state, and behavior.
- R47–R49, Symptoms and signs involving speech and voice.
- R50–R69, General symptoms and signs.
- R70–R79, Abnormal findings on examination of blood, without diagnosis.
- R80–R82, Abnormal findings on examination of urine, without diagnosis.
- R83–R89, Abnormal findings on examination of other body fluids, substances, and tissues, without diagnosis.
- R90–R94, Abnormal findings on diagnostic imaging and in function studies, without diagnosis.
- R97, Abnormal tumor markers.
- R99, Ill-defined and unknown cause of mortality.

Coding of Symptoms, Signs, and Abnormal Clinical and Laboratory Findings, Not Elsewhere Classified

Chapter 18 of ICD-9-CM contains codes for signs, symptoms, and ill-defined conditions such as abnormal clinical or laboratory findings that impact the medical care and management of the patient. A **symptom** is reported by the patient and typically is what brings the patient to seek medical attention. A symptom is considered subjective information because it can be evaluated or measured only by the patient. A **sign** is observed by the physician and is objective evidence of a disease. It can be measured or evaluated.

> **EXAMPLE:** Marie Merry presents with itching and burning of the right forearm. Upon examination, a patch of small blisters is noticed. The itching and burning are considered symptoms because they can be described and evaluated only by the patient. The blisters are a sign because they can be observed and evaluated by the physician.

Ill-defined conditions also code to this chapter but should never be used if a more definitive diagnosis has been made. These codes are used when no other diagnosis is found in the available medical information or a code cannot be found in another chapter of ICD-10-CM. Until a specific diagnosis is assigned, the signs and symptoms are coded.

> **EXAMPLE:** Mrs. Marble presents today with her 3-month-old daughter, who is not eating well and is quite fussy. She cries after she has had her bottle and is projectile vomiting. She has

been like this over the last several days, and now Mrs. Marble would like her to be examined. The report is as follows:

> Examination reveals nothing out of the ordinary. This is a normal, 3-month-old baby girl. Heart and lungs are clear; bowel sounds are active and normal. Abdomen is soft with no splenomegaly.

> Diagnosis: Projectile vomiting

> Plan: Will contact the pediatric GI office and set up a consult with possible workup.

The diagnosis in this example is R11.12, Projectile vomiting, because a definitive diagnosis was not made. If the pediatric gastroenterologist (GI) makes a definitive diagnosis, then the diagnosis is *not* R11.12 but whatever diagnosis the gastroenterologist gives.

Before selecting codes from this chapter, the coder should be familiar with the notations in the Tabular List after the chapter heading. The notations explain the purpose and use of the codes found in chapter 18 of ICD-10-CM. The following is an excerpt from the notation.

The conditions and signs or symptoms included in categories R00–R94 consist of:
a) Cases for which no more specific diagnosis can be made even after all facts bearing on the case have been investigated.
b) Signs or symptoms existing at the time of initial encounter that proved to be transient and whose causes could not be determined.
c) Provisional diagnosis in a patient who failed to return for further investigation or care.
d) Cases referred elsewhere for investigation or treatment before the diagnosis was made.
e) Cases in which a more precise diagnosis was not available for any other reason.
f) Certain symptoms, for which supplementary information is provided, that represent important problems in medical care in their own right.

It is common to select codes from chapter 18 for coding outpatient encounters. Outpatients seek care for relief of symptoms, and the results of diagnostic workups are not always available at the time of the encounter. The codes from chapter 18 are used to describe the reason for the encounter when a more definitive diagnosis is not yet available.

Coding Guidelines for Symptoms, Signs, and Abnormal Clinical and Laboratory Findings, Not Elsewhere Classified

The ICD-10-CM Official Guidelines for Coding and Reporting provide the coder with guidance as to when to use codes from chapter 18. These guidelines, at times, are different for inpatient and outpatient encounters; however, some of the guidelines apply to both the inpatient and the outpatient settings.

The first guideline that applies to coding symptoms and signs appears in Section I, B, 4 of the ICD-10-CM. It reads as follows:

ICD-10-CM Official Coding Guidelines

Signs and Symptoms

Codes that describe symptoms and signs, as opposed to diagnoses, are acceptable for reporting purposes when a related definitive diagnosis has not been established (confirmed) by the provider. Chapter 18 of ICD-10-CM, Symptoms, Signs, and Abnormal Clinical and Laboratory Findings, Not Elsewhere Classified (codes R00.0–R99) contain many, but not all codes for symptoms. (See Appendix A, Section I, B, 4)

Guideline for Principal Diagnosis

An additional guideline in Section II, A of the ICD-10-CM Official Guidelines for Coding and Reporting applies to the selection of one or more principal diagnoses for inpatient, short-term, acute care, long-term care, home health agencies, rehabilitative facilities, and psychiatric hospital records.

ICD-10-CM Official Coding Guidelines

A. Codes for symptoms, signs, and ill-defined conditions

Codes for symptoms, signs, and ill-defined conditions from chapter 18 are not to be used as a principal diagnosis when a related definitive diagnosis has been established. (See Appendix A, section II, A.)

This guideline instructs the coder to report a definitive diagnosis when it is established and not use a code from chapter 18. If a definitive diagnosis is not established, then a code from chapter 18 can be used. In an inpatient setting, symptom codes are not sequenced as a principal diagnosis when a related condition has been confirmed unless the patient was admitted for the purpose of treating the symptom and no care, treatment, or evaluation of the underlying disease occurred. For example, if a patient is admitted with intractable renal colic known to be caused by kidney stones and only pain management occurs, the code for renal colic, N23, is used. Therefore, the symptom can be coded as a principal diagnosis if the patient is being treated for only the symptom and not for the underlying condition. If there is any question about sequencing, the coder should always go back to the reason for the encounter.

Guideline for Symptoms Followed by Contrasting or Comparative Diagnoses

The following guideline applies to the selection of a principal diagnosis for inpatient, short-term, acute care, and long-term care hospitals.

ICD-10-CM Official Coding Guidelines

When a symptom(s) is followed by contrasting/comparative diagnoses, the symptom code is sequenced first. All the contrasting/comparative diagnoses should be coded as additional diagnoses. (See Appendix A, Section II, E.)

EXAMPLE: A patient is experiencing right lower abdominal pain, and the physician records the statement "abdominal pain due to appendicitis versus renal colic." All the contrasting or comparative diagnoses are coded as additional codes, with the symptom code listed first. R10.31 is sequenced first for the right lower quadrant pain. Then codes K35.9 (for the appendicitis) and N23 (renal colic) are the second and third codes.

This guideline applies only to the selection of principal diagnoses, not to the reporting of secondary diagnosis. If the physician lists the same statement as a secondary diagnosis, only the abdominal pain is reported.

Symptoms and Signs as Secondary Codes

The ICD-10-CM Official Guidelines for Coding and Reporting state the following in relation to reporting signs and symptoms as additional diagnoses. This guideline applies to both inpatient and outpatient settings.

ICD-10-CM Official Coding Guidelines

Conditions that are an integral part of a disease process

Signs and symptoms that are associated routinely with a disease process should not be assigned as additional codes unless otherwise instructed by the classification. (See Appendix A, Section I, B, 5.)

The coder must have clinical documentation, as well as reference materials available, to properly code patient admissions and encounters in which signs and symptoms are documented in addition to a disease process. The coder must be able to identify the signs and symptoms that are implicit in a diagnostic statement because, according to the Official Coding Guidelines, these signs and symptoms are not coded separately. For example, if a patient presents with abdominal pain, and it is determined that the patient has gastroenteritis, the abdominal pain is not coded because the abdominal pain is an integral part of the gastroenteritis.

However, when a patient presents with signs and symptoms that are not routinely associated with a disease, the following coding guideline applies.

ICD-10-CM Official Coding Guidelines

Conditions that are not an integral part of a disease process

Additional signs and symptoms that may not be associated routinely with a disease process should be coded when present. (See Appendix A, Section I, B, 6.)

Difference Between Inpatient and Outpatient Coding Guidelines

For inpatient hospital visits, suspected, rule-out, and possible diagnoses can be coded. For outpatient or office visits, suspected, rule-out, and possible diagnoses cannot be coded. Therefore, often in the outpatient setting, codes from chapter 18 of ICD-10-CM are used until a physician can establish a definitive diagnosis. The following guideline applies to outpatient settings and is found in Section IV of the ICD-10-CM Official Guidelines for Coding and Reporting.

ICD-10-CM Official Coding Guidelines

Uncertain diagnoses

Do not code diagnoses documented as "probable," "suspected," "questionable," "rule out," or "working diagnosis" or other similar terms indicating uncertainty. Rather, code the conditions(s) to the highest degree of certainty for that encounter/visit, such as symptoms, signs, abnormal test results, or other reason for the visit.

Please note: This differs from the coding practices used by short-term, acute care, long-term care, and psychiatric hospitals. (See Appendix A, Section IV, H.)

EXAMPLE: Patty Patient presents to the ER with acute rebound tenderness in the lower right quadrant and a fever of 99. The ER doctor orders a lab workup to be done to rule out appendicitis. The diagnosis on lab order is rebound tenderness, fever, possible appendicitis.

The coding is going to hinge on the fact that this patient is being seen in the emergency room and is therefore still considered an outpatient. The diagnosis of "possible appendicitis" cannot be coded. In the outpatient setting, the symptoms of rebound tenderness, R10.823, and fever, R50.9, are coded because these are the reasons the patient presented to the emergency room.

The coder should reference other coding guidelines before assigning codes from this chapter. As we move through the chapter-specific categories, we will reference the applicable guidelines further.

Symptoms and Signs Involving the Circulatory and Respiratory Systems (Category Codes R00–R09)

The codes in this range include those for shortness of breath, hemoptysis, cardiac murmur, and snoring. This code range also includes elevated blood pressure without a diagnosis of hypertension. Documenting the distinction "without a diagnosis of hypertension" is important so that patients are not diagnosed with hypertension when they are not suffering from it.

Symptoms and Signs Involving the Digestive System and Abdomen (Category Codes R10–R19)

For any abdominal pain, whether it is abdominal tenderness, localized or generalized pain, or rebound pain, the codes are found in these categories. The extensive Excludes note at the beginning of the block of codes should be referenced before the code is assigned.

Symptoms and Signs Involving the Skin and Subcutaneous Tissue (Category Codes R20–R23)

This block of codes reports disturbances of skin sensation, rash and other nonspecific skin eruptions, and other skin changes. Also included is hypoesthesia of the skin, pallor, and scaling of the skin.

Symptoms and Signs Involving the Nervous and Musculoskeletal Systems (Category Codes R25–R29)

Tremors, abnormal reflexes, and paralytic gait are included in this range of codes, as well as loss of heat and facial weakness. The Excludes notes specifies various disorders that are not coded from these codes. Documentation has to be referenced to identify the history of the condition being coded.

Symptoms and Signs Involving the Genitourinary System (Category Codes R30–R39)

Hematuria, urinary retention, oliguria, polyuria, and urgency are all coded to this code range. The instructional notation for category R39.1 instructs the coder to "Code, if applicable, any causal condition first, such as: enlarged prostate (N40.1)."

Symptoms and Signs Involving Cognition, Perception, Emotional State, and Behavior (Category Codes R40–R46)

A **coma** is a condition in which the person is in a deep state of unconsciousness. There is usually no spontaneous eye movement or response to painful stimuli. In **altered states of consciousness**, such as transient alteration of awareness, the patient does not lose consciousness completely but may stare or have a loss of awareness. When assigning a code from this category for a coma, a seventh character is necessary to complete each category in the coma scale.

General Symptoms and Signs (Category Codes R50–R69)

Syncope is coded to this category. **Syncope**, also known as fainting, is a condition in which there is a brief loss of consciousness due to a lack of oxygen to the brain. When no specific disease process is identified as causing the condition, syncope in any form is coded to R55.

Nonspecific Abnormal Findings on Examination of Blood and Urine Without Diagnosis (Category Codes R70–R82)

Conditions that are classified as abnormal findings without a definitive diagnosis are coded from this range of codes. Such conditions can be located in the Alphabetic Index under entries such as "Findings, abnormal, without diagnosis," "Elevation," and "Abnormal, abnormality, abnormalities." If the documentation implies but does not specifically state a diagnosis, clarification from the provider is needed; if the physician clarifies the documentation, an addendum is added to it.

A problem that is frequently encountered in a primary care office is a patient who presents with elevated blood glucose but no history of diabetes mellitus. Nothing in the history or examination indicates that this is a chronic condition. Category R73 is used to report the elevated blood glucose. If this same patient presents to the office with elevated blood glucose, is a diagnosed diabetic, and is on medication to control the diabetes, the code for diabetes is used and not the R73 category.

Abnormal Findings on Examination of Other Body Fluids, Substances, and Tissues, Without Diagnosis (Category Codes R83–R89)

Abnormal microbiological findings, abnormal levels of hormones, abnormal levels of enzymes, and abnormal histological findings are coded from these category codes. These codes are used if no definitive diagnosis is found. Coders have to refer to the documentation to be sure that there is not information supporting a diagnosis found in another chapter of ICD-10-CM.

Abnormal Findings on Diagnostic Imaging and in Function Studies, Without Diagnosis (Category Codes R90–R99)

Morbidity refers to a diseased state; **mortality**, to death. Conditions such as sudden infant death syndrome (SIDS) and unattended deaths are coded to this section of the chapter. Before assigning these codes, the coder needs to review all the available medical documentation to ensure that a more definitive diagnosis has not been determined. If a definitive diagnosis is given, then it is coded. As always, coders must review all the medical documentation on hand at the time of the patient encounter to ensure coding accuracy.

Comparing ICD-9-CM to ICD-10-CM

The ICD-10-CM chapter for symptoms, signs, and abnormal findings has been expanded by the addition of new categories and the use of additional characters at the fourth-, fifth-, and sixth-character levels. Expansions include the following:

- Fourth and fifth characters to identify flatulence and related conditions, R14.

- Disturbances of skin sensation, R20, is expanded at the fourth-character level.

- Abnormal findings, R83 to R89, have been expanded to identify the specimen site and other specific information.

- Coma, R40.2, has been greatly expanded. The codes are differentiated at the fourth-, fifth-, and sixth-character levels. Seventh-character extensions are added to some of the codes.

Summary

- Chapter 18 of ICD-10-CM, "Symptoms, Signs and Abnormal Clinical and Laboratory Findings, Not Elsewhere Classified," contains codes for symptoms and signs that affect the medical care and management of the patient.

- Abnormal findings and ill-defined conditions are also coded to chapter 18 of ICD-10-CM.

- Codes from this chapter should not be used if a more definitive diagnosis is available.
- Until a specific diagnosis is assigned, the signs and symptoms are coded.
- Symptoms are not usually sequenced as a principal diagnosis when a related condition has been confirmed.
- Suspected, rule-out, and possible diagnoses cannot be coded in an outpatient setting.

Chapter Review

True/False: Indicate whether each statement is true (T) or false (F).

1. _____ A symptom is objective and a sign is subjective.

2. _____ Diagnosis codes from chapter 18 of ICD-10-CM are not used if a definitive diagnosis is given.

3. _____ In an outpatient setting, rule-out diagnoses can be coded.

4. _____ Symptoms involving the respiratory and digestive systems are coded to the same categories of codes.

5. _____ Ascites is reported with code R18.8.

Fill-in-the-Blank: Enter the appropriate term(s) to complete each statement.

6. Until a specific diagnosis is assigned, the _____ and _____ are coded instead.

7. Another term for fainting is _____.

8. A _____ is a condition in which the person is in a deep state of unconsciousness.

9. The term _____ refers to death.

10. An acronym for sudden infant death syndrome is _____.

Coding Assignments

Instructions: Using an ICD-10-CM code book, assign the proper diagnosis code to the following diagnostic statements.

Diagnosis   *Code*

1. palpitations   _____

2. left lower quadrant abdominal tenderness   _____

3. hypoesthesia of skin   _____

4. nausea and vomiting   _____

5. painful respirations   _____

6. periumbilical rebound tenderness   _____

7. meningismus   _____

8. cardiac bruit   _____

9. ataxia   _____

10. loss of height   _____

11. orthopnea   _____

12. elevated blood pressure reading without
    diagnosis of hypertension   _____

13. epigastric pain   _____

14. tendency to fall   _____

15. eructation   _____

16. cyanosis   _____

17. auditory hallucinations   _____

18. restlessness   _____

19. painful urination   _____

20. malaise   _____

21. failure to thrive, child   _____

22. cardiogenic shock   _____

23. poor urinary stream   _____

24. retrograde amnesia   _____

25. abnormal glucose in a nondiabetic   _____

Case Studies

Instructions: Review each case study and select the correct ICD-10-CM diagnostic code.

CASE 1

Physician Office Visit

CHIEF COMPLAINT: Patient fell walking up her steps last night. She states that she is also having a severe headache since the fall.

PHYSICAL EXAMINATION:

HEENT: Normal

CHEST: Normal

On examination, there is no swelling of the ankles and no other areas of pain reported. The patient was instructed to go to the hospital radiology department for a CT of the skull. Tylenol 3 was ordered for her headache. Patient will be contacted following results of CT.

ICD-10-CM Code Assignment: _____

(continued)

CASE 2

Emergency Room Visit—Physician's Note

S: This 75-year-old patient was shoveling snow when he became short of breath. His wife insisted that he come to the emergency room to be evaluated. He states that he has had no other symptoms.

O: HEENT: Normal

CHEST: Normal heart rate, no significant findings; EKG normal

LUNGS: Clear, no congestion

ABDOMEN: Soft, nontender; no organ enlargement

LABS: All returned normal.

A: Shortness of breath, ruled out MI.

P: Instructed patient to see his primary care provider for full physical examination.

ICD-10-CM Code Assignment: _____

CASE 3

Physician Office Note

The patient is a 72-year-old male who presents today with complaints of abdominal discomfort, some shortness of breath, and pain "in my gut." The patient denied any recent injury or trauma to the abdomen. He says he feels fine otherwise. Social history is positive for alcohol × 6 per day, and cigarette smoking × 1 pack per day.

Examination reveals an obese Caucasian male who has a distended abdomen. No palpable masses in the abdomen.

SKIN: Skin color is normal; no bruises or discoloration

HEENT: No significant findings

HEART: Normal rate and rhythm

Lab results reveal WBC count to be at 400 cells/milliliter.

The diagnosis at this time is generalized ascites. The patient has been counseled on limiting sodium intake and is now taking Aldactone.

ICD-10-CM Code Assignment: _____

CASE 4

Physician Office Visit

Marcus is an 8-year-old male who presented yesterday to the nurse's office at school with a nosebleed that occurred on the playground after Marcus and another student collided on the swing set. Other than the nosebleed, he was fine and able to go back to class. Today Marcus presents to this office with another nosebleed after he fell out of his bed while wrestling with his brother. His mother is concerned because of the two incidents happening so close together and because she had a bit of difficulty getting this nosebleed to stop.

On examination, Marcus is a normal, healthy, 8-year-old male in NAD with evidence of a recent nosebleed. At this time, there is a slight trickle of blood coming from the right nare. Internal exam reveals no serious problems. Marcus does not complain of a headache, blurred vision, or any other pain in the head and neck. We packed the nostril and told the mother to return if any further bleeding occurs.

Diagnosis for today's visit is nosebleed. We will continue to follow him to rule out possible chronic blood disorders.

ICD-10-CM Code Assignment: _____

CASE 5

Physician Clinic Note

Mrs. Black presents today with complaints of "feeling tired" all the time. Upon questioning, she notes that for the most part her routine has not changed very much. She is a 56-year-old female who has 2 grown children who do not live with her. Her husband is 57 years old and semiretired. She said that her husband helps her around the house and also that she helps him around the yard. When asked if she is sleeping all right, she said she is getting up once or twice a night but falls right back to sleep. At this time, I advised Mrs. Black that maybe she should try to get a good walk in during the day and also watch her diet. If the malaise and fatigue don't subside or do not improve over the next two months with these changes, we will do further testing. Labs were drawn today to look at levels.

EXAM:

HEENT: Normal

ABDOMEN: Nondistended, no masses

HEART: RRR

EXTREMITIES: Normal

Oriented to time, person, and place

No significant physical findings noted.

ICD-10-CM Code Assignment: _____

CHAPTER 24

Injury, Poisoning, and Certain Other Consequences of External Causes

Chapter Outline

Objectives

At the conclusion of this chapter, the learner should be able to:

1. Identify when to assign combination codes for injuries.
2. Explain the various types of fractures.
3. Differentiate among abrasions, contusions, and superficial and complex injuries.
4. Describe the types of open wounds.
5. Discuss the specific coding guidelines that relate to injuries and poisoning.
6. Select and code diagnoses from case studies.

Key Terms

adverse effect	closed fracture	compound fracture	depressed fracture
anterior	comminuted fracture	compression fracture	dislocation
avulsion	complete fracture	concussion	first-degree burn
burn	complicated fracture	corrosions	fissured fracture

Reminder

As you work through this chapter, you will need to have a copy of the ICD-10-CM coding book to reference.

fracture (Fx)	medicaments	second-degree burn	subluxation
greenstick fracture	open fracture	simple fracture	third-degree burn
impacted fracture	paralysis	spiral fracture	underdosing
lateral	poisoning	sprain	vault of the skull
luxation	posterior	strain	vertebral column
medial	reduction	stress fracture	

Introduction

This chapter is quite different from the chapters encountered to this point. This chapter is not confined to one part of the body or to one body system. It is an eclectic collection of injuries that can occur in almost any area of the body. The injuries range from fractures and crush injuries to burns, spinal cord injuries, and late effects of injuries.

Injuries are coded according to the type of injury first and then to its location. Coders must use the Tabular List in conjunction with the Alphabetic Index because Includes and Excludes notes are used extensively. Correct code assignments cannot be made if the notes are not followed and if the documentation is not clear.

The block of codes in this chapter are as follows:

- S00–S09, Injuries to head
- S10–S19, Injuries to neck
- S20–S29, Injuries to the thorax
- S30–S39, Injuries to the abdomen, lower back, lumbar spine, pelvis, and external genitals
- S40–S49, Injuries to shoulder and upper arm
- S50–S59, Injuries to the elbow and forearm
- S60–S69, Injuries to wrist and hand
- S70–S79, Injuries to hip and thigh
- S80–S89, Injuries to knee and lower leg
- S90–S99, Injuries to the ankle and foot
- T07, Unspecified multiple injuries
- T14, Injury of unspecified body region
- T15–T19, Effects of foreign body entering through natural orifice
- T20–T32, Burns and corrosions
- T33–T34, Frostbite
- T36–T50, Poisoning by, adverse effect of, and underdosing of drugs, medicaments, and biological substances
- T51–T65, Toxic effects of substances chiefly nonmedicinal as to source
- T66–T78, Other and unspecified effects of external causes
- T79, Certain early complications of trauma
- T80–T88, Complications of surgical and medical care, not elsewhere classified

> **Note:**
>
> *The injury code blocks begin at the head and work their way down the body. This sequence can help you determine that you are coding from the correct section in a chapter.*

In this chapter, the S codes are used for coding different types of injuries related to single body regions. T codes reflect injuries to unspecified body regions, as well as poisoning and certain other consequences of external causes.

Coding Guidelines

The ICD-10-CM Official Guidelines for Coding and Reporting provides many guidelines and much guidance for the coding of injuries and poisoning. Since more than one injury can occur at the same time, the official guidelines state the following:

ICD-10-CM Official Coding Guidelines

b. When coding injuries, assign a separate code for each injury unless a combination code is provided, in which case the combination code is assigned. Multiple injury codes are provided in ICD-10-CM but should not be assigned unless information for a more specific code is not available. These traumatic injury codes (S00–T14.9) are not to be used for normal, healing surgical wounds or to identify complications of surgical wounds.

The code for the most serious injury, as determined by the provider, is sequenced first.

1. Superficial injuries

Superficial injuries such as abrasions or contusions are not coded when associated with more severe injuries of the same site.

2. Primary injury with damage to nerves/blood vessels

When a primary injury results in minor damage to peripheral nerves or blood vessels, the primary injury is sequenced first with additional code(s) for injuries to nerves and spinal cord (such as category S04), and/or injury to blood vessels (such as category S15). When the primary injury is to the blood vessels or nerves, that injury should be sequenced first. (See Appendix A, Section I, C19, b.)

Terminology

Terminology is very important when coding from this chapter. Knowledge of the terminology allows the coder to make a more accurate code selection.

Fractures

Fractures, sometimes seen in a provider note as **Fx**, are broken bones resulting from undue force or pathological changes. Malunions or nonunions are not found in this chapter. These types of fractures were described in the chapter "Diseases of the Musculoskeletal System and Connective Tissue."

Knowing whether the fracture is open or closed is the starting point for coding fractures. An **open fracture**, also known as a **compound fracture**, is a fracture that has broken through the skin at the fracture site. The bone may or may not be protruding through the skin, but an open wound is always associated with this type of fracture. Because the tissues are exposed, these fractures present a high risk for infection. Surgery is almost always required. Foreign bodies, or "missiles," may need to be surgically removed from the tissues.

A **closed fracture** is a type of fracture in which the bone is broken but not the skin. This type of fracture is also known as a **complete** or **simple fracture**.

The following quick reference for terminology related to closed fractures is not comprehensive. If you encounter a term that is not listed here, seek clarification from the provider. If the fracture is not specified as open or closed and you cannot get any further information from the provider, code it as closed.

Type of Closed Fracture	Definition
Comminuted	Bone is crushed, may be splintered.
Compression	Bone is pressed on itself.
Depressed	Relating to skull, bone is broken but pushed inward.
Fissured	Bone has a narrow split that does not go through to the other side.
Greenstick	As with a greenstick of a tree, the bone bends as well as breaks.
Impacted	One end of the broken bone is wedged into the other end.
Spiral	Severe twisting motion caused bone to twist apart.
Stress	Excessive impact on bone causes small hairline crack in the bone.

Figure 24-1 illustrates types and patterns of fractures. If an internal organ has been injured as a direct result of the fracture, it is called a **complicated fracture**. Either the bone itself or just a fragment of the bone may cause the injury.

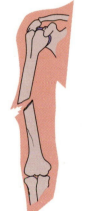
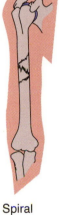

Closed (simple, complete)   Open (compound)   Greenstick (incomplete)   Transverse   Oblique   Spiral

Comminuted   Depressed   Compression   Avulsion   Impacted

Fracture

Figure 24-1   Types and patterns of fractures (From Hegner BR, Acello B, Caldwell E. *Nursing Assistant: A Nursing Process Approach*, 9th ed. Clifton Park, NY: Delmar, Cengage Learning, 2001, p. 644.)

Coders should also be aware of the following guidelines.

ICD-10-CM Official Coding Guidelines

c. Coding of Traumatic Fractures

The principles of multiple coding of injuries should be followed in coding fractures. Fractures of specified sites are coded individually by site in accordance with both the provisions within categories S02, S12, S22, S32, S42, S49, S52, S59, S62, S72, S79, S82, S89, S92, and the level of detail furnished by medical record content.

A fracture not indicated as open or closed should be coded to closed. A fracture not indicated whether displaced or not displaced should be coded to displaced.

More specific guidelines are as follows:

1) Initial vs. Subsequent Encounter for Fractures

Traumatic fractures are coded using the appropriate 7th character extension for initial encounter (A, B, C) while the patient is receiving active treatment for the fracture. Examples of active treatment are: surgical treatment, emergency department encounter, and evaluation and treatment by a new physician.

Fractures are coded using the appropriate 7th character extension for subsequent care for encounters after the patient has completed active treatment of the fracture and is receiving routine care for the fracture during the healing or recovery phase. Examples of fracture aftercare are: cast change or removal, removal of external or internal fixation device, medication adjustment, and follow up visits following fracture treatment.

Care for complications of surgical treatment for fracture repairs during the healing or recovery phase should be coded with the appropriate complication codes.

Care of complications of fractures, such as malunion and nonunion, should be reported with the appropriate 7th character extensions for subsequent care with nonunion (K, M, N,) or subsequent care with malunion (P, Q, R).

A code from category M80, not a traumatic fracture code, should be used for any patient with known osteoporosis who suffers a fracture, even if that patient had a minor fall or trauma, if that fall or trauma would not usually break a normal, healthy bone. See Section I.C.13. Osteoporosis.

The aftercare Z codes should not be used for aftercare for injuries. For aftercare of an injury, assign the acute injury code with the 7th character "D" (subsequent encounter).

2) Multiple fractures sequencing

Multiple fractures are sequenced in accordance with the severity of the fracture. The provider should be asked to list the fracture diagnoses in the order of severity.

(See Appendix A, Section I, C19, c.)

Should the coder identify a situation that indicates both open and closed fractures in the same site, the open fracture is coded because it takes priority over the closed fracture. A patient who might present with multiple fractures after an accident may have both open and closed fractures. In this case, as stated in the guidelines, the fractures are sequenced according to severity.

S Codes

Injuries to the Head (Category Codes S00–S09)

The injuries that are coded from this block include superficial injuries, contusions, open wounds, fractures of the neck and trunk, and concussions. This code range includes codes for injuries that occur from the scalp down to just past the jaw. Some knowledge of anatomy is necessary to navigate through these sections when coding for injuries of the teeth, tongue, gums, and oral cavity.

The **vault of the skull** is made up of three bones: the two parietal bones and the frontal bone. The chapter identifies different types of fractures of the head and face.

These categories classify intracranial injury, such as concussions. A **concussion** is a violent shaking or jarring of the brain. The main axis for coding concussions hinges on whether the patient lost consciousness and, if so, to what degree.

Injuries to the Neck (Category Codes S10–S19)

The next section reports injuries to the neck. The injuries found in this code block include superficial injuries, contusions, open wounds, and fractures. This code block includes fractures of the cervical vertebra. The **vertebral column**, which shields the spinal column, is made up of cervical, thoracic, and lumbar vertebra. To properly code an injury to the spinal column or a vertebra, you need to know the location of the injury. An injury to this area of the body can cause **paralysis**, which is the loss of sensation or voluntary motion. This loss may be permanent or temporary, depending on the type and site of the injury.

Dislocation of some of the vertebrae is coded in this category. The term **dislocation** means that a body part has moved out of place, in this case a bone. The bone has moved or displaced completely from where it should be. A synonymous term for dislocation is **luxation**. In cases of a partial dislocation, or **subluxation**, only part of the joint surface has moved away from where it should be.

Like fractures, dislocations can be open or closed. An open dislocation is prone to infection. A **reduction** is the usual procedure needed to put the joint back into place whether the dislocation is open or closed.

The coding of dislocations requires knowing whether the dislocation is open or closed, as well as the location of the displaced bone in relation to where its proper placement should be in the joint. The terms to look for in provider documentation are "anterior," "posterior," "lateral," and/or "medial."

- **Anterior** means "in front of" or "forward of."
- **Posterior** is the opposite of anterior and means "in back of" or "behind."
- **Medial** is closest or nearest to the midline of a structure.
- **Lateral** means "away from midline" toward the side.

Dislocations can be very serious when major joints are involved, specifically the shoulders, knees, and hips. Vascular complications can occur with these types of dislocations, which can have long lasting or even permanent adverse affects.

When a dislocation occurs with a fracture, the dislocation is included in the code for the fracture and is not coded separately. This category of codes is used when no fracture is present. As with fractures, dislocations are coded as closed unless the provider has specifically stated that the dislocation is open.

Sometimes the terms *sprain* and *strain* are used interchangeably. They are not the same, and coders should seek clarification if there is any question about the condition. A **sprain** is an injury to a joint, specifically the ligament of the joint, which becomes stretched. A **strain** is not an injury at the joint site but to the muscle or to the tendon attachment. In provider documentation, the coder may note that the severity of sprain or strain has been graded or typed, with type I as the least severe through type III as the most severe. When there are multiple sprains or strains, the typing of these sprains and strains is helpful in determining which site to code first.

Commonly a patient is prescribed RICE therapy (rest, ice, compression, and elevation) to treat strains and sprains.

> **Note:**
>
> In the Alphabetic Index, not a lot of sites are listed under the main term strain, but the term sprain has a large range of anatomical sites.

Injuries to the Thorax (Category Codes S20–29)

Injuries to this block of codes includes the breast, chest wall, and the interscapular area. The type of injuries included in this code range are superficial injuries, abrasions, open wounds, fractures, subluxation and dislocations, and crush injuries.

Injuries to the Abdomen, Lower Back, Lumbar Spine, Pelvis, and External Genitals (Category Codes S30–S39)

The anatomy included in this section includes the abdominal wall, anus, buttock, external genitalia, flank, and groin. As in other categories, superficial injuries, contusions, open wounds, and lacerations are coded from this code range, as well as fractures and dislocations of the lumbar spine and pelvis.

This code range also includes injuries to the intra-abdominal organs including the kidneys, the ureters, the bladder, the fallopian tubes, and the uterus. Attention to the specific anatomical sites injured helps with code selection. Documentation must support the codes selected.

Injuries to the Shoulder and Arm, Elbow, Wrist, and Hand (Category Codes S40–S69)

Injuries to all areas from the shoulder to the tip of the fingers are included in this code range, which distinguishes between right and left sides. Refer to the documentation for the correct site of the injury. Superficial wounds, lacerations, open wounds, and fractures are reported from this code range, as well as injuries to the muscle, fascia, and tendons of the shoulder area.

The note at the start of this section includes open wounds caused by animal bites, cuts, lacerations, puncture wounds, and traumatic amputations. Also included here are avulsions. An **avulsion** is a ripping or tearing away. Avulsions are usually documented in reference to fingernails or toenails or a portion of an organ, but they can also occur on arms or legs. Sometimes the coder encounters the term *complicated*, referring to an open wound, such as "complicated open wound of the back."

Injuries to the Hip, Thigh, Knee, Lower Leg, Ankle, Foot, and Toes (Category Codes S70–S99)

The injuries in this code range include dislocations, fractures, and muscle injuries. Refer to the documentation for the necessary details to assign a code. This range of codes contains many Includes and Excludes notations, which must be referenced before code assignment is made.

Exercise 24.1 – Fractures, Dislocation, Sprains, and Strains

True/False: Indicate whether each statement is true (T) or false (F).

1. _____ Injuries are coded according to location first, then type of injury.

2. _____ Sprains and strains are not the same type of injury.

3. _____ When coding fractures, attention to the type of fracture and the location is necessary for proper code assignment.

4. _____ To properly code fractures, the coder needs to know whether the fracture is dislocated or not.

5. _____ The vertebral column shields the spinal cord.

Fill-in-the-Blank: Enter the appropriate term(s) to complete each statement.

6. "Fx" in a provider note refers to a _____.

7. A _____ is an injury to a ligament of the joint, whereas a _____ is an injury to a muscle.

8. Comminuted is a type of _____ fracture.

9. A synonymous term for luxation is _____.

10. A _____ fracture occurs when a bone is pressed on itself.

Instructions: Using an ICD-9-CM coding book, select the code for each diagnostic statement.

Diagnosis	Code
11. comminuted right ankle fracture, initial encounter	_____
12. nondisplaced fracture of the lower epiphysis of the right femur, initial encounter	_____
13. initial encounter for sprain of the sternoclavicular joint	_____
14. initial encounter for fracture of the proximal end of the left tibia	_____
15. closed dislocation of the C6/C7 vertebrae, initial visit	_____
16. open fracture, sternum, initial care	_____
17. nondisplaced closed avulsion fracture of the ilium, initial visit	_____
18. initial care for closed displaced fracture of lateral malleolus of right fibula	_____
19. initial visit for open dislocation of the right carpometacarpal joint	_____
20. initial care for nondisplaced condyle fracture of lower end of right femur	_____

T Codes

As stated earlier, T codes reflect injuries to unspecified body regions, as well as poisoning and certain other consequences of external causes. T codes contain many instructional notations, so any codes found in the Alphabetic Index need to be referenced in the Tabular List to pick up the instructional notations before making a code selection.

Injuries Involving Unspecified Multiple Body Regions (Category Code T07)

This is one of the few three-character codes found in ICD-10-CM. This code is used to identify unspecified multiple injuries. The coder should note that this code is used only when no documentation is available to identify the specific injury or site of injury. This code is not acceptable in the inpatient setting.

Injury of Unspecified Body Region (Category Code T14)

T14 is the only code in this category but, unlike the T07 code, requires fourth- or fifth-digit assignment. However, like the T07 code, T14 is not appropriate for use in the inpatient setting.

Effects of Foreign Body Entering Through Natural Orifice (Category Codes T15–T19)

The T codes in this range reflect foreign bodies in the ear and multiple parts of the eye. It also includes codes for foreign bodies in the respiratory and alimentary tracts.

Pay careful attention to the details of the documentation because the codes in this range do not need an additional external cause code if the external cause is included in the code description.

EXAMPLE: Mary suffered a sore throat due to a chicken bone getting caught in the trachea. The code is T17.428, Food in trachea causing other injury. The Includes note under the T17.42 code identifies bones and seeds in the trachea. For this reason, no additional code is needed.

Burns and Corrosions (Category Codes T20–T32)

Coding for burns can be very difficult and confusing if the coding guidelines are not followed. A **burn** is an injury to body tissue as a result of heat, flame, sun, chemicals, radiation, or electricity. Coding a burn is determined by its severity, or degree, and its location. Codes from the T31 or T32 category are used to identify the extent of body surfaced involved. The code descriptions are very detailed, and the documentation supporting code selection needs to be detailed as well.

Burns are classified as first, second, and third degree.

- **First-degree burns** do not present a danger to the patient and are limited to the outer layer of the epidermis. An example is a mild sunburn.

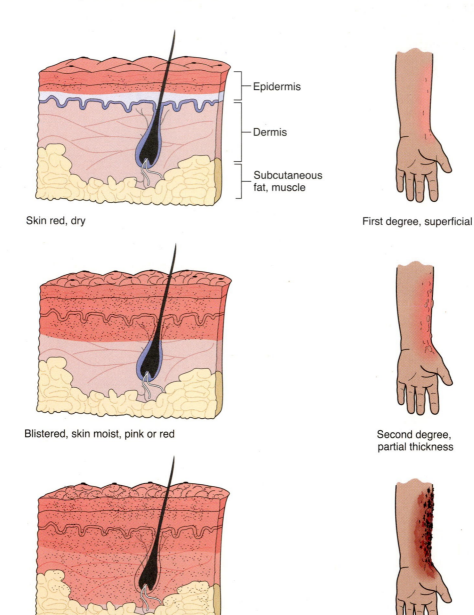

Skin red, dry

First degree, superficial

Blistered, skin moist, pink or red

Second degree, partial thickness

Charring, skin black, brown, red

Third degree, full thickness

Epidermis

Dermis

Subcutaneous fat, muscle

Figure 24-2   First-, second-, and third-degree burns (From Ehrlich A, Schroeder CL. *Medical Terminology for Health Professionals*, 4th ed. Clifton Park, NY: Delmar, Cengage Learning, 2001, p. 264.)

- **Second-degree burns** are partial-thickness burns, which form blisters. A second-degree burn, not properly treated, can result in an infection at the burn site.

- **Third-degree burns** are full-thickness burns and affect the epidermis, dermis, and subcutaneous layers. This type of burn can lead to necrosis and even the loss of the body part.

Because a burn is the destruction of the skin, which protects the body from infection, the patient must receive proper treatment. Infection is a very serious problem in burn victims, as is the loss of blood supply to the areas of third-degree burns. Without blood supply to the area, necrosis can occur. Figure 24-2 illustrates the types of burns.

ICD-10-CM Official Coding Guidelines

Coding of Burns and Corrosions

The ICD-10-CM distinguishes between burns and corrosions. The burn codes are for thermal burns, except sunburns, that come from a heat source, such as a fire or hot appliance. The burn codes are also for burns resulting from electricity and radiation. **Corrosions** are burns due to chemicals. The guidelines are the same for burns and corrosions.

Current burns (T20–T25) are classified by depth, extent and by agent (X code). Burns are classified by depth as first degree (erythema), second degree (blistering), and third degree (full-thickness involvement). Burns of the eye and internal organs (T26–T28) are classified by site, but not by degree.

1) Sequencing of burn and related condition codes

Sequence first the code that reflects the highest degree of burn when more than one burn is present.

a. When the reason for the admission or encounter is for treatment of external multiple burns, sequence first the code that reflects the burn of the highest degree.

b. When a patient has both internal and external burns, the circumstances of admission govern the selection of the principal diagnosis or first-listed diagnosis.

c. When a patient is admitted for burn injuries and other related conditions such as smoke inhalation and/or respiratory failure, the circumstances of admission govern the selection of the principal or first-listed diagnosis.

2) Burns of the same local site

Classify burns of the same local site (three-digit category level, T20–T28) but of different degrees to the subcategory identifying the highest degree recorded in the diagnosis.

3) Non-healing burns

Non-healing burns are coded as acute burns. Necrosis of burned skin should be coded as a non-healed burn.

4) Infected Burn

For any documented infected burn site, use an additional code for the infection.

5) Assign separate codes for each burn site

When coding burns, assign separate codes for each burn site. Category T30, Burn and corrosion, body region unspecified is extremely vague and should rarely be used.

6) Burns and Corrosions Classified According to Extent of Body Surface Involved

Assign codes from category T31, Burns classified according to extent of body surface involved, or T32, Corrosions classified according to extent of body surface involved, when the site of the burn is not specified or when there is a need for additional data. It is advisable to use category T31 as additional coding when needed to provide data for evaluating burn mortality, such as that needed by burn units. It is also advisable to use category T31 as an additional code for reporting purposes when there is mention of a third-degree burn involving 20 percent or more of the body surface.

Categories T31 and T32 are based on the classic "rule of nines" in estimating body surface involved: head and neck are assigned nine percent, each arm nine percent, each leg 18 percent, the anterior trunk 18 percent, posterior trunk 18 percent, and genitalia one percent. Providers may change these percentage assignments where necessary to accommodate infants and children who have proportionately larger heads than adults, and patients who have large buttocks, thighs, or abdomen that involve burns.

(continued)

7) Encounters for treatment of late effects of burns

Encounters for the treatment of the late effects of burns or corrosions (i.e., scars or joint contractures) should be coded with a burn or corrosion code with the 7th character "S" or sequela.

8) Sequelae with a late effect code and current burn

When appropriate, both a code for a current burn or corrosion with 7th character extension "A" or "D" and a burn or corrosion code with extension "S" may be assigned on the same record (when both a current burn and sequelae of an old burn exist). Burns and corrosions do not heal at the same rate and a current healing wound may still exist with sequela of a healed burn or corrosion.

9) Use of an external cause code with burns and corrosions

An external cause code should be used with burns and corrosions to identify the source and intent of the burn, as well as the place where it occurred.

(See Appendix A, Section I, C19, d.)

With these few guidelines in mind, this example helps to illustrate how they are applied.

> **EXAMPLE:** A 56-year-old male presents to the ER with first- and second-degree burns on the right arm. The right leg contains third-degree burns to the thigh, knee, and calf area.
>
> To properly code this example, attention is directed to the area of the right thigh because the third-degree burns are the most severe of the burns to be coded Reference Category T24, Burn and corrosion of lower limb, except ankle and foot. To report the most severe burns, use Code T24.391A, Burn of third degree of multiple sites of right lower limb, except ankle and foot, initial encounter. To report the next severe burn, use Code T22.291A, Burn of second degree of multiple sites of right shoulder and upper limb, except wrist and hand, initial encounter.

The extent of the body surface burned is coded according to the rule of nines. This rule is based on the premise that the adult body can be divided into anatomic regions with surface area percentages that are multiples of nine. The rule of nines breaks down as follows:

* Head and neck, 9%
* Arms, 9% each
* Legs, 18% each
* Anterior trunk, 18%
* Posterior trunk, 18%
* Genitalia, 1%

Section I, C19,d, 6 of the ICD-10-CM Official Guidelines for Coding and Reporting presents the complete details.

There is an instructional notation that an additional code is needed to identify the external source and intent of the burn. If the place is known, add the Y92 code. Be sure to reference the Tabular Listing to see whether a seventh character is needed.

Frostbite (Category Codes T33–T34)

This code range is not referenced if the diagnosis is hypothermia. The site of the frostbite is the first point of reference. The coder then refers to the documentation to find whether the frostbite is superficial or deep and if necrosis has set in.

Poisoning by Adverse Effects of and Underdosing of Drugs, Medicaments, and Biological Substances (Category Codes T36–T50)

ICD-10-CM defines **poisoning** as an overdose of substances or a wrong substance given or taken in error. When the substance is not used as prescribed or not used properly, this is poisoning. If the documentation does not state specifically that the situation is a poisoning, then it is coded as an adverse effect. **Medicaments** is a term for medicine.

An **adverse effect** is defined as *hypersensitivity*, *reaction*, etc. to a correct substance properly administered. The coder may encounter certain terms that indicate an adverse effect, for example, *allergic reaction, paradoxical, synergistic,* or *idiosyncratic reaction*. Also seen in the documentation are phrases like *hypersensitivity to drugs, toxicity, toxic effect, or intoxication due to prescription drugs,* and the like.

Underdosing is defined as taking less of a medication than what is prescribed or instructed by the physician or the manufacturer, whether deliberately or inadvertently. When coding a possible poisoning, the coder needs to determine whether it was actually a poisoning or just an adverse effect.

Refer to the Official Coding Guidelines when there is any question as to how to code these conditions.

ICD-10-CM Official Coding Guidelines

e. Adverse Effects, Poisoning , Underdosing and Toxic Effects

Codes in categories T36–T65 are combination codes that include the substances related to adverse effects, poisonings, toxic effects and underdosing, as well as the external cause. No additional external cause code is required for poisonings, toxic effects, adverse effects, and underdosing codes. A code from categories T36–T65 is sequenced first, followed by the code(s) that specify the nature of the adverse effect, poisoning, or toxic effect. Note: This sequencing instruction does not apply to underdosing codes (fifth or sixth character "6", for example T36.0x6-).

1) Do not code directly from the Table of Drugs

Do not code directly from the Table of Drugs and Chemicals. Always refer back to the Tabular List.

2) Use as many codes as necessary to describe

ICD-10-CM Official Guidelines for Coding and Reporting Effective October 1, 2008.

Use as many codes as necessary to describe completely all drugs, medicinal, or biological substances.

3) If the same code would describe the causative agent

If the same code would describe the causative agent for more than one adverse reaction, poisoning, toxic effect, or underdosing, assign the code only once.

4) If two or more drugs, medicinal, or biological substances

If two or more drugs, medicinal, or biological substances are reported, code each individually unless the combination code is listed in the Table of Drugs and Chemicals.

5) The occurrence of drug toxicity is classified in ICD-10-CM as follows:

(a) Adverse Effect

Assign the appropriate code for adverse effect (for example, T36.0x5-) when the drug was correctly prescribed and properly administered. Use additional code(s) for all manifestations of adverse effects. Examples of manifestations are tachycardia, delirium, gastrointestinal hemorrhaging, vomiting, hypokalemia, hepatitis, renal failure, or respiratory failure.

(b) Poisoning

When coding a poisoning or reaction to the improper use of a medication (e.g., overdose, wrong substance given or taken in error, wrong route of administration), assign the appropriate code from categories T36–T50. Poisoning codes have an associated intent: accidental, intentional self-harm, assault, and undetermined. Use additional code(s) for all manifestations of poisonings.

(continued)

If there is also a diagnosis of abuse or dependence on the substance, the abuse or dependence is coded as an additional code.

Examples of poisoning include:

(i) Error was made in drug prescription

Errors made in drug prescription or in the administration of the drug by provider, nurse, patient, or other person.

(ii) Overdose of a drug intentionally taken

If an overdose of a drug was intentionally taken or administered and resulted in drug toxicity, it would be coded as a poisoning.

(iii) Nonprescribed drug taken with correctly prescribed and properly administered drug

If a nonprescribed drug or medicinal agent was taken in combination with a correctly prescribed and properly administered drug, any drug toxicity or other reaction resulting from the interaction of the two drugs would be classified as a poisoning.

(iv) Interaction of drug(s) and alcohol

When a reaction results from the interaction of a drug(s) and alcohol, this would be classified as poisoning.

See Section I.C.4. if poisoning is the result of insulin pump malfunctions.

(c) Underdosing

Underdosing refers to taking less of a medication than is prescribed by a provider or a manufacturer's instruction. For underdosing, assign the code from categories T36–T50 (fifth or sixth character "6").

Codes for underdosing should never be assigned as principal or first-listed codes. If a patient has a relapse or exacerbation of the medical condition for which the drug is prescribed because of the reduction in dose, then the medical condition itself should be coded.

Noncompliance (Z91.12–, Z91.13–) or complication of care (Y63.61, Y63.8–Y63.9) codes are to be used with an underdosing code to indicate intent, if known.

(Refer to the complete guideline located in Appendix A, Section 1, C19, e.)

If the situation is actually a poisoning, the coder refers to the Table of Drugs and Chemicals. The table is located at the end of the Alphabetic Index, right after the neoplasm table.

The first column in the table is labeled Poisoning, Accidental (unintentional). When a statement of poisoning, overdose, wrong substance given or taken, or intoxication is used in the diagnosis and identified as such in the medical record, these codes are used.

Also found in the Table of Drugs and Chemicals are columns labeled Poisoning Intentional, self-harm, Poisoning, Assault, Poisoning Unintentional, Adverse Effect, and Undercoding. All columns will contain T codes.

Toxic Effects of Substances Chiefly Nonmedicinal as to Source (Category Codes T51–T65)

As with other blocks of codes, ICD-10-CM has official guidelines related to toxic effects.

ICD-10-CM Official Coding Guidelines

(d) Toxic Effects

When a harmful substance is ingested or comes in contact with a person, this is classified as a toxic effect. The toxic effect codes are in categories T51–T65.

Toxic effect codes have an associated intent: accidental, intentional self-harm, assault, and undetermined.

(Refer to the complete guideline located in Appendix A, Section 1, C19, e.)

This code range includes toxic effects of ethanol, methanol, benzen, and tetrachloroethylene. Most of the categories in this range require a 7th character. The Tabular List needs to be referenced before a code is assigned so that, if a 7th character needs to be applied, the coder is aware of it.

Other and Unspecified Effects of External Causes (Category Codes T66–T78)

Radiation sickness, the effects of heat and light, heatstroke and sunstroke, heat exhaustion, and heat edema are conditions coded to this range. These codes are also used to report hypothermia and asphyxiation due to plastic bags and pillows.

Included in the categories T74, Adult and child abuse, neglect, and other maltreatment, confirmed and T76, Adult and child abuse, neglect, and other maltreatment suspected, are neglect, abandonment, sexual abuse, physical abuse, and psychological abuse. The diagnosis must be confirmed by the physician or provider documentation to support assignment of a T74 code. Additional codes should be applied to identify any associated current injury or to identify the perpetrator, if known. If the abuse is suspected but not yet confirmed, reference the T76 code range. These codes should never be used without a confirmation from the physician/provider.

Official Coding Guidelines address the rules for code assignment in cases of abuse.

ICD-10-CM Official Coding Guidelines

f. Adult and child abuse, neglect, and other maltreatment Sequence first the appropriate code from categories T74.– or T76.– for abuse, neglect, and other maltreatment, followed by any accompanying mental health or injury code(s).

If the documentation in the medical record states abuse or neglect it is coded as confirmed. It is coded as suspected if it is documented as suspected.

For cases of confirmed abuse or neglect an external cause code from the assault section (X92–Y08) should be added to identify the cause of any physical injuries. A perpetrator code (Y07) should be added when the perpetrator of the abuse is known. For suspected cases of abuse or neglect, do not report external cause or perpetrator code.

If a suspected case of abuse, neglect, or mistreatment is ruled out during an encounter code Z04.71, Suspected adult physical and sexual abuse, ruled out, or code Z04.72, Suspected child physical and sexual abuse, ruled out, should be used, not a code from T76.

(Refer to the complete guideline located in Appendix A, Section 1, C19, f.)

Many instructional notations require a second code assignment, and coders must follow these instructional notations. A seventh-character assignment might also be necessary, but unless the Tabular Listing is referenced, the coder would not know this.

Complications of Surgical and Medical Care, Not Elsewhere Classified (Category Codes T80–T88)

This code range contains a wide range of codes and complications. It is not referenced if more specific codes can be found elsewhere. An additional code from the Y62–Y82 range may be needed to identify devices involved and details of circumstances. Included in this code range are codes for Rh incompatibility reaction, disruption of an operation wound, or even an obstruction due to a foreign body accidentally left in the body following a procedure. The code range finishes with complications of organ transplants, grafts, and infections.

Comparing ICD-9-CM to ICD-10-CM

The codes found in chapter 19 of ICD-10-CM are very specific. The coder needs to read all the available medical documentation to gather all the necessary information for code selection. Most codes have been expanded to indicate laterality and other specific conditions. Seventh characters are used to identify initial encounters, subsequent encounters, or sequela. Numerous notations throughout the chapter instruct the coder to assign codes for associated injuries. All of the codes have a greater degree of specificity than did ICD-9-CM.

Internet Links

For more information on fractures and the different types of fractures, visit *http://www.orthoinfo.aaos.org*

For more information on types of sprains and strains, go to *http://www.orthopedics.about.com/cc/sprainsstrains/HA/sprain_2.htm*

Summary

- When coding injuries, assign a separate code for each injury unless a combination code is provided.

- When coding from chapter 19, follow the ICD-10-CM Official Guidelines for injuries, poisoning, and other consequences of external causes.

- When a dislocation occurs with a fracture, include the dislocation in the code for the fracture.

- A sprain is an injury to a joint, and a strain is an injury to the muscle or the tendon attachment.

- Intracranial injuries that are diagnosed with cerebral lacerations are coded with a combination code.

- Seven digits are commonly used when coding injuries of the thorax, abdomen, and pelvis.

- A burn is an injury to body tissue as a result of heat, flame, sun, chemicals, radiation, or electricity.

- Burns are classified by the severity: first, second, or third degree.

- The extent of the body surface burned is coded according to the rule of nines.

- An adverse effect occurs when a drug or other substance is used as prescribed or correctly according to directions.

- A seventh-digit character may or may not be needed; refer to the instructional notations before assigning codes.

Chapter Review

True/False: Indicate whether the statement is true (T) or false (F).

1. _____ The codes S00–T14.9 are used for normal, healing surgical wounds or to identify complications of puncture wounds.

2. _____ A fracture that is not specified as displaced or not displaced should be coded to displaced.

3. _____ There is a time limit on when a late effect code can be assigned.

4. _____ The rule of nines is used to figure the total percentage of body surface burned.

5. _____ When a harmful substance is ingested or comes in contact with a person, this is classified as a toxic effect.

Fill-in-the-Blank: Enter the appropriate term(s) to complete each statement.

6. The term _____ means that a body part has moved out of place.

7. The first column listed in the Table of Drugs and Chemicals is _____.

8. A violent shaking or jarring of the brain is known as _____.

9. A substance that causes an allergic reaction even though it is used correctly is called a(n) _____.

10. According to the rule of nines, each arm is valued at _____%.

Coding Assignments

Instructions: Using an ICD-10-CM code book, assign the proper diagnosis code to the following diagnostic statements. (Do not code procedures at this time.)

Diagnosis	*Code*
1. initial visit of laceration with foreign body, abdominal wall	_____
2. surfer's knot, initial encounter	_____
3. infection of the right lower leg amputation stump, first visit	_____
4. initial care for corneal transplant rejection	_____
5. exhaustion due to exposure, initial care	_____
6. Alpine sickness, subsequent care	_____
7. first-degree corrosion of the neck, first visit (no Y code at this time)	_____
8. anaphylactic shock due to properly administered substance, aspirin	_____
9. initial care for open wound of left middle finger with splinter that had to be removed	_____
10. external constriction of the right upper arm, initial visit	_____
11. subsequent encounter for crush injury of the skull	_____
12. second-degree burn of the chest wall (no Y code at this time)	_____
13. traumatic subdural hemorrhage with loss of consciousness for 2 hours	_____
14. first visit for seasickness	_____
15. late effect of 0.5 cm laceration of left eyelid and periocular area	_____
16. spiral displaced fracture of the shaft of the right femur, initial care	_____

17. toxic effect of natural gas (subsequent visit) _____

18. underdosing of tetracycline, initial care _____

19. initial care for superficial frostbite of right hand _____

20. toxic effect of ingested mushrooms, accidental, initial care _____

21. mechanical breakdown of infusion catheter _____

22. bone graft failure _____

23. complex tear of right medical meniscus, current _____

24. heart-lung transplant failure _____

25. epidural hemorrhage with loss of consciousness, <30 minutes _____

Case Studies

Instructions: Review each case study and select the correct ICD-10-CM diagnostic code.

CASE 1

Physician Office Note

S: The patient's wife brought the patient to my office after the patient tried to separate a raccoon and their dog, which were fighting. While trying to separate the animals, the patient was bitten. He is not sure whether the raccoon or the dog bit him.

EXAM:

The patient's left forearm has bite marks on it. The wound is bleeding and is deep, and there is tendon involvement.

The nurse cleaned the wound, and a tetanus shot was given. Because the wound is deep and there is tendon involvement, I called Dr. Black for a surgical consult. The wound was dressed to control the bleeding.

ICD-10-CM Code Assignment: _____

CASE 2

ER Note

CHIEF COMPLAINT: This 2-year-old patient presents with a cut on his face.

History of the present illness: Patient fell off a kitchen chair and struck his face on the seat of the chair.

VITAL SIGNS: Pulse 117, Respirations 28, BP 103/43

RESPIRATORY: Airway clear

BREATH SOUNDS: Clear

SKIN: 1.5-cm laceration to the forehead.

LACERATION REPAIR NOTE: The patient was papoosed with his mother's knowledge and presence. The wound was injected with 2% plain Lidocaine, and the wound edges were approximated with three #6-0 nylon sutures.

The patient was sent for an X-ray to rule out any facial bone fractures.

PLAN: Follow up with family physician in 1 week.

ICD-10-CM Code Assignment: _____

CASE 3

Physician Office Note

CHIEF COMPLIANT: Pain in right arm.

HISTORY OF PRESENT ILLNESS: This 39-year-old female was carrying groceries into her house when she slipped on ice and fell. She landed on her right side and on her arm.

EXAM: EXTREMITIES: Her right arm is swollen, and it appears to be broken due to its abnormal appearance.

An in-office X-ray was completed that showed a complete fracture of the shaft of the humerus. Patient was referred to Dr. Break, the orthopedic surgeon on call. Patient was sent to Dr. Break's office.

ICD-10-CM Code Assignment: _____

CASE 4

Clinic Visit Note

This is a 63-year-old type II diabetic male who presents 4 weeks after left foot amputation due to his diabetes. The patient presented to this office at the time of the injury due to concerns he had regarding possible complications stemming from his amputation as his stump is quite red.

Upon examination, there was no streaking at this time, but some clear drainage is noted. The patient is afebrile, and other vital signs are within normal limits.

The diagnosis at this time is infection of amputation stump, left lower leg. We are starting the patient on antibiotics and have also treated and dressed the wound.

ICD-10-CM Code Assignment: _____

CASE 5

Emergency Department Note

This patient is a 27-year-old male who was brought to the emergency department by ambulance after being bitten by a rattlesnake while hiking in the desert. The bite is located just above the ankle. The patient was wearing sneakers instead of hiking boots. The area of the bite is now red and a bit swollen.

The patient says the pain is about 9 out of 10 on the pain scale. The exact type of snake is not known because the patient wasn't sure.

Examination reveals two small puncture marks on the medial side of the lower leg above the ankle.

Vital signs are within normal limits. The skin is swollen, red, and warm to touch. Patient was given a shot of antivenom and admitted for 24-hour observation.

ICD-10-CM Code Assignment: _____

External Causes of Morbidity

Chapter Outline

Objectives

At the conclusion of this chapter, the learner should be able to:

1. Understand what "external cause" means and when it is appropriately assigned.
2. Discuss sequencing of the V, W, X, and Y codes.
3. Discuss the specific coding guidelines related to chapter 20.
4. Select and code V, W, X, or Y codes for case studies given.

Key Terms

animate object	inanimate object	pedal cycle	terrorism
assault	morbidity	pedestrian	

> **Reminder**
>
> *As you work through this chapter, you will need to have a copy of the ICD-10-CM coding book to reference.*

Introduction

The codes found in the code range V01 through Y99 are used to describe external causes of morbidity. **Morbidity** is another way of saying "diseased state." The codes are used as secondary codes to describe further how an injury happened or what caused a particular health condition.

Some payers do not recognize or require the use of these codes. Medicare is one such payer. The data provided by the use of these codes assists in the evaluation and research of the cause and prevention strategies of injuries or certain health conditions. Also conveyed with this code range is whether the conditional is intentionally inflicted and the place where the injury or the event occurred. The external causes of morbidity codes can be used with any of the other codes from the A0.00–T88.0 range, as well as with the other supplemental code category Z00–Z99.

The following blocks are found in this chapter:

- V00–X58, Accidents
- V00–V99, Transport accidents
- V00–V09, Pedestrian injured in transport accident
- V10–V19, Pedal cyclist injured in transport accident
- V20–V29, Motorcycle rider injured in transport accident
- V30–V39, Occupant of three-wheeled motor vehicle injured in transport accident
- V40–V49, Car occupant injured in transport accident
- V50–V59, Occupant of pickup truck or van injured in transport accident
- V60–V69, Occupant of heavy transport vehicle injured in transport accident
- V70–V79, Bus occupant injured in transport accident
- V80–V89, Other land transport accidents
- V90–V94, Water transport accidents
- V95–V97, Air and space transport accidents
- V98–V99, Other and unspecified transport accidents
- W00–X58, Other external causes of accidental injury
- W00–W19, Slipping, tripping, stumbling, and falls
- W20–W49, Exposure to inanimate mechanical forces
- W50–W64, Exposure to animate mechanical forces
- W65–W74, Accidental drowning and submersion
- W85–W99, Exposure to electric current, radiation, and extreme ambient air temperature and pressure
- X00–X08, Exposure to smoke, fire, and flames
- X10–X19, Contact with heat and hot substances
- X30–X39, Exposure to forces of nature
- X52, X58, Accidental exposure to other specified factors
- X71–X83, Intentional self-harm
- X92–Y08, Assault
- Y21–Y33, Event of undetermined intent

- Y35–Y38, Legal intervention, operations of war, military operations, and terrorism
- Y62–Y84, Complications of medical and surgical care
- Y62–Y69, Misadventures to patients during surgical and medical care
- Y70–Y82, Medical devices associated with adverse incidents in diagnostic and therapeutic use
- Y83–Y84, Surgical and other medical procedures as the cause of abnormal reaction of the patient, or of later complication, without mention of misadventure at the time of the procedure
- Y90–Y99, Supplementary factors related to causes of morbidity classified elsewhere

Coding External Causes of Morbidity

As previously stated, the codes found in the V01–Y99 range are never used as a principal or first listed diagnosis. They are applicable in any health-care setting and are used in research and statistical gathering of data.

The Alphabetic Index to External Causes is located immediately after the Table of Drugs and Chemicals and immediately before the Tabular List of Disease and Injuries.

The main terms include *accident, contact*, and *place of occurrence*.

No code from this code range should ever be used unless the provider documentation clearly states the specifics of an injury or accident, which support the V01–Y99 code choice.

The codes found in this code range can contain up to seven characters. The seventh character indicates the type of encounter, whether it is initial or subsequent, for which the patient is being seen. This character adds another level of detail to the information being reported. Keep in mind that more than one code from this code range may be necessary to accurately paint the picture of the person's accident or illness. The coder should pay close attention to the course of events, as documented in the medical record, before making the decision to use two codes or one combination code.

> **EXAMPLE:** Nina was on a college campus walking to her next class with a friend when they came upon a fight already in progress. As they were trying to get around the fight, one of the campus security persons accidentally kicked Nina in the course of trying to break up the fight. The blow landed on the left thigh and caused her to fall down two concrete steps hitting her head. She was brought to the emergency department with multiple abrasions and contusions.
>
> If we break this down by the course of events, we would reference the Alphabetic Index as follows:
>
> - Place of occurrence—college campus, Y92.214
>
> - Kicked by—person, in fight injuring bystander, Y35.892A (In this case, Nina was not one of the people involved in the fight; so the fact that security was trying to break up the fight and that she was an injured bystander is conveyed with this one code.)
>
> - Fall—fell down two concrete steps, W10.9xxA

Coders must check the codes found in the Alphabetic Index against the Tabular List to be sure they have selected the correct code. Reference all necessary instructional notations and be sure all characters necessary to accurately report the incident have been identified.

To locate a code from the V01–Y99 range, refer to the Index to External Causes, located after the Alphabetic Index. The codes are then referenced in sequence in the Tabular List.

> **EXAMPLE:** In the case of Nina's injury:
>
> - Code Y92.214—College as the place of occurrence of the external cause
>
> - Code Y35.892A—Legal intervention involving other specified means, bystander injured (requires the seventh-character suffix)

- Code W10.9—Fall (on)(from) other stairs and steps (In this case we need to select the appropriate seventh character. This code is four characters, so we need to put in the placeholders to make this W10.9xxA. We know this only if we go to the Tabular List.)

OUR FINAL EXTERNAL CAUSE CODE ASSIGNMENT IS:

- W10.9xxA—assigned first because this code best identifies how the actual injury occurred
- Y92.214
- Y35.892A

The Official Coding Guidelines instruct the coder on how to sequence the external cause codes in Section I.C.20, f, Multiple External Cause Coding Guidelines.

ICD-10-CM Official Coding Guidelines

Multiple External Cause Coding Guidelines

More than one external cause code is required to fully describe the external cause of an illness, injury, or poisoning. The assignment of external cause codes should be sequenced in the following priority:

If two or more events cause separate injuries, an external cause code should be assigned for each cause. The first listed external cause code will be selected in the following order:

External codes for child and adult abuse take priority over all other external cause codes.

See Section I.C.19., Child and Adult abuse guidelines.

External cause codes for terrorism take priority over all other external cause codes except child and adult abuse.

External cause codes for cataclysmic events take priority over all other external cause codes except child and adult abuse and terrorism.

External cause codes for transport accidents take priority over all other external cause codes except cataclysmic events, child and adult abuse, and terrorism.

Activity and external cause status codes are assigned following all causal (intent) external cause codes.

The first-listed external cause code should correspond to the cause of the most serious diagnosis due to an assault, accident, or self-harm, following the order of hierarchy listed above.

Exercise 25.1 – Introduction Summary

Complete the following statements.

1. The codes found in chapter 20 are used as _____ codes in addition to codes from other chapters in ICD-10-CM.

2. _____ is one of the payers that do not recognize this range of codes.

3. Water transport accidents are coded from the _____ code range.

4. Misadventures to patients during surgical and medical care are coded from the _____ range.

5. There is the potential for up to _____ characters in the V01–Y99 code range.

Transport Accidents (Category Codes V00–V99)

This block of codes is broken down into 12 groups. Each group identifies whether the accident was on land or in the water and then further identifies the mode of transportation. The most important issue to identify is the type of vehicle involved and whether the injured person is a passenger, driver, or bystander. The first two characters of the code are used as the identifier of the code block, and the remaining characters note the specifics. Definitions of the different transport vehicles are found at the beginning of chapter 20, in the tabular listing that allows for a more accurate code assignment.

> **EXAMPLE:**
> - V00–V09, Pedestrian injured in a transport accident
> - V10–V19, Pedal cyclist rider injured in transport accident

A **pedestrian** is defined as any person involved in an accident who was not at the time of the accident riding in or on any type of motor or wheeled form of transportation. This definition includes riding an animal such as horseback.

Pedestrian Injured in Transport Accident (Category Codes V00–V09)

To be coded as a transport accident, the vehicle involved must be used for transport purposes, moving, or running at the time of the accident. Coders need to see the Includes and Excludes notes before codes are assigned. At the beginning of this block, in the instructional notation for this section, the appropriate seventh-character assignments are listed:

- A, Initial encounter
- D, Subsequent encounter
- S, Sequela—indicates a late effect

This code range is quite extensive. Pedestrian conveyance accidents, rolling-type pedestrian conveyance accidents, and gliding-type pedestrian conveyance accidents are found at the beginning of the code range. The codes become very detailed regarding the pedestrian colliding with skateboards and scooters and other types of transports.

Pedal Cycle Rider Injured in Transport Accident (Category Codes V10–V19)

A **pedal cycle** is operated by a person who is operating the vehicle without the help of a motor. An accident involving a person who might be riding in a sidecar or a trailer that is attached to a pedal cycle is categorized to this code range unless the sidecar or trailer is animal drawn.

Codes found in this code range include a person injured in a collision with a two- or three-wheeled motor vehicle; a pedal cycle rider injured in a collision with a car, pickup truck, or van; and a pedal cycle rider injured in a collision with railway train or railway vehicle. Pedal cycle riders injured in a noncollision transport accident, which would include a fall from a pedal cycle whether the person was thrown or the pedal cycle overturned, are coded from the V18 category.

Motorcycle Rider Injured in Transport Accident (Category Codes V20–V29)

Included in this code range are motorcycle riders and passengers on a motorcycle, including those seated in a sidecar. Other included vehicles are mopeds, motorized bicycles, and motor scooters. A three-wheeled motor vehicle is excluded. The motor vehicles in this code range are exclusively two-wheeled motor vehicles with a riding saddle. If the sidecar is attached to the motorcycle, it is considered part of the motorcycle.

Occupant of Three-Wheeled Motor Vehicle Injured in Transport Accident (Category Codes V30–39)

This category of codes includes motorized tricycles, rickshaws, or three-wheeled motor cars. Fourth characters are assigned to identify the driver, passenger, or unspecified occupant. Appropriate seventh-character assignment is also needed.

Exercise 25.2 – Category Codes V00–V39

Using an ICD-10-CM code book, assign a code from the V00–V39 code range.

Diagnosis   *Code*

1. a passenger on a motorcycle who was injured in an accident in which a bear ran into the road and hit the motorcycle (subsequent encounter)   _____

2. person on roller skates injured in a collision with a bike in a nontraffic accident (initial encounter)   _____

3. an ice-skater who collided with a railroad tie that was set along side the pond (initial encounter)   _____

4. person on a bicycle injured after being sideswiped by a bus on a busy street (subsequent encounter)   _____

5. person walking on the sidewalk hit by a car backing out of a driveway (initial encounter)   _____

Car Occupant Injured in Transport Accident (Category Codes V40–V49)

This code range is primarily used to report accidents occurring in a four-wheeled motor vehicle designed to carry passengers. A trailer or camper that is being pulled by an automobile is also included in this range. The following box further explains the V40–V49 code block.

Code	Description
V40, Car occupant injured in collision with pedestrian or animal	This category is used to report a driver or passenger injured in a collision. The distinction is made as to the type of accident and who was injured, the driver or passenger.
V41, Car occupant injured in collision with pedal cycle	A car collision with a bicycle either in or out of traffic is reported with this category. The person injured may be a passenger or the driver injured in the vehicle or entering or leaving the vehicle.
V42, Car occupant injured in collision with two- or three-wheeled motor vehicle	As with previous code categories, the driver or passenger of the car needs to be identified. The place of the accident has to be identified, as well as whether the accident was in or out of traffic.
V43, Car occupant injured in collision with car, pickup truck, or van	The driver or passenger needs to be identified before code selection can occur. The identification of the other vehicle needs to be made because the code selection depends on whether the accident occurred with a car, pickup truck, van, or sport utility vehicle and on whether the accident was a traffic or nontraffic accident.

The remainder of the code categories, V44–V49, involve car accidents involving buses, trains, railway vehicles, or cars in an accident with a stationary object. Careful attention to the details of the documentation indicating who was injured, what the vehicle might have hit, and whether the accident happened in traffic are necessary to assign the proper code.

Occupant of Pickup Truck or Van Injured in Transport Accident (Category Codes V50–V59)

This series of codes includes four- or six-wheel motor vehicles that primarily carry passengers and are able to haul some property but are much smaller than an 18-wheeler or a truck that is able to carry large loads. The information needed to code from this range is the same as previous categories. Knowing whether the driver or passenger was injured in a traffic accident is necessary to choose a correct code.

Occupant of Heavy Transport Vehicle Injured in Transport Accident (Category Codes V60–V69)

Heavy transport vehicles are designed for carrying property, meeting local criteria for classification as a heavy goods vehicle in terms of weight and requiring a special driver's license, such as a commercial driver's license (CDL). This definition includes armored cars, panel trucks, and 18-wheelers. Injury of a driver or passenger in or out of traffic is the information necessary to properly assign a code.

Bus Occupant Injured in Transport Accident (Category Codes V70–V79)

A bus transport is a vehicle that is designed to carry more than 10 passengers and that requires a special license to operate. A motorcoach falls into this category as well. The coder must know whether the patient is the driver or a passenger who was injured in the bus accident. The type of accident and the knowledge of whether the accident happened as part of a traffic or nontraffic accident are also necessary information in determining a code.

Other Land Transport Accident (Category Codes V80–V89)

The land transport vehicles that fall into this category include animal, animal-drawn vehicles, and all-terrain vehicles. The specific codes are chosen from this category just as they are selected from other codes in the transport accident blocks of codes. Passengers, drivers, and the type of accident are all considerations that need to be determined prior to code selection.

Exercise 25.3 – Category Codes V40–V89

Using an ICD-10-CM code book, assign the proper code for the accident described.

Diagnosis   *Code*

1. driver of a car injured when a deer jumped out of the woods into the road in front of the moving vehicle (initial encounter)   _____

2. person on the outside of a car who is injured in a collision with an SUV as part of a traffic accident (subsequent encounter)   _____

3. passenger in a pickup truck injured in a collision with a bus in a traffic accident (initial encounter)   _____

4. passenger in a dune buggy injured in an accident on the dunes (initial encounter)   _____

5. person injured in a farm accident involving the driver of a tractor who was injured when he was lost his footing while getting off the tractor out in the field (initial encounter)   _____

Water Transport Accidents (Category Codes V90–V94)

Within ICD-10-CM, watercraft accidents include boats, ships, hovercrafts, and any other transportation that works on the water. The included incidents are drowning due to an accident on the water, crush injuries involving watercraft, burns and falls encountered on the water or involving watercrafts, and injuries or accidents involving machinery on board a watercraft. Inflatable watercraft such as rafts and inner tubes are included in the code choices under V94, Other and unspecified water transport accidents.

There are many Excludes notes throughout this category. The coder needs to pay close attention to these notes in order to properly assign the correct code. The documentation needs to contain as many specifics of the accident as possible to support the code selection.

Air and Space Transport Accidents (Category Codes V95–V97)

The definition of aircraft includes any vehicle used to transport persons or goods in the air. This includes any aircraft except for military aircraft, which are covered in the Y codes. The following further explains the V95–V97 code block.

Code	Description
V95, Accident to powered aircraft causing injury to occupant	This code category includes helicopter accidents, ultralight or microlight, or powered-glider, and fixed-wing aircraft. Also included are codes for spacecraft accidents.
V96, Accident to nonpowered aircraft causing injury to occupant	This category includes accidents that involve balloons, hang gliders, and other nonpowered aircraft accidents.
V97, Other specified air transport accidents	This category includes occupants of aircrafts who might fall in or from an aircraft. Parachute accidents are also coded to this section.

Other and Unspecified Transport Accidents (Category Codes V98–V99)

This range contains codes used to report accidents involving a cable car not on rails, land yacht, ice yacht, and ski lift. The codes in this section are looked at after all other code choices have been exhausted.

Other External Causes of Accidental Injury (Category Codes W00–X58)

Slipping, Tripping, Stumbling, and Falls (Category Codes W00–W19)

The external cause codes found in this code range begin with falls due to ice and snow; falls from a curb; and falls from a wheelchair, bed, chair, playground equipment, tree, ladder, and scaffolding. The majority of the codes found in the W00–W16.4 range are falls *from, into*, or *off* of something. The coder must be able to make that distinction because the next range of codes, beginning with W16.5, describe *jumping* into something.

The W00–W16.4 code range includes falling into a swimming pool, into a natural body of water, or into a bathtub. Once the category of code is chosen, the coder needs to make the determination from the documentation provided as to whether the patient was injured due to striking the water or another structure in the water.

> **EXAMPLE:** Roger was playing in the pool with his cousin when he fell from its side into the water, landing flat on his stomach. He hit the water so hard it knocked the wind out of him, and he had to have help getting to the ladder. Once on the ladder, he caught his breath but felt dizzy, so his mother took him to the doctor to be checked out. He did have some bruising on the anterior trunk. We would assign external cause code W16.012A, Fall into swimming pool striking water surface causing other injury. At the beginning of the category, there is an instructional notation that a character is needed to indicate the status of the encounter. The seventh character of A is chosen because it is the initial encounter for this problem.

Category W16.5 begins the code range for jumping or diving into a swimming pool, lake, or other body of water. The coder needs to determine whether the patient was submerged, drowned, or injured. Refer to the documentation for this information.

Category W17 is referenced for falls from one level to another, such as down an embankment or into a hole or well.

Categories W18 and W19 finish the code range with codes used to indicate slipping, tripping, and/or stumbling. If the type of fall is not found in the previous code categories, these categories are referenced.

Also found in this range of external cause codes are falls due to bumping against an object, such as glass or sports equipment, and falls in the shower or bathtub.

These categories specify slipping, tripping, and stumbling without falling. Refer to the documentation for verification of a fall. Never assume that, because patients are injured due to slipping, tripping, or stumbling, they actually fell. This is not always the case. If the documentation is not clear on this point, query the originator of the documentation.

> **EXAMPLE:** Lisa got up from the couch to get a drink of water. On her way from the living room to the kitchen, her heel caught on the carpet and she stumbled forward, twisting her ankle. She caught herself on the side of the door before she actually fell. Even though Lisa stumbled, she did not fall; so the code assignment is W18.49XA, Other slipping, tripping, and stumbling without falling, initial encounter.

Exposure to Inanimate Mechanical Forces (Category Codes W20–W49)

An **inanimate object** is one that is not alive or able to move (animate) on its own power. The beginning of this category of codes contains an Excludes 1 note that this category does not include assault, contact, or collision with animals or persons; exposure to inanimate mechanical forces involving the military; or intentional self-harm. Reference these injuries elsewhere.

This code range does, however, include being struck by thrown or projected objects, such as cave-ins, or by sports equipment (e.g., footballs, baseballs, volleyballs, etc.). A patient might present with an injury caused by a cleat or skate blade. These incidents are found in the W21 category.

Category W22, Striking against or struck by other objects includes such objects as walls, furniture, and airbags. The code range contains some Exclude notations that should be addressed before codes are assigned.

Crush and contact injuries are found in the code range for exposure to inanimate mechanical forces. The documentation must clearly state what caused the injury so that the coder can determine the correct code.

The W23–W31 categories are referenced for these types of injuries. Contact codes are quite detailed and include contact with glass, knives, garden tools, kitchen utensils, and paper cutters. These categories contain further detail that needs to be referenced after the documentation is reviewed.

The W32–W34 categories contain codes that reflect the external cause codes for the accidental discharge of a weapon. The weapons include firearms such as handguns, pistols, revolvers, pellet guns, rifles, and air guns. The codes become more specific, identifying guns specifically as hunting rifles and machine guns.

Moving from firearms to explosives, the W35–W40 codes break down as illustrated in the following box.

Codes	Description
W35, Explosion and rupture of boiler	This code includes the explosion and/or rupture of a boiler in a structure. A rupture of a boiler on a watercraft is coded to V93.4- instead of this code.
W36, Explosion and rupture of gas cylinder	This code range includes aerosol cans, air tanks, pressurized gas tanks, and gas cylinders.
W37, Explosion and rupture of pressurized tire, pipe, or hose	Included in this code range are car or bicycle tires.
W38, Explosion and rupture of other specified pressurized devices	This is one of the few three-digit codes and is used only if there is no further detail available to obtain a more specific code.
W39, Discharge of firework	An injury related to the discharge of fireworks is reported with the code for the injury and this W code as an additional descriptor.
W40, Explosion of other materials	This range of codes includes blasting material such as blasting caps, detonators, and dynamite. This range also includes explosive gases and other explosive material.

The remaining codes in this block are a somewhat eclectic mix of "contact" issues. There are external cause codes reflecting foreign bodies or objects entering through the skin such as a nail, paper, or lid of a can. Other codes report contact with a hypodermic needle and exposure to abnormal gravitational forces (G force).

Exposure to Animate Mechanical Forces (Category Codes W50–W64)

An **animate object** is a living being capable of movement on its own. The code range includes:

- Accidental injuries by another person, distinguished according to how the injury took place (i.e. hitting, kicking, biting, or scratching).
- Being crushed by a crowd.
- Injury caused by contact with rodents, dogs, cats, horses, or other mammals.
- Contact with reptiles, venomous or nonvenomous.

Accidental Drowning and Submersion (Category Codes W65–W74)

This is not a very extensive code range. Found here are codes for accidental drowning and submersion while in the bathtub or other water but *not* due to a fall.

Exposure to Electric Current, Radiation, and Extreme Ambient Air Temperature and Pressure (Category Codes W85–W99)

This code range contains Includes and Excludes notes that need to be reviewed prior to code selection. This code range is referenced for exposure to broken power lines, to industrial or residential wiring, and to the wiring of appliances that might have caused injury.

The detail extends to injury caused by exposure to the ultraviolet light of a welding light or tanning bed. Also found is contact with heating appliances, with hot engines, machinery, and tools, and with hot metal.

One of the unique features of this chapter is the category for exposure to high and low air pressure changes, which include injuries occurring in the air, in deep water, or due to other rapid changes in air pressure. Like other codes in the external cause chapter, a seventh character assignment is necessary for most of the codes in this block.

Exercise 25.4 – Coding from the W Code Section

Using an ICD-10-CM code book, assign a W code.

Diagnosis   *Code*

1. exposure to infrared radiation (late effect)   _____

2. bitten by a parrot (initial encounter)   _____

3. explosion of propane (initial encounter)   _____

4. contact with a lathe (subsequent encounter)   _____

5. fall from the toilet, striking head on the vanity   _____
     (initial encounter)

Exposure to Smoke, Fire, and Flames (Category Codes X00–X08)

The X codes are actually a continuation of the exposure codes, so they are not broken out into their own section within the external cause chapter of ICD-10-CM. Even though there are more than 68,000 codes in ICD-10-CM, many sections leave room for expansion. The W and X codes are two such blocks.

The X codes begin with X00, Exposure to uncontrolled fire in building or structure. The codes found in the X00–X08 range are also referenced when reporting exposure to flames in a controlled or uncontrolled building or structure fire, as well as the ignition of highly flammable material such as gasoline, kerosene, or even melting clothing. Exposure to ignition of plastic jewelry, bed fires, and other furniture fires is also reported from this code range.

Contact with Heat and Hot Substances (Category Codes X10–X19)

Unfortunately, many people are burned each year. The causes vary from hot water, to flames, to hot air, to appliances. This code range has very specific forms of contact injuries for reporting these exposures.

EXAMPLE: Marcy got home late from work and was very tired. She decided to have a toasted bagel with a little peanut butter and a cup of tea, and call it a night. She was heating water on her hot plate for some tea while the bagel was toasting. When the bagel popped up from the toaster, she went to prepare it. As she was reaching for the knife to apply peanut butter to her bagel, her hand went down on the hotplate by accident. Even though she tried to take care of it, she ended up at the emergency room and had silver nitrate applied to her hand for the second-degree burn she received due to contact with the hot plate.

The burn is the primary diagnosis. How Marcy obtained the burn is reported with X15.2XXA, Contact with hotplate, initial encounter.

Exposure to Forces of Nature (Category Codes X30–X39)

Exposure to forces of nature include exposure to sunlight, earthquake, volcanic eruption, hurricane, tornado, blizzard, and dust storm. These codes are used to report any type of incident that is considered caused by nature but exclude human-made heat or radiation.

Accidental Exposure to Other Specified Factors (Category Codes X52, X58)

This category contains two codes. Code X52 is for prolonged stay in a weightless environment. This is reported by astronauts after prolonged exposure in a training environment or after an extended stay in space. Code X58, Exposure to other specified factors, is used if nothing more specific can be found.

Intentional Self-Harm (Category Codes X71–X83)

This block includes codes for identifying suicide attempts and self-inflicted injuries done on purpose. In some instances, a person causes self-harm just for the attention, without trying to commit suicide. The coder should *never* assign a code for suicide or a suicide attempt unless the physician or provider has been queried and confirms the diagnosis.

Reported from this range of codes is intentional self-harm by drowning, by shotgun or other firearm, or by smoke, fire, flames, or sharp object. Like the other blocks in this chapter, the appropriate seventh character needs to be added when indicated to make the code as specific as possible.

Assault (Category Codes X92–Y08)

Assault is a violent crime committed against another. This block of codes is used to identify various types of assault including homicide or injuries inflicted by another with the intent to injure or kill. The Excludes notation identifies injuries due to legal intervention, operations of war, or terrorism. These incidents are reported using the X92–Y08 codes referenced.

Assault by smoke, fire, or flames, steam, hot vapors, hot objects, and firearms or sharp objects are found in the X94–X99 code range. The Y codes begin with Y00, Assault by blunt object.

The codes for Y07, Perpetrator of assault, maltreatment, and neglect, are very specific and should be used cautiously. The *only* time a coder includes one of these codes on a claim form is if there is a confirmed case of abuse and the person has been positively identified with supporting documentation. Use of this code without such documentation can leave the door open to a defamation of character suit and cause a legal nightmare for the coder, the provider, and the employing organization.

Note:

The codes cross over from X to Y for assault.

Event of Undetermined Intent (Category Codes Y20–Y33)

This code block is referenced when no determination is documented as to the intent of the injury. The coder needs to reference accidental or unintentional events if the intent is documented.

Found in this code block are drowning; the discharge of firearms; contact with explosive materials or sharp objects; and exposure to smoke, fire, and flames. Again, the documentation must state that the intent of the injury could not be determined.

Legal Intervention, Operations of War, Military Operations, and Terrorism (Category Codes Y35–Y38)

This code block includes codes for injuries received as a result of an encounter with law enforcement officials serving on or off duty in any capacity at the time of an encounter. The following box further explains these codes and when to use them.

Y35, Legal intervention	This block of codes is extensive in the types of legal intervention injuries. The category begins with firearm discharge codes and goes through pellet rifle and hand guns. Injuries also obtained by exposure to tear gas or blunt objects can be found here. The codes identify law enforcement personnel, suspects, and bystanders. Refer to the documentation for the support of the proper code selection and determination of who was injured.
Y36, Operation of war	The code block identifies injuries received by military personnel, as well as civilians, that are caused by war and/or civil insurrection. Such occurrences include explosions of marine weapons and military watercraft or aircraft, as well as fragments from a bomb, artillery shell, grenade, land mine, or shrapnel. Codes for the secondary effects of nuclear weapons during war operations are also found in this category. The distinctions among codes in this category are made by the documentation stating whether the injury was due to friendly fire or enemy fire and whether the person injured was a civilian or a member of the military.
Y37, Military operation	Sometimes injuries occur on military property, such as base of operations, during routine military operations. This block of codes identifies such injuries involving military personnel or civilians. In this case, military property does *not* extend to military vehicles, including aircraft or watercraft, involved in transport accidents or other accidents with civilian vehicles; these are reported with codes from the V code section.
Y38, Terrorism	ICD-10-CM guides the coder with the following note at the beginning of this code block, which is the FBI definition of **terrorism**: "These codes are for use to identify injuries resulting from the unlawful use of force or violence against persons or property to intimidate or coerce a Government, the civilian population, or any segment, thereof, in furtherance of political or social objective." An additional code from the Y92 category is needed to indicate the place of occurrence. The codes distinguish among a public safety official, a civilian, or a terrorist being injured. When the cause of the injury is clearly identified by the federal government (FBI) as terrorism, the Y38 code should always be sequenced first. If, however, the cause is suspected terrorism, the injury is identified with a code from the assault code set. Code Y38.9-, Terrorism, secondary effects, is used for conditions occurring after the terrorist event and may be used with other Y38 codes.

Complications of Medical and Surgical Care (Category Codes Y62–Y84)

The blocks of codes that are found in this section of chapter 20 include:

- Misadventures to Patients During Surgical and Medical Care (Category Codes Y62–Y69).

- Medical Devices Associated with Adverse Incidents in Diagnostic and Therapeutic Use (Category Codes Y70–Y82).

- Surgical and Other Medical Procedures as the Cause of Abnormal Reaction of the Patient, or of Later Complication, Without Mention of Misadventure at the Time of the Procedure (Category Codes Y83–Y84).

Included in this block of codes are complications of medical devices, surgical and medical procedures as the cause of an abnormal reaction of the patient, or of later complication, without mention of misadventure at the time of the procedure.

The code selections found in the Y62–Y69 range include failure of sterile precautions for organ transplant, bypass or graft surgery, amputation of a limb, or reconstruction, to name a few.

> **Note:**
>
> *Beginning with this block of codes, a seventh character assignment may or may not be appropriate. Coders need to refer to the Tabular Listing to be sure that they are assigning an accurate code containing all the characters necessary to process a claim.*

Supplementary Factors Related to Causes of Morbidity Classified Elsewhere (Category Codes Y90–Y99)

This block of codes is not used except in conjunction with other codes. Details surrounding the codes are outlined in the following box.

Code	Description
Y90, Evidence of alcohol involvement determined by blood alcohol level	The Y90.0–Y90.9 codes indicate blood alcohol levels that have been determined by an actual blood test. The levels range from less than 20 mg/100 ml to 240 mg/100 ml. There is a "Code First" note indicating that a code from the F10 codes for alcohol-related disorders should be coded before a code from the Y90 series.
Y92, Place of occurrence of the external cause	These codes are used with an activity code to identify the place of occurrence of the external cause. Place of occurrence codes are used only for the initial encounter and are not repeated at subsequent visits. Place of occurrence codes include, but are not limited to, private driveways, private garages, gardens, mobile homes, apartments, institutional residence, nursing homes, and military bases.
Y93, Activity code	The activity code block contains codes that indicate the activity of the injured person at the time of the injury. These codes are used when a person suffers a health condition, such as a stroke or heart attack, and the activity being performed at the time of the heart attack or stroke needs to be reported. A couple of things to note for this category: • The codes can be used for both acute injuries and conditions due to long-term cumulative activities. • The codes are appropriate for use with external cause codes for cause and intent, if identifying the activity provides additional information on the event.

Comparing ICD-9-CM to ICD-10-CM

External causes of morbidity have been expanded ICD-10-CM. Fourth, fifth, and sixth characters are commonly used. Seventh characters are added to further define the case. Numerous new categories have been added throughout the chapter that include categories Y62–Y84, Complications of medical and surgical care. Category Y93 is added to identify the patient's activity at the time of injury and are considered secondary codes.

Summary

- This chapter is referenced to code environmental and other circumstances as the cause of injury and other adverse effects.

- Use the appropriate seventh character, where appropriate, to indicate the length of treatment.

- Codes from this chapter are never used as the primary diagnosis code.

- More than one code may be assigned from this chapter, though sequencing of the codes is important, as outlined in the Official Coding Guidelines.

- Use a late effect external cause code for subsequent visits when a late effect of the initial injury is being treated.

- Late effects are indicated by use of the seventh character S.

- Codes for injuries due to accidents, terrorism, and complications of medical and surgical care are reported from chapter 20.

Chapter Review

Multiple Choice

Select the best answer that completes the statement or answers the question.

1. The external causes of morbidity codes are codes used to:
   a. code an acute medical condition such as pharyngitis.
   b. code a better description of how an injury happened.
   c. code an evaluation and management service to report the service rendered.
   d. indicate what family members might be doing while a patient is in the hospital.

2. The codes from chapter 20 capture the _____, the _____, and the _____ of the event that brought the patient to the facility.
   a. complication, location, duration
   b. location, functioning, injury
   c. intent, location, complication
   d. cause, intent, location

3. Other land transport accidents are reported using:
   a. V98–V99.
   b. V90–V94.
   c. V80–V89.
   d. V70–V79.

4. Another way of saying "diseased state" is to use the term:
   a. *morbidity.*
   b. *mortality.*
   c. *toxic effect.*
   d. *external cause.*

5. Which of the following reflects the proper sequencing if more than one code from chapter 20 is necessary for reporting an encounter?
   a. W45.2-, Y04.1-, Y92.215
   b. W45.2-, Y92.215, Y04.1-
   c. Y04.1-, Y92.215, W45.2-
   d. Y04.1-, W45.2-, Y92.215

6. Which of the following reflects the proper sequencing if more than one code from chapter 20 is necessary for reporting an encounter?
   a. V96.01-, X36.1-, Y38.892-
   b. X36.1-, V96.01-, Y38.892-
   c. Y38.892-, V96.01-, X36.1-
   d. Y38.892-, X36.1-, V96.01-

7. A _____ is defined as a person who was not riding or driving in any form of motor or wheeled transportation.
   a. pediatrician
   b. podiatrist
   c. pedestrian
   d. pharmacist

8. In ICD-10-CM, a late effect is indicated by the seventh character:
   a. *A.*
   b. *B.*
   c. *D.*
   d. *S.*

9. A child is an example of:
    a. an inanimate object.
    b. an animate object.
    c. morbidity.
    d. none of the above.

10. A violent crime committed against another is known as:
    a. assault.
    b. battery.
    c. liable.
    d. slander.

Coding Assignments

Instructions: Using an ICD-10-CM code book, assign the proper external cause code to the following statements. (Assume initial encounter unless otherwise specified.)

1. exposure to sound waves _____

2. bitten by an alligator _____

3. explosion of aerosol can _____

4. fall into well _____

5. fall from bed _____

6. contact with a nonvenomous toad _____

7. subsequent encounter for injury due to fall into a well _____

8. driver of a fire engine injured in a nontraffic accident _____

9. walked into a coffee table _____

10. fell into empty swimming pool _____

11. accidental discharge of a paintball gun _____

12. fall due to collision between two fishing boats _____

13. fall from a nonmotorized scooter _____

14. contact with sharp glass, undetermined intent _____

15. hypodermic needle stick _____

16. civilian injured in terrorist attack involving firearms _____

17. fall on escalator _____

18. contact with hot tap water _____

19. subsequent visit after being struck by a brick from a collapsing building _____

20. drowning after fall in bath tub _____

21.   subsequent visit after contact injury with a chisel   _____

22.   fall from grocery cart   _____

23.   exposure to a broken power line   _____

24.   fall from scaffolding, subsequent encounter   _____

25.   dog bite   _____

Case Studies

Instructions: Review each case study and select the correct ICD-10-CM diagnostic code.

CASE 1

Emergency Department Note

Justin was brought to the emergency room with a broken left tibia. Justin was sky diving and due to a wind shift, he landed in a tree. After a complete examination and scans, the broken tibia is the only injury found. The final diagnosis is a displaced fracture of lateral condyle of left tibia due to a parachutist landing in a tree.

ICD-10-CM Code Assignment: _____

CASE 2

Emergency Department Note

This is a 3-year-old patient who was playing outside and received a cut by slipping and falling on an icy sidewalk and landing on a piece of broken glass on the ground.

EXAM: There is a 1-cm laceration of the right hand. The wound was cleaned and searched for any remaining pieces of glass. No foreign body was found.

PROCEDURE: Dermabond glue was used to repair the laceration

PLAN: Patient will follow up with her pediatrician in one week to check on healing.

ICD-10-CM Code Assignment: _____

CASE 3

Physician Office Note

This is a 27-year old male who is here for follow-up visit after falling into the bathtub full of water and causing a contusion of the right shoulder. He said the pain level is down to a level 2 from a 10 on his last visit. There was a follow-up x-ray done and no fracture or other irregularities are noted. He will continue with ibuprofen as needed.

ICD-10-CM Code Assignment: _____

Factors Influencing Health Status and Contact with Health Services

CHAPTER

26

Chapter Outline

Objectives

At the conclusion of this chapter, the learner should be able to:

1. Explain the purpose of Z codes.
2. Identify key terms that are used to locate Z codes in the Alphabetic Index.
3. Describe and identify encounters for which Z codes are used.
4. Explain the differences between the blocks outlined in the ICD-10-CM code book.
5. Discuss the specific coding guidelines that relate to Z codes.
6. Identify similarities and differences between the ICD-9-CM V codes and the ICD-10-CM Z codes.
7. Select the appropriate Z code for the case studies.

Key Terms

aftercare visits

body mass index

diagnostic examinations

resuscitation

screening examinations

Z codes

Reminder

As you work through this chapter, you will need to have a copy of the ICD-10-CM coding book to reference.

Introduction

ICD-10-CM has replaced the supplementary V codes used in ICD-9-CM with Z codes. **Z codes** are to be used to report encounters when the circumstances surrounding the encounter are for something other than disease or injury. These codes are used to report problems or other factors that might have had an influence on care but that are not themselves a current illness or injury.

> **EXAMPLE:** Melanie was submitting an application for adoption. The application required a physical examination to support the fact that she was physically healthy. The doctor performed the physical and signed the papers, verifying that there were no health problems to report.

The doctor reports Z02.82, Encounter for adoption services, to identify the service performed.

The Z codes apply to any health-care setting and may be used as either a first-listed diagnosis code or as a secondary code depending on the circumstances of the visit.

Introduction to Z Codes

The majority of ICD-10-CM codes require up to seven alphanumeric characters to be valid, but Z codes can contain only three to six characters. Z codes can be located in the Alphabetic Index by referencing some common terms such as *encounter, contact,* and *status post,* though other terms also lead a coder to the correct code assignment.

> **EXAMPLE:** Kate was coding the diagnostic statement of "presence of cochlear implant device." At first, she was confused as to where to find this diagnosis because the patient did not have an implant procedure performed in the office. Kate decided to reference the word *presence* and came up with code Z96.21 for the presence of a cochlear implant device.

This chapter contains the following blocks:

- Z00–Z13, Persons encountering health services for examination
- Z14–Z15, Genetic carrier and genetic susceptibility to disease
- Z16, Infection with drug-resistant microorganisms
- Z17, Estrogen receptor status
- Z20–Z28, Persons with potential health hazards related to communicable diseases
- Z30–Z39, Persons encountering health services in circumstances related to reproduction
- Z40–Z53, Persons encountering health services for specific procedures and health care
- Z55–Z65, Persons with potential health hazards related to socioeconomic and psychosocial circumstances
- Z66, Do not resuscitate (DNR) status
- Z67, Blood type
- Z68, Body mass index (BMI)
- Z69–Z76, Persons encountering health services in other circumstances
- Z77–Z99, Persons with potential health hazards related to family and personal history of certain conditions influencing health status

Each of these blocks is discussed in this chapter.

Persons Encountering Health Services for Examinations (Category Codes Z00–Z13)

Notes throughout this section need to be referenced before code assignment is completed. At the start of this block of codes, a note appears that states "nonspecific abnormal findings disclosed at the time of these examinations are classified to categories R70–R74." An Excludes instructional note also appears that has information about examinations related to pregnancy and reproduction.

Routine physicals in ICD-10-CM are distinguished by an encounter with or without abnormal findings. If an abnormal finding is identified during this encounter, the code for general medical examination with abnormal findings is coded first; then a secondary code that identifies the abnormal finding is second.

> **EXAMPLE:** Jackson was brought to the doctor by his mother for a well-baby check. Jackson is a 2-year-old male who appears to be quite healthy. After his vitals were checked, Jackson was put through the normal age-appropriate developmental screening, and it was determined that he is a very healthy, well-developed 2-year-old. No abnormalities were found.
>
> Code Z00.129 is used to report this encounter because the code reflects a routine exam for a child without abnormal findings. If an abnormal finding had been addressed or discovered, code Z00.121 would have been used, along with a code to identify the abnormal finding per the instructional notations.

Screening examinations are used to "screen" or to look for diseases. These codes are listed first on a claim form. **Diagnostic examinations** are used to confirm or rule out a suspected diagnosis due to signs and symptoms that the patient has experienced. An additional diagnosis may be assigned if a condition is discovered as a result of the screening. This chapter of ICD-10-CM provides codes for encounters for screenings such as infectious and parasitic diseases, malignant neoplasms, eye disorders, diseases of the blood and blood-forming organs, among others.

Routine gynecological examinations are coded to the Z01.4 category. This category has instructional notations regarding additional screenings such as the following:

Use additional code:
for screening for human papillomavirus, if applicable, (Category Codes Z11.51)
for screening vaginal pap smear, if applicable (Category Codes Z12.72)
to identify acquired absence of uterus, if applicable (Category Codes Z90.71-)

Attention to detail in the documentation is critical because many of the encounter codes distinguish among those where problems were encountered and those where the findings were within normal limits.

Genetic Carrier and Genetic Susceptibility to Disease (Category Codes Z14–Z15)

This code set offers much more detail regarding genetic carrier status. Certain diseases can be identified through testing or family history that may be indicative of a carrier of a gene associated with a specific disease. The knowledge that a person may be a carrier of a disease allows the person to know whether their offspring may be at risk or susceptible to the disease.

If a patient is presenting for genetic counseling, code Z31.5, Encounter for genetic counseling, is sequenced first; the code from category Z15, Genetic susceptibility, is the secondary code. If there are applicable codes for family history of a certain disease, they are also listed after the Z31.5 code.

If the patient is being seen for treatment of a specific disease or birth defect, the code for the specific disease or birth defect is assigned instead of a code from this category. The same is true for follow-up visits after a disease has been cured.

Infection with Drug-Resistant Microorganisms (Category Code Z16)

This is the only code in this code block. The instructional notation under this code reads:

> This category is intended for use as an additional code for infectious conditions classified elsewhere to indicate the presence of drug-resistance of the infectious organism
>
> Code first the infection

Estrogen Receptor Status (Category Code Z17)

The two codes in this category are used to report positive and negative status. The malignant neoplasm of the breast is coded first.

Persons with Potential Health Hazards Related to Communicable Diseases (Category Codes Z20–Z28)

This code block represents codes that indicate exposure to or contact with communicable diseases. No signs or symptoms of disease are evident at the time of the visit, but exposure to or contact with an infected individual has caused concern for the patient. These codes might also be referenced if the patient presents for an encounter after living in disease epidemic area. The codes from the Z20 code set might be reported first or, in some cases, second to identify a potential risk.

> **EXAMPLE:** Sylvia, a nurse, presented because she was concerned about a fingerstick she received from a needle that was used by an HIV-infected person. Because the needlestick caused direct exposure, we did a blood test to check for HIV exposure. The doctor assigns code Z20.6, Contact with and exposure to human immunodeficiency virus (HIV).

The Z28 code category represents codes for encounters for immunizations not carried out because of contraindications or because of the patient's religious reasons or group pressure. This is a new code category that was not represented in ICD-9-CM coding. For proper code selection, the documentation must reflect the reason that the immunization was not given.

If the prophylactic immunization is given during a routine health exam, a Z23 code is assigned as a secondary code as part of the visit. A procedure code is necessary to accurately identify the actual type of immunization given.

Persons Encountering Health Services in Circumstances Related to Reproduction (Category Codes Z30–Z39)

This code range is referenced when a patient presents for an encounter related to contraceptive management. This includes sterilization, fertility testing, and procreative management.

Also found within this code range are codes related to pregnancy. The pregnancy-related Z codes found here replace some of the V22 codes series found in ICD-9-CM, but additional codes more specifically report multiple births such as triplets and quintuplets. This range of Z codes for pregnancy is used only when none of the problems or complications would lead the coder to the obstetrics chapter. The Z codes are not used in conjunction with the codes from the obstetrics chapter.

Encounters for Other Specific Health Care (Category Codes Z40–Z53)

This code range is where aftercare codes are found. **Aftercare visits** reflect services provided during the healing or recovery time of a disease. Some consequences of disease processes are also found here. These codes are not referenced if the disease process is still ongoing or acute. Occasionally these codes are found in the secondary position, but usually they are positioned first on the claim.

There are also Z codes for fitting and adjustments for things like vascular access devices and adjustment of a cardiac pacemaker. The code assignment depends on the documentation. There is a detailed list of codes that involve aftercare following specific organ transplants. The proper code assignment is essential to reflect the severity of the condition the patient is experiencing.

Exercise 26.1 – Category Codes Z00–Z53

Using an ICD-10-CM code book, assign the proper code for the diagnostic statements given.

Diagnosis   *Code*

  1. encounter for allergy test   _____

  2. encounter for examination of potential donor of
        organ tissue   _____

  3. encounter for screening for osteoporosis   _____

  4. encounter for screening for respiratory tuberculosis   _____

  5. contact with exposure to rabies   _____

  6. encounter for Rh incompatibility status   _____

  7. immunization not carried out because of
        immune-compromised state of the patient   _____

  8. carrier of viral hepatitis C   _____

  9. encounter for ear piercing   _____

  10. encounter for fitting and adjustment of an orthodontic device   _____

Persons with Potential Health Hazards Related to Socioeconomic and Psychosocial Circumstances (Category Codes Z55–Z65)

This code range identifies the diagnosis of conditions associated with education, such as problems with literacy and maladjustment with teachers and classmates.

The code range also allows for coding for an encounter related to problems with the workplace, the environment, and poverty or economic conditions.

The problems related to negative life events in childhood are coded from Z61. Specific code assignment depends on documentation. The provider's documentation must support code assignments from this code range.

Do Not Resuscitate Status (Category Code Z66)

The medical procedure performed to restore cardiac and/or respiratory function is known as **resuscitation**. When a patient makes the decision not to have this procedure performed and puts the decision in writing, it is known as a "Do Not Resuscitate (DNR)" order. The only code in this category is Z66, which indicates a DNR status.

Blood Type (Category Code Z67)

This category is referenced when the indication needs to be made as to the patient's blood type. Type A, B, O, and AB are coded from this category. The code selection is based on what blood type is necessary to report and also if the patient is Rh negative or Rh positive.

Body Mass Index (BMI) (Category Code Z68)

The **body mass index** is figured by taking a person's weight and height and figuring the index of fat in relation to these elements. A BMI for an adult is calculated differently than a BMI for a child. The code selection is based on age. The adult codes reflect BMI of patients 21 years and older. Pediatric BMI codes are for patients between 2 and 20 years of age.

Persons Encountering Health Services in Other Circumstances (Category Codes Z69–Z76)

This range of codes deals with mental health issues and counseling services. The counseling services include codes for drug, alcohol, and tobacco abuse counseling. The routine dependence of these substances is coded in other areas of ICD-10-CM, so codes from this category are not chosen for this reason.

Behavioral, sleep, and inadequate social skills are found in this code range. Due to the impact that the code assignment has on a person's ability to get life insurance, the medical record must be reviewed carefully before codes are assigned.

Persons with Potential Health Hazards Related to Family and Personal History and Certain Conditions Influencing Health Status (Category Codes Z79–Z99)

This code range has codes for the long-term use of steroids and anticoagulants. These codes are referenced when a patient is on Coumadin, steroids, or insulin. These codes are necessary, in some instances, to support medical necessity for lab testing.

Family history codes are found in this code range. Family history codes are also used to support medical necessity for certain tests that might be ordered.

> **EXAMPLE:** Jack presented to the doctor's office for a routine physical exam. His doctor was obtaining a medical history and found out that Jack's father had died at age 57 from prostate cancer. Even though Jack is only 50 years old, he is at high risk for prostate cancer, so the doctor orders a screening PSA for prostate cancer.
>
> The Z80.42, Family history of malignant neoplasm of the prostate, is assigned to the order for the lab test for the prostate screening. This supports the medical necessity for a PSA even though Jack is only 50 years old.

In addition to family history codes, personal history codes are also found in this range. The personal history codes not only include personal history of cancer but also personal history of different types of medical conditions and treatment, such as surgery. The code would code first any follow-up examination after treatment.

The codes in the Z94 category are used to report the status codes for transplanted organs. Other codes in the Z95 category represent the presence of implants and grafts.

Many notes are found in the Z code section of ICD-10-CM. The best resources to follow when locating or assigning codes from ICD-10-CM are the official coding guidelines. Numerous coding guidelines impact the selection of Z codes. The comprehensive listing of ICD-10-CM Guidelines related to Z codes is found in Appendix A of this textbook starting in section I, C, chapter 21.

Comparing ICD-9-CM and ICD-10-CM

Z codes in ICD-10-CM can be compared to the V codes in ICD-9-CM. Z codes have been expanded to provide specificity for exam codes, expansion for specific procedures, more specificity of health hazards related to socioeconomic and psychological factors, greater specificity for types of counseling, and increased specificity for the reporting of personal and family history codes.

Internet Links

For more information on cancer screenings, visit *http://www.cancer.gov/cancertopics/factsheet*, which brings you to the National Cancer Institute's Web site.

For more information on how to calculate a BMI visit, *http://www.nhlbisupport.com/bmi/*

Summary

- Screening examinations are used to screen or look for diseases.

- Diagnostic examinations are used to confirm or rule out a suspected diagnosis due to signs and symptoms that the patient has experienced.

- If the patient is being seen for treatment of a specific disease or birth defect, the code for the specific disease or birth defect is assigned instead of a code from the Z14–Z15 code range.

- Aftercare visits reflect services provided during the healing or recovery time of a disease.

- There are Z codes for fitting and adjustments for things like vascular access devices and adjustments of a cardiac pacemaker.

- The body mass index is figured by taking a person's weight and height and figuring the index of fat in relation to these elements.

Chapter Review

Fill-in-the-Blank: Enter the appropriate term(s) to complete each statement.

1. Codes that might indicate an influence on care but that are not themselves a current illness or injury are called _____.

2. To locate a code for a person suffering from a psychosocial problem, the coder references the _____ code range.

3. In determining the proper code for a routine physical exam, the coder must know whether there were or were not _____.

4. When coding for a patient who presents for an annual gynecological exam, including pap, the code assignment is_____.

5. When coding for genetic counseling, _____ is sequenced first, and a code from the _____ category is next if the purpose of the encounter is associated with procreative management.

6. A patient presenting for a vasectomy prompts the coder to reference code range _____ to find a code associated with contraceptive management.

7. Diagnostic _____ are used to confirm or rule out a suspected diagnosis due to signs and symptoms.

8. The code needed to reflect a patient who has blood type AB+ is_____.

9. A BMI, or _____, for an adult is calculated _____ than for a child.

10. Leslie suffered from breast cancer five years ago. At her annual physical she noted this as a part of her past medical history. A code from the _____ range is assigned in addition to a code for her physical exam.

Coding Assignments

Instructions: Using an ICD-10-CM code book, assign the proper diagnosis code to the following diagnostic statements. (Assume initial encounter unless otherwise specified.)

Diagnosis   *Code*

1.   status post ileostomy   _____

2.   adjustment and fitting of prosthetic leg   _____

3.   encounter for Rh typing   _____

4.   presence of an IUD   _____

5.   immunization not done because of patient's religious belief   _____

6.   status post cholecystectomy   _____

7.   cervical pap smear (not part of a gyn exam)   _____

8.   encounter of disability determination   _____

9.   dietary counseling for colitis   _____

10. presence of prosthetic heart valve   _____

11. suspected carrier of diphtheria   _____

12. removal of right breast implant   _____

13. blood type O–   _____

14. counseling for medical advice   _____

15. genetic susceptibility to malignant neoplasm of ovary   _____

16. encounter for testing of male partner of habitual aborter   _____

17. positive status for estrogen receptor   _____

18. examination for summer camp   _____

19. burn out   _____

20. counseling for tobacco abuse without nicotine dependence   _____

21. bad sleep habits   _____

22. victim of torture   _____

23. family history of arthritis   _____

24. healthy person accompanying sick person   _____

25. presence of right artificial wrist joint   _____

Case Studies

Instructions: Review each case study and select the correct ICD-10-CM diagnostic code. Assign only the appropriate Z code in the studies given.

CASE 1

This is a 28-year-old patient who presents today expressing anxiety over the fact that his father was just diagnosed with Crohn's disease. His father is 60 years old and has had GI problems for many years. The patient says that he is experiencing some of the same problems his father had prior to this diagnosis, and he would like a complete physical exam to rule out Crohn's disease. A complete physical was performed with no abnormal findings.

ICD-10-CM Code Assignment: _____

CASE 2

While traveling out of state, Joan was injured after a fall down six concrete steps. She went to the emergency room at the local hospital and received 13 sutures in her left thigh. Joan now presents to her PCP, who will remove the sutures. After exam of the area, which was without infection, redness, or oozing, the stitches were successfully removed.

ICD-10-CM Code Assignment: _____

CASE 3

Joe is an 82-year-old male who presents today for a fitting and adjustment of his hearing aid. He has had marked hearing loss in the left ear, and his doctor prescribed a hearing aid. We ordered the aid, and now Joe will try it to see if we need to make any adjustments to the way it fits.

ICD-10-CM Code Assignment: _____

CHAPTER

27

Introduction to ICD-10-PCS

Chapter Outline

Objectives
Key Terms
Introduction
Code Structure

Format
Summary
Chapter Review

Objectives

At the conclusion of this chapter, the learner should be able to:

1. Define key terms related to the implementation of ICD-10-PCS.

2. Explain what ICD-10-PCS is and what it is used for.

3. Identify the purpose of ICD-10-PCS codes.

4. Understand the format used in ICD-10-PCS.

5. Explain the different sections contained within ICD-10-PCS.

6. Understand how to build an ICD-10-PCS procedure code.

Key Terms

device
International
    Classification of
    Diseases, Tenth
    Revision, Procedure
    Coding System
    (ICD-10-PCS)

procedure
qualifier
root operation

> **Reminder**
>
> *As you work through this chapter, you will need to have a copy of the ICD-10-PCS coding book to reference.*

Introduction

ICD-10-PCS, or the **International Classification of Diseases, Tenth Revision, Procedure Coding System**, has been developed as a replacement for ICD-9-CM volume 3–Procedure codes. ICD-9-CM volume 3 has been used for facility reporting since January 1979 with the first revision taking place in 1986. It became apparent quite quickly that, with the current four-digit system and the constant evolution in the procedural forum, the code system would not be able to support these changes for long. A newer, larger, more comprehensive procedural coding system was devised by 3M Health Information Systems, and that system is ICD-10-PCS.

One of the goals set forth by the Centers for Medicare and Medicaid Services (CMS), which funded the three-year contract with 3M, was to develop a new coding system that would improve accuracy. The uniqueness of the latest procedures needed to be reflected with unique codes, and the new procedure codes needed to be able to be expanded. Because new procedures are always being developed, new codes need to be developed to reflect the evolution of newer technology.

It was determined that the ICD-10-PCS codes also needed to be consistent, and each of the individual character positions needed to retain its meaning across broad ranges of codes. Therefore a seven-character axis was developed, which is explained further in this chapter. The terminology used in ICD-10-PCS is therefore standardized. Definitions are included in ICD-10-PCS codes for this reason. Understanding these definitions is key in selecting the correct code assignment for procedures performed in a facility.

In development of ICD-10-PCS, the following general principles were followed:

- Procedure descriptions do not contain any diagnostic information. A disease or disorder is reflected in the diagnosis coding, not in the procedure coding.

- Explicit NOS (not otherwise specified) options are not provided in ICD-10-PCS.

- NEC (not elsewhere classified) has limited options in ICD-10-PCS. NEC codes may need to be referenced when a new procedure is performed that has not yet been assigned a proper ICD-10-PCS code.

- Procedures currently in use and being performed can be specified in the ICD-10-PCS code book with the use of a seven-character code.

Code Structure

Seven is the lucky number when it comes to ICD-10-PCS codes. The ICD-10-PCS codes contain seven characters, which can be letters or numbers. Each alphanumeric character has a specific meaning or value depending on its place in the lineup. Each code is made up of any one of the ten digits 0–9 and any one of 24 letters A–H, J–N, and P–Z. The letters *O* and *I* were left out so as not to be confused with the numbers *0* and *1*.

ICD-10-PCS defines the term **procedure** to mean the complete specification of the seven characters. Each procedure is divided into specific sections that identify the general type of procedure with the first character, either a number or letter, designating the section. The sections and their corresponding section identifier (number or letter) are listed here.

Section	Section Identifier
Medical and Surgical	0
Obstetrics	1
Placement	2

(continued)

Administration	3
Measurement and Monitoring	4
Extracorporeal Assistance and Performance	5
Extracorporeal Therapies	6
Osteopathic	7
Other Procedures	8
Chiropractic	9
Imaging	B
Nuclear Medicine	C
Radiation Oncology	D
Physical Rehabilitation and Diagnostic Audiology	F
Mental Health	G
Substance Abuse Treatment	H

Exercise 27.1 – ICD-10-PCS Sections

Match the identifier to the section to its corresponding section.

_____	**1.** D	**a.** Chiropractic
_____	**2.** 1	**b.** Mental Health
_____	**3.** 9	**c.** Obstetrics
_____	**4.** 7	**d.** Imaging
_____	**5.** H	**e.** Radiation Oncology
_____	**6.** 8	**f.** Measurement and Monitoring
_____	**7.** 4	**g.** Substance Abuse Treatment
_____	**8.** 0	**h.** Other Procedures
_____	**9.** G	**i.** Medical and Surgical
_____	**10.** B	**j.** Osteopathic

Format

To locate a code in ICD-10-PCS, the coder needs to understand the overall format of the book. The ICD-10-PCS is divided into three parts: Index, Tables, and List of Codes.

Index

The Index is a starting point. The Index is a guide to the Tables, which contain the specific characters needed to formulate the code. Commonly used terms or general types of procedures are found in the Index, which supplies the first three or four positions. From there the coder moves to the proper Table to identify the correct code.

Each character position in the Table has a specific meaning. Characters 1–7 are listed here along with the meaning of each position.

Character Position	Meaning
1	Section
2	Body system
3	**Root operation**—the objective of the procedure, such as bypass, drainage, fluoroscopy, MRI, etc.
4	Body part
5	Approach
6	**Device**—a device that remains in the body after completion of a procedure, such as an IUD, a skin graft, a pacemaker, or radioactive implant.
7	**Qualifier**—additional information unique to the individual procedure being performed, such as full or partial thickness, diagnostic, etc.

Given this system, it makes sense that the characters change from section to section in the book even though the actual positions of the characters are the same.

EXAMPLE: The patient is undergoing open extraction of the bursa in the right elbow. If you reference the term *extraction* in the Index, you find:

Extraction
Bursae and Ligaments
Elbow
Left 0MD4
Right 0MD3

Extraction of the bursa of the right elbow is found in Table 0MD. Once you locate this table, you can finish constructing your code selection: 0MD30ZZ. The character meanings are as follows:

- 0—Medical and surgical section
- M—The body system, the bursae and ligaments
- D—The root operation, the extraction
- 3—The body part, in this case, elbow bursa and ligament, right
- 0—The approach, in this case, the procedure was done as an open procedure
- ZZ—(the sixth and seventh spaces), no device or qualifier needed

Tables

When coding in ICD-10-PCS, tables were used to identify groups of codes and to organize them in a way that made it easy to select a code. ICD-10-PCS also uses tables to allow the coder to build their codes. The Tables are a starting point for code assignment.

The specific Tables in the sections in ICD-10-PCS (e.g., Medical and Surgical, Obstetrics, etc.) are identified by the first character just above the table.

EXAMPLE:

- 0, Medical and Surgical

- 3, Upper Arteries

- L, Occlusion: Completely closing an orifice or lumen of a tubular body part

EXAMPLE: In the preceding example, the character 0 identifies the Medical and Surgical section of ICD-10-PCS. Directly above the table is 03L. What this means is that not only is this table part of the Medical and Surgical section, but the second character identifies the upper arteries. The third character *L* identifies that we are opening an occlusion. The lower portion of the table offers the options for the remaining characters in positions four through seven.

There are numerous possibilities for how the code combinations can be built.

In some instances, the coder will notice a split in the rows. In this case, the coder is able to build a code with only the characters in the same row.

EXAMPLE:

- 0, Medical and Surgical

- 2, Heart and Great Vessels

- L, Occlusion

Body Part Character 4	Approach Character 5	Device Character 6	Qualifier Character 7
R Pulmonary artery, left	0 Open 3 Percutaneous 4 Percutaneous endoscopic	C Extraluminal device D Intraluminal device Z No device	T Ductus arteriosus
S Pulmonary vein, right T Pulmonary vein, left V Superior vena cava	0 Open 3 Percutaneous 4 Percutaneous endoscopic	C Extraluminal device D Intraluminal device Z No device	Z No qualifier

As illustrated in the example, characters in the seventh position can be matched up only with characters found in the same row. So R in the fourth position can be reported only with T for character seven. For S and T (fourth position), the only seventh character position to be reported is Z.

Summary

- The goals of ICD-10-PCS are to offer a complete way to report the service rendered, to be able to expand on the codes to accommodate new procedures, to be multiaxial, and to standardize terminology.

- Diagnostic information is not included in the description of the procedures.

- Not otherwise specified and not elsewhere classified codes are used as little as possible.

- ICD-10-PCS codes contain seven alphanumeric characters. The letters *O* and *I* have been excluded so as not to cause confusion with the numbers *0* and *1*.

- There are sections instead of chapters, and each section is identified with either a letter or a number.

- The sections lead to Tables. Codes are built from the information in the Tables.

Chapter Review

Multiple Choice

Select the best answer that completes the statement or answers the question.

1. ICD-9-CM volume 3 was replaced with ICD-10-PCS because ICD-9-CM volume 3:
   a. is newer but harder to use.
   b. contains too many codes.
   c. was an antiquated, four-digit system that needed to be updated.
   d. contained diagnoses as well as procedures that were too confusing.

2. It was _____ who actually funded the new ICD-10-PCS program.
   a. 3M
   b. CMS
   c. WHO
   d. AMA

3. One of the goals of the new coding system is to:
   a. introduce new terminology.
   b. improve accuracy.
   c. confuse coders with more change.
   d. standardize a new six-digit code set.

4. The section identifier for Radiation Oncology is:
   a. B.
   b. C.
   c. D.
   d. F.

5. The body part or system on which a procedure is performed is reported in which character position in the code?
   a. 1
   b. 2
   c. 3
   d. 4

Fill-in-the-Blank: Enter the appropriate term(s) to complete each statement.

6. The _____ is unique to the individual procedure being performed.

7. ICD-10-PCS defines _____ to mean the complete specification of the seven characters.

8. The letters _____ and _____ were left out of ICD-10-PCS so that they would not be confused with _____ and _____.

9. The _____ is also known as the objective of the procedure.

10. The description of procedures does not include _____ information.

In the following codes given, identify the underlined character as either the Section (S), Body System (BS), Root Operations (RO), Body Part (BP), Approach (A), Device (D), or Qualifier (Q). Then identify the procedure. The first two are done for you.

Code	Character Identification	Code Description
11. 01N33ZZ	RO	Percutaneous release of brachial plexus
12. 07WM00Z	BP	Open revision of drainage device of thymus

13. 05<u>L</u>Y0ZZ   _____   _____

14. <u>0</u>CTN0ZZ   _____   _____

15. 09Q<u>F</u>0ZZ   _____   _____

16. BL4<u>2</u>ZZZ   _____   _____

17. 0RPWX<u>0</u>Z   _____   _____

18. 0WJ8<u>X</u>ZZ   _____   _____

19. 0W<u>W</u>833Z   _____   _____

20. 0<u>U</u>WM00Z   _____   _____

Medical and Surgical Section

Chapter Outline

Objectives

Key Terms

Introduction

Selecting a Code

Principles for the Medical and
  Surgical Section

Internet Links

Summary

Chapter Review

Coding Assignments

Case Studies

Objectives

At the conclusion of this chapter, the learner should be able to:

1. Define key terms found in this chapter.
2. Understand how to locate a code in the Medical and Surgical Section of ICD-10-PCS.
3. Explain the code arrangement of the Medical and Surgical Section of ICD-10-PCS.
4. Describe how the code selection is made and how to build a code from the information given.

Key Terms

access location	destruction	extirpation	map
alteration	detachment	extraction	method
approach	dilation	fragmentation	occlusion
bypass	division	fusion	open
change	drainage	insertion	percutaneous
control	excision	inspection	percutaneous
creation	external	instrumentation	endoscopic

Reminder

As you work through this chapter, you will need to have a copy of the ICD-10-PCS coding book to reference.

qualifier	replacement	supplement	via natural or artificial opening endoscopic
reattachment	reposition	transfer	via natural or artificial opening with percutaneous endoscopic assistance
release	resection	transplantation	
removal	restriction	tubular body parts	
repair	revision	via natural or artificial opening	

Introduction

The medical and surgical codes constitute the bulk of codes reported in an inpatient setting. Each surgical procedure is associated with a definition, allowing for uniform code assignment. There is no doubt among coders as to what a particular term means.

EXAMPLE:

- 0, Medical and Surgical

- 0, Central Nervous System

- T, Resection—Cutting out or off, without replacement, all of a body part.

In the Tables of ICD-10-PCS, the definition for *replacement* is given right next to the term so that the procedure can be verified before a code is assigned. If there is any question regarding the definition, consult the physician or provider performing the procedure for clarification or an explanation of the procedure to assure proper code assignment.

Selecting a Code

Section

The first character for the codes reported from the Medical and Surgical section is 0. All tables from which codes are reported that begin with the number 0 identify the code as being pulled from the Medical and Surgical section of ICD-10-PCS.

EXAMPLE:

- **089**, Drainage of the eye

- **08B**, Excision of the eye

As previously explained, the second character indicates the body system. The third character references the root operation, and the fourth character indicates the specific body part on which the procedure is performed. The fifth character identifies the approach used to perform the procedure. The sixth character represents any device that was used and remains at the end of the procedure. The seventh character is a qualifier that may have meaning specific to the limited range of the procedure being reported. Not all procedures require a device or qualifier, so the value of Z is used to represent no qualifier.

Body Systems

The second character represents body system. The Medical and Surgical section of ICD-10-PCS contains 31 possible characters for the second position. The possible character assignments for the second position are as follows:

Character	Body System
0	Central nervous system
1	Peripheral nervous system
2	Heart and great vessels
3	Upper arteries
4	Lower arteries
5	Upper veins
6	Lower veins
7	Lymphatic and hemic system
8	Eye
9	Ear, nose, sinus
B	Respiratory system
C	Mouth and throat
D	Gastrointestinal system
F	Hepatobiliary system and pancreas
G	Endocrine system
H	Skin and breast
J	Subcutaneous tissue and fascia
K	Muscles
L	Tendons
M	Bursae and ligaments
N	Head and facial bones
P	Upper bones
Q	Lower bones
R	Upper joints
S	Lower joints
T	Urinary system
U	Female reproductive system
V	Male reproductive system
W	Anatomical regions, general
X	Anatomical regions, upper extremities
Y	Anatomical regions, lower extremities

With so many characters available, coders can formulate more detailed codes than ever. Seven character positions allow for countless possibilities and leaves room for additional descriptors to be added as new techniques evolve.

Root Operations

Root Operations reflect the objective of the procedure and are specified in the third character position. As previously stated, each root operation has an exact definition located next to the term in the Table section of ICD-10-PCS.

The root operation selections are as follows:

- **Alteration**—Modifying the anatomical structure of a body part without affecting the function of the body part. The purpose of this type of procedure is to change and improve appearance such as a face-lift. (value of 0)

- **Bypass**—Altering the route of passage of the contents of a tubular body part. During these procedures, the rerouting of the contents of a body part occurs such as when a colostomy formation or cystostomy is completed or when coronary bypass surgery is performed. Figure 28-1 illustrates a cystostomy. (value of 1)

- **Change**—Taking out or taking off a device from a body part and putting back an identical or similar device in or on the same body part without cutting or puncturing the skin or a mucous membrane. An example is a urinary catheter change. (value of 2)

- **Control**—Stopping or attempting to stop postprocedural bleeding. An example is the completion of a procedure to control a posthysterectomy hemorrhage. (value of 3)

- **Creation**—Making a new genital structure that does not take over the function of a body part. These procedures are used only for sex change operations. (value of 4)

- **Destruction**—Physical eradication of all or a portion of a body part by the direct use of energy, force, or a destructive agent. An example is cautery of a benign skin lesion. (value of 5)

- **Detachment**—Cutting off all or a portion of an upper or lower extremity. An example is a left leg below the knee amputation. (value of 6)

- **Dilation**—Expanding an orifice or the lumen of a tubular body part. A dilation of the esophagus using an intraluminal device is an example. (value of 7)

- **Division**—Cutting into a body part, without draining fluids and/or gases from the body part, to separate or transect a body part. All or a portion of the body part is separated into two or more portions, such as when an osteotomy is performed. (value of 8)

- **Drainage**—Taking or letting out fluids and/or gases from a body part. An incision and drainage of an abscess is an example. (value of 9)

- **Excision**—Cutting out or off, without replacement, a portion of a body part. A partial nephrectomy is an example. (value of B)

- **Extirpation**—Taking or cutting out solid matter from a body part. During these procedures, the solid matter that is taken may be an abnormal by-product of a biological function or a foreign body. The material can be imbedded in a body part or in the lumen of a tubular body part. The matter may or may not have been previously broken into pieces. An example is a thrombectomy. (value of C)

- **Extraction**—Pulling or stripping out or off all or a portion of a body part by the use of force. Vein stripping is an example. (value of D)

- **Fragmentation**—Breaking solid matter in a body part into pieces. During these procedures physical force, such as a manual force or ultrasound, is applied directly or indirectly to break up solid matter into pieces. The solid matter may be an abnormal byproduct of a biological function or a foreign body. The pieces that are fragmented are not taken out. An example is extracorporeal shockwave lithotripsy. (value of F)

- **Fusion**—Joining together portions of an articular body part rendering the articular body part immobile. A fixation device, bone graft, or other means is used to join the body part, such as in a spinal fusion. (value of G)

- **Insertion**—Putting in a nonbiological appliance that monitors, assists, performs, or prevents a physiological function but does not physically take the place of a body part. An example is an insertion of a central venous catheter. (value of H)

- **Inspection**—Visually and/or manually exploring a body part The visual inspection can occur with or without optical instrumentation. A bronchoscopy is a type of inspection. Figure 28-2 illustrates a bronchoscopy. (value of J)

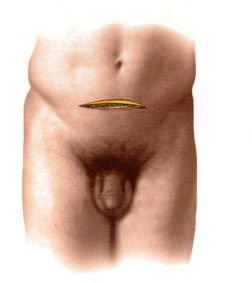
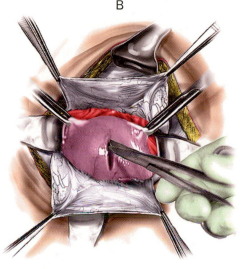
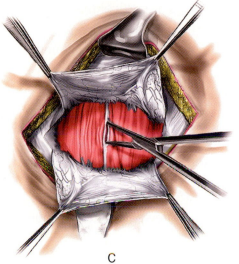
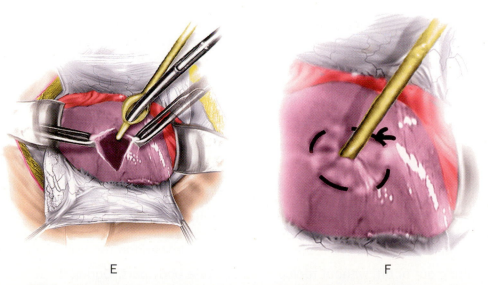

Figure 28-1 Open cystostomy: (A) incision site; (B) fascia incised; (C) muscle split; (D) bladder incised; (E) cystostomy tube inserted; (F) cystostomy tube secured with pursestring suture (From Price P, Frey KB, Jung TL. *Surgical Technology fro the Surgical Technologist: A Positive Care Approach*, 2nd ed. Clifton Park, NY: Delmar, Cengage Learning, 2004, p. 766.)

Figure 28-2 Rigid bronchoscopy (From Price P, Frey KB, Jung TL. *Surgical Technology fro the Surgical Technologist: A Positive Care Approach*, 2nd ed. Clifton Park, NY: Delmar, Cengage Learning, 2004, p. 887.)

- **Map**—Locating the route of passage of electrical impulses and/or locating functional areas in a body part. This root operation is applicable only to the cardiac conduction mechanism and the central nervous system. Examples include cardiac mapping and cortical mapping. (value of K)

- **Occlusion**—Completely closing an orifice or lumen of a tubular body part. The orifice can be a natural orifice or an artificially created one. An example is a fallopian tube ligation. (value of L)

- **Reattachment**—Putting back in or on all or a portion of a separated body part to its normal location or other suitable locations. During these procedures, vascular circulation and nervous pathways may or may not be reestablished. A reattachment of a left great toe or a reattachment of the tongue are examples. (value of M)

- **Release**—Freeing of a body part from an abnormal physical constraint. During these procedures, some of the restraining tissue may be taken out, but none of the body part is taken out. Examples are lysis of adhesions and release of anal sphincter. (value of N)

- **Removal**—Taking out or off a device from a body part. This root operation reports only procedures for taking out a device. If a device is taken out and a similar device is put in without cutting or puncturing the skin or mucous membrane, the procedure is coded to the root operation of change. Examples of removal procedures include cardiac pacemaker removal and removal of esophageal airway device. (value of P)

- **Repair**—Restoring, to the extent possible, a body part to its normal anatomic structure and function. This root operation is used only when the method to accomplish the repair is not part of the other root operations. Examples of repair operations are the suturing of a laceration of the right upper arm or an aortic valve repair. (value of Q)

- **Replacement**—Putting in or on biological or synthetic material that physically takes the place and/or function of all or a portion of a body part The body part may have been taken out or replaced, or it may be taken out, physically eradicated, or rendered nonfunctional during the Replacement procedure. Examples include a total knee replacement, mitral valve replacement, or a free skin graft. Figure 28-3 illustrates a mitral valve replacement. (value of R)

- **Reposition**—Moving to its normal location, or other suitable location, all or a portion of a body part. During these procedures, the body part is moved to a new location from an abnormal location or from a normal location where it is not functioning correctly. During the procedure, the body part may or may not be cut out or off to be repositioned to the new location. Examples are a reduction of a fracture of the left tibia and the repositioning of an undescended testicle. (value of S)

- **Resection**—Cutting out or off, without replacement, all of a body part. During these procedures the entire body part is removed, such as a complete cholecystectomy, a complete appendectomy, or a total transurethral resection of the prostate. Figure 28-4 illustrates a transurethral resection of the prostate. (value of T)

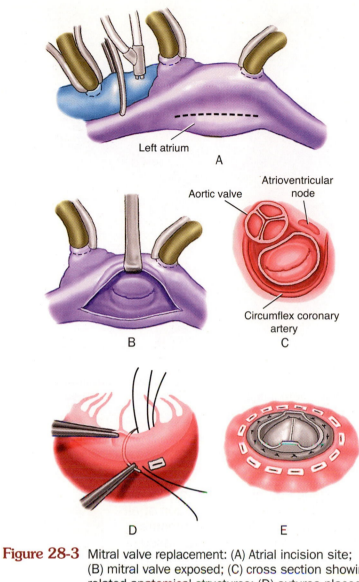

Figure 28-3 Mitral valve replacement: (A) Atrial incision site; (B) mitral valve exposed; (C) cross section showing related anatomical structures; (D) sutures placed in the annulus; (E) prosthesis in place (From Price P, Frey KB, Jung TL. *Surgical Technology fro the Surgical Technologist: A Positive Care Approach*, 2nd ed. Clifton Park, NY: Delmar, Cengage Learning, 2004, p. 917.)

- **Restriction**—Partially closing an orifice or lumen of a tubular body part. The orifice can be a natural orifice or an artificially created one. An example is a restriction of the thoracic duct with a intraluminal stent or a trans-vaginal intraluminal cervical cerclage. (value of V)

- **Revision**—Correcting to the extent possible, a portion of a malfunctioning device or the position of a displaced device. The revision can include the correcting of a malfunctioning or displaced device by taking out and/or putting in part of the device. Adjustment of a pacemaker lead or the external repositioning of a Foley catheter to the bladder are examples. (value of W)

- **Supplement**—Putting in or on biological or synthetic material that physically reinforces and/or augments the function of a portion of a body part. The biological material is nonliving or living and from the same individual. The Supplement procedure is performed to physically reinforce and/or

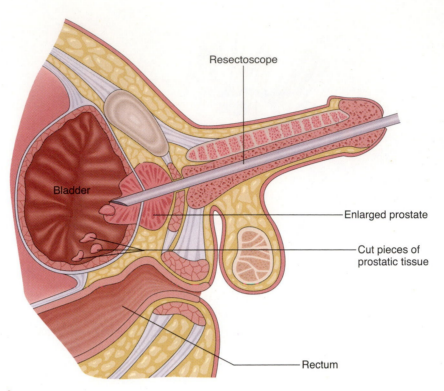

Figure 28-4 Transurethral resection of the prostate (From Ehrlich A, Schroeder CL. *Medical Terminology for Health Professions,* 4th ed. Clifton Park, NY: Delmar, Cengage Learning, 2001, p. 299.)

augment the function of the replaced body part. The body part may have been previously replaced. A herniorrhaphy using mesh and a free nerve graft is an example. (value of U)

- **Transfer**—Moving, without taking out, all or a portion of a body part to another location to take over the function of all or a portion of a body part. During the Transfer procedure, the body part transferred remains connected to its vascular and nervous supply, such as in a tendon transfer or skin pedicle flap transfer. (value of X)

- **Transplantation**—Putting in or on all or a portion of a living body part taken from another individual or animal to physically take the place and/or function of all or a portion of a similar body part. And example is a heart-lung transplant or a kidney transplant. (value of Y)

> **Note:**
>
> *The root operation is used to define the objective of the procedure. The terms are sharply defined, allowing for very precise coding assignments. Appendices A and B in the ICD-10-PCS book provide more explanation and examples of the medical and surgical root operations.*

Exercise 28.1 – Root Operations

Match the root operation with the corresponding value.

_____	**1.** transplantation	**a.** L
_____	**2.** occlusion	**b.** 7
_____	**3.** detachment	**c.** D

_____ **4.** restriction   **d.** J

_____ **5.** dilation   **e.** 3

_____ **6.** extraction   **f.** Y

_____ **7.** map   **g.** 6

_____ **8.** control   **h.** N

_____ **9.** release   **i.** K

_____ **10.** inspection   **j.** V

Body Part

The fourth character for the Medical and Surgical codes represents the body part, the specific part of the body system on which the procedure is performed (e.g., pancreas, colic artery, auditory ossicle). The fourth-character assignments in this section get as detailed as auditory ossicle, right or auditory ossicle, left. The coder will notice in some Tables the term _tubular body parts_. **Tubular body parts** are defined in ICD-10-PCS as hollow body parts that provide a route of passage for solids, liquids, or gases. Vessels for blood flow, the intestines for the flow of waste, and the respiratory tract for the flow of oxygen are examples. (See Figure 28-5 for an illustration of the tubular structures of the lungs.).

Approach

The fifth character place for Medical and Surgical codes are for the identification of the approach used in the procedure. An **approach** is the way in which the surgeon, physician, or provider performs a procedure. The following approaches are used in ICD-10-PCS for the Medical and Surgical Section:

- **External**—Procedures performed directly on the skin or mucous membrane and procedures performed indirectly by the application of external force through the skin or mucous membrane (value of X)

- **Open**—Cutting through the skin or mucous membrane and any other body layers necessary to expose the site of the procedure (value is 0)

- **Percutaneous**—Entry, by puncture or minor incision, of instrumentation through the skin or mucous membrane and any other body layers necessary to reach the site of the procedure (value is 3)

- **Percutaneous endoscopic**—Entry, by puncture or minor incision of instrumentation through the skin or mucous membrane and any other body layers necessary to reach and _visualize_ the site of the procedure (value is 4)

- **Via natural or artificial opening**—Entry of instrumentation through a natural or artificial external opening to reach the site of the procedure (value is 7)

- **Via natural or artificial opening endoscopic**—Entry of instrumentation through a natural or artificial external opening to reach and _visualize_ the site of the procedure (value is 8)

- **Via natural or artificial opening with percutaneous endoscopic assistance**—Insertion of instrumentation through a natural or artificial external opening and entry, by puncture or minor incision, of instrumentation through the skin or mucous membrane and any other body layers necessary to aid in the performance of the procedure (value of F)

Three components make up the approach: the access location, the method, and the type of instrumentation used.

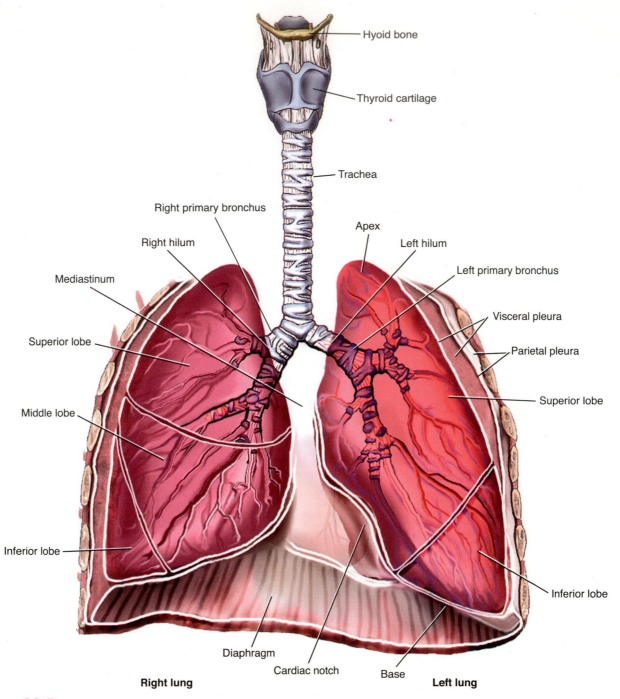

Right lung   Left lung

Figure 28-5 Anterior view of lungs (From Lazo DL. *Fundamentals of Sectional Anatomy: An Imaging Approach*. Clifton Park, NY: Delmar, Cengage Learning, 2005, p. 125.)

Access Location

There are typically two types of general **access locations**: (1) skin or mucous membranes, which can be punctured or cut to reach the site, and (2) external orifices such as the mouth, nares of the nose, or a stoma. For procedures performed on any internal body part, the access location specifies the external site used to access the site of the procedure. Open and percutaneous approach values use the skin or mucous membranes as the access location.

Method

The **method** specifies how the external access location was entered when a procedure is performed on an internal body part. The open method identifies some type of cutting through the skin or mucous membrane and any other body layer necessary to reach the site of the procedure. A puncture does not constitute an open approach because it does not expose the site of the procedure.

Multiple methods can be defined in the approach. For example, the open endoscopic approach includes both the open method to expose the body part and the introduction of instrumentation into the body part to perform the procedure.

Type of Instrumentation

Instrumentation is the specialized equipment used to perform a procedure on an internal body part. Other than the basic open approach, instrumentation is used in all internal approaches and may or may not include the capacity to visualize the procedure site. A needle biopsy of the liver or breast does not allow for visualization with the instrumentation used in these procedures; however, a colonoscopy allows for visualization.

Some method descriptions contain the term *endoscopic*. This term is used when the approach values refer to the instrumentation that allows a site to be visualized through a scope.

The procedures performed directly on the skin or mucous membrane are identified by the external approach (e.g., skin excision). Procedures performed indirectly by the application of external force are also identified by the external approach (e.g., closed reduction of a fracture).

Exercise 28.2 – Approach

Using an ICD-10-PCS code book, identify the approach used and the procedure performed for each of the following examples. The first one is done for you.

Code	Approach	Description
1. 0SS00ZZ	Open	Open reposition of lumbar vertebral joint
2. 07JK0ZZ	_____	_____
3. 0UJ33ZZ	_____	_____
4. 00K83ZZ	_____	_____
5. 0UVC7DZ	_____	_____

Device

The sixth character position indicates the device. This character is used only to specify devices that remain after a procedure is completed. There are four general types of devices:

- Biological or synthetic material that takes the place of all or a portion of the body part. This category includes joint prosthesis or skin grafts.

- Biological or synthetic material that assists or prevents a physiological function. An example of this is an IUD or a stent.

- Therapeutic material that is not absorbed by, eliminated by, or incorporated into a body part. This category includes radioactive implants.

- Mechanical or electronic appliances used to assist, monitor, take the place of, or prevent a physiological function, such as a cardiac pacemaker or an orthopedic pin.

All devices can be removed; however, some devices cannot be removed unless another device replaces it. The specific device values can be coded according to the following root operations: alteration, bypass, creation, dilation, drainage, fusion, occlusion, reposition, and restriction. Scopes or other instruments used in visualization are not specified in the device value because they are specified in the approach.

Keep in mind the objective of the procedure. If the objective of a procedure is to insert something, then the root operation is insertion. If the objective of the procedure is to remove something and to insert a drainage device or other appliance, then the Table is referenced for such a device and the appropriate character assignment is made.

Qualifier

The last character in a Medicine and Surgical code is the qualifier. The **qualifier** is the information that identifies a unique value being reported for the individual procedure. If a qualifier is not needed in a code, the Table indicates that a *Z* is to be added as a placeholder to make the seven-character code.

Principles for the Medical and Surgical Section

The Medical and Surgical Section was developed around four basic principles.

- *Composite terms are not root operations*—The objective of the procedure is the only component of the procedure specified in the root operation. Terms such as *tonsillectomy* and *laryngoscopy* are not root operations because they are specifying many components of a procedure.

  - Laryngoscopy is the *inspection* of the *larynx* using a scope to visualize through a natural or artificial opening endoscopic. The root operation is the inspection, identified by character 3 in the code. Character 4 of the same code would identify the body part, the larynx, and the approach is identified by character 5.

  - Tonsillectomy is the *excision* of the *tonsils*. The root operation is identified as the excision of a body part, the tonsils.

If these terms are referenced in the Index, the coder is then sent to the Tables with the first three characters of the code leading the coder to select the correct root operation and body system from within the Tables.

- *Root operations are based on the objective of the procedure*—As explained, the root operation is based on the objective of the procedure. The root operation is selected based on the procedure that the physician or provider actually performed. The intent of the service might or might not be the procedure performed, but for any number of reasons needs to be modified.

  - For example, the intended procedure might have been a femoral artery bypass. Once the bypass is performed, the blood flow is not producing the desired results; so an arterectomy is performed instead. The arterectomy is now reported because it is the procedure actually performed.

- *Combination procedures are coded separately*—In some cases multiple procedures are defined by distinct objectives. These multiple procedures may be performed during one operative session. If this is the case, multiple codes are used.

  - Endoscopy of bilateral stripping of maxillary sinus, codes 09DQ4ZZ and 09DR4ZZ. Because the procedure was performed bilaterally and the fourth character indicates the body part, we need to use *Q* for the right maxillary sinus and *R* for the left maxillary sinus to reflect the bilateral procedure.

- *The redo of procedures is necessary*—Procedures that need to be performed again, whether partially or completely, are coded to the root operation performed, *not* to the root operation *revision*. Revision is referenced if the procedure was being done to correct a malfunctioning or displaced device.

  - A patient may need to have a total knee replacement for the second time. The new prosthetic knee replacement is coded to the root operation replacement.

  - A patient might have trouble with the timing of a cardiac pacemaker. The doctor needs to go in and reset the pacemaker. In this case, revision is the correct place to reference because the cardiac pacemaker is malfunctioning.

Internet Links

To learn more about surgery and surgical coding of the musculoskeletal system, visit *http://www.omni.ac.uk* or *http://www.fpnotebook.com*

To learn more about surgical coding, visit *http://www.aafp.org* or *http://www.healthsquare.com*

To learn more about surgical coding relating to ICD-10-PCS, visit *http://www.cms.hhs.gov/ICD10* or *http://www.library.ahima.org/xpedio/groups/public/documents/ahima/bok3_004938.hcsp*

Summary

- The Medical and Surgical Section of ICD-10-PCS contains the majority of the codes used in procedure reporting.
- The ICD-10-PCS codes are made up of seven characters.
- The 0 is used to identify the Medical and Surgical Section of ICD-10-PCS.
- The third character position in the codes for Medical and Surgical indicates the root operation, such as detachment, division, excision, removal, and replacement.
- The different types of approaches are specified by the fifth character in the Medical and Surgical Section code.
- In developing the Medical and Surgical Section of ICD-10-PCS, four specific principles were followed.

Chapter Review

True/False: Indicate whether each statement is true (T) or false (F).

1. _____ The third character in a medical and surgical code specifies the objective of the procedure.

2. _____ Completely closing an orifice or lumen of a tubular body part is extirpation.

3. _____ Making a new structure that does not physically take the place of a body part is fragmentation.

4. _____ The root operation of Control is the stopping or attempting to stop postprocedural bleeding.

5. _____ A percutaneous procedure is a puncture or small incision of instrumentation through the skin to reach the site of the procedure.

Coding Assignments

Instructions: Using an ICD-10-PCS code book, assign the proper procedure code to the following procedural statements.

Procedure	Code
1. exploratory arthrotomy of left knee (open)	_____
2. incision with removal of K-wire fixation, right first metatarsal	_____
3. open bilateral breast augmentation with silicone implants	_____
4. intraoperative cardiac mapping during open heart surgery	_____
5. DIP, low joint amputation of right thumb	_____
6. excision of basal cell carcinoma of lower lip	_____
7. open resection of papillary muscle	_____
8. percutaneous division of right foot tendon	_____
9. percutaneous destruction of right retina	_____
10. percutaneous biopsy of right gastrocnemius muscle	_____
11. closure of open wound of neck	_____
12. incision and removal of right lacrimal duct stone	_____
13. open adrenalorrhaphy of left adrenal gland	_____
14. release of scar contracture, skin of right ear	_____
15. reattachment of severed right ear	_____
16. percutaneous ligation of right renal vein	_____
17. open resection of ventricular septum	_____
18. open division of anal sphincter	_____
19. open dilation of old anastomosis, splenic artery	_____
20. digital rectal exam	_____

Case Studies

Instructions: Review each case study and select the correct ICD-10-PCS code.

CASE 1

Patient is a 10-year-old male who presents today with right wrist pain. Patient was riding his skateboard when he hit a crack in the sidewalk and fell forward. His arms were outstretched when he hit the concrete. He denies loss of consciousness, which was confirmed by witnesses. He has not had any vomiting, abdominal pain, or dizziness.

X-ray of the right arm and wrist reveals a dislocation of the right wrist. A closed reduction of the distal radioulnar joint was performed. Follow-up x-ray revealed that the bones are now in place. The child was fitted for a splint and shoulder immobilizer, which are to be worn for the next 10 days. We will see him back at the end of the 10 days to reevaluate the injury.

ICD-10-PCS Code Assignment: _____

CASE 2

This is a healthy 21-year-old female who presents today for removal of an impacted molar, lower left side. The panoramic radiograph shows the tooth to be in a good position now, but due to the pain it is causing the patient and the slight movement of the existing teeth, surgical intervention is needed to get the tooth out before any further movement can occur.

PROCEDURE: The patient was given Versed and conscious sedation was achieved. The lower jaw area was also injected with 2% Lidocaine. The gingiva was removed from the surface with an elevator. A #15 blade was used to incise the gum line. The soft tissue was dissected to expose the impacted tooth and could be removed in whole. The area was then rinsed and all debris removed before two sutures were placed with 4-0 silk. The patient was in good condition when returned to the recovery suite.

ICD-10-PCS Code Assignment: _____

CASE 3

This 30-year-old patient was placed in supine position and the left ear was examined using an operating microscope with a complaint of ear pain. The tympanic membrane was assessed after all debris was removed from the area. There was also noted to be a small, dark colored foreign object, almost resembling a bead. The object was removed and antibiotic solution was placed in the ear canal. The patient was awoken and transferred to the recovery room in excellent condition.

ICD-10-PCS Code Assignment: _____

CHAPTER

29 Obstetrics Section

Chapter Outline

Objectives
Key Terms
Introduction
Obstetrics Section of the ICD-10-PCS
Procedure Highlights

Internet Links
Summary
Chapter Review
Coding Assignments
Case Studies

Objectives

At the conclusion of this chapter, the learner should be able to:

1. Identify the character meanings used for the ICD-10-PCS Obstetrics Section.
2. Discuss the root operations used for the ICD-10-PCS Obstetrics Section.
3. List the body-part values in the ICD-10-PCS Obstetrics Section.
4. Identify the approach, device, and qualifiers used the ICD-10-PCS Obstetrics Section.
5. Code procedures in the ICD-10-PCS Obstetrics Section.

Key Terms

abortion	drainage	inspection	repair
amniocentesis	extraction	obstetrics	reposition
change	forceps delivery	products of conception	resection
delivery	insertion	removal	transplantation

> **Reminder**
>
> *As you work through this chapter, you will need to have a copy of the ICD-10-PCS coding book to reference.*

Introduction

The second section found in ICD-10-PCS is "Obstetrics." **Obstetrics** is the specialty that deals with women during pregnancy, childbirth, and the period immediately after childbirth. This section of ICD-10-PCS is used to build codes for procedures performed on the products of conception, not only the pregnancy. The term **products of conception** is defined as all the physical components of a pregnancy and includes the fetus, amnion, umbilical cord, and the placenta. The codes do not differentiate the gestational age of the products of conception, which is defined in the selection of an ICD-10-CM diagnostic code.

Obstetrics Section of the ICD-10-PCS

The seven characters in this section have the same meaning as they do in the Medical and Surgical Section.

1	2	3	4	5	6	7
Section	Body system	Root operation	Body part	Approach	Device	Qualifier

Section

The first character value indicating obstetric procedure codes is 1. Any codes that relate to obstetrics can be identified with the use of this character value.

Body System

The second character value in this chapter indicating the body system is always going to be 0, Pregnancy.

Root Operation

One of the 12 root operations for the Obstetrics Section of ICD-10-PCS is selected to fill the third-character position. The root operations include the following:

- **Abortion**—Artificially terminating a pregnancy (value of A)
- **Change**—Taking out or off a device from a body part and putting back an identical or similar device in or on the same body part without cutting or puncturing the skin or mucous membrane (value of 2)
- **Delivery**—Assisting the passage of the products of conception from the genital canal (value of E)
- **Drainage**—Taking or letting out fluids and/or gases from a body part (value of 9)
- **Extraction**—Pulling or stripping out or off all or a portion of a body part (value of D)
- **Insertion**—Putting in a nonbiological appliance that monitors, assists, performs, or prevents a physiological function but does not physically take the place of a body part (value of H)
- **Inspection**—Visually and/or manually exploring a body part (value of J)
- **Removal**—Taking out or off a device from a body part, region, or orifice (value of P)
- **Repair**—Restoring, to the extent possible, a body part to its normal anatomic structure and function (value of Q)

- **Reposition**—Moving to its normal location or other suitable location all or a portion of a body part (value of S)

- **Resection**—Cutting out or off, without replacement, all of a body part (value of T)

- **Transplantation**—Putting in or on all or a portion of a living body part taken from another individual or animal to physically take the place and/or function of all or a portion of a similar body part (value of Y)

   EXAMPLE: If a coder were selecting a code for a delivery, the first three characters would be 10E. If a coder were selecting a code for the drainage of amniotic fluid, the first three characters would be 109.

Body Part

The fourth character values in the Obstetrics Section are:

- Products of conception (value of 0)

- Products of conception, retained (value of 1)

- Products of conception, ectopic (value of 2)

Approach

There are seven approach values for the fifth character for the Obstetrics Section.

- Open (value of 0)

- Open endoscopic (value of 2)

- Percutaneous (value of 3)

- Percutaneous endoscopic (value of 4)

- Via natural or artificial opening (value of 7)

- Via natural or artificial opening endoscopic (value of 8)

- External (value of X)

These approach definitions are the same as in the Medical and Surgical Section.

Device

The sixth character represents the device. The device values for Obstetrics are:

- Monitoring electrode (value of 3)

- Other device (value of Y)

- No device (value of Z)

Qualifier

The seventh character represents the qualifier. There are numerous qualifier values for Obstetrics, as shown in Figure 29-1, which summarizes the values for the fifth, sixth, and seventh characters. The qualifiers are used to identify the specific type of an operation, such as a low forceps (value of 3), or the type of fluid removed during a drainage vacuum, such as fetal blood (value of 9).

1: OBSTETRICS

0: PREGNANCY

Approach Chapter 5	Device Character 6	Qualifier Character 7

0 Open
   Open Endoscopic
3 Percutaneous
4 Percutaneous Endoscopic
7 Via Natural of Artificial
   Opening
8 Via Natural or Artificial
   Opening Endoscopic
X External
	3 Monitoring Electrode
	Y Other Device
	Z No Device
		0 Classical
		1 Low Cervical
		2 Extraperitoneal
		3 Low Forceps
		4 Mid Forceps
		5 High Forceps
		6 Vacuum
		7 Internal Version
		8 Other
		9 Fetal Blood
		A Fetal Cerebrospinal Fluid
		B Fetal Fluid, Other
		C Amniotic Fluid, Therapeutic
		D Fluid, Other
		E Nervous System
		F Cardiovascular System
		G Lymphatics and Hermic
		H Eye
		J Ear, Nose, and Sinus
		K Respiratory System
		L Mouth and Throat
		M Gastrointestinal System
		N Hepatobiliary and Pancreas
		P Endocrine System
		Q Skin
		R Musculoskeletal System
		S Urinary System
		T Female Reproductive System
		U Amniotic Fluid, Diagnostic
		V Male Reproductive System
		W Laminaria
		X Abortifacient
		Y Other Body System
		Z No Qualifier

Figure 29-1 Qualifier values for the Obstetrics Section

Not all of the seventh-character values are used for each root operation. Coders must reference the Obstetric tables to determine the seventh-character values that are applicable to each root operation. Figure 29-2 shows the tables for the following root operations: change, drainage, and abortion. Note that each operation has its own set of qualifiers. The root operation of change, for instance, has only the qualifier of Z, whereas the root operation of drainage has a number of qualifier values: 9, A, B, C, D, and U.

1: OBSTETRICS
0: PREGNANCY
2: CHANGE: Taking out or off a device from a body part and putting back an identical or similar device in or on the same body part without cutting or puncturing the skin or a mucous membrane

Body Part Character 4	Approach Character 5	Device Character 6	Qualifier Character 7
0 Products of Conception	7 Via Natural or Artificial Opening	3 Monitoring Electrode Y Other Device	Z No Qualifier

1: OBSTETRICS
0: PREGNANCY
9: DRAINAGE: Taking or letting out fluids and/or gases from a body part

Body Part Character 4	Approach Character 5	Device Character 6	Qualifier Character 7
0 Products of Conception	0 Open 3 Percutaneous 4 Percutaneous Endoscopic 7 Via Natural or Artificial Opening 8 Via Natural or Artificial Opening Endoscopic	Z No Device	9 Fetal Blood A Fetal Cerebrospinal Fluid B Fetal Fluid, Other C Amriotic Fluid, Therapeutic D Fluid, Other U Amnlotic Fluid, Diagnostic

1: OBSTETRICS
0: PREGNANCY
A: ABORTION: Artificially terminating a pregnancy

Body Part Character 4	Approach Character 5	Device Character 6	Qualifier Character 7
0 Product of Conception	0 Open 2 Open Endoscopic 3 Percutaneous 4 Percutaneous Endoscopic 8 Via Natural or Artificial Opening Endoscopic	Z No Device	Z No Qualifier
0 Products of Conception	7 Via Natural or Artificial Opening	Z No Device	6 Vacuum W Laminaria X Abortifacient Z No Qualifier

Figure 29-2 Tables for change, drainage, and abortion

Exercise 29.1 – Identifying Qualifiers

Using an ICD-10-PCS book, for each of the root operations listed, identify the qualifiers that are applicable to the root operation in the Obstetrics Section. The first one is completed for you.

Root Operation	Qualifiers
1. change	Z
2. abortion	_____
3. insertion	_____
4. repair	_____
5. transplantation	_____

Procedure Highlights

The following are some of the common procedures coded to this section of the code book.

Amniocentesis

Amniocentesis is a procedure in which a needle is inserted into the amniotic sac to withdraw fluid for examination. Figure 29-3 illustrates an amniocentesis and the preparation of a specimen for analysis.

> **EXAMPLE:** To code the statement "endoscopic percutaneous amniocentesis for drainage of amniotic fluid for diagnostic purposes" the coder references the term *amniocentesis* in the Index of ICD-10-PCS. Here the coder finds 1090. Referring to this table, the coder then selects the following values: 10904ZU. Note that an amniocentesis is a type of drainage.

Delivery

A normal delivery includes the stages of labor, as illustrated in Figure 29-4.

> **EXAMPLE:** To code a delivery, the coder references the term *delivery* in the index. Here coder finds "delivery," then "products of conception." The index then lists 10E0XZZ. This table is then referenced. ICD-10-PCS codes a normal delivery as 10E0XZZ.

Forceps Extraction

During some deliveries, the use forceps is necessary. A **forceps delivery** occurs when an instrument is used to grasp the fetus to assist in delivery. When forceps are used during a delivery, the procedure is considered a type of extraction because the baby is being pulled through the birth canal.

> **EXAMPLE:** The coder references the term *extraction* in the index, then "by body part," then "products of conception." Here the coder finds 10D0 and refers to the table. From that table, the following code should be selected for a low forceps delivery: 10D07Z3.

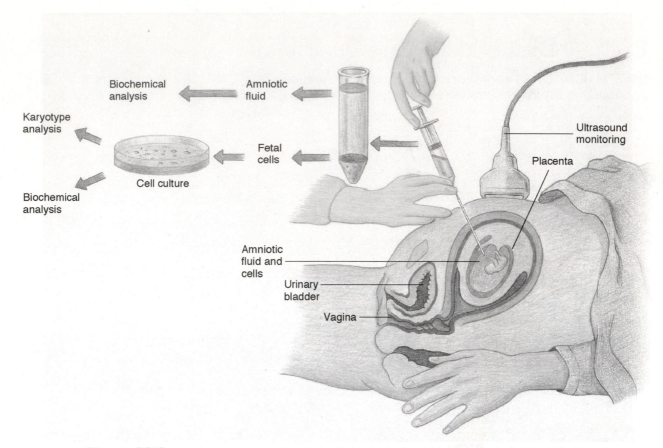

Figure 29-3 Amniocentesis and preparation of specimen for amniotic fluid analysis

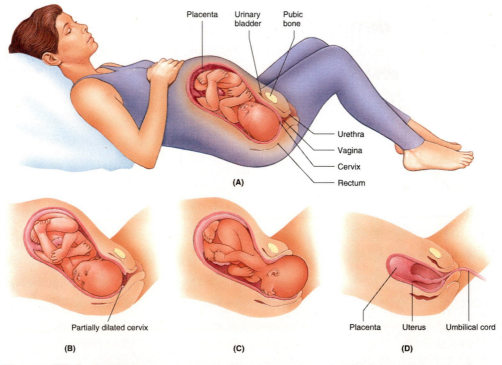

Figure 29-4 Stages of labor: (A) Position of the fetus before labor; (B) first stage of labor, cervical dilation; (C) second stage of labor, fetal delivery; (D) third stage of labor, delivery of placenta

Internet Links

To learn more about types of deliveries, visit the National Women's Health Resource Center at
http://www.healthywomen.org

To learn more about procedures that pertain to obstetrics, visit *http://www.mayoclinic.org/obstetrics*

Summary

- The first character value for obstetric procedure codes is 1.
- The second character value for the body system is pregnancy, with a value of 0.
- Represented in the third-character position is one of 12 root operations for the Obstetrics Section of ICD-10-PCS.
- The fourth-character values in the Obstetrics Section are 0, 1, and 2 for the body parts.
- The fifth character represents the approach, and there are seven different approach values.
- The sixth character represents the device, with three possible values.
- The seventh character represents the qualifiers.

Chapter Review

True/False: Indicate whether each statement is true (T) or false (F).

1. _____ The Obstetrics Section of ICD-10-PCS is used to build codes for procedures performed on the products of conception, not only on the pregnant female.

2. _____ The Obstetric Section codes differentiate the gestational age of the products of conception.

3. _____ A forceps delivery occurs when an instrument is used to grasp the fetus to assist in delivery.

4. _____ In the third character for root operation, the letter *K* is used to represent inspection.

5. _____ When amniotic fluid is extracted for a therapeutic reason, the correct qualifier to report is *C*.

Coding Assignments

Instructions: For each procedure, select the correct ICD-10-PCS code.

1. open approach to drain fetal blood from fetus _____

2. removal of retained placenta via birth canal _____

3. delivery with high forceps _____

4. drainage of fetal cerebrospinal fluid, open approach _____

5. induced abortion, percutaneous endoscopic approach _____

6. open incision to inspect fetal development _____

7. drainage of amniotic fluid for diagnostic review via open approach _____

8. vacuum extraction of products of conception _____

9. extraperitoneal extraction of fetus, open approach _____

10. drainage of fetal blood from fetus at 21 weeks gestation, percutaneous approach _____

11. therapeutic drainage of amniotic fluid, via incision _____

12. resection of ectopic pregnancy, open approach _____

13. open insertion of monitoring electrode into fetus _____

14. diagnostic percutaneous endoscopic drainage of amniotic fluid _____

15. endoscopic extraction of retained products of conception via birth canal _____

Case Studies

Instructions: Review each case study and select the correct ICD-10-PCS code.

CASE 1

INDICATIONS FOR PROCEDURE: This is a 29-year-old gravida 1, para 0, who is 37 weeks' gestational age by dates and ultrasound. She has presented with elevated blood pressure of 151/103. Lab values showed platelet count of 54,000, normal liver function test, a hematocrit of 35.0, and normal PT and PTT. It was felt that the patient was suffering from preeclampsia when examination revealed intrauterine growth retardation and hematemesis. Contractions were occurring but not regularly. Patient was dilated 3 cm, but due to the problems presented, we felt delivery could not wait. Patient was advised that an emergency cesarean was needed, and she agreed.

PROCEDURE: This 29-year-old female was brought to the OR, after which epidural anesthesia was administered. Once patient showed no response to sensitivity, we proceeded. Patient was supine and right hip was slightly elevated to keep pressure off the vena cava. A low transverse incision with a #10 blade was carried to the level of the fascia. Mayo scissors were used to open the incision laterally. The posterior fascia was dissected bluntly from the rectus abdominus muscle. The aponeurosis was cut superiorly near the umbilicus and inferiorly to the symphysis pubis. Clamps were placed, and Metzenbaum scissors were then used to make a longitudinal peritoneal incision and extend the fascial opening. At this point, we were able to palpate the uterus, and fetal position was good. The bladder was freed from the uterus and retracted, a small transverse incision was made in the lower uterine segment, and the amniotic sac was exposed and incised. I then manipulated the fetus from the uterus. The infant female was drawn out, and the mouth and nose were immediately suctioned. The umbilical cord was clamped and cut, and cord samples were sent for pathology. The placenta was then recovered, and then a laparotomy sponge was used to clean the interior before a layered closure was performed: 2-0 absorbable sutures were used when closing the uterus. 3-0 Vicryl was used to close the bladder. The skin was closed with staples. Patient tolerated procedure well; mother and baby were fine.

ICD-10-PCS Code Assignment: _____

CASE 2

INDICATIONS FOR SURGERY: A 34-year-old female presents with severe abdominal pain. After examination was completed and ultrasound results were reviewed, it was determined that patient had an ectopic pregnancy and surgical intervention was needed.

PROCEDURE: Patient was taken to the operating room, and after general anesthesia was induced, she was prepped and draped in the usual sterile fashion. Examination was performed after anesthesia, which showed a normal-sized, nontender uterus, a left adnexal mass, and a fullness in the vagina, all consistent with hyperperitoneum. A 10-mm trocar was inserted directly into the abdomen through a small incision in the umbilicus. Using 3.5 liters of carbon dioxide, a pneumoperitoneum was created. The hemoperitoneum was noticed, and another 10-mm trocar was placed in a small suprapubic incision. Two 5-mm ports were also placed under direct visualization in both the right and left lower quadrants. With an irrigator and aspirator, the hemoperitoneum was reduced. The left fallopian tube was noted to be almost to the point of rupture due to a mass in the tube. The fallopian tube was distended beyond repair; so this needed to be removed. The tube was tied off and removed with its contents through an Endo Catch bag through the 10-mm port. Inspection of the abdomen noted no other problems; adequate hemostasis was noted, and ports were removed. Defects were closed with 0 Vicryl, and the skin was closed with 4-0 Dexon. She was sent to the recovery room in stable condition.

ICD-10-PCS Code Assignment: _____

CASE 3

DIAGNOSIS: False labor without delivery, antepartum complication

This patient is a 20-year-old female who presents today dilated 7 cm with contractions occurring every 3–4 minutes lasting 30–40 seconds. This mother is also an admitted cocaine addict who is worried about how her baby will be when born. At this time we are going to try to obtain a blood sample of the fetus to determine whether we need to have any special services on standby in the NICU.

The fetal monitor is showing a stable heart rate at this time. The amniotic sac is broken, and the amnioscope is inserted through the vagina. A 0.05-mm incision is made in the scalp, and a blood sample is aspirated into a tube for a STAT to the lab. Contractions stopped, and the baby was not delivered at this time.

Procedure completed was an endoscopic drainage via the vagina for fetal blood sample.

ICD-10-PCS Code Assignment: _____

CHAPTER 30

Placement Section

Chapter Outline

Objectives

Key Terms

Introduction

Placement Section of the ICD-10-PCS

Procedure Highlights

Internet Links

Summary

Chapter Review

Coding Assignments

Case Studies

Objectives

At the conclusion of this chapter, the learner should be able to:

1. Identify the character meanings used for the ICD-10-PCS Placement Section.
2. Discuss the root operations used for the ICD-10-PCS Placement Section.
3. List the body-part values in the ICD-10-PCS Placement Section.
4. Identify the approach, device, and qualifiers used the ICD-10-PCS Placement Section.
5. Code procedures in the ICD-10-PCS Placement Section.

Key Terms

change	dressing	packing	traction
compression	immobilization	removal	

Reminder

As you work through this chapter, you will need to have a copy of the ICD-10-PCS coding book to reference.

Introduction

The third section found in ICD-10-PCS is "Placement." Placement procedures include those in which a device is put on or into a body region. The devices are placed to pack, immobilize, stretch, or compress an area.

Placement Section of the ICD-10-PCS

The seven characters in this section have the same meanings as in the Medical and Surgical Section:

1	2	3	4	5	6	7
Section	Body system	Root operation	Body part	Approach	Device	Qualifier

Section

The first character value for placement procedure codes is 2.

Body System: Regions and Orifices

The second character value for the anatomical regions/orifices has two values: anatomical regions with a value of W and anatomical orifices with a value of Y.

Root Operation

There are seven root operations for the Placement Section of ICD-10-PCS; they are selected for the third character:

- **Change**—Taking out or off a device from a body part and putting back an identical or similar device in or on the same body part without cutting or puncturing the skin or mucous membrane (value of 0)

- **Compression**—Putting pressure on a body region (value of 1)

- **Dressing**—Putting material on a body region for protection (value of 2)

- **Immobilization**—Limiting or preventing motion of a body region (value of 3)

- **Packing**—Putting material in a body region or orifice (value of 4)

- **Removal**—Taking out or off a device from a body part (value of 5)

- **Traction**—Exerting a pulling force on a body region in a distal direction (value of 6)

Body Part: Regions and Orifices

The fourth-character values in the Placement Section are:

- Body regions—30 values, used only with the body system character of W, Anatomical regions

- Natural orifices—6 values, are used only with the body system character of Y, Anatomical orifices.

See Figure 30-1 for the list of the values for the fourth character, the body system character *W*. Figure 30-2 is a list of the values for the body system character of *Y*. Note that the fourth-character values are different depending on whether you are coding for the body system character of *W* or *Y*.

2: PLACEMENT

W: ANATOMICAL REGIONS

Operation – Character 3	Body Region – Character 4
0 Change	0 Head
1 Compression	1 Face
2 Dressing	2 Neck
3 Immobilization	3 Abdominal Wall
4 Packing	4 Chest Wall
5 Removal	5 Back
6 Traction	6 Inguinal Region, Right
	7 Inguinal Region, Left
	8 Upper Extremity, Right
	9 Upper Extremity, Left
	A Upper Arm, Right
	B Upper Arm, Left
	C Lower Arm, Right
	D Lower Arm, Left
	E Hand, Right
	F Hand, Left
	G Thumb, Right
	H Thumb, Left
	J Finger, Right
	K Finger, Left
	L Lower Extremity, Right
	M Lower Extremity, Left
	N Upper Leg, Right
	P Upper Leg, Left
	Q Lower Leg, Right
	R Lower Leg, Left
	S Foot, Right
	T Foot, Left
	U Toe, Right
	V Toe, Left

Figure 30-1 Values for the body system character *W*

2: PLACEMENT

Y: ANATOMICAL ORIFICES

Operation – Character 3	Body Region – Character 4
0 Change	0 Mouth and Pharynx
4 Packing	1 Nasal
5 Removal	2 Ear
	3 Anorectal
	4 Female Genital Tract
	5 Urethra

Figure 30-2 Values for the body system character *Y*

Approach

There is only one approach value: X, External. This is because all placement procedures are performed in one of two manners:

- By direct application on the skin or mucus membrane
- By indirectly applying external force through the skin or mucous membrane

Device

The devices used are specified by the sixth character.

The device values for Placement are different for the W and Y body systems. The device characters for the W body system are:

- 0, Traction apparatus
- 1, Splint
- 2, Cast
- 3, Brace
- 4, Bandage
- 5, Packing material
- 6, Pressure dressing
- 7, Intermittent pressure device
- 8, Stereotactic apparatus
- 9, Wire
- Y, Other device

For the Y body system, there is only one value: 5, Packing material.

Coders must carefully reference the Tables to review the assignment of the sixth character because there is differentiation among the tables.

Qualifier

The seventh character represents the qualifier. For the Placement Section of ICD-10-CM there is only one value used: Z, No qualifier.

Exercise 30.1 – Identifying Device Characters

Using an ICD-10-PCS book, for each of the operation blocks, identify the device characters from the Placement Section that are applicable. The first one is completed for you.

Operation Block	Possible Device Characters
1. 2W00X	0, 1, 2, 3, 4, 5, 6, 7, 8, Y
2. 2W02X	_____
3. 2W14X	_____
4. 2W44X	_____
5. 2W33X	_____

Procedure Highlights

Here are of the some common procedures that are coded to this section of the code book.

Cast Application

When a bone is broken or when a body part needs to be immobilized, various devices can be applied to immobilize the area. Body regions can be immobilized by splints, cast, braces, stereotactic apparatus, and other devices. The placement of these devices is coded by using Table 2W3 in the Placement Section. To select codes, the coder first locates the term *immobilization* in the Index. This Index entry is then further divided by body region.

> **EXAMPLE:** A cast application on the upper right leg is coded to 2W3NX2Z.

Dressing Application

At times wounds have to be dressed, that is, covered. When dressings are applied, the 2W2 table is used. To locate *dressing application* in the Index reference the term *dressing*. The Index is then further divided by body region.

> **EXAMPLE:** The code for a dressing application on the left foot is 2W2TX4Z.

Packing

When an area is bleeding, it may need to be packed with packing material. Table 2W4 is used to report the packing of body regions, and Table 2Y4 is used to report the packing of a body orifice. To report packing, the term to reference in the Index is *packing*. The entry is then subdivided into the various body regions or orifice.

> **EXAMPLE:** To code a packing of the nose, assign the code 2Y41X5Z.

Internet Links

To learn about the placement of casts, splints, braces, and the like, visit *http://www.righthealth.com/topic/orthopedic*, and search on the type of device.

Summary

- The first-character value for placement procedure codes is 2.
- The second-character value for the body system has two values: W and Y.
- There are seven root operations for the Placement Section of ICD-10-PCS.
- The fourth character has 30 values for the W anatomical regions and 6 values for the Y anatomical orifices.
- There is only one approach value for the fifth character: X, External.
- The sixth character specifies the devices used.
- The seventh character always means "no qualifier," represented by the character *Z*.

Chapter Review

True/False: Indicate whether each statement is true (T) or false (F).

1. _____ The Placement Section of ICD-10-PCS is used to build codes for procedures performed only on the bones.

2. _____ Compression is exerting a pulling force on a body region in a distal direction.

3. _____ Packing is putting material into a body region or orifice.

4. _____ In the third character for root operation, for anatomical region, the number 2 is used for dressing.

5. _____ When a pressure dressing is used during compression, the sixth-character value is 6.

Coding Assignments

Instructions: Review each case study and select the correct ICD-10-PCS code.

1. splint change, head _____

2. bandage change for open wound on neck _____

3. replacement of packing material on right chest wall _____

4. replacement cast applied on left upper extremity _____

5. brace change on left lower extremity due to patient growth _____

6. pressure dressing applied for compression of left foot _____

7. bandage dressing application on left inguinal region _____

8. brace immobilization of head due to skull fracture _____

9. compression of right toe using intermittent pressure device _____

10. splint immobilization of right foot due to sprain _____

11. cast application right foot _____

12. splint applied to left toe for immobilization _____

13. abdominal wall packing using sterile packing material _____

14. removal of traction apparatus on head _____

15. removal of packing material from wound on head _____

16. traction apparatus removal on device on face _____

17. placement of traction apparatus on left toe _____

18. packing of anorectal region using packing material _____

19. removal of urethra packing material _____

20. packing of ear with sterile packing _____

Case Studies

Instructions: Review each case study and select the correct ICD-10-PCS code.

CASE 1

Patient is a 9-year-old male who presents today with pain in his right arm after falling off his bike. He was not unconscious at any time. His right arm is swollen, and the pain is increased when his arm is moved. X-ray of the right arm showed a fracture in the upper extremity. The fracture is well aligned and no alignment is necessary. A cast was placed on the right upper extremity.

ICD-10-PCS Code Assignment: _____

CASE 2

Mrs. Smith was admitted to the nursing home on Thursday, and the nursing staff noted that she has a 2-by-3-cm wound on her back on the left side. Today I applied a sterile dressing to the area to protect it from infection.

ICD-10-PCS Code Assignment: _____

CASE 3

Emergency Room Note

This 78-year-old male patient presents with a nose bleed for the last 4 hours. The bleeding has increased over the last hour. He has a platelet disorder, which is treated by Dr. Young. I packed the nasal area to stop the bleeding. I instructed him to follow up with Dr. Young in one day.

ICD-10-PCS Code Assignment: _____

Administration Section

Chapter Outline

Objectives

At the conclusion of this chapter, the learner should be able to:

1. Identify the character meanings used for the ICD-10-PCS Administration Section.
2. Discuss the root operations used for the ICD-10-PCS Administration Section.
3. List the body part values in the ICD-10-PCS Administration Section.
4. Identify the approach, device, and qualifiers used in the ICD-10-PCS Administration Section.
5. Code procedures in the ICD-10-PCS Administration Section.

Key Terms

introduction   irrigation   transfusion

Reminder

As you work through this chapter, you will need to have a copy of the ICD-10-PCS coding book to reference.

Introduction

The section titled "Administration" is the fourth section found in ICD-10-PCS. This section reports procedures in which a therapeutic, prophylactic, protective, diagnostic, nutritional, or physiological substance is put into or on the body.

Administration Section of the ICD-10-PCS

The seven characters in this section have the following meanings:

1	2	3	4	5	6	7
Section	Body system: Physiological systems and anatomical regions	Root operation	Body/system region	Approach	Substance	Qualifier

Section

The first character value used to identify the Administration Section is 3.

Body System: Physiological Systems and Anatomical Regions

The second character for the physiological systems and anatomical regions has three values:

- Circulatory system—used for reporting transfusion procedures (value of 0)
- Indwelling device—(value of C)
- Physiological systems and anatomical regions—(value of E)

Root Operation

There are three root operations for the Administration Section of ICD-10-PCS:

- **Introduction**—Putting in or on a therapeutic, diagnostic, nutritional, physiological, or prophylactic substance except blood or blood products with a character representation of 0
- **Irrigation**—Putting in or on a cleansing substance, with a character representation of 1
- **Transfusion**—Putting in blood or blood products, with a character representation of 2

Body Region

The fourth character value in the Administration Section defines the site where the substance is administered. The character values vary according to the physiological system and anatomical regions. The fourth-character values are as follows:

- Circulatory body region—five values:
  - Peripheral veins (value of 3)
  - Central vein (value of 4)
  - Peripheral arteries (value of 5)
  - Central artery (value of 6)
  - Products of conception, circulatory (value of 7)

- For indwelling devices, there is only one value of Z for the whole body.

- For physiological systems and anatomical regions, there are 33 values. See Figure 31-1 for the list of the values.

Remember the fourth character identifies the site in which the substance is administered, not the site where the substance administered takes effect.

Approach

The fifth character identifies the approach. The approaches of intradermal, subcutaneous, and intramuscular injections or introductions are all considered percutaneous approaches. The placement

3: ADMINISTRATION	
E: PHYSIOLOGICAL SYSTEMS AND ANATOMICAL REGIONS	
Operation – Character 3	**Body System / Region – Character 4**
0 Introduction 1 Irrigation	0 Skin and Mucous Membranes 1 Subcutaneous Tissue 2 Muscle 3 Peripheral Vein 4 Central Vein 5 Peripheral Artery 6 Central Artery 7 Coronary Artery 8 Heart 9 Nose A Bone Marrow B Ear C Eye D Mouth and Pharynx E Products of Conception F Respiratory Tract G Upper GI H Lower GI J Biliary and Pancreatic Tract K Genitourinary Tract L Pleural Cavity M Peritoneal Cavity N Male Reproductive P Female Reproductive Q Cranial Cavity and Brain R Spinal Canal S Epidural Space T Peripheral Nerves and Plexi U Joints V Bones W Lymphatics X Cranial Nerves Y Pericardial Cavity

Figure 31-1 List of values for physiological systems and anatomical regions

of a catheter into an internal site is also considered a type of percutaneous approach. The approach values are as follows:

- Open (value of 0)
- Percutaneous (value of 3)
- Via natural or artificial opening (value of 7)
- Via natural or artificial opening endoscopic (value of 8)
- External (value of X)

The Tables need to be referenced to locate the value that is valid for each physiological system and anatomical region based on the documentation.

Substance

The sixth character identifies the substance (instead of device) being introduced into the body. The values vary according the physiological system and anatomical region. See Figure 31-2 for the sixth-character values used for the circulatory system associated with Table 302. This table needs to be referenced to determine which substance character is relevant for circulatory transfusion into the peripheral veins and arteries, as well as for products of conception as they relate to the circulatory system. The documentation needs to be referenced to determine which substance character is relevant for each body system character.

Figure 31-3 lists the sixth-character values for physiological systems and anatomical regions. Tables 3E0 and 3E1 need to be referenced for character assignment based on the documentation and the procedure performed.

Coders must carefully reference the tables to review the assignment of the sixth character because there is differentiation among the tables. Attention to the procedure being performed and to the body area involved are essential to proper code assignment.

Qualifier

The seventh character represents the qualifier. For the Administration Section of ICD-10-PCS, the values for this character vary according to the table being used. For Table 302, three qualifiers are used: Z, No qualifier; 0, Autologous; and 1, Nonautologous. For Table 3C1, the only qualifier is Z. See Figure 31-4 for a list of the values for Tables 3E0 and Table 3E1.

Exercise 31.1 – Identifying Qualifier Characterss

Using an ICD-10-PCS book, for each of the operation blocks, identify the qualifier(s) that are applicable in the Administration Section. The first one is completed for you.

Operation Block	Possible Qualifier Characters
1. 3E1CX82	X, Z
2. 3E0E30	
3. 30233A	
4. 3C1ZX8	
5. 3E0130	

3: ADMINISTRATION
0: CIRCULATORY
2: TRANSFUSION: Putting in blood or blood products

Body System / Region Character 4	Approach Character 5	Substance Character 6	Qualifier Character 7
3 Peripheral Vein 4 Central Vein	0 Open 3 Percutaneous	A Stem Cells, Embryonic	Z No Qualifier
3 Peripheral Vein 4 Central Vein	0 Open 3 Percutaneous	G Bone Marrow H Whole Blood J Serum Albumin K Frozen Plasma L Fresh Plasma M Plasma Cryoprecipitate N Red Blood Cells P Frozen Red Cells Q White Cells R Platelets S Globulin T Fibrinogen V Antihemophilic Factors W Factor IX X Stem Cells, Cord Blood Y Stem Cells, Hematopoietic	0 Autologous 1 Nonautologous
5 Peripheral Artery 6 Central Artery	0 Open 3 Percutaneous	G Bone Marrow H Whole Blood J Serum Albumin K Frozen Plasma L Fresh Plasma M Plasma Cryoprecipitate N Red Blood Cells P Frozen Red Cells Q White Cells R Platelets S Globulin T Fibrinogen V Antihemophilic Factors W Factor IX X Stem Cells, Cord Blood Y Stem Cells, Hematopoietic	0 Autologous 1 Nonautologous
7 Products of Conception, Circulatory	3 Percutaneous 7 Via Natural or Artificial Opening	H Whole Blood J Serum Albumin K Frozen Plasma L Fresh Plasma M Plasma Cryoprecipitate N Red Blood Cells P Frozen Red Cells Q White Cells R Platelets S Globulin T Fibrinogen V Antihemophilic Factors W Factor IX	1 Nonautologous

Figure 31-2 Sixth-character values used for the circulatory system associated with Table 302

3: ADMINISTRATION
E: PHYSIOLOGICAL SYSTEMS AND ANATOMICAL REGIONS

Approach Character 5	Substance Character 6	Qualifier Character 7

0 Open
3 Percutaneous
7 Via Natural or Artificial
   Opening
8 Via Natural or Artificial
   Opening Endoscopic
X External
	0 Antineoplastic
	1 Thrombolytic
	2 Anti-infective
	3 Anti-inflammatory
	4 Serum, Toxoid and Vaccine
	5 Adhesion Barrier
	6 Nutritional Substance
	7 Electrolytic and Water Balance
	   Substance
	8 Irrigating Substance
	9 Dialysate
	A Stem Cells, Embryonic
	B Local Anesthetic
	C Regional Anesthetic
	D Inhalation Anesthetic
	E Stem Cells, Somatic
	F Intracirculatory Anesthetic
	G Other Therapeutic Substance
	H Radioactive Substance
	J Contrast Agent
	K Other Diagnostic Substance
	L Sperm
	M Pigment
	N Analgesics, Hypnotics, Sedatives
	P Platelet Inhibitor
	Q Fertilized Ovum
	R Antiarrhythmic
	S Gas
	T Destructive Agent
	U Pancreatic Islet Cells
	V Hormone
	W Immunotherapeutic
	X Vasopressor
		0 Autologous
		1 Nonautologous
		2 High-dose Interleukin-2
		3 Low-dose Interleukin-2
		4 Liquid Brachytherapy
		   Radioisotope
		5 Other Antineoplastic
		6 Recombinant Human-activated
		   Protein C
		7 Other Thrombolytic
		8 Oxazolidinones
		9 Other Anti-infective
		B Recombinant Bone
		   Morphogenetic Protein
		C Other Substance
		D Nitric Oxide
		F Other Gas
		G Insulin
		H Human B-type Natriuretic
		   Peptide
		J Other Hormone
		K Immunostimulator
		L Immunosuppressive
		M Monoclonal Antibody
		N Blood Brain Barrier Disruption
		X Diagnostic
		Z No Qualifier

Figure 31-3 Sixth-character values for physiological systems and anatomical regions

3: ADMINISTRATION
E: PHYSIOLOGICAL SYSTEMS AND ANATOMICAL REGIONS
0: INTRODUCTION: (*continued*)
   Putting in or on a therapeutic, diagnostic, nutritional, physiological, or prophylactic substance except blood or blood products

Body System / Region Character 4	Approach Character 5	Substance Character 6	Qualifier Character 7
W Lymphatics	3 Percutaneous	2 Anti-infective	8 Oxazolidinones 9 Other Anti-infective
W Lymphatics	3 Percutaneous	3 Anti-inflammatory 6 Nutritional Substance 7 Electrolytic and Water Balance Substance B Local Anesthetic H Radioactive Substance J Contrast Agent K Other Diagnostic Substance N Analgesics, Hypnotics, Sedatives T Destructive Agent	Z No Qualifier
W Lymphatics	3 Percutaneous	G Other Therapeutic Substance	C Other Substance

3: ADMINISTRATION
E: PHYSIOLOGICAL SYSTEMS AND ANATOMICAL REGIONS
1: IRRIGATION: Putting in or on a cleansing substance

Body System / Region Character 4	Approach Character 5	Substance Character 6	Qualifier Character 7
0 Skin and Mucous Membranes C Eye	3 Percutaneous X External	8 Irrigating Substance	X Diagnostic Z No Qualifier
9 Nose B Ear F Respiratory Tract G Upper GI H Lower GI J Biliary and Pancreatic Tract K Genitourinary Tract N Male Repoductive P Female Repoductive	3 Percutaneous 7 Via Natural or Artificial Opening 8 Via Natural or Artificial Opening Endoscopic	8 Irrigating Substance	X Diagnostic Z No Qualifier
L Pleural Cavity Q Cranial Cavity and Brain R Spinal Canal S Epidural Space U Joints Y Pericardial Cavity	3 Percutaneous	8 Irrigating Substance	X Diagnostic Z No Qualifier
M Peritoneal Cavity	3 Percutaneous	8 Irrigating Substance	X Diagnostic Z No Qualifier
M Peritoneal Cavity	3 Percutaneous	9 Dialysate	Z No Qualifier

Figure 31-4 Seventh-character values for Table 3E1

Summary

- The first character value for Administration procedure codes is 3.
- The second character value for the body system has three values: 0, C, or E.
- There are three root operations for the Administration Section of ICD-10-PCS.
- The fourth character values in the Administration Section vary according to the physiological system and anatomical regions.
- The fifth character identifies the approach and includes values of 0, 3, 7, and X.
- The sixth character identifies the substance being introduced into the body.
- The seventh character is a qualifier and the values vary according to the table used.

Chapter Review

True/False: Indicate whether each statement is true (T) or false (F).

1. _____ There are three root operations for the Administration Section of ICD-10-PCS.

2. _____ The sixth character identifies the device being used to introduce the substance into the body.

3. _____ Intradermal, subcutaneous, and intramuscular injections or introductions are all considered percutaneous approaches.

4. _____ In the circulatory body region, there are five values.

5. _____ For indwelling devices, there is only one value of Z for whole body for the fourth character.

Coding Assignments

Instructions: For each procedure, select the correct ICD-10-PCS code.

1. transfusion of embryonic stem cells into peripheral vein, open approach   _____

2. transfusion of nonautologous frozen plasma into peripheral vein, open approach   _____

3. transfusion of nonautologous platelets into peripheral vein, open approach   _____

4. transfusion of autologous hematopoietic stem cells into peripheral vein, open approach   _____

5. transfusion of nonautologous frozen red cells into peripheral vein, percutaneous approach   _____

6. transfusion of autologous bone marrow into central vein, open approach   _____

7. introduction of contrast agent into central artery, open approach   _____

8. introduction of serum, toxoid, and vaccine into central artery, percutaneous approach

   _____

9. introduction of platelet inhibitor into central artery, percutaneous approach

   _____

10. introduction of blood brain barrier disruption substance into central vein, percutaneous approach

    _____

11. transfusion of nonautologous antihemophiliac factors into products of conception, circulatory, via natural or artificial opening

    _____

12. irrigation of indwelling device using irrigating substance, external approach

    _____

13. introduction of oxazolidinones into skin and mucous membranes, external approach

    _____

14. introduction of contrast agent into ear, external approach

    _____

15. introduction of analgesics into ear, external approach

    _____

16. introduction of liquid brachytherapy radioisotope antineoplastic into eye, percutaneous approach

    _____

17. introduction of monoclonal antibody into eye via natural opening

    _____

18. introduction of liquid brachytherapy radioisotope into pharynx, external approach

    _____

19. introduction of serum, toxoid, and vaccine into mouth, percutaneous approach

    _____

20. introduction of monoclonal antibody into products of conception, via artificial opening

    _____

Case Studies

Instructions: Review each case study and select the correct ICD-10-PCS code.

CASE 1

Transfusion Unit Note

This 67-year-old female is diagnosed with leukemia and presents today for a nonautologous transfusion of platelets due to a low platelet count. The transfusion was completed in the left arm in a peripheral vein percutaneously. The patient tolerated the procedure well and was told to follow up with her physician in four days.

ICD-10-PCS Code Assignment: _____

CASE 2

Skilled Nursing Care Note

This 79-year-old male patient has an indwelling catheter, and today it was irrigated per standard nursing protocol. The catheter was cleansed with an irrigating substance.

ICD-10-PCS Code Assignment: _____

CASE 3

This 9-year-old patient presents with an inflamed left eye. His mother states that he has gotten "something" in this eye and it has become irritated. His left eye is red and the conjunctiva is inflamed. I felt it best to irrigate the eye with ophthalmic irrigating solution. I also gave the patient a prescription for ophthalmic antibiotics. He is to follow up with me in 10 days or call if the eye becomes worse.

ICD-10-PCS Code Assignment: _____

CHAPTER

Measurement and Monitoring Section

32

Chapter Outline

Objectives

At the conclusion of this chapter, the learner should be able to:

1. Identify the character meanings used for the ICD-10-PCS Measurement and Monitoring Section.
2. Discuss the root operations used for the ICD-10-PCS Measurement and Monitoring Section.
3. List the body system values in the ICD-10-PCS Measurement and Monitoring Section.
4. Identify the approach, function, and qualifiers used for the ICD-10-PCS Measurement and Monitoring Section.
5. Code procedures in the ICD-10-PCS Measurement and Monitoring Section.

Key Terms

measurement   monitoring

> **Reminder**
>
> *As you work through this chapter, you will need to have a copy of the ICD-10-PCS coding book to reference.*

Introduction

"Measurement and Monitoring" is the fifth section found in ICD-10-PCS. This section is referenced to report procedures in which a physiological or physical function is measured or monitored.

Measurement and Monitoring Section of the ICD-10-PCS

The seven characters in this section have the following meanings:

1	2	3	4	5	6	7
Section	Body system	Root operation	Body system	Approach	Function	Qualifier

Section

The first character value for measurement and monitoring procedure codes is 4. All tables in this section begin with this character value.

Body System

The second character value for the measurement and monitoring section is either A, Physiological systems, or B, Physiological devices.

Root Operation

Two root operations are identified for the Measurement and Monitoring Section of ICD-10-PCS:

- **Measurement**—Determining the level of a physiological or physical function at a point in time (value of 0)

- **Monitoring**—Determining the level of a physiological or physical function repetitively over a period of time (value of 1)

Body System

The fourth-character values in the Measurement and Monitoring Section identify the body system that is measured or monitored. The values vary according to the table used for the root operation. See Figure 32-1 for the appropriate value of the fourth character for physiological systems and Figure 32-2 for the fourth-character values for physiological devices.

Approach

The fifth character identifies the approach used for the procedure and is similar to those used in the Medical and Surgical Section. The approaches are external, open, percutaneous, percutaneous endoscopic, via natural or artificial opening, and via natural or artificial opening endoscopic.

The tables need to be referenced to locate the values that are valid for each body system. Figure 32-3 lists the fifth, sixth, and seventh characters for physiological systems, and Figure 32-4 lists the fifth, sixth, and seventh characters for physiological devices.

4: MEASUREMENT AND MONITORING
A: PHYSIOLOGICAL SYSTEMS

Operation – Character 3	Body System – Character 4
0 Measurement 1 Monitoring	0 Central Nervous 1 Peripheral Nervous 2 Cardiac 3 Arterial 4 Venous 5 Circulatory 6 Lymphatic 7 Visual 8 Olfactory 9 Respiratory B Gastrointestinal C Biliary D Urinary F Musculoskeletal H Products of Conception, Cardiac J Products of Conception, Nervous Z None

Figure 32-1 Fourth-character values for physiological systems

4: MEASUREMENT AND MONITORING
B: PHYSIOLOGICAL DEVICES

Operation – Character 3	Body System – Character 4
0 Measurement	0 Central Nervous 1 Peripheral Nervous 2 Cardiac 9 Respiratory F Musculoskeletal

Figure 32-2 Fourth-character values for physiological devices

Function

The sixth character identifies the physiological or physical function being measured or monitored. The character values can be obtained from Figures 32-3 and 32-4. Note that not all characters are valid for all tables in the Measurement and Monitoring Section, so the tables need to be referenced for the correct character assignments.

4: MEASUREMENT AND MONITORING
A: PHYSIOLOGICAL SYSTEMS

Approach Character 5	Function / Device Character 6	Qualifier Character 7
0 Open	0 Acuity	0 Central
3 Percutaneous	1 Capacity	1 Peripheral
4 Percutaneous Endoscopic	2 Conductivity	2 Portal
7 Via Natural or Artificial	3 Contractility	3 Pulmonary
Opening	4 Electrical Activity	4 Stress
8 Via Natural or Artificial	5 Flow	5 Ambulatory
Opening Endoscopic	6 Metabolism	6 Right Heart
X External	7 Mobility	7 Left Heart
	8 Motility	8 Bilateral
	9 Output	9 Sensory
	B Pressure	B Motor
	C Rate	C Coronary
	D Resistance	D Intracranial
	F Rhythm	F Other Thoracic
	G Secretion	Z No Qualifier
	H Sound	
	J Pulse	
	K Temperature	
	L Volume	
	M Total Activity	
	N Sampling and Pressure	
	P Action Currents	
	Q Sleep	
	R Saturation	

Figure 32-3 Fifth, sixth, and seventh characters for physiological systems

4: MEASUREMENT AND MONITORING
B: PHYSIOLOGICAL DEVICES

Approach Character 5	Function / Device Character 6	Qualifier Character 7
X External	S Pacemaker T Defibrillator V Stimulator	Z No Qualifier

Figure 32-4 Fifth, sixth, and seventh characters for physiological devices

Qualifier

The seventh character represents the qualifier. See Figures 32–3 and 32–4 for the seventh-character values, which identify the specific body part or a variation of the procedure performed.

Summary

- The first-character value for Measurement and Monitoring procedure codes is 4.

- The second-character value for the body system has two values: A or B.

- There are two root operations for this section of ICD-10-PCS: measurement and monitoring.

- The fourth-character values in the Measurement and Monitoring Section vary according to the physiological system or physiological device.

- The fifth character identifies the approach.

- The sixth character identifies the physiological or physical function being measured or monitored.

- The seventh character is a qualifier, and its values vary according to the table being used.

Chapter Review

True/False: Indicate whether each statement is true (T) or false (F).

1. _____ There are three root operations for the Measurement and Monitoring Section of ICD-10-PCS.

2. _____ The third character identifies the root operation.

3. _____ The second-character value represents either the physiological system or the physiological device.

4. _____ *Measurement* is defined as determining the level of physiological or physical function over a period of time.

5. _____ Conductivity is a type of physiological function.

Coding Assignments

Instructions: For each procedure, select the correct ICD-10-PCS code.

1. monitoring of arterial pressure, peripheral, external approach _____

2. monitoring of pulmonary venous pressure, open approach _____

3. monitoring of portal venous flow, percutaneously _____

4. monitoring of venous saturation, portal, open approach _____

5. monitoring of lymphatic flow, open approach _____

6. monitoring of respiratory flow, via nose _____

7. monitoring of gastrointestinal secretion, via artificial opening _____

8. endoscopic monitoring of gastrointestinal pressure _____

9. monitoring of urinary flow _____

10. fetal monitoring of cardiac electrical activity via natural opening _____

11. endoscopic monitoring of fetal cardiac rhythm _____

12. external measurement of cardiac pacemaker _____

13. measurement of cardiac defibrillator, external approach _____

14. measurement of respiratory pacemaker, external approach _____

15. monitoring of cardiac stress, external approach _____

Case Studies

Instructions: Review each case study and select the correct ICD-10-PCS code.

CASE 1

Cardiac Unit Note

This 75-year-old female is diagnosed with cardiac abnormalities. She is brought to the cardiac unit to monitor her cardiac output using an external monitor. Full report to follow.

ICD-10-PCS Code Assignment: _____

CASE 2

Respiratory Care Unit

This 80-year-old female patient is having difficulty breathing, and her respiratory rate varies. She is brought to this unit to externally monitor her respiratory rate. She is to follow up for results with Dr. Kana.

ICD-10-PCS Code Assignment: _____

CASE 3

This 23-week pregnant female is brought to the unit to monitor the cardiac sounds of her child. The sounds were monitored using an endoscopic vaginal monitor.

ICD-10-PCS Code Assignment: _____

Extracorporeal Assistance and Performance and Extracorporeal Therapies Sections

CHAPTER

33

Chapter Outline

Objectives
Key Terms
Introduction
Extracorporeal Assistance and
   Performance Section of ICD-10-PCS

Extracorporeal Therapies Section of
   ICD-10-PCS
Summary
Chapter Review
Coding Assignments

Objectives

At the conclusion of this chapter, the learner should be able to:

1. Identify the character meanings used for Section 6, Extracorporeal Assistance and Performance, and for Section 7, Extracorporeal Therapies of ICD-10-PCS.
2. Discuss the root operations used for these two sections of ICD-10-PCS.
3. List the body system values in these sections of ICD-10-PCS.
4. Identify the duration, function, and qualifiers used in these sections.
5. Code procedures from these ICD-10-PCS sections.

Key Terms

assistance	extracorporeal	pheresis	ultrasound therapy
atmospheric control	hyperthermia	phototherapy	ultraviolet light
decompression	hypothermia	restoration	therapy
electromagnetic therapy	performance	shock wave therapy	

Reminder

As you work through this chapter, you will need to have a copy of the ICD-10-PCS coding book to reference.

Introduction

The sections titled "Extracorporeal Assistance and Performance" and "Extracorporeal Therapies" are the sixth and seventh sections found in ICD-10-PCS. Codes in the Extracorporeal Assistance and Performance Section report procedures in which a physiological or physical function is performed by equipment outside the body. Codes in the Extracorporeal Therapies Section report procedures in which equipment is used for therapy. The term **extracorporeal** means something that is outside of the body.

Extracorporeal Assistance and Performance Section of ICD-10-PCS

The seven characters in this section have the following meanings:

1	2	3	4	5	6	7
Section	Body system	Root operation	Body system	Duration	Function	Qualifier

Section

The first character value for the codes on the Extracorporeal Assistance and Performance Section tables is 5.

Physiological System

The second-character value, for body system, in the Extracorporeal Assistance and Performance section is A for physiological systems—the only second position value for these tables.

Root Operation

There are three root operations for the Extracorporeal Assistance and Performance Section of ICD-10-PCS:

- **Assistance**—Taking over a portion of a physiological function by extracorporeal means (value of 0)

- **Performance**—Completely taking over a physiological function by extracorporeal means (value of 1)

- **Restoration**—Returning or attempting to return a physiological function to its natural state by extracorporeal means (value of 2)

In the Extracorporeal Therapies section, the tables have similar characters (explained later in this chapter), but the root operations have different values.

Body System

The fourth-character values in the Extracorporeal Assistance and Performance Section identify the body system in which the assistance is occurring:

- Cardiac (value of 2)
- Circulatory (value of 5)
- Respiratory (value of 9)
- Biliary (value of C)
- Urinary (value of D)

Reference Tables 5A0, 5A1, and 5A2 in ICD-10-PCS to determine the values that are relevant to each table and to each situation.

Duration

The fifth character identifies the duration of the procedure. Figure 33-1 lists the values for the fifth character.

5: EXTRACORPOREAL ASSISTANCE AND PERFORMANCE
A: PHYSIOLOGICAL SYSTEMS

Duration Character 5	Function Character 6	Qualifier Character 7
0 Single	0 Filtration	0 Balloon Pump
1 Intermittent	1 Output	1 Hyperbaric
2 Continuous	2 Oxygenation	2 Manual
3 Less than 24 Consecutive Hours	3 Pacing	3 Membrane
4 24-96 Consecutive Hours	4 Rhythm	4 Nonmechanical
5 Greater than 96 Consecutive Hours	5 Ventilation	5 Pulsatile Compression
6 Multiple		6 Other Pump
		7 Continuous Positive Airway Pressure
		8 Intermittent Positive Airway Pressure
		9 Continuous Negative Airway Pressure
		B Intermittent Negative Airway Pressure
		C Supersaturated
		D Impellar Pump
		Z No Qualifier

Figure 33-1 Values for the fifth character in the Extracorporeal Assistance and Performance Section

Exercise 33.1 – Duration Characters

For each table, identify the fifth-character. You might have to reference the Extracorporeal Assistance and Performance tables. The first one is done for you.

Table	Fifth Characters
1. 5A0	1, 2, 3, 4, 5
2. 5A2	_____
3. 5A1	_____

Function

The sixth character identifies the physiological function being assisted or performed. See Figure 33-1 for the values.

Qualifier

The seventh character represents the qualifier that specifies the type of equipment used. Figure 33-1 lists the values for the seventh character.

Extracorporeal Therapies Section of ICD-10-PCS

The seven characters in this section have the following meanings:

1	2	3	4	5	6	7
Section	Body system	Root operation	Body system	Duration	Function	Qualifier

Section

The first character value for extracorporeal therapies procedure codes is 6. This character value distinguishes therapies from assistance and performance.

Physiological System

The second character value, for physiological systems, in the Extracorporeal Therapies Section is A. As in the assistance and performance tables, the *A* is the only second position value used.

Root Operation

There are ten root operations for the Extracorporeal Therapies Section of ICD-10-PCS:

- **Atmospheric Control**—Extracorporeal control of atmospheric pressure and composition (value of 0)
- **Decompression**—Extracorporeal elimination of undissolved gas from body fluids (value of 1)
- **Electromagnetic therapy**—Extracorporeal treatment by electromagnetic rays (value of 2)
- **Hyperthermia**—Extracorporeal raising of body temperature (value of 3)
- **Hypothermia**—Extracorporeal lowering of body temperature (value of 4)
- **Pheresis**—Extracorporeal separation of blood products (value of 5)
- **Phototherapy**—Extracorporeal treatment by light rays (value of 6)
- **Ultrasound therapy**—Extracorporeal treatment by ultrasound (value of 7)
- **Ultraviolet light therapy**—Extracorporeal treatment by ultraviolet light (value of 8)
- **Shock wave therapy**—Extracorporeal treatment by shock waves (value of 9)

Body System

The fourth-character values in the Extracorporeal Therapies Section identify the body system in which the therapy is performed:

- Skin (value of 0)
- Urinary (value of 1)
- Central nervous (value of 2)
- Musculoskeletal (value of 3)
- Circulatory (value of 5)
- None (value of Z)

Reference Tables 6A0 through 6A9 in the ICD-10-PCS to determine the values relevant to each situation. Attention to documentation is essential for proper character value assignment.

Duration

The fifth character identifies the duration of the procedure. The two values are 0 for single and 1 for multiple.

Function

The sixth character is not specified for Extracorporeal Therapies and always has a value of Z.

Qualifier

The seventh character is Z for all the tables in this section except for the root operation of pheresis and ultrasound therapy. Here the seventh character is used to specify the blood component on which pheresis is performed or the anatomical structure on which the ultrasound therapy is performed. See Figure 33-2 for the values of the seventh character.

6: EXTRACORPOREAL THERAPIES
A: PHYSIOLOGICAL SYSTEMS

Duration Character 5	Function Character 6	Qualifier Character 7
0 Single 1 Multiple	Z No Qualifier	0 Erythrocytes 1 Leukocytes 2 Platelets 3 Plasma 4 Head and Neck Vessels 5 Heart 6 Peripheral Vessels 7 Other Vessels T Stem Cells, Cord Blood V Stem Cells, Hematopoietic Z No Qualifier

Figure 33-2 Values of the seventh character in the Extracorporeal Therapies Section

Summary

- The first-character value for Extracorporeal Assistance and Performance procedure codes is 5.

- The second-character value for the body system is A.

- There are three root operations for the Extracorporeal Assistance and Performance Section of the ICD-10-PCS: assistance, performance, and restoration.

- The fourth-character values in the Extracorporeal Assistance and Performance Section identify the body system.

- The fifth character in the Extracorporeal Assistance and Performance Section identifies the duration of the procedure.

- The sixth character in the Extracorporeal Assistance and Performance Section identifies the physiological function assisted or performed.

- The seventh character in the Extracorporeal Assistance and Performance Section is a qualifier, and the values vary according to the table used.
- The first character for Extracorporeal Therapies is 6.
- The second character for Extracorporeal Therapies is A.
- The third character for Extracorporeal Therapies identifies one of 10 root operations.
- The fourth character for Extracorporeal Therapies specifies the body system.
- The fifth character for Extracorporeal Therapies specifies the duration.
- The sixth character for Extracorporeal Therapies is always Z.
- The seventh character for Extracorporeal Therapies is always Z except for pheresis and ultrasound therapy.

Chapter Review

True/False: Indicate whether each statement is true (T) or false (F).

1. _____ There are three root operations for the Extracorporeal Assistance and Performance Section of the ICD-10-PCS.

2. _____ The fifth character in the Extracorporeal Assistance and Performance Section identifies the root operation.

3. _____ The second character in the Extracorporeal Assistance and Performance Section is for the duration of the procedure.

4. _____ *Atmospheric control* is defined as the extracorporeal control of atmospheric pressure and composition.

5. _____ Hyperthermia is the extracorporeal lowering of body temperature.

6. _____ The fourth character in the Extracorporeal Therapies Section is to report the body system in which the therapy is performed.

7. _____ In the Extracorporeal Therapies Section, the seventh-character value is always Z.

8. _____ Pheresis is the extracorporeal separation of blood products.

9. _____ In Table 6A7, the following values can represent the fifth character: 0, 1, and 2.

10. _____ In Table 6A5, the only fourth-character value is 5, Skin.

Coding Assignments

Instructions: For each procedure, select the correct ICD-10-PCS code.

1. atmospheric control of whole body single therapy _____

2. electromagnetic therapy of urinary system, single treatment _____

3. multiple electromagnetic therapy of central nervous system _____

4. hyperthermia of whole body, single treatment _____

5. multiple treatments for hypothermia of whole body   _____

6. pheresis of platelets, single duration   _____

7. multiple pheresis of erythrocytes   _____

8. pheresis of cord blood stem cells, multiple   _____

9. multiple treatment of phototherapy of skin   _____

10. single ultrasound therapy of heart   _____

11. single treatment of ultraviolet light therapy of skin   _____

12. single shock wave therapy for musculoskeletal system   _____

13. continuous assistance with cardiac output using pulsatile compression   _____

14. extracorporeal membrane oxygenation assistance, intermittent   _____

15. assistance with respiratory ventilation, less than 24 consecutive hours, intermittent positive airway pressure   _____

16. assistance with respiratory ventilation, for 48 consecutive hours, with continuous positive airway pressure   _____

17. assistance with respiratory ventilation, for 110 consecutive hours with continuous negative airway pressure   _____

18. manual, single performance of cardiac output   _____

19. respiratory ventilation for 10 consecutive hours   _____

20. single urinary filtration   _____

CHAPTER 34

Osteopathic, Chiropractic, and Other Procedure Sections

Chapter Outline

Objectives

At the conclusion of this chapter, the learner should be able to:

1. Define key terms presented in this chapter.
2. Discuss the root operations used for the Osteopathic, Other Procedures, and Chiropractic Sections of the ICD-10-PCS.
3. Identify the character meanings used for the Osteopathic, Other Procedures, and Chiropractic Sections of the ICD-10-PCS.
4. Identify the approach, devices, and qualifiers used in the Osteopathic, Other Procedures, and Chiropractic Sections of the ICD-10-PCS.
5. Code procedures from the Osteopathic, Other Procedures, and Chiropractic Sections of ICD-10-PCS.

Key Terms

chiropractor

osteopathic manipulation therapy (OMT)

other procedures

treatment

> **Reminder**
>
> *As you work through this chapter, you will need to have a copy of the ICD-10-PCS coding book to reference.*

Introduction

The Osteopathic, Other Procedures, and Chiropractic sections of the ICD-10-PCS are discussed here as a group due to the size of the sections and the nature of the procedures. Each section is discussed individually.

Osteopathic Section

Osteopathic services are sometimes referred to as **osteopathic manipulation therapy (OMT)**. OMT is manually guided therapy that is performed by a doctor of osteopathic medicine (DO) to improve physiological function.

The Osteopathic Section of the ICD-10-PCS is made up of one table. Osteopathic procedures are valued with the number 7 as the first character, the section identifier, for this group of codes.

Anatomical Region and Root Operation

The second position is identified as anatomical region and has a value of W. The third position is the root operation, of which there is only one: treatment. **Treatment** is defined by the ICD-10-PCS in the Osteopathic Table as manual treatment to eliminate or alleviate somatic dysfunction and related disorders. The treatment has a value of 0.

Body Region

For osteopathic manipulation, the body region or body area needs to be identified in the fourth-character position. The following notes the body regions and their values for this particular section:

- Head (value of 0)
- Cervical (value of 1)
- Thoracic (value of 2)
- Lumbar (value of 3)
- Sacrum (value of 4)
- Pelvis (value of 5)
- Lower extremities (value of 6)
- Upper extremities (value of 7)
- Rib cage (value of 8)
- Abdomen (value of 9)

Approach, Method, and Qualifier

For the fifth character position, the approach is always external because osteopathic services are noninvasive. The value is X in the fifth-character position.

The sixth character denotes the method. The method varies depending on the service rendered and appear in the table as follows:

- Articulatory—raising (value of 0)
- Fascial release (value of 1)
- General mobilization (value of 2)

- High velocity—low amplitude (value of 3)
- Indirect (value of 4)
- Low velocity—high amplitude (value of 5)
- Lymphatic pump (value of 6)
- Muscle energy—isometric (value of 7)
- Muscle energy—isotonic (value of 8)
- Other method (value of 9)

Any DO performing OMT services should clearly document the method used. Query the physician before assigning a character from the table if you have any doubt about which method was used.

The seventh-character position is not specified in the Osteopathic Section of the ICD-10-PCS, so the value for this position is Z, None.

Exercise 34.1 – Body Region/Method

For each code, identify the body region and the method of treatment. The first one is done for you.

Code	Body Region	Method
1. 7W00X1Z	head	fascial release
2. 7W08X2Z		
3. 7W03X8Z		
4. 7W05X6Z		
5. 7W01X4Z		

Other Procedures

In the section titled "Other Procedures," there are two tables. The first character, identifying the section, is 8.

The second characters have a value of C for indwelling device or E for physiological systems and anatomical regions.

Root Operation

In the tables for other procedures, the third-character position value is 0. The definition given in ICD-10-PCS for **Other Procedures** is methodologies that attempt to remediate or cure a disorder or disease.

Body Region

In the tables for other procedures, the body region character is in the fourth position. Tables 8C0 and 8E0 include values that are unique to each table.

Approach

The fifth-character value represents the approach. For Table 8C0, there is only one option for the fifth character, value X for external. For Table 8E0, the following approach values are used:

- X, External
- 0, Open
- 3, Percutaneous
- 4, Percutaneous endoscopic
- 7, Via natural or artificial opening
- 8, Via natural or artificial open endoscopic

Method

The tables for other procedures contain various methods not seen in other sections. For Table 8C0, in the sixth-character position, there is only one value used: 6, meaning collection. For Table 8E0, the following values are used in the sixth position:

- 0, Acupuncture
- 1, Therapeutic massage
- 6, Collection
- B, Computer assisted procedure
- C, Robotic assisted procedure
- D, Near infrared spectroscopy
- Y, Other Method

The use of these values is dependent on the procedure completed, and applicable values vary according to body region.

Qualifier

Character position 7 is the qualifier position. These alphanumeric character values identify additional information that clarifies the service rendered. For Table 8C0, the following values are used:

- J, Cerebrospinal fluid
- K, Blood
- L, Other fluid

For Table 8E0, many different values are used depending on the procedures completed.

Exercise 34.2 – Other Procedures

Define the code. The first one is done for you.

Code	Description
1. 8E09XY8	suture removal, head and neck region
2. 8E0VX63	_____
3. 8C01X6J4	_____
4. 8E0HXY9	_____
5. 8E0YXY8	_____

Chiropractic Section

A **chiropractor**, a doctor of chiropractic medicine, believes that all body functions are connected. For this reason, healing involves the entire body. Like the osteopathic and other procedure tables, the chiropractic table is very small. Chiropractic services are recognized by the first character value of 9. The second-character position is identified by a W, Anatomical region.

Root Operation

There is only one root operation in the chiropractic table: manipulation. This is identified in the third-character position with a value of B. Manipulation is a manual procedure that involves a directed thrust to move a joint past the physiological range of motion, without exceeding the anatomical limit.

Body Region

The fourth character indicates the body region on which the chiropractic manipulation is performed. The following body regions are noted in the chiropractic table:

- Head (value of 0)
- Cervical (value of 1)
- Thoracic (value of 2)
- Lumbar (value of 3)
- Sacrum (value of 4)
- Pelvis (value of 5)
- Lower extremities (value of 6)
- Upper extremities (value of 7)
- Rib cage (value of 8)
- Abdomen (value of 9)

Approach, Method, Qualifier

The approach in the Chiropractic Table in the ICD-10-PCS always has a value of X because the approach is always external. The approach is located in the fifth position.

The method of manipulation is identified in the sixth-character position. Several methods coded from this table are categorized as nonmanual, indirect visceral, extra-articular, direct visceral, long lever specific contact, short lever specific contact, long and short lever specific contact, mechanically assisted, and other method. The documentation should clearly state the method of manipulation.

The qualifier for the seventh position is always represented by *Z,* denoting no qualifier.

Internet Links

For definitions of osteopathic procedures and a better understanding of OMT, visit *http://www.osteopathic.org*

For more information on chiropractic medicine, visit *http://www.spineuniverse.com*

Summary

- Osteopathic services are sometimes referred to as osteopathic manipulation therapy (OMT).
- Osteopathic and chiropractic treatment services are defined differently in the ICD-10-PCS.

- For osteopathic manipulation, body region needs to be identified in the fourth-character position.
- The Other Procedures Section is identified by the first-character value of 8.
- Suture removal, piercings, and therapeutic massage are coded from the Other Procedures Tables.
- A chiropractor, or doctor of chiropractic medicine, believes that all body functions are connected. For this reason, healing involves the entire body.
- The method of chiropractic manipulation is identified in the sixth-character position.

Chapter Review

True/False: Indicate whether each statement is true (T) or false (F).

1. _____ A value of 8 is used to denote the Osteopathic Section of ICD-10-PCS.

2. _____ There are two tables for the Osteopathic Section.

3. _____ A value of 9 denotes the Chiropractic Section of ICD-10-PCS.

4. _____ In Table 9WB, many values are used for the seventh-character position.

5. _____ In code 8E0XXY8, the 8 denotes suture removal.

Coding Assignments

Instructions: For each procedure, select the correct ICD-10-PCS code.

Diagnosis   *Code*

1. low velocity-high amplitude for osteopathic treatment
    of the pelvis   _____

2. examination of female reproductive system   _____

3. lymphatic pump, osteopathic treatment of the left arm   _____

4. fascial release using osteopathic manipulation of the wrist   _____

5. ear piercing (ear lobe)   _____

6. chiropractic extra-articular treatment of shoulder region   _____

7. acupuncture   _____

8. suture removal, left eyebrow   _____

9. chiropractic treatment of lumbar region using long lever
    specific contact   _____

10. osteopathic manipulation of the lumbar spine using
    general mobilization   _____

11. chiropractic manipulation of the pelvic region, indirect
    visceral   _____

12. therapeutic massage   _____

13. nonmanual chiropractic manipulation of the head   _____

14. suture removal, right thigh   _____

15. indirect OMT of sacrum   _____

Case Studies

Instructions: Review each case study and select the correct ICD-10-PCS code.

CASE 1

Lucy is a 40-year-old female who has been suffering with severe headaches and low back pain for the past month. She has tried ibuprophen and acetominophin without success. Her doctor prescribed medication for migraine headaches, but she still has much pain. She has decided to try acupuncture. No contraindications are noted, so we proceeded.

Procedure: 20 needles with electrical stimulation for 30 minutes.

ICD-10-PCS Code Assignment: _____

CASE 2

Chris is a 5-year-old male who presents today to have 4 stitches removed from his forehead. Ten days ago he was playing on his swing set and fell off the slide, hitting his head on the side of the slide and lacerating the site. He was taken to the emergency room, where 4 stitches were placed. He is here in the office now to have the wound checked and sutures removed.

The wound is 2.5 cm long and healed nicely. No redness, infection, or drainage is noticed. The 4 sutures were removed without a problem.

ICD-10-PCS Code Assignment: _____

Imaging, Nuclear Medicine, and Radiation Oncology Sections

CHAPTER

35

Chapter Outline

Objectives
Key Terms
Introduction
Imaging Section
Nuclear Medicine Section
Radiation Oncology Section

Internet Links
Summary
Chapter Review
Coding Assignments
Case Studies

Objectives

At the conclusion of this chapter, the learner should be able to:

1. Understand the key terms presented in this chapter.
2. Describe the codes associated with the Imaging, the Nuclear Medicine, and the Radiation Oncology Sections of the ICD-10-PCS.
3. Identify the seven-character codes and the differences among the sections of radiology.
4. List the types of imaging procedures noted in the ICD-10-PCS.
5. Code procedures from the Imaging, the Nuclear Medicine, and the Radiation Oncology Sections of the ICD-10-PCS.

Key Terms

computerized tomography (CT scan)

contrast material

fluoroscopy

high osmolar contrast material (HOCM)

isotope

low osmolar contrast material (LOCM)

magnetic resonance imaging (MRI)

modality

nonimaging nuclear medicine assay

Reminder

As you work through this chapter, you will need to have a copy of the ICD-10-PCS coding book to reference.

nonimaging nuclear medicine probe

nonimaging nuclear medicine uptake

nuclear medicine

plain radiography

planar nuclear medicine imaging

positron emission tomographic imaging (PET)

radiation oncology (rad onc)

radioactive isotopes

radiologic technician

radiologist

radiology

radionuclide

radiopharmaceutical

systemic nuclear medicine therapy

tomographic nuclear medicine imaging (tomo)

ultrasonography

Introduction

Radiology is the study of X-rays, high-frequency sound waves, and high-strength magnetic fields, and it sometimes includes the use of radioactive compounds to diagnose and/or treat disease or injuries. A **radiologist** is the doctor whose specialty is radiology. The person who is specially trained to use the equipment that generates the pictures or studies is known as a **radiologic technician**.

Unlike ICD-9-CM Volume 3, the ICD-10-PCS has broken down the radiology services into three distinct sections with their own tables: the Imaging Section, the Nuclear Medicine Section, and the Radiation Oncology Section. We discuss each section separately in this chapter.

Imaging Section

The imaging procedure codes include codes for plain X-ray services, ultrasounds, fluoroscopy, CT scans, and MRI scans. The ICD-10-PCS Imaging Section codes begin with the letter *B* in the first character position to identify imaging codes.

Body System and Type

The second character for the Imaging codes identifies the body system on which the service is performed.

The third character is the type or the root type of imaging procedure. The types of imaging procedures are as follows:

- **Plain radiography**—Standard X-ray, with planar display of an image. The image is captured and the image developed on photographic or photoconductive plates (value of 0).

- **Computerized tomography (CT scan)**—Multiplanar images that have been computer reformatted. The multiple images develop from the capture of multiple exposures of external ionizing radiation (value of 2).

- **Ultrasonography**—A real-time display of images of anatomy or flow information developed from the capture of reflected and attenuated high-frequency sound waves (value of 4).

- **Fluoroscopy**—External ionizing radiation on a fluorescent screen captures a single plane or biplane, real-time image that can also be stored by digital or analog means (value of 1).

- **Magnetic resonance imaging (MRI)**—Multiplanar images developed from the capture of radio frequency signals emitted by nuclei in a particular body site excited within a magnetic field that can produce a computer-formatted digital display of the images (value of 3).

The various types are referenced in the ICD-10-PCS Index to locate the appropriate table to be referenced for a code selection.

Exercise 35.1 – Tables

From the Imaging Section, identify the table to be referenced. The first one is done for you.

Imaging Section	*Table*
1. CT scan of the heart	B22, Reference CT scan
2. fluoroscopy of the veins	_____
3. ultrasound of the CNS	_____
4. plain radiography of the skull and facial bones	_____
5. MRI of the urinary system	_____

Body Part

The fourth-character position identifies the body part being worked on. Attention to detail is important in this value choice because very specific sites are noted in this column of the tables for the Imaging Section.

Contrast

Contrast material might be injected when some of the imaging services are performed. The use of **contrast material** in the imaging facilitates the identification of abnormalities in the body due to image density. The fifth character identifies whether contrast material is used and whether the material was **high osmolar contrast material (HOCM)** or **low osmolar contrast material (LOCM)**. High osmolar contrast material has a higher level of particle concentration than normal body fluids. The low osmolar contrast material has a lower-level particle concentration than normal body fluids.

Qualifier

The sixth- and seventh-character values identify further detail as needed. Character value 6 may identify unenhanced followed by enhanced, or laser. Typically for this section, the value is Z, None. The character value for the seventh position is always Z, None for the Imaging Section.

Exercise 35.2 – Imaging

Match the item in column 1 with the definition or description in column 2.

_____ **1.** radiologist	**a.** single- or biplane real-time images that can be stored digitally or by analog means
_____ **2.** Imaging Section	**b.** Imaging Section is denoted with this
_____ **3.** CT scans	**c.** always Z
_____ **4.** character 4 in the Imaging Section character	**d.** multiplanar images that have been computer reformatted to capture multiple images

(continued)

_____ **5.** Value of B	**e.** lower levels of particle concentration than normal body fluids
_____ **6.** HOCM	**f.** doctor who specializes in radiology
_____ **7.** LOCM	**g.** might be injected at the time an imaging service is performed
_____ **8.** fluoroscopy	**h.** body part being worked on
_____ **9.** contrast material	**i.** codes for ultrasounds are found here
_____ **10.** character 7 in the Imaging Section	**j.** higher levels of particle concentration than in normal body fluids

Nuclear Medicine Section

Nuclear medicine treats and diagnoses diseases using small amounts of radioactive material called **radioactive isotopes**, which create an image. The value identifying the Nuclear Medicine Section is the letter C.

Body System

The body system on which a nuclear medicine procedure is performed is identified by the second-character position. The value depends on the part of the body being tested and the table being referenced.

Type

The third character in the code identifies the type of procedure being performed. The following identifies the types used in the Nuclear Medicine Section, along with their values.

- **Planar nuclear medicine imaging**—Introduction of radioactive materials into the body for single-plane display of images, developed from the capture of radioactive emissions (value of 1).

- **Tomographic (tomo) nuclear medicine imaging**—Introduction of radioactive materials into the body for three-dimensional display of images, developed from the capture of radioactive emissions (value of 2).

- **Positron emission tomographic (PET) imaging**—Introduction of radioactive materials into the body for three-dimensional display of images, developed from the simultaneous capture, 180 degrees apart, of radioactive emissions (value of 3).

- **Nonimaging nuclear medicine uptake**—Introduction of radioactive material into the body for measurements of organ function, from the detection of radioactive emissions (value of 4).

- **Nonimaging nuclear medicine probe**—Introduction of radioactive materials into the body for the study of distribution and fate of certain substances by the detection of radioactive emissions; or alternatively, measurement of absorption of radioactive emissions from an external source (value of 5).

- **Nonimaging nuclear medicine assay**—Introduction of radioactive materials into the body for the study of body fluids and blood elements, by the detection of radioactive emissions (value of 6).

- **Systemic nuclear medicine therapy**—Introduction of radioactive material into the body for treatment (value of 7).

Body Part or Region

The fourth character in the Nuclear Medicine Section identifies the body part or region being studied. The values for each body part or region vary depending on the table being referenced, but it is the same within one body system or region.

EXAMPLE: In the cardiovascular system, the heart is valued in the fourth position as a 6.

C, Nuclear medicine

2, Heart

1, Planar nuclear medicine imaging

Body Part: Character 4	Radionuclide: Character 5	Qualifier: Character 6	Qualifier: Character 7
6, Heart, right and left	1, Technetium 99m (Tc-99m)	Z, None	Z, None
	Y, Other radionuclide		

In the gastrointestinal system, a value of 6, in the fourth character position, identifies the liver and spleen.

C, Nuclear medicine

F, Hepatobiliary system and pancreas

1, Planar nuclear medicine imaging

Body Part: Character 4	Radionuclide: Character 5	Qualifier: Character 6	Qualifier: Character 7
4, Gallbladder	1, Technetium 99m (Tc-99m)	Z, None	Z, None
5, Liver	Y, Other radionuclide		
6, Liver and spleen			
C, Hepatobiliary system, all			

Radionuclide

A **radionuclide**, also called a radioactive isotope, or **radiopharmaceutical**, is a radioactive substance that can either be found in nature or human-made and that is the source of the radiation causing the emissions so that an image can be produced. These radionuclides indicate the location, size, or function of organs, tissues, or vessels. Radioactive material is used to aid in the determinations made with regard to the patient's condition. The radionuclides are represented in the fifth-character position in the nuclear medicine tables. Some of the radionuclides currently being used are:

- Technetium 99m (Tc-99m, value of 1).
- Cobalt 58 (Co-58, value of 7).
- Indium 111 (In-111, value of D).
- Iodine 125 (I-125, value of H).
- Chromium (Cr-51, value of W).

The Y value in the tables presented in the Nuclear Medicine Section indicates Other radionuclide. This value is provided for the newly approved radionuclides that have not yet been assigned a value. Reference the tables for the specific character values applicable to each table.

Qualifier

The sixth- and seventh-character positions are both qualifiers. For the Nuclear Medicine Section of the ICD-10-PCS, a Z value is always in these positions because there are no specified qualifiers for this section at this time.

Exercise 35.3 – Nuclear Medicine

Indicate whether each statement is true (T) or false (F).

1. _____ Images found in a nuclear medicine test can also be treated by nuclear medicine.

2. _____ The body system being treated with nuclear medicine is valued at Z as a placeholder.

3. _____ A nonimaging uptake introduces radioactive materials into the body so that simultaneous images can be captured.

4. _____ PET stands for positron emission testing.

5. _____ Radioactive seeds planted in the prostate to treat prostate cancer are considered systemic therapy and are coded to the Nuclear Medicine Section of the ICD-10-PCS.

6. _____ Character 4 in a nuclear medicine code indicates the body system or region being treated.

7. _____ The value of each body part or region varies depending on the table being referenced.

8. _____ I-111 is a radiopharmaceutical.

9. _____ Code CB221ZZ indicates a PET scan of the chest.

10. _____ Code C72YYZX indicates that Tc-99 was used in a tomo of the spleen.

Radiation Oncology Section

Radiation oncology (rad onc) is a form of radiology that is therapeutic as opposed to diagnostic in nature. The patient is typically undergoing treatment for a malignant neoplasm; the aim is for the radiation to eradicate or shrink the neoplasm or obstruction, relieving pain. Radiation oncology codes begin with the section value of D.

Body System

The second character identifies the body system being treated:

- Central and peripheral nervous system (value of 0)
- Lymphatic and hematologic system (value of 7)
- Eye (value of 8)
- Ear, nose, mouth, and throat (value of 9)
- Respiratory system (value of B)

- Gastrointestinal system (value of D)
- Hepatobiliary system and pancreas (value of F)
- Endocrine system (value of G)
- Skin (value of H)
- Breast (value of M)
- Musculoskeletal system (value of P)
- Urinary system (value of T)
- Female reproductive system (value of U)
- Male reproductive system (value of V)
- Anatomical regions (value of W)

Modality

Modality in medicine means a certain protocol, therapeutic method, or agent, such as chemotherapy, brachytherapy, or stereotactic radiosurgery. Modalities are valued in the third-character position.

Body Part

The fourth character identifies the specific body part in the system that was identified in the second position and that is the target of the radiation therapy.

EXAMPLE:

Body System: Character 2	Body Part: Character 4
0, Central and peripheral nervous system	0, Brain
	1, Brain stem
	6, Spinal cord
	7, Peripheral nerve
7, Lymphatic and hematologic system	0, Bone marrow
	1, Thymus
	2, Spleen
	3, Lymphatics, neck
	4, Lymphatics, axillary
	5, Lymphatics, thorax
	6, Lymphatics, abdomen
	7, Lymphatics, pelvis
	8, Lymphatics, inguinal

The fourth-character value changes as the body system changes.

EXAMPLE: The value of 0 in the central and peripheral nervous system indicates the brain, whereas in the lymphatic and hematologic system, the value of 0 indicates bone marrow.

Modality Qualifier

The fifth position is for the modality qualifier. This position further clarifies the radiation modality, as identified in the third character. Examples include the following.

EXAMPLE:

Modality Qualifier: Character 5
0, Photons < 1 MeV (mega-electron volt)
1, Photons 1–10 MeV
2, Photons > 10 MeV
3, Electrons
4, Heavy particles (protons, ions)
5, Neutrons

Isotope

Character 6 identifies the isotope. An **isotope** is one of two or more atoms that contain the same atomic number (protons) but have different mass numbers (neutrons) in the nucleus. The same radioactive isotopes discussed in the Nuclear Medicine Section are found in the Radiation Oncology Section, and they are identified in the sixth-character position.

Qualifier

Character 7 is a qualifier position. There is no specified qualifier for the radiation oncology section, so the value is always none, indicated by the letter Z.

Internet Links

For more information on nuclear medicine, diagnostic radiology, or interventional radiology, visit *http://www.radiologyinfo.org*

For more information on nuclear medicine, visit *http://www.interactive.snm.org*

For more information on radiation oncology, visit *http://www.cancercenter.com* and search the term *radiation oncology*.

Summary

- A radiologist is the medical doctor whose specialty is radiology.

- The imaging procedure codes include codes for plain X-ray services, ultrasounds, fluoroscopy, CT scans, and MRI scans.

- The use of contrast material in the imaging facilitates the identification of abnormalities in the body due to image density.

- Nuclear medicine treats and diagnoses diseases using small amounts of radioactive material called radioactive isotopes.

- Radiation oncology is a form of radiology that is therapeutic as opposed to diagnostic in nature.

- The patient is typically undergoing treatment for a malignant neoplasm; the aim of the radiation therapy is to eradicate or shrink the neoplasm or obstruction, relieving pain.

Chapter Review

Multiple Choice

Select the best answer that completes the statement or answers the question.

1. Which of the following is the study of X-rays, high-frequency sound waves, and high-strength magnetic fields that sometimes involves the use of radioactive compounds to diagnose and/or treat disease or injuries?
   - a. Nuclear medicine
   - b. Radiotherapy
   - c. Radiology
   - d. Radiation oncology

2. The character value B indicates which section of the ICD-10-PCS?
   - a. Radiation Oncology
   - b. Nuclear Medicine
   - c. Imaging
   - d. Radiotherapy

3. A(n) _____ is a real-time display of images of anatomy developed from the capture of reflected and attenuated high-frequency sound waves.
   - a. CT scan
   - b. ultrasonography
   - c. fluoroscopy
   - d. MRI scan

4. _____ treat(s) and diagnose(s) diseases using small amounts of radioactive material called_____, which create(s) an image.
   - a. Radiopharmaceuticals, radiation
   - b. Radioactive isotopes, radiation
   - c. Radiopharmaceuticals, nuclear medicine
   - d. Nuclear medicine, radioactive isotopes

5. Which of the following is a single-plane display of images, developed from the capture of radioactive emissions after the introduction of radioactive materials?
   - a. planar imaging
   - b. tomo
   - c. PET
   - d. nonimaging assay

6. A(n) _____ is a three-dimensional display of images produced after introduction of radioactive materials. The radioactive materials allow the capture of radioactive emissions to produce these images.
   - a. nonimaging probe
   - b. tomo
   - c. PET
   - d. nonimaging assay

7. Which of the following is a form of radiology that is therapeutic as opposed to diagnostic in nature?
   - a. oncology
   - b. chemotherapy
   - c. radiation oncology
   - d. isotope therapy

8. In a patient being treated with stereotactic other photon radiosurgery of the ovaries, the modality qualifier is:

    a. C.
    b. D.
    c. F.
    d. G.

9. Brachytherapy is a type of:

    a. isotope.
    b. qualifier.
    c. modifier.
    d. modality.

10. In the Radiation Oncology Section of the ICD-10-PCS, the respiratory system is represented by the character value _____, and the diaphragm is represented by the character value _____.

    a. 9, B
    b. B, 9
    c. D, 8
    d. B, 8

Coding Assignments

Instructions: For each procedure, select the correct ICD-10-PCS code.

Diagnosis	Code
1. routine fetal ultrasound, first trimester, single fetus	_____
2. CT scan of the lumbar spine, no contrast	_____
3. MRI of the pelvis, no contrast	_____
4. portable X-ray study of the right radius/ulna shaft, standard series	_____
5. upper GI scan with Tc-99m	_____
6. nonimaging assay of blood using I-125	_____
7. beam radiation of the brain stem, photons 1-10 meV	_____
8. stereotactic gamma beam radiosurgery of the larynx	_____
9. ultrasound of the scrotum	_____
10. X-ray of the lumbosacral joint	_____
11. fluoroscopy of the upper GI tract and small bowel with contrast	_____
12. bilateral CT scan of the lungs with densitometry and high osmolar contrast	_____
13. uniplanar scan of the spine using technetium 99m	_____
14. tomo scan of parathyroid gland using T1-201	_____

15. hyperthermia radiation treatment of the pelvic region   _____

16. carbon 11 PET scan of the brain with qualification   _____

17. nonimaging probe of lower extremities   _____

18. PET scan of the brain using technetium 99m   _____

19. whole body phosphorus 32 administration with risk to
    hematopoetic system   _____

20. MRI of the thyroid, no contrast   _____

Case Studies

Instructions: Review each case study and select the correct ICD-10-PCS code.

CASE 1

This is a 38-year-old-male who presents with a diagnosis of Kaposi's sarcoma, lungs and the diaphragm. The patient will be receiving two separate treatments today.

TREATMENT: Radiation therapy

PROCEDURE PERFORMED: Radiation treatment delivery

INDICATIONS FOR PROCEDURE: Kaposi's sarcoma, lung, with mets to diaphragm

PROCEDURE: Two separate treatment areas, right lung and the diaphragm. Each area was properly marked, and beam radiation of 20 MeV photons was delivered to each area, first the lungs, then the diaphragm.

Patient tolerated his treatment well and will return in two days for the next treatment.

ICD-10-PCS Code Assignment: _____

CASE 2

Mr. Afina presents today with a very painful, barky cough. He said this has been going on for the last two days and he feels terrible. He has been running a fever and is feeling weak. After a physical exam, Dr. Divine ordered a chest X-ray with AP/PA and lateral views. This X-ray confirmed the diagnosis of pneumonia, and Mr. Afina was sent to the hospital immediately.

ICD-10-PCS Code Assignment: _____

CASE 3

Caryn is a 40-year-old female who presented to the doctor's office with a recent change in her mental status. Her doctor wants an MRI of the brain with and without contrast—STAT.

Multiplanar, multisequence imaging of the brain was performed. There is an abnormality of the right frontal region. Postadministration of gadolinium contrast, there is an increased signal on T2 weighted images within the left basal ganglia. The appearance is typical of a focal basal ganglionic infarct on the left.

IMPRESSION: 2-cm lesion of right frontal area

Basal ganglia, likely ischemic in nature, left

ICD-10-PCS Code Assignment: _____

Chapter Outline

Objectives

At the conclusion of this chapter, the learner should be able to:

1. Define the key terms used in the ICD-10-PCS Physical Rehabilitation and Diagnostic Audiology Section.
2. Identify the character meanings used in the Physical Rehabilitation and Diagnostic Audiology Section.
3. Discuss the root types used in this section.
4. Identify the body system and body region to which the Physical Rehabilitation and Diagnostic Audiology codes apply.
5. Code procedures found in the ICD-10-PCS Physical Rehabilitation and Diagnostic Audiology Section.

Key Terms

assessment
caregiver training
fittings
treatment
type

> **Reminder**
>
> *As you work through this chapter, you will need to have a copy of the ICD-10-PCS coding book to reference.*

Introduction

Physical rehabilitation encompasses physical therapy, occupational therapy, and speech-language pathology. The focuses of these rehabilitation areas are different, but they are grouped under the physical rehabilitation title. Because different specialties are involved, the codes reflect different forms of treatment. Diagnostic audiology is included in this section because of the nature of the services provided, such as device fitting and rehabilitative treatment for cochlear implant patients. Careful attention to detail when coding from this section is critical.

> **Note:**
>
> *Osteopathic and chiropractic procedures are located in separate sections and are not discussed in this chapter.*

Physical Rehabilitation and Diagnostic Audiology Section

All codes found in the ICD-10-PCS Physical Rehabilitation and Diagnostic Audiology Section begin with the first character of F. To locate a table in the Index, the coder references either *rehabilitation* or *diagnostic audiology.*

Section Qualifier

The section qualifier, the second character in the coding for this section, is the value that determines whether one is coding for rehabilitation or for diagnostic audiology. At this time, the value 0 indicates rehabilitation, and the diagnostic audiology value is 1.

Type

The third character in this section designates type. The **type** is similar to the root operation in the Medicine and Surgery Section. Because these procedures are rehabilitative or diagnostic, the root *operation* does not apply but the idea is the same.

There are 14 root type values in the Physical Rehabilitation and Diagnostic Audiology Section, and they can be classified into four basic categories:

- **Treatment**—The use of specific, clearly defined activities or methods that are designed to improve and/or restore the performance of necessary functions, compensate for dysfunction, and/or reduce debilitating conditions

- **Caregiver training**—Educational in nature, the teaching of the caregiver skills and knowledge necessary to interact with and properly assist the patient

- **Fittings**—Fabricating, modifying, and/or designing a splint, orthotics, prosthesis, hearing aid, or other rehabilitative device for application

- **Assessment**—The initial and follow-up evaluations of the patient's diagnosis, care plan, need for treatment, and documentation related to these services

Some of the 14 root types include motor and/or nerve function assessment, activities of daily living assessment, motor treatment, device fitting, and hearing aid assessment. As with other sections in the ICD-10-PCS, the definitions for this character position are given next to each of the root types and should be referenced before a code is assigned.

Body System and Region

The fourth-character number identifies the body region and/or system on which the procedure is performed. This character position of the ICD-10-PCS must always be valued. A specific body part may not be identified within the table, but the character place still needs to be identified. The character Z is used if this is the case. The body part or region is identified, if applicable. However, in some cases the code description does not single out just one body system or region but encompasses the body as a whole.

EXAMPLE: A person is going through occupational therapy to be able to go back to work after an injury. The coder references this table:

F, Physical rehabilitation and diagnostic audiology

0, Rehabilitation

8, Activities of daily living treatment: Exercise or activities to facilitate functional competence for activities of daily living.

Body System and Region: Character 4	Type Qualifier: Character 5	Equipment: Character 6	Qualifier: Character 7
Z, None	7, Vocational activities and functional community or work reintegration skills	B, Physical agents C, Mechanical D, Electrotherapeutic E, Orthosis F, Assistive, adaptive, supportive, or protective G, Aerobic endurance and conditioning U, Prosthesis Y, Other equipment Z, None	Z, None

The code assignment for the patient is F08Z7ZZ. Character 4 for the body system or region does not apply because the therapist is treating the whole body.

Type Qualifier

The fifth character denotes the type qualifier and identifies the procedure performed in more detail.

EXAMPLE: Code F13ZHZZ indicates:

- F, Physical rehabilitation and diagnostic audiology

- 1, Diagnostic audiology

- 3, Hearing assessment—measurement of hearing and related functions

- Z, Body system and region—no character identified because it is inferred that the ear is the region being evaluated

- H, Acoustic reflex threshold—the procedure being performed

- Z, No equipment

- Z, No further qualifier needed

Equipment and Qualifier

Character 6 identifies the equipment used in the therapy performed. There is no defined value for the equipment used, but broad categories are specified.

EXAMPLE: In Table F06, the value M indicates augmentative/alternative communication, whereas P indicates computer and K, audiovisual. This is the same in Table F01. The tables need to be referenced for additional values.

Character 7 is always Z in the Rehabilitative and Diagnostic Audiology Section because the qualifier always has a value of none.

Internet Links

For more information on physical therapy, visit *http://www.apta.org/AM/Template.cfm* or *http://www.physicaltherapy.about.com*

Summary

- Physical, occupational, and speech-language pathology are coded to this section of the ICD-10-PCS.
- The coder needs to reference *rehabilitation* or *diagnostic audiology* to locate the appropriate table for code assignment.
- The section value for the Physical Rehabilitation and Diagnostic Audiology Section is F.
- Section qualifier, root type, body system and region, type qualifier, equipment, and qualifier are the remaining values identified in the seven-digit code.
- There are four basic categories of rehabilitation and diagnostic audiology procedures.
- The seventh character for the codes in this section is always Z.

Chapter Review

Completion: For the underlined character in each code, identify the character type and state the meaning. The first one is done for you.

Code	Character Type	Meaning
1. F14Z3PZ	Type qualifier	Binaural hearing aid
2. F0DZ3MZ		
3. F09Z1KZ		
4. F06Z4QZ		
5. F07B6CZ		
6. F00Z02Z		
7. F026GYZ		
8. F01G0UZ		
9. F0DZ05Z		
10. F14Z65Z		

Coding Assignments

Instructions: For each procedure, select the correct ICD-10-PCS code.

1. pure tone audiometry, air and bone _____

2. Bekesy audiometry assessment using audiometer _____

3. cerumen management _____

4. voice analysis of voice prosthetic _____

5. verbal assessment of patient pain level _____

6. treatment of motor speech using voice analysis _____

7. motor treatment of shoulders and upper back using weights (therapeutic exercise) _____

8. individual fitting of left eye prosthesis _____

9. speech assessment, distorted speech _____

10. electrophysiologic facial nerve function assessment _____

11. physical therapy for range of motion and mobility of right hip, no equipment used _____

12. biosensory feedback, perpetual processing assessment _____

13. voice analysis _____

14. auditory processing treatment using computer _____

15. speech word recognition assessment _____

16. assessment of electrophysiologic auditory evoked potentials _____

17. vestibular treatment for musculoskeletal system, postural control _____

18. tone decay hearing assessment using tympanometer _____

19. electrotherapeutic wheelchair mobility, motor treatment _____

20. mechanical gait training _____

Case Studies

Instructions: Review each case study and select the correct ICD-10-PCS code.

CASE 1

This is an 81-year-old female who had a CVA 3 weeks ago. She is here for a speech assessment.

ASSESSMENT: Patient underwent testing for receptive/expressive language function. Levels were evaluated. She is showing vast improvement from our last testing, done 12 days ago. Formal report to follow.

Total time with this patient was 60 minutes

ICD-10-PCS Code Assignment: _____

CASE 2

This 78-year-old male is status post hip replacement 6 days ago. He is now at the Sunny Hill Rehabilitation Center where we are currently working on physical and occupational therapy so that he will be able to live at home and function normally.

This patient is working on being able to groom and dress himself. He is very anxious to able to use the shower but would be unable to get into his tub unassisted. Today we worked on walking to the closet/dresser, walking back to the bed, and getting his clothes on unassisted. He did very well, though he tired easily, and we did not get to the bathroom to brush teeth or wash up. The assessment took 60 minutes.

ICD-10-PCS Code Assignment: _____

CASE 3

Patient presents today for therapy for medial meniscus tear, left knee.

Therapy at today's visit included gait and functional ambulation training.

Total time of visit, 35 minutes. Patient tolerated well and was given exercises to perform at home. Looking for increase in strength and ROM at next visit in 2 days.

ICD-10-PCS Code Assignment: _____

Mental Health and Substance Abuse Treatment

Chapter Outline

Objectives

At the conclusion of this chapter, the learner should be able to:

1. Define key terms presented in this chapter.
2. Discuss the root operations used for the Mental Health and Substance Abuse Sections of the ICD-10-PCS.
3. Identify the character meanings used for the Mental Health and Substance Abuse Sections.
4. Code procedures from these sections.

Key Terms

abuse

addiction

Diagnostic and Statistical Manual of Mental Disorders (DSM-IV-TR)

mental disorders

psychiatrist

psychiatry

Reminder

As you work through this chapter, you will need to have a copy of the ICD-10-PCS coding book to reference.

Introduction

Mental disorders are disorders that affect the ability of a person to function in a healthy, socially acceptable way. **Psychiatry** is the branch of medicine that deals with mental disorders, which include emotional and behavioral disorders. The **psychiatrist** is a medical doctor who administers treatment for patients with mental, emotional, and behavioral disorders. Psychologists and social workers also counsel and treat people with mental disorders in a variety of health-care settings, but these health-care professionals are not able to prescribe medications.

The **Diagnostic and Statistical Manual of Mental Disorders (DSM-IV-TR)** is the main reference guide for mental health professionals when assigning a diagnosis code to a patient encounter. A mental disorder can manifest itself at different levels of severity in different patients. The DSM-IV-TR helps define conditions for health-care professionals to appropriately identify a disorder.

Both the Mental Health Section and the Substance Abuse Treatment Section are presented in this chapter, and they are discussed separately.

Mental Health Section

The Mental Health Section of the ICD-10-PCS is identified with the first-character value of G. All services coded from this section begin with this letter.

Although the second-character place is usually identified with a value identifying specific data, in the mental health tables, this value is always Z, None. The second character position needs to be held, but a specific value in the position does not apply in this section.

EXAMPLE:

G, Mental health

Z, None

1, Psychological tests: The administration and interpretation of standardized psychological tests and measurement instruments for the assessment of psychological function.

Type

The type holds the third position in the codes. In the case of mental health, the type is the type of service provided, such as counseling, family psychotherapy, individual psychotherapy, or crisis intervention, to name a few. Each of these procedure types has a character value, and the definition is provided next to the type.

EXAMPLE:

G, Mental health

Z, None

3, Medication management: Monitoring and adjusting the use of medications for the treatment of mental disorders.

The value 3, Medication management, is the root type, and the description that follows it is the definition assigned to the term *medical management* in the ICD-10-PCS.

Type Qualifier

The fourth character in the Mental Health Section of the ICD-10-PCS is the type qualifier. The type qualifier, the fourth character of a code, is used to indicate more information about the procedure type, the third character of a code.

EXAMPLE: Stan came in today for vocational counseling, which lasted 30 minutes.

G, Mental health

Z, None

6, Counseling

Type Qualifier: Character 4	Qualifier: Character 5	Qualifier: Character 6	Qualifier: Character 7
0 Educational 1 Vocational 3 Other counseling	Z None	Z None	Z None

Reference the main term *counseling* in the Index, which guides you to Table GZ6. Character 4 lists the options: 0, Educational; 1, Vocational; 3, Other Counseling. Stan is receiving vocational counseling; so you identify the type of counseling with the type qualifier of 1 for vocational counseling.

> **Note:**
>
> *The type qualifier character 4 is different for each table. In Table GZ1, for instance, the type qualifier of 0 identifies developmental psychological tests. In Table GZ5, the type qualifier of 0 identifies interactive individual psychotherapy.*

Qualifier

Characters 5, 6, and 7 are not specified in the Mental Health Section, and they always carry a value of Z, None, at this time. The *Z* must be used as a placeholder because all codes are reported with seven characters.

Exercise 37.1 – Mental Health Coding

Match the ICD-10-PCS code in column one with the code description given in column two.

ICD-10-PCS Code

_____ **1.** GZ60ZZZ

_____ **2.** GZFZZZZ

_____ **3.** GZGZZZZ

_____ **4.** GZ3ZZZZ

_____ **5.** GZB2ZZZ

Code Description

a. bilateral electroconvulsive therapy for single seizure

b. hypnosis

c. medication management for depression

d. educational counseling

e. narcosynthesis

Substance Abuse Treatment Section

In general **abuse** is described as the use of a substance (e.g., alcohol, drugs, or tobacco) in excess without having a physical dependence. The abuse may or may not be to the point where it is having an impact on the patient's daily life. **Addiction** is described as abuse to the point where a person cannot get by without the substance of choice (e.g., alcohol, drugs, or tobacco); the body has become physically dependent on the substance. Patients seek care for both abuse and addiction.

The section identifier for the Substance Abuse Treatment Section is H. This means that the H is located in the first-character position.

The second character value is for the body type. Because this value does not apply in this section, the value of none is indicated by Z.

Type

Like the third-character position in the Mental Health Section, the type in the Substance Abuse Treatment Section identifies the service performed. These services include detoxification services, individual counseling, group counseling, individual psychotherapy, family counseling, medication management, and pharmacotherapy. The definition of each service is provided in the tables, just as discussed in the Mental Health Section.

Type Qualifier

The type qualifier, the fourth character, further explains the type, the third character.

> **EXAMPLE:** Carrie has been coming in for the past two months to take part in our behavioral group counseling session. The group addresses tobacco abuse. This would be reported using the following:
>
> H Substance abuse treatment
>
> Z None
>
> 4 Group Counseling

Type Qualifier: Character 4	Qualifier: Character 5	Qualifier: Character 6	Qualifier: Character 7
0 Cognitive	Z None	Z None	Z None
1 Behavioral			
2 Cognitive-behavioral			
3 12-Step			
4 Interpersonal			
5 Vocational			
6 Psychoeducation			
7 Motivational enhancement			
8 Confrontational			
9 Continuing care			
B Spiritual			
C Pre/Post-test infectious disease			

The service provided to Carrie is coded as HZ41ZZZ to reflect behavioral group counseling.

Qualifiers

Characters 5, 6, and 7 are not specified in the Substance Abuse Treatment Section and always carry a value of Z, None, at this time. The Z must be used as a placeholder because all codes are reported with seven characters.

Internet Links

For information on different types of abuse, visit *http://www.nlm.nih.gov/medlineplus/ substanceabuseproblems.html*

For more information on mental disorders, visit *http://www.apa.org*, the homepage of the American Psychiatric Association.

Summary

- Mental disorders are disorders that affect the ability of a person to function in a healthy, socially acceptable way.

- A similar mental disorder can manifest itself in different levels of severity in different patients.

- The Mental Health Section of the ICD-10-PCS is identified with the first character value of G.

- Characters 5, 6, and 7 are not specified in the Mental Health and Substance Abuse Treatment sections. The place values always carry a value of Z, None, at this time. The Z must be used as a placeholder because all codes are reported with seven characters.

- Abuse, in this case, is described as the use of a substance (e.g., alcohol, drugs, or tobacco) in excess without physical dependency.

- Addiction is described as abuse to the point where a person cannot get by without the substance of choice (e.g., alcohol, drugs, or tobacco). The body has become physically dependent on the substance.

- The section identifier for the Substance Abuse Treatment Section is H.

Chapter Review

Multiple Choice

Select the best answer that completes the statement or answers the question.

1. _____ are disorders that impact the ability of a person to function in a healthy, socially acceptable way.
   a. Diagnostic disorders
   b. Mental disorders
   c. Health-care disorders
   d. Medical disorders

2. A _____ is able to treat and prescribe medication in a psychiatric facility.
   a. psychologist
   b. psychiatrist
   c. social worker
   d. nurse

3. The application of controlled electrical voltages to treat mental health disorders is the ICD-10-PCS definition of:
   a. narcosynthesis.
   b. light therapy.
   c. pharmacotherapy.
   d. electroconvulsive therapy.

4. The use of replacement medications for the treatment of addiction is the ICD-10-PCS definition of:
    a. narcosynthesis.
    b. light therapy.
    c. pharmacotherapy.
    d. electroconvulsive therapy.

5. Sylvia was extremely sick when she entered the hospital detox program. Dr. Mallet said that her body was reacting to the lack of drugs it had become accustomed to receiving. This is an example of:
    a. abuse.
    b. addiction.
    c. mental disorder.
    d. cravings.

6. Of the following, which identifies a type of substance abuse treatment as identified in the ICD-10-PCS?
    a. biofeedback
    b. light therapy
    c. hypnosis
    d. pharmacotherapy

7. As part of the rehab program at the abuse and addiction center, John was offered vocational training to help him find a job after he finished the program. Which *type qualifier* is assigned for this type of counseling?
    a. 1
    b. 3
    c. 5
    d. 7

8. Of the following tables, which is referenced if the patient is reporting for methadone maintenance?
    a. HZ2
    b. HZ4
    c. HZ6
    d. HZ8

9. Sam was concerned that he may have been exposed to an STD prior to going to rehab and wanted to get tested to be sure this was not the case. The doctor explained that the counseling performed at this time was the pretest counseling; however, there would also be post-test counseling when he received the results of the test. The counseling is reported from which table?
    a. HZ3
    b. HZ4
    c. HZ5
    d. HZ6

10. Jenny's family had been worried about her state of mind. She was depressed and sad for the past week, but she would not talk about why or what had happened to get her to this point. They decided to have an intervention done before she did something drastic. Which code best describes a crisis intervention?
    a. GZJZZZZ
    b. HZ2ZZZZ
    c. GZ60ZZZ
    d. GZ2ZZZZ

Coding Assignments

Instructions: For each procedure, select the correct ICD-10-PCS code.

1.   light therapy   _____

2.   interactive individual psychotherapy   _____

3.   12-Step group counseling   _____

4.   individual spiritual counseling for substance abuse   _____

5.   narcosynthesis   _____

6.   neurobehavioral and cognitive testing   _____

7.   clonidine management for substance abuse   _____

8.   substance abuse detoxification services   _____

9.   family counseling due to substance abuse   _____

10. psychophysiological psychotherapy, individual   _____

11. vocational counseling   _____

12. cognitive-behavioral substance abuse counseling, individual _____

13. individual interpersonal psychotherapy for drug abuse   _____

14. hypnosis   _____

15. developmental psychological testing   _____

16. pharmacotherapy treatment, bupropion   _____

17. electroconvulsive therapy, bilateral multiple seizures   _____

18. family psychotherapy   _____

19. motivational group counseling for substance abuse   _____

20. psychodynamic psychotherapy for drug dependent patient   _____

Case Studies

Instructions: Review each case study and select the correct ICD-10-PCS code.

CASE 1

Detox Care Unit Discharge Summary

Patient: Zack J. Johns

Age: 42

Zack was brought in by ambulance. He was at a party and had been drinking vodka for 4 hours and then passed out. He began to vomit, and witnesses said that it looked like "he might have had a seizure" but they were not sure. Zack's wife accompanied him to the emergency room and said that Zack does have a drinking problem and thinks he should be admitted for detoxification. Zack was admitted for detox and was moved to the detox unit. Detox was completed.

ICD-10-PCS Code Assignment: _____

CASE 2

Counseling Note

This is a 68-year-old female who is being seen today because she feels "tired and very depressed." She states that she has lost her appetite for the past month and has not been able to sleep well. Her medical doctor requested she see a counselor so that we can do some counseling, see if we can get her back on track, and make life more pleasurable for her again.

At this time, she denies any substance abuse. She denies any suicidal thoughts or tendencies. She is oriented to time, person, and surroundings with no confusion. She cannot, at this time, identify any situation that might have triggered this state, but she does state that her youngest child just moved out of the area. When asked if this might be the trigger, she did affirm that the timing would be right and it was possible.

She has agreed to meet with me twice a week to talk and see if we can get her back on track.

ICD-10-PCS Code Assignment: _____

Appendix: ICD-10-CM Official Guidelines for Coding and Reporting 2010

Narrative changes appear in bold text
Items <u>underlined</u> have been moved within the guidelines since the 2009 version
Italics **are used to indicate revisions to heading changes**

The Centers for Medicare and Medicaid Services (CMS) and the National Center for Health Statistics (NCHS), two departments within the U.S. Federal Government's Department of Health and Human Services (DHHS) provide the following guidelines for coding and reporting using the International Classification of Diseases, 10th Revision, Clinical Modification (ICD-10-CM). These guidelines should be used as a companion document to the official version of the ICD-10-CM as published on the NCHS website. The ICD-10-CM is a morbidity classification published by the United States for classifying diagnoses and reason for visits in all health care settings. The ICD-10-CM is based on the ICD-10, the statistical classification of disease published by the World Health Organization (WHO).

These guidelines have been approved by the four organizations that make up the Cooperating Parties for the ICD-10-CM: the American Hospital Association (AHA), the American Health Information Management Association (AHIMA), CMS, and NCHS.

These guidelines are a set of rules that have been developed to accompany and complement the official conventions and instructions provided within the ICD-10-CM itself. **The instructions and conventions of the classification take precedence over guidelines.** These guidelines are based on the coding and sequencing instructions in Volumes I, and II of ICD-10-CM, but provide additional instruction. Adherence to these guidelines when assigning ICD-10-CM diagnosis codes is required under the Health Insurance Portability and Accountability Act (HIPAA). The diagnosis codes (Volumes 1-2) have been adopted under HIPAA for all healthcare settings. A joint effort between the healthcare provider and the coder is essential to achieve complete and accurate documentation, code assignment, and reporting of diagnoses and procedures. These guidelines have been developed to assist both the healthcare provider and the coder in identifying those diagnoses and procedures that are to be reported. The importance of consistent, complete documentation in the medical record cannot be overemphasized. Without such documentation accurate coding cannot be achieved. The entire record should be reviewed to determine the specific reason for the encounter and the conditions treated.

The term encounter is used for all settings, including hospital admissions. In the context of these guidelines, the term provider is used throughout the guidelines to mean physician or any qualified health care practitioner who is legally accountable for establishing the patient's diagnosis. Only this set of guidelines, approved by the Cooperating Parties, is official.

The guidelines are organized into sections. Section I includes the structure and conventions of the classification and general guidelines that apply to the entire classification, and chapter-specific guidelines that correspond to the chapters as they are arranged in the classification. Section II includes guidelines for selection of principal diagnosis for non-outpatient settings. Section III includes guidelines for reporting additional diagnoses in non-outpatient settings. Section IV is for outpatient coding and reporting. It is necessary to review all sections of the guidelines to fully understand all of the rules and instructions needed to code properly.

Section I. Conventions, general coding guidelines and chapter specific guidelines

The conventions, general guidelines and chapter-specific guidelines are applicable to all health care settings unless otherwise indicated. **The conventions and instructions of the classification take precedence over guidelines.**

A. Conventions for the ICD-10-CM

<u>The conventions for the ICD-10-CM are the general rules for use of the classification independent of the guidelines. These conventions are incorporated within the Index and Tabular of the ICD-10-CM as instructional notes.</u>

1. The Alphabetic Index and Tabular List

The ICD-10-CM is divided into the Index, an alphabetical list of terms and their corresponding code, and the Tabular List, a chronological list of codes divided into chapters based on body system or condition. The Index is divided into two parts, the Index to Diseases and Injury, and the Index to External Causes of Injury. Within the Index of Diseases and Injury there is a Neoplasm Table and a Table of Drugs and Chemicals.

See Section I.C2. General guidelines
See Section I.C.19. Adverse effects, poisoning, underdosing and toxic effects

2. Format and Structure:

The ICD-10-CM Tabular List contains categories, subcategories and codes. Characters for categories, subcategories and codes may be either a letter or a number. All categories are 3 characters. A three-character category that has no further subdivision is equivalent to a code. Subcategories are either 4 or 5 characters. Codes may be 4, 5, 6 or 7 characters. That is, each level of subdivision after a category is a subcategory. The final level of subdivision is a code. All codes in the Tabular List of the official version of the ICD-10-CM are in bold. Codes that have applicable 7th characters are still referred to as codes, not subcategories. A code that has an applicable 7th character is considered invalid without the 7th character.

The ICD-10-CM uses an indented format for ease in reference

3. Use of codes for reporting purposes

For reporting purposes only codes are permissible, not categories or subcategories, and any applicable 7th character is required.

4. Placeholder character

The ICD-10-CM utilizes a placeholder character "X". The "X" is used as a 5th character placeholder at certain 6 character codes to allow for future expansion. An example of this is at the poisoning, adverse effect and underdosing codes, categories T36-T50. Where a placeholder exists, the X must be used in order for the code to be considered a valid code.

5.   7th Characters

Certain ICD-10-CM categories have applicable 7th characters. The applicable 7th character is required for all codes within the category, or as the notes in the Tabular List instruct. The 7th character must always be the 7th character in the data field. If a code that requires a 7th character is not 6 characters, a placeholder X must be used to fill in the empty characters.

6.   Abbreviations

a.   Index abbreviations

NEC   "Not elsewhere classifiable"
This abbreviation in the Index represents "other specified". When a specific code is not available for a condition, the Index directs the coder to the "other specified" code in the Tabular.

b.   Tabular abbreviations

NEC   "Not elsewhere classifiable"
This abbreviation in the Tabular represents "other specified". When a specific code is not available for a condition the Tabular includes an NEC entry under a code to identify the code as the "other specified" code.

NOS   "Not otherwise specified"
This abbreviation is the equivalent of unspecified.

7.   Punctuation

[ ]   Brackets are used in the tabular list to enclose synonyms, alternative wording or explanatory phrases. Brackets are used in the Index to identify manifestation codes.

( )   Parentheses are used in both the Index and Tabular to enclose supplementary words that may be present or absent in the statement of a disease or procedure without affecting the code number to which it is assigned. The terms within the parentheses are referred to as nonessential modifiers.

:   Colons are used in the Tabular List after an incomplete term which needs one or more of the modifiers following the colon to make it assignable to a given category.

8.   Use of "and"

When the term "and" is used in a narrative statement it represents and/or.

9.   **Other and Unspecified codes**

    a.   **"Other" codes**

Codes titled "other" or "other specified" are for use when the information in the medical record provides detail for which a specific code does not exist. Index entries with NEC in the line designate "other" codes in the Tabular. These Index entries represent specific disease entities for which no specific code exists so the term is included within an "other" code.

    b.   **"Unspecified" codes**

Codes (usually a code with a 4th digit 9 or 5th digit 0 for diagnosis codes) titled "unspecified" are for use when the information in the medical record is insufficient to assign a more specific code. For those categories for which an unspecified code is not provided, the "other specified" code may represent both other and unspecified.

10.   **Includes Notes**

This note appears immediately under a three-digit code title to further define, or give examples of, the content of the category.

11.   **Inclusion terms**

List of terms is included under some codes. These terms are the conditions for which that code is to be used. The terms may be synonyms of the code title, or, in the case of "other specified" codes, the terms are a list of the various conditions assigned to that code. The inclusion terms are not necessarily exhaustive. Additional terms found only in the Index may also be assigned to a code.

12.   **Excludes Notes**

The ICD-10-CM has two types of excludes notes. Each type of note has a different definition for use but they are all similar in that they indicate that codes excluded from each other are independent of each other.

    a.   **Excludes1**

A type 1 Excludes note is a pure excludes note. It means "NOT CODED HERE!" An Excludes1 note indicates that the code excluded should never be used at the same time as the code above the Excludes1 note. An Excludes1 is used when two conditions cannot occur together, such as a congenital form versus an acquired form of the same condition.

    b.   **Excludes2**

A type 2 excludes note represents "Not included here". An excludes2 note indicates that the condition excluded is not part of the condition represented by the code, but a patient may have both conditions at the same time. When an Excludes2 note appears under a code, it is acceptable to use both the code and the excluded code together, when appropriate.

13.   Etiology/manifestation convention ("code first", "use additional code" and "in diseases classified elsewhere" notes)

Certain conditions have both an underlying etiology and multiple body system manifestations due to the underlying etiology. For such conditions, the ICD-10-CM has a coding convention that requires the underlying condition be sequenced first followed by the manifestation. Wherever such a combination exists, there is a "use additional code" note at the etiology code, and a "code first" note at the manifestation code. These instructional notes indicate the proper sequencing order of the codes, etiology followed by manifestation.

In most cases the manifestation codes will have in the code title, "in diseases classified elsewhere." Codes with this title are a component of the etiology/ manifestation convention. The code title indicates that it is a manifestation code. "In diseases classified elsewhere" codes are never permitted to be used as first listed or principal diagnosis codes. They must be used in conjunction with an underlying condition code and they must be listed following the underlying condition. See category F02, Dementia in other diseases classified elsewhere, for an example of this convention.

There are manifestation codes that do not have "in diseases classified elsewhere" in the title. For such codes a "use additional code" note will still be present and the rules for sequencing apply.

In addition to the notes in the Tabular, these conditions also have a specific Index entry structure. In the Index both conditions are listed together with the etiology code first followed by the manifestation codes in brackets. The code in brackets is always to be sequenced second.

An example of the etiology/manifestation convention is dementia in Parkinson's disease. In the index, code G20 is listed first, followed by code F02.80 or F02.81 in brackets. Code G20 represents the underlying etiology, Parkinson's disease, and must be sequenced first, whereas codes F02.80 and F02.81 represent the manifestation of dementia in diseases classified elsewhere, with or without behavioral disturbance.

"Code first" and "Use additional code" notes are also used as sequencing rules in the classification for certain codes that are not part of an etiology/ manifestation combination.

See Section I.B.7. Multiple coding for a single condition.

14. "And"

The word "and" should be interpreted to mean either "and" or "or" when it appears in a title.

15. "With"

The word "with" in the Alphabetic Index is sequenced immediately following the main term, not in alphabetical order.

16. "See" and "See Also"

The "see" instruction following a main term in the Index indicates that another term should be referenced. It is necessary to go to the main term referenced with the "see" note to locate the correct code.

A "see also" instruction following a main term in the index instructs that there is another main term that may also be referenced that may provide additional index entries that may be useful. It is not necessary to follow the "see also" note when the original main term provides the necessary code.

17. "Code also note"

A "code also" note instructs that two codes may be required to fully describe a condition, but this note does not provide sequencing direction.

18. Default codes

A code listed next to a main term in the ICD-10-CM Index is referred to as a default code. The default code represents that condition that is most commonly associated with the main term, or is the unspecified code for the condition. If a condition is documented in a medical record (for example, appendicitis) without any additional information, such as acute or chronic, the default code should be assigned.

19. Syndromes

Follow the Alphabetic Index guidance when coding syndromes. In the absence of index guidance, assign codes for the documented manifestations of the syndrome.

B. General Coding Guidelines

1. Locating a code in the ICD-10-CM

To select a code in the classification that corresponds to a diagnosis or reason for visit documented in a medical record, first locate the term in the Index, and then verify the code in the Tabular List. Read and be guided by instructional notations that appear in both the Index and the Tabular List.

It is essential to use both the Index and Tabular List when locating and assigning a code. The Index does not always provide the full code. Selection of the full code, including laterality and any applicable 7th character can only be done in the Tabular list. A dash (-) at the end of an Index entry indicates that additional characters are required. Even if a dash is not included at the Index entry, it is necessary to refer to the Tabular list to verify that no 7th character is required.

2.   Level of Detail in Coding

Diagnosis codes are to be used and reported at their highest number of digits available.

ICD-10-CM diagnosis codes are composed of codes with 3, 4, 5, 6 or 7 digits. Codes with three digits are included in ICD-10-CM as the heading of a category of codes that may be further subdivided by the use of fourth and/or fifth digits, which provide greater detail.

A three-digit code is to be used only if it is not further subdivided. A code is invalid if it has not been coded to the full number of characters required for that code, including the 7th character, if applicable.

3.   Code or codes from A00.0 through T88.9, Z00-Z99.8

The appropriate code or codes from A00.0 through T88.9, Z00-Z99.8 must be used to identify diagnoses, symptoms, conditions, problems, complaints or other reason(s) for the encounter/visit.

4.   Signs and symptoms

Codes that describe symptoms and signs, as opposed to diagnoses, are acceptable for reporting purposes when a related definitive diagnosis has not been established (confirmed) by the provider. Chapter 18 of ICD-10-CM, Symptoms, Signs, and Abnormal Clinical and Laboratory Findings, Not Elsewhere Classified (codes R00.0 - R99) contains many, but not all codes for symptoms.

5.   Conditions that are an integral part of a disease process

Signs and symptoms that are associated routinely with a disease process should not be assigned as additional codes, unless otherwise instructed by the classification.

6.   Conditions that are not an integral part of a disease process

Additional signs and symptoms that may not be associated routinely with a disease process should be coded when present.

7.   Multiple coding for a single condition

In addition to the etiology/manifestation convention that requires two codes to fully describe a single condition that affects multiple body systems, there are other single conditions that also require more than one code. "Use additional code" notes are found in the Tabular at codes that are not part of an etiology/manifestation pair where a secondary code is useful to fully describe a condition. The sequencing rule is the same as the etiology/manifestation pair, "use additional code" indicates that a secondary code should be added.

For example, for bacterial infections that are not included in chapter 1, a secondary code from category B95, Streptococcus, Staphylococcus, and Enterococcus, as the cause of diseases classified elsewhere, or B96, Other bacterial agents as the cause of diseases classified elsewhere, may be required to identify the bacterial organism causing the infection. A "use additional code" note will normally be found at the infectious disease code, indicating a need for the organism code to be added as a secondary code.

"Code first" notes are also under certain codes that are not specifically manifestation codes but may be due to an underlying cause. When there is a "code first" note and an underlying condition is present, the underlying condition should be sequenced first.

"Code, if applicable, any causal condition first", notes indicate that this code may be assigned as a principal diagnosis when the causal condition is unknown or not applicable. If a causal condition is known, then the code for that condition should be sequenced as the principal or first-listed diagnosis.

Multiple codes may be needed for late effects, complication codes and obstetric codes to more fully describe a condition. See the specific guidelines for these conditions for further instruction.

8.   Acute and Chronic Conditions

If the same condition is described as both acute (subacute) and chronic, and separate subentries exist in the Alphabetic Index at the same indentation level, code both and sequence the acute (subacute) code first.

9.   Combination Code

A combination code is a single code used to classify:
Two diagnoses, or
A diagnosis with an associated secondary process (manifestation)
A diagnosis with an associated complication

Combination codes are identified by referring to subterm entries in the Alphabetic Index and by reading the inclusion and exclusion notes in the Tabular List.

Assign only the combination code when that code fully identifies the diagnostic conditions involved or when the Alphabetic Index so directs. Multiple coding should not be used when the classification provides a combination code that clearly identifies all of the elements documented in the diagnosis. When the combination code lacks necessary specificity in describing the manifestation or complication, an additional code should be used as a secondary code.

10.   Late Effects (Sequela)

A late effect is the residual effect (condition produced) after the acute phase of an illness or injury has terminated. There is no time limit on when a late effect code can be used. The residual may be apparent early, such as in cerebral infarction, or it may occur months or years later, such as that due to a previous injury. Coding of late effects generally requires two codes sequenced in the following order: The condition or nature of the late effect is sequenced first. The late effect code is sequenced second.

An exception to the above guidelines are those instances where the code for late effect is followed by a manifestation code identified in the Tabular List and title, or the late effect code has been expanded (at the fourth, fifth or sixth character levels) to include the manifestation(s). The code for the acute phase of an illness or injury that led to the late effect is never used with a code for the late effect.

See Section I.C.9. Sequelae of cerebrovascular disease
See Section I.C.15. Sequelae of complication of pregnancy, childbirth and the puerperium
See Section I.C.19. Code extensions

11.   Impending or Threatened Condition

Code any condition described at the time of discharge as "impending" or "threatened" as follows:

> If it did occur, code as confirmed diagnosis.
> If it did not occur, reference the Alphabetic Index to determine if the condition has a subentry term for "impending" or "threatened" and also reference main term entries for "Impending" and for "Threatened."
> If the subterms are listed, assign the given code.
> If the subterms are not listed, code the existing underlying condition(s) and not the condition described as impending or threatened.

12.   Reporting Same Diagnosis Code More than Once

Each unique ICD-10-CM diagnosis code may be reported only once for an encounter. This applies to bilateral conditions **when there are no distinct codes identifying laterality** or two different conditions classified to the same ICD-10-CM diagnosis code.

13.   Laterality

For bilateral sites, the final character of the codes in the ICD-10-CM indicates laterality. An unspecified side code is also provided should the side not be identified in the medical record.   If no bilateral code is provided and the condition is bilateral, assign separate codes for both the left and right side.

14. **Documentation for BMI and Pressure Ulcer Stages**

For the Body Mass Index (BMI) and pressure ulcer stage codes, code assignment may be based on medical record documentation from clinicians who are not the patient's provider (i.e., physician or other qualified healthcare practitioner legally accountable for establishing the patient's diagnosis), since this information is typically documented by other clinicians involved in the care of the patient (e.g., a dietitian often documents the BMI and nurses often documents the pressure ulcer stages). However, the associated diagnosis (such as overweight, obesity, or pressure ulcer) must be documented by the patient's provider. If there is conflicting medical record documentation, either from the same clinician or different clinicians, the patient's attending provider should be queried for clarification.

The BMI codes should only be reported as secondary diagnoses. As with all other secondary diagnosis codes, the BMI codes should only be assigned when they meet the definition of a reportable additional diagnosis (see Section III, Reporting Additional Diagnoses).

C. Chapter-Specific Coding Guidelines

In addition to general coding guidelines, there are guidelines for specific diagnoses and/or conditions in the classification. Unless otherwise indicated, these guidelines apply to all health care settings. Please refer to Section II for guidelines on the selection of principal diagnosis.

1. **Chapter 1: Certain Infectious and Parasitic Diseases (A00-B99)**

    a. **Human Immunodeficiency Virus (HIV) Infections**

       1) **Code only confirmed cases**

          Code only confirmed cases of HIV infection/illness. This is an exception to the hospital inpatient guideline Section II, H.

          In this context, "confirmation" does not require documentation of positive serology or culture for HIV; the provider's diagnostic statement that the patient is HIV positive, or has an HIV-related illness is sufficient.

2)   Selection and sequencing of HIV codes

(a)   Patient admitted for HIV-related condition

If a patient is admitted for an HIV-related condition, the principal diagnosis should be B20, followed by additional diagnosis codes for all reported HIV-related conditions.

(b)   Patient with HIV disease admitted for unrelated condition

If a patient with HIV disease is admitted for an unrelated condition (such as a traumatic injury), the code for the unrelated condition (e.g., the nature of injury code) should be the principal diagnosis. Other diagnoses would be B20 followed by additional diagnosis codes for all reported HIV-related conditions.

(c)   Whether the patient is newly diagnosed

Whether the patient is newly diagnosed or has had previous admissions/encounters for HIV conditions is irrelevant to the sequencing decision.

(d)   Asymptomatic human immunodeficiency virus

Z21, Asymptomatic human immunodeficiency virus [HIV] infection status, is to be applied when the patient without any documentation of symptoms is listed as being "HIV positive," "known HIV," "HIV test positive," or similar terminology. Do not use this code if the term "AIDS" is used or if the patient is treated for any HIV-related illness or is described as having any condition(s) resulting from his/her HIV positive status; use B20 in these cases.

(e)   Patients with inconclusive HIV serology

Patients with inconclusive HIV serology, but no definitive diagnosis or manifestations of the illness, may be assigned code R75, Inconclusive laboratory evidence of human immunodeficiency virus [HIV].

(f)   Previously diagnosed HIV-related illness

Patients with any known prior diagnosis of an HIV-related illness should be coded to B20. Once a patient has developed an HIV-related illness, the patient should always be assigned code B20 on every subsequent admission/encounter. Patients previously diagnosed with any HIV illness (B20) should never be assigned to R75 or Z21, Asymptomatic human immunodeficiency virus [HIV] infection status.

(g) **HIV Infection in Pregnancy, Childbirth and the Puerperium**

During pregnancy, childbirth or the puerperium, a patient admitted (or presenting for a health care encounter) because of an HIV-related illness should receive a principal diagnosis code of O98.7-, Human immunodeficiency [HIV] disease complicating pregnancy, childbirth and the puerperium, followed by B20 and the code(s) for the HIV-related illness(es). Codes from Chapter 15 always take sequencing priority.

Patients with asymptomatic HIV infection status admitted (or presenting for a health care encounter) during pregnancy, childbirth, or the puerperium should receive codes of O98.7- and Z21.

(h) **Encounters for testing for HIV**

If a patient is being seen to determine his/her HIV status, use code Z11.4, Encounter for screening for human immunodeficiency virus [HIV]. Use additional codes for any associated high risk behavior.

If a patient with signs or symptoms is being seen for HIV testing, code the signs and symptoms. An additional counseling code Z71.7, Human innunodeficiency virus [HIV] counseling, may be used if counseling is provided during the encounter for the test.

When a patient returns to be informed of his/her HIV test results and the test result is negative, use code Z71.7, Human immunodeficiency virus [HIV] counseling.

If the results are positive, see previous guidelines and assign codes as appropriate.

b. **Infectious agents as the cause of diseases classified to other chapters**

Certain infections are classified in chapters other than Chapter 1 and no organism is identified as part of the infection code. In these instances, it is necessary to use an additional code from Chapter 1 to identify the organism. A code from category B95, Streptococcus, Staphylococcus, and Enterococcus as the cause of diseases classified to other chapters, B96, Other bacterial agents as the cause of diseases classified to other chapters, or B97, Viral agents as the cause of diseases classified to other chapters, is to be used as an additional code to identify the organism. An instructional note will be found at the infection code advising that an additional organism code is required.

c.   Infections resistant to antibiotics

Many bacterial infections are resistant to current antibiotics. It is necessary to identify all infections documented as antibiotic resistant. Assign code Z16, Infection with drug resistant microorganisms, following the infection code for these cases.

d.   Sepsis, Severe Sepsis, and Septic Shock

1)   Coding of Sepsis and Severe Sepsis

(a)   Sepsis

For a diagnosis of sepsis, assign the appropriate code for the underlying systemic infection. If the type of infection or causal organism is not further specified, assign code A41.9, Sepsis, unspecified.

A code from subcategory R65.2, Severe sepsis, should not be assigned unless severe sepsis or an associated acute organ dysfunction is documented.

(i)   Negative or inconclusive blood cultures and sepsis

Negative or inconclusive blood cultures do not preclude a diagnosis of sepsis in patients with clinical evidence of the condition, however, the provider should be queried.

(ii)   Urosepsis

The term urosepsis is a nonspecific term. It is not to be considered synonymous with sepsis. It has no default code in the Alphabetic Index. Should a provider use this term, he/she must be queried for clarification.

(iii)   Sepsis with organ dysfunction

If a patient has sepsis and associated acute organ dysfunction or multiple organ dysfunction

(MOD), follow the instructions for coding severe sepsis.

(iv)   Acute organ dysfunction that is not clearly associated with the sepsis

If a patient has sepsis and an acute organ dysfunction, but the medical record documentation indicates that the acute organ dysfunction is related to a medical condition other than the sepsis, do not assign a code from subcategory R65.2, Severe sepsis. An acute organ dysfunction must be associated with the sepsis in order to assign the severe sepsis code. If the documentation is not clear as to whether an acute organ dysfunction is related to the sepsis or another medical condition, query the provider.

(b)   Severe sepsis

The coding of severe sepsis requires a minimum of 2 codes: first a code for the underlying systemic infection, followed by a code from subcategory R65.2, Severe sepsis. If the causal organism is not documented, assign code A41.9, Sepsis, unspecified, for the infection. Additional code(s) for the associated acute organ dysfunction are also required.

Due to the complex nature of severe sepsis, some cases may require querying the provider prior to assignment of the codes.

2)   Septic shock

Septic shock is circulatory failure associated with severe sepsis, and therefore, it represents a type of acute organ dysfunction. For all cases of septic shock, the code for the underlying systemic infection should be sequenced first, followed by code R65.21, Severe sepsis with septic shock. Any additional codes for the other acute organ dysfunctions should also be assigned.

Septic shock indicates the presence of severe sepsis. Code R65.21, Severe sepsis with septic shock, must be assigned if septic shock is documented in the medical record, even if the term severe sepsis is not documented.

3)   Sequencing of severe sepsis

If severe sepsis is present on admission, and meets the definition of principal diagnosis, the underlying systemic infection should be assigned as principal diagnosis followed by the appropriate code from subcategory R65.2 as required by the sequencing rules in the Tabular List. A code from subcategory R65.2 can never be assigned as a principal diagnosis.

When severe sepsis develops during an encounter (it was not present on admission) the underlying systemic infection and the appropriate code from subcategory R65.2 should be assigned as secondary diagnoses.

Severe sepsis may be present on admission but the diagnosis may not be confirmed until sometime after admission. If the documentation is not clear whether severe sepsis was present on admission, the provider should be queried.

4)   Sepsis and severe sepsis with a localized infection

If the reason for admission is both sepsis or severe sepsis and a localized infection, such as pneumonia or cellulitis, a code(s) for the underlying systemic infection should be assigned first and the code for the localized infection should be assigned as a secondary diagnosis. If the patient has severe sepsis, a code from subcategory R65.2 should also be assigned as a secondary diagnosis. If the patient is admitted with a localized infection, such as pneumonia, and sepsis/severe sepsis doesn't develop until after admission, the localized infection should be assigned first, followed by the appropriate sepsis/severe sepsis codes.

5)   Sepsis due to a postprocedural infection

Sepsis resulting from a postprocedural infection is a complication of medical care. For such cases, the postprocedural infection code, such as, T80.2, Infections following infusion, transfusion, and therapeutic injection, T81.4, Infection following a procedure, T88.0, Infection following immunization, or O86.0, Infection of obstetric surgical wound, should be coded first, followed by the code for the specific infection. If the patient has severe sepsis the appropriate code from subcategory R65.2 should also be assigned with the additional code(s) for any acute organ dysfunction.

6)   Sepsis and severe sepsis associated with a noninfectious process (condition)

In some cases a noninfectious process (condition), such as trauma, may lead to an infection which can result in sepsis or severe sepsis. If sepsis or severe sepsis is documented as associated with a noninfectious condition, such as a burn or serious injury, and this condition meets the definition for principal diagnosis, the code for the noninfectious condition should be sequenced first, followed by the code for the resulting infection. If severe sepsis, is present a code from subcategory R65.2 should also be assigned with any associated organ dysfunction(s) codes. It is not necessary to assign a code from subcategory R65.1, Systemic inflammatory response syndrome (SIRS) of non-infectious origin, for these cases.

If the infection meets the definition of principal diagnosis it should be sequenced before the non-infectious condition. When both the associated non-infectious condition and the infection meet the definition of principal diagnosis either may be assigned as principal diagnosis.

Only one code from category R65, Symptoms and signs specifically associated with systemic inflammation and infection, should be assigned. Therefore, when a non-infectious condition leads to an infection resulting in severe sepsis, assign the appropriate code from subcategory R65.2, Severe sepsis. Do not additionally assign a code from subcategory R65.1, Systemic inflammatory response syndrome (SIRS) of non-infectious origin.

See Section I.C.18. SIRS due to non-infectious process

7)   Sepsis and septic shock complicating abortion, pregnancy, childbirth, and the puerperium

See Section I.C.15. Sepsis and septic shock complicating abortion, pregnancy, childbirth and the puerperium

8)   Newborn sepsis

See Section I.C.16. Newborn sepsis

2.   ## Chapter 2: Neoplasms (C00-D49)

General guidelines

Chapter 2 of the ICD-10-CM contains the codes for most benign and all malignant neoplasms. Certain benign neoplasms, such as prostatic adenomas, may be found in the specific body system chapters. To properly code a neoplasm it is necessary to determine from the record if the neoplasm is benign, in-situ, malignant, or of uncertain histologic behavior. If malignant, any secondary (metastatic) sites should also be determined.

The neoplasm table in the Alphabetic Index should be referenced first. However, if the histological term is documented, that term should be referenced first, rather than going immediately to the Neoplasm Table, in order to determine which column in the Neoplasm Table is appropriate. For example, if the documentation indicates "adenoma," refer to the term in the Alphabetic Index to review the entries under this term and the instructional note to "see also neoplasm, by site, benign." The table provides the proper code based on the type of neoplasm and the site. It is important to select the proper column in the table that corresponds to the type of neoplasm. The Tabular should then be referenced to verify that the correct code has been selected from the table and that a more specific site code does not exist. *See Section I.C.21. Factors influencing health status and contact with health services, Status, for information regarding Z15.0, codes for genetic susceptibility to cancer.*

a.   ### Treatment directed at the malignancy

If the treatment is directed at the malignancy, designate the malignancy as the principal diagnosis.

The only exception to this guideline is if a patient admission/encounter is solely for the administration of chemotherapy, immunotherapy or radiation therapy, assign the appropriate Z51.-- code as the first-listed or principal diagnosis, and the diagnosis or problem for which the service is being performed as a secondary diagnosis.

b.   ### Treatment of secondary site

When a patient is admitted because of a primary neoplasm with metastasis and treatment is directed toward the secondary site only, the secondary neoplasm is designated as the principal diagnosis even though the primary malignancy is still present.

c.   ### Coding and sequencing of complications

Coding and sequencing of complications associated with the malignancies or with the therapy thereof are subject to the following guidelines:

1) Anemia associated with malignancy

When admission/encounter is for management of an anemia associated with the malignancy, and the treatment is only for anemia, the appropriate code for the malignancy is sequenced as the principal or first-listed diagnosis followed by code D63.0, Anemia in neoplastic disease).

2) Anemia associated with chemotherapy, immunotherapy and radiation therapy

When the admission/encounter is for management of an anemia associated with **an adverse effect of** chemotherapy, immunotherapy or radiotherapy and the only treatment is for the anemia, **the appropriate adverse effect code should be sequenced first, followed by the appropriate codes for the anemia and neoplasm.**

3) Management of dehydration due to the malignancy

When the admission/encounter is for management of dehydration due to the malignancy or the therapy, or a combination of both, and only the dehydration is being treated (intravenous rehydration), the dehydration is sequenced first, followed by the code(s) for the malignancy.

4) Treatment of a complication resulting from a surgical procedure

When the admission/encounter is for treatment of a complication resulting from a surgical procedure, designate the complication as the principal or first-listed diagnosis if treatment is directed at resolving the complication.

d.   Primary malignancy previously excised

When a primary malignancy has been previously excised or eradicated from its site and there is no further treatment directed to that site and there is no evidence of any existing primary malignancy, a code from category Z85, Personal history of primary and secondary malignant neoplasm, should be used to indicate the former site of the malignancy. Any mention of extension, invasion, or metastasis to another site is coded as a secondary malignant neoplasm to that site. The secondary site may be the principal or first-listed with the Z85 code used as a secondary code.

e.   **Admissions/Encounters involving chemotherapy, immunotherapy and radiation therapy**

  1)   **Episode of care involves surgical removal of neoplasm**

  When an episode of care involves the surgical removal of a neoplasm, primary or secondary site, followed by adjunct chemotherapy or radiation treatment during the same episode of care, the neoplasm code should be assigned as principal or first-listed diagnosis, using codes in the C00-D49 series or where appropriate in the C83-C90 series.

  2)   **Patient admission/encounter solely for administration of chemotherapy, immunotherapy and radiation therapy**

  If a patient admission/encounter is solely for the administration of chemotherapy, immunotherapy or radiation therapy assign code Z51.0, Encounter for antineoplastic radiation therapy, or Z51.11, Encounter for antineoplastic chemotherapy, or Z51.12, Encounter for antineoplastic immunotherapy as the first-listed or principal diagnosis. If a patient receives more than one of these therapies during the same admission more than one of these codes may be assigned, in any sequence.

  The malignancy for which the therapy is being administered should be assigned as a secondary diagnosis.

  3)   **Patient admitted for radiation therapy, chemotherapy or immunotherapy and develops complications**

  When a patient is admitted for the purpose of radiotherapy, immunotherapy or chemotherapy and develops complications such as uncontrolled nausea and vomiting or dehydration, the principal or first-listed diagnosis is Z51.0, Encounter for antineoplastic radiation therapy, or Z51.11, Encounter for antineoplastic chemotherapy, or Z51.12, Encounter for antineoplastic immunotherapy followed by any codes for the complications.

f.   **Admission/encounter to determine extent of malignancy**

  When the reason for admission/encounter is to determine the extent of the malignancy, or for a procedure such as paracentesis or thoracentesis, the primary malignancy or appropriate metastatic site is designated as the principal or first-listed diagnosis, even though chemotherapy or radiotherapy is administered.

g. Symptoms, signs, and abnormal findings listed in Chapter 18 associated with neoplasms

Symptoms, signs, and ill-defined conditions listed in Chapter 18 characteristic of, or associated with, an existing primary or secondary site malignancy cannot be used to replace the malignancy as principal or first-listed diagnosis, regardless of the number of admissions or encounters for treatment and care of the neoplasm.
See section I.C.21. Factors influencing health status and contact with health services, Encounter for prophylactic organ removal.

h. Admission/encounter for pain control/management

See Section I.C.6. for information on coding admission/encounter for pain control/management.

i. Malignancy in two or more noncontiguous sites

A patient may have more than one malignant tumor in the same organ. These tumors may represent different primaries or metastatic disease, depending on the site. Should the documentation be unclear, the provider should be queried as to the status of each tumor so that the correct codes can be assigned.

j. Disseminated malignant neoplasm, unspecified

Code C80.0, Disseminated malignant neoplasm, unspecified, is for use only in those cases where the patient has advanced metastatic disease and no known primary or secondary sites are specified. It should not be used in place of assigning codes for the primary site and all known secondary sites.

k. Malignant neoplasm without specification of site

Code C80.1, Malignant neoplasm, unspecified, equates to Cancer, unspecified. This code should only be used when no determination can be made as to the primary site of a malignancy. This code should rarely be used in the inpatient setting.

l. Sequencing of neoplasm codes

1) Encounter for treatment of primary malignancy

If the reason for the encounter is for treatment of a primary malignancy, assign the malignancy as the principal/first listed diagnosis. The primary site is to be sequenced first, followed by any metastatic sites.

2) Encounter for treatment of secondary malignancy

When an encounter is for a primary malignancy with metastasis and treatment is directed toward the metastatic (secondary) site(s) only, the metastatic site(s) is designated as the principal/first listed diagnosis. The primary malignancy is coded as an additional code.

3)   **Malignant neoplasm in a pregnant patient**

Codes from chapter 15, Pregnancy, childbirth, and the puerperium, are always sequenced first on a medical record. A code from subcategory O94.1-, Malignant neoplasm complicating pregnancy, childbirth, and the puerperium, should be used first, followed by the appropriate code from Chapter 2 to indicate the type of neoplasm.

4)   **Encounter for complication associated with a neoplasm**

When an encounter is for management of a complication associated with a neoplasm, such as dehydration, and the treatment is only for the complication, the complication is coded first, followed by the appropriate code(s) for the neoplasm.

The exception to this guideline is anemia. When the admission/encounter is for management of an anemia associated with the malignancy, and the treatment is only for anemia, the appropriate code for the malignancy is sequenced as the principal or first-listed diagnosis followed by code D63.0, Anemia in neoplastic disease.

5)   **Complication from surgical procedure for treatment of a neoplasm**

When an encounter is for treatment of a complication resulting from a surgical procedure performed for the treatment of the neoplasm, designate the complication as the principal/first listed diagnosis. See guideline regarding the coding of a current malignancy versus personal history to determine if the code for the neoplasm should also be assigned.

6)   **Pathologic fracture due to a neoplasm**

When an encounter is for a pathological fracture due to a neoplasm, if the focus of treatment is the fracture, a code from subcategory M84.5, Pathological fracture in neoplastic disease, should be sequenced first, followed by the code for the neoplasm.

If the focus of treatment is the neoplasm with an associated pathological fracture, the neoplasm code should be sequenced first, followed by a code from M84.5 for the pathological fracture. The "code also" note at M84.5 provides this sequencing instruction.

m. Current malignancy versus personal history of malignancy

When a primary malignancy has been excised but further treatment, such as an additional surgery for the malignancy, radiation therapy or chemotherapy is directed to that site, the primary malignancy code should be used until treatment is completed.

When a primary malignancy has been previously excised or eradicated from its site, there is no further treatment (of the malignancy) directed to that site, and there is no evidence of any existing primary malignancy, a code from category Z85, Personal history of primary and secondary malignant neoplasm, should be used to indicate the former site of the malignancy.

See Section I.C.21. Factors influencing health status and contact with health services, History (of)

n. Leukemia in remission versus personal history of leukemia

The categories for leukemia, and category C90, Multiple myeloma, have codes for in remission. There are also codes Z85.6, Personal history of leukemia, and Z85.79, Personal history of other malignant neoplasms of lymphoid, hematopoietic and related tissues. If the documentation is unclear, as to whether the patient is in remission, the provider should be queried.

See Section I.C.21. Factors influencing health status and contact with health services, History (of)

o. Aftercare following surgery for neoplasm

See Section I.C.21. Factors influencing health status and contact with health services, Aftercare

p. Follow-up care for completed treatment of a malignancy

See Section I.C.21. Factors influencing health status and contact with health services, Follow-up

q. Prophylactic organ removal for prevention of malignancy

See Section I.C. 21, Factors influencing health status and contact with health services, Prophylactic organ removal

r.   Malignant neoplasm associated with transplanted organ

A malignant neoplasm of a transplanted organ should be coded as a transplant complication. Assign first the appropriate code from category T86.-, Complications of transplanted organ, followed by code C80.2, Malignant neoplasm associated with transplanted organ. Use an additional code for the specific malignancy.

3.   Chapter 3: Disease of the blood and blood-forming organs and certain disorders involving the immune mechanism (D50-D89)

Reserved for future guideline expansion

4.   Chapter 4: Endocrine, Nutritional, and Metabolic Diseases (E00-*E89*)

a.   Diabetes mellitus

The diabetes mellitus codes are combination codes that include the type of DM, the body system affected, and the complications affecting that body system. As many codes within a particular category as are necessary to describe all of the complications of the disease may be used. They should be sequenced based on the reason for a particular encounter. Assign as many codes from categories E08 – E13 as needed to identify all of the associated conditions that the patient has.

1)   Type of diabetes

The age of a patient is not the sole determining factor, though most type 1 diabetics develop the condition before reaching puberty. For this reason type 1 diabetes mellitus is also referred to as juvenile diabetes.

2)   Type of diabetes mellitus not documented

If the type of diabetes mellitus is not documented in the medical record the default is E11.-, Type 2 diabetes mellitus.

3)   Diabetes mellitus and the use of insulin

If the documentation in a medical record does not indicate the type of diabetes but does indicate that the patient uses insulin, code E11, Type 2 diabetes mellitus, should be assigned for type 2 patients who routinely use insulin, code Z79.4, Long-term (current) use of insulin, should also be assigned to indicate that the patient uses insulin. Code Z79.4 should not be assigned if insulin is given temporarily to bring a type 2 patient's blood sugar under control during an encounter.

4)   Diabetes mellitus in pregnancy and gestational diabetes

See Section I.C.15. Diabetes mellitus in pregnancy.
See Section I.C.15. Gestational (pregnancy induced) diabetes

5)   Complications due to insulin pump malfunction

(a)   Underdose of insulin due insulin pump failure

An underdose of insulin due to an insulin pump failure should be assigned to a code from subcategory T85.6, Mechanical complication of other specified internal and external prosthetic devices, implants and grafts, that specifies the type of pump malfunction, as the principal or first listed code, followed by code T38.3x6-, Underdosing of insulin and oral hypoglycemic [antidiabetic] drugs. Additional codes for the type of diabetes mellitus and any associated complications due to the underdosing should also be assigned.

(b)   Overdose of insulin due to insulin pump failure

The principal or first listed code for an encounter due to an insulin pump malfunction resulting in an overdose of insulin, should also be T85.6-, Mechanical complication of other specified internal and external prosthetic devices, implants and grafts, followed by code T38.3x1-, Poisoning by insulin and oral hypoglycemic [antidiabetic] drugs, accidental (unintentional).

6)   Secondary Diabetes Mellitus

Codes under category E08, Diabetes mellitus due to underlying condition, and E09, Drug or chemical induced diabetes mellitus, identify complications/manifestations associated with secondary diabetes mellitus. Secondary diabetes is always caused by another condition or event (e.g., cystic fibrosis, malignant neoplasm of pancreas, pancreatectomy, adverse effect of drug, or poisoning).

(a)   Secondary diabetes mellitus and the use of insulin

For patients who routinely use insulin, code Z79.4, Long-term (current) use of insulin, should also be assigned. Code Z79.4 should not be assigned if insulin is given temporarily to bring a patient's blood sugar under control during an encounter.

(b)   Assigning and sequencing secondary diabetes codes and its causes

The sequencing of the secondary diabetes codes in relationship to codes for the cause of the diabetes is based on the tabular instructions for categories E08 and E09. For example, for category E08, Diabetes mellitus due to underlying condition, code first the underlying condition; for category E09, Drug or chemical induced diabetes mellitus, code first the drug or chemical (T36-T65).

(i)   Secondary diabetes mellitus due to pancreatectomy

For postpancreatectomy diabetes mellitus (lack of insulin due to the surgical removal of all or part of the pancreas), assign code E89.1, Postsurgical hypoinsulinemia. Assign a code from category E08 and code Z79.4, Other acquired absence of organ, as additional codes.

(ii)   Secondary diabetes due to drugs

Secondary diabetes may be caused by an adverse effect of correctly administered medications, poisoning or late effect of poisoning.
See section I.C.19.e for coding of adverse effects and poisoning, and section I.C.20 for external cause code reporting.

5.   Chapter 5: Mental and behavioral disorders (F01 – F99)

a.   Pain disorders related to psychological factors

Assign code F45.41, for pain that is exclusively psychological. Code F45.41, Pain disorder with related psychological factors, should be used following the appropriate code from category G89, Pain, not elsewhere classified, if there is documentation of a psychological component for a patient with acute or chronic pain.

See Section I.C.6. Pain

6.   **Chapter 6: Diseases of Nervous System and Sense Organs (G00-G99)**

a.   **Dominant/nondominant side**

Codes from category G81, Hemiplegia and hemiparesis, and subcategories, G83.1, Monoplegia of lower limb, G83.2, Monoplegia of upper limb, and G83.3, Monoplegia, unspecified, identify whether the dominant or nondominant side is affected. Should this information not be available in the record, **and the classification system does not indicate a default,** the default should be dominant. For ambidextrous patients, the default should also be dominant.

b.   **Pain - Category G89**

1)   **General coding information**

Codes in category G89, Pain, not elsewhere classified, may be used in conjunction with codes from other categories and chapters to provide more detail about acute or chronic pain and neoplasm-related pain, unless otherwise indicated below.

If the pain is not specified as acute or chronic, post-thoracotomy, postprocedural, or neoplasm-related, do not assign codes from category G89.

A code from category G89 should not be assigned if the underlying (definitive) diagnosis is known, unless the reason for the encounter is pain control/ management and not management of the underlying condition.

When an admission or encounter is for a procedure aimed at treating the underlying condition (e.g., spinal fusion, kyphoplasty), a code for the underlying condition (e.g., vertebral fracture, spinal stenosis) should be assigned as the principal diagnosis. No code from category G89 should be assigned.

(a)   **Category G89 Codes as Principal or First-Listed Diagnosis**

Category G89 codes are acceptable as principal diagnosis or the first-listed code:
- When pain control or pain management is the reason for the admission/encounter (e.g., a patient with displaced intervertebral disc, nerve impingement and severe back pain presents for

injection of steroid into the spinal canal). The underlying cause of the pain should be reported as an additional diagnosis, if known.

- When a patient is admitted for the insertion of a neurostimulator for pain control, assign the appropriate pain code as the principal or first listed diagnosis. When an admission or encounter is for a procedure aimed at treating the underlying condition and a neurostimulator is inserted for pain control during the same admission/encounter, a code for the underlying condition should be assigned as the principal diagnosis and the appropriate pain code should be assigned as a secondary diagnosis.

(b)   Use of Category G89 Codes in Conjunction with Site Specific Pain Codes

(i)   Assigning Category G89 and Site-Specific Pain Codes

Codes from category G89 may be used in conjunction with codes that identify the site of pain (including codes from chapter 18) if the category G89 code provides additional information. For example, if the code describes the site of the pain, but does not fully describe whether the pain is acute or chronic, then both codes should be assigned.

(ii)   Sequencing of Category G89 Codes with Site-Specific Pain Codes

The sequencing of category G89 codes with site-specific pain codes (including chapter 18 codes), is dependent on the circumstances of the encounter/admission as follows:

- If the encounter is for pain control or pain management, assign the code from category G89 followed by the code identifying the specific site of pain (e.g., encounter for pain management for acute neck pain from trauma is assigned code G89.11, Acute pain due to trauma, followed by code M54.2, Cervicalgia, to identify the site of pain).

- If the encounter is for any other reason except pain control or pain management, and a related definitive diagnosis has not been established (confirmed) by the provider, assign the code for the specific site of pain first, followed by the appropriate code from category G89.

2)   Pain due to devices, implants and grafts

See Section I.C.19. Pain due to medical devices

3)   Postoperative Pain

The provider's documentation should be used to guide the coding of postoperative pain, as well as *Section III. Reporting Additional Diagnoses* and *Section IV. Diagnostic Coding and Reporting in the Outpatient Setting.*

The default for post-thoracotomy and other postoperative pain not specified as acute or chronic is the code for the acute form.

Routine or expected postoperative pain immediately after surgery should not be coded.

(a)   Postoperative pain not associated with specific postoperative complication

Postoperative pain not associated with a specific postoperative complication is assigned to the appropriate postoperative pain code in category G89.

(b)   Postoperative pain associated with specific postoperative complication

Postoperative pain associated with a specific postoperative complication (such as painful wire sutures) is assigned to the appropriate code(s) found in Chapter 19, Injury, poisoning, and certain other consequences of external causes. If appropriate, use additional code(s) from category G89 to identify acute or chronic pain (G89.18 or G89.28).

4)   Chronic pain

Chronic pain is classified to subcategory G89.2. There is no time frame defining when pain becomes chronic pain. The provider's documentation should be used to guide use of these codes.

5)   **Neoplasm Related Pain**

Code G89.3 is assigned to pain documented as being related, associated or due to cancer, primary or secondary malignancy, or tumor. This code is assigned regardless of whether the pain is acute or chronic.

This code may be assigned as the principal or first-listed code when the stated reason for the admission/encounter is documented as pain control/pain management. The underlying neoplasm should be reported as an additional diagnosis.

When the reason for the admission/encounter is management of the neoplasm and the pain associated with the neoplasm is also documented, code G89.3 may be assigned as an additional diagnosis. It is not necessary to assign an additional code for the site of the pain.

See Section I.C.2 for instructions on the sequencing of neoplasms for all other stated reasons for the admission/encounter (except for pain control/pain management).

6)   **Chronic pain syndrome**

Central pain syndrome (G89.0) and chronic pain syndrome (G89.4) are different than the term "chronic pain," and therefore codes should only be used when the provider has specifically documented this condition.

See Section I.C.5. Pain disorders related to psychological factors

7.   **Chapter 7: Diseases of Eye and Adnexa (H00-H59)**

Reserved for future guideline expansion

8.   **Chapter 8: Diseases of Ear and Mastoid Process (H60-H95)**

Reserved for future guideline expansion

9.   **Chapter 9: Diseases of Circulatory System (I00-I99)**

a.   **Hypertension**

1)   **Hypertension with Heart Disease**

Heart conditions classified to I50.- or I51.4-I51.9, are assigned to, a code from category I11, Hypertensive heart disease, when a causal relationship is stated (due to hypertension) or implied (hypertensive). Use an additional code from category I50, Heart failure, to identify the type of heart failure in those patients with heart failure.

The same heart conditions (I50.-, I51.4-I51.9) with hypertension, but without a stated causal relationship, are coded separately. Sequence according to the circumstances of the admission/encounter.

2)   **Hypertensive Chronic Kidney Disease**

Assign codes from category I12, Hypertensive chronic kidney disease, when both hypertension and a condition classifiable to category N18, Chronic kidney disease (CKD), are present. Unlike hypertension with heart disease, ICD-10-CM presumes a cause-and-effect relationship and classifies chronic kidney disease with hypertension as hypertensive chronic kidney disease.
The appropriate code from category N18 should be used as a secondary code with a code from category I12 to identify the stage of chronic kidney disease.

See Section I.C.14. Chronic kidney disease.

If a patient has hypertensive chronic kidney disease **and acute** renal failure, an additional code for the acute renal failure is required.

3)   **Hypertensive Heart and Chronic Kidney Disease**

Assign codes from combination category I13, Hypertensive heart and chronic kidney disease, when both hypertensive kidney disease and hypertensive heart disease are stated in the diagnosis. Assume a relationship between the hypertension and the chronic kidney disease, whether or not the condition is so designated. If heart failure is present, assign an additional code from category I50 to identify the type of heart failure.

The appropriate code from category N18, Chronic kidney disease, should be used as a secondary code with a code from category I13 to identify the stage of chronic kidney disease.

See Section I.C.14. Chronic kidney disease.

The codes in category I13, Hypertensive heart and chronic kidney disease, are combination codes that include hypertension, heart disease and chronic kidney disease. The Includes note at I13 specifies that the conditions included at I11 and I12 are included together in I13. If a patient has hypertension, heart disease and chronic kidney disease then a code from I13 should be used, not individual codes for hypertension, heart disease and chronic kidney disease, or codes from I11 or I12.

For patients with both acute renal failure and chronic kidney disease an additional code for acute renal failure is required.

4) **Hypertensive Cerebrovascular Disease**

For hypertensive cerebrovascular disease, first assign the appropriate code from categories I60-I69, followed by the appropriate hypertension code.

5) **Hypertensive Retinopathy**

Code H35.0, Hypertensive retinopathy, should be used with code I10, Essential (primary) hypertension, to include the systemic hypertension. The sequencing is based on the reason for the encounter.

6) **Hypertension, Secondary**

Secondary hypertension is due to an underlying condition. Two codes are required: one to identify the underlying etiology and one from category I15 to identify the hypertension. Sequencing of codes is determined by the reason for admission/encounter.

7) **Hypertension, Transient**

Assign code R03.0, Elevated blood pressure reading without diagnosis of hypertension, unless patient has an established diagnosis of hypertension. Assign code O13.-, Gestational [pregnancy-induced] hypertension without significant proteinuria, or O14.-, Gestational [pregnancy-induced] hypertension with significant proteinuria, for transient hypertension of pregnancy.

8)   Hypertension, Controlled

This diagnostic statement usually refers to an existing state of hypertension under control by therapy. Assign code I10.

9)   Hypertension, Uncontrolled

Uncontrolled hypertension may refer to untreated hypertension or hypertension not responding to current therapeutic regimen. In either case, assign code I10.

b.   Atherosclerotic coronary artery disease and angina

ICD-10-CM has combination codes for atherosclerotic heart disease with angina pectoris. The subcategories for these codes are I25.11, Atherosclerotic heart disease of native coronary artery with angina pectoris and I25.7, Atherosclerosis of coronary artery bypass graft(s) and coronary artery of transplanted heart with angina pectoris.

When using one of these combination codes it is not necessary to use an additional code for angina pectoris. A causal relationship can be assumed in a patient with both atherosclerosis and angina pectoris, unless the documentation indicates the angina is due to something other than the atherosclerosis.

If a patient with coronary artery disease is admitted due to an acute myocardial infarction (AMI), the AMI should be sequenced before the coronary artery disease.

See Section I.C.9. Acute myocardial infarction (AMI)

c.   Intraoperative and Postprocedural cerebrovascular accident

Medical record documentation should clearly specify the cause-and-effect relationship between the medical intervention and the cerebrovascular accident in order to assign a code for intraoperative or postprocedural cerebrovascular accident. Proper code assignment depends on whether it was an infarction or hemorrhage and whether it occurred intraoperatively or postoperatively. If it was a cerebral hemorrhage, code assignment depends on the type of procedure performed.

d.   Sequelae of Cerebrovascular Disease

1)   Category I69, Sequelae of Cerebrovascular disease

Category I69 is used to indicate conditions classifiable to categories I60-I67 as the causes of late effects (neurologic deficits), themselves classified elsewhere. These "late effects" include neurologic deficits that persist after initial onset of conditions classifiable to categories I60-I67. The neurologic deficits caused by cerebrovascular disease may be present from the onset or may arise at any time after the onset of the condition classifiable to categories I60-I67.

2)   Codes from category I69 with codes from I60-I67

Codes from category I69 may be assigned on a health care record with codes from I60-I67, if the patient has a current cerebrovascular accident (CVA) and deficits from an old CVA.

3)   Code Z86.73

Assign code Z86.73, Personal history of transient ischemic attack (TIA), and cerebral infarction without residual deficits (and not a code from category I69) as an additional code for history of cerebrovascular disease when no neurologic deficits are present.

e.   Acute myocardial infarction (AMI)

1)   ST elevation myocardial infarction (STEMI) and non ST elevation myocardial infarction (NSTEMI)

The ICD-10-CM codes for acute myocardial infarction (AMI) identify the site, such as anterolateral wall or true posterior wall. Subcategories I21.0-I21.2 and code I21.4 are used for ST elevation myocardial infarction (STEMI). Code I21.4, Non-ST elevation (NSTEMI) myocardial infarction, is used for non ST elevation myocardial infarction (NSTEMI) and nontransmural MIs.

2)   Acute myocardial infarction, unspecified

Code I21.3, ST elevation (STEMI) myocardial infarction of unspecified site, is the default for the unspecified term acute myocardial infarction. If only STEMI or transmural MI without the site is documented, query the provider as to the site, or assign code I21.3.

3)   AMI documented as nontransmural or subendocardial but site provided

If an AMI is documented as nontransmural or subendocardial, but the site is provided, it is still coded as a subendocardial AMI. If NSTEMI evolves to STEMI, assign the STEMI code.

If STEMI converts to NSTEMI due to thrombolytic therapy, it is still coded as STEMI.

See Section I.C.21.3 for information on coding status post administration of tPA in a different facility within the last 24 hours.

4)   **Subsequent acute myocardial infarction**

A code from category I22, Subsequent ST elevation (STEMI) and non ST elevation (NSTEMI) myocardial infarction, is to be used when a patient who has suffered an AMI has a new AMI within the 4 week time frame of the initial AMI. A code from category I22 must be used in conjunction with a code from category I21.

The sequencing of the I22 and I21 codes depends on the circumstances of the encounter. Should a patient who is in the hospital due to an AMI have a subsequent AMI while still in the hospital code I21 would be sequenced first as the reason for admission, with code I22 sequenced as a secondary code. Should a patient have a subsequent AMI after discharge for care of an initial AMI, and the reason for admission is the subsequent AMI, the I22 code should be sequenced first followed by the I21. An I21 code must accompany an I22 code to identify the site of the initial AMI, and to indicate that the patient is still within the 4 week time frame of healing from the initial AMI.

The guidelines for assigning the correct I22 code are the same as for the initial AMI.

10.   **Chapter 10: Diseases of Respiratory System (J00-J99)**

a.   **Chronic Obstructive Pulmonary Disease [COPD] and Asthma**

1)   **Acute exacerbation of chronic obstructive bronchitis and asthma**

The codes in categories J44 and J45 distinguish between uncomplicated cases and those in acute exacerbation. An acute exacerbation is a worsening or a decompensation of a chronic condition. An acute exacerbation is not equivalent to an infection superimposed on a chronic condition, though an exacerbation may be triggered by an infection.

b.   Acute Respiratory Failure

1)   Acute respiratory failure as principal diagnosis

Code J96.0, Acute respiratory failure, or code J96.2, Acute and chronic respiratory failure, may be assigned as a principal diagnosis when it is the condition established after study to be chiefly responsible for occasioning the admission to the hospital, and the selection is supported by the Alphabetic Index and Tabular List. However, chapter-specific coding guidelines (such as obstetrics, poisoning, HIV, newborn) that provide sequencing direction take precedence.

2)   Acute respiratory failure as secondary diagnosis

Respiratory failure may be listed as a secondary diagnosis if it occurs after admission, or if it is present on admission, but does not meet the definition of principal diagnosis.

3)   Sequencing of acute respiratory failure and another acute condition

When a patient is admitted with respiratory failure and another acute condition, (e.g., myocardial infarction, cerebrovascular accident, aspiration pneumonia), the principal diagnosis will not be the same in every situation. This applies whether the other acute condition is a respiratory or nonrespiratory condition. Selection of the principal diagnosis will be dependent on the circumstances of admission.   If both the respiratory failure and the other acute condition are equally responsible for occasioning the admission to the hospital, and there are no chapter-specific sequencing rules, the guideline regarding two or more diagnoses that equally meet the definition for principal diagnosis *(Section II, C.)* may be applied in these situations.

If the documentation is not clear as to whether acute respiratory failure and another condition are equally responsible for occasioning the admission, query the provider for clarification.

c.   Influenza due to *certain identified influenza* influenza *viruses*

Code only confirmed cases of avian influenza **(code J09.0-, Influenza due to identified avian influenza virus) or novel H1N1 or swine flu, code J09.1-**. This is an exception to the hospital inpatient guideline Section II, H. (Uncertain Diagnosis).

In this context, "confirmation" does not require documentation of positive laboratory testing specific for avian **or novel H1N1 (H1N1 or swine flu)** influenza. However, coding should be based on the provider's diagnostic statement that the patient has avian influenza.

If the provider records "suspected or possible or probable avian influenza," the appropriate influenza code from category J10, Influenza due to other influenza virus, should be assigned. **A code from category** J09, Influenza due to **certain identified** influenza virus**es**, should not be assigned.

11. **Chapter 11: Diseases of Digestive System (K00-K94)**

Reserved for future guideline expansion

12. **Chapter 12: Diseases of Skin and Subcutaneous Tissue (L00-L99)**

a. **Pressure ulcer stage codes**

1) **Pressure ulcer stages**

Codes from category L89, Pressure ulcer, are combination codes that identify the site of the pressure ulcer as well as the stage of the ulcer.

The ICD-10-CM classifies pressure ulcer stages based on severity, which is designated by stages 1-4, unspecified stage and unstageable .

Assign as many codes from category L89 as needed to identify all the pressure ulcers the patient has, if applicable.

2) **Unstageable pressure ulcers**

Assignment of the code for unstageable pressure ulcer (L89.--0) should be based on the clinical documentation. These codes are used for pressure ulcers whose stage cannot be clinically determined (e.g., the ulcer is covered by eschar or has been treated with a skin or muscle graft) and pressure ulcers that are documented as deep tissue injury but not documented as due to trauma. This code should not be confused with the codes for unspecified stage (L89.--9). When there is no documentation regarding the stage of the pressure ulcer, assign the appropriate code for unspecified stage (L89.--9).

3)   **Documented pressure ulcer stage**

Assignment of the pressure ulcer stage code should be
guided by clinical documentation of the stage or
documentation of the terms found in the index. For clinical
terms describing the stage that are not found in the index,
and there is no documentation of the stage, the provider
should be queried.

4)   **Patients admitted with pressure ulcers documented as
healed**

No code is assigned if the documentation states that the
pressure ulcer is completely healed.

5)   **Patients admitted with pressure ulcers documented as
healing**

Pressure ulcers described as healing should be assigned the
appropriate pressure ulcer stage code based on the
documentation in the medical record. If the documentation
does not provide information about the stage of the healing
pressure ulcer, assign the appropriate code for unspecified
stage.

If the documentation is unclear as to whether the patient
has a current (new) pressure ulcer or if the patient is being
treated for a healing pressure ulcer, query the provider.

6)   **Patient admitted with pressure ulcer evolving into
another stage during the admission**

If a patient is admitted with a pressure ulcer at one stage
and it progresses to a higher stage, assign the code for the
highest stage reported for that site.

13.   **Chapter 13: Diseases of the Musculoskeletal System and
Connective Tissue (M00-M99)**

a.   **Site and laterality**

Most of the codes within Chapter 13 have site and laterality
designations. The site represents either the bone, joint or the muscle
involved. For some conditions where more than one bone, joint or
muscle is usually involved, such as osteoarthritis, there is a "multiple
sites" code available. For categories where no multiple site code is
provided and more than one bone, joint or muscle is involved, multiple
codes should be used to indicate the different sites involved.

1) Bone versus joint

For certain conditions, the bone may be affected at the upper or lower end, (e.g., avascular necrosis of bone, M87, Osteoporosis, M80, M81). Though the portion of the bone affected may be at the joint, the site designation will be the bone, not the joint.

b. Acute traumatic versus chronic or recurrent musculoskeletal conditions

Many musculoskeletal conditions are a result of previous injury or trauma to a site, or are recurrent conditions. Bone, joint or muscle conditions that are the result of a healed injury are usually found in chapter 13. Recurrent bone, joint or muscle conditions are also usually found in chapter 13. Any current, acute injury should be coded to the appropriate injury code from chapter 19. Chronic or recurrent conditions should generally be coded with a code from chapter 13. If it is difficult to determine from the documentation in the record which code is best to describe a condition, query the provider.

c. Coding of Pathologic Fractures

7th character A is for use as long as the patient is receiving active treatment for the fracture. Examples of active treatment are: surgical treatment, emergency department encounter, evaluation and treatment by a new physician. 7th character, D is to be used for encounters after the patient has completed active treatment. The other 7th characters, listed under each subcategory in the Tabular List, are to be used for subsequent encounters for treatment of problems associated with the healing, such as malunions, nonunions, and sequelae.
Care for complications of surgical treatment for fracture repairs during the healing or recovery phase should be coded with the appropriate complication codes.

See Section I.C.19. Coding of traumatic fractures.

d. Osteoporosis

Osteoporosis is a systemic condition, meaning that all bones of the musculoskeletal system are affected. Therefore, site is not a component of the codes under category M81, Osteoporosis without current pathological fracture. The site codes under category M80, Osteoporosis with current pathological fracture, identify the site of the fracture, not the osteoporosis.

1) Osteoporosis without pathological fracture

Category M81, Osteoporosis without current pathological fracture, is for use for patients with osteoporosis who do not currently have a pathologic fracture due to the osteoporosis, even if they have had a fracture in the past. For patients with a history of osteoporosis fractures, status code Z87.31, Personal history of osteoporosis fracture, should follow the code from M81.

2) **Osteoporosis with current pathological fracture**

Category M80, Osteoporosis with current pathological fracture, is for patients who have a current pathologic fracture at the time of an encounter. The codes under M80 identify the site of the fracture. A code from category M80, not a traumatic fracture code, should be used for any patient with known osteoporosis who suffers a fracture, even if the patient had a minor fall or trauma, if that fall or trauma would not usually break a normal, healthy bone.

14.   Chapter 14: Diseases of Genitourinary System (N00-N99)

a.   Chronic kidney disease

1) **Stages of chronic kidney disease (CKD)**

The ICD-10-CM classifies CKD based on severity. The severity of CKD is designated by stages I-V. Stage II, code N18.2, equates to mild CKD; stage III, code N18.3, equates to moderate CKD; and stage IV, code N18.4, equates to severe CKD. Code N18.6, End stage renal disease (ESRD), is assigned when the provider has documented end-stage-renal disease (ESRD).

If both a stage of CKD and ESRD are documented, assign code N18.6 only.

2) **Chronic kidney disease and kidney transplant status**

Patients who have undergone kidney transplant may still have some form of **chronic kidney disease** (CKD) because the kidney transplant may not fully restore kidney function. Therefore, the presence of CKD alone does not constitute a transplant complication. Assign the appropriate N18 code for the patient's stage of CKD and code Z94.0, Kidney transplant status. If a transplant complication such as failure or rejection **or other transplant complication** is documented, see section I.C.19.g for information on coding complications of a kidney transplant. If the documentation is unclear as to whether the patient has a complication of the transplant, query the provider.

3) Chronic kidney disease with other conditions

Patients with CKD may also suffer from other serious conditions, most commonly diabetes mellitus and hypertension. The sequencing of the CKD code in relationship to codes for other contributing conditions is based on the conventions in the Tabular List.

See I.C.9. Hypertensive chronic kidney disease.
See I.C.19. Chronic kidney disease and kidney transplant complications.

15. Chapter 15: Pregnancy, Childbirth, and the Puerperium (O00-*O9A*)

a. General Rules for Obstetric Cases

1) Codes from chapter 15 and sequencing priority

Obstetric cases require codes from chapter 15, codes in the range O00-**O9A**, Pregnancy, Childbirth, and the Puerperium. Chapter 15 codes have sequencing priority over codes from other chapters. Additional codes from other chapters may be used in conjunction with chapter 15 codes to further specify conditions. Should the provider document that the pregnancy is incidental to the encounter, then code Z33.1, Pregnant state, incidental, should be used in place of any chapter 15 codes. It is the provider's responsibility to state that the condition being treated is not affecting the pregnancy.

2) Chapter 15 codes used only on the maternal record

Chapter 15 codes are to be used only on the maternal record, never on the record of the newborn.

3) Final character for trimester

The majority of codes in Chapter 15 have a final character indicating the trimester of pregnancy. The timeframes for the trimesters are indicated at the beginning of the chapter. If trimester is not a component of a code it is because the condition always occurs in a specific trimester, or the concept of trimester of pregnancy is not applicable. Certain codes have characters for only certain trimesters because the condition does not occur in all trimesters, but it may occur in more than just one.

Assignment of the final character for trimester should be based on the trimester for the current admission/encounter. This applies to the assignment of trimester for pre-existing conditions as well as those that develop during or are due to the pregnancy.

Whenever delivery occurs during the current admission, and there is an "in childbirth" option for the obstetric complication being coded, the "in childbirth" code should be assigned.

4)   Selection of trimester for inpatient admissions *that encompass more than one trimesters*

In instances when a patient is admitted to a hospital for complications of pregnancy **during one trimester** and remains in the hospital **into a subsequent trimester, the trimester character for** the antepartum complication code should be assigned on the basis of the trimester when the complication developed, **not the trimester of the discharge. If the condition developed prior to the current admission/encounter or represents a pre-existing condition, the trimester character for the trimester at the time of the admission/encounter should be assigned.**

5)   Unspecified trimester

Each category that includes codes for trimester has a code for "unspecified trimester." The "unspecified trimester" code should rarely be used, such as when the documentation in the record is insufficient to determine the trimester and it is not possible to obtain clarification.

b.   Selection of OB Principal or First-listed Diagnosis

1)   Routine outpatient prenatal visits

For routine outpatient prenatal visits when no complications are present, a code from category Z34, Encounter for supervision of normal pregnancy, should be used as the first-listed diagnosis. These codes should not be used in conjunction with chapter 15 codes.

2)   Prenatal outpatient visits for high-risk patients

For routine prenatal outpatient visits for patients with high-risk pregnancies, a code from category O09, Supervision of high-risk pregnancy, should be used as the first-listed diagnosis. Secondary chapter 15 codes may be used in conjunction with these codes if appropriate.

3)   Episodes when no delivery occurs

In episodes when no delivery occurs, the principal diagnosis should correspond to the principal complication of the pregnancy which necessitated the encounter. Should more than one complication exist, all of which are treated or monitored, any of the complications codes may be sequenced first.

4)   When a delivery occurs

When a delivery occurs, the principal diagnosis should correspond to the main circumstances or complication of the delivery. In cases of cesarean delivery, the selection of the principal **diagnosis should be the condition established after study that was responsible for the patient's admission. If the patient was admitted with a condition that resulted in the performance of a cesarean procedure, that condition should be selected as the principal diagnosis. If** the reason for **the** admission/encounter was unrelated to the condition resulting in the cesarean delivery**, the condition related to the reason for the admission/encounter should be selected as the principal diagnosis, even if a cesarean was performed.**

5)   Outcome of delivery

A code from category Z37, Outcome of delivery, should be included on every maternal record when a delivery has occurred. These codes are not to be used on subsequent records or on the newborn record.

c.   Pre-existing conditions versus conditions due to the pregnancy

Certain categories in Chapter 15 distinguish between conditions of the mother that existed prior to pregnancy (pre-existing) and those that are a direct result of pregnancy. When assigning codes from Chapter 15, it is important to assess if a condition was pre-existing prior to pregnancy or developed during or due to the pregnancy in order to assign the correct code.

Categories that do not distinguish between pre-existing and pregnancy-related conditions may be used for either. It is acceptable to use codes specifically for the puerperium with codes complicating pregnancy and childbirth if a condition arises postpartum during the delivery encounter.

d.   Pre-existing hypertension in pregnancy

Category O10, Pre-existing hypertension complicating pregnancy, childbirth and the puerperium, includes codes for hypertensive heart and hypertensive chronic kidney disease. When assigning one of the O10 codes that includes hypertensive heart disease or hypertensive chronic kidney disease, it is necessary to add a secondary code from the appropriate hypertension category to specify the type of heart failure or chronic kidney disease.

See Section I.C.9. Hypertension.

e.   Fetal Conditions Affecting the Management of the Mother

1)   Codes from categories O35 and O36

Codes from categories O35, Maternal care for known or suspected fetal abnormality and damage, and O36, Maternal care for other fetal problems, are assigned only when the fetal condition is actually responsible for modifying the management of the mother, i.e., by requiring diagnostic studies, additional observation, special care, or termination of pregnancy. The fact that the fetal condition exists does not justify assigning a code from this series to the mother's record.

2)   In utero surgery

In cases when surgery is performed on the fetus, a diagnosis code from category O35, Maternal care for known or suspected fetal abnormality and damage, should be assigned identifying the fetal condition. Assign the appropriate procedure code for the procedure performed.

No code from Chapter 16, the perinatal codes, should be used on the mother's record to identify fetal conditions. Surgery performed in utero on a fetus is still to be coded as an obstetric encounter.

f.   HIV Infection in Pregnancy, Childbirth and the Puerperium

During pregnancy, childbirth or the puerperium, a patient admitted because of an HIV-related illness should receive a principal diagnosis from subcategory O98.7-, Human immunodeficiency [HIV] disease complicating pregnancy, childbirth and the puerperium, followed by the code(s) for the HIV-related illness(es).

Patients with asymptomatic HIV infection status admitted during pregnancy, childbirth, or the puerperium should receive codes of O98.7- and Z21, Asymptomatic human immunodeficiency virus [HIV] infection status.

g. **Diabetes mellitus in pregnancy**

Diabetes mellitus is a significant complicating factor in pregnancy. Pregnant women who are diabetic should be assigned a code O24, Diabetes mellitus in pregnancy, childbirth, and the puerperium, first, followed by the appropriate diabetes code(s) (E08-E13) from Chapter 4.

h. **Long term use of insulin**

Code Z79.4, Long-term (current) use of insulin, should also be assigned if the diabetes mellitus is being treated with insulin.

i. **Gestational (pregnancy induced) diabetes**

Gestational (pregnancy induced) diabetes can occur during the second and third trimester of pregnancy in women who were not diabetic prior to pregnancy. Gestational diabetes can cause complications in the pregnancy similar to those of pre-existing diabetes mellitus. It also puts the woman at greater risk of developing diabetes after the pregnancy. Codes for gestational diabetes are in subcategory O24.4, Gestational diabetes mellitus. No other code from category O24, Diabetes mellitus in pregnancy, childbirth, and the puerperium, should be used with a code from O24.4

The codes under subcategory O24.4 include diet controlled and insulin controlled. If a patient with gestational diabetes is treated with both diet and insulin, only the code for insulin-controlled is required. Code **Z79.4**, Long-term (current) use of insulin, should **not** be assigned **with codes from subcategory O24.4**.

An abnormal glucose tolerance in pregnancy is assigned a code from subcategory O99.81, Abnormal glucose complicating pregnancy, childbirth, and the puerperium.

j. **Sepsis and septic shock complicating abortion, pregnancy, childbirth and the puerperium**

When assigning a chapter 15 code for sepsis complicating abortion, pregnancy, childbirth, and the puerperium, a code for the specific type of infection should be assigned as an additional diagnosis. If severe sepsis is present, a code from subcategory R65.2, Severe sepsis, and code(s) for associated organ dysfunction(s) should also be assigned as additional diagnoses.

k.   Puerperal sepsis

Code O85, Puerperal sepsis, should be assigned with a secondary code to identify the causal organism (e.g., for a bacterial infection, assign a code from category B95-B96, Bacterial infections in conditions classified elsewhere). A code from category A40, Streptococcal sepsis, or A41, Other sepsis, should not be used for puerperal sepsis. If applicable, use additional codes to identify severe sepsis (R65.2-) and any associated acute organ dysfunction.

l.   Alcohol and tobacco use during pregnancy, childbirth and the puerperium

1)   Alcohol use during pregnancy, childbirth and the puerperium

Codes under subcategory O99.31, Alcohol use complicating pregnancy, childbirth, and the puerperium, should be assigned for any pregnancy case when a mother uses alcohol during the pregnancy or postpartum. A secondary code from category F10, Alcohol related disorders, should also be assigned.

2)   Tobacco use during pregnancy, childbirth and the puerperium

Codes under subcategory O99.33, Smoking (tobacco) complicating pregnancy, childbirth, and the puerperium, should be assigned for any pregnancy case when a mother uses any type of tobacco product during the pregnancy or postpartum. A secondary code from category F17, Nicotine dependence, or code Z72.0, Tobacco use, should also be assigned.

m.   Poisoning, toxic effects, adverse effects and underdosing in a pregnant patient

A code from subcategory O9A.2, Injury, poisoning and certain other consequences of external causes complicating pregnancy, childbirth, and the puerperium, should be sequenced first, followed by the appropriate poisoning, toxic effect, adverse effect or underdosing code, and then the additional code(s) that specifies the condition caused by the poisoning, toxic effect, adverse effect or underdosing.

See Section I.C.19. Adverse effects, poisoning, underdosing and toxic effects.

n.   **Normal Delivery, Code O80**

1)   **Encounter for full term uncomplicated delivery**

Code O80 should be assigned when a woman is admitted for a full-term normal delivery and delivers a single, healthy infant without any complications antepartum, during the delivery, or postpartum during the delivery episode. Code O80 is always a principal diagnosis. It is not to be used if any other code from chapter 15 is needed to describe a current complication of the antenatal, delivery, or perinatal period. Additional codes from other chapters may be used with code O80 if they are not related to or are in any way complicating the pregnancy.

2)   **Uncomplicated delivery with resolved antepartum complication**

Code O80 may be used if the patient had a complication at some point during the pregnancy, but the complication is not present at the time of the admission for delivery.

3)   **Outcome of delivery for O80**

Z37.0, Single live birth, is the only outcome of delivery code appropriate for use with O80.

o.   **The Peripartum and Postpartum Periods**

1)   **Peripartum and Postpartum periods**

The postpartum period begins immediately after delivery and continues for six weeks following delivery. The peripartum period is defined as the last month of pregnancy to five months postpartum.

2)   **Peripartum and postpartum complication**

A postpartum complication is any complication occurring within the six-week period.

3)   **Pregnancy-related complications after 6 week period**

Chapter 15 codes may also be used to describe pregnancy-related complications after the peripartum or postpartum period if the provider documents that a condition is pregnancy related.

4)   **Admission for routine postpartum care following delivery outside hospital**

When the mother delivers outside the hospital prior to admission and is admitted for routine postpartum care and no complications are noted, code Z39.0, Encounter for care and examination of mother immediately after delivery, should be assigned as the principal diagnosis.

5)   Pregnancy associated cardiomyopathy

Pregnancy associated cardiomyopathy, code O90.3, is unique in that it may be diagnosed in the third trimester of pregnancy but may continue to progress months after delivery. For this reason, it is referred to as peripartum cardiomyopathy. Code O90.3 is only for use when the cardiomyopathy develops as a result of pregnancy in a woman who did not have pre-existing heart disease.

p.   Code O94, Sequelae of complication of pregnancy, childbirth, and the puerperium

1)   Code O94

Code O94, Sequelae of complication of pregnancy, childbirth, and the puerperium, is for use in those cases when an initial complication of a pregnancy develops a sequelae requiring care or treatment at a future date.

2)   After the initial postpartum period

This code may be used at any time after the initial postpartum period.

3)   Sequencing of Code O94

This code, like all late effect codes, is to be sequenced following the code describing the sequelae of the complication.

q. Abortions

1)   Abortion with Liveborn Fetus

When an attempted termination of pregnancy results in a liveborn fetus assign a code from subcategory O60.1, Preterm labor with preterm delivery, **and a code from** category Z37, Outcome of Delivery. The procedure code for the attempted termination of pregnancy should also be assigned.

2)   Retained Products of Conception following an abortion

Subsequent encounters for retained products of conception following a spontaneous abortion or elective termination of pregnancy are assigned the appropriate code from category O03, Spontaneous abortion, or code Z33.2, Encounter for elective termination of pregnancy. This advice is appropriate even when the patient was discharged previously with a discharge diagnosis of complete abortion.

16.   Chapter 16: Newborn (Perinatal) Guidelines (P00-P96)

For coding and reporting purposes the perinatal period is defined as before birth through the 28th day following birth. The following guidelines are provided for reporting purposes

a.   General Perinatal Rules

1)   Use of Chapter 16 Codes

Codes in this chapter are <u>never</u> for use on the maternal record. Codes from Chapter 15, the obstetric chapter, are never permitted on the newborn record. Chapter 16 code may be used throughout the life of the patient if the condition is still present.

2)   Principal Diagnosis for Birth Record

When coding the birth episode in a newborn record, assign a code from category Z38, Liveborn according to place of birth and type of delivery, as the principal diagnosis. A code from category Z38 is assigned only once, to a newborn at the time of birth. If a newborn is transferred to another institution, a code from category Z38 should not be used at the receiving hospital.

A code from category Z38 is used only on the newborn record, not on the mother's record.

3)   Use of Codes from other Chapters with Codes from Chapter 16

Codes from other chapters may be used with codes from chapter 16 if the codes from the other chapters provide more specific detail. Codes for signs and symptoms may be assigned when a definitive diagnosis has not been established. If the reason for the encounter is a perinatal condition, the code from chapter 16 should be sequenced first.

4)   Use of Chapter 16 Codes after the Perinatal Period

Should a condition originate in the perinatal period, and continue throughout the life of the patient, the perinatal code should continue to be used regardless of the patient's age.

5)   Birth process or community acquired conditions

If a newborn has a condition that may be either due to the birth process or community acquired and the documentation does not indicate which it is, the default is due to the birth process and the code from Chapter 16 should be used.   If the condition is community-acquired, a code from Chapter 16 should not be assigned.

6)   Code all clinically significant conditions

All clinically significant conditions noted on routine newborn examination should be coded. A condition is clinically significant if it requires:
- clinical evaluation; or
- therapeutic treatment; or
- diagnostic procedures; or
- extended length of hospital stay; or
- increased nursing care and/or monitoring; or
- has implications for future health care needs

Note: The perinatal guidelines listed above are the same as the general coding guidelines for "additional diagnoses", except for the final point regarding implications for future health care needs. Codes should be assigned for conditions that have been specified by the provider as having implications for future health care needs.

b. Observation and Evaluation of Newborns for Suspected Conditions not Found

Assign a code from categories P00-P04 to identify those instances when a healthy newborn is evaluated for a suspected condition that is determined after study not to be present. Do not use a code from categories P00-P04 when the patient has identified signs or symptoms of a suspected problem; in such cases, code the sign or symptom.

c. Coding Additional Perinatal Diagnoses

1) Assigning codes for conditions that require treatment

Assign codes for conditions that require treatment or further investigation, prolong the length of stay, or require resource utilization.

2) Codes for conditions specified as having implications for future health care needs

Assign codes for conditions that have been specified by the provider as having implications for future health care needs.

Note: This guideline should not be used for adult patients.

d. Prematurity and Fetal Growth Retardation

Providers utilize different criteria in determining prematurity. A code for prematurity should not be assigned unless it is documented. Assignment of codes in categories P05, Disorders of newborn related to slow fetal growth and fetal malnutrition, and P07, Disorders of newborn related to short gestation and low birth weight, not elsewhere classified, should be based on the recorded birth weight and estimated gestational age. Codes from category P05 should not be assigned with codes from category P07.

When both birth weight and gestational age are available, two codes from category P07 should be assigned, with the code for birth weight sequenced before the code for gestational age.

e. Low birth weight and immaturity status

Codes from subcategory Z91.7, Low birth weight and immaturity status, are for use as personal status codes for a child or adult who was premature or had a low birth weight as a newborn and this is affecting the patient's current health status.

See Section I.C.21. Factors influencing health status and contact with health services, Status.

f.   Bacterial Sepsis of Newborn

Category P36, Bacterial sepsis of newborn, includes congenital sepsis. If a perinate is documented as having sepsis without documentation of congenital or community acquired, the default is congenital and a code from category P36 should be assigned. If the P36 code includes the causal organism, an additional code from category B95, Streptococcus, Staphylococcus, and Enterococcus as the cause of diseases classified elsewhere, or B96, Other bacterial agents as the cause of diseases classified elsewhere, should **not** be assigned. If the P36 code does not include the causal organism, assign an additional code from category B96. If applicable, use additional codes to identify severe sepsis (R65.2-) and any associated acute organ dysfunction.

g.   Stillbirth

Code P95, Stillbirth, is only for use in institutions that maintain separate records for stillbirths. No other code should be used with P95. Code P95 should not be used on the mother's record.

17.   Chapter 17: Congenital malformations, deformations, and chromosomal abnormalities (Q00-Q99)

Assign an appropriate code(s) from categories Q00-Q99, Congenital malformations, deformations, and chromosomal abnormalities when a malformation/deformation or chromosomal abnormality is documented. A malformation/deformation/or chromosomal abnormality may be the principal/first listed diagnosis on a record or a secondary diagnosis.

When a malformation/deformation/or chromosomal abnormality does not have a unique code assignment, assign additional code(s) for any manifestations that may be present.

When the code assignment specifically identifies the malformation/deformation/or chromosomal abnormality, manifestations that are an inherent component of the anomaly should not be coded separately. Additional codes should be assigned for manifestations that are not an inherent component.

Codes from Chapter 17 may be used throughout the life of the patient. If a congenital malformation or deformity has been corrected, a personal history code should be used to identify the history of the malformation or deformity. Although present at birth, malformation/deformation/or chromosomal abnormality may not be identified until later in life. Whenever the condition is diagnosed by the physician, it is appropriate to assign a code from codes Q00-Q99.

For the birth admission, the appropriate code from category Z38, Liveborn infants, according to place of birth and type of delivery, should be sequenced as the principal diagnosis, followed by any congenital anomaly codes, Q00-Q89.

18.   **Chapter 18: Symptoms, signs, and abnormal clinical and laboratory findings, not elsewhere classified (R00-R99)**

Chapter 18 includes symptoms, signs, abnormal results of clinical or other investigative procedures, and ill-defined conditions regarding which no diagnosis classifiable elsewhere is recorded. Signs and symptoms that point to a **specific** diagnosis have been assigned to a category in other chapters of the classification.

a.   **Use of symptom codes**

Codes that describe symptoms and signs are acceptable for reporting purposes when a related definitive diagnosis has not been established (confirmed) by the provider.

b.   **Use of a symptom code with a definitive diagnosis code**

Codes for signs and symptoms may be reported in addition to a related definitive diagnosis when the sign or symptom is not routinely associated with that diagnosis, such as the various signs and symptoms associated with complex syndromes. The definitive diagnosis code should be sequenced before the symptom code.

Signs or symptoms that are associated routinely with a disease process should not be assigned as additional codes, unless otherwise instructed by the classification.

c.   **Combination codes that include symptoms**

ICD-10-CM contains a number of combination codes that identify both the definitive diagnosis and common symptoms of that diagnosis. When using one of these combination codes, an additional code should not be assigned for the symptom.

d.   **Repeated falls**

Code R29.6, Repeated falls, is for use for encounters when a patient has recently fallen and the reason for the fall is being investigated.

Code Z91.81, History of falling, is for use when a patient has fallen in the past and is at risk for future falls. When appropriate, both codes R29.6 and Z91.81 may be assigned together.

e. **Glasgow coma scale**

The Glasgow coma scale codes (R40.2-) can be used in conjunction with traumatic brain injury codes or sequelae of cerebrovascular accident codes. These codes are primarily for use by trauma registries, but they may be used in any setting where this information is collected. The coma scale codes should be sequenced after the diagnosis code(s).

These codes, one from each subcategory, are needed to complete the scale. The 7th character indicates when the scale was recorded. The 7th character should match for all three codes.

At a minimum, report the initial score documented on presentation at your facility. This may be a score from the emergency medicine technician (EMT) or in the emergency department. If desired, a facility may choose to capture multiple Glasgow coma scale scores.

f. **Functional quadriplegia**

Functional quadriplegia (code R53.2) is the lack of ability to use one's limbs or to ambulate due to extreme debility. It is not associated with neurologic deficit or injury, and code R53.2 should not be used for cases of neurologic quadriplegia. It should only be assigned if functional quadriplegia is specifically documented in the medical record.

g. **SIRS due to Non-Infectious Process**

The systemic inflammatory response syndrome (SIRS) can develop as a result of certain non-infectious disease processes, such as trauma, malignant neoplasm, or pancreatitis. When SIRS is documented with a noninfectious condition, and no subsequent infection is documented, the code for the underlying condition, such as an injury, should be assigned, followed by code R65.10, Systemic inflammatory response syndrome (SIRS) of non-infectious origin without acute organ dysfunction, or code R65.11, Systemic inflammatory response syndrome (SIRS) of non-infectious origin with acute organ dysfunction. If an associated acute organ dysfunction is documented, the appropriate code(s) for the specific type of organ dysfunction(s) should be assigned in addition to code R65.11. If acute organ dysfunction is documented, but it cannot be determined if the acute organ dysfunction is associated with SIRS or due to another condition (e.g., directly due to the trauma), the provider should be queried.

g.   Death NOS

Code R99, Ill-defined and unknown cause of mortality, is only for use in the very limited circumstance when a patient who has already died is brought into an emergency department or other healthcare facility and is pronounced dead upon arrival. It does not represent the discharge disposition of death.

19.   Chapter 19: Injury, poisoning, and certain other consequences of external causes (S00-T88)

a.   Code Extensions

Most categories in chapter 19 have 7th character extensions that are required for each applicable code. Most categories in this chapter have three extensions (with the exception of fractures): A, initial encounter, D, subsequent encounter and S, sequela.

Extension "A", initial encounter is used while the patient is receiving active treatment for the injury. Examples of active treatment are: surgical treatment, emergency department encounter, and evaluation and treatment by a new physician.

Extension "D" subsequent encounter is used for encounters after the patient has received active treatment of the injury and is receiving routine care for the injury during the healing or recovery phase. Examples of subsequent care are: cast change or removal, removal of external **or** internal fixation device, medication adjustment, other aftercare and follow up visits following injury treatment.

The aftercare Z codes should not be used for aftercare for injuries. For aftercare of an injury, assign the acute injury code with the 7th character "D" (subsequent encounter).

Extension "S", sequela, is for use for complications or conditions that arise as a direct result of an injury, such as scar formation after a burn. The scars are sequelae of the burn. When using extension "S", it is necessary to use both the injury code that precipitated the sequela and the code for the sequela itself. The "S" is added only to the injury code, not the sequela code. The "S" extension identifies the injury responsible for the sequela. The specific type of sequela (e.g. scar) is sequenced first, followed by the injury code.

b.   **Coding of Injuries**

When coding injuries, assign separate codes for each injury unless a combination code is provided, in which case the combination code is assigned. Multiple injury codes are provided in ICD-10-CM, but should not be assigned unless information for a more specific code is not available. These **traumatic injury** codes (S00-T14.9) are not to be used for normal, healing surgical wounds or to identify complications of surgical wounds.

The code for the most serious injury, as determined by the provider and the focus of treatment, is sequenced first.

1)   **Superficial injuries**

Superficial injuries such as abrasions or contusions are not coded when associated with more severe injuries of the same site.

2)   **Primary injury with damage to nerves/blood vessels**

When a primary injury results in minor damage to peripheral nerves or blood vessels, the primary injury is sequenced first with additional code(s) for injuries to nerves and spinal cord (such as category S04), and/or injury to blood vessels (such as category S15). When the primary injury is to the blood vessels or nerves, that injury should be sequenced first.

c.   **Coding of Traumatic Fractures**

The principles of multiple coding of injuries should be followed in coding fractures. Fractures of specified sites are coded individually by site in accordance with both the provisions within categories S02, S12, S22, S32, S42, **S49,** S52, **S59,** S62, S72, **S79,** S82, **S89,** S92 and the level of detail furnished by medical record content.

A fracture not indicated as open or closed should be coded to closed. A fracture not indicated whether displaced or not displaced should be coded to displaced.

More specific guidelines are as follows:

1)   **Initial vs. Subsequent Encounter for Fractures**

Traumatic fractures are coded using the appropriate 7th character extension for initial encounter (A, B, C) while the patient is receiving active treatment for the fracture.   Examples of active treatment are: surgical treatment, emergency department encounter, and evaluation and treatment by a new physician.

Fractures are coded using the appropriate 7th character extension for subsequent care for encounters after the patient has completed active treatment of the fracture and is receiving routine care for the fracture during the healing or recovery phase. Examples of fracture aftercare are: cast change or removal, removal of external or internal fixation device, medication adjustment, and follow-up visits following fracture treatment.

Care for complications of surgical treatment for fracture repairs during the healing or recovery phase should be coded with the appropriate complication codes.

Care of complications of fractures, such as malunion and nonunion, should be reported with the appropriate 7th character extensions for subsequent care with nonunion (K, M, N,) or subsequent care with malunion (P, Q, R).

A code from category M80, not a traumatic fracture code, should be used for any patient with known osteoporosis who suffers a fracture, **even if the patient had a minor fall or trauma, if that fall or trauma would not usually break a normal, healthy bone.**
See Section I.C.13. Osteoporosis.

The aftercare Z codes should not be used for aftercare for injuries. For aftercare of an injury, assign the acute injury code with the 7th character "D" (subsequent encounter).

2)   Multiple fractures sequencing

Multiple fractures are sequenced in accordance with the severity of the fracture. The provider should be asked to list the fracture diagnoses in the order of severity.

d.   Coding of Burns and Corrosions

The ICD-10-CM distinguishes between burns and corrosions. The burn codes are for thermal burns, except sunburns, that come from a heat source, such as a fire or hot appliance. The burn codes are also for burns resulting from electricity and radiation. Corrosions are burns due to chemicals. The guidelines are the same for burns and corrosions.

Current burns (T20-T25) are classified by depth, extent and by agent (X code). Burns are classified by depth as first degree (erythema), second degree (blistering), and third degree (full-thickness involvement). Burns of the eye and internal organs (T26-T28) are classified by site, but not by degree.

1)   Sequencing of burn and related condition codes

Sequence first the code that reflects the highest degree of burn when more than one burn is present.

a. When the reason for the admission or encounter is for treatment of external multiple burns, sequence first the code that reflects the burn of the highest degree.

b. When a patient has both internal and external burns, the circumstances of admission govern the selection of the principal diagnosis or first-listed diagnosis.

c. When a patient is admitted for burn injuries and other related conditions such as smoke inhalation and/or respiratory failure, the circumstances of admission govern the selection of the principal or first-listed diagnosis.

2)   Burns of the same local site

Classify burns of the same local site (three-digit category level, T20-T28) but of different degrees to the subcategory identifying the highest degree recorded in the diagnosis.

3)   Non-healing burns

Non-healing burns are coded as acute burns.
Necrosis of burned skin should be coded as a non-healed burn.

4)   Infected Burn

For any documented infected burn site, use an additional code for the infection.

5)   Assign separate codes for each burn site

When coding burns, assign separate codes for each burn site. Category T30, Burn and corrosion, body region unspecified is extremely vague and should rarely be used.

6)   Burns and Corrosions Classified According to Extent of Body Surface Involved

Assign codes from category T31, Burns classified according to extent of body surface involved, or T32, Corrosions classified according to extent of body surface involved, when the site of the burn is not specified or when there is a need for additional data. It is advisable to use category T31 as additional coding when needed to provide data for evaluating burn mortality, such as that needed by burn units. It is also advisable to use category T31 as an additional code for reporting purposes when there is mention of a third-degree burn involving 20 percent or more of the body surface.

Categories T31 and T32 are based on the classic "rule of nines" in estimating body surface involved: head and neck are assigned nine percent, each arm nine percent, each leg 18 percent, the anterior trunk 18 percent, posterior trunk 18 percent, and genitalia one percent. Providers may change these percentage assignments where necessary to accommodate infants and children who have proportionately larger heads than adults, and patients who have large buttocks, thighs, or abdomen that involve burns.

7) Encounters for treatment of late effects of burns

Encounters for the treatment of the late effects of burns or corrosions (i.e., scars or joint contractures) should be coded with a burn or corrosion code with the 7th character "S" or sequela.

8) Sequelae with a late effect code and current burn

When appropriate, both a code for a current burn or corrosion with 7th character extension "A" or "D" and a burn or corrosion code with extension "S" may be assigned on the same record (when both a current burn and sequelae of an old burn exist). Burns and corrosions do not heal at the same rate and a current healing wound may still exist with sequela of a healed burn or corrosion.

9) Use of an external cause code with burns and corrosions

An external cause code should be used with burns and corrosions to identify the source and intent of the burn, as well as the place where it occurred.

e. Adverse Effects, Poisoning , Underdosing and Toxic Effects

Codes in categories T36-T65 are combination codes that include the substances related to adverse effects, poisonings, toxic effects and underdosing, as well as the external cause. No additional external cause code is required for poisonings, toxic effects, adverse effects and underdosing codes.

A code from categories T36-T65 is sequenced first, followed by the code(s) that specify the nature of the adverse effect, poisoning, or toxic effect. **Note: This sequencing instruction does not apply to** underdosing codes (fifth or sixth character "6", for example T36.0x6-).

1)   Do not code directly from the Table of Drugs

Do not code directly from the Table of Drugs and Chemicals. Always refer back to the Tabular List.

2)   Use as many codes as necessary to describe

Use as many codes as necessary to describe completely all drugs, medicinal or biological substances.

3)   If the same code would describe the causative agent

If the same code would describe the causative agent for more than one adverse reaction, poisoning, toxic effect or underdosing, assign the code only once.

4)   If two or more drugs, medicinal or biological substances

If two or more drugs, medicinal or biological substances are reported, code each individually unless the combination code is listed in the Table of Drugs and Chemicals.

5)   The occurrence of drug toxicity is classified in ICD-10-CM as follows:

(a)   Adverse Effect

Assign the appropriate code for adverse effect (for example, T36.0x5-) when the drug was correctly prescribed and properly administered. Use additional code(s) for all manifestations of adverse effects. Examples of manifestations are tachycardia, delirium, gastrointestinal hemorrhaging, vomiting, hypokalemia, hepatitis, renal failure, or respiratory failure.

(b)   Poisoning

When coding a poisoning or reaction to the improper use of a medication (e.g., overdose, wrong substance given or taken in error, wrong route of administration), assign the appropriate code from categories T36-T50. Poisoning codes have an associated intent: accidental, intentional self-harm, assault and undetermined. Use additional code(s) for all manifestations of poisonings.

If there is also a diagnosis **of abuse or dependence on** the substance, the abuse or dependence is coded as an additional code.

Examples of poisoning include:

(i)   Error was made in drug prescription

Errors made in drug prescription or in the administration of the drug by provider, nurse, patient, or other person.

(ii)   Overdose of a drug intentionally taken

If an overdose of a drug was intentionally taken or administered and resulted in drug toxicity, it would be coded as a poisoning.

(iii)   Nonprescribed drug taken with correctly prescribed and properly administered drug

If a nonprescribed drug or medicinal agent was taken in combination with a correctly prescribed and properly administered drug, any drug toxicity or other reaction resulting from the interaction of the two drugs would be classified as a poisoning.

(iv)   Interaction of drug(s) and alcohol

When a reaction results from the interaction of a drug(s) and alcohol, this would be classified as poisoning.

See Section I.C.4. if poisoning is the result of insulin pump malfunctions.

(c)   **Underdosing**

Underdosing refers to taking less of a medication than is prescribed by a **provider** or a manufacturer's instruction. For underdosing, assign the code from categories T36-T50 **(fifth or sixth character "6")**.

Codes for underdosing should never be assigned as principal or first-listed codes. If a patient has a relapse or exacerbation of the medical condition for which the drug is prescribed because of the reduction in dose, then the medical condition itself should be coded.

Noncompliance (Z91.12-, Z91.13-) or complication of care (Y63.61, Y63.8-Y63.9) codes are to be used with an underdosing code to indicate intent, if known.

(d)   Toxic Effects

When a harmful substance is ingested or comes in contact with a person, this is classified as a toxic effect. The toxic effect codes are in categories T51-T65.

Toxic effect codes have an associated intent: accidental, intentional self-harm, assault and undetermined.

f.   Adult and child abuse, neglect and other maltreatment

Sequence first the appropriate code from categories T74.- or T76.- for abuse, neglect and other maltreatment, followed by any accompanying mental health or injury code(s).

If the documentation in the medical record states abuse or neglect it is coded as confirmed. It is coded as suspected if it is documented as suspected.

For cases of confirmed abuse or neglect an external cause code from the assault section (X92-Y08) should be added to identify the cause of any physical injuries. A perpetrator code (Y07) should be added when the perpetrator of the abuse is known. For suspected cases of abuse or neglect, do not report external cause or perpetrator code.

If a suspected case of abuse, neglect or mistreatment is ruled out during an encounter code Z04.71, Suspected adult physical and sexual abuse, ruled out, or code Z04.72, Suspected child physical and sexual abuse, ruled out, should be used, not a code from T76.

g.   Complications of care

1)   Complications of care

(a)   Documentation of complications of care

As with all procedural or postprocedural complications, code assignment is based on the provider's documentation of the relationship between the condition and the procedure.

2)   Pain due to medical devices

Pain associated with devices, implants or grafts left in a surgical site (for example painful hip prosthesis) is assigned to the appropriate code(s) found in Chapter 19, Injury, poisoning, and certain other consequences of external causes. Specific codes for pain due to medical devices are found in the T code section of the ICD-10-CM. Use additional code(s) from category G89 to identify acute or chronic pain due to presence of the device, implant or graft (G89.18 or G89.28).

3)   Transplant complications

(a)   Transplant complications other than kidney

Codes under category T86, Complications of transplanted organs and tissues, are for use for both complications and rejection of transplanted organs. A transplant complication code is only assigned if the complication affects the function of the transplanted organ. Two codes are required to fully describe a transplant complication: the appropriate code from category T86 and a secondary code that identifies the complication.

Pre-existing conditions or conditions that develop after the transplant are not coded as complications unless they affect the function of the transplanted organs.

See I.C.21.c.3 for transplant organ removal status
See I.C.2.r for malignant neoplasm associated with transplanted organ.

(b)   Chronic kidney disease and kidney transplant complications

Patients who have undergone kidney transplant may still have some form of chronic kidney disease (CKD) because the kidney transplant may not fully restore kidney function. Code T86.1- should be assigned for documented complications of a kidney transplant, such as transplant failure or rejection or other transplant complication. Code T86.1- should not be assigned for post kidney transplant patients who have chronic kidney (CKD) unless a transplant complication such as transplant failure or rejection is documented. If the documentation is unclear as to whether the patient has a complication of the transplant, query the provider.

For patients with CKD following a kidney transplant, but who do not have a complication such as failure or rejection, *see section I.C.14. Chronic kidney disease and kidney transplant status*.

4) **Complication codes that include the external cause**

As with certain other T codes, some of the complications of care codes have the external cause included in the code. The code includes the nature of the complication as well as the type of procedure that caused the complication. No external cause code indicating the type of procedure is necessary for these codes.

5) **Complications of care codes within the body system chapters**

Intraoperative and postprocedural complication codes are found within the body system chapters with codes specific to the organs and structures of that body system. These codes should be sequenced first, followed by a code(s) for the specific complication, if applicable.

6) **Ventilator associated pneumonia**

(a) **Documentation of Ventilator associated Pneumonia**

As with all procedural or postprocedural complications, code assignment is based on the provider's documentation of the relationship between the condition and the procedure.

Code J95.851, Ventilator associated pneumonia, should be assigned only when the provider has documented ventilator associated pneumonia (VAP). An additional code to identify the organism (e.g., Pseudomonas aeruginosa, code B96.5) should also be assigned. Do not assign an additional code from categories J12-J18 to identify the type of pneumonia.

Code J95.851 should not be assigned for cases where the patient has pneumonia and is on a mechanical ventilator but the provider has not specifically stated that the pneumonia is ventilator-associated pneumonia.

If the documentation is unclear as to whether the patient has a pneumonia that is a complication attributable to the mechanical ventilator, query the provider.

(b)   Patient admitted with pneumonia and develops VAP

A patient may be admitted with one type of pneumonia (e.g., code J13, Pneumonia due to Streptococcus pneumonia) and subsequently develop VAP. In this instance, the principal diagnosis would be the appropriate code from categories J12-J18 for the pneumonia diagnosed at the time of admission. Code J95.851, Ventilator associated pneumonia, would be assigned as an additional diagnosis when the provider has also documented the presence of ventilator associated pneumonia.

20.   Chapter 20: External Causes of Morbidity (V01- Y99)

Introduction: These guidelines are provided for the reporting of external causes of morbidity codes in order that there will be standardization in the process. These codes are secondary codes for use in any health care setting.

External cause codes are intended to provide data for injury research and evaluation of injury prevention strategies. These codes capture how the injury or health condition happened (cause), the intent (unintentional or accidental; or intentional, such as suicide or assault), the place where the event occurred the activity of the patient at the time of the event, **and the person's status (e.g., civilian, military)**.

a.   General External Cause Coding Guidelines

1)   Used with any code in the range of A00.0-T88.9, Z00-Z99

An external cause code may be used with any code in the range of A00.0-T88.9, Z00-Z99, classification that is a health condition due to an external cause. Though they are most applicable to injuries, they are also valid for use with such things as infections or diseases due to an external source, and other health conditions, such as a heart attack that occurs during strenuous physical activity.

2)   External cause code used for length of treatment

Assign the external cause code, with the appropriate 7th character (initial encounter, subsequent encounter or sequela) for each encounter for which the injury or condition is being treated.

3)   Use the full range of external cause codes

Use the full range of external cause codes to completely describe the cause, the intent, the place of occurrence, **and if applicable,** the activity of the patient at the time of the event, **and the patient's status,** for all injuries, and other health conditions due to an external cause.

4)   Assign as many external cause codes as necessary

Assign as many external cause codes as necessary to fully explain each cause. If only one external code can be recorded, assign the code most related to the principal diagnosis.

5)   The selection of the appropriate external cause code

The selection of the appropriate external cause code is guided by the Index to External Causes, which is located after the Alphabetical Index to diseases and by Inclusion and Exclusion notes in the Tabular List.

6)   External cause code can never be a principal diagnosis

An external cause code can never be a principal (first listed) diagnosis.

7)   Combination external cause codes

Certain of the external cause codes are combination codes that identify sequential events that result in an injury, such as a fall which results in striking against an object. The injury may be due to either event or both. The combination external cause code used should correspond to the sequence of events regardless of which caused the most serious injury.

8)   No external cause code needed in certain circumstances

No external cause code from Chapter 20 is needed if the external cause and intent are included in a code from another chapter (e.g. T360x1- Poisoning by penicillins, accidental (unintentional)).

b.   Place of Occurrence Guideline

Codes from category Y92, Place of occurrence of the external cause, are secondary codes for use after other external cause codes to identify the location of the patient at the time of injury or other condition.

A place of occurrence code is used only once, at the initial encounter for treatment. No 7th characters are used for Y92. Only one code from Y92 should be recorded on a medical record. A place of occurrence code should be used in conjunction with an activity code, Y93.

Do not use place of occurrence code Y92.9 if the place is not stated or is not applicable.

c.   **Activity Code**

Assign a code from category Y93, Activity code, to describe the activity of the patient at the time the injury **or other health condition occurred**.

An activity code is used only once, at the initial encounter for treatment. Only one code from Y93 should be recorded on a medical record. An activity code should be used in conjunction with a place of occurrence code, Y92.

If a patient is a student but is injured while performing an activity for income, use 7th character "2", work related activity.
A work related activity is any activity for which payment or income is received.

The activity codes are not applicable to poisonings, adverse effects, misadventures or late effects.

Do not assign Y93.9, Unspecified activity, if the activity is not stated.

d.   **Place of Occurrence, Activity, *and Status* Codes Used with other External Cause Code**

When applicable, place of occurrence, activity, **and external cause status codes** are sequenced after the main external cause code(s). Regardless of the number of external cause codes assigned, there should be only one place of occurrence code, one activity code, **and one external cause status code** assigned to an encounter.

e.   **If the Reporting Format Limits the Number of External Cause Codes**

If the reporting format limits the number of external cause codes that can be used in reporting clinical data, **report the code for the cause/intent** most related to the principal diagnosis. **If the format permits capture of additional external cause codes, the cause/intent, including medical misadventures, of the additional events should be reported rather than the codes for place, activity, or external status.**

f.   Multiple External Cause Coding Guidelines

More than one external cause code is required to fully describe the external cause of an illness, injury or poisoning. The assignment of external cause codes should be sequenced in the following priority:

If two or more events cause separate injuries, an external cause code should be assigned for each cause. The first listed external cause code will be selected in the following order:

External codes for child and adult abuse take priority over all other external cause codes.

See Section I.C.19., Child and Adult abuse guidelines.

External cause codes for terrorism events take priority over all other external cause codes except child and adult abuse.

External cause codes for cataclysmic events take priority over all other external cause codes except child and adult abuse and terrorism.

External cause codes for transport accidents take priority over all other external cause codes except cataclysmic events, child and adult abuse and terrorism.

Activity and external cause status codes are assigned following all causal (intent) external cause codes.

The first-listed external cause code should correspond to the cause of the most serious diagnosis due to an assault, accident, or self-harm, following the order of hierarchy listed above.

g.   Child and Adult Abuse Guideline

Adult and child abuse, neglect and maltreatment are classified as assault. Any of the assault codes may be used to indicate the external cause of any injury resulting from the confirmed abuse.

For confirmed cases of abuse, neglect and maltreatment, when the perpetrator is known, a code from Y07, Perpetrator of maltreatment and neglect, should accompany any other assault codes.

See Section I.C.19. Adult and child abuse, neglect and other maltreatment

h.   Unknown or Undetermined Intent Guideline

If the intent (accident, self-harm, assault) of the cause of an injury or other condition is unknown or unspecified, code the intent as accidental intent. All transport accident categories assume accidental intent.

1) Use of undetermined intent

External cause codes for events of undetermined intent are only for use if the documentation in the record specifies that the intent cannot be determined

i.   Late Effects of External Cause Guidelines

1) Late effect external cause codes

Late effects are reported using the external cause code with the 7th character extension "S" for sequela. These codes should be used with any report of a late effect or sequela resulting from a previous injury.

2) Late effect external cause code with a related current injury

A late effect external cause code should never be used with a related current nature of injury code.

3) Use of late effect external cause codes for subsequent visits

Use a late effect external cause code for subsequent visits when a late effect of the initial injury is being treated. Do not use a late effect external cause code for subsequent visits for follow-up care (e.g., to assess healing, to receive rehabilitative therapy) of the injury or poisoning when no late effect of the injury has been documented.

j.   Terrorism Guidelines

1) Cause of injury identified by the Federal Government (FBI) as terrorism

When the cause of an injury is identified by the Federal Government (FBI) as terrorism, the first-listed external cause code should be a code from category Y38, Terrorism. The definition of terrorism employed by the FBI is found at the inclusion note at the beginning of category Y38. Use additional code for place of occurrence (Y92.-). More than one Y38 code may be assigned if the injury is the result of more than one mechanism of terrorism.

2) Cause of an injury is suspected to be the result of terrorism

When the cause of an injury is suspected to be the result of terrorism a code from category Y38 should not be assigned. Suspected cases should be classified as assault.

3)   Code Y38.9, Terrorism, secondary effects

Assign code Y38.9, Terrorism, secondary effects, for conditions occurring subsequent to the terrorist event. This code should not be assigned for conditions that are due to the initial terrorist act.

It is acceptable to assign code Y38.9 with another code from Y38 if there is an injury due to the initial terrorist event and an injury that is a subsequent result of the terrorist event.

k.   External cause status

A code from category Y99, External cause status, should be assigned whenever any other external cause code is assigned for an encounter, including an Activity code, except for the events noted below. Assign a code from category Y99, External cause status, to indicate the work status of the person at the time the event occurred. The status code indicates whether the event occurred during military activity, whether a non-military person was at work, whether an individual including a student or volunteer was involved in a non-work activity at the time of the causal event.

A code from Y99, External cause status, should be assigned, when applicable, with other external cause codes, such as transport accidents and falls. The external cause status codes are not applicable to poisonings, adverse effects, misadventures or late effects.
Do not assign a code from category Y99 if no other external cause codes (cause, activity) are applicable for the encounter.

Do not assign code Y99.9, Unspecified external cause status, if the status is not stated.

21.   Chapter 21: Factors influencing health status and contact with health services (Z00-Z99)

Note: The chapter specific guidelines provide additional information about the use of Z codes for specified encounters.

a.   Use of Z codes in any healthcare setting

Z codes are for use in any healthcare setting. Z codes may be used as either a first listed (principal diagnosis code in the inpatient setting) or secondary code, depending on the circumstances of the encounter. Certain **Z** codes may only be used as first listed or principal diagnosis.

b.   Z Codes indicate a reason for an encounter

Z codes are not procedure codes. A corresponding procedure code must accompany a Z code to describe the procedure performed.

c.   Categories of Z Codes

1)   Contact/Exposure

Category Z20 indicates contact with, **and suspected** exposure to, communicable diseases. These codes are for patients who do not show any sign or symptom of a disease but **are suspected to** have been exposed to it by close personal contact with an infected individual or are in an area where a disease is epidemic.

Category Z77, indicates contact with and suspected exposures hazardous to health.

Contact/exposure codes may be used as a first listed code to explain an encounter for testing, or, more commonly, as a secondary code to identify a potential risk.

2)   Inoculations and vaccinations

Code Z23 is for encounters for inoculations and vaccinations. It indicates that a patient is being seen to receive a prophylactic inoculation against a disease. Procedure codes are required to identify the actual administration of the injection and the type(s) of immunizations given. Code Z23 may be used as a secondary code if the inoculation is given as a routine part of preventive health care, such as a well-baby visit.

3)   Status

Status codes indicate that a patient is either a carrier of a disease or has the sequelae or residual of a past disease or condition. This includes such things as the presence of prosthetic or mechanical devices resulting from past treatment. A status code is informative, because the status may affect the course of treatment and its outcome. A status code is distinct from a history code. The history code indicates that the patient no longer has the condition.

A status code should not be used with a diagnosis code from one of the body system chapters, if the diagnosis code includes the information provided by the status code. For example, code Z94.1, Heart transplant status, should not be used with a code from subcategory T86.2, Complications of heart transplant. The status code does not provide additional information. The complication code indicates that the patient is a heart transplant patient.

For encounters for weaning from a mechanical ventilator, assign code J96.1, Chronic respiratory failure, followed by code Z99.11, Dependence on respirator [ventilator] status.

The status Z codes/categories are:

Z14   Genetic carrier
          Genetic carrier status indicates that a person carries a gene, associated with a particular disease, which may be passed to offspring who may develop that disease. The person does not have the disease and is not at risk of developing the disease.

Z15   Genetic susceptibility to disease
          Genetic susceptibility indicates that a person has a gene that increases the risk of that person developing the disease.

          Codes from category Z15 should not be used as principal or first-listed codes. If the patient has the condition to which he/she is susceptible, and that condition is the reason for the encounter, the code for the current condition should be sequenced first. If the patient is being seen for follow-up after completed treatment for this condition, and the condition no longer exists, a follow-up code should be sequenced first, followed by the appropriate personal history and genetic susceptibility codes. If the purpose of the encounter is genetic counseling associated with procreative management, code Z31.5, Encounter for genetic counseling, should be assigned as the first-listed code, followed by a code from category Z15. Additional codes should be assigned for any applicable family or personal history.

Z16   Infection with drug-resistant microorganisms
This code indicates that a patient has an infection that is resistant to drug treatment. Sequence the infection code first.

Z17   Estrogen receptor status

Z21   Asymptomatic HIV infection status
This code indicates that a patient has tested positive for HIV but has manifested no signs or symptoms of the disease.

Z22   Carrier of infectious disease
Carrier status indicates that a person harbors the specific organisms of a disease without manifest symptoms and is capable of transmitting the infection.

Z28.3   **Underimmunization status**

Z33.1   Pregnant state, incidental
This code is a secondary code only for use when the pregnancy is in no way complicating the reason for visit. Otherwise, a code from the obstetric chapter is required.

Z66   Do not resuscitate

Z67   Blood type

Z68   Body mass index (BMI)

Z74.01   Bed confinement status

Z76.82   Awaiting organ transplant status

Z78   **Other specified health status**

Z79   Long-term (current) drug therapy
Codes from this category indicate a patient's continuous use of a prescribed drug (including such things as aspirin therapy) for the long-term treatment of a condition or for prophylactic use. It is not for use for patients who have addictions to drugs. This subcategory is not for use of medications for detoxification or maintenance programs to prevent withdrawal symptoms in patients with drug dependence (e.g., methadone maintenance for opiate dependence). Assign the appropriate code for the drug dependence instead.

Assign a code from Z79 if the patient is receiving a medication for an extended period as a prophylactic measure (such as for the prevention of deep vein thrombosis) or as treatment of a chronic condition (such as arthritis) or a disease requiring a lengthy course of treatment (such as cancer). Do not assign a code from category Z79 for medication being administered for a brief period of time to treat an

	acute illness or injury (such as a course of antibiotics to treat acute bronchitis).
Z88	Allergy status to drugs, medicaments and biological substances
	Except: Z88.9, Allergy status to unspecified drugs, medicaments and biological substances status
Z89	Acquired absence of limb
Z90	Acquired absence of organs, not elsewhere classified
Z91.0-	Allergy status, other than to drugs and biological substances
Z92.82	**Status post administration of tPA (rtPA) in a different facility within the last 24 hours prior to admission to a current facility**
	Assign code Z92.82, Status post administration of tPA (rtPA) in a different facility within the last 24 hours prior to admission to current facility, as a secondary diagnosis when a patient is received by transfer into a facility and documentation indicates they were administered tissue plasminogen activator (tPA) within the last 24 hours prior to admission to the current facility.
	This guideline applies even if the patient is still receiving the tPA at the time they are received into the current facility.
	The appropriate code for the condition for which the tPA was administered (such as cerebrovascular disease or myocardial infarction) should be assigned first.
	Code Z92.82 is only applicable to the receiving facility record and not to the transferring facility record.
Z93	Artificial opening status
Z94	Transplanted organ and tissue status
Z95	Presence of cardiac and vascular implants and grafts
Z96	Presence of other functional implants
Z97	Presence of other devices
Z98	Other postprocedural states
	Assign code Z98.85, Transplanted organ removal status, to indicate that a transplanted organ has been previously removed. This code should not be assigned for the encounter in which the

transplanted organ is removed. The complication necessitating removal of the transplant organ should be assigned for that encounter.

See section I.C19.g.3. for information on the coding of organ transplant complications.

Z99   Dependence on enabling machines and devices, not elsewhere classified

                Note: Categories Z89-Z90 and Z93-Z99 are for use only if there are no complications or malfunctions of the organ or tissue replaced, the amputation site or the equipment on which the patient is dependent.

4)   **History (of)**

There are two types of history Z codes, personal and family. Personal history codes explain a patient's past medical condition that no longer exists and is not receiving any treatment, but that has the potential for recurrence, and therefore may require continued monitoring.

Family history codes are for use when a patient has a family member(s) who has had a particular disease that causes the patient to be at higher risk of also contracting the disease.

Personal history codes may be used in conjunction with follow-up codes and family history codes may be used in conjunction with screening codes to explain the need for a test or procedure. History codes are also acceptable on any medical record regardless of the reason for visit. A history of an illness, even if no longer present, is important information that may alter the type of treatment ordered.

The history Z code categories are:

Z80   Family history of primary malignant neoplasm

Z81   Family history of mental and behavioral disorders

Z82   Family history of certain disabilities and chronic diseases (leading to disablement)

Z83   Family history of other specific disorders

Z84   Family history of other conditions

Z85   Personal history of malignant neoplasm

Z86   Personal history of certain other diseases

Z87   Personal history of other diseases and conditions

Z91.4-   Personal history of psychological trauma, not elsewhere classified

Z91.5   Personal history of self-harm

Z91.8-   Other specified personal risk factors, not elsewhere classified

Z92   Personal history of medical treatment
Except: Z92.0, Personal history of contraception
Except: Z92.82, Status post administration of tPA (rtPA) in a different facility within the last 24 hours prior to admission to a current facility

5)   Screening

Screening is the testing for disease or disease precursors in seemingly well individuals so that early detection and treatment can be provided for those who test positive for the disease (e.g., screening mammogram).

The testing of a person to rule out or confirm a suspected diagnosis because the patient has some sign or symptom is a diagnostic examination, not a screening. In these cases, the sign or symptom is used to explain the reason for the test.

A screening code may be a first listed code if the reason for the visit is specifically the screening exam. It may also be used as an additional code if the screening is done during an office visit for other health problems. A screening code is not necessary if the screening is inherent to a routine examination, such as a pap smear done during a routine pelvic examination.

Should a condition be discovered during the screening then the code for the condition may be assigned as an additional diagnosis.

The Z code indicates that a screening exam is planned. A procedure code is required to confirm that the screening was performed.

The screening Z codes/categories:

Z11   Encounter for screening for infectious and parasitic diseases

Z12   Encounter for screening for malignant neoplasms

Z13   Encounter for screening for other diseases and disorders
Except: Z13.9, Encounter for screening, unspecified

Z36   Encounter for antenatal screening for mother

6)   Observation

There are two observation Z code categories. They are for use in very limited circumstances when a person is being observed for a suspected condition that is ruled out. The observation codes are not for use if an injury or illness or any signs or symptoms related to the suspected condition are present. In such cases the diagnosis/symptom code is used with the corresponding external cause code.

The observation codes are to be used as principal diagnosis only. Additional codes may be used in addition to the observation code but only if they are unrelated to the suspected condition being observed.

Codes from subcategory Z03.7 Encounter for suspected maternal and fetal conditions ruled out, may either be used as a first listed or as an additional code assignment depending on the case. They are for use in very limited circumstances on a maternal record when an encounter is for a suspected maternal or fetal condition that is ruled out during that encounter (for example, a maternal or fetal condition may be suspected due to an abnormal test result). These codes should not be used when the condition is confirmed. In those cases, the confirmed condition should be coded. In addition, these codes are not for use if an illness or any signs or symptoms related to the suspected condition or problem are present. In such cases the diagnosis/symptom code is used.

Additional codes may be used in addition to the code from subcategory Z03.7, but only if they are unrelated to the suspected condition being evaluated.

Codes from subcategory Z03.7 may not be used for encounters for antenatal screening of mother. *See Section I.C.21.c.5, Screening.*

For encounters for suspected fetal condition that are inconclusive following testing and evaluation, assign the appropriate code from category O35, O36, O40 or O41.
The observation Z code categories:

Z03   Encounter for medical observation for suspected diseases and conditions ruled out
Z04   Encounter for examination and observation for other reasons

Except: Z04.9, Encounter for examination and
observation for unspecified reason

7)   **Aftercare**

Aftercare visit codes cover situations when the initial treatment
of a disease has been performed and the patient requires
continued care during the healing or recovery phase, or for the
long-term consequences of the disease. The aftercare Z code
should not be used if treatment is directed at a current, acute
disease. The diagnosis code is to be used in these cases.
**Exceptions to this rule are codes Z51.0, Encounter for
antineoplastic radiation therapy, and codes from
subcategory Z51.1, Encounter for antineoplastic
chemotherapy and immunotherapy. These codes are to be
first listed, followed by the diagnosis code when a patient's
encounter is solely to receive radiation therapy,
chemotherapy, or immunotherapy for the treatment of a
neoplasm. If the reason for the encounter is more than one
type of antineoplastic therapy, code Z51.0 and a code from
subcategory Z51.1 may be assigned together, in which case
one of these codes would be reported as a secondary
diagnosis.**

The aftercare Z codes should also not be used for aftercare for
injuries. For aftercare of an injury, assign the acute injury code
with the 7th character "D" (subsequent encounter).

The aftercare codes are generally first listed to explain the
specific reason for the encounter. An aftercare code may be
used as an additional code when some type of aftercare is
provided in addition to the reason for admission and no
diagnosis code is applicable. An example of this would be the
closure of a colostomy during an encounter for treatment of
another condition.

Aftercare codes should be used in conjunction with other
aftercare codes or diagnosis codes to provide better detail on
the specifics of an aftercare encounter visit, unless otherwise
directed by the classification. Should a patient receive multiple
types of antineoplastic therapy during the same encounter, code
Z51.0, Encounter for antineoplastic radiation therapy, and
codes from subcategory Z51.1, Encounter for antineoplastic
chemotherapy and immunotherapy, may be used together on a
record. The sequencing of multiple aftercare codes **depends on
the circumstances of the encounter.**

Certain aftercare Z code categories need a secondary diagnosis code to describe the resolving condition or sequelae. **For** others, the condition is **included** in the code title.

Additional Z code aftercare category terms include fitting and adjustment, and attention to artificial openings.

Status Z codes may be used with aftercare Z codes to indicate the nature of the aftercare. For example code Z95.1, Presence of aortocoronary bypass graft, may be used with code Z48.812, Encounter for surgical aftercare following surgery on the circulatory system, to indicate the surgery for which the aftercare is being performed. A status code should not be used when the aftercare code indicates the type of status, such as using Z43.0, Encounter for attention to tracheostomy, with Z93.0, Tracheostomy status.

The aftercare Z category/codes:

Z42	**Encounter for plastic and reconstructive surgery following medical procedure or healed injury**
Z43	Encounter for attention to artificial openings
Z44	Encounter for fitting and adjustment of external prosthetic device
Z45	Encounter for adjustment and management of implanted device
Z46	Encounter for fitting and adjustment of other devices
Z47	Orthopedic aftercare
Z48	Encounter for other postprocedural aftercare
Z49	Encounter for care involving renal dialysis
Z51	Encounter for other aftercare

8)   Follow-up

The follow-up codes are used to explain continuing surveillance following completed treatment of a disease, condition, or injury. They imply that the condition has been fully treated and no longer exists. They should not be confused with aftercare codes, or injury codes with 7th character "D," that explain ongoing care of a healing condition or its sequelae. Follow-up codes may be used in conjunction with history codes to provide the full picture of the healed condition and its treatment. The follow-up code is sequenced first, followed by the history code.

A follow-up code may be used to explain **multiple** visits. Should a condition be found to have recurred on the follow-up visit, then the code for the condition should be assigned as an additional diagnosis.

The follow-up Z code categories:

Z08   Encounter for follow-up examination after completed treatment for malignant neoplasm

Z09   Encounter for follow-up examination after completed treatment for conditions other than malignant neoplasm

Z39   Encounter for maternal postpartum care and examination

9) Donor

Codes in category Z52, Donors of organs and tissues, are used for living individuals who are donating blood or other body tissue. These codes are only for individuals donating for others, not for self-donations. They are not used to identify cadaveric donations.

10) Counseling

Counseling Z codes are used when a patient or family member receives assistance in the aftermath of an illness or injury, or when support is required in coping with family or social problems. They are not used in conjunction with a diagnosis code when the counseling component of care is considered integral to standard treatment.

The counseling Z codes/categories:

Z30.0-   Encounter for general counseling and advice on contraception

Z31.5   Encounter for genetic counseling

Z31.6-   Encounter for general counseling and advice on procreation

Z32.2   Encounter for childbirth instruction

Z32.3   Encounter for childcare instruction

Z69   Encounter for mental health services for victim and perpetrator of abuse

Z70   Counseling related to sexual attitude, behavior and orientation

Z71   Persons encountering health services for other counseling and medical advice, not elsewhere classified

Z76.81   Expectant mother prebirth pediatrician visit

11) Encounters for Obstetrical and Reproductive Services

See Section I.C.15. Pregnancy, Childbirth, and the Puerperium, for further instruction on the use of these codes.

Z codes for pregnancy are for use in those circumstances when none of the problems or complications included in the codes from the Obstetrics chapter exist (a routine prenatal visit or postpartum care). Codes in category Z34, Encounter for supervision of normal pregnancy, are always first listed and are not to be used with any other code from the OB chapter.

The outcome of delivery, category Z37, should be included on all maternal delivery records. It is always a secondary code. Codes in category Z37 should not be used on the newborn record.

Z codes for family planning (contraceptive) or procreative management and counseling should be included on an obstetric record either during the pregnancy or the postpartum stage, if applicable.

Z codes/categories for obstetrical and reproductive services:

Z30	Encounter for contraceptive management
Z31	Encounter for procreative management
Z32.2	Encounter for childbirth instruction
Z32.3	Encounter for childcare instruction
Z33	Pregnant state
Z34	Encounter for supervision of normal pregnancy
Z36	Encounter for antenatal screening of mother
Z37	Outcome of delivery
Z39	Encounter for maternal postpartum care and examination
Z76.81	Expectant mother prebirth pediatrician visit

12)   Newborns and Infants

See Section I.C.16. Newborn (Perinatal) Guidelines, for further instruction on the use of these codes.

Newborn Z codes/categories:

Z76.1	Encounter for health supervision and care of foundling
Z00.1-	Encounter for routine child health examination
Z38	Liveborn infants according to place of birth and type of delivery

13)   Routine and administrative examinations

The Z codes allow for the description of encounters for routine examinations, such as, a general check-up, or, examinations for administrative purposes, such as, a pre-employment physical. The codes are not to be used if the examination is for diagnosis of a suspected condition or for treatment purposes. In such cases the diagnosis code is used. During a routine exam, should a diagnosis or condition be discovered, it should be coded as an additional code. Pre-existing and chronic conditions and history codes may also be included as additional codes as long as the examination is for administrative purposes and not focused on any particular condition.

Some of the codes for routine health examinations distinguish between "with" and "without" abnormal findings. Code assignment depends on the information that is known at the time the encounter is being coded. For example, if no abnormal findings were found during the examination, but the encounter is being coded before test results are back, it is acceptable to assign the code for "without abnormal findings." When assigning a code for "with abnormal findings," additional code(s) should be assigned to identify the specific abnormal finding(s).

Pre-operative examination **and pre-procedural laboratory examination** Z codes are for use only in those situations when a patient is being cleared for **a procedure or** surgery and no treatment is given.

The Z codes/categories for routine and administrative examinations:

Z00   Encounter for general examination without complaint, suspected or reported diagnosis
Z01   Encounter for other special examination without complaint, suspected or reported diagnosis
Z02   Encounter for administrative examination Except: Z02.9, Encounter for administrative examinations, unspecified
Z32.0-   Encounter for pregnancy test

14)   Miscellaneous Z codes

The miscellaneous Z codes capture a number of other health care encounters that do not fall into one of the other categories. Certain of these codes identify the reason for the encounter; others are for use as additional codes that provide useful information on circumstances that may affect a patient's care and treatment.

Prophylactic Organ Removal

For encounters specifically for prophylactic removal of an organ (such as prophylactic removal of breasts due to a genetic susceptibility to cancer or a family history of cancer), the principal or first listed code should be a code from category Z40, Encounter for prophylactic surgery, followed by the appropriate codes to identify the associated risk factor (such as genetic susceptibility or family history).

If the patient has a malignancy of one site and is having prophylactic removal at another site to prevent either a new primary malignancy or metastatic disease, a code for the malignancy should also be assigned in addition to a code from subcategory Z40.0, Encounter for prophylactic surgery for risk factors related to malignant neoplasms. A Z40.0 code should not be assigned if the patient is having organ removal for treatment of a malignancy, such as the removal of the testes for the treatment of prostate cancer.

Miscellaneous Z codes/categories:

Z28	Immunization not carried out
	Except: Z28.3, Underimmunization status
Z40	Encounter for prophylactic surgery
Z41	Encounter for procedures for purposes other than remedying health state
	Except: Z41.9, Encounter for procedure for purposes other than remedying health state, unspecified
Z53	Persons encountering health services for specific procedures and treatment, not carried out
Z55	Problems related to education and literacy
Z56	Problems related to employment and unemployment
Z57	Occupational exposure to risk factors
Z58	Problems related to physical environment
Z59	Problems related to housing and economic circumstances
Z60	Problems related to social environment
Z62	Problems related to upbringing
Z63	Other problems related to primary support group, including family circumstances
Z64	Problems related to certain psychosocial circumstances
Z65	Problems related to other psychosocial circumstances
Z72	Problems related to lifestyle
Z73	Problems related to life management difficulty

Z74	Problems related to care provider dependency Except: Z74.01, Bed confinement status
Z75	Problems related to medical facilities and other health care
Z76.0	Encounter for issue of repeat prescription
Z76.3	Healthy person accompanying sick person
Z76.4	Other boarder to healthcare facility
Z76.5	Malingerer [conscious simulation]
Z76.89	Persons encountering health services in other specified circumstances
Z91.1-	Patient's noncompliance with medical treatment and regimen
Z91.89	Other specified personal risk factors, not elsewhere classified

15) Nonspecific Z codes

Certain Z codes are so non-specific, or potentially redundant with other codes in the classification, that there can be little justification for their use in the inpatient setting. Their use in the outpatient setting should be limited to those instances when there is no further documentation to permit more precise coding. Otherwise, any sign or symptom or any other reason for visit that is captured in another code should be used.

Nonspecific Z codes/categories:

Z02.9	Encounter for administrative examinations, unspecified
Z04.9	Encounter for examination and observation for unspecified reason
Z13.9	Encounter for screening, unspecified
Z41.9	Encounter for procedure for purposes other than remedying health state, unspecified
Z52.9	Donor of unspecified organ or tissue
Z88.9	Allergy status to unspecified drugs, medicaments and biological substances status
Z92.0	Personal history of contraception

16) Z Codes That May Only be Principal/First-Listed Diagnosis

The following Z codes/categories may only be reported as the principal/first-listed diagnosis, except when there are multiple encounters on the same day and the medical records for the encounters are combined:

| Z00 | Encounter for general examination without complaint, suspected or reported diagnosis |

Z01	Encounter for other special examination without complaint, suspected or reported diagnosis
Z02	Encounter for administrative examination
Z03	Encounter for medical observation for suspected diseases and conditions ruled out
Z33.2	Encounter for elective termination of pregnancy
Z31.81	Encounter for male factor infertility in female patient
Z31.82	Encounter for Rh incompatibility status
Z31.83	Encounter for assisted reproductive fertility procedure cycle
Z31.84	**Encounter for fertility preservation procedure**
Z34	Encounter for supervision of normal pregnancy
Z39	Encounter for maternal postpartum care and examination
Z38	Liveborn infants according to place of birth and type of delivery
Z42	**Encounter for plastic and reconstructive surgery following medical procedure or healed injury**
Z51.0	Encounter for antineoplastic radiation therapy
Z51.1-	Encounter for antineoplastic chemotherapy and immunotherapy
Z52	Donors of organs and tissues Except: Z52.9, Donor of unspecified organ or tissue
Z76.1	Encounter for health supervision and care of foundling
Z76.2	Encounter for health supervision and care of other healthy infant and child
Z99.12	Encounter for respirator [ventilator] dependence during power failure

Section II. Selection of Principal Diagnosis

The circumstances of inpatient admission always govern the selection of principal diagnosis. The principal diagnosis is defined in the Uniform Hospital Discharge Data Set (UHDDS) as "that condition established after study to be chiefly responsible for occasioning the admission of the patient to the hospital for care."

The UHDDS definitions are used by hospitals to report inpatient data elements in a standardized manner. These data elements and their definitions can be found in the July 31, 1985, Federal Register (Vol. 50, No, 147), pp. 31038-40.

Since that time the application of the UHDDS definitions has been expanded to include all non-outpatient settings (acute care, short term, long term care and psychiatric hospitals; home health agencies; rehab facilities; nursing homes, etc).

In determining principal diagnosis the coding conventions in the ICD-10-CM, Volumes I and II take precedence over these official coding guidelines.
(See Section I.A., Conventions for the ICD-10-CM)

The importance of consistent, complete documentation in the medical record cannot be overemphasized. Without such documentation the application of all coding guidelines is a difficult, if not impossible, task.

A. Codes for symptoms, signs, and ill-defined conditions

Codes for symptoms, signs, and ill-defined conditions from Chapter 18 are not to be used as principal diagnosis when a related definitive diagnosis has been established.

B. Two or more interrelated conditions, each potentially meeting the definition for principal diagnosis.

When there are two or more interrelated conditions (such as diseases in the same ICD-10-CM chapter or manifestations characteristically associated with a certain disease) potentially meeting the definition of principal diagnosis, either condition may be sequenced first, unless the circumstances of the admission, the therapy provided, the Tabular List, or the Alphabetic Index indicate otherwise.

C. Two or more diagnoses that equally meet the definition for principal diagnosis

In the unusual instance when two or more diagnoses equally meet the criteria for principal diagnosis as determined by the circumstances of admission, diagnostic workup and/or therapy provided, and the Alphabetic Index, Tabular List, or another coding guidelines does not provide sequencing direction, any one of the diagnoses may be sequenced first.

D. Two or more comparative or contrasting conditions.

In those rare instances when two or more contrasting or comparative diagnoses are documented as "either/or" (or similar terminology), they are coded as if the diagnoses were confirmed and the diagnoses are sequenced according to the circumstances of the admission. If no further determination can be made as to which diagnosis should be principal, either diagnosis may be sequenced first.

E. A symptom(s) followed by contrasting/comparative diagnoses

When a symptom(s) is followed by contrasting/comparative diagnoses, the symptom code is sequenced first. All the contrasting/comparative diagnoses should be coded as additional diagnoses.

F. Original treatment plan not carried out

Sequence as the principal diagnosis the condition, which after study occasioned the admission to the hospital, even though treatment may not have been carried out due to unforeseen circumstances.

G. Complications of surgery and other medical care

When the admission is for treatment of a complication resulting from surgery or other medical care, the complication code is sequenced as the principal diagnosis. If the complication is classified to the T80-T88 series and the code lacks the necessary specificity in describing the complication, an additional code for the specific complication should be assigned.

H. Uncertain Diagnosis

If the diagnosis documented at the time of discharge is qualified as "probable", "suspected", "likely", "questionable", "possible", or "still to be ruled out", or other similar terms indicating uncertainty, code the condition as if it existed or was established. The bases for these guidelines are the diagnostic workup, arrangements for further workup or observation, and initial therapeutic approach that correspond most closely with the established diagnosis.

Note: This guideline is applicable only to inpatient admissions to short-term, acute, long-term care and psychiatric hospitals.

I. Admission from Observation Unit

1. Admission Following Medical Observation

When a patient is admitted to an observation unit for a medical condition, which either worsens or does not improve, and is subsequently admitted as an inpatient of the same hospital for this same medical condition, the principal diagnosis would be the medical condition which led to the hospital admission.

2. Admission Following Post-Operative Observation

When a patient is admitted to an observation unit to monitor a condition (or complication) that develops following outpatient surgery, and then is subsequently admitted as an inpatient of the same hospital, hospitals should apply the Uniform Hospital Discharge Data Set (UHDDS) definition of principal diagnosis as "that condition established after study to be chiefly responsible for occasioning the admission of the patient to the hospital for care."

J. Admission from Outpatient Surgery

When a patient receives surgery in the hospital's outpatient surgery department and is subsequently admitted for continuing inpatient care at the same hospital, the following guidelines should be followed in selecting the principal diagnosis for the inpatient admission:

- If the reason for the inpatient admission is a complication, assign the complication as the principal diagnosis.

- If no complication, or other condition, is documented as the reason for the inpatient admission, assign the reason for the outpatient surgery as the principal diagnosis.
- If the reason for the inpatient admission is another condition unrelated to the surgery, assign the unrelated condition as the principal diagnosis.

Section III. Reporting Additional Diagnoses

GENERAL RULES FOR OTHER (ADDITIONAL) DIAGNOSES

For reporting purposes the definition for "other diagnoses" is interpreted as additional conditions that affect patient care in terms of requiring:

> clinical evaluation; or
> therapeutic treatment; or
> diagnostic procedures; or
> extended length of hospital stay; or
> increased nursing care and/or monitoring.

The UHDDS item #11-b defines Other Diagnoses as "all conditions that coexist at the time of admission, that develop subsequently, or that affect the treatment received and/or the length of stay. Diagnoses that relate to an earlier episode which have no bearing on the current hospital stay are to be excluded." UHDDS definitions apply to inpatients in acute care, short-term, long term care and psychiatric hospital setting. The UHDDS definitions are used by acute care short-term hospitals to report inpatient data elements in a standardized manner. These data elements and their definitions can be found in the July 31, 1985, Federal Register (Vol. 50, No, 147), pp. 31038-40.

Since that time the application of the UHDDS definitions has been expanded to include all non-outpatient settings (acute care, short term, long term care and psychiatric hospitals; home health agencies; rehab facilities; nursing homes, etc).

The following guidelines are to be applied in designating "other diagnoses" when neither the Alphabetic Index nor the Tabular List in ICD-10-CM provide direction. The listing of the diagnoses in the patient record is the responsibility of the attending provider.

A. Previous conditions

If the provider has included a diagnosis in the final diagnostic statement, such as the discharge summary or the face sheet, it should ordinarily be coded. Some providers include in the diagnostic statement resolved conditions or diagnoses and status-post procedures from previous admission that have no bearing on the current stay. Such conditions are not to be reported and are coded only if required by hospital policy.

However, history codes (categories Z80-Z87) may be used as secondary codes if the historical condition or family history has an impact on current care or influences treatment.

B. Abnormal findings

Abnormal findings (laboratory, x-ray, pathologic, and other diagnostic results) are not coded and reported unless the provider indicates their clinical significance. If the findings are outside the normal range and the attending provider has ordered other tests to evaluate the condition or prescribed treatment, it is appropriate to ask the provider whether the abnormal finding should be added.

Please note: This differs from the coding practices in the outpatient setting for coding encounters for diagnostic tests that have been interpreted by a provider.

C. Uncertain Diagnosis

If the diagnosis documented at the time of discharge is qualified as "probable", "suspected", "likely", "questionable", "possible", or "still to be ruled out" or other similar terms indicating uncertainty, code the condition as if it existed or was established. The bases for these guidelines are the diagnostic workup, arrangements for further workup or observation, and initial therapeutic approach that correspond most closely with the established diagnosis.

Note: This guideline is applicable only to inpatient admissions to short-term, acute, long-term care and psychiatric hospitals.

Section IV. Diagnostic Coding and Reporting Guidelines for Outpatient Services

These coding guidelines for outpatient diagnoses have been approved for use by hospitals/ providers in coding and reporting hospital-based outpatient services and provider-based office visits.

Information about the use of certain abbreviations, punctuation, symbols, and other conventions used in the ICD-10-CM Tabular List (code numbers and titles), can be found in Section IA of these guidelines, under "Conventions Used in the Tabular List." Information about the correct sequence to use in finding a code is also described in Section I.

The terms encounter and visit are often used interchangeably in describing outpatient service contacts and, therefore, appear together in these guidelines without distinguishing one from the other.

Though the conventions and general guidelines apply to all settings, coding guidelines for outpatient and provider reporting of diagnoses will vary in a number of instances from those for inpatient diagnoses, recognizing that:

The Uniform Hospital Discharge Data Set (UHDDS) definition of principal diagnosis applies only to inpatients in acute, short-term, long-term care and psychiatric hospitals.

Coding guidelines for inconclusive diagnoses (probable, suspected, rule out, etc.) were developed for inpatient reporting and do not apply to outpatients.

A. Selection of first-listed condition

In the outpatient setting, the term first-listed diagnosis is used in lieu of principal diagnosis.

In determining the first-listed diagnosis the coding conventions of ICD-10-CM, as well as the general and disease specific guidelines take precedence over the outpatient guidelines.

Diagnoses often are not established at the time of the initial encounter/visit. It may take two or more visits before the diagnosis is confirmed.

The most critical rule involves beginning the search for the correct code assignment through the Alphabetic Index. Never begin searching initially in the Tabular List as this will lead to coding errors.

1.   Outpatient Surgery

When a patient presents for outpatient surgery (same day surgery), code the reason for the surgery as the first-listed diagnosis (reason for the encounter), even if the surgery is not performed due to a contraindication.

2.   Observation Stay

When a patient is admitted for observation for a medical condition, assign a code for the medical condition as the first-listed diagnosis.

When a patient presents for outpatient surgery and develops complications requiring admission to observation, code the reason for the surgery as the first reported diagnosis (reason for the encounter), followed by codes for the complications as secondary diagnoses.

B. Codes from A00.0 through T88.9, Z00-Z99

The appropriate code(s) from A00.0 through T88.9, Z00-Z99 must be used to identify diagnoses, symptoms, conditions, problems, complaints, or other reason(s) for the encounter/visit.

C. Accurate reporting of ICD-10-CM diagnosis codes

For accurate reporting of ICD-10-CM diagnosis codes, the documentation should describe the patient's condition, using terminology which includes specific diagnoses as well as symptoms, problems, or reasons for the encounter. There are ICD-10-CM codes to describe all of these.

D. Codes that describe symptoms and signs

Codes that describe symptoms and signs, as opposed to diagnoses, are acceptable for reporting purposes when a diagnosis has not been established (confirmed) by the provider. Chapter 18 of ICD-10-CM, Symptoms, Signs, and Abnormal Clinical and Laboratory Findings Not Elsewhere Classified (codes R00-R99) contain many, but not all codes for symptoms.

E. Encounters for circumstances other than a disease or injury

ICD-10-CM provides codes to deal with encounters for circumstances other than a disease or injury. The Factors Influencing Health Status and Contact with Health Services codes (Z00-99) is provided to deal with occasions when circumstances other than a disease or injury are recorded as diagnosis or problems.
See Section I.C.21. Factors influencing health status and contact with health services.

F. Level of Detail in Coding

1.   ICD-10-CM codes with 3, 4, or 5 digits

ICD-10-CM is composed of codes with either 3, 4, 5, 6 or 7 digits. Codes with three digits are included in ICD-10-CM as the heading of a category of codes that may be further subdivided by the use of fourth fifth digits, sixth or seventh digits which provide greater specificity.

2.   Use of full number of digits required for a code

A three-digit code is to be used only if it is not further subdivided. A code is invalid if it has not been coded to the full number of characters required for that code, including the 7th character extension, if applicable.

G. ICD-10-CM code for the diagnosis, condition, problem, or other reason for encounter/visit

List first the ICD-10-CM code for the diagnosis, condition, problem, or other reason for encounter/visit shown in the medical record to be chiefly responsible for the services provided. List additional codes that describe any coexisting conditions. In some cases the first-listed diagnosis may be a symptom when a diagnosis has not been established (confirmed) by the physician.

H. Uncertain diagnosis

Do not code diagnoses documented as "probable", "suspected," "questionable," "rule out," or "working diagnosis" or other similar terms indicating uncertainty. Rather, code the condition(s) to the highest degree of certainty for that encounter/visit, such as symptoms, signs, abnormal test results, or other reason for the visit.

Please note: This differs from the coding practices used by short-term, acute care, long-term care and psychiatric hospitals.

I. Chronic diseases

Chronic diseases treated on an ongoing basis may be coded and reported as many times as the patient receives treatment and care for the condition(s)

J. Code all documented conditions that coexist

Code all documented conditions that coexist at the time of the encounter/visit, and require or affect patient care treatment or management. Do not code conditions that were previously treated and no longer exist. However, history codes (categories Z80-Z87) may be used as secondary codes if the historical condition or family history has an impact on current care or influences treatment.

K. Patients receiving diagnostic services only

For patients receiving diagnostic services only during an encounter/visit, sequence first the diagnosis, condition, problem, or other reason for encounter/visit shown in the medical record to be chiefly responsible for the outpatient services provided during the encounter/visit. Codes for other diagnoses (e.g., chronic conditions) may be sequenced as additional diagnoses.

For encounters for routine laboratory/radiology testing in the absence of any signs, symptoms, or associated diagnosis, assign Z01.89, Encounter for other specified special examinations. If routine testing is performed during the same encounter as a test to evaluate a sign, symptom, or diagnosis, it is appropriate to assign both the V code and the code describing the reason for the non-routine test.

For outpatient encounters for diagnostic tests that have been interpreted by a physician, and the final report is available at the time of coding, code any confirmed or definitive diagnosis(es) documented in the interpretation. Do not code related signs and symptoms as additional diagnoses.

Please note: This differs from the coding practice in the hospital inpatient setting regarding abnormal findings on test results.

L. Patients receiving therapeutic services only

For patients receiving therapeutic services only during an encounter/visit, sequence first the diagnosis, condition, problem, or other reason for encounter/visit shown in the medical record to be chiefly responsible for the outpatient services provided during the encounter/visit. Codes for other diagnoses (e.g., chronic conditions) may be sequenced as additional diagnoses.

The only exception to this rule is that when the primary reason for the admission/encounter is chemotherapy or radiation therapy, the appropriate Z code for the service is listed first, and the diagnosis or problem for which the service is being performed listed second.

M. Patients receiving preoperative evaluations only

For patients receiving preoperative evaluations only, sequence first a code from subcategory Z01.81, Encounter for pre-procedural examinations, to describe the pre-op consultations. Assign a code for the condition to describe the reason for the surgery as an additional diagnosis. Code also any findings related to the pre-op evaluation.

N. Ambulatory surgery

For ambulatory surgery, code the diagnosis for which the surgery was performed. If the postoperative diagnosis is known to be different from the preoperative diagnosis at the time the diagnosis is confirmed, select the postoperative diagnosis for coding, since it is the most definitive.

O. Routine outpatient prenatal visits

See Section I.C.15. Routine outpatient prenatal visits.

P. Encounters for general medical examinations with abnormal findings

The subcategories for encounters for general medical examinations, Z00.0-, provide codes for with and without abnormal findings. Should a general medical examination result in an abnormal finding, the code for general medical examination with abnormal finding should be assigned as the first listed diagnosis. A secondary code for the abnormal finding should also be coded.

Q. Encounters for routine health screenings

See Section I.C.21. Factors influencing health status and contact with health services, Screening

Glossary

A

Abortion artificially terminating a pregnancy

Abruptio placentae a premature sudden separation of the placenta from the uterus prior to or during labor

Abscess a localized collection of pus and indicates tissue destruction

Abuse use of a substance in excess without having a physical dependence

Acariasis being run over or infested with mites or acariads

Access locations skin or mucous membranes that can be punctured or cut to reach the site; external orifices such as the mouth, nares of the nose, or a stoma

Accessory organs secondary organs

Accrediting Bureau of Health Education Schools (ABHES) accredits graduates of an accredited medical assisting program

Acquired conditions conditions that occur during a person's life

Acquired Immunodeficiency Syndrome (AIDS) a condition in which the body's immune system deteriorates

Acute bronchitis inflammation of the bronchus that lasts for a short period of time

Acute renal failure the sudden interruption of renal function

Addiction abuse to the point that a person cannot get by without the substance of choice

Administration Simplification aspect of the Health Insurance Portability and Accountability Act of 1996 that developed standards for the electronic exchange of health-care data by administrative and financial transactions

Adnexa a term for the accessory or appendage of an organ

Adult onset diabetes the body is unable to produce sufficient amounts of insulin within the pancreas; patient might be insulin dependent or not; also known as Type II diabetes

Adverse effect hypersensitivity or reaction to a correct substance properly administered

Aftercare visits services provided during healing or recovery

Agammaglobulinemia a hereditary disorder in which the immunoglobulin (immune proteins) are extremely low, leaving the person open to infection

Agranulocytes cells that do not have a granular appearance

Alcohol abuse drinking alcohol to excess but not having a physical dependence on it

Alcohol dependence a person becomes dependent on alcohol and is unable to stop drinking even though the alcoholism has negative effects on the person's health, social relationships, and normal daily activities such as work; also known as alcoholism

Alcoholism a person becomes dependent on alcohol and is unable to stop drinking even though the alcoholism has negative effects on the person's health, social relationships, and normal daily activities such as work; also known as alcohol dependence

Alimentary canal another name for the digestive system

Alopecia hair loss

Alpha thalassemia condition in which there is a deficiency in the alpha protein being produced

Alteration modifying the anatomical structure of a body part without affecting its function

Altered state of consciousness transient alteration of awareness; altered loss of awareness

Alzheimer's disease a disease in which brain structure changes lead to memory loss, personality changes, and ultimately impaired ability to function

American Academy of Professional Coders (AAPC) organization founded in an effort to elevate the standards of medical coding

American Association of Medical Assistants (AAMA) association that represents individuals trained in performing routine administrative and clinical jobs that keep medical offices and clinics running efficiently and smoothly

American Health Information Management Association (AHIMA) organization that represents the health information professionals who manage, organize, process, and manipulate patient data

American Medical Technologists (AMT) professional association for medical technicians

Amniocentesis a procedure in which a needle is inserted into the amniotic sac to withdraw fluid for examination

Anemia condition marked by a decrease in red blood cells, hemoglobin, hematocrit, or a combination thereof

Angina pectoris severe chest pain caused by an insufficient amount of blood reaching the heart

Angiohemophilia a deficiency in the clotting factor and platelet function; also known as Von Willebrand disease

Animate object an object capable of moving on its own

Ankylosing spondylitis form of rheumatoid arthritis in which there is a chronic inflammation of the spine and sacroiliac joints that leads to the stiffening of the spine

Ankylosis complete fusion of the vertebrae

Anomaly a deviation from what is normal in the development of a structure or organ

Antepartum the time before childbirth

Anterior forward or front

Anterior chamber a chamber located in front of the lens of the eye

Anxiolytic sedative that relieves anxiety

Aplastic anemia failure of bone marrow to produce blood components

Aporosity Swiss cheese appearance of the bones, creating a decrease in bone mass

Appendicitis inflammation of the appendix

Appendix a wormlike structure that is found at the blind end of the cecum

Approach the way in which the surgeon, physician, or provider performs a procedure

Aqueous humor fluid that fills the two cavities of the interior of the eye

Arteries vessels that carry oxygen-rich blood from the heart to the body

Arthritis inflammation of a joint

Arthropods organisms that include insects, ticks, spiders, and mites

Aspiration pneumonia occurs when a solid or liquid is inhaled into the lung

Assault a violent crime committed against another

Assessment initial and follow-up evaluations of the patient's diagnosis, care plan, need for treatment, and documentation related to the patient's care

Assistance taking over a portion of a physiological function by extracorporeal means

Atmospheric extracorporeal control of atmospheric pressure and composition

Auditory ossicles the three small bones that transmit sound waves

Auditory tube connects the bony structures of the middle ear to the pharynx; also known as eustachian tube

Auricle known as the pinna or earlobe

Autonomic nervous system the part of the nervous system that regulates the activities of the cardiac muscle, smooth muscle, and glands

Avulsion a ripping or tearing away

B

Bacteria one-celled organisms named according to their shapes and arrangements

Bed wetting incontinence of urine that occurs at night; also known as nocturnal enuresis

Bedsore a sore resulting from continuous pressure in an area that eventually limits or stops circulation and oxygen flow to an area; also known as decubitus ulcer, pressure ulcer, or pressure sore

Benign noncancerous growth of cells

Benign prostatic hypertrophy (BPH) an abnormal enlargement of the prostate

Beta thalassemia condition in which there is a lack of beta protein being produced

Bile chemical secreted by the liver to help in digestion

Biopsy removal of tissue or cells for pathological examination

Birth defect a deviation from what is normal in the development of a structure or organ; also called an anomaly

Blepharitis inflammation of the eyelids

Blepharochalasis atrophy of the intercellular tissue that causes relaxation of the skin of the eyelid

Body mass index figured by taking a person's weight and height and figuring the index of fat in relation to these elements

Bones dense, porous, calcified connective tissue that protect the internal organs and form the framework of the body

Bony labyrinth consists of bones that make up the inner ear

Brackets used in the Tabular Listing and Alphabetic Index to enclose synonyms, alternative wording, abbreviations, or explanatory phrases

Bronchi formed when the trachea branches off in the chest

Bronchitis inflammation of the bronchus

Burn an injury to body tissue as a result of heat, flame, sun, and/or chemicals, radiation, or electricity

Bursa synovial-fluid-filled sac that works as a cushion to assist in movement

Bursitis an inflammation of the bursa

Bypass altering the route of passage of the contents of a tubular body part

C

Calculus a stone in the kidney or ureter

Cancer condition that is characterized by malignant neoplasm

Cancerous growth a condition in which cancer cells multiply; also called a malignant neoplasm

Candidiasis fungal infections caused by the *Candida* fungus; also known as moniliasis

Canthus inner edge of the eye

Carbuncles furuncles cluster and form a puslike sac

Carcinoma cancer of epithelial cells of connective tissue

Carcinoma in situ (ca in situ, CIS) neoplastic cells that are undergoing malignant changes confined to the original epithelium site without invading surrounding tissues; also called transitional cell carcinoma, noninfiltrating carcinoma, noninvasive carcinoma, and preinvasive carcinoma

Cardiomyopathy diseases of the heart muscle

Caregiver training educational in nature, teaching the caregiver skills and knowledge necessary to interact with and properly assist the patient

Cartilage smooth, nonvascular connective tissue that comprises the more flexible parts of the skeleton

Cataracts the abnormal loss of transparency of the lens of the eye

Cecum the end of the ileum and the start of the large intestine

Cellulitis a type of infection that develops in the layers of the skin

Centers for Medicare and Medicaid Services (CMS) a government agency responsible for maintaining the procedure codes ICD-CM, which are found in volume 3 of the ICD system

Central nervous system (CNS) the part of the nervous system made up of the brain and spinal cord

Cerebral hemorrhage bleeding in the brain or layers of brain lining

Cerebral palsy a disorder in which the motor function of the brain is impaired; present at birth, chronic, and nonprogressive

Cerebrovascular accident (CVA) disruption in the normal blood supply to the brain; also called a stroke

Cerebrovascular disease abnormal nontraumatic conditions that affect the cerebral arteries

Certified Medical Assistant (CMA) certification for the medical assisting profession

Certified Professional Coder (CPC) certification for coders offered by the American Academy of Professional Coders

Certified Professional Coder, Hospital Based (CPC-H) certification for coders in a hospital setting

Cerumen honey-colored, thick, waxy substance; also known as earwax

Ceruminous gland   sweat glands found in the external auditory canal

Chalazion   a small tumor of the eyelid caused by the retention of secretions of the meibomian gland

Change   taking out or taking off a device from a body part and putting back an identical or similar device in or on the same body part without cutting or puncturing the skin or a mucous membrane

Childbirth   the delivery of one or more infants

Chiropractor   a doctor who believes all body functions are connected

Chlamydia   a type of bacteria that lives inside host cells

Choclear duct   a membranous structure that is found in the inner ear and aids in the hearing process

Cholecystitis   inflammation of the gallbladder

Cholelithiasis   formation or presence of gallstones

Choroids   layer just beneath the sclera containing capillaries that provide the blood supply and nutrients to the eye

Chronic bronchitis   prolonged inflammation lasting for more than three months and occurring for two consecutive years

Chronic kidney disease (CKD)   progressive disease in which renal failure increases, causing multisystem problems

Chronic renal failure   progressive disease in which renal failure increases, causing multisystem problems

Chronic sinusitis   prolonged inflammation of one or more of the sinus cavities

Cilia   tiny hairs along the external auditory canal

Ciliary body   muscles responsible for adjusting the lens

Cleft lip   congenital defect that results in a deep groove or opening of the lip running upward to the nose; also called a harelip

Cleft palate   a congenital groove or opening of the palate that involves the hard palate, soft palate, or both, as well as the upper lip.

Closed fracture   a fracture in which the bone is broken but the skin has not been broken; also known as a complete or simple fracture

Cochlea   snail-shaped, bony structure in the ear that transmits sound

Code also   instructs the coder that two codes may be needed to fully code the diagnostic phrase being coded; no sequencing directions are provided

Code first   notes appearing in the Tabular section of ICD-10-CM and identifying for the coder the sequence of the code assignment

Coding   the assignment of numerical or alphanumerical characters to specify diagnostic and procedural phrases

Colitis   an inflammation of the colon

Colles' fracture   a wrist fracture that typically occurs when a person tries to break a fall by extending the arm

Colon   used in the Tabular listing after a term that is modified by one or more terms following the colon

Coma   a deep state of unconsciousness

Combination code   a single code used to classify two diagnoses, a diagnosis with an associated secondary process, or a diagnosis with an associated complication

Comminuted   the bone is crushed and may be splintered

Commission on Accreditation of Allied Health Education Programs (CAAHEP)   accredits medical assisting programs in both public and private postsecondary institutions throughout the United States

Complete fracture   a fracture in which the bone is broken but the skin has not been broken; also known as a closed or simple fracture

Complete placenta previa   occurs when the placenta entirely covers the cervical os

Complete prolapse   entire uterus descends and protrudes beyond the introitus, and the vagina becomes inverted

Complicated fracture   an internal organ injured as a direct result of the fracture

Compound fracture   a fracture that has broken through the skin at the fracture site; also known as an open fracture

Compression   the bone is pressed on itself and may exert pressure on a body region

Compression fractures of the spine   the vertebrae in the spine become weak and collapse under low stress

Computerized tomography (CT scan)   multiplanar images that have been computer reformatted

Concussion   a violent shaking or jarring of the brain

Congenital anomaly   a disorder that exists at the time of birth and may be a result of genetic factors, agents causing defects in the embryo, or both

Conjunctiva   colorless mucous membrane that lines the anterior part of the eye

Constitutional aplastic anemia   congenital or hereditary anemia

Contrast material   material injected into the patient to allow for quicker identification of abnormalities in the body due to image density

Control   stopping, or attempting to stop, postprocedural bleeding

Conventions   a group of instructional notes, punctuation marks, abbreviations, and symbols

Conversion disorders   conditions occurring when a patient represses emotional conflicts; sensory, motor, or visceral symptoms occur

Cornea   a transparent nonvascular structure located on the anterior portion of the sclera

Corrosion   a burn due to chemicals

Creation   making a new structure that does not physically take the place of a body part

Crohn's disease   a form of inflammatory bowel disease that can cause the thickening and scarring of the abdominal wall; also know as regional enteritis

Culture and sensitivity Test (C&S)   a test that identifies the type of organism causing the infection (the culture), and the sensitivity identifies the antibiotic that should be used to treat the infection

Cushing's syndrome   condition that results from the excessive and chronic production of cortisol by the adrenal cortex or by the administration of glucocorticoids in large doses for a period of several weeks or longer

Cutane   skin

Cystitis   an inflammation of the bladder

D

Dacryoadenitis inflammation of the lacrimal gland

Decompression extracorporeal elimination of undissolved gas from body fluids

Decubitus ulcer sore resulting from continuous pressure in an area that eventually limits or stops circulation and oxygen flow to an area; also known as pressure sore, pressure ulcer, or bedsore

Deformity a problem in the structure or form that may or may not be disfiguring

Degenerative joint disease a type of osteoarthritis

Delivery assisting the passage of the products of conception from the genital canal

Depressed fracture the skull bone is broken and pushed inward

Dermatitis an inflammation of the upper layer of the skin

Dermis the thick layer of tissue located directly below the epidermis

Destruction eradicating all or a portion of a body part

Detachment cutting off of all or a portion of an extremity

Developmental dyspraxia defined as an impaired ability to perform coordinated movements in the absence of any defect in sensory or motor functions

Device an object that is suppose to remain in the body after the completion of a procedure, such as a pacemaker

Diabetes mellitus chronic problem resulting from problems with the pancreas

Diagnostic and Statistical Manual of Mental Disorders, Fourth Revision (DSM-IV) psychiatric disorders diagnosed by psychiatrists most commonly are recorded using the nomenclature established by the American Psychiatric Association

Diagnostic examinations used to confirm or rule out a suspected diagnosis due to signs and symptoms that the patient has experienced

Diastolic blood pressure the pressure on the arterial walls during relaxation of the heart muscle

Dilation expanding an orifice or the lumen of a tubular body part

Direct inguinal hernia a protrusion in the groin area

Dislocation a body part has moved out of place; also known as luxation

Dissociative disorders characterized by emotional conflicts of which the patient represses the emotions in such a manner that a separation in the personality occurs

Diverticula pouches or sacs in the lining of the intestine that cause diverticulitis if the sacs become inflamed

Diverticulitis inflammation of the diverticula

Diverticulosis abnormal condition of the pouches or sacs in the lining of the intestine known as diverticula

Division separating, without taking out, a body part

Dorsopathies disorders of the back

Dowager's hump an abnormal curvature in the upper thoracic spine

Drainage taking or letting out fluids and/or gases from a body part

Dressing putting material on a body region for protection

Drug abuse taking drugs to excess but not having a dependence on them

Drug dependence the chronic use of drugs that creates a compulsion to take them in order to experience their effects

Duodenal ulcer an ulcer that occurs in the upper part of the small intestine

Duodenum the start of the small intestine at the end of the stomach

Dysplasia an abnormal development or growth of cells

E

Ear lobe the flexible cartilaginous flap that has a bottom portion known as the pinna

Ectopic pregnancy a pregnancy that occurs outside the uterus

Electromagnetic therapy extracorporeal treatment by electromagnetic rays

Embryo the developing child from conception through the eighth week of pregnancy

Emphysema the loss of lung function due to progressive decrease in the number of alveoli in the bronchus of the lung

Encapsulated surrounded by a capsule; confined to an area within a capsule; not able to metastasize

Encephalitis an inflammation of the brain

Encephalomyelitis inflammation of both the brain and spinal cord

Encopresis the involuntary passage of feces

End-Stage Renal Disease (ESRD) the late stage of chronic renal failure

Endocarditis the inflammation of the inner layer of the heart

Endocrine system consists of several different internal groups of glands and structures that produce or secrete hormones

Endolymph one of the auditory fluids found in the cochlea that aid in hearing

Endometriosis an abnormal growth of the endometrium outside the uterus

Enteritis an inflammation of the intestines

Entropion the turning inward of the border of the eyelid against the eyeball

Enuresis incontinence of urine

Eosinophilia a condition in which the eosinophil white blood cell is found in excess in the blood or body tissues

Epidermis the outermost layer of the skin

Epilepsy a transient disturbance of cerebral function that is recurrent and characterized by episodes of seizures

Epiphora tearing of the eyes

Erythrocytes red blood cells that are formed in the bone marrow

Escherichia coli (E. coli) rod-shaped bacillus found in the large intestine of humans

Esophagitis an inflammation of the esophagus

Esophagus structure that connects the throat to the stomach

Eustachian tube connects the bony structures of the middle ear to the pharynx; also known as the auditory tube

Excision cutting out or off, without replacement, a portion of a body part

Excludes notes used to signify that the conditions listed are not assigned to the category or block of category codes

Excludes 1 the diagnostic terms listed are not coded to the category or subcategory; therefore, the two conditions are mutually exclusive

Excludes 2   used to signify that the diagnostic terms listed after the note are not part of the condition(s) represented by the code or code block

External auditory canal   the canal that allows sound waves to travel to the inner part of the ear; also known as the external auditory meatus

External auditory meatus   the canal that allows sound waves to travel to the inner part of the ear; also known as the external auditory canal

External ear   the visible part of the ear, not within the structure of the skull

Extirpation   the taking or cutting out of solid matter from a body part

Extracorporeal   something that is outside of the body

Extraction   pulling or stripping out or off all or a portion of a body part

Eyelashes   located along the edge of the eyelids to protect the eye from foreign material

Eyelids (upper and lower)   the lids that protect the eyes and help to keep the surface of the eyeball lubricated

F

Factitious disorders   characterized by a patient exhibiting disease symptoms caused by the patient's deliberate actions to gain attention

Fascia   connective tissue that not only covers but supports and separates muscle

Female genital prolapse   downward displacement of the genital organs

Female genitalia   the female reproductive organs

Fetus   the developing child from the ninth week until birth

First-degree burns   burns that do not present a danger to the patient because they are limited to the outer layer of the epidermis

Fissured fracture   the bone has a narrow split that does not go through to the other side

Fitting(s)   necessary to fabricate, modify, and/or design a splint, orthosis, prosthesis, hearing aid, or other rehabilitative device for application

Fluoroscopy   external ionizing radiation on a fluorescent screen captures a single-plane or biplane, real-time image, which can also be stored by digital or analog means

Folate   a water-soluble B vitamin most commonly found in food

Folate deficient anemia   insufficient amounts of folic acid, which is needed for proper cell reproduction and growth

Forceps delivery   an instrument is used to grasp the fetus to assist in the delivery

Fracture (fx)   broken bones resulting from undue force or pathological changes

Fragmentation   breaking solid matter in a body part into pieces

Fungi   microscopic plant life that lack chlorophyll and are not able to manufacture their own food

Fusion   the joining of portions of an articular body part, rendering the part immobile

G

Gallbladder   stores bile secreted by the liver

Gastric ulcer   an ulcer that occurs in the stomach

Gastroesophageal reflux disease (GERD)   the reflux of stomach acid and pepsin into the esophagus, causing inflammation

Gastrointestinal (GI) tract   the digestive system

Gastrojejunal ulcer   an ulcer that occurs in the stomach and the jejunum

Geographic tongue   on the tongue, irregularly shaped patches that resemble landforms on a map

Glaucoma   disease of the eye marked by increased pressure in the eyeball that may result in damage to the optic nerve, causing the gradual loss of vision

Glomerulonephritis   inflammation of the glameruli of the kidneys

Glucose   needed for the cells to properly supply energy for the body's metabolic functions

Goiter   a condition in which the thyroid becomes enlarged even though hormone secretions fall within normal limits

Grand mal   severe seizure

Granularity   the level of detail

Granulocytes   cells with a granular appearance

Greenstick fracture   as with a greenstick of a tree, the bone bends as well as breaks

H

Hair   a form of protection used by the body to keep foreign material from entering through the skin

Hallucinogens   substances that induce a perception of visual image or a sound that is not present

Harelip   a congenital defect that results in a deep groove or opening of the lip running upward to the nose; also called a cleft lip

Healed myocardial infarction   identifies a history of a heart attack in the past

Health Insurance Portability and Accountability Act of 1996 (HIPAA)   law passed by Congress in 1996 that mandates how paper and electronic health information is cared for and monitored

Heart   a muscular organ that pumps blood throughout the body

Heart attack   occurs when there is inadequate blood supply to a section or sections of the heart; also known as myocardial infarction

Heart failure   a decreased ability of the heart to pump a sufficient amount of blood to the body's tissue

Helminths   organisms that include flatworms, roundworms, and flukes

Hemiparesis   a condition in which one side of the body is paralyzed due to brain hemorrhage, cerebral thrombosis, embolism, or a tumor of the cerebrum; a synonym for hemiplegia

Hemiplegia   a condition in which one side of the body is paralyzed due to brain hemorrhage, cerebral thrombosis, embolism, or a tumor of the cerebrum; a synonym for hemiparesis

Hemoglobin   absorbs oxygen and transports it to the tissues of the body; also seen as Hgb

Hemolytic anemia   occurs when red blood cells are broken down at a faster rate than bone marrow can produce them

Hemorrhoids   enlarged veins in or near the anus

Hepatic   pertaining to the liver

Hereditary factor VIII deficiency   a form of hemophilia

Hernia a protrusion or bulge through the tissue that normally contains the structure

Herniated disc the result of the rupture of the nucleus pulposus, or the material in the center of the disc

Hiatal hernia the sliding of part of the stomach into the chest cavity

High osmolar contrast material (HOCM) material that has a higher level of particle concentration than normal body fluids

Hirsutism excessive hair growth

Hives urticaria

Hordeolum commonly known as a sty

Hormones chemical substances produced by the body to keep organs and tissues functioning properly

Host supports a parasite

Human immunodeficiency virus (HIV) the virus that leads to AIDS

Hydrocephalus an accumulation of fluid in the cranial meninges

Hyperparathyroidism an abnormal condition of the parathyroid glands in which there is an excessive secretion of parathyroid hormone

Hypertension an increase in systolic pressure, diastolic pressure, or both

Hyperthermia the raising of body temperature

Hyperthyroidism the thyroid is producing excessive amounts of thyroid hormones

Hypnotics sleep-inducing agents

Hypoparathyroidism the abnormal or insufficient secretion of parathyroid hormone by the parathyroid glands, caused by a primary parathyroid dysfunction or elevated serum calcium level

Hypotension low blood pressure

Hypothermia the lowering of body temperature

Hypothyroidism the thyroid is not operating as efficiently as it could be due to a deficiency of hormone secretion

I

ICD-10 Procedure Coding System (ICD-10-PCS) the most recent version of the ICD coding system set up to replace volume 3 of the ICD-9-CM system

Idiopathic aplastic anemia a condition in which the bone marrow is not able, for unknown reasons, to produce cells properly

Ileum the last part of the small intestine, starting at the end of the jejunum

Immobilization limiting or preventing motion of a body region

Immune system the body's defense mechanism against disease and other foreign materials

Impacted fracture one end of the broken bone is wedged into the other bone

Impulse disorders characterized by a sudden desire or urge to act without consideration of consequences that may result

In Diseases Classified Elsewhere applies to the etiology/manifestation conventions

In situ neoplasms neoplastic cells that are undergoing malignant changes confined to the original epithelium site without invading surrounding tissues; also known as carcinoma in situ, ca in situ, or CIS

Inanimate object object that is not alive or able to move (animate) on its own power

Includes note used to define and/or give examples of the content of a particular category or a block of category codes

Incomplete prolapse the uterus descends into the introitus

Incus anvil-shaped bone of the middle ear; one of the auditory ossicles

Indirect inguinal hernia a protrusion that has moved to the scrotum

Infectious arthropathies disorders of the joints that are caused by an infectious agent

Infectious disease diseases that occur when a microorganism invades the body and causes disease

Influenza highly contagious respiratory disease

Inguinal hernia part of the intestine passes through a weak point or tear in the abdominal wall

Inhalants substances that are inhaled for their euphoric effect

Insertion putting in a nonbiological appliance that monitors, assists, performs, or prevents a physiological function but does not physically take the place of a body part

Inspection visually and/or manually exploring a body part

Instrumentation the specialized equipment used to perform a procedure on an internal body part

Insulin used by the body to process glucose

Insulin-dependent diabetes mellitus a diabetic patient that requires insulin injections to survive; may be a Type I or a Type II diabetic; also known as IDDM

Integumentary covering or outer layer

International Classification of Diseases, Tenth Revision, Clinical Modification (ICD-10-CM) an arrangement of classes or groups of diagnoses and procedures by systemic division

Introduction putting in or on a therapeutic, diagnostic, nutritional, physiological, or prophylactic substance other than blood or blood products

Iris the colored portion of the eye

Irrigation putting in or on a cleansing substance

Ischemic heart disease an inadequate supply of blood to the heart caused by an occlusion

Isotope one of two or more atoms that contain the same atomic number but have different mass numbers in the nucleus

J

Jejunum starts at the end of the duodenum and is the middle section of the small intestine

Joints allow for bending and rotating movements

Juvenile diabetes insufficient amount of insulin secretions, requiring insulin injections; also known as Type I diabetes mellitus

K

Kidneys bilateral organs located against the dorsal wall that filter blood to constantly to remove waste

Kleptomania pathological stealing

L

Labor and delivery process of childbirth

Labyrinth bony and membranous structures of the inner ear

Lacrimal duct the duct that drains the tears from the eye through the eye and that is located at the inner edge of the eye

Lacrimal gland the gland that produces tears

Lagophthalmos the inability of the eye to close completely

Larynx made up of cartilage and ligaments that compose the vocal cords or voice box

Late effect a condition produced after the acute phase of an illness or injury has terminated

Lateral away from the midline toward the side

Laterality for bilateral sites ICD-10-CM indicates the specific site

Legally induced abortion termination of a pregnancy that is done by medical personnel working within the law

Lens a colorless structure that allows the eye to focus on images

Leukemia cancer of the blood-forming organs

Leukocytes white blood cells that protect the body from disease

Ligaments bands of connective tissue that connect the joints

Lipoma a benign neoplasm of adipose tissue

Liver considered an accessory organ of the digestive system that filters red blood cells, produces glycogen, and secretes bile

Low osmolar contrast material (LOCM) material with a lower level of particle concentration than normal body fluids

Lungs the main organs of the respiratory system

Lupus a disease in which the body produces too many antibodies, which begin to turn against the patient's own body, attacking body organs, joints, and muscles

Luxation a body part has moved out of place; also known as dislocation

Lymphadenitis inflammation of the lymph nodes

Lymphoma cancer of the lymph nodes and immune system

M

Magnetic resonance imaging (MRI) multiplanar images developed from the capture of radio frequency signals emitted by nuclei in a particular body site excited within a magnetic field that can produce a computer-formatted digital display of the images

Male genitalia made up of the scrotum, testicles, and the penis

Malignant neoplasm cancerous growth

Malignant primary refers to the originating site of a malignant tumor

Malignant secondary refers to the site of tumor metastasis

Malleus hammer-shaped bone found in the middle ear; one of the auditory ossicles

Malunion fracture the fracture site is misaligned

Map locating the route of passage of electrical impulses and/or the functional areas in a body part

Measurement determining the level of something at a point in time

Medial closest or nearest to the midline of a structure

Medicaments term for medicine

Melanocytes cells that produce dark pigment

Melanoma fast-growing cancer of melanin-producing cells

Membranous labyrinth a term used to describe the structures in the inner ear that are not bony structures

Meningitis the inflammation of the membranes, or meninges, of the spinal cord or brain

Menopause the time in a woman's life when her menstrual cycle ceases

Mental disorders disorders that affect the ability of a person to function in a healthy, socially acceptable way

Mental retardation a condition in which the mind of the patient never fully develops

Metabolism the rate at which energy is used by the body and at which body functions occur

Metastasize the growing and spreading of cancer to other body parts

Methemoglobinemia a disorder of the hemoglobin in which oxygen is not able to be transported by the cells

Method specifies how the external access location was entered when a procedure is performed on an internal body part

Micturate voiding or urinating

Middle ear also known as the tympanic cavity, the middle ear found in the temporal bone and housing the auditory ossicles

Mild mental retardation an IQ of 50-55 to approximately 70

Missed abortion the fetus has died before the completion of 22 weeks gestation, with the retention of the dead fetus or products of conception for up to four weeks after demise

Modality in medicine, a certain protocol, therapeutic method, or agent

Moderate mental retardation an IQ of 35-40 to 50-55

Molar pregnancy a blighted ovum in the uterus that develops into a mole or benign tumor

Moniliasis a fungal infection that can affect various sites; also called candidiasis

Monitoring determining the level of something over a period of time

Morbidity the rate or frequency of disease; diseased state

Morphology the form and structure of neoplastic growth of cells

Mortality the rate or frequency of death

Multiple sclerosis a demyelinating disorder in which patches of hardened tissue form in the brain or spinal cord and cause partial or complete paralysis and muscle tremors

Muscle holds the body erect and allows movement

Myelitis an inflammation of the spinal cord

Myelopathy any disorder of the spinal cord

Myelophthisis severe form of anemia in which certain bone marrow material shows up in the peripheral blood

Myocardial infarction (MI) occurs when there is inadequate blood supply to a section or sections of the heart; also called a heart attack

Myocarditis inflammation of the heart muscle

Myositis inflammation of the muscle

N

Nails hardened cells of the epidermis

National Center for Health Statistics (NCHS) organization responsible for maintaining the diagnostic codes that are found in volume 1 and 2 of the ICD-CM manual

Neoplasms   uncontrolled abnormal growth of cells; also called tumors

Neoplasms of uncertain behavior   neoplasms in which cells are not histologically confirmed even after pathological investigation

Neoplasms of unspecified behavior   tumors in which the morphology and behavior of the neoplasm is not specified in the patient's medical record

Nephritis   the inflammation of the kidneys

Nephrons   found in the kidneys and used to filter, reabsorb, and secrete urine

Nephropathy   a disease or disorder of the kidney

Nephrosis   a disease or disorder of the kidney

Nervous system   system that controls all bodily activities and is made up of the central nervous system and the peripheral nervous system

Neutropenia   an abnormal decrease of granular leukocytes in the blood

Nicotine   a poisonous alkaloid found in tobacco

Nocturnal enuresis   incontinence of urine that occurs at night; also known as bed wetting

Nonessential modifiers   the terms found in the parentheses that do not change code assignment

Nonimaging assay   after the introduction of radioactive materials, the detection of radioactive emissions are identified and measured in the body fluids and blood elements

Nonimaging probe   after the introduction of radioactive materials into the body, there is a study of the distribution and fate of certain substances by the detection of the radioactive emissions

Nonimaging uptake   after the introduction of radioactive materials into the body, organ function can be determined from the detection of radioactive emissions

Noninfiltrating carcinoma   neoplastic cells that are undergoing malignant changes confined to the original epithelium site without invading surrounding tissues; also known as transitional cell carcinoma, carcinoma in situ, noninvasive carcinoma, and preinvasive carcinoma in situ

Noninsulin-dependent diabetes mellitus   a diabetic patient who does not require insulin injections to survive; the diabetic might be controlled by diet, exercise, or other medications outside of insulin, usually a Type II diabetic; also known as NIDDM

Noninvasive carcinoma   neoplastic cells undergoing malignant changes that are confined to the original epithelium site without invading surrounding tissues; also called transitional cell carcinoma, noninfiltrating carcinoma, carcinoma in situ, and preinvasive carcinoma

Nonmalignant tumor   not life-threatening, benign

Nonunion fracture   fracture fragments fail to unite

Not elsewhere classified (NEC)   used to signal coders that the term being coded is considered a general term

Not otherwise specified (NOS)   codes are not specific and should be used only after the coder has clarified with the physician that a more specific code is not available

Nuclear medicine   treats and diagnoses diseases using small amounts of radioactive material to create an image

O

Obsessive-compulsive disorder   a psychoneurotic disorder where the patient has obsessions or compulsions and suffers extreme anxiety or depression that can interfere with the patient's ability to function occupationally, interpersonally, or socially

Obstetrics   medical care that occurs during pregnancy and childbirth

Occlusion   complete closure of an orifice or lumen of a tubular body part, such as a vessel

Occlusion of cerebral and precerebral arteries   the blocking of arteries

Old myocardial infarction   identifies a history of a heart attack in the past

Omphalitis   the inflammation of the navel

Open   cutting through the skin or mucous membrane and any other body layers necessary to expose the site of the procedure

Open fracture   a fracture that has broken through the skin at the fracture site; also known as a compound fracture

Open with percutaneous endoscopic assistance   cutting through the skin or mucous membrane and any other body layers necessary to expose the site of the procedure, along with entry by puncture or minor incision of instrumentation through the skin or mucous membrane and any other body layers necessary to aid in the performance of the procedure

Optic disc   the blind spot on the optic nerve that is the point of entry for the artery supplying blood to the retina

Optic nerve   the nerve that transmits impulses to the brain from the eye

Organ of Corti   the true organ of hearing found in the cochlea

Osteoarthritis (OA)   most common form of arthritis; causes the degeneration of the articular cartilage

Osteopathic manipulation therapy   manually guided therapy that is performed to improve physiological function

Osteoporosis   the reduction in bone mass that is responsible for different conditions affecting a person's health

Otalgia   earache

Other procedures   a methodology that attempts to remediate or cure a disorder or disease

Otitis externa   the inflammation of the external auditory canal

Otorrhagia   hemorrhage from the ear

Otorrhea   a discharge from the external ear

Otosclerosis   a growth of spongy bone in the inner ear

Oval window   what separates the middle ear and inner ear

Ovarian cysts   an encapsulated sac of the ovary that is filled with semisolid or liquid material

P

Packing   putting material in a body region

Pancreas   anatomically located under the stomach in the upper abdomen; performs various physiological functions

Pancytopenia   a decrease in the number of platelets, white blood cells, and red blood cells

Paralysis   the loss of sensation or voluntary motion

Paraphilias   sexual perversions or deviations

Parasite   lives within another organism and may or may not cause disease

Parasitic disease   a disease caused by an organism that lives within another organism and that can cause illness

Parentheses   used in both Tabular List and Alphabetic Index around terms providing additional information about the main diagnostic term

Parkinson's disease a progressive disease characterized by a masklike facial expression, weakened muscles, tremors, and involuntary movement

Partial placenta previa occurs when the placenta covers part of the cervical os

Pathogen a microorganism that can cause disease in humans

Pathologic factures a break of diseased bone that occurs from a minor stress or injury that would not normally occur in healthy bone

Pedal cycle type of transportation operated by a person without the help of a motor

Pedestrian any person who is not riding in or on any type of motor or wheeled form of transportation

Pediculosis an infestation of lice

Penis the male organ that functions in both the urinary and reproductive systems

Peptic ulcer an ulcer that occurs in an unspecified site of the GI tract

Percutaneous entry, by puncture or minor incision, of instrumentation through the skin or mucous membrane and/or any other body layers necessary to reach the site of the procedure

Percutaneous endoscopic entry, by puncture or minor incision, of instrumentation through the skin our mucous membrane and/or any other body layers necessary to reach and visualize the site of the procedure

Performance completely taking over a physiological function by extracorporeal means

Periapical abscess an infection of the pulp and surrounding tissue

Pericarditis the inflammation of the outer layers of the heart

Perilymph one of two auditory fluids found in the inner ear that aid in the transmission of sound

Perimenopausal when symptoms of menopause begin

Perinatal period the time surrounding the birth of the child and up to 28 days after birth

Peripheral nervous system (PNS) the part of the nervous system that directly branches off the central nervous system

Peritonitis inflammation of the lining of the abdominal cavity

Pernicious anemia an autoimmune disorder in which the stomach is unable to produce intrinsic factor needed to absorb vitamin B_{12}

Petit mal a seizure, less severe than a grand mal

Pharyngitis a sore throat

Pharyngotympanic tube connects the bony structures of the middle ear to the pharynx; also known as the eustachian tube

Pharynx the throat

Pheresis the separation of blood products

Phlebitis the inflammation of a vein

Phototherapy treatment by light rays

Pica a person has an abnormal craving and eating of substances that are not normally eaten by humans

Pinna flexible cartilaginous flap that has a bottom portion known as the ear lobe

Placenta previa the abnormal positioning of the placenta in the lower uterus so that the cervical os is partially or completely covered

Plain radiography standard X-ray, with planar display of an image

Planar imaging single-plane display of images after the introduction of radioactive materials

Pneumonia a condition in which liquid, known as exudates, and pus infiltrate the lung and cause inflammation

Point dash a signal to the coder that the code contains a list of options at a level of specificity past the three-character category

Poisoning an overdose of a substance or the intake of a wrong substance given or taken in error

Polycystic kidney disease an inherited disorder in which the kidneys gradually lose the ability to function due to the grapelike clusters of cysts that form

Polymorphonuclear neutrophils white blood cells found in the peripheral blood

Polysubstance drug use indiscriminate use of multiple drugs

Portal vein thrombosis a blood clot in the main vein of the liver

Positron emission tomographic Imaging (PET) a three-dimensional image is produced after the introduction of radioactive materials but the images are simultaneously captured 180 degrees apart

Posterior back or behind

Posterior chamber a chamber located behind the lens of the eye

Postmenopausal when a woman has not had a period for at least one year until the time she celebrates her 100th birthday

Postpartum from birth until six weeks after the birth

Preinvasive carcinoma neoplastic cells undergoing malignant changes that are confined to the original epithelium site without invading surrounding tissues; also called transitional cell carcinoma, noninfiltrating carcinoma, noninvasive carcinoma, and carcinoma in situ

Premenopausal the time right before menopause

Pressure sore sore resulting from continuous pressure in an area that eventually limits or stops circulation and oxygen flow to an area; also known as decubitus ulcer, pressure ulcer, or bedsore

Pressure ulcer sore resulting from continuous pressure in an area that eventually limits or stops circulation and oxygen flow to an area; also known as decubitus ulcer, pressure sore, or bedsore

Principal diagnosis the condition defined after study as the main reason for admission of a patient to the hospital

Procedure the complete specification of the seven characters to identify what service was performed

Products of conception all the physical components of a pregnancy, including the fetus, amnion, umbilical cord, and the placenta

Profound mental retardation IQ below 20-25

Prostate gland secretes fluid that is part of the semen and also aids in the motility of the sperm in the male

Protozoa one-celled organisms that live on living matter and are classified by the way they move

Psychiatrist a medical doctor who administers treatment for patients with mental, emotional, and behavioral disorders

Psychiatry the branch of medicine that deals with mental disorders

Pterygium a benign growth over the conjunctiva of the eye

Puerperium the postpartum period beginning from birth until six weeks after birth

Pulp the center of a tooth

Pulpitis an abscess of the pulp

Pupil the center of the iris that controls the amount of light entering the eye

Pure red cell aplasia a condition in which precursors to the red blood cells are affected in the bone marrow and eventually cease to be produced

Purpura the accumulation of blood under the skin that forms multiple pinpoint hemorrhages

Pyromania an impulse disorder characterized by the desire to set fires

Q

Qualifier additional information unique to the individual procedure being performed

R

Radiation oncology (rad onc) a form of radiology that is therapeutic as opposed to diagnostic

Radioactive isotopes radioactive material used to create an image

Radiologic technician a person specially trained to use the equipment unique to the radiology department

Radiologist a doctor whose specialty is radiology

Radiology the study of X-rays, high-frequency sound waves, and high-strength magnetic fields, which sometimes include the use of radioactive compounds to diagnose and/or treat disease or injuries

Radionuclide a radioactive substance that can be found in nature, that can be human-made, and that is the source of the radiation causing the emissions for the image to be produced; also called a radioactive isotope or radiopharmaceutical

Radiopharmaceutical a radioactive substance that can be found in nature, that can be human-made, and that is the source of the radiation causing the emissions for the image to be produced; also called a radioactive isotope or radionuclide

Reattachment putting back in or on all or a portion of a separated body part to its normal location or other suitable locations

Red blood cells (RBC) disc-shaped cells formed in the bone marrow that contain hemoglobin

Reduction the act of putting something back into its proper place

Regional enteritis a form of inflammatory bowel disease that can cause the thickening and scarring of the abdominal wall; also know as Crohn's disease

Registered Health Information Administrator (RHIA) certification offered by AHIMA to members who have obtained their bachelor's degree from an accredited program

Registered Health Information Technician (RHIT) certification offered by AHIMA to members who have obtained their associate's degree from an accredited program

Registered Medical Assistant (RMA) professional credentials for a medical technician

Release the freeing of a body part

Removal taking out or off a device from a body part

Renal colic acute pain caused by the passage of a kidney stone from the kidney through the ureter

Repair restoring, to the extent possible, a body part to its normal anatomic structure and function

Replacement putting in or on a biological or synthetic material that physically takes the place of all or a portion of a body part

Reposition moving to its normal location or other suitable location all or a portion of a body part

Resection cutting out or off, without replacement, all of a body part

Respiratory system the system containing structures that exchange oxygen and carbon dioxide in the body

Restoration the return or the attempt to return a physiological function to its natural state by extracorporeal means

Restriction partially closing an orifice or lumen of a tubular body part

Resuscitation procedure performed to restore cardiac and/or respiratory function

Retina the nerve cell layer of the eye that changes light rays into nerve impulses

Revision correcting, to the extent possible, a malfunctioning or displaced device

Rheumatism the general term for the deterioration and inflammation of connective tissue, including muscles, tendons, synovium, and bursa

Rheumatoid arthritis (RA) an autoimmune disease in which the synovial membranes are inflamed and thickened

Rickettsioses a bacterial infection that might also be referred to as typhus or a form of spotted fever

Root operation the objective of the procedure, such as bypass, drainage, fluoroscopy, and the like

Rumination disorder of infancy when a person regurgitates and chews previously swallowed food

S

Saccule membranous sac that aids in maintaining balance

Sarcoma cancer of supportive tissue, such as blood vessels, bones, cartilage, and muscles

Schizophrenia a psychotic disorder characterized by disruptive behavior, hallucinations, delusions, and disorganized speech

Sclera the white portion of the eye that maintains the shape of the eyeball

Screening examinations examinations used to screen, or look, for diseases

Sebaceous glands glands of the skin that produce an oily secretion to condition the skin

Second-degree burn a partial-thickness burn that forms blisters

Secondary diagnoses conditions that are not responsible for admission but that exist at the time of treatment

Secondary hypertension high arterial blood pressure due to another disease, such as vascular disease

Sedatives drugs that induce a relaxed state and calm or tranquilize a patient

See used in the Alphabetic Index and instructs the coder to cross-reference the term or diagnosis following the notation

See also refers the coder to another location in the Alphabetic Index when the initial listing does not contain all the necessary information to select an accurate code

Semicircular canals bony structures filled with fluid that help maintain balance

Semicircular ducts found in the middle ear; aid in balance

Sepsis   a life-threatening bacterial infection that causes clots to form, which block blood flow to vital organs

Severe mental retardation   IQ of 20-25 to 35-40

Severe sepsis   a septic infection with associated acute organ dysfunction or failure

Shock wave therapy   treatment by shock waves

Sickle-cell anemia   genetic disorder in which the development of an abnormal type of hemoglobin in red blood cells causes decreased oxygenation in the tissues

Sickle-cell trait   an asymptomatic condition in which the patient receives the genetic trait from only one parent

Sideropenic dysphagia   a type of iron-deficiency anemia that becomes so severe that the patient has difficulty swallowing in addition to the other symptoms of anemia; also known as Plummer-Vinson syndrome

Sign   observed by the physician/provider and objective evidence of disease

Simple fracture   a fracture in which the bone is broken but not the skin; also known as a closed or complete fracture

Sinusitis   the inflammation of the sinus cavity

Somatoform disorders   characterized by symptoms that suggest a physical illness or disease but for which there are no organic causes or physiologic dysfunctions

Spina bifida   a congenital condition in which the spinal canal fails to close around the spinal cord

Spiral fracture   a severe twisting motion causes the bone to twist apart

Spirochetal   a gram-negative bacteria made up of spiral-shaped cells

Spleen   located in the upper left quadrant of the abdomen; the site of lymphocyte and monocyte formation and erythrocyte storage

Spondylitis   an inflammation of the vertebrae

Sprain   an injury to a joint, specifically the ligament of the joint that becomes stretched

Stapes   stirrup-shaped bone that is part of the middle ear; one of the auditory ossicles

Stomach   pouchlike structure at the end of the esophagus

Strain   an injury at the joint site to a muscle or tendon

Stress fracture   excessive impact on the bone causes small hairline crack in it

Stroke   the disruption in the normal blood supply to the brain; also called a cerebrovascular accident

Subluxation   part of the joint surface has moved away from where it should be; also called a partial dislocation

Supplement   putting in or on biological or synthetic material that physically reinforces and/or augments the function of a portion of a body part

Suspensory ligaments   ligaments that attach to the lens and hold it in place

Symptom   the reason that brings a patient to seek medical attention; the subjective information

Syncope   a condition in which there is a brief loss of consciousness due to lack of oxygen to the brain; also known as fainting

Synovia   the fluid that acts as a lubricant for joints, tendon sheath, or bursa

Systemic blood pressure   the pressure on the arterial walls during the heart muscle contraction

Systemic therapy   the introduction of unsealed radioactive material into the body for treatment; does not include the encapsulated radioactive material used in cancer treatment

Systolic blood pressure   the pressure on the arterial walls during the heart muscle contraction

T

Tendons   connect muscle to bone

Teratogens   agents that cause defects in an embryo

Terrorism   the unlawful use of force or violence against persons or property to intimidate or coerce a government, the civilian population, or any segment thereof in the furtherance of political or social objectives

Thalassemia   red blood cells are not formed or functioning properly, and the globulin gene arrangement is affected

Third-degree burn   full-thickness burn affecting the epidermis, dermis, and subcutaneous layers

Thrombocytopenia   an abnormal decrease in platelet count that causes purpural hemorrhages

Thrombolytic therapy   the intravenous administration of thrombolytic agents, often completed to open the coronary artery occlusion and to restore blood flow to the cardiac tissue

Thrombophilia   a condition in which the patient is predisposed to develop thromboses

Thrombophlebitis   the inflammation of a vein with the formation of a thrombus

Thyroid gland   secretes hormones that regulate growth and metabolism

Thyrotoxic crisis   symptoms of hyperthyroidism that are so severe as to threaten the patient's life; also known as thyrotoxic storm

Thyrotoxic storm   symptoms of hyperthyroidism that are so severe as to threaten the patient's life; also known as thyrotoxic crisis

Tic disorder   a repetitive involuntary muscle spasm that is usually psychogenic and that can increase due to stress or anxiety

Tomographic imaging (tomo)   a three-dimensional display of images, developed from the capture of radioactive emissions

Tonsils   protect the entrance to the respiratory system

Trachea   the windpipe

Traction   exerting a pulling force on a body region in a distal direction

Transcobalamin II deficiency   a rare autosomal recessive disease

Transfer   moving, without taking out, all or a portion of a body part

Transfusion   putting in blood or blood products

Transient hypertension   elevated blood pressure but not identified as chronic hypertension

Transitional cell carcinoma   neoplastic cells undergoing malignant changes and confined to the original epithelium site without invading surrounding tissues; also called carcinoma in situ, noninfiltrating carcinoma, noninvasive carcinoma, and preinvasive carcinoma

Transplantation   putting in or on all or a portion of a living body part taken from another individual or animal to physically take the place and/or function of all or portion of a similar body part

Treatment   manual treatment to eliminate or alleviate somatic dysfunction and related disorders

Trichiasis   the turning inward of the eyelashes

Trichotillomania   an impulse disorder characterized by the desire to pluck hair

Tubular body parts   hollow body parts that provide a route of passage for solids, liquids, or gases

Tumor   the uncontrolled abnormal growth of cells; also called a neoplasm

Tympanic cavity   the middle ear found in the temporal bone and housing the auditory ossicles and the eustachian tube

Tympanic membrane   the eardrum

Type   similar to root operation

Type I diabetes mellitus   insufficient amount of insulin secretion, requiring insulin injections; also known as juvenile diabetes

Type II diabetes mellitus   the body is unable to produce sufficient amounts of insulin in the pancreas; patient might be insulin dependent or not; also known as adult onset diabetes

U

Ulcerative colitis   the colon becomes inflamed, and ulcers develop in the lining of the intestine

Ulcers   erosions of the skin in which tissue becomes inflamed and then lost

Ultrasonography   the real-time display of images of anatomy, developed from the capture of reflected and attenuated high-frequency sound waves

Ultrasound therapy   treatment by ultrasound

Ultraviolet light therapy   treatment by ultraviolet light

Underdosing   taking less of a medication than what is prescribed or instructed by the physician or the manufacturer, whether deliberately or inadvertently

Unstable angina   an accelerating, or crescendo, pattern of chest pain that occurs at rest or during mild exertion, typically lasting longer than angina pectoris and not responsive to medication

Ureters   very narrow tubes that conduct urine from the kidneys to the bladder

Urethra   a small tube extending from the bladder to outside the body

Urethral stricture   a narrowing of the urethra

Urethritis   an inflammation of the urethra

Urinary bladder   holds urine until it moves to the urethra

Urinary system   the system that maintains the balance of the contents of the fluids in the body

Urinary tract infection (UTI)   the abnormal presence of microorganisms in the urine

Urine   fluid waste

Urticaria   hives

Use additional code   instructs the coder to use an additional code to identify the manifestation that is present

Uterus   the organ that sits above the cervix and houses a fetus until birth

Utricle   the structure of the inner ear that aids in maintaining balance

V

Valgus deformity of feet   congenital outward turning of the feet

Varicose veins   dilated superficial veins of the legs

Varus deformity of feet   congenital inward turning of the feet

Vault of the skull   made up of the two parietal bones and the frontal bone

Veins   vessels that carry deoxygenated blood from the body back to the heart

Vertebral column   shields the spinal column and is made up of cervical, thoracic, and lumbar vertebra

Vestibule   the central portion of the inner ear

Via natural or artificial opening   the entry of instrumentation through a natural or artificial external opening to reach the site of the procedure

Virus   the smallest of infectious pathogens

Vitamin B_{12} deficient anemia   anemia due to an insufficient dietary intake of vitamin B_{12} or the inability of the body to absorb the vitamin B_{12} appropriately

Vitreous humor   a clear, jellylike fluid that fills the posterior chamber of the eye and that helps to shape the eye

Vocal cords   ligaments that produce sound or speech when air passes through them

Voiding   urination or micturating

Volkmann's deformity   congenital dislocation of the tibiotarsal

Von Willebrand disease   the most common of the hereditary bleeding disorders in which the clotting process is not working properly

W

White blood cells   protect the body from disease; also called leukocytes

World Health Organization (WHO)   responsible for preparing and publishing the revisions to ICD system; based in Geneva, Switzerland

Z

Z codes   used to report encounters when the circumstances surrounding the encounter are for something other than disease or injury

Index

Note: An "f" after the page number indicates a figure.